AF814431

QUE Bee

From Doubts to Distinction
Your ICSE 2026 Exams Partner

GIST OF THE TEXTBOOK
Crisp & Complete Theory - No need to go back to textbooks!

ALL TYPES OF LATEST PATTERN QUESTIONS
MCQs | Case-based | Assertion-Reason | Fill ups; All in one place!

KEY WORDS HIGHLIGHTED
Important points and formulae neatly highlighted, never miss what matters

10 YEARS' PYQS SOLUTIONS
Coverage of Previous Years' Questions with Solutions

COUNCIL-STYLE ANSWERS
Write responses like an examiner expects

SAMPLE & SPECIMEN PAPERS
Practice in real-exam mode. Perfect your timing, strategy and confidence.

arihant
SUCCESS AND NOTHING LESS

ARIHANT PRAKASHAN
(School Division Series)

ADMINISTRATIVE & PRODUCTION OFFICES

Regd. Office
'Ramchhaya' 4577/15, Agarwal Road, Darya Ganj, New Delhi -110002
Tele: 011- 47630600, 43518550; Fax: 011- 23280316

Head Office
Kalindi, TP Nagar, Meerut (UP) - 250002, Tel: 0121-7156203, 7156204

SALES & SUPPORT OFFICES
Agra, Ahmedabad, Bengaluru, Bareilly, Chennai, Delhi, Guwahati, Hyderabad, Jaipur, Jhansi, Kolkata, Lucknow, Nagpur & Pune.

PO No : TXT-XX-XXXXXXX-X-XX

Published By Arihant Publications (India) Ltd.

For further information about the books published by Arihant, log on to www.arihantbooks.com or e-mail at info@arihantbooks.com

Follow us on

PRICE ₹ 300.00

PRODUCTION TEAM

Publishing Manager
Keshav Mohan

Project Head
Akansha Tomar

Cover Designer
Bilal Hashmi

Inner Designer
Ankit Tyagi

Page Layouting
Sanjay Yadav

Proof Reader
Nisha Verma, Sarthak Sharma

QUE Bee

ICSE CHEMISTRY Class 10

Types of Questions & their Respective Number

Types of Questions	Total Number
Multiple Choice Questions (MCQs)	306
Assertion-Reason (A-R)	63
Fill in the Blanks	132
Correct the Incorrect Statement	67
Matching Type Questions	19
Identify the following	105
Short Answer Type I Questions (SA-I)	183
Short Answer Type II Questions (SA-II)	145
Long Answer Type Questions (LA)	136
Case Based Questions	30
TOTAL NO. OF QUESTIONS	**1186**

Created by

Dr. Arun Sharma

M.Sc., Ph.D

PGT, St. Francis' Convent School, Meerut

Contributor

Tarnija Midha

From Learner to Leader

Step-Into the Spotlight

QUE Bee is more than just a book - it's a platform for young achievers like you to guide future toppers. If you've cracked the code to smart study or have insights that can make learning easier for others, this is your moment to shine!

What Can You Share?

- Your study techniques, time management tips, or motivation hacks
- Feedback or suggestions to make QUE Bee even better
- Real experiences that can guide other students through the exam maze

What's in It for You?

- Your name will be featured in our exclusive Student Panel in the next edition
- Win exciting & surprise rewards for impactful suggestions
- **Get published** - your photo, Ideas-or even interviews can be featured in the book
- **Become a student icon** - recognized and followed by peers across schools

Let your learning become someone else's ladder.
Be remembered. Be featured. Be the guide.

SCAN TO SHARE YOUR IDEA

Index

Latest
Course Structure

*There will be one paper of **two hours** duration of 80 marks and Internal Assessment of practical work carrying 20 marks.*

***Note:** All chemical process/reactions should be studied with reference to the reactants, products, conditions, observations, the (balanced) equations and diagrams.*

1. PERIODIC PROPERTIES AND VARIATIONS OF PROPERTIES - PHYSICAL AND CHEMICAL

(i) Periodic properties and their variations in groups and periods.

Definitions and trends of the following periodic properties in groups and periods should be studied:

- *atomic size*
- *metallic character*
- *non-metallic character*
- *ionisation potential*
- *electron affinity*
- *electronegativity*

(ii) Periodicity on the basis of atomic number for elements.

- The study of modern periodic table up to period 3 (students to be exposed to the complete modern periodic table but no questions will be asked on elements beyond period 3 - Argon);
- Periodicity and other related properties to be explained on the basis of nuclear charge and shells (not orbitals).

Special reference to the alkali metals and halogen groups.

2. CHEMICAL BONDING

Electrovalent, covalent and co-ordinate bonding, structures of various compounds, Electron dot structure.

(i) Electrovalent bonding

- *Electron dot structure of Electrovalent compounds NaCl, $MgCl_2$, CaO.*
- *Characteristic properties of electrovalent compounds – state of existence, melting and boiling points, conductivity (heat and electricity), dissociation in solution and in molten state to be linked with electrolysis.*

(ii) Covalent Bonding

- *Electron dot structure of covalent molecules on the basis of duplet and octet of electrons (example: hydrogen, chlorine, nitrogen, ammonia, carbon tetrachloride, methane.*
- *Polar Covalent compounds based on difference in electronegativity:*
  Examples - HCl and H_2O including structures.
- *Characteristic properties of Covalent compounds – state of existence, melting and boiling points, conductivity (heat and electricity), ionisation in solution.*

Comparison of Electrovalent and Covalent compounds.

(iii) Coordinate Bonding

- *Definition*
- *The lone pair effect of the oxygen atom of the water molecule and the nitrogen atom of the ammonia molecule to explain the formation of H_3O^+ and OH^- ions in water and NH_4^+ ion.*

The meaning of lone pair; the formation of hydronium ion and ammonium ion must be explained with the help of electron dot diagrams.

3. STUDY OF ACIDS, BASES AND SALTS

(i) Simple definitions in terms of the molecules and their characteristic properties.

(ii) Ions present in mineral acids, alkalis and salts and their solutions; use of litmus and pH paper to test for acidity and alkalinity.

- *Examples with equation for the ionisation/dissociation of ions of acids, bases and salts.*
- *Acids form hydronium ions (only positive ions) which turn blue litmus red, alkalis form hydroxyl ions (only negative ions) with water which turns red litmus blue.*

- *Salts are formed by partial or complete replacement of the hydrogen ion of an acid by a metal. (To be explained with suitable examples).*
- *Introduction to pH Scale to test for acidity, neutrality and alkalinity by using pH paper or Universal indicator.*

(iii) Definition of salt; types of salts.
Types of salts: normal salts, acid salt, basic salt, definition and examples.

(iv) Action of dilute acids on salts.
Decomposition of hydrogen carbonates, carbonates, sulphites and sulphides by appropriate acids with heating if necessary. (Relevant laboratory work must be done.)

(v) Methods of preparation of Normal salts with **relevant equations.** (Details of apparatus or procedures not required.
Methods included are:
- *Direct combination*
- *Displacement*
- *Precipitation (double decomposition)*
- *Neutralisation of insoluble base*
- *Neutralisation of an alkali (titration)*
- *Action of dilute acids on carbonates and bi-carbonates.*

4. ANALYTICAL CHEMISTRY

(i) Action of Ammonium Hydroxide and Sodium Hydroxide on solution of salts: colour of salt and its solution; formation and colour of hydroxide precipitated for solutions of salts of Ca, Fe, Cu, Zn and Pb; special action of ammonium hydroxide on solutions of copper salt & sodium hydroxide on ammonium salts.
On solution of salts:
- *Colour of salt and its solution.*
- *Action on addition of Sodium Hydroxide to solution of Ca, Fe, Cu, Zn and Pb salts drop by drop in excess. Formation and colour of hydroxide precipitated to be highlighted with the help of equations.*
- *Action on addition of Ammonium Hydroxide to solution of Ca, Fe, Cu, Zn and Pb salts drop by drop in excess. Formation and colour of hydroxide precipitated to be highlighted with the help of equations.*
- *Special action of Ammonium Hydroxide on solutions of copper salts and sodium hydroxide on ammonium salts.*

(ii) Action of alkalies (NaOH, KOH) on certain metals, their oxides and hydroxides.
The metals must include aluminium, zinc and lead, their oxides and hydroxides, which react with caustic alkalies (NaOH, KOH), showing the amphoteric nature of these substances.

5. MOLE CONCEPT AND STOICHIOMETRY

(i) Gay Lussac's Law of Combining Volumes; Avogadro's Law.
- *Idea of mole – a number just as a dozen, a gross (Avogadro's number).*
- *Avogadro's Law statement and explanation.*
- *Gay Lussac's Law of Combining Volumes– Statement and explanation.*
- *Understanding molar volume- "the mass of 22.4 litres of any gas at S.T.P. is equal to its molar mass". (Questions will not be set on formal proof but may be taught for clear understanding).*
- *Simple calculations based on the molar volume and Gay Lussac 's law.*

(ii) Refer to the atomicity of hydrogen, oxygen, nitrogen and chlorine (proof not required).
The explanation can be given using equations for the formation of HCl, NH_3 and NO.

(iii) Vapour Density and its relation to relative molecular mass:
- *Molecular mass = 2× vapour density (formal proof not required)*
- *Deduction of simple (empirical) and molecular formula from:*
  - *(a) the percentage composition of a compound.*
  - *(b) the masses of combining elements.*

(iv) Mole and its relation to mass.
- *Relating mole and atomic mass; arriving at gram atomic mass and then gram atom; atomic mass is a number dealing with one atom; gram atomic mass is the mass of one mole of atoms.*
- *Relating mole and molecular mass arriving at gram molecular mass and gram molecule– molecular mass is a number dealing with a molecule, gram molecular mass is the mass of one mole of molecules.*
- *Simple calculations based on relation of mole to mass, volume and Avogadro's number.*

(v) Simple calculations based on chemical equations

Related to weight and/or volumes of both reactants and products.

6. ELECTROLYSIS

(i) Electrolytes and non-electrolytes.
Definitions and examples.

(ii) Substances containing molecules only, ions only, both molecules and ions.

- *Substances containing molecules only ions only, both molecules and ions.*
- *Examples; relating their composition with their behaviour* ***as strong and weak electrolytes as well as non-electrolytes.***

(iii) Definition and explanation of electrolysis, electrolyte, electrode, anode, cathode, anion, cation, oxidation and reduction (on the basis of loss and gain of electrons).

(iv) An elementary study of the migration of ions, with reference to the factors influencing selective discharge of ions (reference should be made to the activity series as indicating the tendency of metals, e.g. (Na, Mg, Fe, Cu) to form ions) illustrated by the electrolysis of:

- *Molten lead bromide*
- *Acidified water with platinum electrodes*
- *Aqueous copper (II) sulphate with copper electrodes; electron transfer at the electrodes.*

The above electrolytic processes can be studied in terms of electrolyte used, electrodes used, ionization reaction, anode reaction, cathode reaction, use of selective discharge theory, wherever applicable.

(v) Applications of electrolysis:

- *Electroplating with nickel and silver, choice of electrolyte for electroplating.*
- *Electro refining of copper;*

Reasons and conditions for electroplating, names of the electrolytes and the electrodes used should be given. Equations for the reactions at the electrodes should be given for electroplating, refining of copper.

7. METALLURGY

(i) Occurrence of metals in nature:

- *Mineral and ore - Meaning only.*
- *Common ores of iron, aluminium and zinc.*

(ii) Stages involved in the extraction of metals:

(a) Dressing of the ore – hydrolytic method, magnetic separation, froth flotation method.

(b) Conversion of concentrated ore to its oxide– roasting and calcination (definition, examples with equations).

(c) Reduction of metallic oxides–some can be reduced by hydrogen, carbon and carbon monoxide (e.g. copper oxide, lead (II) oxide, iron (III) oxide and zinc oxide) and some cannot (e.g. Al_2O_3, MgO)– refer to activity series). Active metals by electrolysis e.g. sodium, potassium and calcium. (reference only).

Equations with conditions should be given.

(d) Electrorefining – reference only

(iii) Extraction of Aluminium.

(a) Chemical method for purifying bauxite by using NaOH - Baeyer's Process.

(b) Electrolytic extraction - Hall Heroult's process: Structure of electrolytic cell - the various components as part of the electrolyte, electrodes and electrode reactions.

Description of the changes occurring, purpose of the substances used and the main reactions with their equations.

(iv) Alloys – composition and uses
Stainless steel, duralumin, brass, bronze, fuse metal/solder.

8. STUDY OF COMPOUNDS

(i) **Hydrogen Chloride**

Hydrogen chloride: preparation of hydrogen chloride from sodium chloride; refer to the density and solubility of hydrogen chloride (fountain experiment); reaction with ammonia; acidic properties of its solution.

- *Preparation of hydrogen chloride from sodium chloride; the laboratory method of preparation can be learnt in terms of reactants, product, condition, equation, diagram or setting of the apparatus, procedure, observation, precaution, collection of the gas and identification.*
- *Simple experiment to show the density of the gas (Hydrogen Chloride) -heavier than air.*
- *Solubility of hydrogen chloride (fountain experiment); setting of the apparatus, procedure, observation, inference.*

- *Method of preparation of hydrochloric acid by dissolving the gas in water– the special arrangement and the mechanism by which the back suction is avoided should be learnt.*
- *Reaction with ammonia*
- *Acidic properties of its solution – reaction with metals, their oxides, hydroxides and carbonates to give their chlorides; decomposition of carbonates, hydrogen carbonates, sulphides, sulphites.*
- *Precipitation reactions with silver nitrate solution and lead nitrate solution.*

(ii) **Ammonia**

Ammonia: its laboratory preparation from ammonium chloride and collection; ammonia from nitrides like Mg_3N_2 and AlN and ammonium salts. Manufacture by Haber's Process; density and solubility of ammonia (fountain experiment); aqueous solution of ammonia; its reactions with hydrogen chloride and with hot copper (II) oxide and chlorine; the burning of – ammonia in oxygen; uses of ammonia.

- *Laboratory preparation from ammonium chloride and collection; (the preparation to be studied in terms of, setting of the apparatus and diagram, procedure, observation, collection and identification).*
- *Ammonia from nitrides like Mg_3N_2 and AlN using warm water.*

  Ammonia from ammonium salts using alkalies.

The reactions to be studied in terms of reactants, products, conditions and equations.

- *Manufacture by Haber's Process.*
- *Density and solubility of ammonia (fountain experiment).*
- *The burning of ammonia in oxygen.*
- *The catalytic oxidation of ammonia (with conditions and reaction).*
- *Its reactions with hydrogen chloride and with hot copper (II) oxide and chlorine (both chlorine in excess and ammonia in excess).*

All these reactions may be studied in terms of reactants, products, conditions, equations and observations.

- *Aqueous solution of ammonia – reaction with sulphuric acid, nitric acid, hydrochloric acid and solutions of iron(III) chloride, iron(II) sulphate, lead nitrate, zinc nitrate and copper sulphate.*
- *Uses of ammonia – manufacture of fertilisers, explosives, nitric acid, refrigerant gas (Chlorofluro carbon and its suitable alternatives which are non-ozone depleting) and cleansing* agents.

(iii) **Nitric Acid**

Nitric Acid: one laboratory method of preparation of nitric acid from potassium nitrate or sodium nitrate. Large scale preparation. Nitric acid as an oxidising agent.

- *Laboratory preparation of nitric acid from potassium nitrate or sodium nitrate; the laboratory method to be studied in terms of reactants, products, conditions, equations, setting up of apparatus, diagram, precautions, collection and identification.*
- *Manufacture of Nitric acid by Ostwald's process (Only equations with conditions where applicable).*
- *As an oxidising agent: its reaction with copper, carbon, sulphur.*

(iv) **Sulphuric Acid**

Large scale preparation, its behaviour as an acid when dilute, as an oxidising agent when concentrated – oxidation of carbon and sulphur; as a dehydrating agent – dehydration of sugar and copper (II) sulphate crystals; its non-volatile nature.

- *Manufacture by Contact process Equations with Conditions where applicable).*
- *Its behaviour as an acid when dilute – reaction with metal, metal oxide, metal hydroxide, metal carbonate, metal bicarbonate, metal sulphite, metal sulphide.*
- *Concentrated sulphuric acid as an oxidizing agent – the oxidation of carbon and sulphur.*
- *Concentrated sulphuric acid as a dehydrating agent– (a) the dehydration of sugar (b) Copper (II) sulphate crystals.*
- *Non-volatile nature of sulphuric acid reaction with sodium or potassium chloride and sodium or potassium nitrate.*

9. ORGANIC CHEMISTRY

(i) **Introduction to Organic compounds.**

- *Unique nature of Carbon atom - tetra-valency, catenation.*
- *Formation of single, double and triple bonds, straight chain, branched chain, cyclic compounds (only benzene).*

(ii) **Structure and Isomerism**

- *Structure of compounds with single, double and triple bonds.*
- *Structural formulae of hydrocarbons. Structural formula must be given for: alkanes, alkenes, alkynes up to 5 carbon atoms.*
- *Isomerism – structural (chain, position).*

(iii) **Homologous series** – characteristics with examples.

Alkane, alkene, alkyne series and their gradation in properties and the relationship with the molecular mass or molecular formula.

(iv) **Simple nomenclature**

Simple nomenclature – of the hydrocarbons with simple functional groups – (double bond, triple bond, alcoholic, aldehydic, carboxylic group) longest chain rule and smallest number for functional groups rule – trivial and IUPAC names (compounds with only one functional group).

(v) **Hydrocarbons** alkanes, alkenes, alkynes.

- *Alkanes – general formula; methane (greenhouse gas) and ethane – methods of preparation from sodium ethanoate (sodium acetate), sodium propanoate (sodium propionate), from iodomethane (methyl iodide) and bromoethane (ethyl bromide). Complete combustion of methane and ethane, reaction of methane and ethane with chlorine through substitution.*
- *Alkenes – (unsaturated hydrocarbons with a double bond); ethene as an example. Methods of preparation of ethene by dehydro halogenation reaction and dehydration reactions.*
- *Alkynes – unsaturated hydrocarbons with a triple bond); ethyne as an example of alkyne; Methods of preparation from calcium carbide and 1,2 dibromoethane ethylene dibromide).*

Only main properties, particularly addition products with hydrogen and halogen namely , Cl_2, Br_2 and I_2 pertaining to alkenes and alkynes.

- *Uses of methane, ethane, ethene, ethyne.*

(vi) Alcohols: ethanol – preparation, properties and uses.

- *Preparation of ethanol by hydrolysis of alkyl halide.*
- *Properties - Physical: Nature, Solubility, Density, Boiling Points. Chemical: Combustion, action with sodium, ester formation with acetic acid, dehydration with conc. Sulphuric acid to prepare ethene.*
- *Denatured and spurious alcohol.*
- *Important uses of Ethanol.*

(vii) Carboxylic acids (aliphatic–monocarboxylic acid): Acetic acid – properties and uses of acetic acid.

- *Structure of acetic acid.*
- *Properties of Acetic Acid: Physical properties – odour (vinegar), glacial acetic acid (effect of sufficient cooling to produce ice like crystals). Chemical properties – action with litmus, alkalis and alcohol (idea of esterification).*
- *Uses of acetic acid.*

INTERNAL ASSESSMENT OF PRACTICAL WORK

Candidates will be asked to observe the effect of reagents and/or of heat on substances supplied to them. The exercises will be simple and may include the recognition and identification of certain gases and ions listed below. The examiners will not, however, be restricted in their choice to substances containing the listed ions.

Gases: Hydrogen, Oxygen, Carbon dioxide, Chlorine, Hydrogen chloride, Sulphur dioxide, Hydrogen sulphide, Ammonia, Water vapour, Nitrogen dioxide.

Ions: Calcium, Copper, Iron, Lead, Zinc and Ammonium, Carbonate, Chloride, Nitrate, Sulphide, Sulphite and Sulphate.

Knowledge of a formal scheme of analysis is not required. Semi-micro techniques are acceptable but candidates using such techniques may need to adapt the instructions given to suit the size of the apparatus being used.

Candidates are expected to have completed the following minimum practical work:

1. Action of heat on the following substances:
   (a) Copper carbonate, zinc carbonate
   (b) zinc nitrate, copper nitrate, lead nitrate
   Make observations, identify the products and make deductions where possible. (equations not required)
2. Make a solution of the unknown substance: add sodium hydroxide solution or ammonium hydroxide solution, make observations and give your deduction. Warming the mixture may be needed. Choose from substances containing Ca^{2+}, Cu^{2+}, Fe^{2+}, Fe^{3+}, Pb^{2+}, Zn^{2+}, NH^{4+}.
3. Supply a solution of a dilute acid and alkali. Determine which is acidic and which is basic, giving two tests for each.
4. Add concentrated hydrochloric acid to each of the given substances, warm, make observations, identify any product and make deductions:
   (a) Copper oxide
   (b) Manganese dioxide.

List of Important Topics

On the basis of analysis of last 8 Years' Board Examination Papers we have identified Important Topics from each chapter.

Chapter 1: Periodic Properties and their Variations

- Periodic Properties and their Variations in Groups and Periods
  (Average Marks is last 8 years ; 2025 - 8 Marks, 2024 - 5 Marks, 2023 - 8 Marks, 2020 - 3 Marks, 2019 - 5 Marks, 2018 - 5 Marks)
- Periodicity
  (Average Marks in last 8 years ; 2025 - 6 Marks, 2024 - 3 Marks, 2020 -1 Mark, 2019 - 1 Mark, 2018 - 1 Mark)

Chapter 2: Chemical Bonding

- Electrovalent Bonding
  (Average Marks in last 8 years ; 2025 - 1 Mark, 2024 - 3 Marks, 2023 - 1 Mark, 2020 - 2 Marks, 2019 - 1 Mark, 2018 -2 Marks)
- Covalent Bonding
  (Average Marks in last 8 years ; 2025 - 3 Marks, 2024 - 7 Marks, 2023 - 3 Marks, 2020 - 4 Marks, 2019 - 4 Marks)
- Coordinate Bonding
  (Average Marks in last 8 years ; 2025 - 2 Marks, 2023 - 1 Mark, 2018 - 3 Marks)

Chapter 3: Acids, Bases and Salts

- Acids and Bases
  (Average Marks in last 8 years ; 2024 - 5 Marks, 2023 - 2 Marks, 2020 - 6 Marks, 2019 - 4 Marks, 2018 - 3 Marks)
- Salts
  (Average Marks in last 8 years ; 2025 - 5 Marks, 2024 - 5 Marks, 2023 - 2 Marks, 2020 - 3 Marks, 2019 - 4 Marks, 2018 - 5 Marks)

Chapter 4: Analytical Chemistry

(Average Marks in last 8 years ; 2025 - 4 Marks, 2024 - 7 Marks, 2023 - 5 Marks, 2020 - 3 Marks, 2019 - 7 Marks, 2018 - 7 Marks)

Chapter 5: Mole concept and Stoichiometry

- Number of Molecules /Moles
  (Average Marks in last 8 years ; 2024 - 3 Marks, 2023 - 1 Mark, 2020 - 2 Marks, 2019 - 2 Marks)
- Vapour Density
  (Average Marks in last 8 years ; 2025 - 3 Marks, 2023 - 2 Marks)
- Percentage Composition
  (Average Marks in last 8 years ; 2023 - 5 Marks, 2020 - 3 Marks, 2018- 2 Marks)
- Empirical and Molecular Formula
  (Average Marks in last 8 years ; 2025 - 4 Marks, 2024 - 2 Marks, 2019 - 6 Marks)
- Stoichiometric Calculations
  (Average Marks in last 8 years ; 2025 - 5 Marks, 2024 - 6 Marks)

Chapter 6: Electrolysis

- Electrolytes and Non-electrolytes
  (Average Marks in last 8 years ; 2025 - 7 Marks, 2024 - 5 Marks, 2023 - 3 Marks, 2020 - 7 Marks, 2019 - 6 Marks, 2018 -11 Marks)
- Application of Electrolysis
  (Average Marks in last 8 years ; 2025 - 1 Mark, ; 2024 - 5 Marks, 2023 - 4 Marks, 2020 - 6 Marks)

Latest
Course Structure

Chapter 7: Metallurgy

- Extraction of Metals
  (Average Marks in last 8 years ; 2025 - 5 Marks, ; 2024 - 6 Marks, 2023 - 6 Marks, 2020 - 3 Marks, 2019 - 6 Marks , 2018 - 5 Marks)
- Alloys and Use of Metals
  (Average Marks in last 8 years ; 2024 - 3 Marks, 2023- 4 Marks, 2020 - 2 Marks, 2019 - 5 Marks , 2018 - 2 Marks)

Chapter 8: Study of Compounds

- Hydrogen Chloride
  (Average Marks in last 8 years ; 2025 - 6 Marks, 2024 - 5 Marks, 2023 -5 Marks, 2020 - 8 Marks, 2019 - 2 Marks , 2018 - 7 Marks)
- Ammonia
  (Average Marks in last 8 years ; 2025 - 10 Marks, ; 2024 - 4 Marks, 2023 - 9 Marks, 2020 -3 Marks, 2019 - 9 Marks , 2018 - 8 Marks)
- Nitric Acid
  (Average Marks in last 8 years ; 2025 - 6 Marks, ; 2024 - 1 Mark, 2023 - 3 Marks, 2020 - 3 Marks, 2019 - 4 Marks , 2018 -4 Marks)
- Sulphuric Acid
  (Average Marks in last 8 years ; 2025 - 8 Marks, ; 2024 - 6 Marks, 2023 4 Marks, 2020 2 Marks, 2019 - 4 Marks , 2018 - 3 Marks)

Chapter 9: Organic Chemistry

- Organic Compounds
  (Average Marks in last 8 years ; 2025 - 2 Marks, ; 2023 - 6 Marks, 2020 - 2 Marks, 2019 - 1 Mark , 2018 - 9 Marks)
- Nomenclature of Organic Compounds
  (Average Marks in last 8 years ; 2025 - 5 Marks, ; 2024 - 6 Marks, 2023 - 2 Marks, 2020 - 5 Marks, 2018 -3 Marks, 2019 - 2 Marks)
- Hydrocarbons - Alkanes, Alkenes and Alkynes
  (Average Marks in last 8 years ; 2025 - 4 Marks, ; 2024 - 7 Marks, 2023 - 6 Marks, 2020 - 6 Marks, 2019 - 12 Marks)
- Alcohols and Carboxylic Acids
  (Average Marks in last 8 years ; 2025 - 4 Marks, ; 2024 - 3 Marks)

01

PERIODIC PROPERTIES AND THEIR VARIATIONS

Modern Periodic Law and Periodic Table

Modern Periodic Law states that "physical and chemical properties of the elements are a periodic function of their atomic number". When the elements were arranged in the increasing order of their atomic number, the obtained table is called **Modern Periodic Table.**

Some salient features of modern periodic table are given below.

Groups

- The modern periodic table consists of eighteen vertical columns, called **groups**.
- Each group accommodates elements with the same number of electrons in the outermost shell (**valence electrons**).
- These columns are arranged from left to right in the order:
  IA, IIA, IIIB, IVB, VB, VIB, VIIB, VIII (3 columns), IB, IIB, IIIA, IVA, VA, VIA, VIIA and zero.
- Group 1 elements are called **alkali metals** (except hydrogen). They form strong alkalies with water.
- Group 2 elements are called **alkaline earth metals**. They form weaker alkalies as compared to group 1 and their oxides are sparingly soluble in water.
- The elements of groups 3, 4, 5, 6, 7, 8, 9, 10, 11 and 12 are known as **transition elements**. They have incomplete outermost shells.
- Group 13 elements are known as **boron family**.
- Group 14 elements are known as **carbon family**.
- Group 15 elements are known as **nitrogen family**.
- Group 16 elements are known as **oxygen family** or **chalcogen family** (chalcogen = ore forming).
- Group 17 elements are known as **halogen family**. They form salts.
- Group 18 (zero group) elements are called **noble gases** or **inert gases**. They have stable electronic configuration, due to which, they hardly react with other elements.
- The elements of groups 1, 2, 13, 14, 15, 16 and 17 are known as **main group elements** or **representative elements** or **normal elements**.

Periods

There are seven horizontal rows in the modern periodic table, called **periods**.

The number of shells present in an atom determine its period.

- First period is the shortest period containing only **two elements**, i.e. hydrogen (H) and helium (He).
- Second period is a short period containing **eight elements** (Li, Be, B, C, N, O, F and Ne).
- Third period is also a short period containing **eight elements** (Na, Mg, Al, Si, P, S, Cl and Ar).
- Fourth and fifth periods are long periods, each one containing **eighteen elements** (atomic numbers 19-36 in the fourth period and atomic numbers 37-54 in the fifth period).
- Sixth and seventh periods are longest period, containing **32 elements** each (atomic number 55-86 and 87-118 respectively).

- In group 3 and period 6, the elements of atomic numbers 57-71 are present which are called **lanthanides** (rare earth metals).
- In group 3 and period 7, the elements of atomic numbers 89-103 are present which are called **actinides** (radioactive elements).
- As lanthanides and actinides are large in number, thus they are shown at the bottom of the periodic table. If they are shown in the main body of the table, its shape will be distorted.
- All elements after atomic number 92 (Uranium) are man-made, hence they are called **artificial elements** or **transuranic elements**.

Long or Extended form of Modern Periodic Table

Metals | Metalloids | Non-metals

The *zig-zag* line separates the metals from the non-metals.

s-block elements (groups 1–2) · Transition elements or *d*-block elements (groups 3–12) · *p*-block elements (groups 13–18)

PERIODS	1	2	3	4	5	6	7	8	9	10	11	12	13	14	15	16	17	18
1	1 H Hydrogen																	2 He Helium
2	3 Li Lithium	4 Be Beryllium											5 B Boron	6 C Carbon	7 N Nitrogen	8 O Oxygen	9 F Fluorine	10 Ne Neon
3	11 Na Sodium	12 Mg Magnesium											13 Al Aluminium	14 Si Silicon	15 P Phosphorus	16 S Sulphur	17 Cl Chlorine	18 Ar Argon
4	19 K Potassium	20 Ca Calcium	21 Sc Scandium	22 Ti Titanium	23 V Vanadium	24 Cr Chromium	25 Mn Manganese	26 Fe Iron	27 Co Cobalt	28 Ni Nickel	29 Cu Copper	30 Zn Zinc	31 Ga Gallium	32 Ge Germanium	33 As Arsenic	34 Se Selenium	35 Br Bromine	36 Kr Krypton
5	37 Rb Rubidium	38 Sr Strontium	39 Y Yttrium	40 Zr Zirconium	41 Nb Niobium	42 Mo Molybdenum	43 Tc Technetium	44 Ru Ruthenium	45 Rh Rhodium	46 Pd Palladium	47 Ag Silver	48 Cd Cadmium	49 In Indium	50 Sn Tin	51 Sb Antimony	52 Te Tellurium	53 I Iodine	54 Xe Xenon
6	55 Cs Caesium	56 Ba Barium	57 La* Lanthanum	72 Hf Hafnium	73 Ta Tantalum	74 W Tungsten	75 Re Rhenium	76 Os Osmium	77 Ir Iridium	78 Pt Platinum	79 Au Gold	80 Hg Mercury	81 Tl Thallium	82 Pb Lead	83 Bi Bismuth	84 Po Polonium	85 At Astatine	86 Rn Radon
7	87 Fr Francium	88 Ra Radium	89 Ac** Actinium	104 Rf Rutherfordium	105 Db Dubnium	106 Sg Seaborgium	107 Bh Bohrium	108 Hs Hassium	109 Mt Meitnerium	110 Ds Darmstadtium	111 Rg Roentgenium	112 Cn Copernicium	113 Nh Nihonium	114 Fl Flerovium	115 Mc Moscovium	116 Lv Livermorium	117 Ts Tennessine	118 Og Oganesson

Inner-transition elements or *f*-block elements

*Lanthanides	58 Ce Cerium	59 Pr Praseodymium	60 Nd Neodymium	61 Pm Promethium	62 Sm Samarium	63 Eu Europium	64 Gd Gadolinium	65 Tb Terbium	66 Dy Dysprosium	67 Ho Holmium	68 Er Erbium	69 Tm Thulium	70 Yb Ytterbium	71 Lu Lutetium
*Actinides	90 Th Thorium	91 Pa Protactinium	92 U Uranium	93 Np Neptunium	94 Pu Plutonium	95 Am Americium	96 Cm Curium	97 Bk Berkelium	98 Cf Californium	99 Es Einsteinium	100 Fm Fermium	101 Md Mendelevium	102 No Nobelium	103 Lr Lawrencium

Periodicity

The properties which reappear at regular intervals, or in which there is a gradual variation at regular intervals are called **periodic properties** and the phenomenon is known as **periodicity of elements**.

Variation in Periodic Properties in Periodic Table

Periodic Properties		Depending Factors		Variation in a Group	Variation in a Period
Name	Definition	Number of Shells/Atomic Size	Nuclear Charge		
Atomic Size	It is defined as the distance between the centre of the nucleus and the outermost shell of an isolated gaseous atom.	With increase in the number of shells, the atomic size increases.	With increase in nuclear charge, the size of the atom decreases.	Increases as we move down the group.	Decreases as we move along the period from left to right.
Metallic Character	The tendency of the elements to lose electrons is called metallic character.	Larger the atomic size, lesser is the nuclear pull exerted on electrons. As a result, the electrons can be removed more easily. Thus, making the elements more metallic.	Greater nuclear charge causes the valence electron to be tightly bound. Hence, the electrons cannot be released easily. Thus, metallic nature decreases.	Increases as we move down the group.	Decreases as we move along the period from left to right.
Non-metallic Character	The tendency of the elements to gain electrons, in order to attain octet in their outermost orbit, is considered as non-metallic character.	Smaller the atomic size, greater is the nuclear pull which increases the tendency to gain electron(s). This makes the element more non-metallic in nature.	Greater the nuclear charge, greater is the tendency to gain electron(s). Hence, the element becomes more non-metallic.	Decreases as we move down the group.	Increases as we move along the period from left to right.
Ionisation Potential	This is the energy required to remove an electron from the outermost shell of an atom in its isolated gaseous state and to convert it into a positively charged gaseous ion.	Greater the atomic size, lesser is the force of attraction between the electron(s) of the outermost shell and the nucleus. Thus, the ionisation energy required will be less.	Greater is the nuclear charge, greater is the attraction between the nucleus and the outermost electron(s). Thus, greater energy is required to remove the electron(s).	Decreases as we move down the group.	Increases as we move along the period from left to right.
Electron Affinity	The amount of energy released by the addition of an electron to the outermost shell of an atom in its isolated gaseous state is called electron affinity.	Smaller the atomic size, greater the electron affinity.	Greater the nuclear charge, greater will be the electron affinity.	Decreases as we move down the group.	Increases as we move along the period from left to right.
Electro-negativity	It is the tendency of an atom in a molecule to attract the shared pair of electrons toward itself.	As the atomic size increases, the electronegativity decreases.	As nuclear charge increases, electronegativity of an element also increases.	Decreases as we move down the group.	Increases as we move along the period from left to right.

Summary of the Trends in Periodic Properties in the Periodic Table

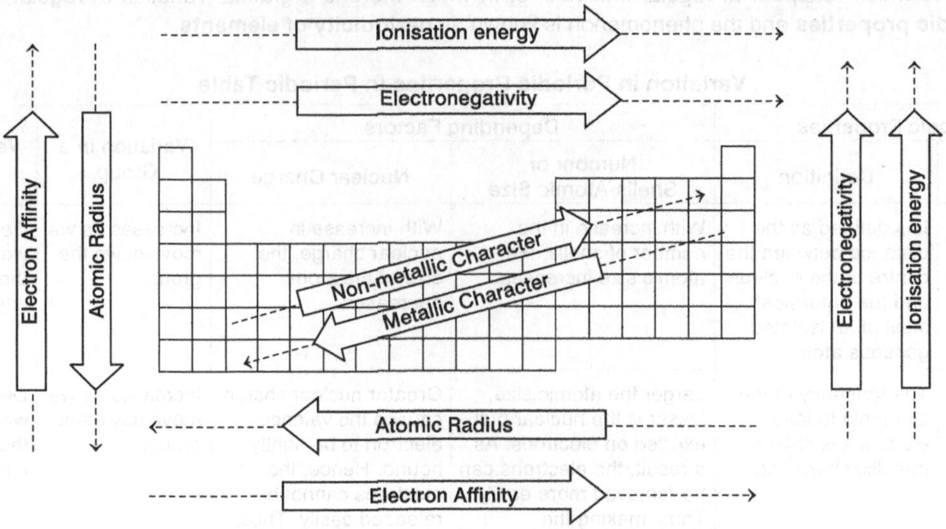

Variation in Periodic Properties of Alkali Metals and Halogens

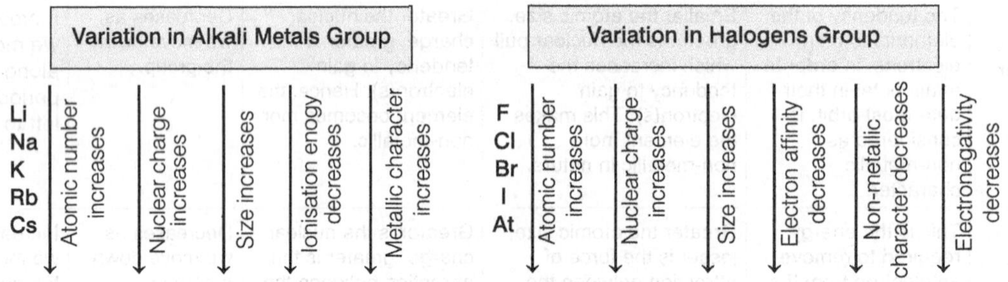

Note Chlorine has more electron affinity than fluorine because in case of fluorine, electron feels lesser attraction as compared to chlorine due to the smaller size and electron-electron repulsion in fluorine.

REVISION NOTES

EXAM ORIENTED QUESTIONS

TYPE - 1 01 Mark

Multiple Choice Questions

Q.1 Given below are four ions: Cl^-, Li^+, Al^{3+}, K^+

Identify the pair of ions which have the same electronic configuration.

[Atomic number: Cl = 17, Li = 3, Al = 13, K = 19] **(ICSE 2025)**

(a) Cl^- and Li^+ (b) Al^{3+} and K^+
(c) Cl^- and K^+ (d) Li^+ and K^+

Ans. (c) **Cl^- and K^+** have the same electronic configuration.

Electronic configuration of Cl = 2, 8, 8

Electronic configuration of Li^+ = 2

Electronic configuration of Al^{3+} = 2, 8

Electronic configuration of K^+ = 2, 8, 8

Q.2 An alkali metal found in period 3 and group 1 is

(a) magnesium (b) lithium **(ICSE Specimen 2023)**
(c) sodium (d) potassium

Ans. (c) **Sodium** is an alkali metal found in period 3 and group 1.

Q.3 On the basis of electronic configuration the period and group of B^9_5 is **(ICSE Specimen 2021-22, Sem-I)**

(a) 2 and IIIA (b) 3 and IIA
(c) 4 and VIA (d) 5 and VIIA

Ans. (a) Electronic configuration of B^9_5 is $1s^2 2s^2 2p^1$

Period no.= 2 Group = IIIA

Q.4 $A \rightarrow A^{+3}; B \rightarrow B^{-1}$

Number of electrons present in the outermost shell of atoms *A* and *B* respectively are **(ICSE Specimen 2024)**

(a) 5, 1 (b) 3, 1
(c) 3, 7 (d) 5, 7

Ans. (c) $\underset{(2,\,8,\,3)}{A} \longrightarrow \underset{(2,\,8)}{A^{+3}};\ \underset{(2,\,7)}{B} \longrightarrow \underset{(2,\,8)}{B^{-1}}$

So, number of electrons present in the outermost shells of *A* and *B* are **3 and 7** respectively.

Q.5 An element belongs to third period and sixteenth group. It will have .... electrons in its valence shell. **(ICSE Specimen 2024)**

(a) 2 (b) 5 (c) 6 (d) 3

Ans. (c) As an element belongs to group 16, the electronic configuration will be 2, 8, 6. It has **6 electrons** in its valence shell.

Q.6 If an element *A* belongs to period 3 and group-II then it will have **(ICSE 2014)**

(a) 3 shells and 2 valence electrons.
(b) 2 shells and 3 valence electrons.
(c) 3 shells and 3 valence electrons.
(d) 2 shells and 2 valence electrons.

Ans. (a) Period number = number of shells and group number = valence electrons. Thus, *A* has **3 shells** and **2 valence electrons**.

Q.7 The number of electrons present in the valence shell of a halogen is

(a) 1 (b) 3
(c) 5 (d) 7

Ans. (d) Group 17 is called halogen family, so group 17 has **7 electrons** in the valence shell.

Q.8 $_1H^2$ is an isotope of hydrogen. In the modern periodic table it will **(ICSE Specimen 2025)**

(a) be placed before hydrogen
(b) be placed after hydrogen
(c) be placed at the same position as hydrogen
(d) not have any position in the Periodic Table

Ans. (c) Isotopes of the same element have the same atomic number, thus they are placed at the same position as the element in the periodic table.

Q.9 Elements with similar valence shell configuration in a periodic table are placed in

(a) different groups **(ICSE Specimen 2021-22, Sem-I)**
(b) same period
(c) different period
(d) same group

Ans. (d) Elements with similar valence shell configuration in a periodic table are placed in **same group**.

Q.10 Alkaline earth metals have the same **(ICSE 2021-22, Sem-I)**

(a) number of valence electrons
(b) number of shells
(c) metallic property
(d) ionisation potential

Ans. (a) Alkaline earth metals have the same number of valence electrons.

Q.11 Which graph shows the number of electrons in the outer shell of an atom, plotted against the proton (atomic) number for the first ten elements in the periodic table?

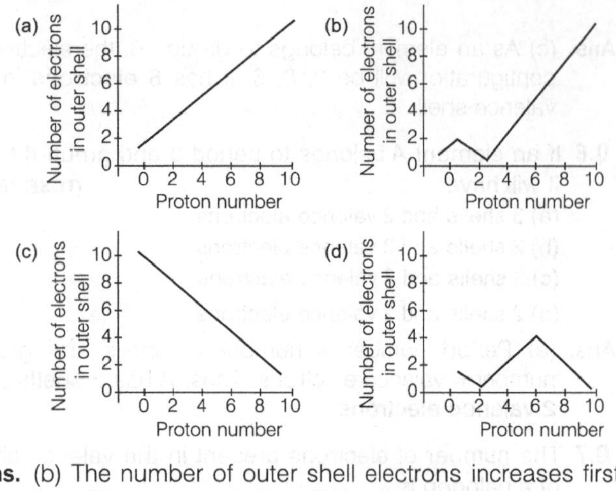

Ans. (b) The number of outer shell electrons increases first from hydrogen to helium then decreases to 1 in case of lithium and then increases regularly by one.

Q.12 Elements with the code letters *Q* and *R* occupy the positions shown in the outline of the periodic table.

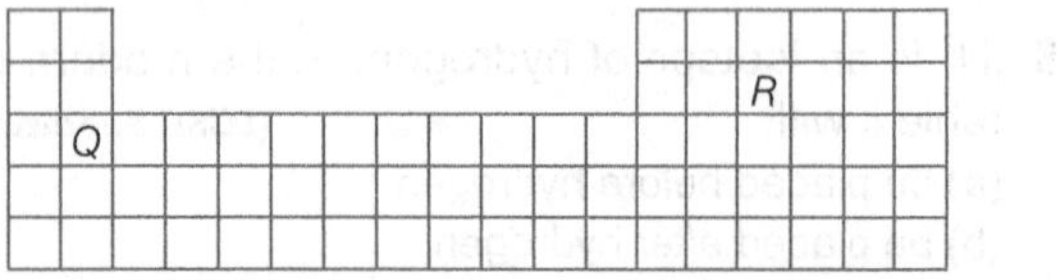

What is the formula of the compound formed between them?

(a) QR_2 (b) Q_2R (c) Q_2R_3 (d) Q_3R_2

Ans. (d) *Q* belongs to group II, so its valency is +2. *R* belongs to group 15 or VA, so its valency is –3 (as it requires 3 electrons to complete its octet). Thus, the formula of the compound formed between *Q* and *R* is Q_3R_2.

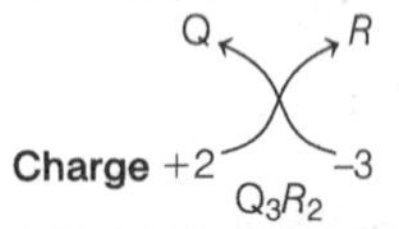

Q.13 The positions of four elements are shown on the outline of part of the periodic table.

Element *X* has a high melting point and is a good conductor of electricity.

It forms chlorides XCl_2 and XCl_3. Which element is *X*?

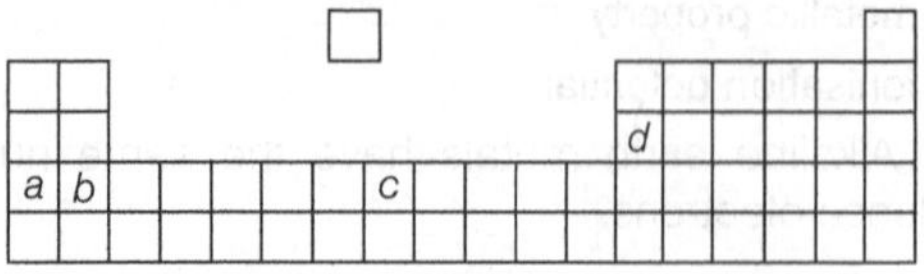

(a) *a* (b) *b* (c) *c* (d) *d*

Ans. (c) Element *X* is a **transition metal** that has variable valency. e.g. $FeCl_2$ and $FeCl_3$.

Q.14 Element '*P*' has electronic configuration 2, 8, 8, 1. The number of chlorine atoms present in the chloride of '*P*' is: **(ICSE Specimen 2025)**

(a) 2 (b) 1
(c) 3 (d) 4

Ans. (b) The valency of element '*P*' is 1 (or it can lose one electron to form P^+). So, it can combine with **one** Cl^- to form *PCl*.

Q.15 An element with largest atomic radius among the following is **(ICSE 2023)**

(a) carbon
(b) nitrogen
(c) lithium
(d) beryllium

Ans. (c) **Lithium** has the largest atomic radius among all the given options.

Q.16

Group Numbers	IA 1	IIA 2	IIIA 13	IVA 14	VA 15	VIA 16	VIIA 17	VIIIA 18
	Li		D			O	J	Ne
	A	Mg	E	Si		H	K	
	B	C		F	G			L

With reference to the portion of the periodic table given above, identify the element having the largest atomic size. **(Competency Based Que.)**

(a) Li (b) B
(c) K (d) L

Ans. (b) B has the largest atomic size as atomic size increases down the group and decreases across a period.

Q.17 The trend in metallic nature of metals as we go from top to bottom in a group **(ICSE Specimen 2021-22, Sem-I)**

(a) increases
(b) decreases
(c) neither increases nor decreases
(d) None of the above

Ans. (a) Metallic character **increases** down a group due to increase in atomic size and nuclear charge.

Q.18 The property which decreases from left to right across the periodic table **(ICSE Specimen 2021-22, Sem-I)**

(a) electron affinity
(b) electronegativity
(c) ionisation energy
(d) metallic character

Ans. (d) **Metallic character** decreases from left to right across the periodic table.

Q.19 *X*, *Y* and *Z* are three metallic atoms in successive order belonging to the same group such that atomic radii of '*X*' is the smallest. Which of the three atoms is the best reducing agent? **(ICSE 2025)**

(a) *X* (b) *Y*
(c) *Z*
(d) All three have the same reducing power

Ans. (c) A metal with larger atomic radii and lower ionisation energy will readily lose electrons, and act as a stronger reducing agent. Among the three metals, Z has largest atomic radii (as atomic radii increases down the group) and it has lowest ionisation energy. Thus, **atom Z** will be the strongest reducing agent.

Q.20 The non-metallic properties of elements from left to right in a periodic table **(ICSE 2021-22, Sem-I)**

(a) increases
(b) decreases
(c) remains same
(d) first increases and then decreases

Ans. (a) Non-metallic character **increases** from left to right in a periodic table due to decrease in atomic size and increase in nuclear charge.

Q.21 Which of the following properties do not match with elements of the halogen family?

(a) They have seven electrons in their valence shell.
(b) They are highly reactive chemically.
(c) They are metallic in nature.
(d) They are diatomic in their molecular form.

Ans. (c) The elements of the halogens family have 7 electrons in their valence shell and thus, they are chemically reactive. They are **non-metals** and diatomic in their molecular form.

Q.22 The basic oxide which is an alkali? **(ICSE Specimen 2021-22, Sem-I)**

(a) Copper oxide (b) Sodium oxide
(c) Ferric oxide (d) Zinc oxide

Ans. (b) As we know, alkali metal forms basic oxides. Hence in the given oxides, **sodium oxide** is a basic oxide which is an alkali.

Q.23 The position of four elements *A*, *B*, *C* and *D* in the modern periodic table are shown below. The element which is most likely to form a basic oxide is

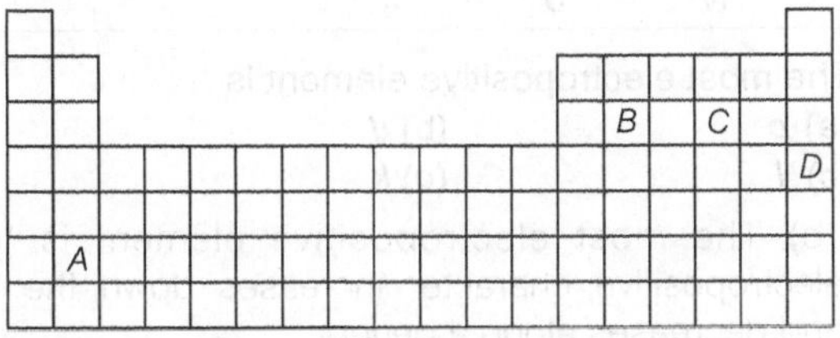

(a) *B* (b) *C* (c) *A* (d) *D*

Ans. (c) The **element *A*** will form a basic oxide while *B*, *C* and *D* will form an acidic oxide. This is because on moving along a period, the acidic character of the oxide increases.

Q.24 Sodium, aluminium and sulphur are in the same period of the periodic table.

Which trend in types of oxide occurs across this period?

	Left	⟶	Right
(a)	Acidic	amphoteric	basic
(b)	Amphoteric	basic	acidic
(c)	Basic	acidic	amphoteric
(d)	Basic	amphoteric	acidic

Ans. (d) Sodium, a metal from 1st group produces basic oxide. Sulphur from VI group is a non-metal, which produces an acidic oxide. Aluminium being from third group is a metalloid and it produces an amphoteric oxide.

Q.25 An element with atomic number .... will form an acidic oxide. **(ICSE Specimen 2024)**

(a) 3 (b) 17
(c) 11 (d) 13

Ans. (b) Non-metals usually form an acidic oxide. From the options, non metal is one which has atomic number 17, which is chlorine.

Q.26 Which of the following about oxides is correct? **(ICSE Specimen 2025)**

(a) A basic oxide is an oxide of a non-metal.
(b) Acidic oxides contain ionic bonds.
(c) Amphoteric oxides contain a metal.
(d) Basic oxides are always gases.

Ans. (c) Metal oxides that can react with both acids and bases are called amphoteric oxides.

e.g. Al_2O_3, ZnO, etc.

Q.27 Element with an atomic number 19 will **(ICSE 2021-22, Sem-I)**

(a) accept an electron and get oxidised.
(b) accept an electron and get reduced.
(c) lose an electron and get oxidised.
(d) lose an electron and get reduced.

Ans. (c) Element with an atomic number 19 belongs to group 1, so it can lose an electron and get oxidised.

Q.28 During ionisation, metals lose electrons. This change can be called **(ICSE Specimen 2021-22, Sem-I)**

(a) oxidation (b) reduction
(c) redox (d) displacement

Ans. (a) During ionisation, metals lose electrons. This change is called **oxidation**.

Q.29 The element with highest ionisation potential is
(a) hydrogen
(b) caesium **(ICSE 2020, 2016)**
(c) radon
(d) helium

Ans. (d) The element with highest ionisation potential is **helium**. Its atomic size is smaller than H, Cs, Ra due to an increase in the nuclear charge and thus, more energy is required to remove the electron.

Q.30 If an element has low ionisation potential, then it is likely to be a **(ICSE 2021-22, Sem-I)**
(a) metal
(b) metalloid
(c) non-metal
(d) inert gas

Ans. (a) **Metals** have the lowest ionisation potential.

Q.31 In a periodic table, the element of period 3 are arranged in the increasing order of ionisation potential as **(ICSE 2021-22, Sem-I)**
(a) B, N,Cl, Ar
(b) Mg, Si, S, Ar
(c) Ar, Si, S, Mg
(d) Si, Ar, Cl, Mg

Ans. (b) The increasing order of ionisation potential is:
Mg < Si < S < Ar.

Q.32 In the 2nd period neon has maximum ionisation potential because **(ICSE 2024)**
(a) it has unstable electronic configuration.
(b) it easily accepts electrons.
(c) it easily loses electrons.
(d) the outermost shell is completely filled.

Ans. (d) The outermost shell is completely filled.

Q.33 Element *Y* is in Group IIA of the Periodic Table. *Y* reacts with element *Q* to form an ionic compound. Which equation shows the process that takes place when Y forms ions? **(Competency Based Que.)**
(a) $Y + 2e^- \longrightarrow Y^{2+}$
(b) $Y - 2e^- \longrightarrow Y^{2-}$
(c) $Y + 2e^- \longrightarrow Y^{2-}$
(d) $Y - 2e^- \longrightarrow Y^{2+}$

Ans. (d) Since, element *Y* is present in Group IIA, so its **valency is 2**. Element *Y* can **lose two electrons** to attain a noble gas configuration.

$\therefore$ $Y \longrightarrow Y^{2+} + 2e^-$

or $Y - 2e^- \longrightarrow Y^{2+}$

Q.34 An element in period 3, whose electron affinity is zero. **(ICSE 2023)**
(a) Neon
(b) Sulphur
(c) Sodium
(d) Argon

Ans. (d) Electron affinity of noble gases is zero. Neon and argon both are noble gases but neon belongs to period 2 and **argon** belongs to period 3.

Q.35 Among the elements of period 2, the element which has high electron affinity is
(a) lithium
(b) carbon
(c) oxygen
(d) fluorine

Ans. (d) Among the period 2 elements, fluorine element has high electron affinity.

Q.36 Electron affinity is maximum in **(ICSE 2024)**
(a) Mg
(b) Ar
(c) Li
(d) Br

Ans. (d) Br. Halogens have maximum electron affinity.

Q.37 Electron affinity is maximum in **(ICSE Specimen 2023, 2019, 2020)**
(a) alkaline earth metals
(b) halogens
(c) inert gases
(d) alkali metals

Ans. (b) Due to their smaller size, **halogens** have maximum electron affinity.

Q.38 The tendency of an atom to attract shared pair of electrons to itself when forming a chemical bond is known as **(ICSE 2021-22, Sem-I)**
(a) electron affinity
(b) electronegativity
(c) ionisation potential
(d) nuclear charge

Ans. (b) **Electronegativity** is the tendency of an atom to attract shared pair of electron toward itself when forming a chemical bond.

Q.39 The most electronegative element is **(ICSE Specimen 2021-22, Sem-I)**
(a) sodium
(b) aluminium
(c) bromine
(d) fluorine

Ans. (d) **Fluorine** is the most electronegative element.

Q.40 Consider the part of periodic table given below:

Group/Period	1	2	13	14	15	16	17	18
I	*a*							*j*
II	*b*	*e*				*g*	*h*	*k*
III	*c*			*f*			*i*	*l*
IV	*d*							

The most electropositive element is
(a) *c*
(b) *d*
(c) *l*
(d) *k*

Ans. (b) The most electropositive element is **'*d*'** as electropositive character increases down the group and decreases along a period.

Q.41 Among the elements given below, the element with the least electronegativity is **(ICSE 2015)**

(a) lithium (b) carbon
(c) boron (d) fluorine

Ans. (a) The element with the least electronegativity is **lithium**.

Q.42 The most electronegative element from the following elements is **(ICSE 2019)**

(a) magnesium (b) chlorine
(c) aluminium (d) sulphur

Ans. (b) Among the given options, **chlorine** (Cl) is the most elecronegative element because it has the maximum tendency to attract the shared pair of electrons towards itself.

Q.43 Which of the following electronic configuration represents the most electropositive element? **(ICSE 2025 Specimen)**

(a) 2, 1 (b) 2, 8, 1 (c) 2, 2 (d) 2, 8, 2

Ans. (b) The elements which have tendency to lose electrons and form positive ions are called electropositive elements. Element with electronic configuration **2, 8, 1** can lose electron most easily to attain a noble gas configuration. Therefore, it is the most electropositive element.

Q.44

Group Numbers	IA	IIA	IIIA	IVA	VA	VIA	VIIA	VIIIA
	1	2	13	14	15	16	17	18
	Li		D			O	J	Ne
	A	Mg	E	Si		H	K	
	B	C		F	G			L

With reference to the portion of the periodic table given above, identify the element having least electronegativity.

(a) Li (b) B (c) K (d) L

Ans. (b) B has the least electronegativity among the given options.

Q.45 Which of the following arrangements is incorrect as per the property stated against it? **(Competency Based Que.)**

(a) Li > Be > N > O (Metallic character)
(b) Cl > F > Br > I (Electron gain enthalpy)
(c) $O^{2-} > F^{-} > Mg^{2+} > Na^{+}$ (Ionic radii)
(d) I > Br > Cl > F (Number of shells)

Ans. (c) $O^{2-} > F^{-} > Mg^{2+} > Na^{+}$ is the incorrect option among the following as it is not the trend of decreasing ionic radii. The correct order is :

$O^{2-} > F^{-} > Na^{+} > Mg^{2+}$ (size decreases with increasing nuclear charge).

TYPE - 2 01 Mark

Assertion-Reason Type Questions

Direction (Q. Nos. 1-10) In the following questions, a statement of Assertion (A) is followed by a statement of Reason (R). Choose the answer based on the codes given below.

(a) Both (A) and (R) are true and (R) is the correct explanation of (A).
(b) Both (A) and (R) are true but (R) is not the correct explanation of (A).
(c) (A) is true but (R) is false.
(d) (A) is false but (R) is true.

Q.1 Assertion (A) Group 2 elements are called alkaline earth metals.

Reason (R) Alkaline earth metals are those metals which do not react with water.

Ans. (c) Group-2 elements are called as alkaline earth metals as their oxides form in the earth and are water soluble. Thus, (A) is true but (R) is false.

Q.2 Assertion (A) Elements in the same vertical column have different properties.

Reason (R) Properties depends upon the number of electrons in the valence shell.

Ans. (d) Elements in the same vertical column (groups) have similar properties as the properties depends upon the number of electrons in the valence shell.

Thus, (A) is false but (R) is true.

Q.3 Assertion (A) Third period consists of 8 elements.

Reason (R) Number of elements in each period is four times the number of atomic orbitals available in the energy level that is being filled.

Ans. (c) Third period consists of 8 elements but the number of elements in each period is not the four times of the number of atomic orbitals available in the energy level, that is being filled.

Thus, (A) is true but (R) is false.

Q.4 Assertion (A) The elements of the different group have similar chemical properties.

Reason (R) It is because they have same number of valence electrons.

Ans. (d) The elements of the same group have similar chemical properties because of the presence of same number of valence electrons.

Thus, (A) is false but (R) is true.

Q.5 Assertion (A) Non-metallic character refers to the tendency of an element to gain electrons, in order to complete its octet to form anion (negative ion).

Reason (R) Non-metallic character decreases down the group.

Ans. (b) Non-metallic character refers to the tendency of an element to gain electrons, in order to complete its octet to form anion (negative ion). Non-metallic character decreases down the group because down the group the effect of increasing atomic size is greater.

Thus, both (A) and (R) are true but (R) is not the correct explanation of (A).

Q.6 Assertion (A) Non-metals usually have high ionisation energy.

Reason (R) Metal and metalloids have high ionisation energy.

Ans. (c) Metals usually have low ionisation energy, while non-metals have high ionisation energy.

Thus, (A) is true but (R) is false.

Q.7 Assertion (A) The tendency of losing electrons increases down the Group.

Reason (R) The most reactive metal is placed at the top of Group 1. **(ICSE 2025)**

Ans. (c) The most reactive metal is not placed at the top of Group 1 because reactivity increases down the group. The reason behind this trend is the increase in tendency to lose electrons down the group to form positive ions. Thus, (A) is true but (R) is false.

Q.8 Assertion (A) The amount of energy released while converting a neutral gaseous isolated atom into a negative charged gaseous ion by addition of electrons is called as electron affinity.

Reason (R) Alkali metals have low electron affinity which further decreases down the group.

Ans. (b) Electron affinity is defined as the amount of energy released while converting a neutral gaseous isolated atom into a negative charged gaseous ion by the addition of electrons. Alkali metals have low electron affinity which decreases down the group.

Thus, both (A) and (R) are true but (R) is not the correct explanation of (A).

Q.9 Assertion (A) The electron affinity of carbon is more than boron.

Reason (R) In a period, from left to right, the electron affinity increases.

Ans. (a) The electron affinity of C is more than B, as the electron affinity increases from left to right in a periodic table. Therefore, both (A) and (R) are true and (R) is the correct explanation of (A).

Q.10 Assertion (A) Alkali metals have lowest electro-negativity in their period.

Reason (R) The electronegativity decreases down the group.

Ans. (b) Atomic number increases down the group, (i.e. nuclear charge increases), but due to addition of extra shells, the atomic size increases. The effect of an increase in the atomic size overcomes the effect of increase in nuclear charge, hence electronegativity decreases down the group. Alkali metals have lowest electronegativity in their period as electronegativity increases on moving left to right along a period.

Thus, Both (A) and (R) are true but (R) is not the correct explanation of (A).

TYPE - 3

01 Mark

Fill in the Blanks

Q.1 Sixth and seventh are the longest periods, containing .... elements each (18/32).

Ans. 32

Q.2 If an element has one electron in the outermost shell then it is likely to have the .... [smallest/largest] atomic size amongst all the elements in the same period. **(ICSE Specimen 2025, 2024)**

Ans. largest

Q.3 The atomic size of boron is 0.88 Å, and that of nitrogen is 0.70 Å. Nitrogen lies to the .... (left/right) of boron. **(Competency Based Que.)**

Ans. right

Q.4 Metals are good .... (oxidising agents/reducing agents). **(ICSE 2016)**

Ans. reducing agents

Q.5 In period 3, the most metallic element is .... (sodium/magnesium). **(ICSE 2019)**

Ans. sodium

Q.6 Across a period, the ionisation potential .... (increases/decreases).

Ans. increases

Q.7 The energy required to remove an electron from a neutral isolated gaseous atom and convert it into a positively charged gaseous ion is called .... (ionisation potential/electronegativity) **(ICSE 2017)**

Ans. ionisation potential

Q.8 If an element has a low ionisation energy then it is likely to be .... (metallic/non-metallic) **(ICSE 2016)**

Ans. metallic

Q.9 Down the group, electron affinity .... (increases decreases).

Ans. decreases

Q.10 The electronegativity of iodine is .... (less/greater) than that of chlorine. **(ICSE 2016)**

Ans. less

TYPE - 4 — 01 Mark

Correct the Incorrect Statement

Q.1 Atomic number 17 in the periodic table correspond to sulphur.

Ans. Atomic number 17 in the periodic table correspond to **chlorine**.

Q.2 Atomic size decreases as we move down the group.

Ans. Atomic size **increases** as we move down the group.

Q.3 Non-metallic oxides are basic in nature.

Ans. Non-metallic oxides are **acidic** in nature.

Q.4 Ionisation potential increases down the group.

Ans. Ionisation potential **decreases** down the group.

Q.5 Chlorine is the most electronegative element in the periodic table.

Ans. **Fluorine** is the most electronegative element in the periodic table.

TYPE - 5 — 01 × 05 = 05 Marks

Matching Type Questions

Q.1 Match the following columns. **(Competency Based Que.)**

Column I	Column II
A. Alkali metals	1. Be, C, O, F
B. Alkaline earth metals	2. F, Cl, Br, I
C. Atomic radius decreases	3. P, Al, Na, S
D. Non-metallic character decreases	4. K, Na, Li, Rb
E. Period 3 elements	5. Ba, Ca, Sr, Ra

Ans. A $\rightarrow$ 4, B $\rightarrow$ 5, C $\rightarrow$ 1, D $\rightarrow$ 2, E $\rightarrow$ 3.

Q.2 Match the following columns.

Column I	Column II
A. Neutral oxide	1. MgO
B. Feebly acidic oxide	2. N_2O
C. Amphoteric oxide	3. Cl_2O_7
D. Most acidic oxide	4. SiO_2
E. Basic oxide	5. Al_2O_3

Ans. A $\rightarrow$ 2, B $\rightarrow$ 4, C $\rightarrow$ 5, D $\rightarrow$ 3, E $\rightarrow$ 1.

Q.3 Match the following columns. **(Competency Based Que.)**

Column I	Column II
A. Increasing number of shells	1. F > Cl > Br
B. Increasing reactivity	2. Cl > F > Be
C. Decreasing electron affinity	3. Ca > Mg > Be
D. Decreasing electronegativity	4. F < Cl < Br
E. Decreasing metallic character	5. Br < Cl < F

Ans. A $\rightarrow$ 4, B $\rightarrow$ 5, C $\rightarrow$ 2, D $\rightarrow$ 1, E $\rightarrow$ 3.

TYPE - 6 — 01 Mark

Identify the Following

Q.1 Name an alkali metal present in the second period.

Ans. **Lithium** is an alkali metal which is present in the second period.

Q.2 Name a metal present in period 3 and group 1 of the periodic table.

Ans. Period 3 indicates that the number of shells is 3 (i.e. *K*, *L*, *M*), and group 1 indicates that number of electron in the outermost shell, i.e., valence shell is 1. So, its electronic configuration is $\underset{2}{K}\,\underset{8}{L}\,\underset{1}{M}$.

So, metal is **sodium (Na)** with atomic number 11.

Q.3 Give the number of the group and the period, of the element having three shells with three electrons in valence shell.

Ans. Three shells indicates **period number 3**. Three electrons in valence shell indicates group number 3, so, electronic configuration is $\underset{2}{K}\,\underset{8}{L}\,\underset{3}{M}$.

So, atomic number is 13. **Group is III A.**

Q.4 An element *X* belongs to 3rd period and Group-2 of the periodic table. State the number of valence electrons present in an element *X*.

Ans. An element *X* has **2 valence electrons** as it is present in Group-2 of the periodic table.

Q.5 Name an inert gas having two electrons in its outermost shell.

Ans. **Helium** is an inert gas having two electrons in its outermost shell.

Q.6 A group of elements in the periodic table are given below.

Boron, aluminium, gallium, indium, thallium

Which element has the most metallic character?

Ans. **Thallium** has the most metallic character as the metallic character increases on moving down the group (B to Tl).

Q.7 Which type of elements have tendency to gain electrons in order to complete their octet.

Ans. Non-metals.

Q.8 Name the energy required to remove an electron from the valence shell of a neutral isolated gaseous atom. **(ICSE Specimen 2025, 2023, 2019)**

Ans. **Ionisation potential** is defined as the energy required to remove an electron from the valence shell of a neutral isolated gaseous atom.

Q.9 State the term for "The energies required to remove the residual electrons one by one".

Ans. Successive ionisation energy.

Q.10 Name the element which has the highest ionisation potential.

Ans. **Helium (He)** will have the highest ionisation energy (or ionisation potential).

Q.11 Name the energy released when an atom in the gaseous state accepts an electron to form an anion. **(ICSE 2018, 2014)**

Ans. **Electron affinity** is defined as the energy released when an atom in the gaseous state accepts an electron to form an anion.

Q.12 State the term for "the tendency of an atom to pull a shared pair of electrons towards itself in a compound". **(ICSE 2025, 2024)**

Ans. **Electronegativity** is defined as the tendency of an atom to pull a shared pair of electrons towards itself in a compound.

TYPE - 7 — 02 Marks

Short Answer Type I Questions

Q.1 An element *Z* has atomic number 16. Answer the following questions.

(i) State the period and group to which *Z* belongs.

(ii) Is *Z* a metal or a non-metal? Give reason. **(ICSE 2016)**

Ans. (i) Atomic number of element, $Z = 16$

Electronic configuration = $\begin{matrix} K & L & M \\ 2 & 8 & 6 \end{matrix}$

Number of shells is 3, (i.e. *K*, *L*, *M*). So, **period is 3** and group number is VIA or **16 group**. **(1)**

(ii) Non-metals usually have 5, 6 or 7 electrons in their outermost shell, so *Z* is a **non-metal**. **(1)**

Q.2 Element '*X*' forms an oxide with the formula X_2O_3 which is a solid with high melting point. '*X*' would most likely be placed in the group of the periodic table as:

(i) (a) Na (b) Mg

(c) Al (d) Si

(ii) Justify your answer in the above question. **(ICSE Specimen 2025)**

Ans. (i) (c) Al **(1)**

(ii) Since element '*X*' forms X_2O_3 oxide, this means '*X*' has a valency of three. Therefore, among the options '*X*' is Al, as it belongs to group-13 and it shows valency of 3. **(1)**

Q.3 (i) Element *X* belongs to period 2 and group 1 of the periodic table. State the formula of the chloride of the element *X*.

(ii) Ionisation energies of 4 elements *A*, *B*, *C* and *D* are 496, 403, 520 and 419 kJ/mol, respectively. If these elements belong to the same group in the Periodic Table, which element will occupy the top position in the group? Justify your answer. **(Competency Based Que.)**

Ans. (i) Since, element *X* belongs to group 1, thus its valency is 1 and it combines with Cl^- to form **XCl**. **(1)**

(ii) Ionisation energy decreases down the group. So, the element with highest ionisation energy, i.e., element *C* will occupy the top position in the group. **(1)**

Q.4 The atomic number of two atoms '*X*' and '*Y*' are 14 and 8 respectively.

State:

(i) the period to which '*X*' belongs.

(ii) the formula of the compound formed between '*X*' and '*Y*' (Do not identify *X* and *Y*) **(ICSE 2025)**

Ans. Atomic number of *X* is 14 so, its electronic configuration is 2, 8, 4. Whereas, atomic number of *Y* is 8 and its electronic configuration is 2, 6.

(i) *X* belongs to **period 3** as its electrons occupy three shells. **(1)**

(ii) The valency of *X* is 4. *Y* has 6 valence electrons, so it needs two more electrons to complete its octet, thus its valency is 2.

Therefore, according to the valencies, *X* and *Y* combines to form **XY_2 compound**. (Here, electrons are shared to complete the octet). **(1)**

Q.5 Given below are two sets of elements from two different periods.

Name the element with the highest ionisation potential in each of the following sets.

(i) Al, Cl, Mg (ii) Ne, O, F **(ICSE 2025)**

Ans. (i) Cl has the highest ionisation potential as the ionisation potential generally increases from left to right across a period. **(1)**

(ii) Ne has the highest ionisation potential as it has a fully filled electronic configuration, making it very stable and difficult to remove an electron. **(1)**

Q.6 Identify the term/substance in each of the following

(i) The tendency of an atom to attract electrons towards itself when combined with a compound.

(ii) The electrons present in the outermost shell of an atom. **(ICSE 2016)**

Ans. (i) Electronegativity (ii) Valence electrons. **(1 × 2 = 2)**

Q.7 Arrange the following as per the instructions given in the brackets:

(i) Fluorine, iodine, bromine, chlorine (increasing order of electronegativity.)

(ii) Sodium, Magnesium, Aluminium, Silicon (decreasing order of non-metallic character).

Ans. (i) Electronegativity decreases as we move down the group. Therefore, the increasing order of electronegativity is:

Iodine < Bromine < Chlorine < Fluorine **(1)**

(ii) Non-metallic character increases as we move along the period from left to right. Therefore, the decreasing order of non-metallic character is :

Silicon > Aluminium > Magnesium > Sodium **(1)**

Q.8 Arrange the following as per the instructions given in the brackets.

(i) Carbon, fluorine, beryllium (decreasing order of atomic size)

(ii) Potassium, lithium, sodium (increasing order of ionisation potential) **(ICSE 2024)**

Ans. (i) Atomic size decreases as we move along the period from left to right. Therefore the decreasing order of atomic size is :

beryllium > carbon > fluorine **(1)**

(ii) Ionisation potential decreases as we move down the group. Therefore, the increasing order of ionisation potential is :

potassium < sodium < lithium **(1)**

Q.9 Define the following terms.

(i) Ionisation potential

(ii) Electron affinity

Ans. (i) The energy required to remove an electron from an isolated gaseous atom and convert it into a positively charged gaseous ion is called **ionisation energy**. **(1)**

(ii) The amount of energy released by the addition of electron to the outermost shell of an atom in its isolated gaseous state is called **electron affinity**. **(1)**

TYPE - 8 03 Marks

Short Answer Type II Questions

Q.1 The diagram shows part of the periodic table.

											He
						B	C	N	O	F	Ne
						Al	Si	P	S	Cl	Ar
	Fe	Co	Ni	Cu	Zn	Ga	Ge	As	Se	Br	Kr
										I	Xe

Answer these questions using only the elements shown in the diagram.

Each element can be used once, more than once or not at all.

Write the symbol for

(i) an element which is in Group 5 and Period 3,

(ii) an element which is used as a gas in balloons,

(iii) two elements which combine to form a compound which causes acid rain.

Ans. (i) P (ii) He (iii) S and O **(1 × 3 = 3)**

Q.2 Atomic number of element *M* is 12 and it forms an ionic compound with element *L*.

(i) Which of the following atomic numbers will match *L*?

(a) 14 (b) 10 (c) 8

(ii) What is the name given to the members of the group to which element *M* belongs?

(iii) **Draw the electron dot structure of the compound formed between *M* and *L*.** **(Competency Based Que.)**

Ans. (i) Atomic number of given element *M* is 12 and it forms ionic compound with element *L*, so according to electronic configuration of *M* (2, 8, 2), it losses its two electron to form a compound with *L* so, element *L* must have vacancy of two electrons to accept. Thus, *L* **have atomic number 8**. Therefore, (iii) 8 is the correct answer. **(1)**

(ii) Alkaline earth metals. **(1)**

(iii) Electron dot structure of the compound formed between *M* and *L* is

$$M^{2+} \overset{\times}{\underset{\times}{}}\ddot{\underset{\cdot\cdot}{L}}:^{2-}$$

(1)

Q.3 Study the table given below. Use only the letters given in the table to answer the questions. Do not identify the elements.

IA	IIA	IIIA	IVA	VA	VIA	VIIA	0
			E		*J*		*Q*
	L			*G*			
	M	*D*				*P*	
	N						

(i) **State the valency of element '*G*'.**

(ii) **Which element can exhibit catenation?**

(iii) **Write the formula of the compound formed between '*M*' and '*P*'.** **(ICSE 2025)**

Ans. (i) Since, '*G*' belongs to group VA (Group 15). Elements in this group has 5 valence electrons, and it needs three electrons to complete its octet, thus its **valency is 3**. **(1)**

(ii) The element which can exhibit catenation is **'*E*'**. **(1)**

(iii) Element '*M*' belongs to group IIA, so it has a valency of two as it can lose two electrons to complete its octet. While, element '*P*' belongs to group VII A, so it has a valency of one as it can gain one electron to achieve octet.

Thus, *M* and *P* can combine to form MP_2 where, '*M*' loses two electrons and two '*P*' atoms gains each electron. **(1)**

Q.4 The metals of group 2 from top to bottom are Be, Mg, Ca, Sr and Ba.

(i) **Which one of these elements will form ions most readily and why?**

(ii) **State the common feature in the electronic configuration of all these elements.** **(ICSE 2015)**

Ans. (i) **Ba element** will form ions most readily. Since, it is more metallic and loses electrons easily.

Ba has two electrons in the outermost shell and it has a tendency to lose valence electrons and form a positive ion. **(2)**

(ii) All these elements have 2 electrons in the outermost shell. **(1)**

Q.5 Identify the following.

(i) **An element in period 1 which can be placed in both group 1 and group 17 of the periodic table.**

(ii) **The element having electronic configuration 2, 8, 6.**

(iii) **The most electronegative element of period 3.** **(ICSE 2024)**

Ans. (i) Hydrogen (ii) Sulphur (iii) Chlorine **(1 × 3 = 3)**

Q.6 An element *X* has atomic number 17. Answer the following questions.

(i) **State the period and group to which it belongs.**

(ii) **Is it a metal or non-metal?**

(iii) **Write the formula between *X* and hydrogen.** **(ICSE Specimen 2023)**

Ans. An element X has atomic number = 17

So, the electronic configuration = 2, 8, 7

(i) The **period is 3** and **group is 17**.

(ii) It is a **non-metal**.

(iii) The formula between X and H is HX (or HCl). **(1 × 3 = 3)**

Q.7 *X* [2, 8, 7] and *Y* [2, 8, 2] are two elements. Using this information complete the following.

(i) **......... is the metallic element.**

(ii) **Metal atoms tend to have a maximum of .... electrons in the outermost shell.**

(iii) **......... is the reducing agent.** **(ICSE Specimen 2025, 2024)**

Ans. (i) *Y* (ii) three (iii) *Y* **(1 × 3 = 3)**

Q.8 Arrange the following as per the instructions given in the brackets.

(i) **Al, K, Mg, Ca (decreasing order of its reactivity)**

(ii) **N, Be, O, C (increasing order of non-metallic character)**

(iii) **P, Si, F, Be (decreasing order of valence electrons)** **(ICSE 2023)**

Ans. (i) Ionisation potential increases on moving left to right in a period and decreases on moving down the group, so chemical reactivity of elements decreases on moving left to right in a period and increases on moving down the group.

So, the correct decreasing order of chemical reactivity is K> Ca > Mg > Al.

(ii) Non-metallic character increases on moving left to right in a period and decreases on moving down the group. So, the correct increasing order of non-metallic character is Be < C < N < O.

(iii) The electrons present in the outermost shell of an atom are called valence electrons.

So, the correct decreasing order of valence electrons is F > P > Si > Be

$(7e^-)$ $(5e^-)$ $(4e^-)$ $(2e^-)$ **(1 × 3 = 3)**

Q.9 Given below is a diagram showing the placement of five different oxides. With respect to the given diagram answer the following questions.

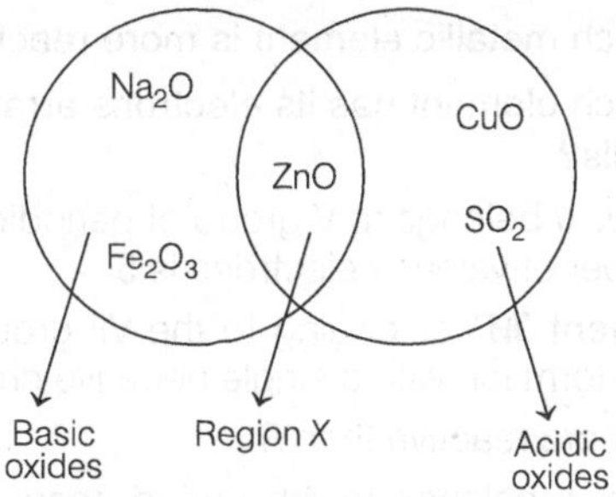

(i) Name the type of oxide represented in region *X* in the diagram.

(ii) Identify the oxide which has been incorrectly placed in the above diagram.

(iii) Name the oxide from the above diagram which will form an alkali when dissolved in water.

(ICSE 2025)

Ans. (i) Region *X* in the diagram represents **amphoteric oxides**. **(1)**

(ii) CuO is a **basic oxide**, but it is incorrectly placed in acidic oxides in the above diagram. **(1)**

(iii) $\mathbf{Na_2O}$ reacts with water to form an alkali (NaOH).

$$Na_2O + H_2O \longrightarrow \underset{\text{(Alkali)}}{2NaOH}$$ **(1)**

Q.10 Give reason for the following statements.

(i) Alkali metals are good reducing agents.

(ii) The oxidising nature of elements increases on moving from left to right along a period in the periodic table.

(iii) Ionisation potential increases across a period, from left to right. **(ICSE 2018)**

Ans. (i) Due to lower values of ionisation potential, alkali metals can easily lose their electrons and hence are good reducing agents.

(ii) On moving across a period, the tendency to gain electron(s) increases due to an increase in nuclear pull and a decrease in the atomic size.

So, non-metallic character increases from left to right in a period and thereby, oxidising nature of elements also increases.

(iii) On moving from left to right in a periodic table, the atomic size decreases due to increase in the nuclear charge.

Thus, more energy is required to remove the electron(s) from outermost shell resulting into increase in ionisation potential across a period.

(1 × 3 = 3)

Q.11 Study the information given in the table below and answer the questions that follow. (**Note** The letters do not represent the actual symbols of the elements)

Element	Electronic configuration	Ionisation energy kJ mol^{-1}
X	2, 2	900
Y	2, 8, 2	738
Z	2, 8, 8, 2	590

(i) Explain why element *X* has highest ionisation energy.

(ii) To which period does *Z* belong?

(iii) Draw the electron dot structure of the compound formed between *Z* and oxygen.

(Competency Based Que.)

Ans. (i) As the number of shells are less, then attraction by the nucleus on the electrons is more.

So, more energy is required to remove the electron from the outermost shell.

(ii) Fourth period.

(iii) 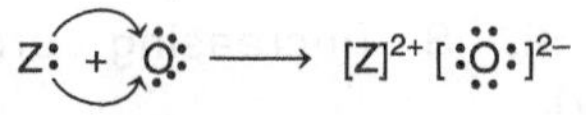 **(1 × 3 = 3)**

Q.12 The electron affinity of an element *X* is greater than that of element *Y*.

(i) How is the oxidising power of *X* likely to compare with that of *Y*?

(ii) How is the electronegativity of *X* likely to compare with that of *Y*?

(iii) State whether *X* is likely to be placed to the left or to the right of *Y* in the periodic table?

(ICSE Specimen 2025, 2024)

Ans. (i) As the electron affinity increases, the amount of energy released when an electron is added to an atom increases which makes an atom stable, and the tendency to gain electrons increases.

So, oxidising property increases with an increase in electron affinity.

Hence, **oxidising power of *X* is greater than *Y*.** **(1)**

(ii) An element that has high electron affinity, has large electronegativity.

So, **electronegativity of *X* is greater than *Y*.** **(1)**

(iii) ***X* is placed to the right of *Y*** because electron affinity increases from left to right in a period. **(1)**

Q.13 In period 3 of the periodic table, element *B* is placed to the left of element *A*. On the basis of this information, choose the correct word from the brackets to complete the following statements.

(i) The element *B* would have (lower/higher) metallic character than *A*.

(ii) The element *A* would probably have (lesser/ higher) electron affinity than *B*.

(iii) The element *A* would have (greater/smaller) atomic size than *B*. **(ICSE 2018)**

Ans. If in period 3 of the periodic table, element *B* is placed to the left of element *A*, then

(i) The element *B* would have **higher** metallic character than *A*. Due to increase in nuclear charge and decrease in atomic size, metallic character decreases across a period. **(1)**

(ii) The element *A* would probably have **higher** electron affinity than *B*. As we move from left to right in the periodic table, the atomic size decreases and the nuclear charge increases, thus the electron affinity increases. **(1)**

(iii) The element *A* would have **smaller** atomic size than *B*. An increase in nuclear charge tends to pull the valence electrons closer to the nucleus and reduces the size of the atom. **(1)**

Q.14 Arrange the following as per the instruction given in the brackets.

(i) Na, K, Cl, Si, S (increasing order of electronegativity).

(ii) Be, Li, F, C, B, N, O (increasing order of metallic character).

(iii) Br, F, I, Cl (increasing order of atomic size).

(ICSE Specimen 2023)

Ans. (i) Since, electronegativity decreases down the group and increases across period. So, the correct increasing order of electronegativity is

K < Na < Si < S < Cl **(1)**

(ii) Since, metallic character decreases across a period on moving from left to right, so the correct increasing order of metallic character is

F < O < N < C < B < Be < Li **(1)**

(iii) Since, atomic size increases down the group. So, the correct increasing order of atomic size is

F < Cl < Br < I **(1)**

TYPE - 9 — 04/05 Marks

Long Answer Type Questions

Q.1 Use the letters only written in the periodic table given below to answer the questions that follow:

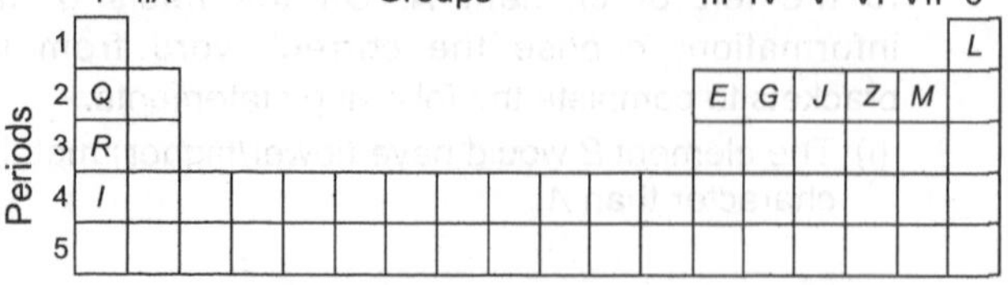

(i) State the number of valence electrons in atom *J*.

(ii) Which element forms ions with a single negative charge?

(iii) Which metallic element is more reactive than *R*?

(iv) Which element has its electrons arranged in four shells? **(ICSE 2016)**

Ans. (i) Since, *J* belongs to V group of periodic table, hence number of valence electrons is **5**.

(ii) **Element '*M*'** belonging to the VII group of periodic table form ion with a single negative charge.

(iii) ***I*** is more reactive than *R*.

(iv) Since, ***I*** belongs to 4th period, therefore, it has its electrons arranged in four shells. **(1 × 4 = 4)**

Q.2 Choose the most appropriate answer from the following list of oxides which fit the description. Each answer may be used only once.

[SO_2, SiO_2, Al_2O_3, MgO, CO, Na_2O]

(i) A basic oxide.

(ii) An oxide which dissolves in water forming an acid.

(iii) An amphoteric oxide.

(iv) A covalent oxide of a metalloid. **(ICSE 2015)**

Ans. (i) Basic oxides: Na_2O, MgO

(ii) SO_2

(iii) Al_2O_3

(iv) SiO_2 **(1 × 4 = 4)**

Q.3 The table below shows the electronic arrangements of six atoms, *A* to *F*.

Atom	A	B	C	D	E	F
Electronic configuration	2, 5	2	2, 6	2, 8, 6	2, 8, 8	2, 8, 3

With respect to the table select the following.

(ICSE 2021-22, Sem-I)

(i) Two atoms from the same group of the periodic table.

(a) *D* and *E* (b) *C* and *D*
(c) *E* and *F* (d) *C* and *E*

(ii) Two noble gases

(a) *A* and *B* (b) *E* and *F*
(c) *B* and *E* (d) *D* and *E*

(iii) The atom which is the most electronegative

(a) *A* (b) *B* (c) *C* (d) *F*

(iv) The atom which has the highest ionisation potential.

(a) *A* (b) *B* (c) *E* (d) *F*

Ans. (i) (b) **Element *C* (2, 6) and *D* (2, 8, 6)** belongs to the same group because these have same valence shell electronic configuration.

(ii) (c) **Element *B* (2) and *E* (2, 8, 8)** are noble gases (He and Ar respectively).

(iii) (c) ***C* (2, 6)** is the most electronegative element.

(iv) (b) **Element *B* (2)** has highest ionisation potential. Element *B* is helium. **(1 × 4 = 4)**

Q.4 Arrange the following as per the instruction given in the brackets.

(i) He, Ar, Ne (Increasing order of the number of electron shells)

(ii) Na, Li, K (Increasing ionisation energy)

(iii) F, Cl, Br (Increasing electronegativity)

(iv) Na, K, Li (Increasing atomic size) **(ICSE 2017)**

Ans. (i) Number of electron shells increases down the group.

He < Ne < Ar

(ii) Ionisation energy decreases down the group.

K < Na < Li

(iii) Electronegativity decreases down the group.

Br < Cl < F

(iv) Atomic size increases down the group.

Li < Na < K **(1 × 4 = 4)**

Q.5 Match the atomic number 2, 4, 8, 15 and 19 with each of the following.

(i) A solid non-metal belonging to the third period.

(ii) A metal of valency 1.

(iii) A gaseous element with valency 2.

(iv) An element belonging to group 2.

(v) A rare gas. **(ICSE 2017)**

Ans. (i) Atomic number - 15 (Phosphorus)

(ii) Atomic number - 19 (Potassium)

(iii) Atomic number - 8 (Oxygen)

(iv) Atomic number - 4 (Beryllium)

(v) Atomic number - 2 (Helium) **(1 × 5 = 5)**

Q.6 For answering the following questions refer to the periodic table.

(i) Name the second last element of the period 3.

(ii) How many elements are in the second period?

(iii) Name the element which has the highest electron affinity.

(iv) Name the element which has the highest electronegativity.

(v) Name the element which may be placed on group 1 but is not a metal. **(ICSE Specimen 2017)**

Ans. (i) **Chlorine** is the second last element of the period 3.

(ii) **Eight elements** are in the second period.

(iii) **Chlorine** has the highest electron affinity.

(iv) **Fluorine** has the highest electronegativity.

(v) **Hydrogen** is not a metal which may be placed in group 1. **(1 × 5 = 5)**

Q.7 Answer any 5 questions.

Group number	IA	IIA	IIIA	IVA	VA	VIA	VIIA	0
Period	1	2	13	14	15	16	17	18
Second	Li		*D*			*O*	*J*	Ne
Third	*A*	Mg	*E*	Si		*H*	*M*	
Fourth	*R*	*T*	*I*		*Q*	*U*		*Y*

Note In this table, *H* does not represent hydrogen. Some elements are given in their own symbol and position in the periodic table. While others are shown with a letter.

With reference to the above table answer the following questions.

(i) Identify the most electronegative element.

(ii) Identify the most reactive element of group 1.

(iii) Identify the element from period 3 with least atomic size.

(iv) How many valence electrons are present in *Q* ?

(v) Which element from group 2 would have the least ionisation energy?

(vi) Identify the noble gas of the fourth period.

Ans. (i) ***J*** is the most electronegative element.

(ii) ***R*** is the most reactive element of group I.

(iii) ***M*** has the least atomic size in period 3.

(iv) *Q* belongs to group VA. So, number of valence electrons in *Q* are **five**.

(v) In group 2, ***T*** will have least ionisation energy.

(vi) ***Y*** is a noble gas of the fourth period. **(1 × 5 = 5)**

Q.8 Consider the part of periodic table given below and answer the following questions.

Group → / Period↓	1	2	13	14	15	16	17	18
1	*a*							*j*
2	*b*	*e*				*g*	*h*	*k*
3	*c*			*f*			*i*	*l*
4	*d*							

(i) The atom of which element is smaller in size *e* or *h*?

(ii) Which element is the most electropositive in nature?

(iii) Which element has only one proton in its atom?

(iv) What is the valency of *g*?

(v) Name the element which is a metalloid.

Ans. (i) *h*

As we move from left to right across a period, atomic size decreases.

(ii) *d*

Electropositive character decreases across a period and increases down the group.

(iii) *a*

Hydrogen atom has only one proton in its atom.

(iv) 2

As '*g*' belongs to 16 group, number of valence electrons it has is '6'. It requires 2 electrons to complete its octet, therefore its valency is 2.

(v) *f*

Element '*f*' is germanium and it is a metalloid. **(1 × 5 = 5)**

TYPE - 10

03 Marks

Case Based Questions

Q.1 Ravi was studying elements of the periodic table and he noticed that some elements which are placed on the left side of the table, have a tendency to lose their valence electrons (electrons of the outermost orbit) and form a positive ion, they are considered as metals. While, some elements are placed on the right side of the periodic table, and they have a tendency to gain electrons in order to attain octet in their outermost orbit, they are considered as non-metals.

(i) Why sodium is a metal and chlorine is a non-metal?

(ii) On which factors metallic character of the elements depend? (explain in brief)

(iii) What are the changes shown in metallic character of the elements while moving down the group?

Ans. (i) Sodium is a metal because it has one electron in its outermost shell (valence electron). It tends to lose this electron easily to achieve a stable configuration, forming a positive ion (Na^+). This tendency to lose electrons and form positive ions is a characteristic of metals.

Chlorine, on the other hand, has seven electrons in its outer shell and needs one more electron to complete its octet. It tends to gain an electron to form a negative ion (Cl^-), which is a characteristic of non-metals. **(1)**

(ii) The metallic character of an element depends on the ease with which it can lose electrons. The more easily an element loses electrons, the more is its metallic character. This is influenced by factors such as the **atomic size** and **ionisation energy**. **(1)**

(iii) As we move down a group in the periodic table, the metallic character **increases**. This happens because the atomic size increases and the outer electrons are farther from the nucleus, making them easier to lose.

Hence, elements down the group are more likely to exhibit metallic properties. **(1)**

Q.2 While studying the formation of ions, Arvind noted the following:

- Potassium (K) is an alkali metal. It has an atomic number of 19 and a mass number of 39. It has one electron in its valence shell.
- Fluorine (F) is a halogen atom. It has an atomic number of 9 and a mass number of 19. It has 7 electrons in its valence shell.

(i) What is the valency of potassium and how does it form an ion?

(ii) What is the valency of fluorine and how does it form an ion?

(iii) How does the atomic number help determine the number of electrons in a neutral atom?

Ans. (i) The valency of potassium is **1** because it has 1 electron in its outermost shell, which it loses to form a K^+ **ion** with a stable electron configuration. **(1)**

(ii) The valency of fluorine is **1** because it needs 1 electron to complete its octet. It gains 1 electron to form an F^- **ion** with a stable electron configuration. **(1)**

(iii) The atomic number is equal to the number of protons in a neutral atom, and since the number of electrons equals the number of protons in a neutral atom, the atomic number also determines the number of electrons. **(1)**

02

CHEMICAL BONDING

Chemical Bond

- The force of attraction that hold different atoms together in a molecule is called **chemical bond**.
- Atoms form chemical bond to attain stable configuration, i.e. to have either 2 or 8 electrons in the outermost shell.
- Atoms can achieve stable electronic configuration in following three ways:
  (i) By **transferring** electrons (donating or accepting) to each other from their outermost shells.
  (ii) By **sharing** the pair of electrons.
  (iii) By **donating** a pair of electrons from one atom to another.
- The number of electrons that an atom lose, gain or share to attain the nearest noble gas electronic configuration in its outermost orbit is called **valency** of an atom.
  – In ionic compounds, it is called **electrovalency**.
  – In covalent compounds, it is called **covalency**.

Types of Chemical Bonds

On the basis of transfer or share of electrons between atoms. These are three types of bond.

(i) **Electrovalent bond** Formed by transfer of electrons from one atom to another.
(ii) **Covalent bond** Formed by sharing the pair of electrons between two or more atoms.
(iii) **Coordinate or dative bond** Formed by donating a pair of electrons from one atom to another.

Electrovalent or Ionic Bond

- These bonds are formed by the complete transfer of electron(s) from one atom to another. Here, one atom loses electrons and other atom gains those electrons. The compounds formed by ionic bonds are called **ionic compounds**. These bonds are easily formed between a metallic atom and a non-metallic atom.
- Metallic atom easily loses electron(s) to form cations (+ve ion) and is called an **electropositive element**. Non-metallic atom easily gains electron(s) to form anions (–ve ion) and is called an **electronegative element**. Thus, ionic bond is formed by ions, i.e. **cations** and **anions**.
- **Group 1** elements are most electropositive and **group 17** elements are most electronegative. Thus, compounds of the elements of these two groups are ionic, e.g. NaCl, CsF, KBr, etc.
- The simple notation to represent the valence electrons of an atom are called **Lewis symbols** or **electron dot formulae**. These symbols were introduced by an American Chemist, G.N. Lewis.
  In these symbols, the valence electrons are represented by placing dot (•) or cross (×) around their symbol.
  e.g. The Lewis symbols for the atoms of second period are

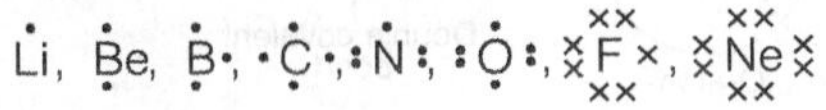

- For the formation of electrovalent bond, metal and non-metal should have large electronegativity difference, metal must have low ionisation energy and non-metal should have high electron affinity.

REVISION NOTES

Electron Dot Structure of Some Electrovalent Compounds

1. Sodium Chloride (NaCl)

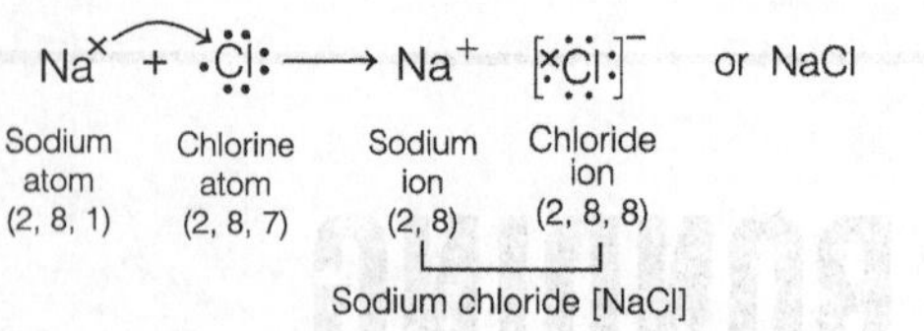

2. Magnesium Chloride ($MgCl_2$)

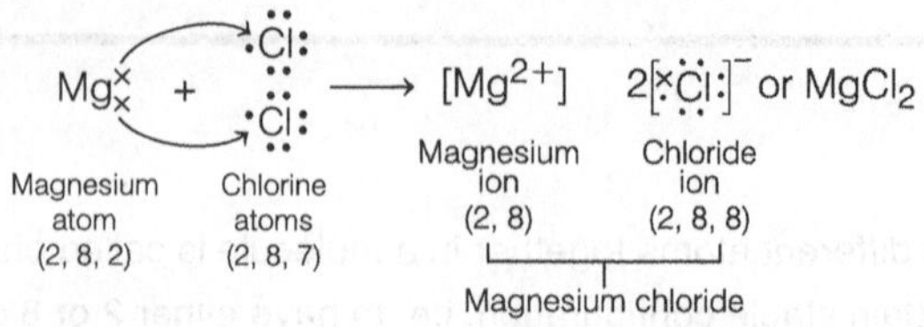

3. Calcium Oxide (CaO)

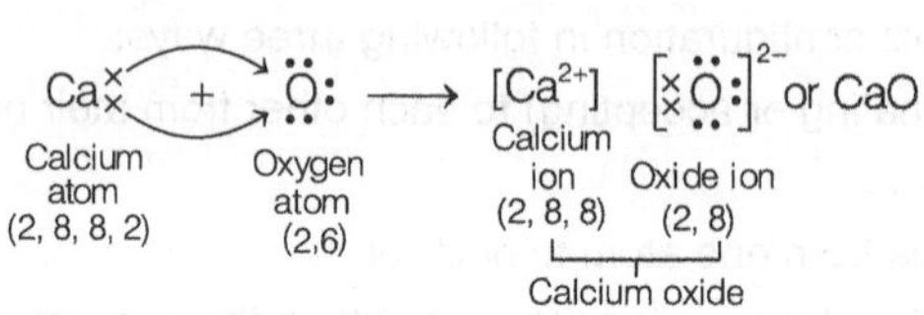

> ***Redox Reaction***
> - **Oxidation** process involves the loss of electrons and **reduction** process involves the gain of electrons.
> - The process in which oxidation and reduction occurs simultaneously is called **redox reaction**.
> - The substance which gains electron(s) is called an **oxidising agent**, whereas, substance which loses electron(s) is called a **reducing agent**.

Covalent Bond or Molecular Bond

- The bond formed by the sharing of electrons between two or more atoms is called the **covalent bond**.
- This bond is generally formed between two electronegative, i.e. non-metallic elements.
- The compounds formed by covalent bonds are called **covalent compounds**.

Types of Covalent Bonds

(i) **Single covalent bond** It is formed by the sharing of one pair of electrons between two atoms. It is represented by a single line (—). e.g

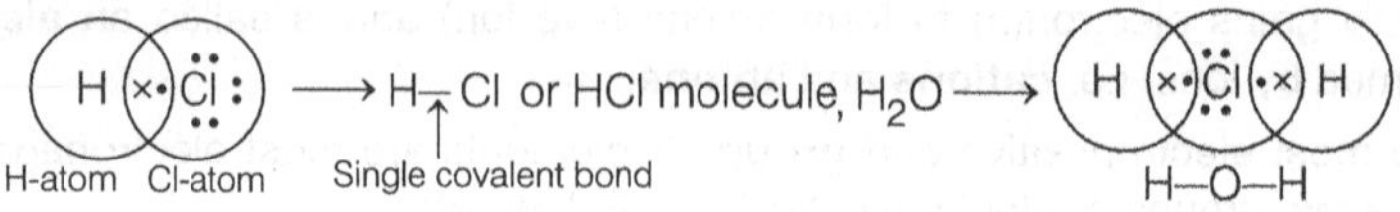

(ii) **Double covalent bond** It is formed by the sharing of two pair of electrons between two atoms. It is represented by a double line (=). e.g.

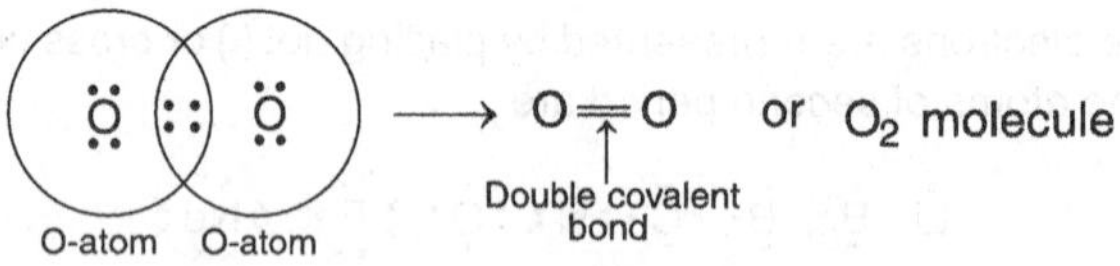

(iii) **Triple covalent bond** It is formed by the sharing of three pair of electrons between two atoms. It is represented by a triple line (≡). e.g.

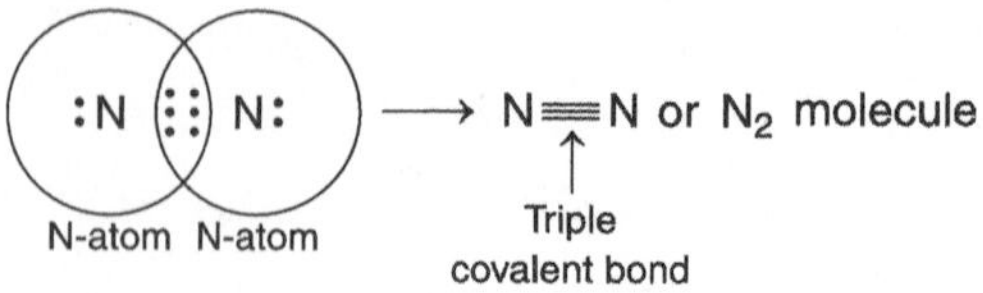

Polar and Non-Polar Covalent Bond

(i) **Polar covalent bond** is formed between two atoms having difference in their electronegativities, and the shared pair of electrons slightly shift towards the more electronegative atoms. e.g. H_2O, NH_3, etc.

(ii) **Non-polar covalent bond** is formed between two atoms having almost same electronegativity and the electrons are equally shared by the two atoms. e.g. H_2, Cl_2, O_2, etc.

Electron Dot Structures of Some Covalent Molecules

1. Hydrogen Molecule (H_2)

A hydrogen atom has one electron in its outermost shell. It needs one more electron to complete its duplet. Thus, hydrogen atom shares its electron with another hydrogen atom to form H_2 molecule.

e.g.

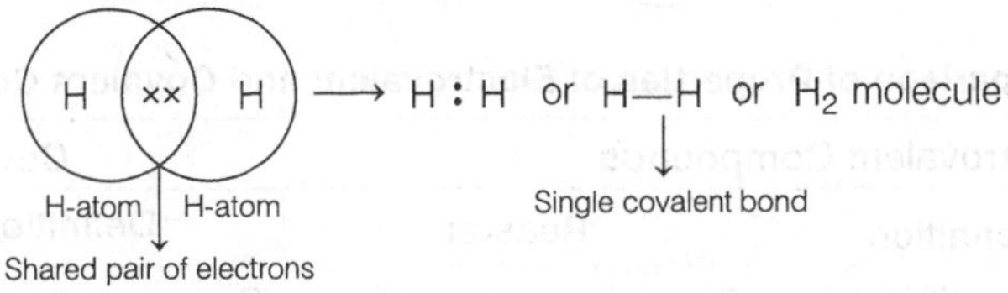

2. Chlorine Molecule (Cl_2)

Chlorine has 7 electrons in its outermost shell, so to complete its octet, it shares one electron with another chlorine atom to form Cl_2 molecule.

e.g.

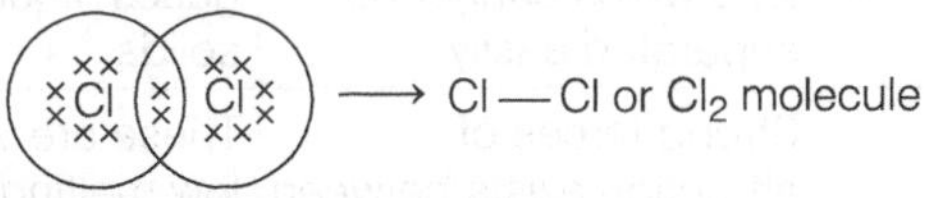

3. Nitrogen Molecule (N_2)

Nitrogen atom has 5 electrons in its outermost shell, to complete its octet, nitrogen needs three electrons. Hence, two N-atoms share three pairs of electrons to form N_2 molecule.

e.g.

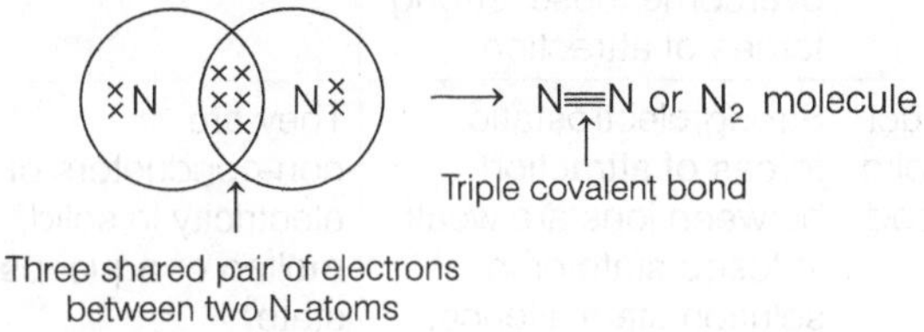

4. Ammonia Molecule (NH_3)

Nitrogen needs 3 electrons to complete its octet, while hydrogen needs one electron to complete its duplet. So, nitrogen shares three electrons with one electron of three hydrogen atoms.

e.g.

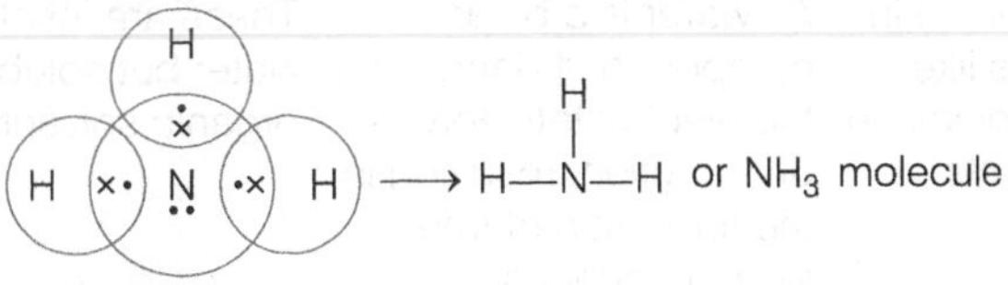

Hence, number of covalent bond in $NH_3 = 3$

5. Carbon Tetrachloride (CCl_4)

Carbon has four electrons in its outermost shell, so to complete its octet, it shares four electrons with one electron of four chlorine atoms.

e.g.

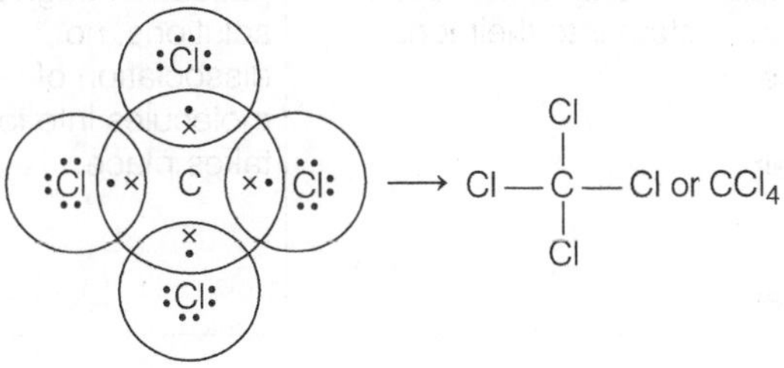

6. Methane (CH_4)

Carbon has four electrons in its outermost shell, so to complete its octet, it shares four electrons with one electron of four hydrogen atoms.

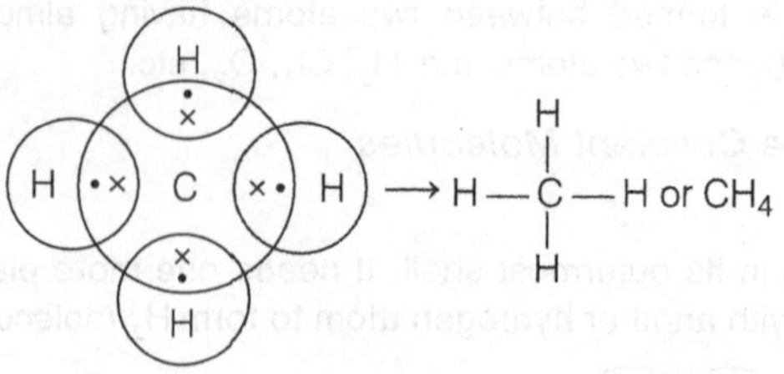

Comparison of Properties of Electrovalent and Covalent Compounds

	Electrovalent Compounds		Covalent Compounds	
Property	**Definition**	**Reason**	**Definition**	**Reason**
Nature	Their constituent particles are ions. They are hard solids.	These have strong electrostatic forces of attraction between their ions which cannot be separated easily.	Their constituent particles are molecules. They are gases, liquids or soft solids.	They have weak forces of attraction between their molecules.
Boiling and Melting Points	These are non-volatile, with high boiling and melting points.	Strong forces of attraction exists between the oppositely charged ions, so, a large amount of energy is required to overcome these strong forces of attraction.	These are volatile with low melting and boiling points.	They have weak forces of attraction between the binding molecules, thus, less energy is required to break this force of attraction.
Conducting Nature (heat and electricity)	They do not conduct electricity in the solid state. They are good conductors of electricity in the fused (or in aqueous) state. They are good conductors of heat.	Strong electrostatic forces of attraction between ions are weak in fused state or in solution state. Hence, ions become mobile.	They are non-conductors of electricity in solid, molten or aqueous state. They are poor conductors of heat.	Due to the absence of free ions.
Solubility	These are soluble in polar solvents like water but insoluble in organic solvents.	As water is a polar compound, it decreases the electrostatic forces of attraction, resulting in the formation of free ions in aqueous solution. Hence, they dissolve.	These are insoluble in water but soluble in organic solvents.	As organic solvents are non-polar, hence, these compounds dissolves in non-polar covalent compounds.
Ionisation/ Dissociation in Solution	When electricity is passed through their aqueous solution or molten state, these compounds dissociate into their ions and the ions migrate to the opposite electrodes.	Compounds dissociate in water or in molten state into their ions.	When electricity is passed through their solutions, no dissociation of molecules into ions takes place.	Covalent compounds do not dissociate because they contain molecules, rather than the ions.

Coordinate Bond or Dative Bond

- The bond which is formed between two atoms by sharing a pair of electrons, provided both of the electrons are contributed by only one of the bonding atoms is called a **coordinate bond** or **dative bond.**
- The atom which provides the electron pair for the formation of a coordinate bond is called **donor** and the other atom is called **acceptor**.
  The bond is shown by an arrow with its head pointing away from the donor to acceptor atom ($\longrightarrow$).
  e.g. Ammonium ion (NH_4^+) and hydronium ion (H_3O^+) contain one coordinate bond each.

1. Formation of Hydronium Ion (H_3O^+)

- The hydronium ion, $[H_3O]^+$ involves water molecule and hydrogen ion.

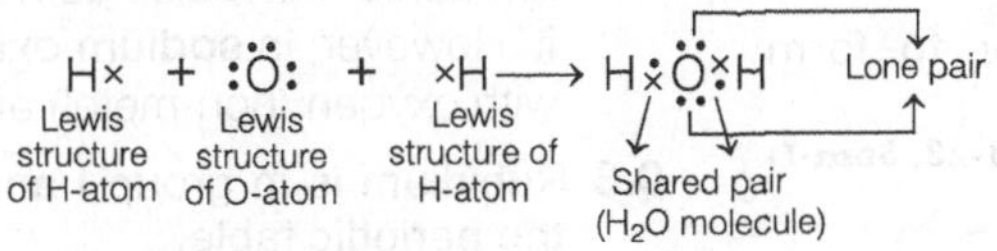

Note A pair of electrons which is not shared with any other atom is called the **lone pair** of electrons.

- Out of these two lone pair of electrons, one lone pair is used to donate to hydrogen ion.

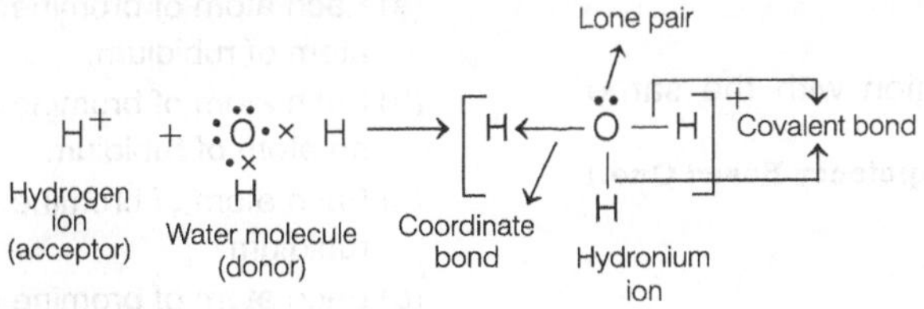

2. Formation of Ammonium Ion (NH_4^+)

- Formation of ammonium ion (NH_4^+) involves ammonia molecule and hydrogen ion. In ammonia, covalent bond formation takes place and one unshared pair of electrons is left which is also called lone pair of electron. It is present on N-atom of ammonia after completing its octet.

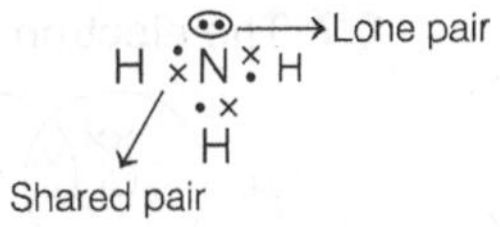

- Hydrogen ion, H^+ (proton) accepts this lone pair of electrons of nitrogen atom leading to the formation of a coordinate bond.

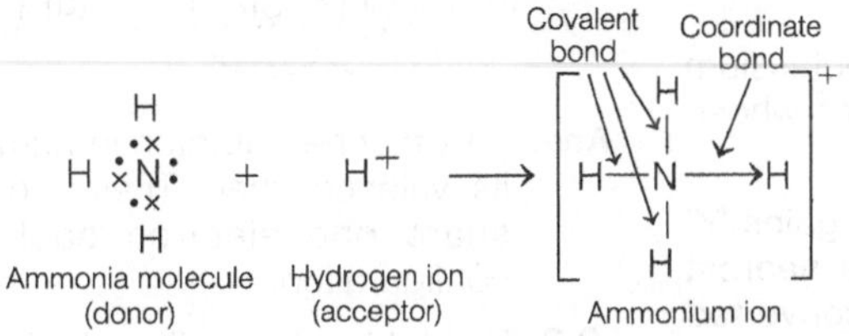

3. Formation of Hydroxyl Ion (OH^-)

Hydroxyl ion or hydroxide ion is formed when one hydrogen ion (H^+) is removed from water molecule. After removing H^+, the shared pair of electron remains with oxygen as it is more electronegative and as a result hydroxyl ion attains negative charge.

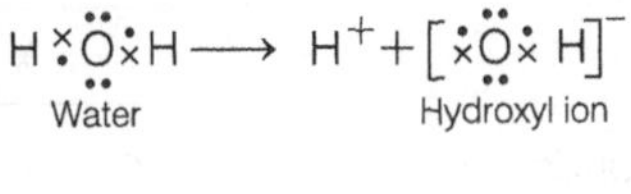

EXAM ORIENTED QUESTIONS

TYPE - 1 01 Mark

Multiple Choice Questions

Q.1 The particles which attract one another to form electrovalent compounds are **(ICSE Specimen 2021-22, Sem-I)**

(a) electrons (b) protons
(c) ions (d) molecules

Ans. (c) The charged particles which attract one another to form electrovalent compounds are **ions**, i.e. cations and anions.

Q.2 Which element forms a stable anion with the same electronic configuration as argon? **(Competency Based Que.)**

(a) Magnesium (b) Fluorine
(c) Chlorine (d) Sodium

Ans. (c) Chlorine

The electronic configuration of argon is = 2, 8, 8
Electronic configuration of magnesium is = 2, 8, 2
Electronic configuration of fluorine is = 2, 7
Electronic configuration of chlorine is = 2, 8, 7
Electronic configuration of sodium is = 2, 8, 1

So, **chlorine** will accept an electron to form an ion with the same electronic configuration as argon.

Q.3 An element with the atomic number 19 will most likely combine chemically with the element whose atomic number is **(ICSE 2016)**

(a) 17 (b) 11 (c) 18 (d) 20

Ans. (a) The element with atomic number 19 is potassium (K), it will react with electronegative element whose atomic number is **17** (chlorine).

Q.4 The electronic configuration of X is 2, 8, 6. It gains 'Y' electrons into its valence shell to attain the nearest noble gas electronic configuration and gets converted to an ion Z. **(Competency Based Que.)**

X, *Y* and *Z*, respectively are

(a) sodium, one, electropositive
(b) beryllium, two, electronegative
(c) oxygen, six, electronegative
(d) sulphur, two, electronegative

Ans. (d) Sulphur, two, electronegative

Element *X* with atomic number 16, corresponds to **sulphur**. It will accept **two electrons** to complete its octet, and it is an **electronegative** ion.

Q.5 Ionic bonding is seen in **(ICSE Specimen 2021-22, Sem-I)**

(a) methane (b) hydrogen
(c) ammonia (d) sodium oxide

Ans. (d) Among the given options, methane, hydrogen and ammonia molecules do not have any metal atoms in it. However, in **sodium oxide**, sodium metal combines with oxygen (non-metal) and an ionic bond is formed.

Q.6 Rubidium is in group I and bromine is in group VII of the periodic table.

How is a compound formed between rubidium and bromine?

(a) Each atom of bromine shares an electron with an atom of rubidium.
(b) Each atom of bromine shares a pair of electrons with an atom of rubidium.
(c) Each atom of bromine gives an electron to an atom of rubidium.
(d) Each atom of bromine receives an electron from an atom of rubidium.

Ans. (d) Generally, Group I metals need to lose one electron to form cation and Group VII non-metals require one electron to form anion. So, bromine receives one electron from rubidium to form ionic bond.

Q.7 The electron dot structure of chlorine molecule is

(a) 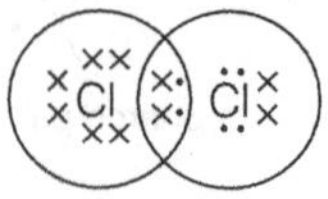

(b) 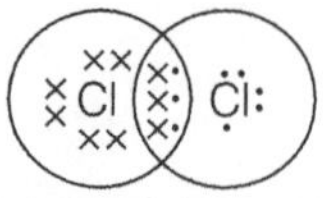

(c) 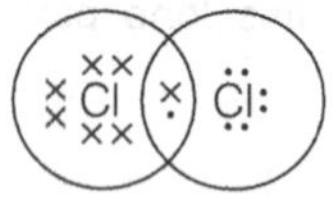

(d) 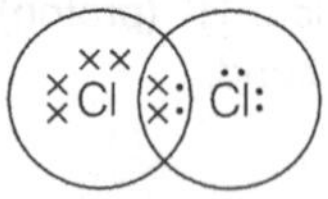

Ans. (c) Chlorine has atomic number 17 and 7 electrons in its valence shell. Therefore, each chlorine atom will share one electron each to achieve noble gas configuration.

Q.8 The table shows the electronic configuration of four elements. **(ICSE 2021-22, Sem-I)**

Element	Electronic configuration
W	2, 6
X	2, 8
Y	2, 8, 1
Z	2, 8, 7

Which pair of atoms will form a covalent compound?

(a) Two atoms of *W*
(b) Two atoms of *X*
(c) An atom of *W* and atom of *X*
(d) An atom of *Y* and an atom of *Z*

Ans. (a) In the given table, configuration of *W* is 2, 6. So, it needs two electrons to complete its octet.
Thus, two *W*-atoms share their two pairs of electrons to form **W_2 covalent compound.**

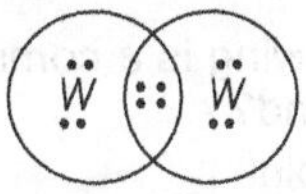

Q.9 Type of bonding present in hydrogen chloride. **(ICSE Specimen 2021-22, Sem-I)**

(a) metallic (b) ionic
(c) covalent (d) coordinate

Ans. (c) **Covalent bond** is present between hydrogen and chlorine as they both are non-metals and form a bond by mutual sharing of electrons.

Q.10 The type of bonding present in the nitrogen molecule **(ICSE Specimen 2021-22, Sem-I)**

(a) single covalent bond
(b) double covalent bond
(c) polar covalent bond
(d) triple covalent bond

Ans. (d) Nitrogen have 5 electrons in its outermost shell and in order to complete its octet, 3 electrons are needed. Hence, it can form **three or triple covalent bonds**.

Q.11 The correct representation of covalent bonding in an oxygen molecule is

(a) 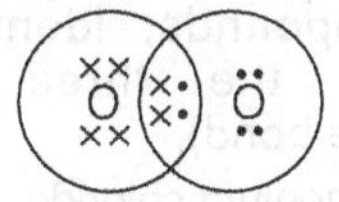
(b) 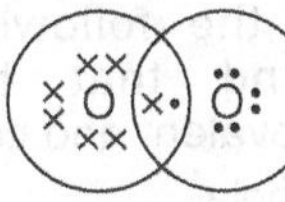
(c) 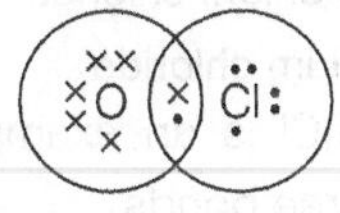
(d) 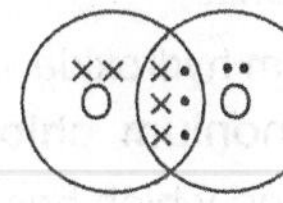

Ans. (a) Oxygen has atomic number 8 and 6 electrons in its valence shell. Therefore, each oxygen atom will share two electrons each to achieve noble gas configuration.

Q.12 The total number of electrons shared in the formation of an ethyne molecule is

(a) 6 (b) 3
(c) 10 (d) 4

Ans. (c) H—C≡C—H

or

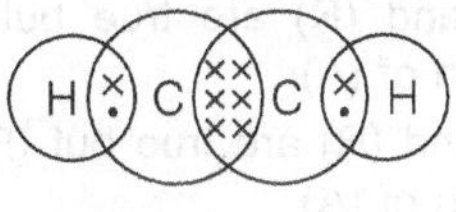

∴ Total number of electrons shared = 10.

Q.13 Ramu makes a detailed study on the values of electronegativity and the formation of compounds. Accordingly, he draws the following conclusion:

The larger the electronegativity (EN) difference between the combining atoms, the more ionic bonds will form. If the EN difference is negligible, covalent bonds will form. So, which of the following values refers to covalent bonds? **(Competency Based Que.)**

P : 3.0 and 3.0
Q : 0.9 and 3.0

(a) Only *P* (b) Only *Q*
(c) Both *P* and *Q* (d) Neither *P* and *Q*

Ans. (a) For covalent bond formation to take place, electronegativity difference between the combining atoms should be negligible. Thus, **only *P*** values refers to covalent bonds formation.

Q.14 Element *X* has the electronic configuration 2, 5 and element *Y* has the electronic configuration 2, 6. What type of bond will be formed between these two elements?

(a) Non-polar covalent (b) Polar covalent
(c) Ionic (d) All of these

Ans. (b) *X* (nitrogen) and *Y* (oxygen) both need electrons to complete their octet. The electronegativity difference between them is significant, so they form a polar covalent bond, where electrons are shared unequally, with oxygen (*Y*) pulling the electrons closer.

Q.15 Which electron arrangement for the outer shell electrons in a covalent compound is correct? **(ICSE 2021-22, Sem-I)**

(a) 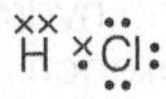
(b) 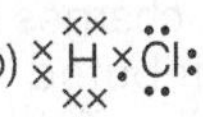
(c) 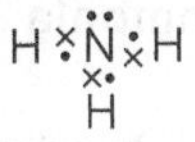
(d) 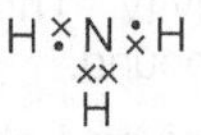

Ans. (c) Nitrogen needs 3 electrons to complete its octet and hydrogen needs 1 electron to complete its duplet. So, in the formation of NH_3 molecule, N and H contribute one electron each to form common shared pair. There are 3 covalent bond (3 N—H) in NH_3.

Q.16 Given below are four covalents compounds

(*A*) H_2O (*B*) CCl_4 (*C*) Cl_2 (*D*) NH_3

Which of the following represents the correct order when they are arranged in their increasing number of covalent bonds? **(Competency Based Que.)**

(a) $B < D < A < C$ (b) $A < C < D < B$
(c) $C < D < A < B$ (d) $C < A < D < B$

Ans. (d) $C < A < D < B$

The structures of the compounds are

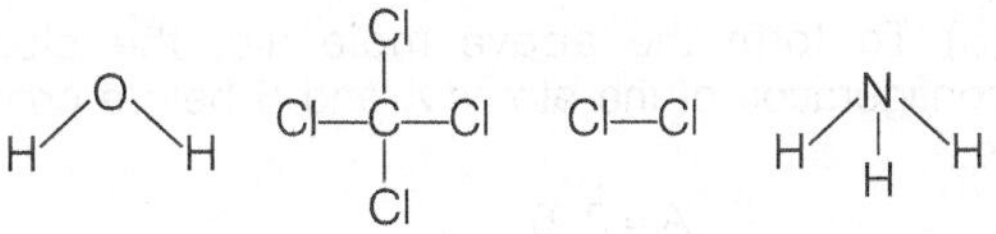

Q.17 The number of lone pair of electrons in the nitrogen atom in ammonia molecule is **(ICSE Specimen 2021-22, Sem-I)**

(a) one (b) two
(c) three (d) four

Ans. (a) The structure of ammonia involves three bond pairs between nitrogen and hydrogen and **one lone pair** of electron present on nitrogen.

Q.18 In the molecule of water, oxygen atom has **(ICSE 2024)**

(a) one shared pair of electrons
(b) three shared pairs of electrons
(c) two lone pairs of electrons
(d) one lone pair of electrons

Ans. (c) **Two lone pairs of electrons** are present on oxygen atom of water molecule.

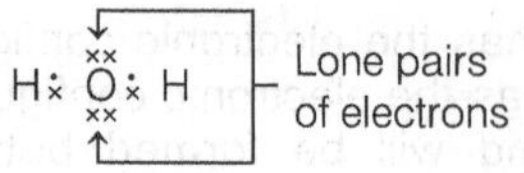

Q.19 Which of the following has two sets of lone pair of electron in them? **(ICSE 2021-22, Sem-I)**

(a) Ammonia (b) Methane
(c) Water (d) Ammonium ion

Ans. (c) **Water** (H_2O) molecule consists of two bond pairs and two lone pairs.

Q.20 A polar covalent compound is **(ICSE Specimen 2023)**

(a) methane (b) ammonia
(c) nitrogen (d) chlorine

Ans. (b) In ammonia, charges on nitrogen and hydrogen are unequally distributed due to difference in their electronegativity. This makes **ammonia** a polar covalent compound.

Q.21 The diagram given below shows the bonding in the covalent molecule AB_2.

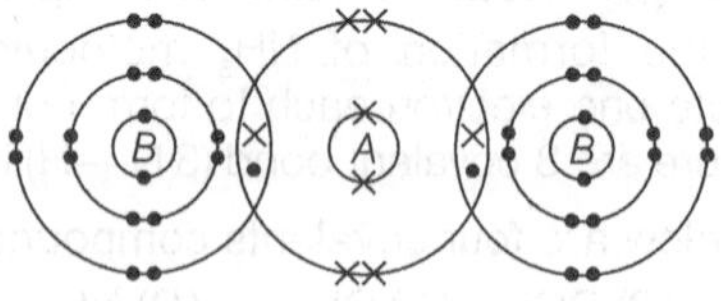

Which option represents the correct electronic configuration of atoms A and B before combining together to form the above molecule?

	A	B
(a)	2, 4	2, 8, 6
(b)	2, 4	2, 8, 7
(c)	2, 8	2, 8, 8
(d)	2, 6	2, 8, 7

Ans. (d) To form the above molecule, the electronic configuration of the atoms A and B before combining is

$$A = 2, 6$$
$$B = 2, 8, 7$$

Q.22 Which of the following is not a typical property of an ionic compound?

(a) High melting point.
(b) Conducts electricity in the molten and in the aqueous solution state.
(c) They are insoluble in water.
(d) They exist as oppositely charged ions even in the solid state.

Ans. (c) Ionic compounds are **soluble in water.**

Q.23 Which of the following is a common characteristic of a covalent compound? **(ICSE 2017)**

(a) High melting point.
(b) Consists of molecules.
(c) Always soluble in water.
(d) Conducts electricity, when it is in the molten state.

Ans. (b) The constituent particles of covalent compounds are **molecules.**

Q.24 A compound with low boiling point is **(ICSE 2020)**

(a) sodium chloride (b) calcium chloride
(c) potassium chloride (d) carbon tetrachloride

Ans. (d) **Carbon tetrachloride** has low boiling point. Out of the four options given, only carbon tetrachloride is covalent, while the other three are ionic compounds.

Q.25 Bonding in this molecule can be understood to involve coordinate bonding. **(ICSE 2015)**

(a) Carbon tetrachloride (b) Hydrogen
(c) Hydrogen chloride (d) Ammonium chloride

Ans. (d) In **ammonium chloride** (NH_4Cl), there is coordinate bonding.

Q.26 Among the following compounds, identify the compound that has all the three bonds (ionic, covalent and coordinate bond).

(a) Ammonia (b) Ammonium chloride
(c) Sodium hydroxide (d) Calcium chloride

Ans. (b) **Ammonium chloride**, NH_4Cl is an example of a compound which has all the three bonds.

TYPE - 2

01 Mark

Assertion-Reason Questions

Directions (Q. Nos. 1-5) In the following questions, a statement of Assertion (A) is followed by a statement of Reason (R). Choose the answer based on the codes given below.

(a) Both (A) and (R) are true but (R) is the correct explanation of (A).
(b) Both (A) and (R) are true but (R) is not the correct explanation of (A).
(c) (A) is true but (R) is false.
(d) (A) is false but (R) is true.

Q.1 Assertion (A) Caesium fluoride, CsF is the most ionic compound.

Reason (R) Larger the electronegativity difference of two elements, more will be the ionic nature of the resulting compound.

Ans. (a) Caesium is the most electropositive and fluorine is the most electronegative element of the periodic table. The compound, therefore formed by their combination, i.e. CsF is the most ionic compound.

Thus, both (A) and (R) are true and (R) is the correct explanation of (A).

Q.2 Assertion (A) NaCl is an ionic compound.

Reason (R) Both atoms having either high electron affinity or high ionisation energy form ionic compound.

Ans. (c) NaCl is an ionic compound formed by the transfer of electrons.

Ionic compounds are formed when one of the atom has low ionisation energy and other atom has high electron affinity. When both the atoms have either high ionisation energy or high electron affinity then covalent compounds are formed.

Thus, (A) is true but (R) is false.

Q.3 Assertion (A) N_2 molecule contains triple bond.

Reason (R) N_2 conduct electricity due to the presence of free ions.

Ans. (c) Nitrogen molecule contains triple bond.

$$(N \equiv N)$$

N_2 cannot conduct electricity because it is a non-polar covalent compound and does not give free ions in aqueous solution.

Thus, (A) is true but (R) is false.

Q.4 Assertion (A) The bond between nitrogen (N) and hydrogen (H) in ammonia is polar covalent.

Reason (R) Nitrogen is more electronegative than hydrogen, causing the electrons to be shared unevenly.

Ans. (a) The bond in NH_3 is polar covalent because N has higher electronegativity than H, causing the electrons to be shared unevenly.

Thus, both (A) and (R) are true and (R) is the correct explanation of (A).

Q.5 Assertion (A) The formation of ammonium chloride takes place through coordinate bond.

Reason (R) Ammonia molecule contains a lone pair of electron due to which it can form coordinate bond.

Ans. (a) Ammonia molecule contains a lone pair of electron due to which it can form coordinate bond.

Thus, both (A) and (R) are true and (R) is the correct explanation of (A).

TYPE - 3 — 01 Mark

Fill in the Blanks

Q.1 Cations are.........(oxidised/reduced) ions due to the loss of electrons by the neutral atom

Ans. oxidised **(Competency Based Que.)**

Q.2 The compound that does not have a lone pair of electrons is ...... (ammonia/carbon tetrachloride). **(ICSE 2017)**

Ans. carbon tetrachloride, 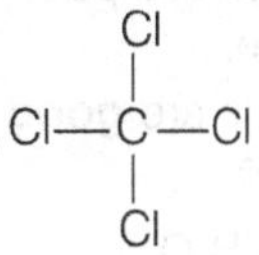

Q.3 Carbon tetrachloride is a .... (polar/non-polar) covalent molecule. **(ICSE 2024)**

Ans. non-polar

Q.4 Electrovalent compounds have .... melting points (high/low). **(ICSE 2016)**

Ans. high

Q.5 Ionic or electrovalent compounds do not conduct electricity in their .... state. (fused/solid) **(ICSE 2018)**

Ans. solid

Q.6 Non-polar covalent compounds are ...... (good/bad) conductors of heat and electricity. **(ICSE 2023)**

Ans. bad

Q.7 The polar covalent compound in gaseous state that does not conduct electricity is .... (ammonia/methane) **(ICSE 2020)**

Ans. ammonia

TYPE - 4 — 01 Mark

Correct the Incorrect Statement

Q.1 One atom with high ionisation potential and other with low electron affinity favours the formation of electrovalent bond.

Ans. One atom with **low** ionisation potential and other with **high** electron affinity favours the formation of electrovalent bond.

Q.2 $CaCl_2$, KBr, $MgCl_2$, CaO are the examples of covalent compounds.

Ans. $CaCl_2$, KBr, $MgCl_2$, CaO are the examples of **ionic** compounds.

Q.3 Methane molecule contains two lone pair of electrons on the carbon atom.

Ans. Methane (CH_4) molecule contains **zero** lone pair of electrons on the carbon atom.

Q.4 NH_3, CCl_4, H_2O and HCl are examples of polar covalent compound.

Ans. NH_3, H_2O and HCl are polar covalent compounds but **CCl_4 is a non-polar covalent compound.**

Q.5 Ethene contains single covalent bond between two carbon atoms.

Ans. Ethene contains **double** covalent bond between two carbon atoms.

Q.6 Ionic compounds are poor conductors of electricity in aqueous state.

Ans. Ionic compounds are **good** conductors of electricity in aqueous state.

Q.7 CH_4 dissolves in H_2O.

Ans. CH_4 **does not** dissolve in H_2O.

Q.8 Water molecule undergo self ionisation to produce hydrogen ion (H^+) and hydroxide ion (OH^-).

Ans. Water molecule undergo self ionisation to produce **hydronium ion (H_3O^+)** and hydroxide ion (OH^-).

Q.9 Hydroxyl ion is formed when H^+ is added to water molecule.

Ans. Hydroxyl ion is formed when H^+ is **removed** from water molecule.

TYPE - 5

01 × 05 = 05 Marks

Matching Type Questions

Q.1 Match the following columns.

Column I	Column II
A. Hydronium ion	1. Non-polar covalent compound
B. Hydrogen chloride	2. Most ionic compound
C. Chlorine molecule	3. Polar covalent compound
D. Caesium fluoride	4. Covalent and coordinate bond
E. Sodium chloride	5. Ionic compound

Ans. A→4, B→3, C→1, D→2, E→5

- Hydronium ion (H_3O^+) contains both covalent and coordinate bond.
- HCl is formed by the combination of atoms having electronegativity difference therefore, it is a polar covalent compound.
- Chlorine molecule consists of atoms of same electronegativity therefore, it is a non-polar covalent compound.
- Caesium fluoride is the most ionic compound because it is formed by the combination of most electropositive and most electronegative element of the periodic table.
- Sodium chloride is an ionic compound because it is formed by the transfer of electrons between sodium and chlorine atoms.

Q.2 Match the following columns.

Column I	Column II
A. Coordinate compound	1. Potassium chloride
B. Electropositive element	2. Chlorine
C. Electrovalent compound	3. Water
D. Electronegative element	4. NH_4^+
E. Polar covalent compound	5. Sodium

Ans. A→4, B→5, C→1, D→2, E→3

Q.3 Match the following columns.

Column I	Column II
A. Ionic compounds	1. Low melting point
B. Fluorine	2. High melting point
C. Neon	3. Incomplete octet
D. Helium	4. Octet
E. Covalent compounds	5. Duplet

Ans. A→2, B→3, D→4, D→5, E→1

Ionic compounds have high melting points and covalent compounds have low melting points.

Fluorine consists of incomplete octet, while helium and neon consists of duplet and octet respectively.

F = 2, 7, He = 2, Ne = 2, 8

TYPE - 6

01 Mark

Identify the Following

Q.1 Name the chemical bond formed by a shared pair of electrons, each bonding atom contributing one electron to the pair. **(ICSE 2020)**

Ans. Covalent bond

Q.2 Write a covalent compound which behaves like an ionic compound in aqueous solution.

Ans. Hydrogen chloride

Q.3 Identify the type of covalent bond in which electrons are shared unequally between the combining atoms. **(ICSE 2025)**

Ans. Polar covalent bond

Q.4 Name a bond formed by a shared pair of electrons with both electrons coming from the same atom. **(ICSE Specimen 2025)**

Ans. Coordinate bond

Q.5 What is the term used for formation of ions from molecules. **(ICSE 2014)**

Ans. Ionisation

TYPE - 7 — 02 Marks

Short Answer Type I Questions

Q.1 There are three elements *E*, *F*, *G* with atomic numbers 19, 8 and 17 respectively. Give the molecular formula of the compound formed between *E* and *G* and state the type of chemical bond in this compound.

Ans. Electronic configuration of elements *E*, *F*, *G* are

E (Atomic number 19): 2, 8, 8, 1

F (Atomic number 8) : 2, 6

G (Atomic number 17) : 2, 8, 7

Thus, *E* and *G* being metals and non-metals respectively, form **ionic or electrovalent compound.**

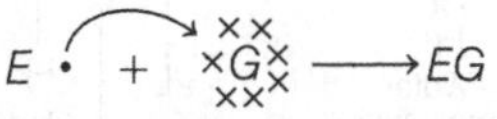

Hence, molecular formula of the compound is ***EG***. **(2)**

Q.2 Element *X* is a metal with a valency 2, *Y* is a non-metal with a valency 3.

(i) Write an equation to show how *Y* forms an ion?

(ii) If *Y* is a diatomic gas, write an equation for the direct combination of *X* and *Y* to form a compound. **(ICSE 2015)**

Ans. *X* - Metal (valency 2)

Y - Non-metal (valency 3)

(i) $Y + 3e^- \longrightarrow Y^{3-}$ **(1)**

(ii) $3X + Y_2 \longrightarrow X_3Y_2$ **(1)**

Q.3 Atom of an element contains five electrons in its valence shell. This element is major component of air. It exists as a diatomic molecule. Identify the element. Draw the electron dot structure of this molecule.

Ans. Nitrogen (N) contains five electrons in its valence shell $\begin{pmatrix} K, & L \\ 2, & 5 \end{pmatrix}$. It is a major component of air and exists as a diatomic molecule (N_2). **(1)**

Electron dot structure of nitrogen molecule is:

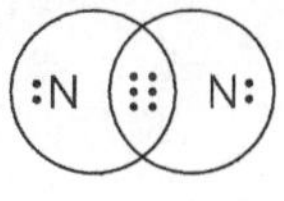

(1)

Q.4 (i) Magnesium ribbon is added to dilute HCl. A gas is liberated along with the formation of a compound. Draw an electron dot diagram to show the structure of the compound that is formed.

(ii) $:\dot{X}: + :\dot{X}: \longrightarrow \square$

The equation given above represents the molecule formation of element *X*. Fill in the box with the electron dot structure of the molecule

(Competency Based Que.)

Ans.

(i)

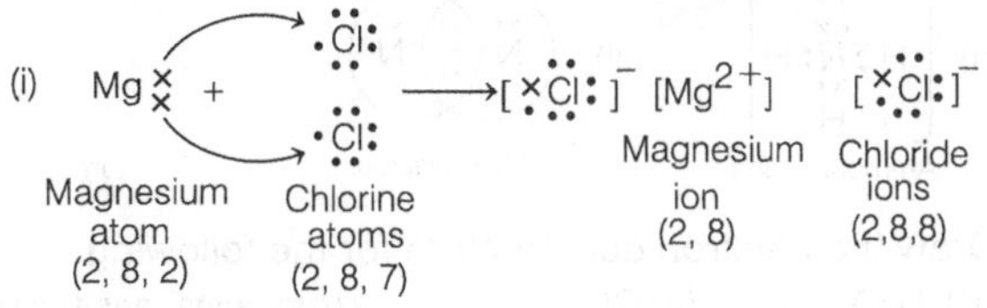

(1)

(ii) $\ddot{X}::\ddot{X}$ **(1)**

Q.5 An element *L* consists of molecules.

(i) What type of bonding is present in the particles that make up *L*?

(ii) When *L* is heated with iron metal, it forms a compound Fe *L*. What chemical term would you use to describe the change undergone by *L*? **(ICSE 2015)**

Ans. (i) Covalent bonding **(1)**

(ii) When *L* is heated with iron metal, it forms Fe*L*. In this case, Fe loses its two electrons and undergoes oxidation whereas, *L* gains two electrons and undergoes reduction. **(1)**

Q.6 Give the appropriate term defined by the statement given below.

(i) The tendency of an atom to attract electrons towards itself, when combined in a covalent compound.

(ii) The covalent bond in which the electrons are shared equally between the combining atoms. **(ICSE 2019)**

Ans. (i) **Electronegativity** is the tendency of an atom in a molecule to attract the shared pair of electrons toward itself. **(1)**

(ii) **Non-polar covalent bond** is formed between two atoms having almost same electronegativity, and electrons are equally shared by the two atoms situated exactly between the two identical nuclei. **(1)**

Q.7 Draw the appropriate structural formula of carbon tetrachloride and state the type of bond present in it.

Ans. Covalent bond **(1)**

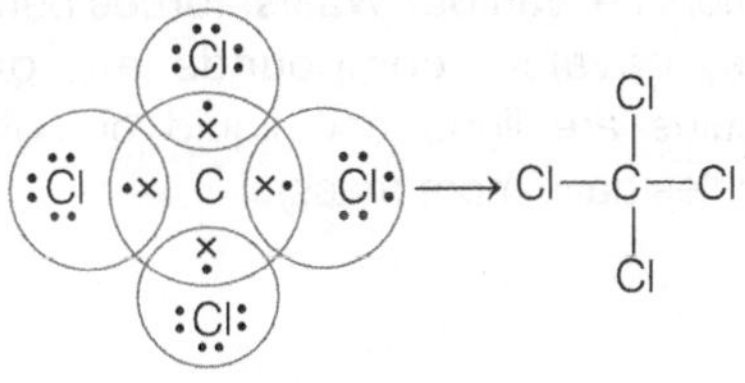

(1)

Q.8 State the type of bonding in the following molecules.
(i) Water
(ii) Calcium oxide **(ICSE 2017)**

Ans. (i) Water (H_2O) - **covalent bonding** **(1)**
(ii) Calcium oxide (CaO)- **ionic bonding** **(1)**

Q.9 Draw the electron dot structure for the following.
(i) Ammonium ion **(ICSE Specimen 2025)**
(ii) A molecule of nitrogen (At. no. N = 7, H = 1) **(ICSE 2023)**

Ans. (i) 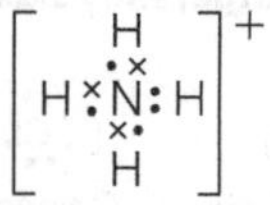
Ammonium ion

(ii) 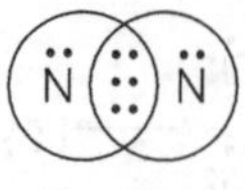
N_2 molecule **(1 × 2 = 2)**

Q.10 Draw the electron dot structure for the following.
(i) H_3O^+ (ii) CH_4 **(ICSE 2023, 2024, 2015)**

Ans. (i) Electron dot structure of H_3O^+.

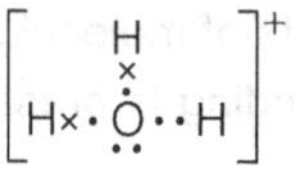
(1)

(ii) Electron dot structure of CH_4.

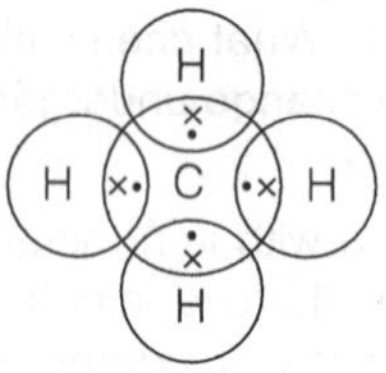
(1)

Q.11 (i) Inert gases do not form ions. Why? **(ICSE specimen 2024, ICSE 2018, 2024)**
(ii) Covalent compounds have a low melting and boiling point.

Ans. (i) Inert gases do not form ions because they have **stable electronic configuration**, i.e. their outermost (valence) shell is complete. These do not lose, gain or share electrons. **(1)**
(ii) Covalent compounds have low melting and boiling points because of the presence of **weak forces of attraction** between the molecules which are easily overcome at low temperatures. **(1)**

Q.12 (i) Why do covalent compounds exist as gases, liquids or soft solids? **(ICSE 2014)**
(ii) Give difference between polar and non-polar covalent compounds. **(ICSE specimen 2019)**

Ans. (i) Covalent compounds have weak forces of attraction. i.e. **van der Waals' forces** between them. Hence, covalent compounds are gaseous (if molecules are light) and liquid or soft solids (if molecules have more mass). **(1)**
(ii) Polar covalent compounds are formed by atoms having significant electronegativity difference, while non-polar covalent compounds are formed by atoms having almost same electronegativity. **(1)**

Q.13 Compare the compounds carbon tetrachloride and sodium chloride with regard to solubility in water and electrical conductivity. **(ICSE 2013)**

Ans.

Sodium Chloride	Carbon Tetrachloride
It does not conduct electricity in solid but a good conductor of electricity in molten or aqueous state.	It does not conduct electricity in solid, molten or aqueous sate.
It is soluble in polar solvents but insoluble in non-polar solvents.	It is soluble in non-polar solvent but insoluble in polar solvents like water.

(2)

Q.14 Draw an electron dot diagram to show the structure of hydronium ion. State the type of bonding present in it.

Ans. Covalent and coordinate bonding **(1)**

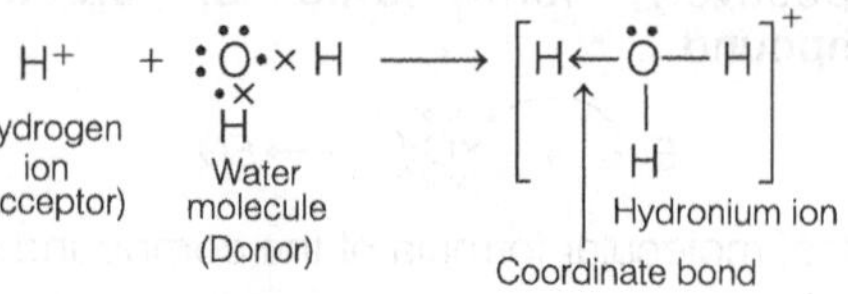

(1)

Q.15 Define the following terms:
(i) Coordinate bond
(ii) Electrovalency **(ICSE 2025)**

Ans. (i) The bond formed between two atoms by sharing a pair of electrons, provided entirely by one of the combining atoms, but shared by both is called a **coordinate bond** or **dative bond**. **(1)**
(ii) The number of electrons that an atom of an element loses or gains to form an electrovalent bond is called **electrovalency**. **(1)**

Q.16 Draw the structure of stable positive ion, when an acid dissolves in water. **(ICSE 2014)**

Ans. When an acid is dissolved in water, **hydronium ion** (H_3O^+) is formed.

$$HA + H_2O \longrightarrow H_3O^+(aq) + A^-(aq)$$

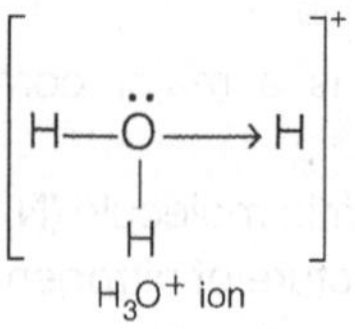
H_3O^+ ion **(2)**

TYPE - 8   03 Marks

Short Answer Type II Questions

Q.1 Choose the kind of chemical bonding (ionic bond, covalent bond, both ionic and covalent bonds) present in the following compounds. Potassium chloride, magnesium oxide, sulphuric acid, ammonium hydroxide, zinc sulphide, phosphorus trichloride (PCl_3).

Ans.

Ionic bond	Covalent bond	Both ionic and covalent bond
(i) Potassium chloride	Phosphorus trichloride	Sulphuric acid
(ii) Magnesium oxide		Ammonium hydroxide
(iii) Zinc sulphide		

(3)

Q.2 A compound has the formula H_2Y? (Y = non-metal). State the following
(i) the valency of Y.
(ii) The outer electronic configuration of Y.
(iii) the bonding present in H_2Y.

Ans. (i) Valency of Y is 2. **(1)**

(ii) For compound H_2Y, valency of Y is 2 ($8 - 6 = 2$). Hence, it has 6 electrons in its valence shell.

Thus, outer electronic configuration of Y is K, L: 2, 6 **(1)**

(iii) As bond formation is through sharing of electrons. These shared electrons belong to the outermost shells of both the atoms and in this way, both atom attain the noble gas configuration. This type of bonding is called **covalent bonding**. **(1)**

Q.3 Draw the electron dot diagram for the compounds given below. Represent the electrons by (•) and (x) in the diagram. **(ICSE 2020)**

[Atomic number Ca = 20, O = 8, Cl = 17, H = 1]
(i) Calcium oxide
(ii) Chlorine molecule
(iii) Water molecule

Ans. (i) CaO

$Ca\overset{\times}{\underset{\times}{}} + :\ddot{O}: \longrightarrow [Ca^{2+}] [\overset{\times}{\underset{\times}{}}\ddot{O}:]^{2-}$ or CaO

Calcium atom (2,8,8,2)   Oxygen atom (2,6)   Calcium ion (2,8,8)   Oxide ion (2,8)

Calcium oxide **(1)**

(ii) Cl_2

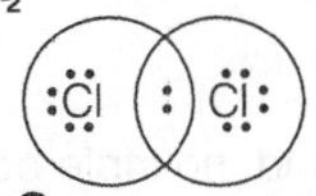

$\equiv$ Cl—Cl or Cl_2 molecule **(1)**

(iii) H_2O

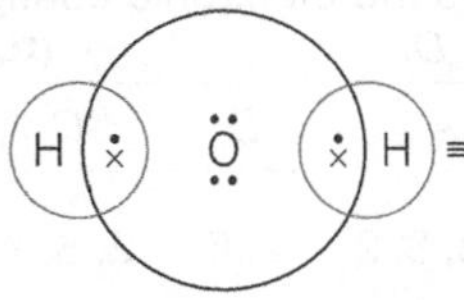

$\equiv$ H—O—H or H_2O molecule **(1)**

Q.4 Draw the electron dot structure of
(i) Nitrogen molecule [N = 7] **(ICSE 2024)**
(ii) Sodium chloride [Na = 11, Cl = 17]
(iii) Ammonium ion [N = 7, H = 1] **(ICSE 2019)**

Ans. (i) Electron dot structure of nitrogen molecule (N_2)

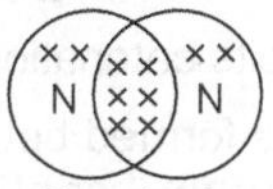

N_2 molecule **(1)**

(ii) Electron dot structure of NaCl

$Na^{\times} + \cdot\ddot{Cl}: \longrightarrow Na^{+} [\overset{\times}{}\ddot{Cl}:]^{-}$

Sodium atom (2, 8, 1)   Chlorine atom (2, 8, 7)   Sodium ion (2, 8)   Chloride ion (2, 8, 8)

Sodium chloride **(1)**

(iii) Electron dot structure of ammonium ion (NH_4^+)

$$\left[\begin{array}{c} H \\ \times\bullet \\ H \overset{\times}{\bullet} N \overset{\bullet}{\times} H \\ \times\bullet \\ H \end{array}\right]^{+}$$

Ammonium ion **(1)**

Q.5 Give the electron dot structure of the following
(i) NH_3 (ii) CH_4 (iii) H_3O^+ **(ICSE 2017)**

Ans. (i) $H \overset{\times}{\bullet} \ddot{N} \overset{\bullet}{\times} H$ with H below   (ii) $H \overset{\times}{\bullet} C \overset{\bullet}{\times} H$ with H above and below   (iii) $[H \overset{\times}{\bullet} \ddot{O} \overset{\bullet}{\times} H]^{+}$ with H below **(1 × 3 = 3)**

Q.6 (i) Show the formation of covalent bond in chlorine by dot diagram.
(ii) What is the condition required for the formation of polar molecule?
(iii) How many single, double and triple bonds are present in ethene molecule?

Ans. (i)

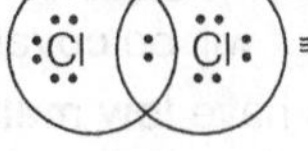

$\equiv$ Cl—Cl or Cl_2 molecule **(1)**

(ii) There should be significant electronegativity difference between the two combining atoms. **(1)**

(iii) 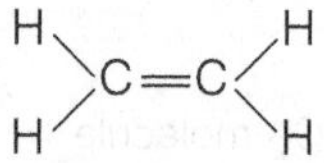

4 single bonds, 1 double bond, no triple bond. **(1)**

Q.7 The following table shows the electronic configuration of the atoms *A*, *B*, *C* and *D*. **(ICSE 2024)**

Element	*A*	*B*	*C*	*D*
Electronic configuration	2, 8, 8, 2	2, 6	2, 8, 7	2, 4

(i) Write the formula of the compound formed between

(a) *A* and *B* (b) *D* and *C*

(ii) Which of the above elements will exhibit catenation?

Ans. (i) (a) ***AB*** (CaO) (b) ***DC***$_4$ (CCl_4) **(2)**

(ii) ***D*** (Carbon exhibits catenation) **(1)**

Q.8 A chemical bond is formed between atoms to achieve a stable electronic configuration, either by transferring, sharing or donating electrons.

(i) In a covalent compound the bond is formed due to .... of electrons (sharing/transfer).

(ii) A molecule which has a single lone pair of electrons .... (NH_3 / H_2O).

(iii) Electrovalent compounds do not conduct electricity in their .... state (molten /solid).

(ICSE Specimen 2023)

Ans. (i) sharing (ii) NH_3 (iii) solid **(1×3=3)**

Q.9 Compound *X* consists of molecules.

Choose the letter corresponding to the correct answer from the choices (a), (b), (c) and (d) given below.

(i) The type of bonding in *X* will be

(a) ionic (b) electrovalent
(c) covalent (d) molecular

(ii) *X* is likely to have a

(a) low melting point and high boiling point.
(b) high melting point and low boiling point.
(c) low melting point and low boiling point.
(d) high melting point and high boiling point.

(iii) In the liquid state, *X* will

(a) become ionic.
(b) be an electrolyte.
(c) conduct electricity.
(d) not conduct electricity.

Ans. (i) (c) Compound *X* consist of molecules. So, the type of bonding in compound *X* will be **covalent**.

(ii) (c) Covalent compounds have **low melting and low boiling points** because they have weak forces of attraction between the binding molecules, thus less energy is required to break the binding force.

(iii) (d) In the liquid state, *X* will **not conduct electricity** because it does not have free ions. **(1×3=3)**

Q.10 The following table represent the elements and the atomic number.

With reference to this, answer the following using only the alphabets given in the table.

Elements	Atomic number
P	13
Q	7
R	10

(i) Which element combines with hydrogen to form a basic gas ?

(ii) Which element has an electron affinity zero ?

(iii) Name the element, which forms an ionic compound with chlorine.

Ans. (i) ***Q*** ($N_2 + 3H_2 \longrightarrow 2NH_3$, ammonia is a basic gas).

(ii) ***R*** (Because neon with atomic number 10 has zero electron affinity). It has fully-filled electronic configuration (2, 8).

(iii) ***P*** (Al with atomic number 13 forms ionic compound, $2Al + 3Cl_2 \longrightarrow 2AlCl_3$). **(1×3=3)**

Q.11 (i) Explain why carbon tetrachloride does not dissolve in water?

(ii) (a) Elements *Q* and *S* react together to form an ionic compound. Under normal conditions, which physical state will the compound *QS* exist in?

(b) Can *Q* and *S*, both be metals? Justify your answer.

Ans. (i) Carbon tetrachloride is a **non-polar covalent compound** and water is a polar solvent. So, carbon tetrachloride does not dissolve in water. **(1)**

(ii) (a) Under normal conditions, an ionic compound exists in solid state. Thus, the compound *QS* will exist in **solid state**. **(1)**

(b) To form an ionic compound if one element give electrons then the other accepts electrons.

Metals can only lose electrons and form positive ions, whereas, non-metals accept electrons and form negative ions.

Therefore, both *Q* and *S* cannot be metal because they form ionic compound with each other. **If *Q* is a metal then *S* will be non-metal or *vice-versa***. **(1)**

Q.12 Give reason for the following statements :

(i) Ionic compounds have a high melting point. **(ICSE 2018)**

(ii) Ionic compounds do not conduct electricity in solid state. **(ICSE 2023)**

(iii) Sodium chloride will conduct electricity only in fused or aqueous solution state. **(ICSE 2016)**

Ans. (i) Ionic compounds have high melting point due to the presence of **strong electrostatic forces of attraction**. It requires a large amount of energy to break these forces of attraction. **(1)**

(ii) In solid state, ionic compounds do not conduct electricity because the **ions are in fixed position** and cannot move. **(1)**

(iii) NaCl gives **free ions** in fused or aqueous state, which are responsible for the conduction of electricity. **(1)**

Q.13 Draw the dot and cross structure of the following:

(i) An ionic compound formed when Mg reacts with the dilute HCl.

(ii) A covalent compound formed when H_2 reacts with Cl_2.

(iii) The positive ion produced when ammonia gas is dissolved in water.

[Atomic number: Mg = 12, Cl = 17, H = 1N = 1]

(ICSE 2025)

Ans. (i) When Mg reacts with the dilute HCl, $\mathbf{MgCl_2}$ is formed as an ionic compound.

$$Mg + \underset{(Dil.)}{2HCl} \longrightarrow MgCl_2 + H_2\uparrow$$ **(1)**

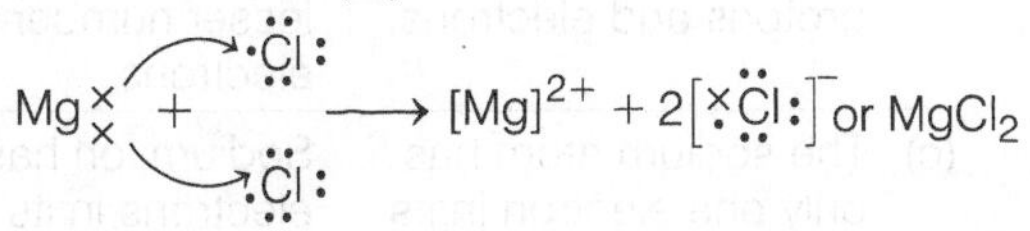

(ii) When H_2 reacts with Cl_2, a covalent compound **HCl** is formed.

$$H_2 + Cl_2 \longrightarrow 2HCl$$

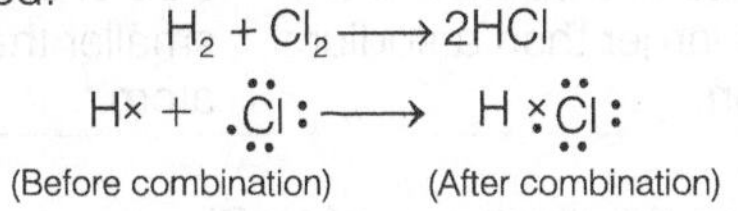

(1)

(ii) When ammonia gas is dissolved in water, **ammonium ion** (NH_4^+) is formed as the positive ion.

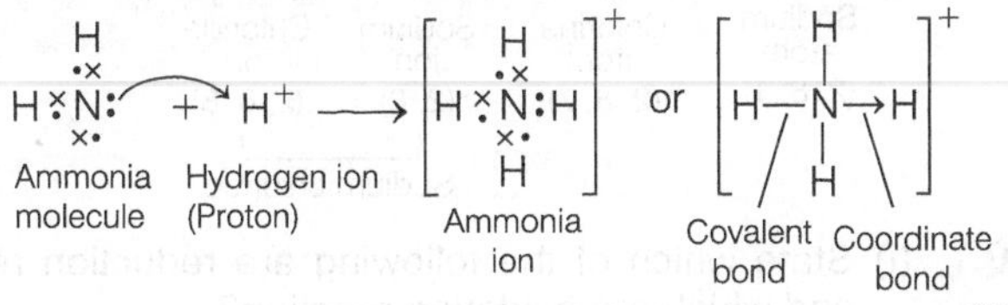

(1)

Q.14 (i) What do you understand by a lone pair of electrons?

(ii) Draw the electron dot diagram of hydronium ion. (H = 1, O = 8) **(ICSE 2018)**

Ans. (i) A lone pair of electrons can be defined as the pair of valence shell electrons that are **not shared** with another atom. **(1)**

(ii) Electronic configuration of H = 1 and O = 2, 6. Hydronium ion is formed by the combination of water molecule and hydrogen ion.

The oxygen atom of a water molecule possesses two lone pair of electrons.

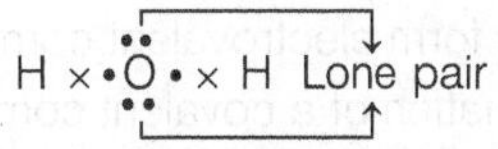

Out of these two lone pair of electrons, one lone pair is used to donate to hydrogen ion.

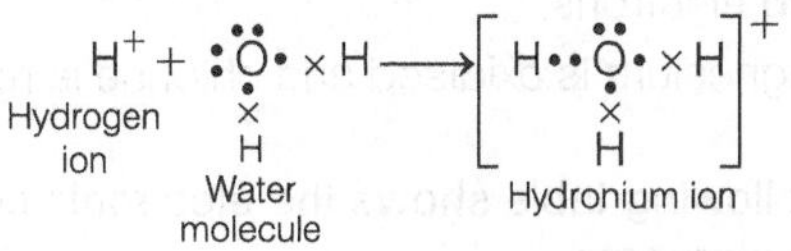

or

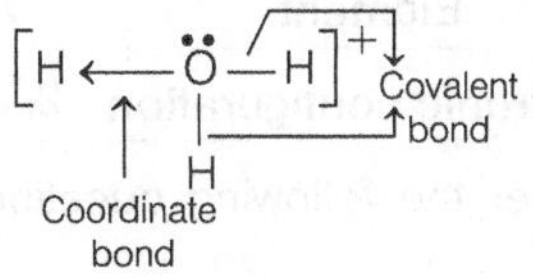

(2)

TYPE - 9 — 04/05 Marks

Long Answer Type Questions

Q.1 Elements *A*, *B* and *C* have atomic number 12, 17 and 10, respectively.

(i) State which one is metal, non-metal and chemically inert?

(ii) Write down the formula of the compound formed by two of the above elements.

Ans. (i) *K L M*

Electronic configuration of *A* : 2, 8, 2.

Electronic configuration of *B* : 2, 8, 7.

Electronic configuration of *C* : 2, 8.

Element *A* is metal.

Element *B* is non-metal.

Element *C* is a noble gas (chemically inert). **(3)**

(ii) $\boldsymbol{B_2A}$ is the formula of the compound formed by *A* and *B* elements. **(1)**

Q.2 (i) Name the charged particles, which attract one another to form electrovalent compounds.

(ii) In the formation of electrovalent compounds, electrons are transferred from one element to another. How are electrons involved in the formation of a covalent compound?

(iii) The electronic configuration of nitrogen is 2, 5. How many electrons in the outershell of a nitrogen atom are not involved in the formation of a nitrogen molecule?

(iv) In the formation of magnesium chloride (by direct combination between magnesium and chlorine), Name the substance that is oxidised and the substance that is reduced.

Ans. (i) **Cations** are positively charged ions and **anions** are negatively charged ions. These ions attract one another to form electrovalent compounds.

(ii) In the formation of a covalent compound, **sharing** of one, two or three pairs of electrons between two atoms takes place.

(iii) **Two** electrons.

(iv) Magnesium is oxidised and chlorine is reduced. **(1 × 4 = 4)**

Q.3 **The following table shows the electronic configuration of the elements.**

Element	*W*	*X*	*Y*	*Z*
Electronic configuration	2, 8, 1	2, 8, 7	2, 5	1

Answer the following questions based on the above table.

(i) What type of bond is formed between

(a) *W* and *X*? **(b) *Y* and *Z*?**

(ii) What is the formula of the compound formed between

(a) *X* and *Z* ? **(b) *W* and *X* ?** **(ICSE 2016)**

Ans. (i) (a) **Electrovalent** bond (b) **Covalent** bond **(2)**

(ii) (a) *X* is chlorine (Cl) and *Z* is hydrogen (H), therefore, formula of the compound is ***XZ*** or HCl.

(b) *W* is sodium (Na) and *X* is chlorine (Cl) therefore, formula of the compound is ***WX*** or NaCl. **(2)**

Q.4 **Draw an electron dot diagram to show the formation of each of the following compounds:**

(i) Methane

(ii) Magnesium chloride [H = 1, C = 6, Mg = 12, Cl = 17] **(ICSE 2017)**

Ans.

(i) 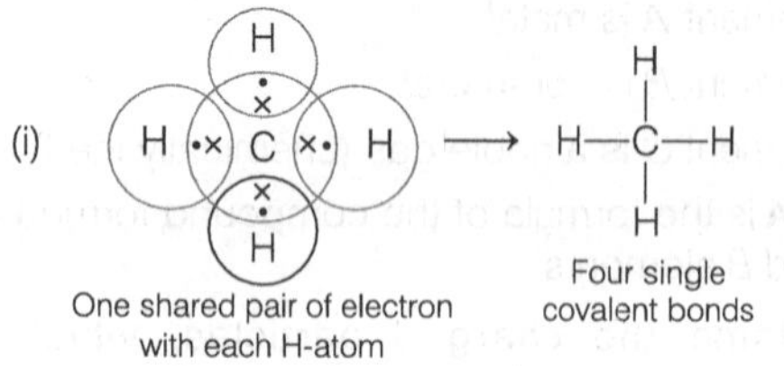

(2)

(ii) 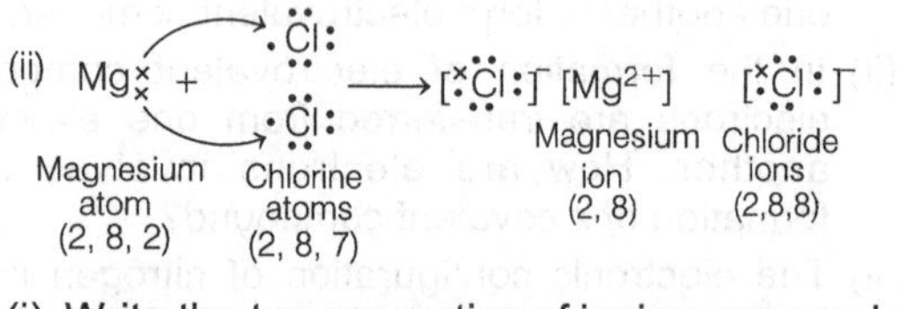

(2)

Q.5 **(i) Write the two properties of ionic compounds.**

(ii) An atom *A* has one electron more than noble gas configuration (neon). Write the formula of its

(a) chloride **(b) oxide**

Ans. (i) (a) Ionic compounds do not conduct electricity in their solid state, as the ions are not free. But they can conduct electricity in their fused, molten and in their aqueous solutions.

(b) Ionic compounds are soluble in water but insoluble in organic solvents. **(2)**

(ii) *A* has one electron more than the noble gas configuration, i.e. neon gas (2, 8). So, its electronic configuration is **2, 8, 1**.

(a) Formula of its chloride is

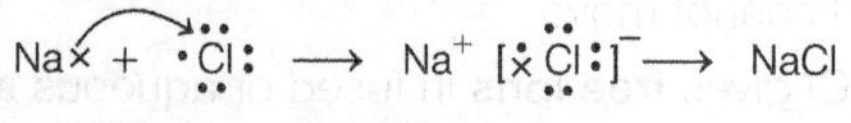

(b) Formula of its oxide is

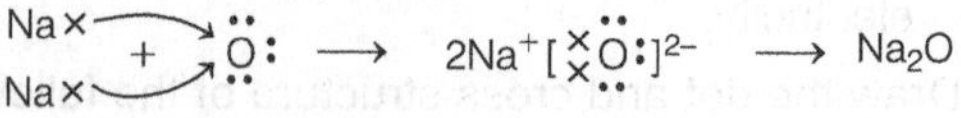

(2)

Q.6 **(i) Give difference between the properties of Na atom and Na^+ ion.**

(ii) Draw the electron dot structure of NaCl.

Ans. (i)

	Sodium atom	Sodium ion
(a)	Sodium atom is electrically neutral.	Sodium ion is positively charged.
(b)	In sodium atom, there are 11 protons and 11 electrons, i.e. an equal number of protons and electrons.	In sodium ion, there are 11 protons but 10 electrons, i.e. sodium ion contains a lesser number of electrons.
(c)	The sodium atom has only one electron in its valence shell.	Sodium ion has 8 electrons in its valence shell.
(d)	Size of a sodium atom is larger than a sodium ion.	Size of a sodium ion is smaller than a sodium atom.

(1 × 4 = 4)

(ii) Electron dot structures of NaCl

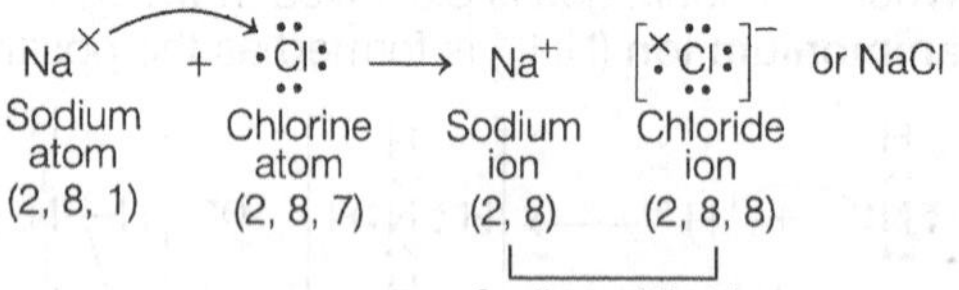

(1)

Q.7 **(i) State which of the following are reduction reaction and which are oxidation reaction?**

(a) $Pb \longrightarrow Pb^{2+} + 2e^-$ **(b) $Fe^{3+} + e^- \longrightarrow Fe^{2+}$**

(c) $Cu \longrightarrow Cu^{2+} + 2e^-$ **(d) $Zn - 2e^- \longrightarrow Zn^{2+}$**

(e) $Na^+ \longrightarrow Na - e^-$ **(f) $Fe^{2+} - e^- \longrightarrow Fe^{3+}$**

(ii) Identify whether the underlined species is an oxidising agent or a reducing agent.

(a) $\underline{Cl} + e^- \longrightarrow Cl^-$ **(b) $\underline{X} - e^- \longrightarrow X^+$**

Ans. (i) (a) Oxidation (as loss of 2 electrons by Pb).

(b) Reduction (as gain of an electron by Fe^{3+}).

(c) Oxidation (as loss of 2 electrons by Cu).

(d) Oxidation (as loss of 2 electrons by Zn).

(e) Reduction (as gain of an electron by Na^+).

(f) Oxidation (as loss of an electron by Fe^{2+}). **(½ × 6 = 3)**

(ii) (a) Cl is an **oxidising agent** as it gains electron (undergoes reduction). **(1)**

(b) *X* is a **reducing agent** as it loses electron (undergoes oxidation). **(1)**

Q.8 (i) Choose the correct species from the given list to answer the following questions.

HCl, O_2, N_2, CCl_4, NH_4^+, NH_3, H_3O^+, H_2O

(a) Name two species having only single covalent bond.

(b) Which two species have multiple covalent bonds?

(c) Name two species which have both coordinate and covalent bond.

(ii) (a) Arrange the following as per instruction given in the bracket.

H_2O, NH_3, H_2 (Increasing order of number of lone pairs)

(b) Why is carbon tetrachloride a non-electrolyte.

Ans. (i) (a) Single covalent bond = HCl and CCl_4. **(1)**

(b) Multiple covalent bond = O_2 and N_2. **(1)**

(c) Both coordinate and covalent bond = NH_4^+ and H_3O^+. **(1)**

(ii) (a) The increasing order of number of lone pairs is

$$H_2 < NH_3 < H_2O$$

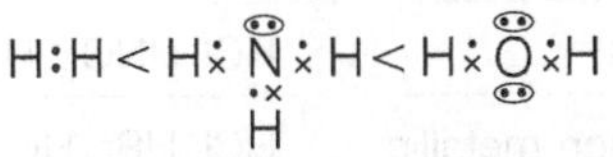

(⊙ = lone pair) **(1)**

(b) Carbon tetrachloride is a **covalent compound** and it does not dissociate into ions in aqueous solution. Therefore, CCl_4 is a non-electrolyte. **(1)**

TYPE - 10 03 Marks

Case Based Questions

Q.1 Reena was studying the electronic configuration of elements. The electronic configuration of magnesium is: 2, 8, 2.

The electronic configuration of aluminium is: 2, 8, 3.

The electronic configuration of silicon is: 2, 8, 4.

The electronic configuration of chlorine is: 2, 8, 7

She observed that magnesium, aluminium and silicon, all three form compounds with chlorine.

(i) State the type of compound formed between magnesium and chlorine.

(ii) State the type of compound formed between silicon and chlorine.

(iii) Draw the lewis dot structure of compound formed by aluminium and chlorine.

Ans. (i) **Electrovalent compound**.

Magnesium loses 2 electrons and two chlorine accepts 1 electron each to form a compound having formula $MgCl_2$. **(1)**

(ii) **Covalent** compound.

Silicon shares its four electrons with four chlorine atoms to form $SiCl_4$. **(1)**

(iii) Aluminium and chlorine form a compound with molecular formula **$AlCl_3$**.

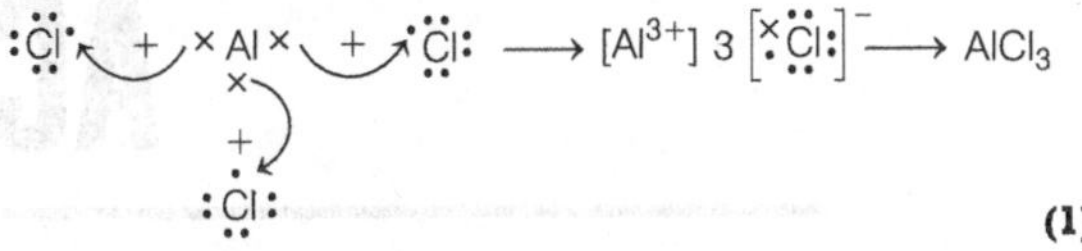

(1)

Q.2 Ramesh was studying the redox reaction. He observed that elements that lie on the far left side of the periodic table undergo oxidation and elements that lie on the right side of the periodic table apart from noble gases undergo reduction.

(i) In the given reaction, identify the oxidation and reduction reaction.

$$A - e^- \rightarrow A^+$$
$$B^{2+} + e^- \rightarrow B^+$$

(ii) Define oxidising agent and reducing agent.

(iii) Identify the elements which undergo oxidation:

K, Mg, Na, Cl, O, F.

Ans. (i) **Oxidation** : $A - e^- \rightarrow A^+$

Reduction : $B^{2+} + e^- \rightarrow B^+$

Oxidation involves loss of electrons.

Reduction involves gain of electrons. **(1)**

(ii) **Oxidising agent**: The substance which accept electrons is called oxidising agent.

Reducing agent: The substance which donate electrons is called reducing agent. **(1)**

(iii) **K, Mg, Na**

The elements which lie on the far left side of the periodic table undergo oxidation. **(1)**

Q.3 Sunita set-up four electrolytic cells using sugar, magnesium chloride, chloroform and alcohol as an electrolyte. She observed that light bulb glows in case of magnesium chloride but not in case of sugar, chloroform and alcohol.

This shows that magnesium chloride can conduct electricity but sugar, chloroform and alcohol cannot.

(i) What type of compound is magnesium chloride?

(ii) What type of compounds are sugar, chloroform and alcohol?

(iii) How magnesium chloride conduct electricity?

Ans. (i) **Ionic or electrovalent** compound. **(1)**

(ii) Covalent compounds. **(1)**

(iii) Magnesium chloride in aqueous solution gives **free ions** which are responsible for the conduction of electricity. **(1)**

ACIDS, BASES AND SALTS

Acids

- Acids are defined as compounds which contain one or more hydrogen atoms and when dissolved in water, they produce hydronium ions (H_3O^+), the only positively charged ions.
- An acid molecule furnishes **hydrogen ion** (or proton), i.e. H^+ ion in aqueous solution.

$$HCl \xrightarrow{H_2O} H^+ + Cl^-$$

But this H^+ ion cannot exist independently. Therefore, it combines with a water molecule to form **hydronium ion (H_3O^+)**.

$$H^+ + H_2O \longrightarrow H_3O^+$$

Classification of Acids

Classification	Acids and their identity	Examples
On the basis of sources of acids	**Organic acids** Derived from plants and animals.	CH_3COOH, $HCOOH$
	Inorganic acids Derived from minerals.	HCl, HNO_3, H_2SO_4
On the basis of molecular composition	**Hydracids** Containing hydrogen and non-metallic element (except oxygen).	HCl, HBr, HI
	Oxyacids Containing hydrogen, oxygen and some other element.	HNO_3, H_2SO_4
On the basis of strength	**Strong acid** Ionised completely in aqueous solution.	HCl, HNO_3, H_2SO_4
	Weak acid Ionised partially in aqueous solution.	CH_3COOH, H_2CO_3, HNO_2
On the basis of concentration	**Concentrated acid** High percentage of acid.	conc. H_2SO_4, conc.HCl
	Dilute acid Low percentage of acid.	Dil. H_2SO_4, dil. HCl
On the basis of basicity	**Monobasic** Contains one replaceable hydrogen ion per acid molecule.	HCl, HBr, CH_3COOH
	Dibasic Contains two replaceable hydrogen ions per acid molecule.	H_2SO_4, H_2CO_3
	Tribasic Contains three replaceable hydrogen ions per acid molecule.	H_3PO_4

Physical Properties of Acids

(i) Sour in taste in aqueous solution.

(ii) Turns blue litmus red.

(iii) Some acids are solids and some are liquids at room temperature.

(iv) All strong mineral acids have corrosive action on the skin and cause painful burns.

(v) They are electrolytes, i.e. they conduct electricity in the aqueous state.

Preparation of Acids

(i) **By direct synthesis**

$$\underset{\text{Hydrogen}}{H_2} + \underset{\text{Chlorine}}{Cl_2} \longrightarrow \underset{\text{Hydrochloric acid}}{2HCl}$$

(ii) **By addition of water to non-metallic or acidic oxides**

$$\underset{\text{Sulphur trioxide}}{SO_3} + H_2O \longrightarrow \underset{\text{Sulphuric acid}}{H_2SO_4}$$

$$\underset{\text{Nitrogen pentoxide}}{N_2O_5} + H_2O \longrightarrow \underset{\text{Nitric acid}}{2HNO_3}$$

(iii) **By the oxidation of non-metals**

$$\underset{\text{Sulphur}}{S} + \underset{\text{Nitric acid}}{6HNO_3} \longrightarrow \underset{\text{Sulphuric acid}}{H_2SO_4} + 2H_2O + \underset{\text{Nitrogen dioxide}}{6NO_2}$$

$$\underset{\text{Phosphorus}}{P} + \underset{\text{Nitric acid}}{5HNO_3} \longrightarrow \underset{\text{Phosphoric acid}}{H_3PO_4} + H_2O + \underset{\text{Nitrogen dioxide}}{5NO_2}$$

(iv) **By displacement**

$$\underset{\text{Sodium chloride}}{NaCl} + \underset{\text{Sulphuric acid}}{H_2SO_4} \xrightarrow{\Delta} \underset{\text{Sodium bisulphate}}{NaHSO_4} + \underset{\text{Hydrochloric acid}}{HCl}$$

Chemical Properties of Acids

(i) **Reaction with active metals** Dilute acids (e.g. HCl and H_2SO_4), react with certain active metals like zinc (Zn), iron (Fe), etc., to evolve H_2 gas.

e.g.

$$\text{Metal} + \text{Acid} \longrightarrow \text{Salt} + \text{Hydrogen gas}$$

$$\underset{\text{Zinc}}{Zn(s)} + \underset{\text{Sulphuric acid}}{H_2SO_4(aq)} \longrightarrow \underset{\text{Zinc sulphate}}{ZnSO_4(aq)} + \underset{\text{Hydrogen}}{H_2(g)}$$

(ii) **Reaction with metal oxides** Acids react with certain metal oxides (basic oxides) to form salt and water.

e.g.

$$\underset{\text{Calcium oxide}}{CaO(s)} + \underset{\text{Hydrochloric acid}}{2HCl(aq)} \longrightarrow \underset{\text{Calcium chloride}}{CaCl_2(aq)} + \underset{\text{Water}}{H_2O(l)}$$

$$\underset{\text{Magnesium oxide}}{MgO(s)} + \underset{\text{Nitric acid}}{2HNO_3(aq)} \longrightarrow \underset{\text{Magnesium nitrate}}{Mg(NO_3)_2(aq)} + \underset{\text{Water}}{H_2O(l)}$$

(iii) **Reaction with chlorides** Generally, chlorides do not react with any dilute acids but reacts with conc. H_2SO_4 to liberate HCl.

$$\underset{\text{Sodium chloride}}{NaCl} + \underset{\text{(Conc.) Sulphuric acid}}{H_2SO_4} \xrightarrow[\text{Heat}]{\text{Below } 200^\circ C} \underset{\text{Sodium hydrogen sulphate}}{NaHSO_4} + \underset{\text{Hydrochloric acid}}{HCl\uparrow}$$

(iv) **Reaction with nitrates** Generally, nitrates do not react with dilute acids but lead nitrate [$Pb(NO_3)_2$] reacts with dil. HCl and dil. H_2SO_4 to form insoluble lead salts.

$$\underset{\text{Lead nitrate}}{Pb(NO_3)_2} + \underset{\text{Hydrochloric acid}}{2HCl} \longrightarrow \underset{\text{Lead chloride}}{PbCl_2} + \underset{\text{Nitric acid}}{2HNO_3}$$

Some other nitrates e.g., KNO_3 reacts with conc. H_2SO_4 on warming to liberate HNO_3.

$$\underset{\text{Potassium nitrate}}{KNO_3} + \underset{\text{(Conc.) Sulphuric acid}}{H_2SO_4} \xrightarrow[\text{Heat}]{\text{Below } 200^\circ C} \underset{\text{Potassium hydrogen sulphate}}{KHSO_4} + \underset{\text{Nitric acid}}{HNO_3}$$

(v) **Reaction with bases - Neutralisation** Acids neutralise bases to form salt and water only.

Basic oxide/hydroxide	+	Acid	$\longrightarrow$	Salt	+	Water
CuO	+	H_2SO_4	$\longrightarrow$	$CuSO_4$	+	H_2O
NaOH	+	HNO_3	$\longrightarrow$	$NaNO_3$	+	H_2O

(vi) **Decomposition of hydrogen carbonates and carbonates** Acids liberate carbon dioxide on reaction with metallic carbonates and bicarbonates.

Carbonate/bicarbonate	+	Acid	$\longrightarrow$	Salt	+	Water	+	Carbon dioxide
$CaCO_3$ Carbonate	+	2HCl	$\longrightarrow$	$CaCl_2$	+	H_2O	+	$CO_2 \uparrow$
$Ca(HCO_3)_2$ Bicarbonate	+	2HCl	$\longrightarrow$	$CaCl_2$	+	$2H_2O$	+	$2CO_2 \uparrow$

(vii) **Decomposition of sulphites and bisulphites** Acids react with sulphites and bisulphites of metals to liberate sulphur dioxide.

Sulphite/bisulphite	+	Acid	$\longrightarrow$	Salt	+	Water	+	Sulphur dioxide
$CaSO_3$ Sulphite	+	2HCl	$\longrightarrow$	$CaCl_2$	+	H_2O	+	$SO_2 \uparrow$
$NaHSO_3$ Bisulphite	+	HCl	$\longrightarrow$	NaCl	+	H_2O	+	$SO_2 \uparrow$

(viii) **Decomposition of sulphides** Acids react with metal sulphides to liberate hydrogen sulphide.

$$\text{Metal sulphide} + \text{Acid} \longrightarrow \text{Salt} + \text{Hydrogen sulphide}$$

$$ZnS + 2HCl \longrightarrow ZnCl_2 + H_2S\uparrow$$

$$FeS + H_2SO_4 \longrightarrow FeSO_4 + H_2S\uparrow$$

Uses

- **Vinegar (Acetic acid)** is used to preserve pickles and chinese foods.
- In stomach, **hydrochloric acid** is released, which makes the medium acidic and leads to coagulation of proteins.
- Cold drinks contain **carbonic acid**.
- **Oxalic acid** is used to remove ink or rust stains.
- **Boric acid** is used as an antiseptic for eye wash.
- **Hydrochloric acid** is used in cleaning of metal items (pickling).
- **Nitric acid** is used in explosives.
- **Sulphuric acid** is used in the manufacture of fertilizers like ammonium sulphate, synthetic fibres, dyes, etc., and in the storage batteries.

Bases

A **base** is defined as *either a metallic oxide or a metallic hydroxide or ammonium hydroxide which reacts with hydronium ions of an acid to form salt and water only.*

e.g. CuO (metallic oxide), $Mg(OH)_2$ (metallic hydroxide), etc.

Basic oxide

A basic oxide is a metallic oxide which contains the ion O^{2-} and reacts with an acid to form salt and water only.

Basic hydroxide

A basic hydroxide is a metallic hydroxide which contains OH^- and will react with an acid to give salt and water only.

Alkali

- An alkali is a compound (basic hydroxide) which when dissolved in water yields hydroxyl ions (OH^-) as the only negatively charged ions. e.g.

$$NaOH(aq) \rightleftharpoons Na^+ + OH^-$$

- An alkali is a base soluble in water. All alkalis furnish OH^- ions in aqueous solution.
- All alkalies are bases but all bases are not alkalies.

Classification of Bases

Classification	Bases and their identity	Examples
On the basis of strength	**Strong base** Ionised completely in aqueous solution.	NaOH, KOH
	Weak base Ionised partially in aqueous solution.	$NH_4OH, Cu(OH)_2$
On the basis of acidity	**Monoacidic** Contains one hydroxyl ion per molecule of base.	$NaOH, NH_4OH$
	Diacidic Contains two hydroxyl ions per molecule of base.	$Ca(OH)_2, Mg(OH)_2$
	Triacidic Contains three hydroxyl ions per molecule of base.	$Al(OH)_3, Fe(OH)_3$

Physical Properties of Bases

- Bases are bitter in taste and soapy to touch.
- They are strong electrolytes and show a mild corrosive action.
- Bases turn red litmus to blue.

Preparation of Bases

(i) **From metals**

$$\underset{\text{Sodium}}{4Na} + \underset{\text{Oxygen}}{O_2} \longrightarrow \underset{\text{Sodium oxide}}{2Na_2O}$$

(ii) **By action of water on reactive metals**

$$\underset{\text{Sodium}}{2Na} + \underset{\text{Water}}{2H_2O} \longrightarrow \underset{\text{Sodium hydroxide}}{2NaOH} + H_2\uparrow$$

(iii) **By action of water on soluble metallic oxide**

$$\underset{\text{Sodium oxide}}{Na_2O} + \underset{\text{Water}}{H_2O} \longrightarrow \underset{\text{Sodium hydroxide}}{2NaOH}$$

(iv) **By double decomposition**

$$\underset{\text{Ferric chloride}}{FeCl_3} + \underset{\text{Sodium hydroxide}}{3NaOH} \longrightarrow \underset{\text{Ferric hydroxide}}{Fe(OH)_3\downarrow} + 3NaCl$$

Chemical Properties of Bases

- Strong alkalis absorb carbon dioxide from air to form carbonates. e.g.

$$\underset{\text{Sodium hydroxide}}{2NaOH} + \underset{\text{Carbon dioxide}}{CO_2} \longrightarrow \underset{\text{Sodium carbonate}}{Na_2CO_3} + \underset{\text{Water}}{H_2O}$$

- They have the capability to neutralise acids to form salt and water.

$$\underset{\text{Base}}{Ca(OH)_2} + \underset{\text{Acid}}{2HCl} \longrightarrow \underset{\text{Salt}}{CaCl_2} + \underset{\text{Water}}{2H_2O}$$

- They are precipitated as insoluble metallic hydroxides when added to the solutions of salts of heavy metals. e.g.

$$\underset{\text{Copper sulphate}}{CuSO_4(aq)} + \underset{\text{Ammonium hydroxide}}{2NH_4OH} \longrightarrow \underset{\text{Ammonium sulphate}}{(NH_4)_2SO_4} + \underset{\text{(Pale blue) Copper hydroxide}}{Cu(OH)_2\downarrow}$$

- When they are warmed with an ammonium salt, ammonia gas is evolved, which can be checked by Nessler's reagent (turns brown).

$$\underset{\text{Ammonium chloride}}{NH_4Cl} + \underset{\text{Sodium hydroxide}}{NaOH} \xrightarrow{\Delta} \underset{\text{Sodium chloride}}{NaCl} + \underset{\text{Water}}{H_2O} + \underset{\text{Ammonia}}{NH_3\uparrow}$$

- Insoluble bases decompose on heating to form metallic oxides and water.

$$\underset{\text{Zinc hydroxide}}{Zn(OH)_2} \xrightarrow{\Delta} \underset{\text{Zinc oxide}}{ZnO} + H_2O$$

Uses

- **Sodium hydroxide** is used in the manufacturing of soap.
- **Potassium hydroxide** is used in the manufacturing of salts and soaps. It is also used in alkaline batteries.
- **Calcium hydroxide** (slaked lime) is used in the manufacturing of bleaching powder and softening of hard water.
- **Magnesium hydroxide** can be used as an antacid.
- **Aluminium hydroxide** acts as a foaming agent in fire extinguishers.

Strength of Acid and Base

The strength of an acid or a base depends upon the number of H^+ ions or OH^- ions produced by them.

Larger the number of H^+ ions produced by an acid, stronger is the acid. Similarly, larger the number of OH^- ions produced by a base, stronger is the base.

pH Value

It represents the strength of acids and alkalis expressed in terms of hydrogen ion concentration.

pH of a solution is the negative logarithm to the base 10 of the hydrogen ion concentration expressed in moles per litre.

$$pH = -\log_{10}[H^+]$$

pH Scale

It is a scale showing the relative strength of acids and alkalis. The normal pH scale ranges from 0 to 14 as shown below.

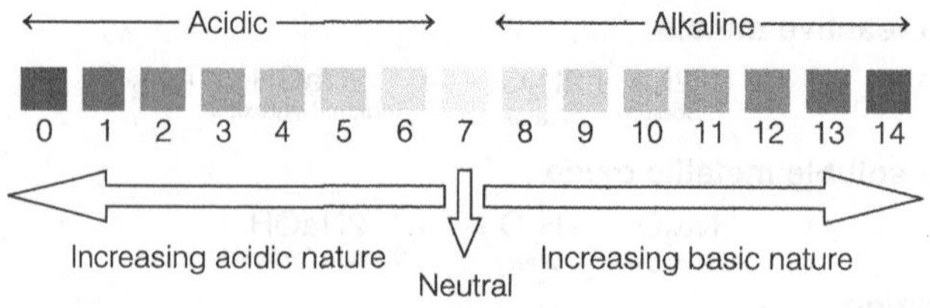

- A solution having high concentration of hydrogen ions has a low pH value.
- A solution having low concentration of hydrogen ions has a high pH value.

From the above scale, it can be easily concluded that:

(i) Neutral substances have a pH of exactly 7.
(ii) Acids have a pH of less than 7.
(iii) Bases have a pH of more than 7.

Indicators

The substances that change their colour or odour when added into an acid or an alkaline solution, to indicate the presence of an acid or a base are called **indicators**. Some types of indicators are given below.

(i) **Natural Indicators** These indicators are obtained from natural sources, e.g. litmus solution is a purple colour dye extracted from the lichen plant (belonging to the division "Thallophyta").

(ii) **Synthetic Indicators** The indicators which are synthesised in the laboratory or in industry and are not obtained by natural sources are known as synthetic indicators. e.g. Methyl orange, phenolphthalein, etc.

Colour Changes by Various Indicators

Indicator	Colour Change		
	Neutral	Acidic	Alkaline
Litmus	Purple	Red	Blue
Methyl orange	Orange	Pink	Yellow
Phenolphthalein	Colourless	Colourless	Pink

(iii) **Universal Indicators** To predict how strong a given acid or base is, an universal indicator is preferred over litmus paper. It is a mixture of several indicators. It shows different colours at different concentrations of hydrogen ion in a solution.

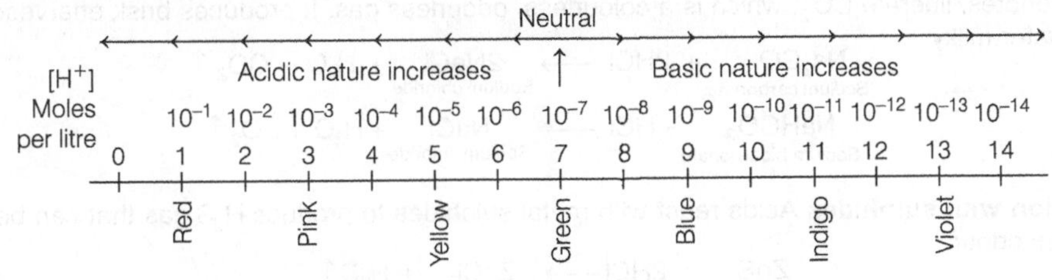

Colour changes in the universal indicator (for different pH values)

(iv) **Olfactory Indicators** Those substances whose odour changes in acidic or basic medium are called olfactory indicators. Vanilla extract, clove and onion can be used as olfactory indicators. The smell of vanilla extract and onion indicators can be detected in presence of an acid only but not in the presence of a base.

Salts

Salt is a compound formed by the partial or total replacement of the ionisable hydrogen atoms of an acid by a metallic ion or an ammonium ion.

Partial Replacement

$$\underset{}{NaNO_3} + \underset{\text{(conc.)}}{H_2SO_4} \xrightarrow{<200^\circ C} \underset{\text{Salt}}{NaHSO_4} + HNO_3$$

Complete Replacement

$$2NaNO_3 + \underset{\text{(conc.)}}{H_2SO_4} \xrightarrow{>200^\circ C} \underset{\text{Salt}}{Na_2SO_4} + 2HNO_3$$

Classification of Salts

(i) **Normal salts** are the salts formed by complete replacement of the ionisable hydrogen ion of an acid molecule by a basic radical (ammonium ion) or metallic ion.

e.g. $$HCl + NaOH \longrightarrow NaCl + H_2O$$

(ii) **Acid salts** are the salts formed by partial replacement of the ionisable hydrogen ion of an acid molecule by a metal or by a basic radical (ammonium ion).

e.g. $$H_2SO_4 + NaOH \xrightarrow{<200^\circ C} \underset{\text{Acid salt}}{NaHSO_4} + H_2O$$

(iii) **Basic salts** are formed by partial replacement of hydroxyl radicals of a diacidic or triacidic base with an acid radical.

e.g. $$Mg(OH)_2 + HCl \longrightarrow \underset{\text{Basic magnesium chloride}}{Mg(OH)Cl} + H_2O$$

Preparation of Normal Salts

I. Soluble Salts

1. **Direct Combination Reaction**

In this method, two elements combines together to form salts, such as:

$$\text{Metal} + \text{Non-metal} \longrightarrow \text{Salt}$$

$$2Na\ (\text{molten}) + Cl_2 \longrightarrow \underset{\text{Sodium chloride}}{2NaCl}$$

2. **Displacement Reaction**

$$\text{Active metal} + \text{Acid} \longrightarrow \text{Salt} + \text{Hydrogen}$$

$$Zn + H_2SO_4 \longrightarrow \underset{\text{Zinc sulphate}}{ZnSO_4} + H_2 \uparrow$$

3. **Decomposition Reaction** (Action of Dilute Acids on Salts)

In this method, the single reactant breaks into two or more elements. Reactions involved are as follows :

(i) **Reaction with metal carbonates and bicarbonates** Acids on reaction with metal carbonates and bicarbonates, liberate CO_2, which is a colourless, odourless gas. It produces brisk effervescence and turns lime water milky.

$$\underset{\text{Sodium carbonate}}{Na_2CO_3} + 2HCl \longrightarrow \underset{\text{Sodium chloride}}{2NaCl} + H_2O + CO_2 \uparrow$$

$$\underset{\text{Sodium bicarbonate}}{NaHCO_3} + HCl \longrightarrow \underset{\text{Sodium chloride}}{NaCl} + H_2O + CO_2 \uparrow$$

(ii) **Reaction with sulphides** Acids react with metal sulphides to produce H_2S gas that can be checked by its foul gas odour.

$$\underset{\text{Zinc sulphide}}{ZnS} + 2HCl \longrightarrow \underset{\text{Zinc chloride}}{ZnCl_2} + H_2S \uparrow$$

(iii) **Reaction with metallic sulphites** Acids on reaction with metallic sulphites liberate a colourless gas, which turns orange acidified potassium dichromate to green, and $KMnO_4$ solution from purple to colourless, i.e. it gets decolourised.

$$\underset{\text{Potassium sulphite}}{K_2SO_3} + 2HCl \longrightarrow \underset{\text{Potassium chloride}}{2KCl} + H_2O + SO_2 \uparrow$$

4. **Neutralisation of an Alkali** (Titration)

$$\underset{\text{Acid}}{HNO_3} + \underset{\text{Base}}{NaOH} \longrightarrow \underset{\text{Salt}}{NaNO_3} + \underset{\text{Water}}{H_2O}$$

5. **Neutralisation of an Acid with an Insoluble Base**

$$\underset{\text{Acid}}{2HCl} + \underset{\text{Insoluble base}}{MgO} \longrightarrow \underset{\text{Salt}}{MgCl_2} + \underset{\text{Water}}{H_2O}$$

6. **Reaction of Metals with Alkali**

On reaction of metals with alkali, evolution of hydrogen gas takes place and their corresponding salts are obtained.

$$Zn + 2NaOH \xrightarrow{\text{Boiling}} \underset{\text{Sodium zincate}}{Na_2ZnO_2} + H_2 \uparrow$$

II. Insoluble Salts

1. **Direct Combination Reaction**

In this method, reactants directly combine to form insoluble salts.

e.g.

$$Pb + S \xrightarrow{\Delta} \underset{\text{Lead sulphide}}{PbS}$$

$$Fe + S \xrightarrow{\Delta} \underset{\text{Ferrous sulphide}}{FeS}$$

2. **By the Combination of an Acidic Oxide with a Basic Oxide**

When acidic oxide reacts with basic oxide, salt is formed.

e.g.

$$\underset{\text{Sulphur dioxide}}{SO_2} + \underset{\text{Calcium oxide}}{CaO} \xrightarrow{\Delta} \underset{\text{Calcium sulphite}}{CaSO_3}$$

$$\underset{\text{Carbon dioxide}}{CO_2} + \underset{\text{Calcium oxide}}{CaO} \xrightarrow{\Delta} \underset{\text{Calcium carbonate}}{CaCO_3}$$

3. **Precipitation Reaction** (By Double Decomposition Reaction)

When soluble salt reacts with acid (or soluble salt), then insoluble salt and acid (or salt) are formed.

e.g.

$$BaCl_2 + H_2SO_4 \longrightarrow \underset{\text{Barium sulphate}}{BaSO_4 \downarrow} + 2HCl$$

$$AgNO_3 + HCl \longrightarrow \underset{\text{Silver chloride}}{AgCl \downarrow} + HNO_3$$

General Properties of Salts

(i) Salts are **electrovalent compounds**. They conduct electricity in their molten state as well as in their aqueous solution [due to their dissociation into ions].

(ii) Salts are **non-volatile solids** that form **crystals**.

(iii) **Solubility of salts**: Most of the salts are soluble in water. Their degree of solubility in water varies with temperature.

(iv) Salt can exhibit neutral, acidic or basic nature based on their reaction.

(v) Some salts unite with a definite quantity of water, which is known as the **water of crystallisation**.

(vi) **Efflorescence** It is the property of some salts to lose wholly, or partly their water of crystallisation when their crystals are exposed to dry air even for a short time. They become powdery. Such substances are called **efflorescent substances**.

(vii) **Hygroscopic substances** Some salts absorb moisture (water vapour) from the atmosphere without dissolving in it. Such substances are called **hygroscopic substances** and the phenomenon is called **hygroscopy**.

(viii) **Deliquescence** Certain water-soluble substances, when exposed to the atmosphere at ordinary temperature, absorb moisture from the atmospheric air to become moist, lose their crystalline form and ultimately dissolve in the absorbed water, forming a saturated solution. Such substances are called **deliquescent substances** and this property is called **deliquescence**.

(ix) **Drying or dessicating agents** Some substances remove moisture from other substances, and are called **dessicants** or **drying agents** or **dessicating agents**.

(x) **Dehydrating agents** These substances remove water molecules even from compounds.

Laboratory Preparation of Some Important Salts

1. Iron (III) Chloride or Ferric chloride ($FeCl_3$)

It is an industrial scale chemical compound. When dissolved in water, it undergoes hydrolysis and evolve heat, which is an exothermic reaction.

Industrially, iron (III) chloride is prepared by the reaction of iron with chlorine.

$$2Fe(s) + 3Cl_2(g) \longrightarrow 2FeCl_3(s)$$

The product is highly deliquescent, so it is kept dry using calcium chloride as drying agent.

2. Copper (II) Sulphate/Blue Vitriol ($CuSO_4 \cdot 5H_2O$)

Copper (II) sulphate can be easily prepared industrially by treating copper hydroxide, copper oxide or copper carbonate with dilute acid (dil. H_2SO_4).

$$Cu(OH)_2 + H_2SO_4 \longrightarrow CuSO_4 + 2H_2O$$

$$CuSO_4 + 5H_2O \longrightarrow \underset{\text{(Blue vitriol)}}{CuSO_4 \cdot 5H_2O}$$

3. Zinc Sulphate/White Vitriol ($ZnSO_4 \cdot 7H_2O$)

Zinc sulphate is produced by treating any zinc containing material with sulphuric acid.

$$Zn(s) + H_2SO_4(aq) \longrightarrow ZnSO_4(aq) + H_2(g)\uparrow$$

$$ZnSO_4 + 7H_2O \longrightarrow \underset{\text{(White vitriol)}}{ZnSO_4 \cdot 7H_2O}$$

4. Calcium Carbonate ($CaCO_3$)

It is formed by three main elements carbon, oxygen and calcium. It is an insoluble salt. It can be prepared by mixing the solutions of calcium chloride and sodium carbonate.

$$CaCl_2 + Na_2CO_3 \longrightarrow \underset{\text{(White ppt.)}}{CaCO_3 \downarrow} + 2NaCl$$

5. Lead Chloride ($PbCl_2$)

It is an inorganic compound with formula, $PbCl_2$ which is a white solid under ambient conditions. It is one of the most important lead-based reagents. It can be obtained by mixing solutions of lead nitrate and dilute hydrochloric acid.

$$Pb(NO_3)_2 + 2HCl \longrightarrow \underset{\text{(White ppt.)}}{PbCl_2 \downarrow} + 2HNO_3$$

6. Sodium Bicarbonate ($NaHCO_3$)

It is a white crystalline solid but often appears as a fine powder. It can be prepared by treating carbon dioxide gas with sodium carbonate solution.

$$Na_2CO_3 + CO_2 + H_2O \longrightarrow 2NaHCO_3$$

7. Iron (II) Sulphate/Green Vitriol ($FeSO_4 \cdot 7H_2O$)

It is prepared by the action of iron with dil. H_2SO_4.

$$Fe(s) + H_2SO_4(aq) \longrightarrow FeSO_4(s) + H_2(g)$$

$$FeSO_4 + 7H_2O \longrightarrow \underset{\text{(Green vitriol)}}{FeSO_4 \cdot 7H_2O}$$

EXAM ORIENTED QUESTIONS

TYPE - 1 01 Mark

Multiple Choice Questions

Q.1 A particular solution contains molecules and ions of the solute, so it is a

(a) weak acid (b) strong acid
(c) strong base (d) salt solution

Ans. (a) **Weak acid** contains molecules and ions of the solute.

Q.2 The acid which can produce carbon from cane sugar is **(ICSE 2020)**

(a) concentrated hydrochloric acid
(b) concentrated nitric acid
(c) concentrated sulphuric acid
(d) concentrated acetic acid

Ans. (c) **Conc. sulphuric acid** can produce carbon from cane sugar.

$$\underset{\text{Cane sugar}}{C_{12}H_{22}O_{11}} \xrightarrow{\text{Conc. } H_2SO_4} \underset{\text{Carbon}}{12C(s)} + 11H_2O$$

Q.3 An organic weak acid is

(a) formic acid (b) sulphuric acid
(c) nitric acid (d) hydrochloric acid

Ans. (a) Formic acid (HCOOH).

Q.4 Hydracids are those acids which contain **(ICSE 2020)**

(a) hydrogen with any metal.
(b) hydrogen, a non-metal and oxygen.
(c) hydrogen and a non-metal other than oxygen.
(d) hydrogen and oxygen only.

Ans. (c) Acids that contain hydrogen and a non-metal, except oxygen are called hydracids.

Q.5 The basicity of acetic acid is **(ICSE Specimen 2024)**

(a) 1 (b) 2
(c) 3 (4) 4

Ans. (a) The number of replaceable hydrogen atoms in an acid is known as basicity. In acetic acid the number of replaceable hydrogen atoms is 1. So, **basicity is 1**.

Q.6 An acid which has two replaceable hydrogen ions **(ICSE Specimen 2023)**

(a) acetic acid (b) hydrochloric acid
(c) phosphoric acid (d) carbonic acid

Ans. (d) **Carbonic acid** is a **dibasic acid** and has two replaceable hydrogen ions.

Q.7 Select the acid which contains four hydrogen atoms in it.

(a) Formic acid (b) Sulphuric acid
(c) Nitric acid (d) Acetic acid

Ans. (d) **Acetic acid** (CH_3COOH) contains four hydrogen atoms in it.

Q.8 Which of the following is a tribasic acid?

(a) H_2SO_4 (b) $Al(OH)_3$ **(ICSE 2021-22, Sem-I)**
(c) H_3PO_4 (d) $Ca(OH)_2$

Ans. (c) $\mathbf{H_3PO_4}$ is a tribasic acid as it can donate its three protons attached to it.

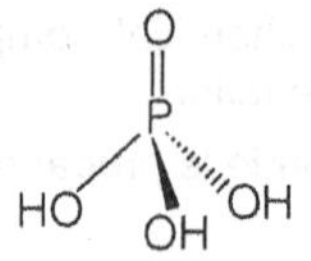

Q.9 The aqueous solution of the following compounds which contains both ions and molecules is

(a) sulphuric acid (b) hydrochloric acid
(c) nitric acid (d) acetic acid

Ans. (d) **Acetic acid** which is a weak acid contains both ions and molecules.

Q.10 When dilute sulphuric acid reacts with iron sulphide, the gas evolved is ....

(a) hydrogen sulphide (b) sulphur dioxide
(c) sulphur trioxide (d) vapour of sulphuric acid

Ans. (a) **Hydrogen sulphide**.

$$\underset{\text{(Dil.)}}{H_2SO_4} + \underset{\text{Iron sulphide}}{FeS} \longrightarrow FeSO_4 + \underset{\text{Hydrogen sulphide}}{H_2S\uparrow}$$

Q.11 Which of the following hydroxides is not an alkali?

(a) Ammonium hydroxide (b) Calcium hydroxide
(c) Copper hydroxide (d) Sodium hydroxide

Ans. (c) **Copper hydroxide** is not an alkali.

Q.12 The basic oxide which is an alkali

(a) copper oxide (b) sodium oxide
(c) ferric oxide (d) zinc oxide

Ans. (b) **Sodium oxide** is an alkali.

Q.13 If the pH of a solution is '2', then the solution is a **(ICSE 2021-22, Sem-I)**

(a) strong acid (b) strong alkali
(c) weak acid (d) weak alkali

Ans. (a) Acids have pH<7 and bases have pH>7.

If the pH of a solution is 2, then the solution is a **strong acid**.

Q.14 Anita added a drop each of diluted acetic acid and diluted hydrochloric acid on pH paper and compared the colours. Which of the following is the correct conclusion?

(a) pH of acetic acid is more than that of hydrochloric acid.
(b) pH of acetic acid is less than that of hydrochloric acid.
(c) Acetic acid dissociates completely in aqueous solution.
(d) Acetic acid is a strong acid.

Ans. (a) pH of acetic acid is more than that of hydrochloric acid because acetic acid is a weak acid while hydrochloric acid is a strong acid.

Q.15 To increase the pH value of a neutral solution, we should add **(ICSE 2017)**

(a) an acid (b) an acid salt
(c) an alkali (d) a salt

Ans. (c) To increase the pH value of a neutral solution, we should add an **alkali**.

Q.16 The pH of the soil is tested and for the better growth of crops, slightly alkaline soil is required. Which ion in the fertilizer will increase the alkalinity of the soil? **(Competency Based Que.)**

(a) Hydronium ion
(b) Hydroxyl ion
(c) Hydrogen ion
(d) Both hydroxyl and hydrogen

Ans. (b) Hydroxyl ion

Q.17 The indicator which changes to pink colour in an alkaline solution is **(ICSE Specimen 2023)**

(a) blue litmus
(b) methyl orange
(c) red litmus
(d) phenolphthalein

Ans. (d) Phenolphthalein

Q.18 An aqueous compound which turns colourless phenolphthalein to pink is **(ICSE Specimen 2023)**

(a) ammonium hydroxide
(b) nitric acid
(c) anhydrous calcium chloride
(d) sulphuric acid

Ans. (a) **Ammonium hydroxide** is a basic salt which turns phenolphthalein from colourless to pink.

Q.19 The colour change observed when the solution of magnesium hydroxide is tested with the following indicators. **(ICSE 2021-22, Sem-I)**

(a) Phenolphthalein turns colourless to pink
(b) Methyl orange remains orange
(c) Phenolphthalein remains colourless
(d) Blue litmus solution turns red

Ans. (a) Magnesium hydroxide is a **basic metal oxide**. So, when phenolphthalein is tested with this basic oxide, it turns colourless to pink.

Q.20 Which of the following observations correctly shows the action of indicator on sodium hydroxide solution? **(Competency Based Que.)**

	Indicator	Methyl orange	Phenolphthalein
(a)	P	orange to yellow	remains colourless
(b)	Q	orange to pink	remains colourless
(c)	R	orange to yellow	colourless to pink
(d)	S	remains orange	remains pink

Ans. (c) R

Q.21 A compound *P* is heated in a test tube with sodium hydroxide solution. A red litmus paper held at the mouth of the test tube turns blue. Which of the following could compound *P* be? **(ICSE Specimen 2025)**

(a) Zinc sulphate (b) Copper sulphate
(c) Ferrous sulphate (d) Ammonium sulphate

Ans. (d) Ammonium sulphate

The reaction is represented as

$$\underset{\text{Ammonium sulphate (P)}}{(NH_4)_2SO_4} + \underset{\text{Sodium hydroxide}}{2NaOH} \longrightarrow \underset{\text{Sodium sulphate}}{Na_2SO_4} + \underset{\text{Water}}{2H_2O} + \underset{\text{Ammonia}}{2NH_3}$$

As, **ammonia is alkaline** in nature. When red litmus paper is held at the mouth of the test tube, it changes the colour of the red litmus paper to blue.

Q.22 A student tests four different solutions with Universal Indicator.

Solution	P	Q	R	S
Colour with Universal Indicator	purple	green	red	yellow

What are the pH values of the four solutions?

	P	Q	R	S
(a)	2	9	4	7
(b)	4	7	8	9
(c)	9	5	12	2
(d)	12	7	2	5

Ans. (d) The colour of the Universal Indicator ranges from red when it is very acidic (pH ≈ 2) to green when it is neutral (pH = 7) and to purple or violet when it is very basic (pH ≈ 12).

Q.23 The products formed when an acid reacts with a base is **(ICSE 2021-22, Sem-I)**

(a) salt and hydrogen (b) salt and oxygen
(c) salt and water (d) salt and carbon dioxide

Ans. (c) When an acid reacts with a base, they neutralise each other's effect, and **salt and water** are formed.

Q.24 The salt formed by partial replacement of hydrogen ion of an acid by a basic radical.

(ICSE Specimen 2022, Sem-I)

(a) Sodium sulphite
(b) Magnesium hydroxide
(c) Potassium sulphate
(d) Zinc hydrogen sulphite

Ans. (d) **Zinc hydrogen sulphite** is formed by the partial replacement of hydrogen ion of an acid by a basic radical.

Q.25 A salt formed by incomplete neutralisation of an acid by a base **(ICSE Specimen 2022, Sem-I)**

(a) basic salt (b) acid salt
(c) normal salt (d) complex salt

Ans. (b) A salt formed by the incomplete neutralisation of an acid by a base is called an **acid salt**.

Q.26 Acidic salts ionise in water solution to give which of the following ions.

(a) H^+ ions (b) H_3O^+ ions
(c) OH^- (d) SO_4^{2-} ions

Ans. (b) Acidic salts ionise in water solution to give **hydronium ions** (H_3O^+) and therefore, show all the properties of an acid.

Q.27 The acid which does not form an acidic salt by a basic radical. **(ICSE 2023)**

(a) H_2CO_3 (b) H_3PO_4
(c) H_2SO_4 (d) CH_3COOH

Ans. (d) **Acetic acid** is a weak acid which does not dissociate completely in water so it does not give an acidic salt.

Q.28 The salt formed when concentrated sulphuric acid reacts with KNO_3 above 200°C. **(ICSE 2023)**

(a) K_2SO_4 (b) K_2SO_3 (c) $KHSO_4$ (d) $KHSO_3$

Ans. (a) $KNO_3(aq) + conc.H_2SO_4(aq) \xrightarrow{\text{Above } 200°C} 2HNO_3(aq) + K_2SO_4(aq)$

Q.29 Which pair of reactants can be best used to produce lead (II) sulphate? **(ICSE 2025)**

(a) Sulphuric acid + Lead
(b) Sulphuric acid + Lead hydroxide
(c) Sodium sulphate + Lead nitrate
(d) Potassium sulphate + Lead oxide

Ans. (c) Insoluble lead (II) sulphate can be prepared by treating **lead nitrate with sodium sulphate**.

$$Pb(NO_3)_2 + Na_2SO_4 \longrightarrow \underset{\text{(Lead (II) sulphate)}}{PbSO_4\downarrow} + 2NaNO_3$$

Q.30 A black colour solid which on reaction with dilute sulphuric acid forms a blue coloured solution is

(a) carbon (b) manganese (IV) oxide
(c) lead (II) oxide (d) copper (II) oxide

Ans. (d) $\underset{\text{Copper (II) oxide}}{CuO} + H_2SO_4 \longrightarrow \underset{\text{Blue colour}}{CuSO_4} + H_2O$

Q.31 The salt which in solution gives a pale green precipitate with sodium hydroxide solution and a white precipitate with barium chloride solution is

(a) iron (III) sulphate
(b) iron (II) sulphate
(c) iron (II) chloride
(d) iron (III) chloride

Ans. (b) **Iron (II) sulphate**, $FeSO_4$.

It gives pale green precipitate with sodium hydroxide solution and white precipitate with barium chloride solution.

$$FeSO_4(aq) + 2NaOH(aq) \longrightarrow \underset{\text{Pale green ppt.}}{Fe(OH)_2(s)\downarrow} + Na_2SO_4(aq)$$

$$FeSO_4(aq) + BaCl_2(aq) \longrightarrow FeCl_2(aq) + \underset{\text{White ppt.}}{BaSO_4(s)\downarrow}$$

TYPE - 2 01 Mark

Assertion-Reason Questions

Directions (Q. Nos. 1-8) In the following questions, a statement of Assertion (A) is followed by a statement of Reason (R). Choose the answer based on the codes given below.

(a) Both (A) and (R) are true and (R) is the correct explanation of (A).
(b) Both (A) and (R) are true but (R) is not the correct explanation of (A).
(c) (A) is true but (R) is false.
(d) (A) is false but (R) is true.

Q.1 Assertion (A) All acids form hydroxyl ion when dissolved in water.

Reason (R) Every acid has hydrogen as the necessary element.

Ans. (d) All acids form **hydronium ions** when dissolved in water and every acid has hydrogen as the necessary element.

Thus, (A) is false but (R) is true.

Q.2 Assertion (A) It is advised that while diluting an acid, one should add water to acid and not acid to water keeping the solution continuously stirred.

Reason (R) The process of dissolving an acid into it water is highly exothermic.

Ans. (d) While diluting an acid, we should add **acid to the water** and not water to the acid as the process of dissolving an acid into water is highly exothermic.

Thus, (A) is false but (R) is true.

Q.3 Assertion (A) Sodium hydroxide reacts with zinc to produce hydrogen gas.

Reason (R) Bases react with active metals to produce hydrogen gas.

Ans. (b) Both (A) and (R) are true but (R) is not the correct explanation of (A). Sodium hydroxide being an strong base, reacts with active metal (zinc) to produce H_2 gas. The reaction is given as follows

$$Zn(s) + 2NaOH(aq) \longrightarrow Na_2ZnO_2(aq) + H_2(g)$$

Q.4 Assertion (A) Acids have a pH of less than 7.

Reason (R) Acids produce hydronium ions as the only positively charged ion in solution.

Ans. (a) Acids have pH in the range 0 to 7. Thus, acids have pH less than 7 and they produce hydronium ions as the only positively charged ion in solution.

Thus, both (A) and (R) both are true and (R) is the correct explanation of (A).

Q.5 Assertion (A) When baking soda is added to fresh milk, it takes a longer time to set as curd.

Reason (R) Baking soda decreases the pH value of fresh milk to below 6.

Ans. (c) When baking soda is added to milk, it takes longer to set as curd because baking soda is a base, thus it **increases the pH value** of fresh milk to above 6. It neutralises the lactic acid produced by bacteria during the curdling process, making the milk slightly basic and hindering the acidic conditions needed for curd formation. Thus, (A) is true but (R) is false.

Q.6 Assertion (A) Alkali is a basic hydroxide.

Reason (R) All alkalis form hydroxyl (OH^-) ion in aqueous solution as the only negative ions. They turn red litmus blue.

Ans. (a) An alkali is a base, soluble in water and all alkalis is a basic hydroxide which when dissolved in water produces **hydroxyl (OH^-) ions** as the only negatively charged ions. They turn red litmus blue.

Therefore, both (A) and (R) are true and (R) is the correct explanation of (A).

Q.7 Assertion (A) All bases react with acids to form salt and water only.

Reason (R) All alkalies are bases but all bases are not alkalies.

Ans. (b) All bases when mixed with acids form salt and water as the product.

e.g. $\underset{\text{(Acid)}}{HCl} + \underset{\text{(Base)}}{NaOH} \longrightarrow \underset{\text{(Salt)}}{NaCl} + \underset{\text{(Water)}}{H_2O}$

Thus, both (A) and (R) are true but (R) is not the correct explanation of (A).

Q.8 Assertion (A) Normal salts are salts formed by the complete replacement of the ionisable hydrogen atoms of an acid by a metallic or an ammonium ion.

Reason (R) Normal salts have no ionisable hydrogen atoms.

Ans. (a) Normal salts are formed by complete replacement of the ionisable hydrogen atoms of an acid, due to which all hydrogen atoms are replaced and there are no further ionisable hydrogen atoms.

Thus, both (A) and (R) are true and (R) is the correct explanation of (A).

TYPE - 3 01 Mark

Fill in the Blanks

Q.1 An acid is a compound which, when dissolved in water give............. (hydronium/ hydroxide) ions as the only positive ions.

Ans. hydronium

Q.2 .... (Lactic acid/Tartaric acid) is an organic acid, which is naturally occuring in grapes, tamarind and apples.

Ans. Tartaric acid

Q.3 Acids which are obtained usually from minerals are referred as .... (organic acids/inorganic acids).

Ans. inorganic acids

Q.4 .... (Formic acid/Carbonic acid) is a weak mineral acid, which turns blue litmus pink. It is non-corrosive and is used in soft drinks.

Ans. Carbonic acid

Q.5 The acid which cannot act as an oxidising agent is ....(conc. H_2SO_4/conc. HCl). **(ICSE 2020)**

Ans. conc. HCl

Q.6 The basicity of acetic acid is .... (3/1). **(ICSE 2014)**

Ans. The basicity of acetic acid is **1** because on ionisation, it gives only one H_3O^+ ion.

$$CH_3COOH + H_2O \rightleftharpoons \underset{\text{Hydronium ion}}{H_3O^+} + \underset{\text{Acetate ion}}{CH_3COO^-}$$

Q.7 The number of .... (hydronium/hydroxide) ions which can be liberated by one molecule of an acid on complete ionisation is called as basicity.

Ans. hydronium

Q.8 A base is a compound which is soluble in water and gives off .... ions. (hydroxide/hydrogen)

Ans. hydroxide

Q.9 An alkali which completely dissociates into ions is .... (ammonium hydroxide/calcium hydroxide) **(ICSE 2020)**

Ans. calcium hydroxide.

$Ca(OH)_2$ is a strong base because it completely dissociates into Ca^{2+} and OH^- ions.

Q.10 When a metallic oxide is dissolved in water, the solution formed has a high concentration of .... ions. (H^+/OH^-) **(ICSE 2017)**

Ans. OH^-

Q.11 The 'p' in the pH stands for .... which means power in German. (*potenz*/neutron)

Ans. potenz

Q.12 pH of acetic acid is greater than dilute sulphuric acid. So, acetic acid contains .... concentration of H^+ ions. (greater/low). **(ICSE 2020)**

Ans. low

Q.13 Higher the pH value of a solution, the more .... (acidic/alkaline) it is. **(ICSE 2023, 2016)**

Ans. alkaline

Q.14 The indicator which does not change colour on passage of HCl gas is .... (moist blue litmus/ phenolphthalein).

Ans. phenolphthalein

Q.15 An .... (alkaline/acidic) solution will turn methyl orange solution pink or red. **(ICSE Specimen 2025)**

Ans. acidic

Q.16 .... (sulphuric acid/ hydrochloric acid) does not form an acid salt. **(ICSE Specimen 2024)**

Ans. Hydrochloric acid

Q.17 Superphosphate is an example of a compound called .... (acidic salt/basic salt)

Ans. acidic salt

Q.18 The salt prepared by the method of direct combination is .... (iron (II) chloride/iron (III) chloride)

Ans. iron (III) chloride **(ICSE 2018, 2024)**

Q.19 The salt that is an insoluble chloride is .... ($AgCl/MgCl_2$) **(ICSE 2015)**

Ans. AgCl is a crystalline white solid. It does not dissolve in water, dilute acids and alcohols.

Q.20 The .... (acidic salts/basic salts) are formed by partial replacement of hydroxyl radicals of a diacidic or triacidic base with an acid radical.

Ans. basic salts

Q.21 The correct formula of sodium sulphate (crystals) is .... ($Na_2SO_4 \cdot 8H_2O$/$Na_2SO_4 \cdot 10H_2O$)

Ans. $Na_2SO_4 \cdot 10H_2O$

TYPE - 4 — 01 Mark

Correct the Incorrect Statement

Q.1 Oxalic acid is present in vinegar.

Ans. **Acetic acid** is present in vinegar.

Q.2 Hydracids contains hydrogen and oxygen.

Ans. Hydracids contains hydrogen and a **non-metallic element** (except oxygen).

Q.3 Phosphoric acid is dibasic acid and it ionise in two steps.

Ans. Phosphoric acid (H_3PO_4) is a **tribasic** acid and it ionise in **three** steps, as shown below.

$$H_3PO_4 + H_2O \rightleftharpoons H_3O^+ + H_2PO_4^-$$

$$H_2PO_4^- + H_2O \rightleftharpoons H_3O^+ + HPO_4^{2-}$$

$$HPO_4^{2-} + H_2O \rightleftharpoons H_3O^+ + PO_4^{3-}$$

Q.4 Magnesium reacts with nitric acid to liberate hydrogen gas.

Ans. Magnesium reacts with **very dilute** nitric acid to liberate hydrogen gas.

Q.5 Sodium chloride reacts with dilute sulphuric acid and on warming, it liberates HCl.

Ans. Sodium chloride reacts with **concentrated** sulphuric acid and on warming, it liberates HCl **gas**.

Q.6 Zinc reacts with sulphuric acid to liberate hydrogen sulphide gas.

Ans. **Zinc sulphide** reacts with sulphuric acid to liberate hydrogen sulphide gas.

Q.7 Weak alkali undergoes almost complete dissociation in aqueous solution to produce a high concentration of OH^-.

Ans. Weak alkali undergoes **only partial** dissociation in aqueous solution to produce a **low** concentration of OH^- in solution.

TYPE - 5 — 01 × 05 = 05 Marks

Matching Type Questions

Q.1 (i) Match the following.

Column I	Column II
A. Acid salt	1. Sodium potassium carbonate
B. Normal salt	2. Sodium carbonate
	3. Sodium zincate
	4. Sodium hydrogen carbonate

(ii) Match the following.

Column I	Column II
A. $ZnCl_2$ from Zn	1. Precipitation
B. KNO_3 from KOH	2. Direct combination
C. $CaCO_3$ from $CaCl_2$	3. Displacement reaction
	4. Neutralisation

(ICSE 2024)

Ans. (i)

Column I	Column II
A. Acid salt	4. Sodium hydrogen carbonate ($NaHCO_3$)
B. Normal salt	2. Sodium carbonate (Na_2CO_3)

A → (4); B → (2)

(ii) A → (3), B → (4), C → (1)

(a) $Zn + 2HCl \longrightarrow ZnCl_2 + H_2$ (Displacement reaction)

(b) $KOH + HNO_3 \longrightarrow KNO_3 + H_2O$ (Neutralisation reaction)

(c) $CaCl_2 + Na_2CO_3 \longrightarrow CaCO_3\downarrow + 2NaCl$ (Precipitation reaction)

Q.2 Match the following.

Column I	Column II
A. Acid salt	1. Ferrous ammonium sulphate
B. Double salt	2. Contains only ions
C. Ammonium hydroxide solution	3. Sodium hydrogen sulphate
D. Dilute hydrochloric Acid	4. Contains only molecules
E. Carbon tetrachloride	5. Contains ions and molecules

Ans. A → (3); B → (1); C → (5); D → (2); E → (4).

Q.3 Match the following. **(ICSE 2016)**

Column I	Column II
A. $Pb(NO_3)_2$ from PbO	1. Simple displacement
B. $MgCl_2$ from Mg	2. Titration
C. $FeCl_3$ from Fe	3. Neutralisation
D. $NaNO_3$ from NaOH	4. Precipitation
E. $ZnCO_3$ from $ZnSO_4$	5. Combination

Ans. A → (3); B → (1); C → (5); D → (2); E → (4).

TYPE - 6

01 Mark

Identify the Following

Q.1 Name an acid which is present in vinegar.

Ans. Acetic acid (CH_3COOH)

Q.2 Find the odd one out.
Formic acid, nitric acid, acetic acid, propanoic acid.

Ans. Nitric acid (all other are organic acids).

Q.3 Name the gas evolved when sodium hydrogen carbonate is added to hydrochloric acid (HCl).

Ans. Carbon dioxide (CO_2) gas.

Q.4 Name the gas produced on reaction of dilute sulphuric acid with a metallic sulphide.

Ans. Hydrogen sulphide (H_2S).

$$\underset{\text{Iron sulphide}}{FeS} + \underset{\text{Sulphuric acid (dil.)}}{H_2SO_4} \longrightarrow FeSO_4 + \underset{\text{Hydrogen sulphide}}{H_2S}$$

Q.5 Name any one base which is soluble in water.

Ans. Sodium hydroxide (NaOH)

Q.6 Write the appropriate term for
"A compound which is soluble in water and the only negative ions in the solution are hydroxide ions".

Ans. Alkali

Q.7 Identify a salt formed by the complete neutralisation of an acid by a base. **(ICSE Specimen 2025)**

Ans. Normal salt
e.g. $HCl + NaOH \longrightarrow NaCl + H_2O$

Q.8 Name a type of salt formed by partial replacement of hydroxyl radicals with an acidic radical. **(ICSE 2023)**

Or A salt formed by the partial replacement of the hydroxyl group of a di-acidic or a tri-acidic base by an acid radical **(ICSE 2025)**

Ans. Basic salt.

Q.9 Give an example of a salt which is formed by the direct combination.

Ans. Ferric chloride ($FeCl_3$)

Q.10 Name "A solid formed by reaction of two gases, one of which is acidic and the other basic in nature". **(ICSE 2017)**

Ans. Salt is formed. e.g. HCl gas is acidic and NH_3 gas is basic in nature. A solid salt NH_4Cl is formed by the reaction of these two gases.

$$NH_3(g) + HCl(g) \longrightarrow NH_4Cl(s)$$

TYPE - 7 02 Marks

Short Answer Type I Questions

Q.1 Write the balanced chemical equation.

(i) Calcium bicarbonate reacts with dilute hydrochloric acid.

(ii) Dilute sulphuric acid is poured over sodium sulphite.

Ans. (i) $Ca(HCO_3)_2 + (Dil.)2HCl \longrightarrow CaCl_2 + 2H_2O + 2CO_2$ **(1)**

(ii) $Na_2SO_3 + H_2SO_4 \longrightarrow Na_2SO_4 + H_2O + SO_2\uparrow$ **(1)**

Q.2 Give the balanced equation for the following.

(i) Potassium hydrogen carbonate and dilute sulphuric acid.

(ii) Copper oxide and dilute hydrochloric acid.

Ans. (i) $2KHCO_3 + H_2SO_4 \longrightarrow K_2SO_4 + 2H_2O + 2CO_2\uparrow$

(ii) $CuO + \underset{(Dil.)}{2HCl} \longrightarrow CuCl_2 + H_2O$ **(1 × 2 = 2)**

Q.3 Arrange the following as per the instructions given in the brackets.

(i) Sulphuric acid, phosphoric acid, acetic acid (increasing order of number of replaceable H^+ ions per molecule) **(ICSE 2024)**

(ii) Aluminium hydroxide, copper hydroxide, sodium hydroxide (increasing order of number of replaceable OH^- ions per molecule).

Ans. (i) Acetic acid < Sulphuric acid < Phosphoric acid. **(1)**

(ii) Sodium hydroxide < Copper hydroxide < Aluminium hydroxide. **(1)**

Q.4 (i) If a few drops of concentrated acid accidentally spills over the hand of a student, what should be done?

(ii) A few drops of liquid X were added to distilled water. It was observed that the pH of the water decreased. What could be the liquid sample X?

Ans. (i) Wash the hand immediately with plenty of water and apply a paste of baking soda ($NaHCO_3$). Baking soda is a mild base. Here, a strong base cannot be used to neutralise the acid due to its corrosive nature. **(1)**

(ii) Distilled water has pH = 7. X could be any **acid** like HCl, therefore when it is added to distilled water, pH becomes less than 7. **(1)**

Q.5 (i) The following table lists the pH values of some substances.

Solutions	pH
Hydrochloric acid	1
Milk	6
Pure water	7
Baking soda	9
Sodium hydroxide	14

What would happen to the pH of an acid and a base when each is diluted (pure distilled water is added to it)?

(ii) Aditi finds that a mixture of an acid and a base does not change the colour of either red or blue litmus paper.

Compare the amount of H^+ and OH^- in the solution.

Ans. (i) On dilution, the pH of an acid will increase and that of a base will decrease. **(1)**

(ii) If the mixture of an acid and a base does not change the colour of either red or blue litmus paper, it means that the solution is **neutral**. In a neutral solution, the amount of H^+ ions is equal to the amount of OH^- ions. **(1)**

Q.6 Three solutions P, Q and R have pH value of 3.5, 5.2 and 12.2, respectively. Which one of these is a

(i) weak acid? (ii) strong alkali? **(ICSE 2018)**

Ans. Three solutions P, Q, R have pH value of 3.5, 5.2 and 12.2, respectively. Thus,

(i) **Solution Q** will behave as a weak acid as acidic solution has pH<7 and with increase in pH, acidity of solution decreases. **(1)**

(ii) **Solution R** will behave as a strong alkali or base because of it has pH>7. It acts as a basic solution and rest of them (P and Q) acts as an acidic solution. **(1)**

Q.7 Mahesh prepared a basic solution X that has a pH 7. How will the pH of the solution X change on addition of the following: **(ICSE Specimen 2024)**

(i) Hydrochloric acid

(ii) A solution of a base

Ans. (i) The hydrogen ion concentration will increase when HCl is added to solution. The pH will **decrease** below 7 because of the increased hydrogen ion concentration. **(1)**

(ii) On addition of a solution of a base, pH will **increase.** It will become a basic solution as pH will be greater than 7. **(1)**

Q.8 (i) Define the following term 'Normal salt'. **(ICSE 2024)**

(ii) How many types of salts can be prepared from orthophosphoric acid?

Ans. (i) The salts which are formed by the complete replacement of hydrogen ion of an acid molecule by a basic radical (metallic or ammonium ion) are called **normal salts.**

$$\underset{\text{Sodium hydroxide}}{2NaOH} + \underset{\text{Sulphuric acid}}{H_2SO_4} \longrightarrow \underset{\text{Sodium sulphate (normal salt)}}{Na_2SO_4} + 2H_2O$$

Both 'H' ions in sulphuric acid are replaced by metallic radical, i.e. sodium. **(1)**

(ii) There are **three** types of salts which can be prepared from orthophosphoric acid (H_3PO_4), two acidic salts and one normal salt. **(1)**

Q.9 Some general rules for the solubility of salts in water are listed.

- Carbonates are insoluble (except ammonium carbonate, potassium carbonate and sodium carbonate).
- Chlorides are soluble (except lead (II) chloride and silver chloride).
- Nitrates are soluble.
- Sulphates are soluble (except barium sulphate, calcium sulphate and lead (II) sulphate).

Which substances produce an insoluble salt when aqueous solutions of them are mixed?

Justify your answer.

(a) Copper nitrate and magnesium chloride

(b) Zinc chloride and ammonium nitrate

(c) Silver nitrate and zinc chloride

(d) Potassium carbonate and sodium sulphate

(Competency Based Que.)

Ans. (c) silver nitrate and zinc chloride. **(1)**

Silver chloride is formed, which is an insoluble precipitate, while for all others, no precipitate is formed. **(1)**

Q.10 State your observations, when

(i) dilute hydrochloric acid is added to lead nitrate solution and the mixture is heated.

(ii) barium chloride solution is mixed with sodium sulphate solution. **(ICSE 2016)**

Ans. (i) **Lead chloride** ($PbCl_2$) gets precipitated in the given reaction.

$$\underset{\text{Lead nitrate}}{Pb(NO_3)_2} + 2HCl \xrightarrow{\Delta} \underset{\text{Lead chloride}}{PbCl_2\downarrow} + \underset{\text{Nitric acid}}{2HNO_3}$$ **(1)**

(ii) White precipitate of **barium sulphate** is formed in the given reaction.

$$BaCl_2 + Na_2SO_4 \longrightarrow \underset{\text{(White ppt.) Barium sulphate}}{BaSO_4\downarrow} + 2NaCl$$ **(1)**

Q.11 Give the balanced equations for the following reactions.

(i) Dilute nitric acid and copper carbonate.

(ii) Silver nitrate solution and sodium chloride solution.

Ans. (i) $CuCO_3 + 2HNO_3 \longrightarrow Cu(NO_3)_2 + CO_2 + H_2O$

(ii) $AgNO_3 + NaCl \longrightarrow AgCl + NaNO_3$ **(1 × 2 = 2)**

Q.12 Write a balanced equation for the preparation of each of the following salts.

(i) Copper sulphate from copper carbonate.

(ii) Zinc carbonate from zinc sulphate. **(ICSE 2018)**

Ans. Following are the balanced chemical equations for the preparation of:

(i) **Copper sulphate from copper carbonate**

$$\underset{\text{Copper carbonate}}{CuCO_3} + H_2SO_4 \longrightarrow \underset{\text{Copper sulphate}}{CuSO_4} + H_2O + CO_2\uparrow$$ **(1)**

(ii) **Zinc carbonate from zinc sulphate**

$$\underset{\text{Zinc sulphate}}{ZnSO_4} + Na_2CO_3 \longrightarrow \underset{\text{Zinc carbonate}}{ZnCO_3} + \underset{\text{Sodium sulphate}}{Na_2SO_4}$$ **(1)**

Q.13 From the formulae listed below, choose one in each case corresponding to the salt having the given descriptions.

$AgCl, CuCO_3, CuSO_4 \cdot 5H_2O, KNO_3, NaCl, NaHSO_4$

(i) An acid salt. (ii) An insoluble chloride.

Ans. (i) Acid salt is **$NaHSO_4$**.

(ii) **AgCl** is an insoluble chloride. **(1 × 2 = 2)**

Q.14 Classify the solutions of the following as acids, bases or salt.

Ammonium hydroxide, Barium chloride, Sodium chloride and HNO_3.

Ans.

Ammonium hydroxide	Base
Barium chloride	Salt
Sodium chloride	Salt
HNO_3	Acid

(½ × 4 = 2)

Q.15 Select from the list given [(*A*) to (*E*)] one substance in each case which matches the description given in parts (i) and (ii).

Note Each substance is used only once in the answer.

(*A*) Nitroso iron (II) sulphate

(*B*) Iron (III) chloride

(*C*) Chromium sulphate

(*D*) Lead (II) chloride

(*E*) Sodium chloride

(i) A compound which is insoluble in cold water, but soluble in hot water.

(ii) A compound whose aqueous solution is neutral in nature.

Ans. (i) (*D*) Lead (II) chloride (ii) (*E*) Sodium chloride

(1 × 2 = 2)

Q.16 The diagram below is to prepare iron (III) chloride in the laboratory.

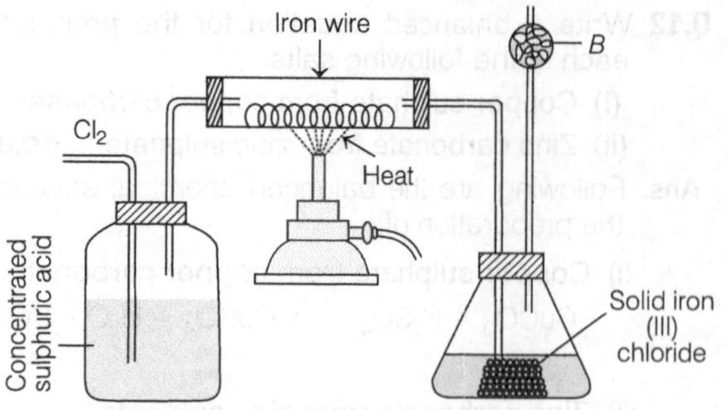

(i) What is substance *B* and what is its purpose?

(ii) Why is iron (III) chloride to be stored in a closed container?

Ans. (i) Substance *B* is **anhydrous calcium chloride**, $CaCl_2$. It is a **drying agent** which does not allow the moisture to enter into the reaction set up. **(1)**

(ii) Iron (III) chloride is **highly deliquescent**. So, it should be kept dry by storing in a closed container. **(1)**

TYPE - 8

03 Marks

Short Answer Type II Questions

Q.1 (i) How is the concentration of hydronium ions, $[H_3O^+]$ affected when a solution of an acid is diluted?

(ii) Why do HCl, HNO_3, etc., show acidic characters in aqueous solutions while solutions of compounds like alcohol and glucose do not show acidic character?

(iii) Why does an aqueous solution of an acid conduct electricity?

Ans. (i) An acid dissociates into hydronium ions $[H_3O^+]$ and anions when dissolved in water. When a solution is diluted, the volume of the solution increases but the number of ions remains the same, so concentration of hydronium ions $[H_3O^+]$ per unit volume **decreases**. **(1)**

(ii) Acidic character of a compound is due to the presence of **replaceable H^+ ions**, which are released in aqueous solution and are responsible for acidic properties. As HCl, HNO_3, etc., have replaceable H^+ ions, they show acidic character, while glucose and alcohol do not have replaceable H^+ ions hence, no acidic character is shown by them. **(1)**

(iii) An acid molecule (*HA*) dissociates in an aqueous solution to produce H^+ [or H_3O^+] ions and corresponding anions (A^-). These free ions carry the electrical charge from one place to other hence, conduct electricity. **(1)**

Q.2 Write the equations for the following reactions.

(i) Dilute sulphuric acid and barium chloride.

(ii) Dilute hydrochloric acid and lead nitrate solution.

(iii) Dilute sulphuric acid and sodium sulphide.

Ans. (i) $H_2SO_4 + BaCl_2 \longrightarrow BaSO_4 + 2HCl$

(ii) $Pb(NO_3)_2 + 2HCl \longrightarrow PbCl_2 + 2HNO_3$

(iii) $Na_2S + Dil.H_2SO_4 \longrightarrow Na_2SO_4 + H_2S\uparrow$ **(1 × 3 = 3)**

Q.3 Study the following observations and name the anions present in each of the reactions. **(ICSE 2023, 2018)**

(i) When a crystalline solid '*P*' is warmed with concentrated H_2SO_4 and copper turnings a reddish brown gas is released.

(ii) When few drops of dilute sulphuric acid is added to salt '*R*' and heated, a colourless gas is released which turns moist lead acetate paper silvery black.

(iii) When few drops of barium nitrate solution is added to the salt solution '*Q*', a white precipitate is formed which is insoluble in HCl.

Ans. (i) When **copper nitrate** (*P*) is warmed with concentrated H_2SO_4 and copper turnings, reddish brown gas is released.

$$Cu(NO_3)_2 + 2H_2SO_4 + Cu \longrightarrow 2CuSO_4 + 2NO_2\uparrow + 2H_2O$$

Anion present is $\mathbf{NO_3^-}$. **(1)**

(ii) When dil. H_2SO_4 is added to **sodium sulphide** salt, Na_2S **(*R*)** and heated, hydrogen sulphide (H_2S) gas is released. Anion is $\mathbf{S^{2-}}$.

$$Na_2S + H_2SO_4 \longrightarrow Na_2SO_4 + H_2S\uparrow$$

$$(CH_3COO)_2Pb + H_2S \longrightarrow \underset{\text{(Black)}}{PbS}\downarrow + 2CH_3COOH$$ **(1)**

(iii) When few drops of barium nitrate solution are added to the **sodium sulphate solution** (*Q*), a white ppt. of $BaSO_4$ is formed. Anion present in *Q* is $\mathbf{SO_4^{2-}}$. **(1)**

Q.4 Complete and balance the following equations

(i) $NH_4Cl + Ca(OH)_2 \longrightarrow$ (ii) $CuSO_4 + NH_4OH \longrightarrow$

(ii) $Cu +$ conc. $HNO_3 \longrightarrow$ **(ICSE 2023)**

Ans. (i) $2NH_4Cl + Ca(OH)_2 \longrightarrow CaCl_2 + 2NH_3 + 2H_2O$

(ii) $CuSO_4 + 2NH_4OH \longrightarrow (NH_4)_2SO_4 + Cu(OH)_2\downarrow$

(iii) $Cu + 4\,conc.HNO_3 \longrightarrow Cu(NO_3)_2 + 2NO_2\uparrow + 2H_2O$

(1 × 3 = 3)

Q.5 Choose the substances given in the box below to answer the following questions.

Iron	Magnesium sulphate	Zinc	Sodium sulphite
Lead	Ferric chloride	Copper	Ferrous sulphate

(i) The metal that will not produce hydrogen gas when reacted with dilute acids.

(ii) The compound that will produce sulphur dioxide gas when reacted with dilute HCl.

(iii) The solution of this compound produces dirty green precipitate with NaOH. **(ICSE 2023)**

Ans. (i) **Copper**

Because copper is present below hydrogen in the reactivity series of metals.

Therefore, it does not react with dilute acids like HCl, H_2SO_4.

(ii) **Sodium sulphite**

$$Na_2SO_3(aq) + 2HCl(aq) \longrightarrow 2NaCl(aq) + SO_2(g)\uparrow + H_2O(l)$$

(iii) **Ferrous sulphate**

$$FeSO_4(aq) + 2NaOH(aq) \longrightarrow Fe(OH)_2(s)\downarrow + Na_2SO_4(aq)$$

(1 × 3 = 3)

Q.6 Choose the answer from the list which fits the description.

[CaO, CO_2, NaOH, $Fe(OH)_3$, CO]

(i) A basic oxide. (ii) An oxide which is acidic.

(iii) An alkali. **(ICSE Specimen 2023)**

Ans. (i) A basic oxide is **CaO** (It forms strong base when reacted with water).

(ii) An oxide which is acidic, is **CO_2** (It dissolves in water to form carbonic acid which is an acid).

(iii) An alkali is **NaOH** (It can dissociate into Na^+ and OH^-). **(1 × 3 = 3)**

Q.7 Name the kind of particles present in

(i) sodium hydroxide solution

(ii) carbonic acid

(iii) sugar solution **(ICSE 2014)**

Ans. (i) **Na^+ and OH^-** ions are present in sodium hydroxide solution.

$$NaOH(aq) \rightleftharpoons Na^+(aq) + OH^-(aq)$$

(1)

(ii) Carbonic acid, H_2CO_3 is a weak acid. So, **ions and molecules** are present.

$$H_2CO_3 + 2H_2O \rightleftharpoons \underset{\text{Hydronium ion}}{2H_3O^+} + \underset{\text{Carbonate ion}}{CO_3^{2-}}$$

(1)

(iii) Sugar solution ($C_{12}H_{22}O_{11}$) does not dissociate, thus **molecules** are present in sugar solution. **(1)**

Q.8 Solution *A* is a sodium hydroxide solution. Solution *B* is a weak acid. Solution *C* is dilute sulphuric acid. Which solution will

(i) liberate sulphur dioxide from sodium sulphite?

(ii) give a white precipitate with zinc sulphate solution?

(iii) contain solute molecules and ions?

Ans. (i) *C* = Dilute sulphuric acid

(ii) *A* = Sodium hydroxide

$$ZnSO_4 + \underset{\text{Sodium hydroxide}}{2NaOH} \longrightarrow Na_2SO_4 + \underset{\text{(White ppt.)}}{Zn(OH)_2\downarrow}$$

(iii) *B* = Weak acid contains molecules and ions.

e.g. $H_2CO_3 + 2H_2O \rightleftharpoons 2H_3O^+ + \underset{\text{Carbonate ion}}{CO_3^{2-}}$ **(1 × 3 = 3)**

Q.9 Mohan has three solutions *P*, *Q* and *R* having a pH of 13, 5 and 2 respectively. Which of the above solutions *P*, *Q* or *R*

(i) will react with magnesium to liberate hydrogen gas?

(ii) will liberate ammonia gas when it reacts with ammonium chloride?

(iii) will contain molecules as well as ions? **(ICSE 2024)**

Ans. (i) **Solution '*R*'** having a pH of 2 is **strongly acidic**. It reacts with Mg to liberate H_2 gas.

$$Mg + \underset{(R)}{2HCl} \longrightarrow MgCl_2 + \underset{\text{Hydrogen gas}}{H_2\uparrow}$$

(1)

(ii) **Solution '*P*'** having a pH of 13 is **strongly alkaline**. It reacts with NH_4Cl to give NH_3 gas.

$$NaOH + NH_4Cl \longrightarrow NaCl + \underset{\text{Ammonia gas}}{NH_3\uparrow} + H_2O$$

(1)

(iii) **Solution '*Q*'** having a pH of 5 is a **weak acid**. Its solution contains ions as well as molecules. e.g.

$$CH_3COOH \rightleftharpoons CH_3COO^- + H^+$$

(1)

Q.10 Mention the colour changes observed when the following indicators are added to acids.

(i) Alkaline phenolphthalein solution

(ii) Methyl orange solution

(iii) Neutral litmus solution

Ans. (i) Colour changes from **pink to colourless**.

(ii) By adding methyl orange solution colour changes from **orange to pink**.

(iii) By adding neutral litmus solution colour changes from **purple to red**. **(1 × 3 = 3)**

Q.11 The pH values of three solutions *A*, *B* and *C* are given in the table. Answer the following questions

Solution	pH value
A	12
B	2
C	7

(i) Which solution will have no effect on litmus solution?
(ii) Which solution will liberate CO_2 when reacted with sodium carbonate?
(iii) Which solution will turn red litmus solution blue?
(ICSE 2019)

Ans. (i) The solution with pH value 7, i.e. **solution [C]**, shows no effect on litmus solution as it has equal number of $[H^+]$ and $[OH^-]$ ions. **(1)**

(ii) Acids liberate carbon dioxide on reaction with metallic carbonates (sodium carbonate).

Therefore, solution with pH = 2, i.e., **solution [*B*]** is acidic in nature and will react with Na_2CO_3 to give CO_2. **(1)**

(iii) Bases turn red litmus to blue. Therefore, solution with pH>7, is basic hence, **solution [*A*]** will turn the red litmus solution blue. **(1)**

Q.12 Give balanced chemical equations for the following conversions A, B and C. **(ICSE 2014)**

$$Fe \xrightarrow{A} FeCl_2 \xrightarrow{B} FeCO_3 \xrightarrow{C} Fe(NO_3)_2$$

Ans. $Fe + \underset{\text{(Hydrochloric acid)}}{\underset{(A)}{2HCl}} \longrightarrow \underset{\text{Ferrous chloride}}{FeCl_2} + H_2\uparrow$

$FeCl_2 + \underset{\text{Sodium carbonate}}{\underset{(B)}{Na_2CO_3}} \longrightarrow FeCO_3 + 2NaCl$

$FeCO_3 + \underset{\text{Nitric acid}}{\underset{(C)}{2HNO_3}} \longrightarrow \underset{\text{Iron (II) nitrate}}{Fe(NO_3)_2} + H_2O + CO_2$ **(1 × 3 = 3)**

Q.13 P, Q, R and S are the different methods of preparation of salts.

P. Simple displacement
Q. Neutralisation by titration
R. Precipitation
S. Direct combination

Choose the most appropriate method to prepare the following salts.

(i) $PbCl_2$
(ii) $FeCl_3$
(iii) Na_2SO_4 **(ICSE 2025)**

Ans. (i) **R** $PbCl_2$ can be prepared by **precipitation** reaction of lead nitrate with hydrochloric acid.

$$Pb(NO_3)_2 + 2HCl \longrightarrow PbCl_2\downarrow + 2HNO_3 \quad \textbf{(1)}$$

(ii) **S** $FeCl_3$ is prepared by **direct combination** of Fe and Cl_2.

$$2Fe + 3Cl_2 \longrightarrow 2FeCl_3 \quad \textbf{(1)}$$

(iii) **Q** Na_2SO_4 is prepared by the method of **neutralisation by titration** of H_2SO_4 (an acid) and NaOH (a soluble base).

$$H_2SO_4 + 2NaOH \longrightarrow Na_2SO_4 + 2H_2O \quad \textbf{(1)}$$

Q.14 Give the balanced chemical equations to prepare the following salts.

(i) Lead sulphate from lead carbonate.
(ii) Sodium sulphate using dilute sulphuric acid.
(iii) Copper chloride using copper carbonate.
(ICSE 2014)

Ans. (i) $\underset{\text{Lead carbonate}}{PbCO_3} + 2HNO_3 \longrightarrow Pb(NO_3)_2 + H_2O + CO_2$

$Pb(NO_3)_2 + H_2SO_4 \longrightarrow \underset{\text{Lead sulphate}}{PbSO_4} + 2HNO_3$

(ii) $2NaCl + H_2SO_4 \xrightarrow{>200\,°C} Na_2SO_4 + 2HCl$

Or

$2NaOH + H_2SO_4 \longrightarrow Na_2SO_4 + 2H_2O$

(iii) $\underset{\text{Copper carbonate}}{CuCO_3} + 2HCl \longrightarrow \underset{\text{Copper chloride}}{CuCl_2} + H_2O + CO_2\uparrow$ **(1 × 3 = 3)**

Q.15 A student prepared a potassium sulphite solution in the lab and added few drops of barium nitrate solution to it. He observed a white precipitate being formed in the test tube. On addition of dilute hydrochloric acid to the white precipitate and mixing it, he observed that the precipitate disappeared. **(Competency Based Que.)**

(i) Name the white precipitate.
(ii) Write a balanced chemical equation for the reaction between dilute hydrochloric acid and the white precipitate.
(iii) Name the gas evolved in the above reaction.

Ans. (i) Barium sulphite **(1)**

(ii) $BaSO_3 + 2HCl \longrightarrow BaCl_2 + H_2O + SO_2\uparrow$ **(1)**

(iii) Sulphur dioxide **(1)**

Q.16 The preparation of lead sulphate from lead carbonate is a two-step process.

(Lead sulphate cannot be prepared by adding dilute sulphuric acid to lead carbonate).

(i) What is the first step that is required to prepare lead sulphate from lead carbonate?
(ii) Write the equation for the reaction that will take place when this first step is carried out.
(iii) Why is the direct addition of dilute sulphuric acid to lead carbonate an impractical method of preparing lead sulphate?

Ans. (i) Lead carbonate is first treated with dilute nitric acid to get lead nitrate.

(ii) $PbCO_3 + 2HNO_3 \longrightarrow Pb(NO_3)_2 + H_2O + CO_2$

(iii) From an insoluble salt, another insoluble salt cannot be prepared by direct addition of dilute acid.

Lead carbonate ($PbCO_3$) and lead sulphate ($PbSO_4$) both are insoluble salts in water. When dilute sulphuric acid is added to lead carbonate, lead sulphate is formed which deposits on the remaining lead carbonate and stops the further reaction to take place. **(1 × 3 = 3)**

Q.17 You are provided with the list of chemicals mentioned below in the box:

Sodium hydroxide solution, copper carbonate, zinc, hydrochloric acid, copper, dilute sulphuric acid, chlorine, iron

Using suitable chemicals from the list given, write balanced chemical equation for the preparation of the salts mentioned below: **(ICSE Specimen 2025)**

(i) copper sulphate
(ii) sodium zincate
(ii) ferric chloride

Ans. (i) $\underset{\text{Copper carbonate}}{CuCO_3} + \underset{\text{Sulphuric acid}}{H_2SO_4} \longrightarrow \underset{\text{Copper sulphate}}{CuSO_4} + H_2O + CO_2$

(ii) $\underset{\text{Zinc}}{Zn} + \underset{\text{Sodium hydroxide}}{2NaOH} \longrightarrow \underset{\text{Sodium zincate}}{Na_2ZnO_2} + H_2$

(iii) $\underset{\text{Iron}}{2Fe} + \underset{\text{Chlorine}}{3Cl_2} \longrightarrow \underset{\text{Ferric chloride}}{2FeCl_3}$ **(1 × 3 = 3)**

TYPE - 9

04/05 Marks

Long Answer Type Questions

Q.1 Solution *A* is a strong acid; solution *B* is a weak acid; solution *C* is a strong alkali.

(i) Which solution contains solute molecules in addition to water molecules?
(ii) Which solution will give a gelatinous white precipitate with zinc sulphate solution? The precipitate disappears when an excess of the solution is added.
(iii) Which solution could be a solution of glacial acetic acid?
(iv) Give an example of solution which is a weak alkali.

Ans. (i) **Solution *B***, weak acid contains solute molecules in addition to water molecules.

(ii) **Solution *C***, strong alkali gives a gelatinous white precipitate with zinc sulphate solution.

(iii) **Solution *B***, weak acid could be a solution of glacial acetic acid.

(iv) **Ammonium hydroxide** solution, NH_4OH. **(1 × 4 = 4)**

Q.2 Copy and complete the following table. Column III has the names of gases to be prepared using the substance you enter in Column I along with dilute or concentrated sulphuric acid as indicated by you in Column II.

Column I	Column II	Column III
Substance reacted with acid	Dilute or concentrated sulphuric acid	Hydrogen gas
		Carbon dioxide

Ans.

Column I	Column II	Column III
Zinc	Dilute sulphuric acid	Hydrogen
Calcium carbonate	Concentrated sulphuric acid	Carbon dioxide

(1 × 4 = 4)

Q.3 Write the balanced equations for the preparation of the following compounds (as the major product) starting from iron and using only one other substance.

(i) Iron (II) chloride
(ii) Iron (III) chloride
(iii) Iron (II) sulphate
(iv) Iron (II) sulphide

Ans. (i) $\underset{\text{Iron metal}}{Fe} + \underset{\text{(Dil.)}}{2HCl} \longrightarrow \underset{\text{Iron (II) chloride}}{FeCl_2} + H_2\uparrow$

(ii) $\underset{\text{Iron}}{2Fe} + 3Cl_2 \longrightarrow \underset{\text{Iron (III) chloride}}{2FeCl_3}$

(iii) $\underset{\text{Iron metal}}{Fe} + H_2SO_4 \longrightarrow \underset{\text{Iron (II) sulphate}}{FeSO_4} + H_2O$

(iv) $\underset{\text{Iron metal}}{Fe} + S \longrightarrow \underset{\text{Iron (II) sulphide}}{FeS}$ **(1 × 4 = 4)**

Q.4 Write balanced equations for following conversions. **(ICSE Specimen 2019)**

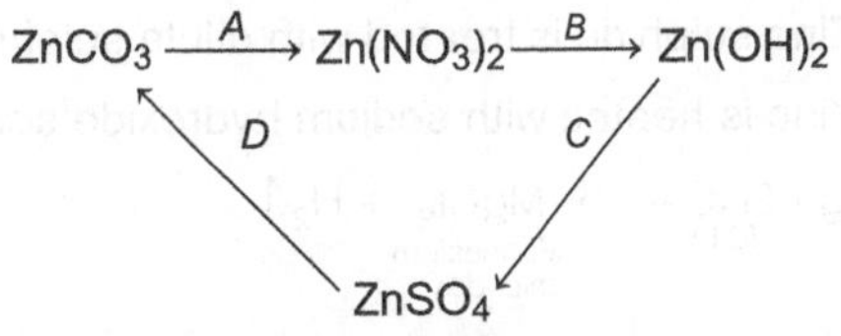

Ans. Balanced chemical equations for the conversions are:

(i) $\underset{\text{Zinc carbonate}}{ZnCO_3} + \underset{(A)}{2HNO_3} \longrightarrow \underset{\text{Zinc nitrate}}{Zn(NO_3)_2} + H_2O + CO_2$

(ii) $Zn(NO_3)_2 + \underset{(B)}{2NaOH} \longrightarrow \underset{\text{Zinc hydroxide}}{Zn(OH)_2} + 2NaNO_3$

(iii) $Zn(OH)_2 \xrightarrow{\Delta} \underset{\text{Zinc oxide}}{ZnO} + H_2O$

$ZnO + \underset{(C)}{H_2SO_4} \longrightarrow ZnSO_4 + H_2O$

(iv) $\underset{\text{Zinc sulphate}}{ZnSO_4} + \underset{\substack{\text{Sodium carbonate}\\(D)}}{Na_2CO_3} \longrightarrow ZnCO_3 + Na_2SO_4$ **(1 × 4 = 4)**

Q.5 Choosing the substances from the list given below, write the balanced chemical equations for the reactions which would be used in the laboratory to obtain the following salts.

Dilute sulphuric acid	Copper, iron, sodium	Copper (II) carbonate, sodium carbonate, sodium chloride, zinc nitrate

(i) Sodium sulphate (ii) Zinc carbonate
(iii) Copper (II) sulphate (iv) Iron (II) sulphate

Ans. (i) Sodium sulphate

$$\underset{\text{Sodium carbonate}}{Na_2CO_3} + \underset{\text{Sulphuric acid}}{H_2SO_4} \xrightarrow{>200°C} \underset{\text{Sodium sulphate}}{Na_2SO_4} + H_2O + CO_2\uparrow$$

(ii) Zinc carbonate

$$\underset{\text{Zinc nitrate}}{Zn(NO_3)_2} + \underset{\text{Sodium carbonate}}{Na_2CO_3} \longrightarrow 2NaNO_3 + \underset{\text{Zinc carbonate}}{ZnCO_3}$$

(iii) Copper (II) sulphate

$$\underset{\text{Copper carbonate}}{CuCO_3} + \underset{\text{Sulphuric acid}}{H_2SO_4} \longrightarrow \underset{\text{Copper (II) sulphate}}{CuSO_4} + H_2O + CO_2\uparrow$$

(iv) Iron (II) sulphate

$$\underset{\text{Iron metal}}{Fe} + \underset{\text{Sulphuric acid}}{H_2SO_4} \longrightarrow \underset{\text{Iron (II) sulphate}}{FeSO_4} + H_2O$$ **(1 × 4 = 4)**

Q.6 Write the balanced chemical equation for reaction,

(i) Magnesium metal is treated with dilute hydrochloric acid.
(ii) Lead nitrate solution is added to sodium chloride solution.
(iii) Zinc is reacted with dilute hydrochloric acid.
(iv) Zinc sulphide is treated with dilute sulphuric acid.
(v) Zinc is heated with sodium hydroxide solution.

Ans. (i) $Mg + \underset{(\text{Dil.})}{2HCl} \longrightarrow \underset{\text{Magnesium chloride}}{MgCl_2} + H_2\uparrow$

(ii) $Pb(NO_3)_2 + 2NaCl \longrightarrow PbCl_2 + 2NaNO_3$

(iii) $Zn + 2HCl \longrightarrow ZnCl_2 + H_2\uparrow$

(iv) $ZnS + H_2SO_4 \longrightarrow \underset{\text{Zinc Sulphate}}{ZnSO_4} + \underset{\text{Hydrogen Sulphide gas}}{H_2S}$

(v) $\underset{\text{Zinc metal}}{Zn} + 2NaOH \longrightarrow \underset{\text{Sodium zincate}}{Na_2ZnO_2} + H_2\uparrow$ **(1 × 5 = 5)**

Q.7 Making use only of substances chosen from those given below.

Dilute sulphuric acid	Sodium carbonate
Zinc	Sodium sulphite
Lead	Calcium carbonate

Give the equations for the reactions by which you could obtain

(i) hydrogen gas (ii) sulphur dioxide
(iii) carbon dioxide
(iv) zinc carbonate (two steps required)

Ans. (i) $Zn + H_2SO_4(\text{dil.}) \longrightarrow ZnSO_4 + H_2\uparrow$ **(1)**

(ii) $Na_2SO_3 + H_2SO_4 \longrightarrow Na_2SO_4 + H_2O + SO_2\uparrow$ **(1)**

(iii) $Na_2CO_3 + H_2SO_4 \longrightarrow Na_2SO_4 + H_2O + CO_2\uparrow$ **(1)**

(iv) (a) $Zn + H_2SO_4(\text{dil.}) \longrightarrow ZnSO_4 + H_2\uparrow$

(b) $ZnSO_4 + Na_2CO_3 \longrightarrow ZnCO_3 + Na_2SO_4$ **(2)**

Q.8 Give the equations for the following conversions (*A*) to (*E*).

$$ZnSO_4 \xrightarrow{(A)} ZnCO_3 \xrightarrow{(B)} Zn(NO_3)_2 \xrightarrow{(C)} Zn(OH)_2 \xrightarrow{(D)} ZnO \xrightarrow{(E)} ZnSO_4$$

Ans. (*A*) $\underset{\text{Zinc sulphate}}{ZnSO_4} + \underset{\text{Sodium carbonate}}{Na_2CO_3} \longrightarrow \underset{\text{Zinc carbonate}}{ZnCO_3} + Na_2SO_4$

(*B*) $\underset{\text{Zinc carbonate}}{ZnCO_3} + \underset{\text{Nitric acid}}{2HNO_3} \longrightarrow \underset{\text{Zinc nitrate}}{Zn(NO_3)_2} + H_2O + CO_2\uparrow$

(*C*) $\underset{\text{Zinc nitrate}}{Zn(NO_3)_2} + \underset{\text{Sodium hydroxide}}{2NaOH} \longrightarrow \underset{\text{Zinc hydroxide}}{Zn(OH)_2} + \underset{\text{Sodium nitrate}}{2NaNO_3}$

(*D*) $\underset{\text{Zinc hydroxide}}{Zn(OH)_2} \xrightarrow{\Delta} \underset{\text{Zinc oxide}}{ZnO} + H_2O$

(*E*) $\underset{\text{Zinc oxide}}{ZnO} + \underset{\text{Sulphuric acid}}{H_2SO_4} \longrightarrow \underset{\text{Zinc sulphate}}{ZnSO_4} + H_2O$ **(1 × 5 = 5)**

Q.9 From the list given below, select the word(s) required to correctly complete blanks (i) to (v) in the following passage. The words from the list are to be used only once. Write the answers as (a) (i), (ii), (iii) and so on. Do not copy the passage

[ammonia, ammonium carbonate, carbon dioxide, hydrogen, hydronium, hydroxide, precipitate, salt, water]

A solution *M* turns blue litmus red, so it must contain (i) .... ions; another solution *O* turns red litmus blue and hence, must contain (ii) .... ions.

When solutions *M* and *O* are mixed together, the products will be (iii) .... and (iv) .... If a piece of magnesium was put into a solution *M*, (v) .... gas would be evolved.

Ans. (i) hydronium $[H_3O^+]$ (ii) hydroxide $[OH^-]$
(iii) salt (iv) water
(v) hydrogen
[Reason Active metal like Mg reacts with acid to liberate hydrogen gas]. **(1 × 5 = 5)**

Q.10 Give the equation for the preparation of each of the following salts from the starting material given below.
(i) Copper sulphate from copper (II) oxide.
(ii) Iron (III) chloride from iron.
(iii) Potassium sulphate from potassium hydroxide solution.
(iv) Lead chloride from lead carbonate (two equations).

Ans. (i) $CuO + H_2SO_4 \longrightarrow CuSO_4 + H_2O$ **(1)**
(ii) $\underset{\text{Iron}}{2Fe} + 3Cl_2 \longrightarrow \underset{\text{Iron (III) chloride}}{2FeCl_3}$ **(1)**
(iii) $2KOH + H_2SO_4 \longrightarrow K_2SO_4 + 2H_2O$ **(1)**
(iv) $PbCO_3 + 2HNO_3 \longrightarrow Pb(NO_3)_2 + H_2O + CO_2$
$Pb(NO_3)_2 + 2HCl \longrightarrow PbCl_2 + 2HNO_3$ **(2)**

TYPE - 10

03 Marks

Case Based Questions

Q.1 Ravi was studying the properties of an element *X*. The element *X* combines with oxygen to form an oxide X_2O_3. This oxide is a good conductor of electricity and can be reduced to its metal only by electrolysis.
(i) Write the equation for the reaction formed when the oxide (X_2O_3) combines with hydrochloric acid.
(ii) How many valence electrons are present in the outermost shell of *X*?
(iii) Will element *X* undergo oxidation or reduction?
(Competency Based Que.)

Ans. (i) $X_2O_3 + 6HCl \longrightarrow 2XCl_3 + 3H_2O$
(ii) 3
(iii) Oxidation **(1 × 3 = 3)**

Q.2 Rohit has solution *X*, *Y* and *Z* that has pH 2, 7 and 13 respectively. Which solution
(i) will liberate sulphur dioxide gas when heated with sodium sulphite?
(ii) will liberate ammonia gas when reacted with ammonium chloride?
(iii) will not have any effect on litmus paper?
(ICSE Specimen 2025)

Ans. (i) Sodium sulphite can react with dilute H_2SO_4 to release SO_2 gas.
$\underset{\text{Sodium sulphite}}{Na_2SO_3} + \underset{(pH = 2)}{H_2SO_4} \longrightarrow Na_2SO_4 + \underset{\text{Sulphur dioxide}}{SO_2 \uparrow} + H_2O$
Thus, **X** will liberate sulphur dioxide gas when heated with sodium sulphite. **(1)**
(ii) Ammonia will be liberated from ammonium salts like ammonium chloride by addition of an alkaline solution like *Z*(pH = 13). **(1)**
(iii) Since, solution **Y** having pH 7 is neither acidic nor basic, so it will have no effect on either of the litmus papers. **(1)**

Q.3 Frothing in Yamuna: The primary reason behind the formation of the toxic foam is high phosphate content in the waste water because of detergents used in dyeing industries, dhobi ghats and households. Yamuna's pollution level is so bad that parts of it have been labelled 'dead' as there is no oxygen in it for aquatic life to survive.

(i) Predict the pH value of the water of river Yamuna, if the reason for froth is high content of detergents dissolved in it.
(ii) What is the nature of detergent (in term of acids/base/salts). How the concentration of hydroxide and hydronium ion changes when detegents are dissolved in water?
(iii) The table provides the pH value of four solutions *P*, *Q*, *R* and *S*.

Solutions	pH value
P	2
Q	9
R	5
S	11

Write the solutions in increasing order of their hydronium ion concentration.

Ans. (i) If high content of detergent is dissolved in water of river Yamuna, then the value of pH of water will be in between 7-14 because nature of detergent is basic. **(1)**

(ii) Almost all detergents are basic in nature and gives OH^- ions in water. When they are dissolved in water, then the concentration of hydroxide ions (OH^-) increases and the concentration of hydronium ion (H_3O^+) decreases. **(1)**

(iii) The value of pH of solution depends on hydronium ion concentration. Lower the value of pH, it means higher the hydronium ion concentration.

Hence, according to given pH values, the increasing order of hydronium ion concentration will be

$S < Q < R < P$ (11 < 9 < 5 < 2). **(1)**

Q.4

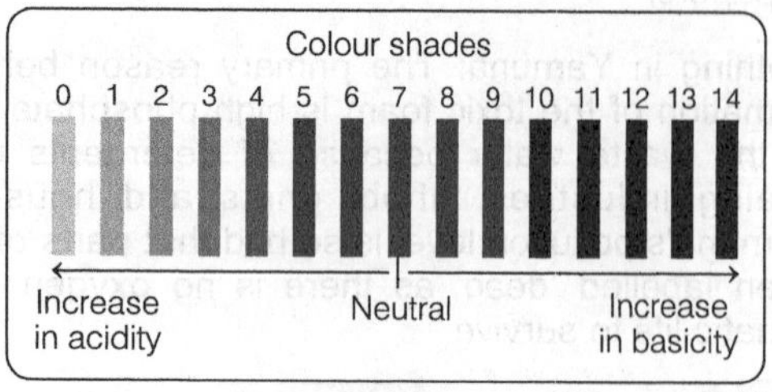

A pH paper changes its colour depending upon the pH value of the substance it is dipped into.

The above picture shows different colours of a pH paper. Leena tested the pH value of four liquids using a pH paper.

The table shows the shade of the pH paper after it is dipped separately in the four liquids.

	Liquid 1	Liquid 2	Liquid 3	Liquid 4
Shade of the pH paper	Colour 9	Colour 12	Colour 5	Colour 3

(i) Leena was advised by her teacher to wear gloves and use forceps while dipping the pH paper in the liquids. What was the reason for this advice?

(ii) What should be the colour of a pH paper after it is dipped in distilled water? Explain your answer.

(ii) Which of these liquid is more basic in nature?

Ans. (i) Leena was advised to wear gloves and use forceps while dipping the pH paper in the liquids because there is a risk that liquids could spill on her hands. They can not only hurt her skin but can also leave stains which may further cause burn or rashes. **(1)**

(ii) Distilled water is neutral with pH close to 7. Thus, the colour of pH paper will **remain the same**. **(1)**

(iii) **Liquid 2** is more basic. Anything which have pH value above 7.0 is alkaline or basic. Also, as the pH value increases, the basic strength increases. **(1)**

04

ANALYTICAL CHEMISTRY

- **Analysis** means determination of the chemical components in a given sample. It is of two types:
  (i) **Qualitative analysis** involves the identification of the unknown substance.
  (ii) **Quantitative analysis** involves the determination of composition of a mixture.
- **Reagent** is a substance that reacts with another substances in order to bring about a chemical change. Alkali such as NaOH (sodium hydroxide), KOH (potassium hydroxide) and NH_4OH (ammonium hydroxide) are important laboratory reagents.
- **Sodium hydroxide** (NaOH) is a strong alkali, whereas **ammonium hydroxide** (NH_4OH) is a weak alkali. These alkalies on reaction with various metal ions gives precipitate and colour of precipitate helps in identification of the metal ions.
- **Precipitation** is the process of formation of an insoluble solid when solutions are mixed. The solid thus formed is called **precipitate**.

Colour of the Salts and their Solution

- The salts of **representative elements**, i.e. the elements of groups 1, 2 and 13 to 17 are generally **colourless** while, salts of **transition elements**, i.e. the elements of group 3 to 12 are generally **coloured.**
- During qualitative analysis, different colours of salts help in their identification.

Some Coloured and Colourless Ions

Colourless Ions		Coloured Ions		
Anion	**Symbol**	**Anion**	**Symbol**	**Colour**
Chloride ion	Cl^-	Permanganate ion	MnO_4^-	Pink or purple
Sulphate ion	SO_4^{2-}			
Carbonate ion	CO_3^{2-}	Dichromate ion	$Cr_2O_7^{2-}$	Orange
Nitrate ion	NO_3^-			
Hydrogen carbonate ion	HCO_3^-	Chromate ion	CrO_4^{2-}	Yellow
Sulphide ion	S^{2-}			
Bromide ion	Br^-			
Acetate ion	CH_3COO^-			
Cation	**Symbol**	**Cation**	**Symbol**	**Colour**
Ammonium ion	NH_4^+	Cupric ion	Cu^{2+}	Blue
Sodium ion	Na^+	Ferrous ion	Fe^{2+}	Light green
Potassium ion	K^+	Ferric ion	Fe^{3+}	Yellowish brown
Calcium ion	Ca^{2+}	Cobalt ion	Co^{2+}	Pink violet
Magnesium ion	Mg^{2+}	Nickel ion	Ni^{2+}	Green
Aluminium ion	Al^{3+}	Chromium ion	Cr^{3+}	Green
Lead ion	Pb^{2+}	Manganese ion	Mn^{2+}	Pink
Zinc ion	Zn^{2+}			

Action of Sodium Hydroxide (NaOH) on Metallic Salt Solutions

Salt Solution	+ Alkali	$\longrightarrow$ Metal Hydroxide (ppt.)	+ Salt formed in Solution	Colour of ppt. and its Solubility in excess of Alkali
1. Calcium Salts [Ca^{2+} ion]				
$Ca(NO_3)_2$	+ 2NaOH	$\longrightarrow$ $Ca(OH)_2 \downarrow$	+ $2NaNO_3$	
Calcium nitrate (Colourless)	+ Caustic soda (Colourless)	$\longrightarrow$ Calcium hydroxide (White precipitate)	+ Sodium nitrate (Colourless)	White Sparingly soluble
2. Iron				
A. Ferrous Salts [Fe^{2+} ion]				
$FeSO_4$	+ 2NaOH	$\longrightarrow$ $Fe(OH)_2 \downarrow$	+ Na_2SO_4	
Ferrous sulphate (Pale green)	+ Caustic soda (Colourless)	$\longrightarrow$ Ferrous hydroxide (Dirty green gelatinous ppt.)	+ Sodium sulphate (Colourless)	Dirty green Insoluble
B. Ferric Salt [Fe^{3+} ion]				
$FeCl_3$	+ 3NaOH	$\longrightarrow$ $Fe(OH)_3 \downarrow$	+ 3NaCl	
Ferric chloride (Yellow)	+ Caustic soda (Colourless)	$\longrightarrow$ Ferric hydroxide (Reddish brown ppt.)	+ Sodium chloride (Colourless)	Reddish brown Insoluble
3. Copper Salts [Cu^{2+} ion]				
$CuSO_4$ (Blue)	+ 2NaOH (Colourless)	$\longrightarrow$ $Cu(OH)_2 \downarrow$ (Pale blue ppt.)	+ Na_2SO_4 (Colourless)	Pale blue Insoluble
4. Zinc Salts [Zn^{2+} ion]				
$ZnSO_4$ (Colourless)	+ 2NaOH (Colourless)	$\longrightarrow$ $Zn(OH)_2 \downarrow$ (White, gelatinous ppt.)	+ Na_2SO_4 (Colourless)	Gelatinous white Soluble
(With excess of NaOH, ppt. dissolves)				
$Zn(OH)_2$	+ 2NaOH (Excess)	$\longrightarrow$ Na_2ZnO_2 Sodium zincate (Colourless)	+ $2H_2O$	
5. Lead Salts [Pb^{2+} ion]				
$Pb(NO_3)_2$ (Colourless)	+ 2NaOH (Colourless)	$\longrightarrow$ $Pb(OH)_2 \downarrow$ (White ppt.)	+ $2NaNO_3$ (Colourless)	Chalky white Soluble
(With excess of NaOH, ppt. dissolves)				
$Pb(OH)_2$	+ 2NaOH (Excess)	$\longrightarrow$ $2Na_2PbO_2$ Sodium plumbite (Colourless)	+ $2H_2O$	

6. Ammonium Salts [NH_4^+ ion]

When sodium hydroxide (or any water soluble base) is heated with ammonium salts, ammonia gas is evolved.

$$NH_4Cl + NaOH \xrightarrow{\Delta} NaCl + H_2O + NH_3$$

$$(NH_4)_2SO_4 + 2NaOH \xrightarrow{\Delta} Na_2SO_4 + 2H_2O + 2NH_3$$

Action of Ammonium Hydroxide on Certain Salt Solutions

Salt Solution	+ Ammonium Hydroxide	⟶ Metal Hydroxide	+ Salt Formed in Solution	Colour of ppt. and its Solubility in excess of Ammonium Hydroxide
1. Calcium Salt				
No precipitation occurs even with addition of excess of NH_4OH. This is because the concentration of OH^- ions from the ionisation of NH_4OH is so low that it cannot precipitate the hydroxide of calcium.				
2. Iron				
A. **Iron (II) Salts [Fe^{2+} ion]**				
$FeSO_4$ (Green)	+ $2NH_4OH$	⟶ $Fe(OH)_2\downarrow$ (Dirty green ppt.)	+ $(NH_4)_2SO_4$ (Colourless in solution)	Dirty green ppt. Insoluble
B. **Iron (III) Salt [Fe^{3+} ion]**				
(i) $FeCl_3$ (Yellow solution)	+ $3NH_4OH$	⟶ $Fe(OH)_3\downarrow$ (Reddish brown ppt.)	+ $3NH_4Cl$ (Colourless in solution)	Reddish brown ppt. Insoluble
(ii) $Fe_2(SO_4)_3$ (Yellow solution)	+ $6NH_4OH$	⟶ $2Fe(OH)_3\downarrow$ (Reddish brown ppt.)	+ $3(NH_4)_2SO_4$ (Colourless in solution)	
3. Copper (II) Salts [Cu^{2+} ion]				
$CuSO_4$ (Blue)	+ $2NH_4OH$	⟶ $Cu(OH)_2\downarrow$ (Pale blue ppt.)	+ $(NH_4)_2SO_4$ (Colourless in solution)	Pale blue ppt.
(With excess of NH_4OH, ppt. dissolves)				
$Cu(OH)_2$ + $(NH_4)_2SO_4$	+ $2NH_4OH$ (Excess)	⟶ $[Cu(NH_3)_4]SO_4$ Tetraamine copper (II) sulphate	+ $4H_2O$	Soluble in excess of NH_4OH and forms deep blue solution
4. Zinc Salts [Zn^{2+} ion]				
$ZnSO_4$ (Colourless solution)	+ $2NH_4OH$	⟶ $Zn(OH)_2\downarrow$ (White, gelatinous ppt.)	+ $(NH_4)_2SO_4$ (Colourless in solution)	Gelatinous white ppt.
(With excess of NH_4OH, ppt. dissolves)				
$Zn(OH)_2$ + $(NH_4)_2SO_4$ Zinc hydroxide	+ $2NH_4OH$ (Excess)	⟶ $[Zn(NH_3)_4]SO_4$ Tetraamine zinc (II) sulphate (colourless solution)	+ $4H_2O$	Soluble in excess of NH_4OH
Or				
$Zn(OH)_2$	+ $4NH_4OH$	⟶ $[Zn(NH_3)_4](OH)_2$ Tetraamine zinc hydroxide	+ $4H_2O$	
5. Lead Salts [Pb^{2+} ion]				
$Pb(NO_3)_2$ (Colourless)	+ $2NH_4OH$	⟶ $Pb(OH)_2\downarrow$ (White ppt.)	+ $4NH_4NO_3$	Chalky white ppt. Insoluble

Action of Alkalis on Certain Amphoteric Metals

Metals which can react with both acids and bases are called **amphoteric metals.** e.g. Zn, Al and Pb.

Metals like Al, Zn and Pb react with hot concentrated **caustic alkali** (NaOH and KOH) to give the corresponding **soluble salt** and liberate **hydrogen gas.**

Aluminium Metal (Al)

It reacts only with boiling and concentrated alkali.

$$\underset{\text{Aluminium}}{2Al} + \underset{\substack{\text{Sodium}\\\text{hydroxide}}}{2NaOH} + 2H_2O \xrightarrow{\Delta} \underset{\substack{\text{Sodium}\\\textit{meta}\text{ aluminate}\\\text{(Colourless)}}}{2NaAlO_2} + 3H_2\uparrow$$

$$\underset{\text{Aluminium}}{2Al} + \underset{\substack{\text{Potassium}\\\text{hydroxide}}}{2KOH} + 2H_2O \xrightarrow{\Delta} \underset{\substack{\text{Potassium}\\\textit{meta}\text{ aluminate}}}{2KAlO_2} + 3H_2\uparrow$$

Zinc Metal (Zn)

It also reacts only with boiling and concentrated alkali.

$$\underset{\text{Zinc}}{Zn} + \underset{\substack{\text{(Hot and conc.)}\\\text{Sodium hydroxide}}}{2NaOH} \xrightarrow{\Delta} \underset{\substack{\text{Sodium zincate}\\\text{(Colourless)}}}{Na_2ZnO_2} + H_2\uparrow$$

$$\underset{\text{Zinc}}{Zn} + \underset{\substack{\text{Potassium}\\\text{hydroxide}}}{2KOH} \xrightarrow{\Delta} \underset{\substack{\text{Potassium}\\\text{zincate}}}{K_2ZnO_2} + H_2\uparrow$$

Lead Metal (Pb)

It also reacts only with boiling and concentrated alkali.

$$\underset{\text{Lead}}{Pb} + \underset{\substack{\text{Sodium}\\\text{hydroxide}}}{2NaOH} \xrightarrow{\Delta} \underset{\substack{\text{Sodium plumbite}\\\text{(Colourless)}}}{Na_2PbO_2} + H_2\uparrow$$

$$\underset{\text{Lead}}{Pb} + \underset{\substack{\text{Potassium}\\\text{hydroxide}}}{2KOH} \xrightarrow{\Delta} \underset{\substack{\text{Potassium}\\\text{plumbite}\\\text{(Colourless)}}}{K_2PbO_2} + H_2\uparrow$$

Amphoteric Nature of Metal Oxides and Hydroxides

Most of the metal oxides are basic in nature and dissolve in water to give hydroxides or alkalies. These metal oxides and hydroxides neutralise acids and do not react with bases.

e.g.

$$\underset{\text{Sodium oxide}}{Na_2O} + \underset{\text{Water}}{H_2O} \longrightarrow \underset{\text{Sodium hydroxide}}{2NaOH}$$

$$Na_2O + \underset{\substack{\text{Hydrochloric}\\\text{acid}}}{2HCl} \longrightarrow \underset{\substack{\text{Sodium}\\\text{chloride}}}{2NaCl} + H_2O$$

$$\underset{\substack{\text{Sodium}\\\text{hydroxide}}}{NaOH} + \underset{\substack{\text{Hydrochloric}\\\text{acid}}}{HCl} \longrightarrow \underset{\substack{\text{Sodium}\\\text{chloride}}}{NaCl} + H_2O$$

But oxides and hydroxides of few metals (like Zn, Al and Pb) are **amphoteric** in nature, i.e., they react with both acids and bases. e.g. Zinc oxide (ZnO) and zinc hydroxide [$Zn(OH)_2$].

- Amphoteric oxide/Hydroxide + Acid ⟶ Salt + Water
- Amphoteric oxide/Hydroxide + Alkali ⟶ Salt + Water

Action of Alkali on Amphoteric Metal Oxides and Hydroxides

Amphoteric Oxide / Hydroxide		Oxide / Hydroxide	+	Alkali	⟶	Salt	+	Water
1. **Zinc oxide/Zinc hydroxide**	(i)	ZnO (White)	+	$2NaOH$	$\xrightarrow{\Delta}$	Na_2ZnO_2 Sodium zincate (Colourless, soluble)	+	H_2O
		$Zn(OH)_2$ (White, gelatinous)	+	$2NaOH$	$\xrightarrow{\Delta}$	Na_2ZnO_2	+	$2H_2O$
	(ii)	ZnO (White)	+	$2KOH$	$\xrightarrow{\Delta}$	K_2ZnO_2 Potassium zincate (Colourless, soluble)	+	H_2O
		$Zn(OH)_2$ (White, gelatinous)	+	$2KOH$	$\xrightarrow{\Delta}$	K_2ZnO_2	+	$2H_2O$
2. **Aluminium oxide / Aluminium hydroxide**	(i)	Al_2O_3 (White)	+	$2NaOH$	$\longrightarrow$	$2NaAlO_2$ Sodium *meta* aluminate	+	H_2O
		$Al(OH)_3$	+	$NaOH$	$\longrightarrow$	$NaAlO_2$	+	$2H_2O$
	(ii)	Al_2O_3 (White)	+	$2KOH$	$\longrightarrow$	$2KAlO_2$ Potassium *meta* aluminate	+	H_2O
		$Al(OH)_3$	+	KOH	$\longrightarrow$	$KAlO_2$	+	$2H_2O$
3. **Lead oxide/ Lead hydroxide**	(i)	PbO (Yellow)	+	$2NaOH$	$\longrightarrow$	Na_2PbO_2 Sodium plumbite (Colourless, soluble)	+	H_2O
		$Pb(OH)_2$ (Chalky white)	+	$2NaOH$	$\longrightarrow$	Na_2PbO_2	+	$2H_2O$
	(ii)	PbO (Yellow)	+	$2KOH$	$\longrightarrow$	K_2PbO_2 Potassium plumbite (Colourless, soluble)	+	H_2O
		$Pb(OH)_2$ (Chalky white)	+	$2KOH$	$\longrightarrow$	K_2PbO_2	+	$2H_2O$

EXAM ORIENTED QUESTIONS

TYPE - 1 01 Mark

Multiple Choice Questions

Q.1 The colour of the precipitate formed after the addition of a small amount of sodium hydroxide solution to an aqueous solution of ferric chloride is **(ICSE 2021-22, Sem-I)**

(a) gelatinous white (b) pale blue
(c) reddish brown (d) dirty green

Ans. (c) When NaOH is added to ferric chloride solution following reaction takes place.

$$3NaOH + FeCl_3 \longrightarrow \underset{\text{Reddish brown ppt.}}{Fe(OH)_3\downarrow} + 3NaCl$$

Q.2 The hydroxide which is soluble in excess of NaOH is **(ICSE Specimen 2023)**

(a) ferric hydroxide (b) lead hydroxide
(c) copper hydroxide (d) calcium hydroxide

Ans. (b) The reaction of lead (II) salt with sodium hydroxide gives white coloured precipitate. This precipitate of **lead hydroxide, $Pb(OH)_2$** is soluble in excess of sodium hydroxide.

Q.3 A compound *P* is heated in a test tube with sodium hydroxide solution. A red litmus paper held at the mouth of the test tube turns blue. **(ICSE Specimen 2024)**
Which of the following could compound *P* be?

(a) Zinc sulphate (b) Copper sulphate
(c) Ferrous sulphate (d) Ammonium sulphate

Ans. (d) The reaction is represented as:

$$(NH_4)_2SO_4 + 2NaOH \longrightarrow Na_2SO_4 + 2H_2O + 2NH_3\uparrow$$

So, **ammonia is alkaline** in nature. When red litmus paper is held at the mouth of test tube it changes the colour of the red litmus paper to blue.

Q.4 The salt which gives a pale green precipitate with sodium hydroxide solution and a white precipitate with barium chloride solution is

(a) iron (III) sulphate (b) iron (II) sulphate
(c) iron (II) chloride (d) iron (III) chloride

Ans. (b) **Iron (II) sulphate** gives a pale green precipitate with sodium hydroxide solution and a white precipitate with barium chloride solution. Reactions are:

$$FeSO_4 + 2NaOH \longrightarrow \underset{\text{Pale green}}{Fe(OH)_2\downarrow} + Na_2SO_4$$

$$FeSO_4 + BaCl_2 \longrightarrow \underset{\text{White ppt.}}{BaSO_4\downarrow} + FeCl_2$$

Q.5 A student added excess of sodium hydroxide solution to each of the salt solution. An insoluble precipitate formed was observed in **(ICSE Specimen 2023)**

(a) calcium nitrate (b) zinc nitrate
(c) lead nitrate (d) sodium nitrate

Ans. (a) When sodium hydroxide reacts with **calcium nitrate**, white precipitate of $Ca(OH)_2$ is obtained. This precipitate is insoluble in excess NaOH.

Q.6 The observation when ammonium chloride reacts with potassium hydroxide. **(ICSE Specimen 2021-22, Sem-I)**

(a) A reddish brown gas.
(b) A colourless gas which turns moist red litmus blue.
(c) A green coloured gas which turns moist blue litmus paper red.
(d) A colourless gas which turns lime water milky.

Ans. (b) On reacting ammonium chloride with potassium hydroxide, a colourless gas with a pungent odour, i.e., **ammonia** is liberated.

$$\underset{\text{Ammonium chloride}}{NH_4Cl} + \underset{\text{Potassium hydroxide}}{KOH} \longrightarrow \underset{\text{Potassium chloride}}{KCl} + \underset{\text{Ammonia}}{NH_3\uparrow} + \underset{\text{Water}}{H_2O}$$

Ammonia gas is alkaline in nature and it turns moist red litmus paper blue.

Q.7 Aqueous lead (II) nitrate can be distinguished from aqueous zinc nitrate by adding any of the following solution in excess except **(ICSE Specimen 2025)**

(a) aqueous potassium chloride
(b) aqueous sodium sulphate
(c) dilute sulphuric acid
(d) sodium hydroxide solution

Ans. (d) Sodium hydroxide solution.

Both $Pb(NO_3)_2$ and $Zn(NO_3)_2$ form white precipitate with NaOH. So, we cannot distinguish them by on adding NaOH.

$$\underset{\text{Lead (II) nitrate}}{Pb(NO_3)_2} + 2NaOH \longrightarrow \underset{\text{White ppt.}}{Pb(OH)_2\downarrow} + 2NaNO_3$$

$$\underset{\text{Zinc (II) nitrate}}{Zn(NO_3)_2} + 2NaOH \longrightarrow \underset{\text{White ppt.}}{Zn(OH)_2\downarrow} + 2NaNO_3$$

Q.8 Ravi was asked to identify the cation present in the salt solution. He added one of the reagents given below and got a reddish-brown precipitate. The reagent that he used is: **(Competency Based Que.)**

(a) silver nitrate solution
(b) barium chloride solution
(c) ammonium hydroxide
(d) calcium chloride solution

Ans. (c) Ammonium hydroxide.

Q.9 Aqueous solution of cupric chloride forms a deep blue solution on addition of **(ICSE 2021-22, Sem-I)**
(a) dropwise sodium hydroxide.
(b) excess sodium hydroxide.
(c) dropwise ammonium hydroxide.
(d) excess ammonium hydroxide.

Ans. (d) On adding **excess ammonium hydroxide** to cupric chloride, a deep blue solution of $[Cu(NH_3)_4]^{2+}$ is formed.

$$CuCl_2 + 2NH_4OH \longrightarrow Cu(OH)_2 \downarrow + 2NH_4Cl$$

$$Cu(OH)_2 + \underset{\text{Excess}}{2NH_4OH} + 2NH_4Cl \longrightarrow [Cu(NH_3)_4]Cl_2 + 4H_2O$$

Q.10 The metallic hydroxide which forms a deep inky blue solution with excess ammonium hydroxide solution is **(ICSE 2023)**
(a) $Fe(OH)_2$ (b) $Cu(OH)_2$
(c) $Ca(OH)_2$ (d) $Fe(OH)_3$

Ans. (b) $Cu(OH)_2 + (NH_4)_2SO_4 + \underset{\text{(Excess)}}{2NH_4OH} \longrightarrow \underset{\text{Deep blue solution}}{[Cu(NH_3)_4]SO_4} + 4H_2O$

Q.11 A nitrate which forms a precipitate with ammonium hydroxide and is also soluble in excess of it is **(ICSE Specimen 2025)**
(a) ferrous nitrate (b) ferric nitrate
(c) lead nitrate (d) copper nitrate

Ans. (d) **Copper nitrate.**
When NH_4OH is added to $Cu(NO_3)_2$ solution in small quantity then ppt. of $Cu(OH)_2$ is formed, but when excess of NH_4OH is added then, the ppt. turns into a solution of **tetraamine copper (II) nitrate.**

Q.12 The hydroxide which is soluble in excess ammonium hydroxide. **(ICSE Specimen 2021-22, Sem-I)**
(a) Lead hydroxide (b) Ferrous hydroxide
(c) Zinc hydroxide (d) Ferric hydroxide

Ans. (c) The hydroxide which is soluble in excess ammonium hydroxide is **zinc hydroxide, $Zn(OH)_2$**.

$$\underset{\text{Zinc nitrate}}{Zn(NO_3)_2} + \underset{\text{Ammonium hydroxide}}{2NH_4OH} \longrightarrow \underset{\text{Zinc hydroxide}}{Zn(OH)_2\downarrow} + \underset{\text{Ammonium nitrate}}{2NH_4NO_3}$$

$$Zn(OH)_2 + 2NH_4NO_3 + \underset{\text{Excess}}{2NH_4OH} \longrightarrow \underset{\text{Tetraamine zinc (II) nitrate}}{[Zn(NH_3)_4](NO_3)_2} + 4H_2O$$

Q.13 The colour of the precipitate formed when ferrous ions react with ammonium hydroxide solution. **(ICSE Specimen 2021-22, Sem-I)**
(a) Blue (b) Reddish brown (c) Dirty green (d) White

Ans. (c) When ammonium hydroxide is added to iron (II) sulphate, the precipitate of ferrous hydroxide is obtained which is **dirty green** in colour.

Q.14 The salt solution which does not react with ammonium hydroxide is **(ICSE 2018)**
(a) calcium nitrate (b) zinc nitrate
(c) lead nitrate (d) copper nitrate

Ans. (a) **Calcium nitrate** does not react with ammonium hydroxide because the concentration of OH^- ions produced by the ionisation of NH_4OH is very low, and it cannot form precipitate of calcium hydroxide.

Q.15 A chloride which forms a precipitate that is soluble in excess of ammonium hydroxide is **(ICSE 2017)**
(a) calcium chloride (b) ferrous chloride
(c) ferric chloride (d) copper chloride

Ans. (d) **Copper chloride** forms a precipitate that is soluble in excess of ammonium hydroxide.

Q.16 Hydroxide of this metal is soluble in sodium hydroxide solution.
(a) Magnesium (b) Lead
(c) Silver (d) Copper

Ans. (b) **Lead hydroxide**, $Pb(OH)_2$ is soluble in excess of sodium hydroxide solution.

Q.17 The metal oxide which can react with acid as well as alkali is
(a) silver oxide (b) copper (II) oxide
(c) aluminium oxide (d) calcium oxide

Ans. (c) **Aluminium oxide** can react with acid as well as alkali, because it is **amphoteric** in nature.

Q.18 The metal hydroxide which reacts with both acids and alkalis to form salt and water is **(ICSE 2024)**
(a) calcium hydroxide (b) magnesium hydroxide
(c) aluminium hydroxide (d) ferric hydroxide

Ans. (c) Aluminium hydroxide.

Acidic nature

$$Al(OH)_3 + NaOH \xrightarrow{\Delta} \underset{\text{(Colourless, soluble)}}{NaAlO_2} + 2H_2O$$

Basic nature

$$Al(OH)_3 + 3HCl(dil.) \longrightarrow \underset{\text{(Salt)}}{AlCl_3} + 3H_2O$$

Q.19 A .... solution is observed after placing magnesium metal in a solution of copper sulphate for half an hour. **(ICSE Specimen 2024)**
(a) blue (b) colourless
(c) reddish brown (d) dirty green

Ans. (b) When magnesium is placed in copper sulphate solution, the blue colour fades as colourless magnesium sulphate is formed and brown bits of copper metal form a precipitate.

$$Mg + CuSO_4 \longrightarrow MgSO_4 + Cu$$

Q.20 A student takes Cu, Al, Fe and Zn strips, separately in four test tubes labellel as I, II, III and IV respectively. He adds 10 ml of freshly prepared ferrous sulphate solution to each test tube and observers the colour of the metal residue in each case. **(ICSE Specimen 2025)**

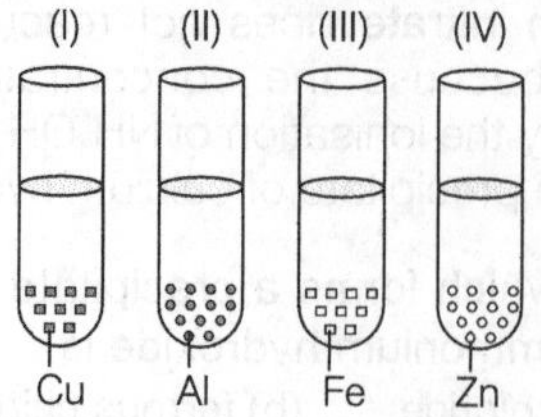

He would observe a black residue in the test tubes:

(a) (I) and (II) (b) (I) and (III)
(c) (II) and (III) (d) (II) and (IV)

Ans. (d) (II) and (IV)

$$2Al + 3FeSO_4 \longrightarrow Al_2(SO_4)_3 + 3Fe$$

$$Zn + FeSO_4 \longrightarrow ZnSO_4 + Fe$$

In both reactions, Al and Zn are more reactive than Fe.

TYPE - 2 01 Mark

Assertion-Reason Questions

Directions (Q. Nos. 1-5) In the following questions, a statement of Assertion (A) is followed by a statement of Reason (R). Choose the answer based on the codes given below.

(a) Both (A) and (R) true and (R) is the correct explanation of (A).
(b) Both (A) and (R) are true but (R) is not the correct explanation of (A).
(c) (A) is true but (R) is false.
(d) (A) is false but (R) is true.

Q.1 **Assertion** (A) When sodium hydroxide is added to solution of copper salt, pale blue precipitate of copper hydroxide is formed.

Reason (R) $Fe(OH)_2$ is precipitated out in dirty green colour. When Fe^{2+} salts are treated with NaOH.

Ans. (b) Sodium hydroxide reacts with copper salt to form a pale blue precipitate of copper hydroxide.

Fe^{2+} salts on treatment with sodium hydroxide gives dirty green colour precipitate of $Fe(OH)_2$.

Thus, both (A) and (R) are true but (R) is not the correct explanation of (A).

Q.2 **Assertion** (A) Zinc reacts with sodium hydroxide to form sodium zincate and hydrogen gas.

Reason (R) Metal oxides or hydroxides which do not react with both acid and alkali are called amphoteric.

Ans. (c) Zinc reacts with sodium hydroxide to form sodium zincate and hydrogen gas. Metal oxides or hydroxides which reacts with both acid and alkali are called amphoteric. Thus, (A) is true but (R) is false.

Q.3 **Assertion** (A) Some metallic hydroxides are soluble in excess of ammonium hydroxide.

Reason (R) With excess of ammonium hydroxide there is formation of soluble amino complexes.

Ans. (a) Some metallic hydroxides are soluble in excess of ammonium hydroxide because in excess of ammonium hydroxide, the precipitate forms a soluble amino complexes and hence they dissolve in the solution.

Thus, both (A) and (R) are true and (R) is the correct explanation of (A).

Q.4 **Assertion** (A) When ferrous sulphate solution is added to ammonium hydroxide, dirty green precipitate is formed.

Reason (R) The dirty green precipitate is due to formation of ferrous hydroxide.

Ans. (a) When green coloured solution of ferrous sulphate is added to ammonium hydroxide, the solution becomes faded due to the formation of dirty green precipitate of ferrous hydroxide.

Thus, both (A) and (R) are true and (R) is the correct explanation of (A).

Q.5 **Assertion** (A) Lead oxide and lead hydroxide both reacts with acid and alkali.

Reason (R) Lead oxide and lead hydroxide are amphoteric in nature.

Ans. (a) Lead oxide and lead hydroxide both reacts with acid and alkali. These are called amphoteric.

Thus, both (A) and (R) are true and (R) is the correct explanation of (A).

TYPE - 3 01 Mark

Fill in the Blanks

Q.1 Salts of .... (representative elements/transition elements) are generally coloured.

Ans. transition elements

Q.2 Calcium hydroxide is a white precipitate which is .... (insoluble/sparingly soluble) in sodium hydroxide solution.

Ans. sparingly soluble

Q.3 ...... (Silver chloride/Lead chloride) is a white precipitate that is soluble in excess of ammonium hydroxide solution. **(ICSE 2023, 2016)**

Ans. Silver chloride

$$AgCl + 2NH_4OH \longrightarrow [Ag(NH_3)_2]Cl + H_2O$$

Silver chloride dissolves in excess of ammonium hydroxide solution due to the formation of diamine silver (I) chloride, which is soluble in water.

Q.4 .... $(Zn(OH)_2 / Pb(OH)_2$, a white precipitate is soluble in excess NH_4OH.

Ans. $Zn(OH)_2$

Q.5 .... [Ferrous chloride/Copper nitrate] solution forms a coloured precipitate with ammonium hydroxide which is soluble in excess of ammonium hydroxide. **(ICSE 2025)**

Ans. Copper nitrate

Q.6 A .... (reddish brown/ dirty green) coloured precipitate is formed when ammonium hydroxide is added to a solution of ferric chloride. **(ICSE Specimen 2024, 2025)**

Ans. reddish brown

Q.7 An alkali which completely dissociates into ions is .... (ammonium hydroxide, calcium hydroxide) **(ICSE 2020)**

Ans. calcium hydroxide

Q.8 The salt formed when ZnO reacts with hot concentrated NaOH is ...... (Sodium zincate/zinc hydroxide) **(ICSE 2025)**

Ans. sodium zincate

TYPE - 4 (01 Mark)

Correct the Incorrect Statement

Q.1 Qualitative analysis involves the determination of composition of a mixture.

Ans. Qualitative analysis involves the **identification of unknown substance** and not the determination of composition of a mixture.

Q.2 Sodium hydroxide is a weak alkali whereas ammonium hydroxide is a strong alkali.

Ans. Sodium hydroxide is a **strong alkali** and ammonium hydroxide is a **weak alkali**.

Q.3 Precipitation is the process of formation of a soluble solid when solutions are mixed.

Ans. Precipitation is the process of formation of an **insoluble** solid when solutions are mixed.

Q.4 NH_4^+, Mg^{2+}, Fe^{2+}, Cu^{2+} and Mn^{2+} are examples of coloured cations.

Ans. Fe^{2+}, Cu^{2+} and Mn^{2+} are **coloured cations** but NH_4^+, Mg^{2+} are **colourless cations**.

Q.5 MnO_4^-, $Cr_2O_7^{2-}$ and CrO_4^{2-} are examples of colourless anions.

Ans. MnO_4^-, $Cr_2O_7^{2-}$ and CrO_4^{2-} are examples of **coloured** anions.

Q.6 Steam is evolved when sodium hydroxide is heated with ammonium salts.

Ans. **Ammonia gas** is evolved sodium hydroxide is heated with ammonia salts.

Q.7 Metals like Zn, Al and Pb can liberate carbon dioxide gas with hot concentrated caustic alkalis.

Ans. Metals like Zn, Al and Pb can liberate **hydrogen gas** with hot concentrated caustic alkalis.

Q.8 ZnO, Al_2O_3 and PbO are examples of acidic oxides.

Ans. ZnO, Al_2O_3 and PbO are examples of **amphoteric** oxides.

TYPE - 5 (01×05=05 Marks)

Matching Type Questions

Q.1 Match the following Column I with Column II. **(ICSE Specimen 2023)**

Column I	Column II
A. Acid salt	1. Black in colour
B. Copper oxide	2. Reddish brown
C. Zinc hydroxide	3. Hydrogen chloride
D. Copper metal	4. Sodium hydrogen carbonate
E. Polar compound	5. Soluble in excess sodium hydroxide

Ans. A→(4), B→(1), C→(5), D→(2), E→(3).

Q.2 Sodium hydroxide is added to the solutions containing the ions mentioned in Column I. Column II gives the details of the precipitate. Match the ions with their coloured precipitates.

Column I	Column II
A. Pb^{2+}	1. Reddish brown
B. Fe^{2+}	2. White insoluble in excess
C. Zn^{2+}	3. Dirty green
D. Fe^{3+}	4. White soluble in excess
E. Cu^{2+}	5. Blue

Ans. A→(2), B→(3), C→(4), D→(1), E→(5).

TYPE - 6   01 Mark

Identify the Following

Q.1 What is the colour of the dichromate ion?

Ans. Orange

Q.2 Write the probable colour of the calcium salts.

Ans. Colourless

Q.3 Identify the substance underlined, in the given case.

'Cation that does not form a precipitate with ammonium hydroxide but forms precipitate with sodium hydroxide.' **(ICSE 2017)**

Ans. Ca^{2+} does not form precipitate with NH_4OH but forms precipitate with NaOH.

Reaction of calcium salt with sodium hydroxide

$$\underset{\text{Calcium nitrate (Colourless)}}{Ca(NO_3)_2} + \underset{\text{Caustic soda (Colourless)}}{2NaOH} \longrightarrow \underset{\text{Calcium hydroxide (White precipitate)}}{Ca(OH)_2 \downarrow} + \underset{\text{Sodium nitrate}}{2NaNO_3}$$

Q.4 Give the appropriate term.

A solution of this compound gives a pale blue precipitate with sodium hydroxide.

Ans. Copper sulphate gives a pale blue precipitate with sodium hydroxide solution.

$$\underset{\text{Copper sulphate (Blue)}}{CuSO_4} + 2NaOH \longrightarrow \underset{\text{Copper hydroxide (Pale blue ppt.)}}{Cu(OH)_2 \downarrow} + Na_2SO_4$$

Q.5 Identify the substance *P*.

The deliquescent salt *P*, turns yellow on dissolving in water and gives a reddish brown precipitate with sodium hydroxide solution.

Ans. The deliquescent salt *P* is **iron (III) chloride ($FeCl_3$)** which turns yellow on dissolving in water and gives a reddish brown ppt. with NaOH solution.

$$\underset{\text{Ferric chloride}}{FeCl_3} + \underset{\text{Sodium hydroxide}}{3NaOH} \longrightarrow \underset{\text{Ferric hydroxide (Reddish brown ppt.)}}{Fe(OH)_3 \downarrow} + \underset{\text{Sodium chloride}}{3NaCl}$$

Q.6 Name a positive non-metallic radical which is basic in nature. **(Competency Based Que.)**

Ans. Ammonium / NH_4^+.

Q.7 Name an oxide which forms salts when it reacts with both acids and alkalis.

Ans. Al_2O_3 (or **ZnO**) form salts when it reacts with both acids and alkalis.

Q.8 Name a yellow monoxide that dissolves in hot and concentrated caustic alkali.

Ans. Lead oxide (PbO)

Q.9 Find the odd one out (Valency is not a criterion).

$Al(OH)_3$, $Pb(OH)_2$, $Mg(OH)_2$, $Zn(OH)_2$

Ans. $Mg(OH)_2$

$Mg(OH)_2$ is purely basic, while other three are amphoteric in nature. $Mg(OH)_3$ neutralises an acid but do not react with bases.

$$Mg(OH)_2 + H_2SO_4 \longrightarrow MgSO_4 + 2H_2O$$
$$Mg(OH)_2 + NaOH \longrightarrow \text{No reaction}$$

Other three neutralises acids as well as bases.

TYPE - 7   02 Marks

Short Answer Type I Questions

Q.1 State one observation.

(i) Sodium hydroxide solution is added to ferric chloride solution at first a little and then in excess.

(ii) When excess sodium hydroxide is added to calcium nitrate solution. **(ICSE 2014)**

Ans. (i) **Reddish brown ppt., insoluble in excess NaOH** is formed.

$$\underset{\text{Ferric chloride (Yellow solution)}}{FeCl_3} + \underset{\text{Caustic soda (Colourless)}}{3NaOH} \longrightarrow \underset{\text{Ferric hydroxide (Reddish brown ppt.) (Insoluble in excess NaOH)}}{Fe(OH)_3 \downarrow} + \underset{\text{Sodium chloride (Colourless)}}{3NaCl} \quad \textbf{(1)}$$

(ii) **White precipitate of calcium hydroxide, sparingly soluble** in excess NaOH is formed.

$$\underset{\text{Calcium nitrate (Colourless)}}{Ca(NO_3)_2} + \underset{\text{Caustic soda (Colourless)}}{2NaOH} \longrightarrow \underset{\text{Calcium hydroxide (White ppt.)}}{Ca(OH)_2 \downarrow} + \underset{\text{Sodium nitrate (Colourless)}}{2NaNO_3} \quad \textbf{(1)}$$

Q.2 From the list of substances given in the box.

Ammonium sulphate, lead carbonate, chlorine, copper nitrate, ferrous sulphate

Choose a solution of the compound which gives a dirty green precipitate with sodium hydroxide. Also give the chemical reaction involved.

Ans. Ferrous sulphate gives a dirty green precipitate with sodium hydroxide (caustic soda). **(1)**

The reaction involved is

$$\underset{\text{(Pale green)}}{FeSO_4} + 2NaOH \longrightarrow \underset{\text{(Dirty green ppt.)}}{Fe(OH)_2 \downarrow} + \underset{\text{(Colourless)}}{Na_2SO_4} \quad \textbf{(1)}$$

Q.3 Give an equation for the following.

(i) Conversion of $Zn(NO_3)_2$ to $Zn(OH)_2$.

(ii) Ammonium chloride is heated with sodium hydroxide.

Ans. (i) $$\underset{\text{Zinc nitrate}}{Zn(NO_3)_2} + 2NaOH \longrightarrow \underset{\text{Zinc hydroxide}}{Zn(OH)_2 \downarrow} + 2NaNO_3 \quad \textbf{(1)}$$

(ii) When sodium hydroxide is heated with ammonium chloride, **ammonia gas** is evolved.

$$\underset{\text{Ammonium chloride}}{NH_4Cl} + \underset{\text{Sodium hydroxide}}{NaOH} \xrightarrow{\Delta} NaCl + H_2O + \underset{\text{Ammonia gas}}{NH_3 \uparrow} \quad \textbf{(1)}$$

Q.4 On adding dilute ammonia solution to a colourless solution of a salt, a white gelatinous precipitate appears. This precipitate, however, dissolves on addition of an excess of ammonia solution.

Identify (choose from Na, Al, Zn, Pb, Fe).

(i) Which metal salt solution was used?

(ii) What is the formula of the white gelatinous precipitate obtained?

Ans. (i) $ZnSO_4$ **(1)**

(ii) $Zn(OH)_2$ **(1)**

Q.5 State your observations when ammonium hydroxide solution is added drop by drop and then in excess to each of the following solutions

(i) Copper sulphate solution

(ii) Zinc sulphate solution **(ICSE 2016)**

Ans. (i) On adding ammonium hydroxide drop by drop to a solution of copper salt, a **pale blue precipitate** is formed, which **dissolves in excess of NH_4OH** to give **deep blue or prussian blue solution**.

$$\underset{\text{Copper sulphate}}{CuSO_4} + \underset{\text{Ammonium hydroxide}}{2NH_4OH} \longrightarrow \underset{\substack{\text{Copper hydroxide}\\\text{(Pale blue ppt.)}}}{Cu(OH)_2} + \underset{\substack{\text{Ammonium sulphate}\\\text{(colourless)}}}{(NH_4)_2SO_4}$$

$$Cu(OH)_2 + (NH_4)_2SO_4 + \underset{\text{(Excess)}}{2NH_4OH} \longrightarrow \underset{\substack{\text{Tetraamine copper (II) sulphate}\\\text{(Deep blue solution)}}}{[Cu(NH_3)_4]SO_4} + 4H_2O$$ **(1)**

(ii) When ammonium hydroxide solution is added drop by drop to $ZnSO_4$ solution, a **gelatinous white precipitate** of zinc hydroxide $[Zn(OH)_2]$ is formed.

$$ZnSO_4 + 2NH_4OH \longrightarrow \underset{\substack{\text{Zinc hydroxide}\\\text{(Gelatinous white ppt.)}}}{Zn(OH)_2} + (NH_4)_2SO_4$$

$Zn(OH)_2$ is **soluble in excess** of NH_4OH.

$$Zn(OH)_2 + \underset{\text{(Excess)}}{NH_4OH} + (NH_4)_2SO_4 \longrightarrow \underset{\substack{\text{Tetraamine zinc (II)}\\\text{sulphate (Colourless solution)}}}{[Zn(NH_3)_4]SO_4} + 4H_2O$$ **(1)**

Q.6 How will you distinguish between ammonium hydroxide and sodium hydroxide using copper sulphate solution? **(ICSE 2017)**

Ans. (i) On adding NaOH drop by drop to a solution of copper salt, **pale blue precipitate** is formed which is **insoluble in excess of sodium hydroxide**.

$$CuSO_4 + NaOH \longrightarrow \underset{\text{(Pale blue ppt.)}}{Cu(OH)_2}\downarrow + Na_2SO_4$$ **(1)**

(ii) On adding ammonium hydroxide drop by drop to a solution of copper salt, a **pale blue precipitate** is formed, which **dissolves in excess of ammonium** hydroxide to give **deep blue or inky blue or prussian blue solution**.

$$\underset{\substack{\text{Copper}\\\text{sulphate}\\\text{(Blue)}}}{CuSO_4} + \underset{\substack{\text{Ammonium}\\\text{hydroxide}}}{2NH_4OH} \longrightarrow \underset{\text{(Pale blue ppt.)}}{Cu(OH)_2}\downarrow + \underset{\substack{\text{Ammonium}\\\text{sulphate}\\\text{(Colourless)}}}{(NH_4)_2SO_4}$$

$$Cu(OH)_2 + (NH_4)_2SO_4 + \underset{\text{(Excess)}}{2NH_4OH} \longrightarrow \underset{\substack{\text{Tetraamine copper (II)}\\\text{sulphate}\\\text{(Deep blue solution)}}}{[Cu(NH_3)_4]SO_4} + 4H_2O$$ **(1)**

Q.7 Distinguish between the following pairs of compounds using the test given with in brackets. **(ICSE 2014)**

(i) A lead salt (Pb^{2+}) and a zinc salt (Zn^{2+}) (using excess ammonium hydroxide).

(ii) Iron (II) sulphate and iron (III) sulphate (using ammonium hydroxide).

Ans. (i) On addition of ammonium hydroxide drop by drop to a solution of lead salt, a **white precipitate** is formed which is **insoluble in excess of ammonium hydroxide**.

$$\underset{\text{Lead nitrate}}{Pb(NO_3)_2} + 2NH_4OH \longrightarrow \underset{\substack{\text{Lead hydroxide}\\\text{(Chalky white ppt.)}}}{Pb(OH)_2}\downarrow + 2NH_4NO_3$$ **(1)**

In case of Zn^{2+} salt, a gelatinous **white precipitate** is formed on addition of NH_4OH, which is **soluble in excess of ammonium hydroxide**.

$$\underset{\text{Zinc sulphate}}{ZnSO_4} + 2NH_4OH \longrightarrow \underset{\substack{\text{Zinc hydroxide}\\\text{(white, gelatinous}\\\text{ppt.)}}}{Zn(OH)_2}\downarrow + (NH_4)_2SO_4$$

$$Zn(OH)_2 + (NH_4)_2SO_4 + 2NH_4OH \longrightarrow \underset{\substack{\text{Tetraamine zinc (II)}\\\text{sulphate (colourless)}}}{[Zn(NH_3)_4]SO_4} + 4H_2O$$

(ii) On addition of NH_4OH to solution of Fe^{2+} salt, **dirty green precipitate** is formed which turns reddish brown after sometime and is **insoluble in excess of NH_4OH**.

$$\underset{\substack{\text{Ferrous sulphate}\\\text{(green)}}}{FeSO_4} + \underset{\substack{\text{Ammonium}\\\text{hydroxide}}}{2NH_4OH} \longrightarrow \underset{\substack{\text{Ferrous hydroxide}\\\text{(Dirty green ppt.)}}}{Fe(OH)_2}\downarrow + \underset{\substack{\text{Ammonium sulphate}\\\text{(colourless)}}}{(NH_4)_2SO_4}$$

In case of Fe^{3+} salt, a **reddish brown precipitate** is formed on addition of NH_4OH, which is **insoluble in excess of NH_4OH**.

$$\underset{\text{Iron (III) sulphate}}{Fe_2(SO_4)_3} + \underset{\substack{\text{Ammonium}\\\text{hydroxide}}}{6NH_4OH} \longrightarrow \underset{\substack{\text{Ferric hydroxide}\\\text{(Reddish brown ppt.)}}}{2Fe(OH)_3}\downarrow + 3(NH_4)_2SO_4$$ **(1)**

Q.8 Name the solution.

(i) Which solution becomes a deep/inky blue colour when excess of ammonium hydroxide is added to it?

(ii) Which solution gives a white precipitate when either dilute hydrochloric acid or dilute sulphuric acid is added to it.

Ans. (i) Copper nitrate $[Cu(NO_3)_2]$ **(1)**

(ii) Lead nitrate $[Pb(NO_3)_2]$ **(1)**

Q.9 Write a balanced chemical equation for the following.

(i) Reduction of copper (II) oxide by hydrogen.

(ii) Ammonium hydroxide is added to ferrous sulphate solution. **(ICSE 2019)**

Ans. (i) Reduction of copper (II) oxide by hydrogen:

$$CuO + H_2 \longrightarrow Cu + H_2O$$ **(1)**

(ii) When ammonium hydroxide is added to ferrous sulphate solution, it gives **insoluble precipitates of ferrous hydroxide that are dirty green** in colour.

$$FeSO_4 + 2NH_4OH \longrightarrow (NH_4)_2SO_4 + \underset{\substack{\text{Dirty green} \\ \text{(Insoluble in excess} \\ \text{of } NH_4OH)}}{Fe(OH)_2\downarrow}$$ **(1)**

Q.10 A student was asked to perform two experiments in the laboratory based on the instructions given:

Observe the picture given below and state one observation for each of the experiments 1 and 2 that you would notice on mixing the given solutions.

(i) Experiment 1 **(ICSE Specimen 2025)**

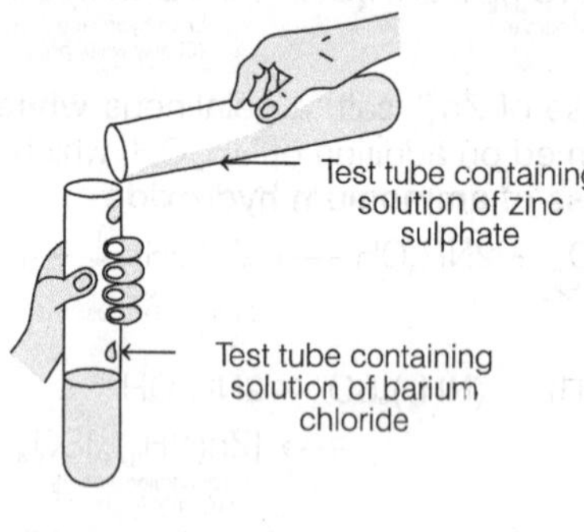

(ii) Experiment 2

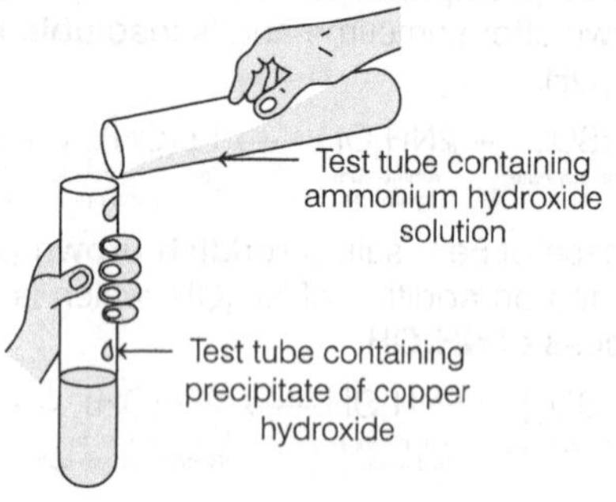

Ans. (i) In experiment 1,

$$\underset{\text{Zinc sulphate}}{ZnSO_4} + \underset{\substack{\text{Barium} \\ \text{chloride}}}{BaCl_2} \longrightarrow \underset{\text{Zinc chloride}}{ZnCl_2} + \underset{\substack{\text{Barium sulphate} \\ \text{(White ppt.)}}}{BaSO_4\downarrow}$$

Observation White ppt. is formed. **(1)**

(ii) In experiment 2,

$$\underset{\substack{\text{Copper hydroxide} \\ \text{(Pale blue ppt.)}}}{Cu(OH)_2} + \underset{\substack{\text{Ammonium} \\ \text{hydroxide}}}{4NH_4OH} \longrightarrow \underset{\substack{\text{Tetraamine copper hydroxide} \\ \text{(deep blue solution) (III)}}}{[Cu(NH_3)_4](OH)_2} + 4H_2O$$

Observation Blue precipitate of $Cu(OH)_2$ dissolves to form an inky blue or deep blue solution. **(1)**

Q.11 State giving reasons if : **(ICSE Specimen 2025, ICSE 2024)**

(i) **Zinc and aluminium can be distinguished by heating the metal powder with concentrated sodium hydroxide solution.**

(ii) **Calcium nitrate and lead nitrate can be distinguished by adding ammonium hydroxide solution to the salt solution.**

Ans. (i) **No**

Metals like zinc and aluminium react with hot and conc. sodium hydroxide to produce hydrogen gas. Zinc (Zn) reacts with NaOH to form sodium zincate with the evolution of hydrogen gas.

The reaction of aluminium with a NaOH also gives a salt and hydrogen gas.

So, Zn and Al cannot be distinguished because both will liberate hydrogen gas and form a colourless salt, which is soluble in excess of sodium hydroxide.

$$Zn + 2NaOH \xrightarrow{\Delta} \underset{\substack{\text{Sodium zincate} \\ \text{(colourless)}}}{Na_2ZnO_2} + H_2\uparrow$$ **(1)**

$$2Al + 2NaOH + 2H_2O \xrightarrow{\Delta} \underset{\substack{\text{Sodium } meta \\ \text{aluminate} \\ \text{(colourless)}}}{2NaAlO_2} + 3H_2\uparrow$$ **(1)**

(ii) **Yes**

Calcium nitrate does not react with ammonium hydroxide because the concentration of OH^- ions produced by the ionisation of NH_4OH is very low, that cannot form ppt. of calcium hydroxide.

$$Ca(NO_3)_2 + NH_4OH \longrightarrow \text{No ppt.}$$

When ammonium hydroxide is added drop by drop to a solution of lead nitrate, a white ppt. is formed which is insoluble in excess of ammonium hydroxide.

$$Pb(NO_3)_2 + 2NH_4OH \longrightarrow \underset{\text{White ppt.}}{Pb(OH)_2\downarrow} + 2NH_4NO_3$$ **(1)**

Q.12 Differentiate between the following pairs of compounds using the regent given in the bracket:

(i) **Ammonium chloride and sodium chloride** (*using an alkali*)

(ii) **Zinc nitrate solution and Calcium nitrate solution** (*using excess sodium hydroxide solution*)

(ICSE 2025)

Ans. (i) When ammonium chloride is heated with sodium hydroxide (alkali), a pungent smelling **ammonia gas** is produced. Whereas, no such reaction takes place when sodium chloride and sodium hydroxide (alkali) are heated together.

$$\underset{\substack{\text{(Ammonium} \\ \text{chloride)}}}{NH_4Cl} + \underset{\text{(Alkali)}}{NaOH} \xrightarrow{\Delta} NaCl + H_2O + \underset{\text{(Ammonia)}}{NH_3\uparrow}$$ **(1)**

(ii) Zinc nitrate solution when reacted with sodium hydroxide solution forms a **gelatinous white precipitate**. This precipitate is **soluble in excess of NaOH** as it forms soluble sodium zincate.

$$\underset{\text{Zinc nitrate}}{Zn(NO_3)_2} + 2NaOH \longrightarrow \underset{\substack{\text{Zinc hydroxide} \\ \text{(White, gelatinous ppt.)}}}{Zn(OH)_2\downarrow} + 2NaNO_3$$

$$Zn(OH)_2 + \underset{\text{(Excess)}}{2NaOH} \longrightarrow \underset{\substack{\text{Sodium zincate} \\ \text{(Colourless)}}}{Na_2ZnO_2} + H_2O$$

Whereas, calcium nitrate forms **calcium hydroxide** (white precipitate) when reacted with NaOH. This precipitate is **sparingly soluble in excess NaOH**.

$$\underset{\text{Calcium nitrate}}{Ca(NO_3)_2} + 2NaOH \longrightarrow \underset{\substack{\text{Calcium hydroxide} \\ \text{(White ppt.)}}}{Ca(OH)_2} + 2NaNO_3$$ **(1)**

Q.13 Answer the following questions.

(i) Identify *A*, *B* and *C* in the given reactions:

$$Zn + 2NaOH \xrightarrow{-H_2} B$$

$$\text{(A)} + 2NaOH \xrightarrow{-H_2O} \text{(B)} \xleftarrow{-2H_2O} \text{(C)} + 2NaOH$$

What is the nature of *A* and *C*.

(ii) Calcium hydroxide solution is used to detect the presence of carbon dioxide gas, while sodium hydroxide is not. Justify. **(Competency Based Que.)**

Ans. (i) $A = ZnO$

$B = Na_2ZnO_2$

$C = Zn(OH)_2$

A and *C* are **amphoteric** in nature. **(1)**

(ii) Carbon dioxide gas forms a white ppt. with calcium hydroxide, while with sodium hydroxide, it does not. **(1)**

Q.14 Distinguish between the following as directed.

(i) Sodium carbonate and sodium sulphate by using dilute HCl. **(ICSE Specimen 2023)**

(ii) Ammonium sulphate and sodium sulphate by using calcium hydroxide.

Ans. (i) Sodium carbonate reacts with dilute HCl to form sodium chloride, water and CO_2 gas. While sodium sulphate does not react with dilute HCl at normal condition.

$$\underset{\substack{\text{Sodium} \\ \text{carbonate}}}{Na_2CO_3} + \text{dil.}2HCl \longrightarrow 2NaCl + H_2O + \underset{\substack{\text{Carbon} \\ \text{dioxide}}}{CO_2\uparrow}$$

$$\underset{\text{Sodium sulphate}}{Na_2SO_4} + \text{dil.}HCl \longrightarrow \text{No reaction}$$ **(1)**

(ii) Ammonium sulphate reacts with calcium hydroxide to form calcium sulphate, water and ammonia gas. While sodium sulphate reacts with calcium hydroxide to form calcium sulphate as a white precipitate and sodium hydroxide.

$$\underset{\substack{\text{Ammonium} \\ \text{sulphate}}}{(NH_4)_2SO_4} + \underset{\substack{\text{Calcium} \\ \text{hydroxide}}}{Ca(OH)_2} \longrightarrow \underset{\text{Ammonia}}{2NH_3\uparrow} + \underset{\substack{\text{Calcium} \\ \text{sulphate}}}{CaSO_4} + 2H_2O$$

$$\underset{\substack{\text{Sodium} \\ \text{sulphate}}}{Na_2SO_4} + \underset{\substack{\text{Calcium} \\ \text{hydroxide}}}{Ca(OH)_2} \longrightarrow \underset{\text{(White ppt.)}}{CaSO_4\downarrow} + \underset{\substack{\text{Sodium} \\ \text{hydroxide}}}{2NaOH}$$ **(1)**

Q.15 (i) Why the alkali is added drop by drop to the salt solution?

(ii) What do you understand by the term amphoteric oxide?

Ans. (i) If an alkali is added too quickly, then it is easy to miss the precipitate that **redissolves** in excess alkali. **(1)**

(ii) Amphoteric oxides are compounds which **react with both acids and alkalis** to form salt and water. **(1)**

Q.16 *A*, *B* and *C* are three elements which undergo chemical reactions according to the following equations:

$$A_2O_3 + 2B \longrightarrow B_2O_3 + 2A$$

$$3CSO_4 + 2B \longrightarrow B_2(SO_4)_3 + 3C$$

$$3CO + 2A \longrightarrow A_2O + 3C$$

Answer the following questions:

(i) Which element is the most reactive?

(ii) Which element is the least reactive?

(Competency Based Que.)

Ans. (i) *B*, because *B* displaces *A* and *C* from their compounds. **(1)**

(ii) *C*, because both *A* and *B* displaces *C* from its compound. **(1)**

TYPE - 8 — 03 Marks

Short Answer Type II Questions

Q.1 Copper sulphate solution reacts with sodium hydroxide solution to form a precipitate of copper hydroxide according to the equation.

$$2NaOH + CuSO_4 \longrightarrow Na_2SO_4 + Cu(OH)_2\downarrow$$

(i) What mass of copper hydroxide is precipitated by using 200 g of sodium hydroxide?

[H = 1, O = 16, Na = 23, S = 32, Cu = 64]

(ii) What is the colour of the precipitate formed?

(ICSE 2019)

Ans. (i) **Given:** $2NaOH + CuSO_4 \longrightarrow Na_2SO_4 + Cu(OH)_2$

Molar mass of $Cu(OH)_2 = 64 + 2(16 + 1)$

$= 64 + 32 + 2 = 98$

Molar mass of NaOH $= 23 + 16 + 1 = 40$

According to given equation:

2 moles of NaOH ≡ 1 mole of $Cu(OH)_2$

∵ 2 × 40 g of NaOH, gives 98 g of $Cu(OH)_2$

∴ 200 g of NaOH gives $\frac{98 \times 200}{80}$ g of $Cu(OH)_2$

$= \mathbf{245\ g\ of\ Cu(OH)_2}$ **(2)**

(ii) $Cu(OH)_2$ precipitate is of **pale greenish-blue colour**. **(1)**

Q.2 State one relevant observation for each of the following reaction.

(i) Lead nitrate solution is treated with sodium hydroxide solution dropwise till it is in excess. **(ICSE 2018)**

(ii) Action of sodium hydroxide solution on ferrous sulphate solution. **(ICSE 2017)**

(iii) Ammonium hydroxide is added to ferrous sulphate solution. **(ICSE Specimen 2023)**

Ans. (i) When sodium hydroxide is added drop by drop to a solution of lead nitrate, a **white precipitate** is formed, which is **soluble in excess of sodium hydroxide**.

$$\underset{\text{Lead nitrate}}{Pb(NO_3)_2} + \underset{\text{Sodium hydroxide}}{2NaOH} \longrightarrow \underset{\text{Lead hydroxide (White ppt.)}}{Pb(OH)_2\downarrow} + \underset{\text{Sodium nitrate}}{2NaNO_3}$$

$$Pb(OH)_2 + \underset{\text{(Excess)}}{2NaOH} \longrightarrow \underset{\text{Sodium plumbite (Soluble salt)}}{Na_2PbO_2} + 2H_2O \quad \textbf{(1)}$$

(ii) On adding sodium hydroxide drop by drop to a solution of ferrous ion, a **dirty green precipitate** is formed which turns reddish brown after sometime and is **insoluble in excess of sodium hydroxide**.

$$\underset{\text{Ferrous sulphate (Pale green)}}{FeSO_4} + \underset{\text{Sodium hydroxide (Colourless)}}{2NaOH} \longrightarrow \underset{\text{Ferrous hydroxide (Dirty green, gelatinous ppt.)}}{Fe(OH)_2\downarrow} + \underset{\text{Sodium sulphate (Colourless)}}{Na_2SO_4} \quad \textbf{(1)}$$

(iii) On adding NH_4OH to ferrous sulphate solution, a **dirty green precipitate** is formed, which is **insoluble in excess of NH_4OH**.

$$FeSO_4 + 2NH_4OH \longrightarrow (NH_4)_2SO_4 + \underset{\text{Dirty green ppt.}}{Fe(OH)_2\downarrow} \quad \textbf{(1)}$$

Q.3 Identify the cations in each of the following case.

(i) NaOH solution when added to the solution *A* gives a reddish brown precipitate.

(ii) NH_4OH solution when added to the solution *B* gives white precipitate which does not dissolve in excess of NH_4OH.

(iii) NaOH solution when added to solution *C* gives white precipitate which is insoluble in excess of NaOH. **(ICSE 2016)**

Ans. (i) **[Fe^{3+} ion]**

$$\underset{\text{Ferric chloride}}{FeCl_3} + \underset{\text{Caustic soda}}{3NaOH} \longrightarrow \underset{\text{Ferric hydroxide (Reddish brown ppt.)}}{Fe(OH)_3\downarrow} + 2NaCl \quad \textbf{(1)}$$

(ii) **[Pb^{2+} ion]**

$$\underset{\text{Lead nitrate}}{Pb(NO_3)_2} + \underset{\text{Ammonium hydroxide}}{2NH_4OH} \longrightarrow \underset{\text{(White ppt.) Lead hydroxide (Insoluble in excess } NH_4OH)}{Pb(OH)_2\downarrow} + 2NH_4NO_3 \quad \textbf{(1)}$$

(iii) **[Ca^{2+} ion]**

$$Ca(NO_3)_2 + 2NaOH \longrightarrow \underset{\text{Calcium hydroxide (White ppt.) (Insoluble in excess NaOH)}}{Ca(OH)_2\downarrow} + 2NaNO_3 \quad \textbf{(1)}$$

Q.4 Answer the following questions.

(i) What would you observe when ammonium hydroxide is first added in a small quantity and then in excess to a solution of copper sulphate?

(ii) Write the observation and balance the equation. Sodium hydroxide is added dropwise till in excess to a solution of zinc sulphate.

(iii) Name the gas evolved on reaction of aluminium with boiling concentrated caustic alkali solution. Write the equation.

Ans. (i) When NH_4OH is added to $CuSO_4$ solution, **a pale blue ppt.** is formed which is **soluble in excess of NH_4OH** and forms **deep blue solution**.

$$\underset{\text{Copper sulphate (Blue)}}{CuSO_4} + \underset{\text{Ammonium hydroxide}}{2NH_4OH} \longrightarrow \underset{\text{Copper hydroxide (Pale blue ppt.)}}{Cu(OH)_2\downarrow} + \underset{\text{Ammonium sulphate (Colourless)}}{(NH_4)_2SO_4}$$

$$\underset{\text{Copper hydroxide}}{Cu(OH)_2} + \underset{\text{Ammonium sulphate}}{(NH_4)_2SO_4} + \underset{\text{(Excess)}}{2NH_4OH} \longrightarrow \underset{\text{Tetraamine copper (II) sulphate (Deep blue solution)}}{[Cu(NH_3)_4]SO_4} + 4H_2O \quad \textbf{(1)}$$

(ii) On adding NaOH drop by drop to solution of zinc salt, a **white precipitate** is formed, which is **soluble in excess of NaOH**.

$$\underset{\text{Zinc sulphate (Colourless)}}{ZnSO_4} + \underset{\text{Sodium hydroxide (Colourless)}}{2NaOH} \longrightarrow \underset{\text{Zinc hydroxide (White ppt.)}}{Zn(OH)_2\downarrow} + \underset{\text{Sodium sulphate (Colourless)}}{Na_2SO_4}$$

$$Zn(OH)_2 + \underset{\text{(Excess)}}{2NaOH} \longrightarrow \underset{\text{Sodium zincate (soluble salt)}}{Na_2ZnO_2} + 2H_2O \quad \textbf{(1)}$$

(iii) **Hydrogen gas**

$$2Al + \underset{\text{(Hot and conc. alkali)}}{2NaOH} + 2H_2O \longrightarrow \underset{\text{Sodium } metaaluminate \text{ (Colourless)}}{2NaAlO_2} + \underset{\text{Hydrogen gas}}{3H_2} \quad \textbf{(1)}$$

Q.5 Consider the following salt solutions:

A. Copper(II) nitrate
B. Iron(II) sulphate
C. Iron(III) chloride
D. Lead nitrate
E. Magnesium sulphate

(i) Which salt solution gives a blue solution when excess ammonium hydroxide is added?

(ii) Which salt solution forms a white precipitate that is insoluble in excess ammonia?

(iii) Which salt solution givs a dirty green precipitate with ammonium hydroxide?

Ans. (i) **Copper(II) nitrate (A)** gives a deep blue solution due to the formation of the $[Cu(NH_3)_4]^{2+}$ complex when excess ammonium hydroxide is added. **(1)**

(ii) **Lead nitrate (D)** forms a white precipitate of $Pb(OH)_2$, which is insoluble in excess ammonia. **(1)**

(iii) **Iron(II) sulphate (B)** gives a dirty green precipitate of $Fe(OH)_2$ when ammonium hydroxide is added. **(1)**

Q.6 State one relevant observation for each of the following reactions.

(i) When excess ammonia is passed through an aqueous solution of lead nitrate. **(ICSE Specimen 2023)**

(ii) Addition of excess ammonium hydroxide into copper sulphate solution. **(ICSE 2020)**

(iii) Ammonium hydroxide is added to ferrous sulphate solution.

Ans. (i) When ammonia is passed through an aqueous solution of lead nitrate, **chalky white precipitate** of **lead hydroxide** is formed which is **insoluble** in **excess of ammonia**. The reactions involved is as follows.

$$\underset{\text{Ammonia}}{NH_3} + H_2O \longrightarrow \underset{\text{Ammonium hydroxide}}{NH_4OH}$$

$$\underset{\text{Lead nitrate}}{Pb(NO_3)_2} + \underset{\text{Ammonium hydroxide}}{2NH_4OH} \longrightarrow \underset{\text{Lead hydroxide}}{Pb(OH)_2\downarrow} + \underset{\text{Ammonium nitrate}}{NH_4NO_3}$$ **(1)**

(ii) When copper sulphate solution reacts with ammonium hydroxide, ammonium sulphate and **copper hydroxide (pale blue ppt.)** are produced.

$$\underset{\text{Copper sulphate}}{CuSO_4(aq)} + \underset{\text{Ammonium hydroxide}}{2NH_4OH} \longrightarrow \underset{\text{Ammonium sulphate}}{(NH_4)_2SO_4} + \underset{\text{Copper hydroxide (pale blue colour)}}{Cu(OH)_2\downarrow}$$ **(1)**

This pale blue precipitate **dissolves in excess of NH_4OH** to give **deep blue** or **inky blue** or **prussian blue solution**.

$$Cu(OH)_2 + (NH_4)_2SO_4 + 2NH_4OH \longrightarrow \underset{\text{Tetraamine copper (II) sulphate (Deep blue solution)}}{[Cu(NH_3)_4]SO_4} + 4H_2O$$

(iii) When ammonium hydroxide is added to ferrous sulphate solution, a **dirty green precipitate** of $Fe(OH)_2$ is obtained.

$$\underset{\text{Ferrous sulphate}}{FeSO_4} + \underset{\text{Ammonium hydroxide}}{2NH_4OH} \longrightarrow \underset{\text{Ammonium sulphate}}{(NH_4)_2SO_4} + \underset{\text{Ferrous hydroxide (Dirty green ppt.)}}{Fe(OH)_2\downarrow}$$ **(1)**

Q.7 Distinguish between the following pairs of compounds using the test given within the brackets.

(i) Calcium sulphite and calcium carbonate (using dil. HCl)

(ii) Calcium nitrate and potassium nitrate (using a flame test)

(iii) Lead nitrate solution and zinc nitrate solution (using an alkali) **(ICSE 2019)**

Ans. (i) On adding dil. HCl to calcium sulphite and calcium carbonate, **SO_2 and CO_2 gas** evolves respectively.

$$\underset{\text{Calcium carbonate}}{CaCO_3} + \underset{\text{(Dil.)}}{2HCl} \longrightarrow \underset{\text{Calcium chloride}}{CaCl_2} + H_2O + \underset{\text{Carbon dioxide}}{CO_2\uparrow}$$

$$\underset{\text{Calcium sulphite}}{CaSO_3} + 2HCl \longrightarrow CaCl_2 + H_2O + \underset{\text{Sulphur dioxide}}{SO_2\uparrow}$$ **(1)**

(ii) On performing flame test, calcium nitrate salt gives **orange-red flame** whereas, potassium nitrate salt gives **magenta** or **lilac flame**. **(1)**

(iii) On adding ammonium hydroxide to lead nitrate solution, a **white precipitate** is formed which is **insoluble** in excess of ammonium hydroxide.

$$\underset{\text{Lead nitrate (Colourless)}}{Pb(NO_3)_2} + 2NH_4OH \longrightarrow \underset{\text{Chalky white ppt.}}{Pb(OH)_2\downarrow} + \underset{\text{Ammonium nitrate}}{2NH_4NO_3}$$

Whereas, on adding ammonium hydroxide to zinc nitrate solution, a white ppt. so formed is soluble in excess of ammonium hydroxide and we get colourless solution.

$$\underset{\text{Zinc nitrate}}{Zn(NO_3)_2} + 2NH_4OH \longrightarrow \underset{\text{White ppt.}}{Zn(OH)_2\downarrow} + \underset{\text{Ammonium nitrate}}{2NH_4NO_3}$$

$$Zn(OH)_2 + \underset{\text{(Excess)}}{2NH_4OH} + 2NH_4NO_3 \longrightarrow [Zn(NH_3)_4](NO_3)_2 + 4H_2O$$ **(1)**

Q.8 Define the following:

(i) Reagent

(ii) Precipitation

(iii) Amphoteric metals

Ans. (i) A **reagent** is a substance that reacts with other substances in order to bring about a chemical change. **(1)**

(ii) **Precipitation** is the process by which an insoluble solid (called a **precipitate**) forms and separates from a solution during a chemical reaction. **(1)**

(iii) **Amphoteric metals** are metals that can react with both acids and bases to form salt and water. **(1)**

TYPE - 9 04/05 Marks

Long Answer Type Questions

Q.1 Write the balanced chemical equation for the following reactions.

(i) Reaction of sodium hydroxide solution with iron (III) chloride solution. **(ICSE 2018)**

(ii) Zinc and sodium hydroxide solution.

(iii) Zinc oxide dissolves in sodium hydroxide.

(iv) Aluminium oxide in sodium hydroxide. **(ICSE 2024)**

Ans. (i) $$\underset{\text{Ferric chloride}}{FeCl_3} + \underset{\text{Sodium hydroxide}}{3NaOH} \longrightarrow \underset{\text{Ferric hydroxide}}{Fe(OH)_3\downarrow} + \underset{\text{Sodium chloride}}{3NaCl}$$ **(1)**

(ii) Zinc metal reacts with sodium hydroxide to form **sodium zincate**.

$$Zn + \underset{\text{(Hot and conc.)}}{2NaOH} \longrightarrow \underset{\text{Sodium zincate}}{Na_2ZnO_2} + H_2\uparrow$$ **(1)**

(iii) $ZnO + 2NaOH \xrightarrow{\Delta} Na_2ZnO_2 + H_2O$
(White) (Conc.) Sodium zincate (Colourless, soluble) **(1)**

(iv) $Al_2O_3 + 2NaOH \longrightarrow 2NaAlO_2 + H_2O$
Aluminium oxide; Sodium *meta* aluminate **(1)**

Q.2 Identify the cation in each of the following cases.

(i) Ammonium hydroxide solution when added to solution *B* gives a white precipitate which does not dissolve in excess of ammonium hydroxide solution.

(ii) Sodium hydroxide solution when added to solution *C* gives a white precipitate which is insoluble in excess of sodium hydroxide solution. **(ICSE 2023)**

(iii) Reddish brown precipitate insoluble in ammonium hydroxide.

(iv) Blue coloured sulphate solution. **(ICSE Specimen 2023)**

Ans. (i) When **lead nitrate (solution *B*)** reacts with ammonium hydroxide (NH_4OH), a white gelatinous precipitate of lead hydroxide is formed which is insoluble in excess of ammonium hydroxide.

$$Pb(NO_3)_2 + 2NH_4OH \longrightarrow Pb(OH)_2\downarrow + 2NH_4NO_3$$

So, cation is $\mathbf{Pb^{2+}}$. **(1)**

(ii) $NaOH(aq) + Ca(NO_3)_2(aq) \longrightarrow Ca(OH)_2(s)\downarrow + 2NaNO_3(aq)$
(Solution *C*) Calcium hydroxide

Calcium hydroxide is a white precipitate which is insoluble in excess of sodium hydroxide solution So, cation present is $\mathbf{Ca^{2+}}$ **ion.** **(1)**

(iii) The name of cation is $\mathbf{Fe^{3+}}$ **ion**.

Involved reaction is as follows:

$$FeCl_3 + 3NaOH \longrightarrow Fe(OH)_3\downarrow + 3NaCl$$

Iron chloride; Sodium hydroxide; Ferric hydroxide (Reddish brown ppt.); Sodium chloride **(1)**

(iv) The name of cation is $\mathbf{Cu^{2+}}$. The compound is $\mathbf{CuSO_4}$. **(1)**

Q.3 Give a chemical test to distinguish between the following pairs of chemicals.

(i) Lead nitrate solution and zinc nitrate solution.

(ii) Sodium chloride solution and sodium nitrate solution. **(ICSE 2018)**

Ans. Following are the chemical tests to distinguish between

(i) **Lead nitrate solution and zinc nitrate solution** On adding ammonium hydroxide drop by drop to a solution of zinc nitrate, a white gelatinous precipitate is formed, which is soluble in excess of ammonium hydroxide.

$$Zn(NO_3)_2 + 2NH_4OH \longrightarrow 2NH_4NO_3 + Zn(OH)_2\downarrow$$

Zinc nitrate; Ammonium hydroxide; Ammonium nitrate; Zinc hydroxide (White gelatinous ppt.)

$$Zn(OH)_2 + 2NH_4NO_3 + 2NH_4OH \longrightarrow [Zn(NH_3)_4](NO_3)_2 + 4H_2O$$

(Excess)

On the other hand, in case of lead nitrate, a white precipitate is formed which is insoluble in excess of ammonium hydroxide.

$$Pb(NO_3)_2 + 2NH_4OH \longrightarrow Pb(OH)_2\downarrow + 2NH_4NO_3$$

Lead nitrate; Ammonium hydroxide; Lead hydroxide (White ppt.); Ammonium nitrate **(2)**

(ii) **Sodium chloride solution and sodium nitrate solution** To a solution of sodium chloride, when few drops of $AgNO_3$ (silver nitrate) solution is added, a white precipitate of AgCl (silver chloride) is obtained, while in case of sodium nitrate, no such reaction takes place.

$$NaCl + AgNO_3 \longrightarrow AgCl\downarrow + NaNO_3$$

(White ppt.)

$$NaNO_3 + AgNO_3 \longrightarrow \text{No reaction}$$ **(2)**

Q.4 Give one chemical test to distinguish between the following compounds.

(i) Iron (III) chloride and copper chloride solution.

(ii) Iron (II) chloride and iron (III) chloride solution.

(iii) Calcium nitrate and zinc nitrate solution.

(iv) Ferrous nitrate and lead nitrate solution.

Ans. (i) Iron (III) chloride gives reddish brown ppt. with NaOH solution and copper chloride gives blue ppt. with NaOH solution.

$$FeCl_3 + 3NaOH \longrightarrow Fe(OH)_3\downarrow + 3NaCl$$

Iron (III) chloride; Ferric hydroxide (Reddish brown ppt.)

$$CuCl_2 + 3NaOH \longrightarrow Cu(OH)_2\downarrow + 2NaCl$$

Copper (II) chloride; Copper (II) hydroxide (blue ppt.) **(1)**

(ii) $FeCl_2 + 2NaOH \longrightarrow Fe(OH)_2\downarrow + 2NaCl$
Ferrous chloride; Ferrous hydroxide (Dirty green ppt.)

$FeCl_3 + 3NaOH \longrightarrow Fe(OH)_3\downarrow + 3NaCl$
Ferric chloride; Ferric hydroxide (Reddish brown ppt.) **(1)**

(iii) Action with NaOH can distinguish $Ca(NO_3)_2$ and $Zn(NO_3)_2$,

(a) $Ca(NO_3)_2 + 2NaOH \longrightarrow Ca(OH)_2\downarrow + 2NaNO_3$
Calcium nitrate (Colourless); Caustic soda (Colourless); Calcium hydroxide (White ppt.) (Sparingly soluble in excess NaOH); Sodium nitrate (Colourless) **(1)**

(b) $Zn(NO_3)_2 + 2NaOH \longrightarrow Zn(OH)_2\downarrow + 2NaNO_3$
Zinc nitrate; Sodium hydroxide Colourless); Zinc hydroxide (White gelatinous ppt.)

$Zn(OH)_2 + 2NaOH \longrightarrow Na_2ZnO_2 + 2H_2O$
Zinc hydroxide; (Excess); Sodium zincate (Soluble salt) (Colourless) **(1)**

(iv) Action with NaOH solution can distinguish $Fe(NO_3)_2$ and $Pb(NO_3)_2$.

(a) $Fe(NO_3)_2 + 2NaOH \longrightarrow Fe(OH)_2\downarrow + 2NaNO_3$
Ferrous nitrate; Caustic soda; Ferrous hydroxide (Dirty green, gelatinous ppt.) (Insoluble in excess NaOH)

(b) $Pb(NO_3)_2 + 2NaOH \longrightarrow Pb(OH)_2\downarrow + 2NaNO_3$
Lead nitrate (Colourless); Caustic soda (Colourless); Lead hydroxide (White ppt.); Sodium nitrate (Colourless)

$Pb(OH)_2 + 2NaOH \longrightarrow Na_2PbO_2 + 2H_2O$
Lead hydroxide; (Excess); Sodium plumbite (Soluble salt) **(1)**

Q.5 The following table shows the tests a student performed on four different aqueous solutions which are *X*, *Y*, *Z* and *W*. Based on the observations provided, identify the cation present.

Chemical test	Observation	Conclusion
To solution *X*, ammonium hydroxide is added in minimum quantity first and then in excess.	A dirty white precipitate is formed which dissolves in excess to form a clear solution.	(i)
To solution *Y*, ammonium hydroxide is added in minimum quantity first and then in excess.	A pale blue precipitate is formed which dissolves in excess to form a clear inky blue solution.	(ii)
To solution *W* a small quantity of sodium hydroxide solution is added and then in excess.	A white precipitate is formed which remains insoluble.	(iii)
To a salt *Z* calcium hydroxide solution is added and then heated.	A pungent smelling gas turning moist red litmus paper blue is obtained.	(iv)

(ICSE 2015)

Ans. (i) Cation present is **zinc (Zn^{2+}ion)** as dirty white precipitate is soluble in excess of ammonium hydroxide.

$ZnSO_4 + 2NH_4OH \longrightarrow Zn(OH)_2\downarrow + (NH_4)_2SO_4$
(White ppt.)

$Zn(OH)_2 + (NH_4)_2SO_4 + 2NH_4OH \longrightarrow [Zn(NH_3)_4]SO_4 + 4H_2O$
(Excess); Tetraamine zinc (II) sulphate (Soluble) **(1)**

(ii) Cation present is **copper (Cu^{2+}ion)** as pale blue precipitate is soluble in excess of ammonium hydroxide.

$CuSO_4 + 2NH_4OH \longrightarrow Cu(OH)_2\downarrow + (NH_4)_2SO_4$
Copper sulphate; (Pale blue ppt.)

$Cu(OH)_2 + (NH_4)_2SO_4 + 2NH_4OH \longrightarrow [Cu(NH_3)_4]SO_4 + 4H_2O$
(Excess); Tetraamine copper (II) sulphate (Inky blue solution) (Soluble) **(1)**

(iii) Cation present is **calcium (Ca^{2+}ion)** as white precipitate remains insoluble in excess sodium hydroxide.

$Cu(NO_3)_2 + 2NaOH \longrightarrow Cu(OH)_2\downarrow + 2NaNO_3$
Calcium nitrate; Calcium hydroxide (White ppt.) (Insoluble) **(1)**

(iv) Cation present is **ammonium ion (NH_4^+)** and the gas evolved is **ammonia**, which turns moist red litmus paper blue. This shows that ammonia gas is alkaline in nature.

$2NH_4Cl + Ca(OH)_2 \longrightarrow CaCl_2 + 2H_2O + 2NH_3\uparrow$
Ammonia gas (Pungent smell) **(1)**

Q.6 Observe the reactions given below and answer the following questions:

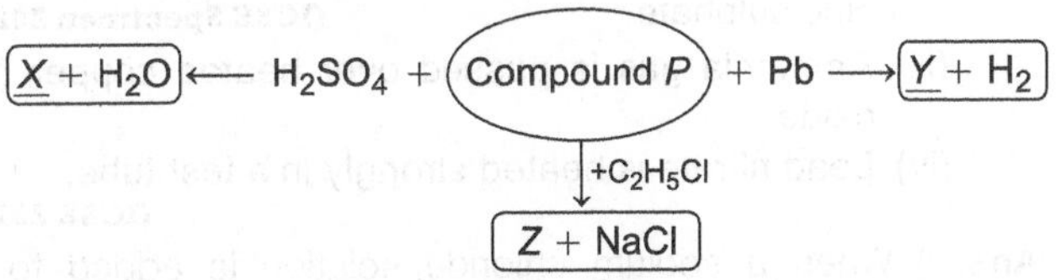

(i) Identify compound *P*.
(ii) Give the chemical formula of *Z*.
(iii) Write the reaction taking place between the identified compound *P* and sulphuric acid.
(iv) Name compound *Y*. **(Competency Based Que.)**

Ans. (i) NaOH (ii) C_2H_5OH
(iii) $NaOH + H_2SO_4 \longrightarrow Na_2SO_4 + H_2O$
(iv) Sodium plumbite **(1 × 4 = 4)**

Q.7 Identify the anion present in each of the following compounds.

(i) When barium chloride solution is added to a solution of compound *B*, a white precipitate insoluble in dilute hydrochloric acid is formed.
(ii) When dilute sulphuric acid is added to compound *D*, a gas is produced which turns lime water milky but has no effect on acidified potassium dichromate solution. **(ICSE Specimen 2023)**
(iii) The compound on heating produces a colourless, odourless gas which turns lime water milky and has no effect on acidified potassium dichromate solution.
(iv) The solution of the compound which on treating with concentrated sulphuric acid and freshly prepared ferrous sulphate solution produces a brown ring. **(ICSE 2024)**

Ans. (i) When barium chloride solution is added to a solution of compound *B*, a white precipitate of **$BaSO_4$** is obtained. It is insoluble in dilute hydrochloric acid. Hence, **SO_4^{2-} ions** are present. **(1)**

(ii) When dilute sulphuric acid is added to compound *D*. Then, the gas evolved that turns lime water milky is CO_2. So, the compound is **Na_2CO_3**. It also does not show any effect on acidified $K_2Cr_2O_7$ solution. Then, anion present in compound *D* is **CO_3^{2-}**. **(1)**

(iii) **CO_3^{2-} (Carbonate ion)**: Carbonate salt (e.g. calcium carbonate) on heating produces CO_2 (colourless, odourless gas) which has no effect on acidified potassium dichromate solution. **(1)**

(iv) **NO_3^- (Nitrate ion)**: Brown ring test is used for a detection of nitrate ions in a solution. **(1)**

Q.8 State one observation in the following cases.

(i) Sodium chloride solution is added to a solution of lead nitrate.

(ii) Barium chloride solution is added to a solution of zinc sulphate. **(ICSE Specimen 2024)**

(iii) Ammonia gas is passed over heated copper (II) oxide.

(iv) Lead nitrate is heated strongly in a test tube. **(ICSE 2019)**

Ans. (i) When a sodium chloride solution is added to a solution of lead nitrate, a **precipitate of lead chloride and sodium nitrate solution** is formed. **(1)**

(ii) When barium chloride solution is added to a solution of zinc sulphate, it gives **zinc chloride solution and barium sulphate precipitate**. **(1)**

(iii) When ammonia gas is passed over heated copper(II) oxide, it gives **reddish brown copper**.

In fact, **ammonia reduces oxide to give metals, water vapour and N_2**.

$$\underset{}{2NH_3} + \underset{\text{Black solid}}{3CuO} \longrightarrow \underset{\text{Reddish brown solid}}{3Cu\downarrow} + 3H_2O + \underset{\text{Gas}}{N_2\uparrow}$$ **(1)**

(iv) On heating lead nitrate [$Pb(NO_3)_2$] strongly in a test tube, we get **lead oxide (PbO), NO_2 and O_2** as decomposition products.

$$2Pb(NO_3)_2 \xrightarrow{\Delta} 2PbO + 4NO_2 + O_2$$ **(1)**

Q.9 State any one observation for each of the following.

(i) Dilute hydrochloric acid is added to silver nitrate solution.

(ii) Concentrated nitric acid is added to copper turnings.

(iii) Mixture of ammonium chloride and sodium hydroxide is heated.

(iv) Ammonium hydroxide solution is added in excess to copper sulphate solution.

(v) NaOH solution is added to calcium nitrate solution. **(ICSE Specimen 2019)**

Ans. (i) On adding dil. HCl to silver nitrate solution, a white **precipitate of silver chloride** is formed.

$$\underset{\text{Silver nitrate}}{AgNO_3} + \underset{\text{(Dil.)}}{HCl} \longrightarrow \underset{\text{Silver chloride ppt.}}{AgCl\downarrow} + HNO_3$$ **(1)**

(ii) On adding conc. HNO_3 to copper turnings, it **oxidises copper to copper nitrate**.

$$\underset{\text{Copper}}{Cu} + \underset{\text{Conc.}}{4HNO_3} \longrightarrow \underset{\text{Copper nitrate}}{Cu(NO_3)_2} + 2H_2O + \underset{\text{Nitrogen dioxide}}{2NO_2}$$ **(1)**

(iii) When sodium hydroxide solution (or any other alkali) is heated with ammonium chloride, **ammonia** gas is evolved.

$$\underset{\text{Ammonium chloride}}{NH_4Cl} + \underset{\text{Caustic soda}}{NaOH} \xrightarrow{\Delta} \underset{\text{Sodium chloride}}{NaCl} + H_2O + \underset{\text{Ammonia gas}}{NH_3\uparrow}$$ **(1)**

(iv) On adding ammonium hydroxide to copper sulphate solution, a pale-blue precipitate is formed, which dissolves in excess of ammonium hydroxide to give **deep blue or inky blue or prussian blue solution**.

$$\underset{\text{Copper sulphate (Blue)}}{CuSO_4} + \underset{\text{Ammonium hydroxide}}{2NH_4OH} \longrightarrow \underset{\text{Pale blue ppt.}}{Cu(OH)_2\downarrow} + \underset{\text{Ammonium sulphate (Colourless)}}{(NH_4)_2SO_4}$$

$$Cu(OH)_2 + \underset{\text{Ammonium sulphate}}{(NH_4)_2SO_4} + \underset{\text{(Excess)}}{2NH_4OH} \longrightarrow \underset{\text{Tetraammine copper (II) sulphate (Deep blue solution)}}{[Cu(NH_3)_4]SO_4} + 4H_2O$$ **(1)**

(v) On adding sodium hydroxide to a solution of calcium nitrate, a **white precipitate** is formed, which is **sparingly soluble in excess of NaOH**.

$$\underset{\text{Calcium nitrate (Colourless)}}{Ca(NO_3)_2} + \underset{\text{Caustic soda (Colourless)}}{2NaOH} \longrightarrow \underset{\text{Calcium hydroxide (White ppt.)}}{Ca(OH)_2\downarrow} + \underset{\text{Sodium nitrate (Colourless)}}{2NaNO_3}$$ **(1)**

Q.10 Sodium hydroxide solution is added first in a small quantity, then in excess to the aqueous salt solutions of copper (II) sulphate, zinc nitrate, lead nitrate, calcium chloride and iron (III) sulphate. Copy the following table and write the colour of the precipitate in (i) to (v) and the nature of the precipitate (soluble or insoluble) in (vi) to (x).

Aqueous salt solution	Colour of precipitate when NaOH is added in a small quantity	Nature of precipitate (soluble or insoluble) when NaOH is added in excess
Copper (II) sulphate	(i)	(vi)
Zinc nitrate	(ii)	(vii)
Lead nitrate	(iii)	(viii)
Calcium chloride	(iv)	(ix)
Iron (III) sulphate	(v)	(x)

Ans.

Aqueous salt solution	Colour of precipitate when NaOH is added in a small quantity	Nature of precipitate when NaOH is added in excess (Soluble or insoluble)
Copper (II) sulphate	(i) Blue	(vi) Insoluble
Zinc nitrate	(ii) White	(vii) Soluble
Lead nitrate	(iii) White	(viii) Soluble
Calcium chloride	(iv) White	(ix) Insoluble
Iron (III) sulphate	(v) Reddish brown	(x) Insoluble

Q.11 The setup shown below is that of the fountain experiment with hydrogen chloride gas in the flask.

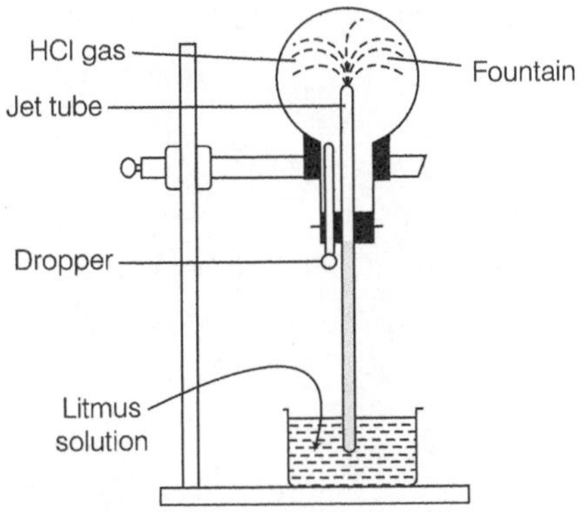

The fountain starts when a few drops of water from the dropper are introduced into the flask. Instead of the drops of water, Pooja started the fountain by introducing a few drops of sodium hydroxide into the flask.

(i) Explain why the litmus solution gets sucked up when sodium hydroxide is used.

(ii) What will be the colour of the fountain when sodium hydroxide is used? Justify your answer.

(iii) If instead of HCl gas, ammonia gas is filled in the flask and water is introduced from the dropper, will there be a different observation? Justify your answer. **(ICSE Specimen 2024)**

Ans. (i) All the hydrogen chloride in the flask dissolves in the sodium hydroxide drops from the pipette, creating a vacuum in the flask. NaOH is sucked up at a great speed from the bowl, creating a spectacular 'fountain' in the flask. **(1)**

(ii) The colour of litmus solution turns blue in basic medium and red in acidic medium. We know that NaOH is basic in nature.

Therefore, in the fountain experiment, the colour of litmus solution turns blue. **(2)**

(iii) The properties of ammonia can be shown in a fountain experiment. A few drops of water are injected into the flask and they dissolve some of the ammonia gas. This decreases the pressure in the flask and sucks in the water from the beaker. The indicator turns blue upon contact with the ammonia solution due to its basic nature. **(2)**

TYPE - 10 — 03 Marks

Case-Based Questions

Q.1 Rita was given an unknown salt for identification. She prepared a solution of the salt and divided it into two parts. To the first part of the salt solution, she added a few drops of ammonium hydroxide and obtained a reddish brown precipitate.

To the second part of the salt solution, she added a few drops of silver nitrate solution and obtained a white precipitate.

Name:

(i) The cation present.

(ii) The anion present in the salt given for identification. **(ICSE 2024)**

(iii) The formula of reddish brown precipitate.

Ans. (i) **Fe^{3+} ion.**

$$\underset{\text{(Salt solution)}}{FeCl_3} + 3NH_4OH \longrightarrow 3NH_4Cl + \underset{\text{Iron (III) hydroxide (Reddish brown ppt.)}}{Fe(OH)_3\downarrow}$$ **(1)**

(ii) **Cl^- ions.**

$$\underset{\text{(Salt solution)}}{FeCl_3} + 3AgNO_3 \longrightarrow \underset{\text{(White ppt.)}}{3AgCl\downarrow} + Fe(NO_3)_4$$ **(1)**

(iii) **$Fe(OH)_3$.** **(1)**

Q.2 In a rural area, local water supply is being tested for hardness, which is a key indicator of water quality. Hard water contains high levels of dissolved minerals, primarily calcium and magnesium ions. Excessive hardness can cause sealing in pipes, reduce the efficiency of soaps and damage household appliances. The water sample is tested using a qualitative analysis to identify the metal ions responsible for the hardness.

The water sample is first treated with sodium hydroxide, and then with ammonium hydroxide (NH_4OH).

(i) What is the observation when sodium hydroxide is added to the water sample containing calcium ions?

(ii) What will you observe when ammonium hydroxide is added to the water sample containing calcium ions?

(iii) What happens if we add excess of ammonium hydroxide to the above solution in part (b)? Explain briefly.

Ans. (i) A white precipitate of calcium hydroxide [$Ca(OH)_2$] is formed.

$$Ca^{2+}(aq) + 2OH^-(aq) \longrightarrow Ca(OH)_2(s)\downarrow \quad \textbf{(1)}$$

(ii) No precipitate is formed when ammonium hydroxide is added to a solution containing calcium ions. **(1)**

(iii) No precipitation occurs even if we add excess of ammonium hydroxide because the concentration of OH^- ions from the ionisation of ammonium hydroxide is so low that it cannot precipitate the hydroxide of calcium. **(1)**

Q.3 Seema takes a blue crystalline salt *P* in a test tube. On heating it produces a white anhydrous powder. *P* is dissolved in water. Zinc is added to one part of the solution and to another part of the solution barium chloride is added. **(ICSE Specimen 2024)**

(i) Name the compound *P*.

(ii) Mention one observation when zinc is added to the solution of *P*.

(iii) State the colour of the precipitate formed when barium chloride is added to the solution of *P*.

Ans. (i) *P* = copper(II) sulphate. **(1)**

(ii) When zinc is added to the copper(II) sulphate solution then solution becomes colourless. **(1)**

(iii) White precipitate of barium sulphate is formed when barium chloride is added to copper sulphate solution. **(1)**

05

MOLE CONCEPT AND STOICHIOMETRY

Gay-Lussac's Law of Combining Volumes

- At the same temperature and pressure, the volume of gases taking part in a chemical reaction are in whole number ratio to one another. e.g. One volume of hydrogen mixed with one volume of chlorine gives two volumes of hydrogen chloride gas, at the same temperature and pressure.

$$\underset{1\text{ vol}}{H_2} + \underset{1\text{ vol}}{Cl_2} \longrightarrow \underset{2\text{ vol}}{2HCl} \quad \text{Simple ratio is } 1:1:2.$$

- Gay-Lussac's law is **applicable only for gases**. The volumes of liquids and solids are considered to be zero.

Note The reactant which is completely used up in a reaction is known as the **limiting reagent**.

Avogadro's Law

- Avogadro's law states that "equal volumes of all gases under similar conditions of temperature and pressure contain the same number of molecules."
- If there are two balloons of equal volumes, one filled with H_2 and other with N_2, then at the same temperature and pressure, number of gas molecules in both the balloons will be same, though the gases are different.

Atomicity

The number of atoms present in a molecule of an element is called its **atomicity**.

(i) **Monoatomic** Molecules consisting of one atom, e.g. He, Ne.

(ii) **Diatomic** Molecules which consists of two identical atoms, e.g. H_2, O_2, N_2, Cl_2.

(iii) **Triatomic** Molecules composed of three identical atoms, e.g. O_3.

(iv) **Tetraatomic** Molecules made up of four identical atoms, e.g. P_4.

(v) **Octaatomic** Molecules composed of eight similar atoms, e.g. S_8.

Homoatomic and Heteroatomic Molecules

Molecules made up of same type of atoms are **homoatomic molecules**, e.g. phosphorus (P_4), ozone (O_3), etc., while molecules made up of different types of atoms are **heteroatomic molecules**, e.g. HCl, NH_3, etc.

Relative Atomic Mass (RAM) (Atomic Weight)

The relative atomic mass or atomic weight of an element is the number of times one atom of the element is heavier than $\frac{1}{12}$ times of the mass of an atom of C-12.

$$\text{Relative Atomic Mass (RAM)} = \frac{\text{Mass of one atom of an element}}{\text{1/12th mass of one C-12 atom}}$$

Atomic mass is expressed in atomic mass units [amu]. **Atomic mass unit** is defined as $\frac{1}{12}$ the mass of carbon atom C-12.

Gram Atomic Mass

The relative atomic mass of an element expressed in grams is known as gram atomic mass or gram atom of that element. e.g. Gram atomic mass of oxygen is 16 gram.

$$\text{Gram atom} = \frac{\text{Mass in grams}}{\text{Relative atomic mass}}$$

Fractional Atomic Mass

The relative atomic mass of any element is the weighted average of the atomic masses of its natural isotopes.

e.g. The average relative atomic mass of chlorine $= \frac{35 \times 3 + 37 \times 1}{4} = 35.5$ (^{35}Cl and ^{37}Cl are in the ratio 3 : 1).

Relative Molecular Mass (RMM) (Molecular Weight)

Relative molecular mass of an element/compound is the number that represents how many times one molecule of the substance is heavier than $\frac{1}{12}$ of the mass of an atom of C-12.

$$\text{Relative molecular mass} = \frac{\text{Mass of one molecule of a substance}}{\text{1/12th mass of one atom of carbon C-12}}$$

Gram Molecular Mass

The relative molecular mass of a substance expressed in grams is known as **gram molecular mass** or **gram molecule** of that element. e.g. Molecular mass of water (H_2O) is 18 amu and its gram molecular mass is 18.00 g.

$$\text{Gram molecule} = \frac{\text{Mass in grams of substance}}{\text{Relative molecular mass}}$$

Vapour Density and its Relation to Relative Molecular Mass

The vapour density of a gas is the ratio between the masses of equal volumes of gas (or vapour) and hydrogen under the same conditions of temperature and pressure.

$$VD = \frac{\text{Mass of volume } (V) \text{ of the gas under similar conditions}}{\text{Mass of volume } (V) \text{ of hydrogen gas under similar conditions}}$$

$$\text{Vapour density (VD)} = \frac{\text{Relative molecular mass of a gas}}{2}$$

Or

The relative molecular mass of a gas or vapour is twice its vapour density.

Mole

A mole is defined as "the amount of a substance containing as many elementary particles (atoms, molecules or ions) as in 12 g of C-12".

- The mole of a substance always contain the same number of entities independent of the nature of the substance taken.
- The mass of one mole of a substance in gram is called its **molar mass**.
- One mole of any gas occupy 22.4 L (dm^3) or 22400 cm^3 (mL) at standard temperature and pressure (STP). This volume is called **molar volume**.

Avogadro's Number

It is defined as the number of atoms present in 12 g (gram atomic mass) of C-12 isotope. It is a constant whose value is 6.022×10^{23}. It is denoted by N_A.

The number of elementary units, i.e., atoms, ions, molecules, etc., present in one mole of a substance is called **Avogadro's number**.

Important Formulae

Mole and Gram Atomic Mass:	One mole of atoms	$= 6.022 \times 10^{23}$ atoms = Gram atomic mass of an element = 1 gram atom of the element
Mole and Gram Molecular Mass:	One mole of molecules	$= 6.022 \times 10^{23}$ molecules = Gram molecular mass = 1 gram molecule of the compound
Mole in terms of volume:	One mole of gas	= 22.4 L at STP

Moles of an element $= \frac{\text{Mass of the element}}{\text{Atomic mass or GAW}}$	**Moles of a compound** $= \frac{\text{Mass of the compound}}{\text{Molecular mass or GMW}}$
Mass of one atom $= \frac{\text{Atomic mass or GAW}}{6.022 \times 10^{23}}$	**Mass of one molecule** $= \frac{\text{Molecular mass or GAW}}{6.022 \times 10^{23}}$
Number of molecules $=$ Moles $\times 6.022 \times 10^{23}$	**Number of atom** $=$ Moles $\times 6.022 \times 10^{23}$

Percentage Composition

Percentage by weight of each element present in a compound is called **percentage composition** of the compound.

$$\text{Percentage of an element in a compound} = \frac{\text{Total weight of the element in one molecule}}{\text{Gram molecular weight of the compound}} \times 100$$

e.g. To find the % of water of crystallisation in $Na_2CO_3 \cdot 10H_2O$

Molecular mass of $Na_2CO_3 \cdot 10H_2O = 23 \times 2 + 12 + 16 \times 3 + 10 \times 18 = 286$

$$\% \text{ of water of crystallisation} = \frac{10 \times 18}{286} \times 100 = 62.9\ \% \text{ of } H_2O$$

Empirical or Simple Formula of a Compound

The empirical formula of a compound is the simplest formula, which shows the **simplest whole number ratio** between the atoms of the elements in the compound. The empirical formula of a compound represents only the **atomic ratio** of the various elements present in its molecule.

Compound	Molecular formula	Whole number ratio	Simplest ratio of empirical formula
Glucose	$C_6H_{12}O_6$	1 : 2 : 1	CH_2O
Benzene	C_6H_6	1 : 1	CH

Molecular Formula of a Compound

The molecular formula of a compound denotes the **actual number of atoms** of different elements present in one molecule of the compound. e.g. Molecular formula of blue vitriol is $CuSO_4 \cdot 5H_2O$. It gives the information that it is made up of 1 atom of Cu, 1 atom of S, 4 atoms of O and five molecules of water of crystallisation.

Compound	Molecular formula	Actual number of atoms present in a compound
Glucose	$C_6H_{12}O_6$	6 atoms of carbon, 12 atoms of hydrogen, 6 atoms of oxygen
Sulphuric acid	H_2SO_4	2 atoms of hydrogen, 1 atom of sulphur, 4 atoms of oxygen

Relationship between Empirical Formula and Molecular Formula

$$\text{Molecular formula} = n \times \text{Empirical formula}$$

$$\text{where, } n = \frac{\text{Molecular mass}}{\text{Empirical formula mass}}$$

Calculations Based on Chemical Equations

Chemical equation is the symbolic representation of a balanced chemical reaction. It gives both qualitative and quantitative information about a chemical reaction. e.g.

$$2KClO_3(s) \xrightarrow{MnO_2,\ \Delta} 2KCl(s) + 3O_2(g)$$

The relationship between the amounts of reactants and products is called **stoichiometry**. The number before the formula unit or molecule used to balance the equations are called **stoichiometric coefficients**.

EXAM ORIENTED QUESTIONS

TYPE - 1 01 Mark

Multiple Choice Questions

Q.1 The Gay-Lussac's law is applicable

(a) only to solids. (b) only to liquids.
(c) to both liquids and gases. (d) only to gases.

Ans. (d) only to gases.

Q.2 A diagram given below shows three containers containing equal volumes of three different gases: O_2, N_2 and CO_2 at the same pressure and temperature.

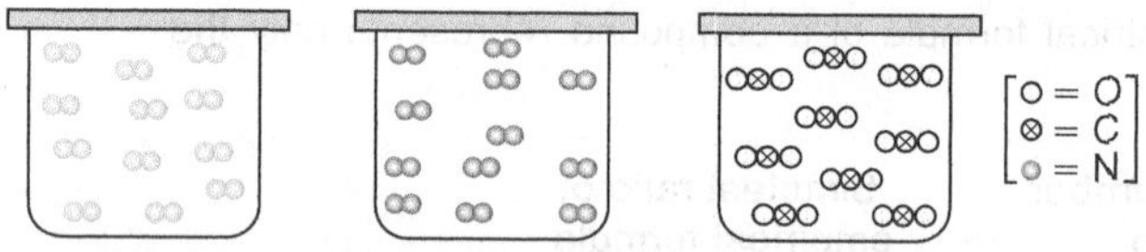

Which of the following statements is correct based on the given figure.

(a) The number of gas molecules in each container is the same.
(b) The mass of gas in each container is the same.
(c) The density of gases in each container is the same.
(d) The number of atoms in each container is the same.

Ans. (a) According to **Avogadro's law**, equal volumes of gases at the same temperature and pressure contain the same number of molecules, regardless of their molecular masses.

Q.3 3.0 dm^3 of sulphur dioxide is reacted with 2.0 dm^3 of oxygen.

$$2SO_2(g) + O_2(g) \longrightarrow 2SO_3(g)$$

Assuming the reaction goes to completion and that all gases are at room temperature and pressure, which volume of sulphur trioxide is formed?

(a) 2.0 dm^3 (b) 3.0 dm^3 (c) 4.0 dm^3 (d) 5.0 dm^3

Ans. (b) In gases, volume is directly proportional to the number of moles.

Moles of $SO_2 = \frac{3}{2} = 1.5$, Moles of $O_2 = \frac{2}{1} = 2.0$

Hence, SO_2 is the limiting reagent and

$$SO_2(g) + \frac{1}{2}O_2(g) \longrightarrow SO_3(g)$$

Mole ratio between SO_2 and SO_3 is 1 : 1 so 3 dm^3 of SO_2 yields 3 dm^3 of SO_3.

Q.4 40 cm^3 of methane (CH_4) is reacted with 60 cm^3 of oxygen.

The equation for the reaction is given below

$$CH_4 + 2O_2 \longrightarrow CO_2 + 2H_2O$$

All volumes are measured at room temperature.

What is the total volume of the gases remaining at the end of the reaction? **(ICSE 2025)**

(a) 60 cm^3
(b) 40 cm^3
(c) 45 cm^3
(d) 50 cm^3

Ans. (b) $\underset{1\text{ vol}}{CH_4} + \underset{2\text{ vol}}{2O_2} \longrightarrow \underset{1\text{ vol}}{CO_2} + 2H_2O$

According to the reaction,

1 vol of CH_4 reacts with 2 vol of O_2

$\therefore$ 40 cm^3 of CH_4 will react with $(40 \times 2) = 80\,cm^3$ of O_2.

But, we have 60 cm^3 of oxygen. Therefore, **oxygen is the limiting reagent**.

$\because$ 2 vol of O_2 reacts with 1 vol of CH_4.

$\therefore$ 60 cm^3 of O_2 will react with $\left(\frac{60}{2}\right) = 30\,cm^3$ of CH_4

Volume of methane remaining at the end of the reaction $= (40 - 30)\,cm^3 = 10\,cm^3$

Also, 2 vol of O_2 gives 1 vol of CO_2

So, 60 cm^3 of O_2 will give 30 cm^3 of CO_2.

Thus, the total volume of the gases at the end of the reaction $= (10 + 30)\,cm^3 = 40\,cm^3$

Q.5 An organic compound has a vapour density of 22. The molecular formula of the organic compound is [Atomic weight: C = 12, H = 1] **(ICSE 2025)**

(a) CH_4 (b) C_2H_4
(c) C_2H_6 (d) C_3H_8

Ans. (d) Molecular mass = 2 × Vapour density
= 2 × 22 = 44

Molecular mass of $CH_4 = 12 + (4 \times 1) = 16$

Molecular mass of $C_2H_4 = (2 \times 12) + (4 \times 1) = 28$

Molecular mass of $C_2H_6 = (2 \times 12) + (6 \times 1) = 30$

Molecular mass of $C_3H_8 = (3 \times 12) + (8 \times 1) = 44$

Thus, the molecular formula of the organic compound is C_3H_8.

Q.6 A gas cylinder of capacity of 20 dm^3 is filled with a gas *X*, the mass of which is 10 g. When the same cylinder is filled with hydrogen gas at the same temperature and pressure the mass of the hydrogen is 2 g, hence the relative molecular mass of the gas is

(a) 5 (b) 10 (c) 15 (d) 20

Ans. (b) Vapour density

$$= \frac{\text{Mass of gas}}{\text{Mass of equal volume of hydrogen gas}} = \frac{10\text{g}}{2\text{ g}} = 5$$

Relative molecular mass of the gas

$= 2 \times \text{vapour density} = 2 \times 5 = 10$

Thus, relative molecular mass of the gas is 10.

Q.7 Twice the vapour density gives **(ICSE Specimen 2021-22, Sem-I)**

(a) actual vapour density
(b) relative vapour density
(c) molecular mass
(d) molar volume

Ans. (c) The **molecular mass** of a gas or liquid is the twice of its vapour density.

Q.8 The vapour density of CH_3OH is ...... (At. wt. C = 12, H = 1, O = 16) **(ICSE 2023)**

(a) 32 (b) 18 (c) 16 (d) 34

Ans. (c) Molecular weight = 2 × vapour density

Molecular weight of $CH_3OH = 12 + (1 \times 3) + 16 + 1$
$= 12 + 3 + 17 = 32$

So, vapour density $= \frac{\text{Molecular weight}}{2} = \frac{32}{2} = 16$

Q.9 If relative molecular mass of butane (C_4H_{10}) is 58, then its vapour density will be **(ICSE 2021-22, Sem-I)**

(a) 5 (b) 29
(c) 32 (d) 16

Ans. (b) Vapour density $= \frac{\text{Relative molecular mass}}{2}$

$= \frac{58}{2} = 29$

Q.10 If the RMM of carbon dioxide is 44, then its vapour density is **(ICSE Specimen 2023)**

(a) 22 (b) 32 (c) 44 (d) 88

Ans. (a) Vapour density $= \frac{\text{RMM}}{2} = \frac{44}{2} = 22$

Q.11 Which of the following would occupy 22.4 L at S.T.P.?

(i) 32 g of oxygen gas
(ii) 2 moles of hydrogen gas
(iii) 6.022×10^{23} molecules of ammonia **(ICSE 2024)**

(a) (i) and (ii) (b) (i) and (iii)
(c) (ii) and (iii) (d) (i), (ii) and (iii)

[Atomic weights: O = 16, H = 1, N = 14]

Ans. (b) (i) and (iii)

Q.12 The table below shows data for different substances:

Substance	Molar mass (g)	Given mass (g)	Moles (n)
Oxygen (O_2)	32	64	?
Carbon dioxide (CO_2)	44	88	?
Water (H_2O)	18	36	?

Which of the following correctly fills the missing moles (*n*) values?

(a) 2, 2, 2 (b) 2, 1, 2 (c) 1, 2, 1 (d) 1, 1, 2

Ans. (a) 2, 2, 2.

Q.13 The ratio between the volumes occupied by 4.4 grams of carbon dioxide and 2 grams of hydrogen gas is **(ICSE Specimen 2025)**

(a) 2.2:1 (b) 1:2.2 (c) 1:10 (d) 10:1

Ans. (c) Volume occupied by 1 mole of gas = 22.4 litre at STP

No. of moles of $CO_2 = \frac{4.4}{44} = 0.1$

No. of moles of $H_2 = \frac{2}{2} = 1$

$$\therefore \frac{\text{Volume occupied by 4.4 g } CO_2}{\text{Volume occupied by 2 g } H_2} = \frac{0.1 \times 22.4}{1 \times 22.4} = 1:10$$

Q.14 The ratio between the number of molecules in 2 g of hydrogen and 32 g of oxygen is
[Atomic mass : H = 1, O = 16] **(ICSE 2016)**

(a) 1 : 2 (b) 1 : 0.01
(c) 1 : 1 (d) 0.01 : 1

Ans. (c) 1 : 1

	H_2	:	O_2
Given mass	2g		32 g
Molecular mass	$2 \times 1 = 2$		$2 \times 16 = 32$

[Given, mass are also in the ratio 2 g : 32 g]

$$\text{Mole} = \frac{\text{Mass of substance (g)}}{\text{Molecular mass of substance (g)}}$$

H_2 and O_2 both have equal number of moles (i.e. 1 : 1).

∴ Ratio of number of molecules is 1 : 1.

Q.15 Which mass of carbon contains the same number of atoms as 16.0 g of sulphur?

(a) 0.5 g (b) 6.0 g (c) 8.0 g (d) 12.0 g

Ans. (b) Moles $= \frac{\text{Mass (g)}}{\text{Molar mass}}$

Moles of sulphur $= \frac{16}{32} = 0.5$ mol

Since, the number of atoms is same, therefore, they have same number of moles.

Mass of carbon $= 0.5 \times 12 = 6.0$ g

Q.16 Which of the following would weigh the least?
(Atomic masses C = 12, O = 16, Na = 23) **(ICSE Specimen 2025)**
(a) 2 gram atoms of oxygen
(b) one mole of sodium
(c) 22.4 litres of carbon dioxide at STP
(d) 6.023×10^{22} atoms of carbon

Ans. (d) 6.023×10^{22} atoms of carbon.
$\Rightarrow$ 1 g atom of O = 1 mole of atom of O
2 g atoms of O = 2 moles of atom of O
2 g atoms of O = mass of 2 moles of O
2 g atoms of O = $2 \times 16 = 32$ g
$\Rightarrow$ Mass of one mole of sodium
= atomic mass of sodium in grams
= 23 g of sodium
$\Rightarrow$ 22.4 L of CO_2 at STP = 1 mole of CO_2
= molecular mass of CO_2 in g
= 44 g of CO_2
$\Rightarrow 6.023 \times 10^{22}$ atoms of carbon
= mass of 0.1 mole of C-atoms
= 1.2 g of C
[$\because$ 6.022×10^{23} atoms of carbon = 1 mole of carbon atoms
$\therefore$ 6.022×10^{22} atoms of carbon = 0.1 mole of carbon atoms]
Hence, among all the given options, 6.023×10^{22} atoms of carbon would weigh the least.

Q.17 The atomic masses of sulphur (S), oxygen (O) and helium (He) are approximately 32, 16 and 4 respectively. **(ICSE Specimen 2024)**
Which of the following statements regarding the number of atoms in 32 g of sulphur, 16 g of oxygen and 4 g of helium is correct?
P. 16 g of oxygen contains four times the number of atoms as 4 g of helium.
Q. 16 g of oxygen contains half the number of atoms as 32 g of sulphur.
(a) Only P (b) Only Q
(c) Both P and Q (d) Neither P nor Q

Ans. (d) No. of moles of O $= \frac{16}{16} = 1$
No. of moles of S $= \frac{32}{32} = 1$
No. of moles of He $= \frac{4}{4} = 1$
Since, all three have same number of moles, so they contain same number of atoms. Therefore, neither *P* nor *Q* statements are correct.

Q.18 The percentage of hydrogen present in NaOH is (Relative molecular mass of NaOH = 40) (At. wt. of H = 1). **(ICSE 2021-22, Sem-I)**
(a) 2.5 (b) 25 (c) 0.25 (d) 0.025

Ans. (a) Molecular mass of NaOH = 40
At. wt. of H = 1
% of element in a compound
$$= \frac{\text{Total wt. of element in one molecule}}{\text{Gram molecular wt. of compound}} \times 100$$
$$= \frac{1}{40} \times 100 = 2.5$$

Q.19 A sample of magnesium hydroxide, $Mg(OH)_2$, is made by adding an excess of aqueous sodium hydroxide to an aqueous solution containing 1.20 g magnesium sulphate, $MgSO_4$. The mass of magnesium hydroxide formed is 0.26 g.
What is the percentage yield of magnesium hydroxide?
(a) 10.5 % (b) 21.7 %
(c) 44.8 % (d) 61.9 %

Ans. (c) $2NaOH + MgSO_4 \longrightarrow Mg(OH)_2 + Na_2SO_4$
Moles of $MgSO_4 = \frac{1.2 \text{ g}}{120} = 0.01$ mol
$MgSO_4 : Mg(OH)_2 = 1:1$
Mass of $Mg(OH)_2 = 0.01 \times 58 = 0.58$ g
% yield $= \frac{0.26}{0.58} \times 100 = 44.8$ %

Q.20 A compound with empirical formula XY_2, has the vapour density equal to its empirical formula weight, its molecular formula is **(ICSE Specimen 2021-22, Sem-I)**
(a) X_2Y_4 (b) X_2Y_2 (c) XY (d) X_4Y_2

Ans. (a) As the molecular weight is twice of its vapour density, hence, it will be twice of its empirical formula weight.
$\therefore$ Molecular formula = $XY_2 \times 2 = X_2Y_4$

Q.21 If the empirical formula of a compound is CH and its vapour density is 13, then its molecular formula will be (At. wt. C = 12, H = 1) **(ICSE 2021-22, Sem-I)**
(a) CH (b) C_2H_2 (c) C_4H_4 (d) C_3H_3

Ans. (b) $n = \frac{2 \times \text{Vapour density}}{\text{Empirical formula wt.}} = \frac{2 \times 13}{13} = 2$
Molecular formula = $n \times$ Empirical formula
$= 2 \times CH = C_2H_2$

Q.22 The molecular formula of an organic compound is $C_6H_{12}O_6$ and the empirical formula is CH_2O, the value of *n* is **(ICSE Specimen 2021-22, Sem-I)**
(a) 2 (b) 6 (c) 1 (d) 12

Ans. (b) Empirical formula $\times\, n$ = Molecular formula
$(CH_2O) \times n = C_6H_{12}O_6$
$(CH_2O)_n = (CH_2O)_6$
$\therefore \quad n = 6$

Q.23 The empirical formula of the compound is CH_2O, the possible molecular formula can be **(ICSE Specimen 2021-22, Sem-I)**

(a) $C_3H_6O_3$ (b) C_2H_4O (c) $C_4H_3O_2$ (d) $C_4H_6O_2$

Ans. (a) In $C_3H_6O_3$, the empirical formula will be CH_2O. C_2H_4O and $C_4H_3O_2$ do not have CH_2O as the empirical formula, and the empirical formula of $C_4H_6O_2$ is C_2H_3O.

Q.24 If the empirical mass of the formula PQ_2 is 10 and the relative molecular mass is 30, then the molecular formula will be **(ICSE 2021-22, Sem-I)**

(a) PQ_2 (b) P_3Q_2 (c) P_6Q_3 (d) P_3Q_6

Ans. (d) $n = \frac{\text{Molecular mass}}{\text{Empirical formula mass}} = \frac{30}{10} = 3$

Molecular formula = $n \times$ Empirical formula
$= 3 \times (PQ_2) = P_3Q_6$

Q.25 The simplest ratio of the atoms of carbon and hydrogen is 1:1. Identify the possible molecular formula. **(ICSE Specimen 2021-22, Sem-I)**

(a) C_6H_6 (b) C_2H_4 (c) C_6H_2 (d) C_3H_4

Ans. (a) The simple ratio of atoms of carbon and hydrogen in C_6H_6 is 1:1.

Q.26 10 g of magnesium carbonate reacts completely with excess dilute hydrochloric acid. What volume of carbon dioxide is formed at room temperature and pressure? [Mg = 24, C = 12, O = 16]
The equation for the reaction is

$$MgCO_3 + 2HCl \longrightarrow MgCl_2 + H_2O + CO_2$$

(Competency Based Que.)

(a) 2.8 dm^3 (b) 2.6 dm^3 (c) 2.2 dm^3 (d) 2.4 dm^3

Ans. (b) 2.6 dm^3

Moles of $MgCO_3 = \frac{10}{84} = 0.119$ mol

1 mole of $MgCO_3$ gives 1 mole of CO_2

$\therefore$ 0.119 mol $MgCO_3$ gives 0.119 mol CO_2

At STP, 1 mole of CO_2 occupies 22.4 dm^3

Volume of 0.119 mol $CO_2 = 0.119 \times 22.4 \approx 2.6\ dm^3$

TYPE - 2   01 Mark

Assertion-Reason Questions

Directions (Q. Nos. 1-5) In the following questions, a statement of Assertion (A) is followed by a statement of Reason (R). Choose the answer based on the codes given below.

(a) Both (A) and (R) are true and (R) is the correct explanation of (A).
(b) Both (A) and (R) are true but (R) is not the correct explanation of (A).
(c) (A) is true but (R) is false.
(d) (A) is false but (R) is true.

Q.1 Assertion (A) The limiting reagent in a reaction determines the maximum amount of product formed.

Reason (R) The excess reagent does not affect the product formation.

Ans. (a) The limiting reagent determines the amount of product formed, while excess reagents remain unused once the limiting reagent is consumed.
Thus, both (A) and (R) are true and (R) is the correct explanation of (A).

Q.2 Assertion (A) The atomic mass of oxygen is 16 amu, therefore, its gram atomic mass is 16g.

Reason (R) The atomic mass of an element expressed in grams is called gram atomic mass.

Ans. (a) The atomic mass of an element expressed in grams is called as gram atomic mass. Thus, the atomic mass of oxygen in 16 a.m.u and hence its gram atomic mass is 16 g.
Thus, both (A) and (R) are true and (R) is the correct explanation of (A).

Q.3 Assertion (A) The molar mass of a compound is the sum of the atomic masses of all its elements.

Reason (R) The atomic mass of each element is found on the periodic table in atomic mass units (amu).

Ans. (b) The molar mass of a compound is the sum of the atomic masses of all its elements. e.g.,

Molar mass of H_2O
$= 2$(atomic mass of H) + (atomic mass of O)
$= 2(1) + 16$
$= 2 + 16$
$= 18$ g

Thus, both (A) and (R) are true but (R) is not the correct explanation of (A).

Q.4 Assertion (A) One mole of any gas at STP occupies 22.4 L.

Reason (R) The volume occupied by one mole of a gas depends on its molar mass.

Ans. (c) The volume of one mole of any ideal gas at STP is always 22.4 L, regardless of its molar mass. Thus, (A) is true but (R) is false.

Q.5 Assertion (A) The empirical formula of a compound represents the actual number of atoms in a molecules.

Reason (R) It shows the simplest whole number ratio of elements in a compound.

Ans. (d) The molecular formula represents the actual number of atoms, while the empirical formula shows only the simplest ratio. Thus, (A) is false but (R) is true.

TYPE - 3 (01 Mark)

Fill in the Blanks

Q.1 Law of .... (combining/same) volumes of gas, states that when gases react together to form other gases, all volumes are in whole number ratio to one another, when measured at the same temperature and pressure.

Ans. combining

Q.2 The relative atomic mass of nitrogen is 14, and that of hydrogen is 1. This means that .... of nitrogen has the same mass as 7 molecules of hydrogen (an atom/a molecule) **(Competency Based Que.)**

Ans. an atom

Q.3 1 mole = ... (22.4 / 11.2) L at STP, if substance is a gas.

Ans. 22.4

Q.4 1 mole of He contains ......(4/2) g of helium.

Ans. 4

Q.5 The number of moles in 18 g of H_2O is .... (1 mole/3 moles).

Ans. 1 mole

Q.6 The number of moles in 11 g of nitrogen gas is .... (0.39/0.49)

Ans. 0.39

Q.7 The number of hydrogen atom present in 1 mole of sulphuric acid and 1 mole of sulphurous acid are (X) and (Y), respectively. Relationship between X and Y is .... ($X = Y$/ cannot compare X and Y). **(Competency Based Que.)**

Ans. $X = Y$

Q.8 A formula which shows the simplest whole number ratio is .... (empirical formula /molecular formula).

Ans. empirical formula

Q.9 Complete the following, $n = \frac{\text{Molecular mass}}{\_\_\_\_}$ (empirical formula mass/molar mass).

Ans. empirical formula mass

Q.10 CH_2O is .... (Empirical formula/a molecular formula) for $C_6H_{12}O_6$.

Ans. empirical formula

TYPE - 4 (01 Mark)

Correct the Incorrect Statement

Q.1 Gay-Lussac's law is valid for solid, liquids and gases.

Ans. Gay-Lussac's law is valid **only for gases**. The volumes of solids and liquids are considered to be zero.

Q.2 The reactant which is completely used up in a reaction is known as excess reagent.

Ans. The reactant which is completely used up in a reaction is known as **limiting reagent**.

Q.3 The number of atoms in a molecule of an element is called its molarity.

Ans. The number of atoms in a molecule of an element is called its **atomicity**.

Q.4 One mole of atom contains 6.022×10^{-23} atoms, having mass equal to its gram atomic mass.

Ans. One mole of atoms contains $\mathbf{6.022 \times 10^{23}}$ atoms, having mass equal to its gram atomic mass.

Q.5 Empirical formula mass of a compound denotes the actual number of atoms of different elements present in one molecule of the compound.

Ans. **Molecular formula** of a compound denotes the actual number of atoms of different elements present in one molecule of the compound.

TYPE - 5 ($01 \times 05 = 05$ Marks)

Matching Type Questions

Q.1 Match the following columns.

Column I (Law/Property)	Column II (Defining character)
A. Gay-Lussac's law	1. Hydrogen
B. Avogadro's law	2. Combining volumes of gases
C. Molar volume	3. Volume molecule relationship
D. Empirical formula	4. 22.4 dm^3
E. Diatomic	5. Simplest ratio

Ans. A → 2, B → 3, C → 4, D → 5, E → 1

Q.2 Match the following columns.

Column I (Molecular formula)	Column II (Empirical formula)
A. C_6H_6	1. BH_2
B. $C_{10}H_{20}Fe_2$	2. CH
C. B_6H_{12}	3. NO_2
D. N_2O_4	4. BH_3
E. B_2H_6	5. $C_5H_{10}Fe$

Ans. A → 2, B → 5, C → 1, D → 3, E → 4

TYPE - 6 — 01 Mark

Identify the Following

Q.1 Name the law which states that equal volumes of all gases, at the same temperature and pressure, have the same number of molecules.

Ans. Avogadro's law

Q.2 What is the term used to define number of atoms present in one molecule of an element?

Ans. Atomicity

Q.3 What is the ratio of mass of 1 atom of the element to the 1/12th the mass of an atom of carbon-12 called?

Ans. Relative atomic mass

Q.4 Name the following. "The ratio of the mass of a certain volume of gas to the mass of an equal volume of hydrogen under the same conditions of temperature and pressure". **(ICSE 2023, 2014)**

Ans. Vapour density

Q.5 State the term used for the "amount of substance which contains the same number of units as the number of atoms in carbon-12". **(ICSE 2024)**

Ans. Mole

Q.6 28 g of nitrogen and 44 g of carbon dioxide at the same conditions of temperature and pressure occupy the same amount of space. What term describes such space occupied by any gas? **(Competency Based Que.)**

Ans. Molar volume

Q.7 What is the formula which represents the simplest ratio between the atoms of elements present in a compound? **(ICSE 2024, 2019)**

Ans. Empirical formula

Q.8 The equation for the burning of octane is

$$2C_8H_{18} + 25O_2 \longrightarrow 16CO_2 + 18H_2O$$

What is the empirical formula of octane?

Ans. C_4H_9

TYPE - 7 — 02 Marks

Short Answer Type I Questions

Q.1 Give reason for the following statements.

(i) The atomic weight of the elements is fractional also.

(ii) The number of atoms in certain volume of hydrogen is twice the number of atoms in same volume of helium at same temperature and pressure.

Ans. (i) The atomic weight of an element is the average relative weight of all naturally occurring isotopes of the given element. Therefore, atomic weight of elements is fractional also. **(1)**

(ii) Same volume of gas occupies same number of molecules. But the atomicity of hydrogen molecule is two, while helium is monoatomic molecule.

Hence, number of atoms of hydrogen is twice the number of atoms of helium. **(1)**

Q.2 Oxygen oxidises ethyne to carbon dioxide and water as shown by the equation.

$$2C_2H_2 + 5O_2 \longrightarrow 4CO_2 + 2H_2O$$

What volume of ethyne gas at STP is required to produce 8.4 dm^3 of carbon dioxide at STP?
[H = 1, C = 12, O = 16] **(ICSE 2014)**

Ans. The reaction involved is given by

$$\underset{2\text{ vol}}{2C_2H_2} + \underset{5\text{ vol}}{5O_2} \longrightarrow \underset{4\text{ vol}}{4CO_2} + \underset{2\text{ vol}}{2H_2O}$$

By Gay-Lussac's law,

If 4 volumes of CO_2 is produced by 2 volumes of C_2H_2 at STP.

∴ 8.4 dm^3 of CO_2 is produced by

$$\frac{2}{4} \times 8.4 = 4.2 \text{ dm}^3 \text{ of ethyne gas.}$$

Thus, the required volume of ethyne gas is 4.2 dm^3. **(2)**

Q.3 67.2 L of hydrogen combines with 44.8 L of nitrogen to form ammonia under specific conditions as

$$N_2(g) + 3H_2(g) \longrightarrow 2NH_3(g)$$

Calculate the volume of ammonia produced. What is the other substance, if any, that remains in the resultant mixture?

Ans. The given equation is

$$\underset{1\text{ vol}}{N_2(g)} + \underset{3\text{ vol}}{3H_2(g)} \longrightarrow \underset{2\text{ vol}}{2NH_3(g)}$$

3 volumes of hydrogen produces 2 volumes of ammonia.

67.2 L of hydrogen produces

$$= \frac{2}{3} \times 67.2 = 44.8 \text{ L of ammonia}$$

3 volumes of hydrogen reacts with 1 volume of nitrogen.

67.2 L of hydrogen reacts with $= \frac{1}{3} \times 67.2 = 22.4$ L

$\therefore$ Nitrogen left = 44.8 – 22.4 = 22.4 L **(2)**

Q.4 What volume of oxygen is required to burn completely a mixture of 22.4 dm³ of methane and 11.2 dm³ of hydrogen into carbon dioxide and steam? Equations of the reactions are given below (Assume that all volumes are measured at STP)

$$CH_4 + 2O_2 \longrightarrow CO_2 + 2H_2O$$

$$2H_2 + O_2 \longrightarrow 2H_2O$$

Ans. $\underset{\substack{1\text{ vol}\\1\times22.4}}{CH_4} + \underset{\substack{2\text{ vol}\\2\times22.4}}{2O_2} \longrightarrow \underset{1\text{ vol}}{CO_2} + \underset{2\text{ vol}}{2H_2O}$

$\therefore$ Volume of oxygen used $= 2 \times 22.4 = 44.8\,dm^3$

$\underset{2\times5.6=11.2}{2H_2} + \underset{5.6}{O_2} \longrightarrow 2H_2O$

$\therefore$ Volume of oxygen used $= 5.6\,dm^3$

Total volume of oxygen used $= 44.8 + 5.6$

$= 50.4\,dm^3$ **(2)**

Q.5 What volume of oxygen is required to burn completely 90 dm³ of butane, under similar condition of temperature and pressure?

$$2C_4H_{10} + 13O_2 \longrightarrow 8CO_2 + 10H_2O$$

Ans. The reaction is

$$2C_4H_{10} + 13O_2 \longrightarrow 8CO_2 + 10H_2O$$

2 volumes of butane is completely burnt by 13 volumes of O_2.

90 volumes of butane is completely burnt by $\frac{13}{2} \times 90$ volumes of O_2.

$\therefore$ Volume of O_2 required $= 13 \times \frac{90}{2} = 585\,dm^3$ **(2)**

Q.6 If 112 cm³ of hydrogen sulphide is mixed with 120 cm³ of chlorine at STP, what mass of sulphur is formed?

$$H_2S + Cl_2 \longrightarrow 2HCl + S$$

Ans. $\underset{1\text{ vol}}{H_2S} + \underset{1\text{ vol}}{Cl_2} \longrightarrow \underset{2\text{ vol}}{2HCl} + S$

1 volume of H_2S reacts with 1 volume of Cl_2.

$\therefore$ 112 cm³ of H_2S is mixed with 120 cm³ of Cl_2 at STP. Only 112 cm³ of Cl_2 will react.

$\therefore$ **H_2S is the limiting reagent.**

1 mole of any gas at STP = 22400 cm³

1 mole of H_2S gives 1 atom of S

22400 cm³ H_2S = 32 g S

112 cm³ $H_2S = \frac{32 \times 112}{22400} = 0.16$ g of S **(2)**

Q.7 560 mL of carbon monoxide is mixed with 500 mL of oxygen and ignited. The chemical equation for the reaction is as follows

$$2CO + O_2 \longrightarrow 2CO_2$$

Calculate the volume of oxygen used and carbon dioxide formed in the above reaction.

Ans. Given, $\underset{2\text{ vol}}{2CO} + \underset{1\text{ vol}}{O_2} \longrightarrow \underset{2\text{ vol}}{2CO_2}$

2 volumes of CO consumes O_2 = 1 vol

$\therefore$ 560 mL of CO consumes $O_2 = \frac{1}{2} \times 560 = 280$ mL

But, we have 500 mL O_2. Thus, **CO is the limiting reagent.**

2 volumes of CO gives CO_2 = 2 vol

$\therefore$ 560 mL of CO give $CO_2 = \frac{2}{2} \times 560 = 560$ mL **(2)**

Q.8 Calcium carbide is used for the artificial ripening of fruits. Actually the fruit ripens because of the heat evolved, while calcium carbide reacts with moisture.

During this reaction calcium hydroxide and acetylene gas is formed. If 200 cm³ of acetylene is formed from a certain mass of calcium carbide, find the volume of oxygen required and carbon dioxide formed during the complete combustion.

The combustion reaction can be represented as below.

$$2C_2H_2(g) + 5O_2(g) \longrightarrow 4CO_2(g) + 2H_2O(g)$$

Ans. $\underset{2\text{ vol}}{2C_2H_2(g)} + \underset{5\text{ vol}}{5O_2(g)} \longrightarrow \underset{4\text{ vol}}{4CO_2(g)} + 2H_2O(g)$

By Gay-Lussac's law,

2 volumes of acetylene requires 5 volumes of oxygen

200 cm³ of acetylene requires $= \frac{5}{2} \times 200$

= 500 cm³ of oxygen

2 volumes of acetylene gives 4 volumes of CO_2

200 cm³ of acetylene gives $= \frac{4}{2} \times 200 = 400$ cm³ of CO_2 **(2)**

Q.9 The reaction $4N_2O + CH_4 \longrightarrow CO_2 + 2H_2O + 4N_2$ takes place in the gaseous state. If all volumes are measured at the same temperature and pressure, calculate the volume of dinitrogen oxide (N_2O) required to give 150 cm³ of steam.

[N = 14, O = 16, C = 12, H = 1]

Ans. $\underset{4\text{ vol}}{4N_2O} + CH_4 \longrightarrow CO_2 + \underset{2\text{ vol}}{2H_2O} + 4N_2$

2 volumes of H_2O are produced by 4 volumes of N_2O

1 volume of H_2O are produced by $= \frac{4}{2} = 2$ volumes of N_2O

$\therefore$ 150 cm³ of H_2O is produced by 2×150

= 300 cm³ of N_2O **(2)**

Q.10 A gas cylinder can hold 150 g of hydrogen under certain conditions of temperature and pressure. If an identical cylinder with the same capacity can hold 450 g of gas 'G' under the same conditions of temperature and pressure, find: **(ICSE 2025)**

(i) the vapour density of the gas '*G*'

(ii) the molecular weight of gas '*G*'

Ans. (i) Vapour density of gas '*G*'

$$= \frac{\text{Mass of gas '}G\text{' under similar conditions}}{\text{Mass of hydrogen gas under similar conditions}}$$

Vapour density of gas '*G*' $= \frac{450}{150} = 3$ **(1)**

(ii) Molecular weight of gas '*G*' $= 2 \times$ Vapour density $= 2 \times 3 = 6$ **(1)**

Q.11 The vapour density of a gas is 8. What would be the volume occupied by 24.0 g of the gas at STP?

Ans. Vapour density of gas = 8

Molecular weight of gas = 2 × Vapour density = 2 × 8 = 16 g

Volume of 16 g of gas = 22.4 L

Volume of 24 g of gas $= \frac{22.4}{16} \times 24 = 33.6$ L **(2)**

Q.12 A gas cylinder contains 12×10^{24} molecules of oxygen gas.

If Avogadro's number is 6×10^{23}, calculate

(i) the mass of oxygen present in the cylinder.

(ii) the volume of oxygen at STP present in the cylinder. [Atomic mass of O = 16] **(ICSE 2016)**

Ans. Number of molecules of oxygen gas $= 12 \times 10^{24}$

Avogadro's number $= 6 \times 10^{23}$

(i) $\frac{\text{Mass of oxygen present}}{\text{Molecular mass of } O_2 \text{ gas } (= 32 \text{ g})} = \frac{\text{Number of molecules of } O_2 \text{ gas}}{\text{Avogadro's number}}$

Mass of oxygen $= \frac{12 \times 10^{24} \times 32}{6 \times 10^{23}} = 640$ g **(1)**

(ii) Number of moles of oxygen $= \frac{\text{Given weight}}{\text{Molecular weight}} = \frac{640}{32} = 20$ mol

Volume occupied by 1 mole of oxygen = 22.4 L

Volume occupied by 20 moles of oxygen = 448 L **(1)**

Q.13 Calculate the mass of

(i) 10^{22} atoms of sulphur.

(ii) 0.1 mole of carbon dioxide.

[Atomic mass : S = 32, C = 12 and O = 16, Avogadro's number $= 6 \times 10^{23}$].

Ans. (i) 6×10^{23} atoms of sulphur = 32 g

∴ Mass of 10^{22} atoms of sulphur $= \frac{32}{6 \times 10^{23}} \times 10^{22} = 0.533$ g **(1)**

(ii) Molar mass of $CO_2 = 12 + (2 \times 16) = 44$ g

1 mole of CO_2 weighs = 44 g

0.1 mole of CO_2 weighs $= \frac{44}{1} \times 0.1 = 4.4$ g **(1)**

Q.14 A gas cylinder contains 24×10^{24} molecules of nitrogen gas. If Avogadro's number is 6×10^{23} and the relative atomic mass of nitrogen is 14, calculate

(i) mass of nitrogen gas in the cylinder.

(ii) volume of nitrogen gas at STP in dm^3.

Ans. (i) 6×10^{23} molecules of nitrogen gas weigh = 2 × 14 = 28 g

∴ 24×10^{24} molecules of nitrogen gas weigh

$$= \frac{2 \times 14 \times 24 \times 10^{24}}{6 \times 10^{23}} = 28 \times 40 = 1120 \text{ g}$$ **(1)**

(ii) Volume of nitrogen gas at STP

∵ 6×10^{23} molecules of N_2 occupy 22.4 L at STP

∴ 24×10^{24} molecules of N_2 occupy

$$= \frac{22.4 \times 24 \times 10^{24}}{6 \times 10^{23}}$$

$= 22.4 \times 40 = 896\ dm^3$ or 896 L **(1)**

Q.15 Calculate the volume of 320 g of SO_2 at STP. [Atomic mass of S = 32 and O = 16].

Ans. Molecular mass of $SO_2 = 32 + 2 \times 16 = 64$ g

Since, 64 g of SO_2 occupies 22.4 L at STP

∴ 320 g of SO_2 occupies $= \frac{22.4}{64} \times 320 = 112$ L **(2)**

Q.16 The mass of 5.6 dm^3 of a certain gas at STP is 12.0 g. Calculate the relative molecular mass of the gas.

Ans. Volume of the gas at STP = 5.6 dm^3 = 5.6 L

Mass of the gas = 12 g

5.6 dm^3 of gas weighs = 12 g

22.4 dm^3 of gas weighs $= \frac{12}{5.6} \times 22.4 = 48$ g

Relative molecular mass of the gas = 48 g **(2)**

Q.17 A certain gas *X* occupies a volume of 100 cm^3 at STP and weighs 0.5 g. Find its relative molecular mass.

Ans. 100 cm^3 of the gas weighs 0.5 g

∴ 22400 cc of gas weighs $= \frac{0.5 \times 22400}{100} = 112$ g **(2)**

Q.18 Calculate

(i) The number of moles in 22 grams of carbon dioxide. **(ICSE Specimen 2024)**

(ii) Gas *M* occupies a volume of 1000 c.c and contains *X* molecules. How many molecules will be present in gas N occupying a volume of 250 c.c? **(Competency Based Que.)**

Ans. (i) Number of moles $= \frac{\text{Given mass}}{\text{Molar mass}} = \frac{22}{44} = 0.5$ moles **(1)**

(ii) $\frac{X}{4}$

Ratio of volumes = Ratio of molecules

$\frac{1000}{250} = \frac{X}{Y}$ (let *Y* be no. of moles of gas *N*)

$Y = \frac{X(250)}{1000} = \frac{X}{4}$ **(1)**

Q.19 Calculate the percentage of nitrogen and oxygen in ammonium nitrate. Relative molecular mass of ammonium nitrate is 80.
[H = 1, N = 14 and O = 16]

Ans. Relative molecular weight of ammonium nitrate $(NH_4NO_3) = 14 + 1 \times 4 + 14 + 3 \times 16 = 80$

Total nitrogen in ammonium nitrate = 2

Molecular weight of two nitrogen $= 2 \times 14 = 28$

% of nitrogen $= \frac{28}{80} \times 100 = 35\%$ **(1)**

Total oxygen in ammonium nitrate = 3

Molecular weight of 3 oxygen $= 16 \times 3 = 48$

% of oxygen $= \frac{48}{80} \times 100 = 60\%$ **(1)**

Q.20 Calculate the percentage of platinum in ammonium chloroplatinate $(NH_4)_2PtCl_6$.
(Give your answer correct to the nearest whole number). (Pt = 195, N = 14, H = 1, Cl = 35.5)

Ans. Relative molecular weight of ammonium chloroplatinate $(NH_4)_2PtCl_6 = 14 \times 2 + 4 \times 1 \times 2 + 195 + 6 \times 35.5 = 444$

Platinum in ammonium chloroplatinate = 1

Molecular weight of 1 Pt $= 1 \times 195 = 195$

% of platinum $= \frac{195}{444} \times 100 = 43.92 \approx 44\%$ **(2)**

Q.21 Find the total percentage of magnesium in magnesium nitrate crystals, $Mg(NO_3)_2 \cdot 6H_2O$.
[Mg = 24, N = 14, O = 16 and H = 1]

Ans. Molecular mass of $Mg(NO_3)_2 \cdot 6H_2O$

$= 24 + (14 + 48) \times 2 + 6 \times 18 = 256$ g **(1)**

Percentage of Mg $= \frac{24}{256} \times 100 = 9.375\%$ **(1)**

Q.22 The percentage composition of a gas is nitrogen-82.38%, hydrogen-17.64%. Find the empirical formula of the gas. [N = 14, H = 1] **(ICSE 2018)**

Ans. Calculation of empirical formula

Element	% by mass	Atomic mass	Relative no. of atoms	Simplest ratio
N	82.38	14	$\frac{82.35}{14} = 5.88$	$\frac{5.88}{5.88} = 1$
H	17.64	1	$\frac{17.64}{1} = 17.64$	$\frac{17.64}{5.88} = 3$ **(1)**

Empirical formula of the gas $= NH_3$ **(1)**

Q.23 Find the empirical formula and molecular formula of an organic compound from the data given below.
C = 75.92%, H = 6.32%, N = 17.76% its vapour density is 39.5. (At.wt. C = 12, H = 1, N = 14)
(ICSE Specimen 2023)

Ans.

Element	% weight	Atomic weight	Relative number of moles	Simple ratio of atoms
C	75.92%	12	$75.92 \div 12 = 6.32$	$6.32 \div 1.26 = 5$
H	6.32%	1	$6.32 \div 1 = 6.32$	$6.32 \div 1.26 = 5$
N	17.76%	14	$17.76 \div 14 = 1.26$	$1.26 \div 1.26 = 1$

Empirical formula of organic compound $= C_5H_5N$

Empirical formula weight of organic compound $= 5 \times 12 + 1 \times 5 + 14 = 79$

Molecular weight of organic compound

$= 2 \times$ vapour density

$= 2 \times 39.5 = 79$ **(1)**

Thus, here empirical formula weight = Molecular formula weight.

So, molecular formula and empirical formula of the compound is C_5H_5N. **(1)**

Q.24 Calculate.

(i) A gas cylinder is filled with hydrogen and it holds 5g of gas. The same cylinder holds 85g of gas *X* under same temperature and pressure. Calculate the vapour density of gas *X*.

(ii) Give the empirical formula of CH_3COOH.

(ICSE Specimen 2023)

Ans. (i) Vapour density

$= \frac{\text{Mass of given volume of gas}}{\text{Mass of same volume of gas at same } T \text{ and } p}$

Vapour density of $X = \frac{85 \text{ g}}{5 \text{ g}} = 17$ **(1)**

(ii) Empirical formula of CH_3COOH is CH_2O.

∵ Simple ratio of whole number of atoms $(C_2:H_4:O_2) = (1:2:1)$ **(1)**

Q.25 Given that the relative molecular mass of copper oxide is 80, what volume of ammonia (measured at STP) is required to completely reduce 120 g of copper oxide?

The equation for the reaction is

$$3CuO + 2NH_3 \longrightarrow 3Cu + 3H_2O + N_2$$

[Volume occupied by 1 mole of gas at STP is 22.4 L]

Ans. $3CuO + 2NH_3 \longrightarrow 3Cu + 3H_2O + N_2$

3 mol 2 mol

3×80 g 2×22.4 L

= 240 g = 44.8 L

For 240 g of CuO, volume of NH_3 consumed = 44.8 L

∴ For 120 g of CuO, volume of NH_3 consumed

$$= \frac{44.8}{240} \times 120 = 22.4 \text{ L}$$ **(2)**

Q.26 Calculate the volume of oxygen required for the complete combustion of 8.8 g of propane (C_3H_8). [Atomic mass of C = 12, O = 16, H = 1, Molar volume = 22.4 dm^3 at STP].

Ans. Balanced chemical equation is

$$C_3H_8 + 5O_2 \longrightarrow 3CO_2 + 4H_2O$$

Molar mass of propane = $3 \times 12 + 8 \times 1 = 44$

44 g of propane require 5×22.4 L of oxygen at STP

8.8 g of propane require = $\frac{5 \times 22.4}{44} \times 8.8 = 22.4$ L **(2)**

Q.27 Commercial sodium hydroxide weighing 30 g has some sodium chloride ink. The mixture on dissolving in water and subsequent treatment with excess silver nitrate solution formed a precipitate weighing 14.3 g. What is the percentage of sodium chloride in the commercial sample of sodium hydroxide? The equation for the reaction is

$$NaCl + AgNO_3 \longrightarrow AgCl + NaNO_3$$

[Relative molecular mass of NaCl = 58 and AgCl = 143]

Ans. Equation is:

$$\underset{23+35=58}{NaCl} + AgNO_3 \longrightarrow \underset{108+35=143}{AgCl} + NaNO_3$$

∵ 143 g of AgCl is obtained from 58 g of NaCl

∴ 14.3 g of AgCl is obtained from $\frac{58 \times 14.3}{143}$

= 5.8 g of NaCl

% of NaCl in the given sample = $\frac{5.8}{30} \times 100 = 19.33\%$ **(2)**

Q.28 The reaction of potassium permanganate (VII) with acidified iron (II) sulphate is given below.

$$2KMnO_4 + 10FeSO_4 + 8H_2SO_4 \longrightarrow K_2SO_4 + 2MnSO_4 + 5Fe_2(SO_4)_3 + 8H_2O$$

If 15.8 g of potassium permanganate (VII) was used in the reaction, calculate the mass of iron (II) sulphate used in the above reaction.

[K = 39, Mn = 55, Fe = 56, S = 32, O = 16]

Ans. $2KMnO_4 + 10FeSO_4 + 8H_2SO_4 \longrightarrow K_2SO_4 + 2MnSO_4 + 5Fe_2(SO_4)_3 + 8H_2O$

Molecular mass of 2 moles of $KMnO_4$

$= 2[39 + 55 + 16 \times 4] = 316$ g

Molecular mass of $10FeSO_4 = 10[56 + 32 + 64]$

= 1520 g

∵ 316 g of $KMnO_4$ reacts with 1520 g of $FeSO_4$

∴ 1 g of $KMnO_4$ reacts with $\frac{1520}{316}$ g of $FeSO_4$

∴ 15.8 g of $KMnO_4$ reacts with $\frac{1520}{316} \times 15.8$

= 76 g of $FeSO_4$ **(2)**

TYPE - 8

03 Marks

Short Answer Type II Questions

Q.1 (i) State Gay-Lussac's law of combining volumes.

(ii) The empirical formula of an organic compound is $CHCl_2$. If its relative molecular mass is 168, what is its molecular formula?

[At. wt. C = 12, H = 1, Cl = 35.5] **(ICSE 2023)**

Ans. (i) According to **Gay-Lussac's law**, when gases react they do so in volumes which bear a simple ratio to one another and to the volumes of gaseous product, provided that all the volumes are measured at the same temperature and pressure. **(1)**

(ii) Empirical formula mass of $CHCl_2$

$= 12 + 1 + 35.5 \times 2 = 84$

$$n = \frac{\text{Relative molecular mass}}{\text{Empirical formula mass}} = \frac{168}{84} = 2$$

Molecular formula = (Empirical formula)$_n$

$= (CHCl_2)_2 = C_2H_2Cl_4$ **(2)**

Q.2 Solve the following numerical problem.

Ethane burns in oxygen according to the chemical equation.

$$2C_2H_6 + 7O_2 \longrightarrow 4CO_2 + 6H_2O$$

If 80 mL of ethane is burnt in 300 mL of oxygen, find the composition of the resultant gaseous mixture when measured at room temperature. **[ICSE 2023]**

Ans. $2C_2H_6 + 7O_2 \longrightarrow 4CO_2 + 6H_2O$

According to equation, 2 moles of ethane react with 7 moles of O_2 to produce 4 moles of CO_2. Also, 2 mL of ethane reacts with 7 mL of O_2 to produce 4 mL CO_2 then, 80 mL of ethane reacts with 280 mL O_2 to give 160 mL of CO_2.

So, here **ethane (C_2H_6) is the limiting reagent** and volume O_2 left = 300 − 280 = 20 mL

So, the composition of resultant gaseous mixture when measured at room temperature will be 20 mL of O_2 and 160 mL of carbon dioxide. **(3)**

Q.3 The volumes of gases A, B, C and D are in the ratio, 1: 2 : 2 : 4 under the same conditions of temperature and pressure.

(i) Which sample of gas contains the maximum number of molecules?

(ii) If the temperature and the pressure of gas *A* are kept constant, then what will happen to the volume of *A*, when the number of molecules is doubled?

(iii) If this ratio of gas volumes refers to the reactants and products of a reaction, which gas law is being observed?

Ans. (i) Sample of **gas *D*** contains the maximum number of molecules.

(ii) When the number of molecules is doubled, then the volume of the gas *A* will get **doubled**.

(iii) Gay-Lussac's law of combining volumes. **(1 × 3 = 3)**

Q.4 (i) A gas cylinder of capacity 40 dm^3 is filled with gas *X* the mass of which is 20 g. When the same cylinder is filled with hydrogen gas at the same temperature and pressure the mass of hydrogen is 2 g. Find the relative molecular mass of the gas. **(ICSE Specimen 2024)**

(ii) Give the atomicity of the following gases.

(a) Ozone gas (b) Nitrogen gas

Ans. (i) Vapour density of gas

$$= \frac{\text{Mass of gas}}{\text{Mass of an equal volume of hydrogen}}$$

$$= \frac{20}{2} = 10$$

$\therefore$ Relative molecular mass = 2 × Vapour density

$$= 2 \times 10 = 20$$

Hence, relative molecular mass of gas *X* is 20 g. **(2)**

(ii) Atomicity of the following gases are:

(a) O_3 (Ozone gas) = 3 (Triatomic)

(b) N_2 (Nitrogen gas) = 2 (Diatomic) **(1)**

Q.5 The equation $4NH_3 + 5O_2 \longrightarrow 4NO + 6H_2O$, represents the catalytic oxidation of ammonia. If 100 cm^3 of ammonia is used, calculate the volume of oxygen required to oxidise the ammonia completely. **(ICSE 2016)**

Ans. The given equation is

$$\underset{4\text{ vol}}{4NH_3} + \underset{5\text{ vol}}{5O_2} \longrightarrow 4NO + 6H_2O$$

5 volumes of O_2 oxidises 4 volumes of NH_3 completely, or we can say 4 volumes of NH_3 is completely oxidised by 5 volumes of O_2,

$\therefore$ 1 volume of NH_3 is completely oxidised by $\frac{5}{4}$ volumes of O_2.

$\therefore$ 100 cm^3 volume of NH_3 is completely oxidised by $\frac{5}{4} \times 100\ cm^3 = 125\ cm^3$ of O_2. **(3)**

Q.6 The gases hydrogen, oxygen, carbon dioxide, sulphur dioxide and chlorine are arranged in order of their increasing relative molecular mass. Given 8 g of each gas at STP, which gas will contain the least number of molecules and which gas the most?

Ans. Moles of a gas $= \frac{\text{given mass}}{\text{molar mass}}$

Moles of $H_2 = \frac{8}{2}$; Moles of $O_2 = \frac{8}{32}$

Moles of $CO_2 = \frac{8}{44}$; Moles of $SO_2 = \frac{8}{64}$

Moles of $Cl_2 = \frac{8}{71}$

Number of molecules ∝ number of moles.

As the given mass is same for every gas, moles are inversely proportional to the molar mass.

Therefore, Cl_2 contains least number of molecules whereas, H_2 contains maximum number of molecules. **(3)**

Q.7 A cylinder contains 68 g of ammonia gas at STP.

(i) What is the volume occupied by this gas?

(ii) How many moles of ammonia are present in the cylinder?

(iii) How many molecules of ammonia are present in the cylinder? [N = 14, H = 1] **(ICSE 2014)**

Ans. (i) Molecular mass of NH_3 gas = 14 + 3 = 17

If 17 g of NH_3 contains 22.4 L at STP

Then, 68g of NH_3 contains $= \frac{22.4}{17} \times 68$

$= 89.60$ L **(1)**

(ii) Number of moles $= \frac{\text{Mass in gram}}{\text{Gram molecular mass}}$

$= \frac{68}{17} = 4$ mol **(1)**

(iii) One mole of NH_3 contains 6.022×10^{23} molecules

$\therefore$ 4 moles of NH_3 contains $= 4 \times 6.022 \times 10^{23}$

$= 2.4088 \times 10^{24}$ molecules **(1)**

Q.8 Calculate the percentage of

(i) fluorine, (ii) sodium and (iii) aluminium in sodium aluminium fluoride [Na_3AlF_6], to the nearest whole number.

[Atomic mass: Na = 23, Al = 27, F = 19] **(ICSE 2020)**

Ans. (i) F % in [Na_3AlF_6] $= \frac{19 \times 6}{23 \times 3 + 27 + 6 \times 19} \times 100$

$= \frac{11400}{210} = 54.29\% = 54\%$ **(1)**

(ii) Na % in $[Na_3AlF_6] = \frac{23 \times 3}{210} \times 100 = \frac{6900}{210}$

$= 32.86\% = 33\%$ **(1)**

(iii) Al % in $[Na_3AlF_6] = \frac{27}{210} \times 100 = \frac{2700}{210}$

$= 12.86\% = 13\%$ **(1)**

Q.9 Calculate:

(i) The percentage of phosphorus in the fertilizer super phosphate $Ca(H_2PO_4)_2$ correct to 1 decimal point. [At. wt. H = 1, P = 31, O = 16 Ca = 40]

(ii) Write the empirical formula of C_8H_{18}. **(ICSE 2023)**

Ans. (i) Molecular mass of $Ca(H_2PO_4)_2$

$= 40 + 2(1 \times 2 + 31 + 16 \times 4)$

$= 234$ amu

% of phosphorus

$= \frac{\text{Mass of phosphorus in one molecule}}{\text{Molecular mass of compound}}$

$= \frac{62}{234} \times 100$

$= 26.496\% \approx 26.5\%$ **(2)**

(ii) Molecular formula = (Empirical formula)$_n$

(C_8H_{18}) = (Empirical formula)$_n$

$(C_4H_9)_2$ = (Empirical formula)$_n$

Comparing both sides, we get

Empirical formula = C_4H_9 **(1)**

Q.10 Determine the empirical formula of a compound containing 47.9% potassium, 5.5% beryllium and 46.6% fluorine by mass.

[Atomic weight of Be = 9, F = 19, K= 39] Work to one decimal place.

Ans. Calculation of empirical formula

Element	%	Atomic mass	Relative no. of atoms	Simplest ratio
K	47.9	39	$\frac{47.9}{39} = 1.2$	$\frac{1.2}{0.6} = 2$
Be	5.5	9	$\frac{5.5}{9} = 0.6$	$\frac{0.6}{0.6} = 1$
F	46.6	19	$\frac{46.6}{19} = 2.4$	$\frac{2.4}{0.6} = 4$

$\therefore$ Empirical formula of compound = K_2BeF_4 **(3)**

Q.11 A gaseous compound of nitrogen and hydrogen contains 12.5% hydrogen by mass. Find the molecular formula of the compound if its relative molecular mass is 37. [N = 14, H = 1]

Ans. Calculation of empirical formula

Element	% by mass	Atomic mass	Relative no. of atoms	Simplest ratio
N	87.5	14	$\frac{87.5}{14} = 6.25$	$\frac{6.25}{6.25} = 1$
H	12.5	1	$\frac{12.5}{1} = 12.5$	$\frac{12.5}{6.25} = 2$

$\therefore$ Empirical formula of compound = NH_2

Empirical formula weight = 14 + 2 = 16

Molecular weight = 37,

$$n = \frac{\text{Molecular weight}}{\text{Empirical formula weight}} = \frac{37}{16} = 2.3 \approx 2$$

Molecular formula = (Empirical formula)$_n$

$= (NH_2)_2 = N_2H_4$ **(3)**

Q.12 The empirical formula of an organic compound is C_3H_4N. Its molecular weight is 108.

Find the amount of carbon in one mole of the compound. Show all the steps involved.

(Atomic weights: C = 12; H = 1; N = 14)

(ICSE Specimen 2024)

Ans. Empirical formula of an organic compound = C_3H_4N

C, H and N are present in 3 : 4 : 1 ratio.

Molecular weight of compound 108 g/mol. The mass of carbon present in one mole (108 g) of compound

$= \frac{108 \times 3}{8} = 40.5$ g **(3)**

Q.13 Calculate.

(i) The number of moles in 12 g of oxygen gas. [O = 16]

(ii) The weight of 10^{22} atoms of carbon. [C = 12, Avogadro's number = 6×10^{23}]

(iii) Molecular formula of a compound is $C_6H_{18}O_3$. Find its empirical formula. **(ICSE 2019)**

Ans. (i) Given, mass of oxygen (w) = 12 g

Molar mass of oxygen gas (M) = 32 g/mol

$\because$ No. of moles $(n) = \frac{w}{M}$

$\therefore \quad n = \frac{12}{32} = 0.375$ mol **(1)**

(ii) Given,

Number of carbon-atoms (N) = 10^{22} atoms

Avogadro's number (N_A) = 6×10^{23}

Molar mass of carbon (M) = 12

∴ Mass of carbon atoms (w) is:

$$\frac{w}{M} = \frac{N}{N_A}$$

or $$w = \frac{N \times M}{N_A}$$

$$\Rightarrow \quad w = \frac{10^{22} \times 12}{6 \times 10^{23}} = 2 \times 10^{-1}$$

Weight of carbon atoms = 0.2 g **(1)**

(iii) Given: Molecular formula $= C_6H_{18}O_3$.

To find empirical formula, we calculate the simplest whole number ratio of $C_6H_{18}O_3$.

∴ Ratio of C, H and O is 6 : 18 : 3.

As '3' is the common divisor; On dividing by (3), we get C_2H_6O.

Simplest ratio is 2 : 6 : 1.

Hence, the empirical formula of $C_6H_{18}O_3$ is $\mathbf{C_2H_6O}$. **(1)**

Q.14 **(i) Calculate the weight of gram atoms in 4.6 g of sodium (Na = 23).**

(ii) Calculate the percentage of water of crystallisation in $CuSO_4 \cdot 5H_2O$.

(H = 1, O = 16, S = 32, Cu = 64)

(iii) A compound of X and Y has the empirical formula XY_2. Its vapour density is equal to its empirical formula weight. Determine its molecular formula. **(ICSE 2017)**

Ans. (i) 1 g atom of sodium weighs = 23 g of sodium

∴ 4.6 g atoms of sodium weighs = 23 × 4.6 g = 105.8 g of Na. **(1)**

(ii) Percentage of an element in a compound

$$= \frac{\text{Total weight of the element in one molecule}}{\text{Gram molecular weight of the compound}} \times 100$$

Molecular mass of $CuSO_4 \cdot 5H_2O$

$= 64 + 32 + (4 \times 16) + 5(2 \times 1 + 16)$

$= 64 + 32 + 64 + 90 = 250$ **(1)**

∴ Percent of water of crystallisation

$$= \frac{5 \times 18}{250} \times 100 = 36\% \text{ of } H_2O$$

(iii) $$n = \frac{2 \times \text{Vapour density}}{\text{Empirical formula weight}} = 2$$

[∵ Vapour density = Empirical formula weight]

Empirical formula = XY_2

Molecular formula = n × empirical formula

∴ Molecular formula = 2 × empirical formula

$= 2 \times XY_2 = X_2Y_4$ **(1)**

Q.15 **A gaseous hydrocarbon contains 82.76% of carbon. Given that its vapour density is 29, find its molecular formula. [Atomic mass: C = 12, H = l]** **(ICSE 2016)**

Ans.

Element	% composition	Atomic mass	Relative no. of atoms	Simplest ratio
C	82.76	12	$\frac{82.76}{12} = 6.89$	$\frac{6.89}{6.89} = 1$
H	100 − 82.76 = 17.24	1	$\frac{17.24}{1} = 17.24$	$\frac{17.24}{6.89} \simeq 2$

Empirical formula of the compound $= CH_2$

Empirical formula weight = 12 + 2 × 1 = 14

Vapour density = 29 (given)

Molecular weight = 2 × vapour density = 2 × 29 = 58

$$n = \frac{\text{Molecular weight}}{\text{Empirical formula weight}} = \frac{58}{14} = 4.14 \approx 4$$

Molecular formula = $(CH_2)_4 = C_4H_8$ **(3)**

Q.16 **A compound made up of two elements X and Y has an empirical formula X_2Y. If the atomic weight of X is 10 and that of Y is 5 and the compound has a vapour density 25, find the molecular formula.** **(ICSE 2014)**

Ans. Empirical formula = X_2Y

Atomic weight of X = 10, Atomic weight of Y = 5

∴ Empirical formula mass = 2 × 10 + 5 = 25

Vapour density (VD) = 25

Molecular mass = 2 × VD = 2 × 25 = 50

$$n = \frac{\text{Molecular mass}}{\text{Empirical formula mass}} = \frac{50}{25} = 2$$

∴ Molecular formula = Empirical formula × 2

$= X_2Y \times 2 = X_4Y_2$ **(3)**

Q.17 **An organic compound with vapour density 94 contains C = 12.67%, H = 2.13% and Br = 85.11%. Find the molecular formula.**

[Atomic mass of C = 12, H = 1, Br = 80]

Ans. Calculation of empirical formula

Element	% composition	Atomic mass	Relative no. of atoms	Simplest ratio
C	12.67	12	$\frac{12.67}{12} = 1$	1
H	2.13	1	$\frac{2.13}{1} = 2$	2
Br	85.11	80	$\frac{85.11}{80} = 1$	1

Empirical formula of compound = CH_2Br

Empirical formula weight = 12 + 2 × 1 + 80 = 94

Vapour density = 94 (given)

Molecular mass = 2 × Vapour density = 2 × 94 = 188

$$n = \frac{\text{Molecular weight}}{\text{Empirical formula weight}} = \frac{188}{94} = 2$$

Molecular formula = $(CH_2Br)_n = C_2H_4Br_2$ **(3)**

Q.18 Calcium carbonate reacts with dilute hydrochloric acid as given below.

$$CaCO_3 + 2HCl \longrightarrow CaCl_2 + H_2O + CO_2$$

(i) What is the mass of 5 moles of calcium carbonate? (Relative molecular mass of calcium carbonate is 100)

(ii) How many moles of HCl will react with 5 moles of calcium carbonate?

(iii) What is the volume of carbon dioxide liberated at STP at the same time? **(ICSE 2024)**

Ans. Reaction of calcium carbonate with dilute hydrochloric acid is:

$$CaCO_3 + 2HCl \longrightarrow CaCl_2 + H_2O + CO_2$$

(i) Mass of 1 mole of calcium carbonate = 100 g

Mass of 5 moles of calcium carbonate

= 5 × 100 g = 500 g **(1)**

(ii) According to the given equation,

1 mole of calcium carbonate reacts with 2 moles of HCl

5 moles of calcium carbonate will react with 2 × 5 = 10 moles of HCl **(1)**

(iii) 1 mole $CaCO_3$ = 1 mole CO_2 = 22.4 L

5 moles $CaCO_3$ = 5 moles CO_2

= 5 × 22.4 L = 112 L CO_2 **(1)**

Q.19 One variety of a household fuel is a mixture of propane (60%) and butane (40%). If 20 L of this mixture is burnt, find the total volume of carbon dioxide gas added to the atmosphere. Combustion reactions can be represented as

$$C_3H_8 + 5O_2 \longrightarrow 3CO_2 + 4H_2O$$
$$2C_4H_{10} + 13O_2 \longrightarrow 8CO_2 + 10H_2O$$

(ICSE Specimen 2025)

Ans. Combustion reactions are

$$C_3H_8 + 5O_2 \longrightarrow 3CO_2 + 4H_2O$$
$$2C_4H_{10} + 13O_2 \longrightarrow 8CO_2 + 10H_2O$$

Given, propane = 60%, butane = 40%,

Volume of mixture = 20 L

Volume of propane = $\frac{60}{100} \times 20 = 12$ L

Volume of butane = $\frac{40}{100} \times 20 = 8$ L

According to equation,

$$\underset{1\text{ vol}}{C_3H_8} + \underset{5\text{ vol}}{5O_2} \longrightarrow \underset{3\text{ vol}}{3CO_2} + 4H_2O$$

1 volume of C_3H_8 (propane) gives 3 volumes of CO_2

12 L of propane gives = $\frac{3}{1} \times 12 = 36$ L of CO_2

According to equation,

$$\underset{2\text{ vol}}{2C_4H_{10}} + 13O_2 \longrightarrow \underset{8\text{ vol}}{8CO_2} + 10H_2O$$

2 volumes of butane (C_4H_{10}) gives 8 volumes of CO_2

∴ 8 L of butane gives = $\frac{8}{2} \times 8 = 32$ L of CO_2

Total volume of CO_2 = 36 L + 32 L = 68 L produced. **(3)**

Q.20 The reaction between concentrated sulphuric acid and magnesium can be represented by the equation given below:

$$Mg + 2H_2SO_4 \longrightarrow MgSO_4 + 2H_2O + SO_2$$

If 60 g of magnesium is used in the reaction, calculate the following:

(i) The mass of sulphuric acid needed for the reaction

(ii) The volume of sulphur dioxide gas liberated at STP. [Atomic weight Mg = 24, H = 1, S = 32, O = 16] **(ICSE 2025)**

Ans. $$\underset{24\text{ g}}{Mg} + \underset{2(2\times1+32+4\times16)=196\text{ g}}{2H_2SO_4} \longrightarrow MgSO_4 + 2H_2O + \underset{22.4\text{ L}}{SO_2}$$

(i) From the reaction, 24 g Mg reacts with 196 g H_2SO_4.

∴ 60 g Mg will react with $\frac{60 \times 196}{24} = 490$ g H_2SO_4

Thus, the mass of sulphuric acid needed for the reaction is **490 g**. **(1)**

(ii) 1 mol of Mg gives 1 mol of SO_2 and at STP 1 mol of SO_2 occupies 22.4 L volume.

⇒ 1 mol or 24 g Mg gives 22.4 L SO_2

∴ 60 g Mg will give $\frac{60 \times 22.4}{24} = 56$ L SO_2

Thus, the volume of SO_2 gas liberated at STP is **56 L**. **(2)**

TYPE - 9

04/05 Marks

Long Answer Type Questions

Q.1 (i) (a) State 'Avogadro's law'. **(ICSE 2025)**

(b) Define vapour density.

(ii) 1250 cc of oxygen was burnt with 300 cc of ethane (C_2H_6). Calculate the volume of the unused oxygen and the volume of the carbon dioxide formed.

$$2C_2H_6 + 7O_2 \longrightarrow 4CO_2 + 6H_2O$$

(ICSE Specimen 2023)

Ans. (i) (a) **Avogadro's law** states that 'equal volumes of all gases under similar conditions of temperature and pressure contain the same number of molecules.' **(1)**

(b) The **vapour density** of a gas is the ratio between the masses of equal volumes of gas and hydrogen under the same conditions of temperature and pressure. **(1)**

(ii) $2C_2H_6 + 7O_2 \longrightarrow 4CO_2 + 6H_2O$
$\underset{2\text{ vol}}{} \quad \underset{7\text{ vol}}{} \quad \underset{4\text{ vol}}{}$

2 moles of C_2H_6 require $O_2 = 7$ vol

$\therefore$ 300 cc of C_2H_6 requires $O_2 = \frac{7}{2} \times 300 = 1050$ cc

Unused oxygen = 1250 cc– 1050 cc = 200 cc

C_2H_6 is the limiting reagent.

Again 2 moles of C_2H_6 produce $CO_2 = 4$ mol

$\therefore$ 300 cc of C_2H_6 produce $CO_2 = \frac{4}{2} \times 300 = 600$ cc **(2)**

Q.2 The volume of gases *A*, *B*, *C* and *D* are in the ratio 1 : 2 : 2 : 4 under same conditions of temperature and pressure.

(i) If the volume of *A* is actually 5.6 dm^3 at STP, calculate the number of molecules in the actual volume of *D* at STP.

[Avogadro's number is 6×10^{23}].

(ii) Using your answer from (i) state the mass *D*, if the gas is dinitrogen oxide (N_2O) [N = 14, O = 16]. **(ICSE 2005)**

Ans. (i)

Gases	*A*	*D*
Volume	1	4
Volume at STP	5.6 dm^3	$4 \times 5.6\ dm^3 = 22.4\ dm^3$ (molar volume)

$\because$ 1 mole of gas occupies 22.4 dm^3 and it contains 6×10^{23} number of molecules.

$\therefore$ 6×10^{23} molecules is Avogadro's number of molecules contained in 22.4 dm^3 of D. **(2)**

(ii) If gas *D* is N_2O.

Molecular mass of $D = 2 \times 14 + 16$
$= 28 + 16 = 44$ g **(2)**

Q.3 (i) **Ammonia burns in oxygen as shown below.**

$4NH_3 + 3O_2 \longrightarrow 2N_2 + 6H_2O$

If 240 cc of ammonia is burnt in 300 cc of oxygen, find out the composition of the resultant gaseous mixture at room temperature. **(ICSE 2024)**

(ii) **In the given reaction, $N_2 + 3H_2 \longrightarrow 2NH_3$.**

Which of the reactant and product species are homoatomic and heteroatomic respectively?

Ans. (i) $\underset{4\text{ vol}}{4NH_3} + \underset{3\text{ vol}}{3O_2} \longrightarrow \underset{2\text{ vol}}{2N_2} + \underset{6\text{ vol}}{6H_2O}$

4 volume of NH_3 at STP requires $O_2 = 3$ vol

240 cc of NH_3 will require $O_2 = \frac{240 \times 3}{4} = 180$ cc

Excess $O_2 = 300$ cc – 180 cc = 120 cc

NH_3 is limiting reagent. It limits the amount of product formed.

4 volume of NH_3 at STP gives = 2 volume N_2

240 cc of NH_3 at STP will give $= \frac{240 \times 2}{4} = 120$ cc N_2

4 volume of NH_3 at STP gives = 6 volume of H_2O

240 cc of NH_3 at STP will give $= \frac{240 \times 6}{4} = 360$ cc H_2O

Composition of resultant gaseous mixture is as follows

Unreacted $O_2 = 120$ cc
$N_2 = 120$ cc
$H_2O = 360$ cc **(3)**

(ii) Homoatomic = N_2 and H_2

Heteroatomic = NH_3 **(1)**

Q.4 A gas cylinder can hold 1 kg of hydrogen at room temperature and pressure.

(i) Find the number of moles of hydrogen present.

(ii) What weight of CO_2 can the cylinder hold under similar conditions of temperature and pressure? (H = 1, C = 12, O = 16)

(iii) If the number of molecules of hydrogen in the cylinder is *X*, calculate the number of CO_2 molecules in the cylinder under the same conditions of temperature and pressure.

(iv) State the law that helped you to arrive at the above result.

Ans. (i) Given, weight of $H_2 = 1$ kg = 1000 g

Number of moles $= \frac{\text{Weight}}{\text{Molecular mass}}$

Molecular mass of $H_2 = 2$ g

$\therefore$ Number of moles of $H_2 = \frac{2}{1000}$ mol

$= 0.002$ mol **(1)**

(ii) According to Avogadro's law, equal volumes of all gases under similar conditions of temperature and pressure contains equal number of molecules.

$\because$ Volume is constant,

$\therefore n_1 = n_2$ or, $n_{H_2} = n_{CO_2} = 0.002$ mol

As we know, number of moles $= \frac{\text{Weight}}{\text{Molecular mass}}$

$\therefore$ Weight of $CO_2 = 0.002 \times 44 = 0.088$ g **(1)**

(iii) Number of molecules of $H_2 = X$

$\therefore$ Number of molecules of $CO_2 = X$ **(1)**

(iv) **Avogadro's law** **(1)**

Q.5 (i) **Calculate the number of moles and the number of molecules present in 1.4 g ethylene gas. What is the volume occupied by the same amount of ethylene?**

(ii) **What is vapour density of ethane?**

[Avogadro's number = 6×10^{23}; Atomic weight of C = 12, H = 1; Molar volume = 22.4 L at STP].

Ans. (i) Molecular weight of ethylene ($CH_2{=\!=}CH_2$)

$$= 12 + 2 + 12 + 2 = 28\text{ g}$$

$$\text{Number of moles} = \frac{\text{Given weight}}{\text{Molecular weight}}$$

$$= \frac{1.4}{28} = 0.05\text{ mol}$$

Number of molecules in 1 mole = 6×10^{23}

∴ Number of molecules in 0.05 mole

$$= 6 \times 10^{23} \times 0.05 = 0.3 \times 10^{23}$$
$$= 3 \times 10^{22}\text{ molecules}$$

Volume occupied by 1 mole = 22 . 4 L

∴ Volume occupied by 0.05 mole

$$= 22.4 \times 0.05 = 1.12\text{ L}$$ **(3)**

(ii) Vapour density (VD)

$$= \frac{\text{Molecular weight}}{2}$$

[∵ Molecular weight of ethane (C_2H_6) = 30 g]

$$= \frac{30}{2} = 15$$ **(1)**

Q.6 Find the empirical formula and the molecular formula of an organic compound from the data given below.
C = 75.92%, H = 6.32% and N = 17.76%
The vapour density of the compound is 39.5.
[C = 12, H = 1 and N = 14] **(ICSE 2019)**

Ans. Given, C = 75.92%, H = 6.32%, N = 17.76%

Vapour density of compound = 39.5

∵ Molecular mass (M) = 2 × Vapour density

$$= 2 \times 39.5 = 79$$

To find empirical formula

Element	% in 100 g of sample (w)	Molar-mass of element (M')	$\left(n = \frac{w}{M'}\right)$	Simplest ratio of atoms
Carbon	75.92	12	$n = \frac{75.92}{12} = 6.32$	$\frac{6.32}{1.268} \approx 5$
Hydrogen	6.32	1	$n = \frac{6.32}{1} = 6.32$	$\frac{6.32}{1.268} \approx 5$
Nitrogen	17.76	14	$n = \frac{17.76}{14} = 1.268$	$\frac{1.268}{1.268} = 1$

On dividing 6.32, 6.32 and 1.268 respectively by 1.268, we get,

$$C = 5, H = 5, N = 1$$

Hence, simple ratio, i.e. empirical formula is C_5H_5N.

Also, empirical formula weight = mass of 5C + 5H + N

$$= 5 \times 12 + 5 \times 1 + 14 = 79$$

and molecular weight = $n' \times$ empirical formula weight.

$$\text{where, } n' = \frac{\text{Molecular weight}}{\text{Empirical formula weight}} = \frac{79}{79} = 1$$

Hence, molecular formula = $1 \times (C_5H_5N)$

$$= C_5H_5N$$ **(4)**

Q.7 An oxide of phosphorus contains 43.7% by mass of phosphorus.

(i) **Show that the empirical formula for this oxide is P_2O_5.**

(ii) **A sample of this oxide has a mass of 2.56 g. The sample contains 0.00901 mol of the oxide. Calculate the relative molecular mass and hence the molecular formula for this oxide of phosphorus.**

Ans. (i)

Element	P	O
Percentage	43.7	56.3
Atomic mass	31	16
No. of moles	$\frac{43.7}{31}$	$\frac{56.3}{16}$
	= 1.41	= 3.52
Simple ratio	$\frac{1.41}{1.41}$	$\frac{3.52}{1.41}$
	= 1	= 2.5

∴ Empirical formula = $P_1O_{2.5}$

$$= (P_1O_{2.5})_2 = P_2O_5$$ **(2)**

(ii) Molecular mass of oxide = $\frac{2.56}{0.00901} = 284.1$

Empirical formula mass of P_2O_5 = (31 × 2) + (16 × 5)
= 142

$$n = \frac{\text{Molecular mass}}{\text{Empirical formula mass}}$$

$$\Rightarrow \quad n = \frac{284.1}{142} \approx 2$$

∴ Molecular formula = $(P_2O_5)_2 = P_4O_{10}$ **(2)**

Q.8 An organic compound 'X' contains carbon, oxygen and hydrogen only. The percentage of carbon and hydrogen are 47.4% and 10.5% respectively. The relative molecular formula of 'X' is 76. Find the empirical formula and the molecular formula of 'X'.

[Atomic weight C = 12, O = 16, H = 1] **(ICSE 2025)**

Ans.

Element	Percentage composition	Atomic mass	Atomic ratio	Simplest ratio	Whole number ratio
C	47.4	12	$\frac{47.4}{12} = 3.95$	$\frac{3.95}{2.63} = 1.5$	$1.5 \times 2 = 3$
H	10.5	1	$\frac{10.5}{1} = 10.5$	$\frac{10.5}{2.63} = 4$	$4 \times 2 = 8$
O	100 – (47.4 +10.5) = 42.1	16	$\frac{42.1}{16} = 2.63$	$\frac{2.63}{2.63} = 1$	$1 \times 2 = 2$

The empirical formula is $C_3H_8O_2$.

Empirical formula mass

$= (3 \times 12) + (8 \times 1) + (2 \times 16) = 76$

Molecular mass = 76 (given)

$$n = \frac{\text{Molecular mass}}{\text{Empirical formula mass}} = \frac{76}{76} = 1$$

∴ Molecular formula = Empirical formula × n

$= C_3H_8O_2$ **(4)**

Q.9 8.2 grams of calcium nitrate is decomposed by heating according to the equation

$$2Ca(NO_3)_2 \longrightarrow 2CaO + 4NO_2 + O_2$$

Calculate the following: **(ICSE Specimen 2025, 2024)**

(i) Volume of nitrogen dioxide obtained at STP.

(ii) Mass of CaO formed.

[Atomic weights: Ca = 40, N = 140, O = 16]

Ans. $2Ca(NO_3)_2 \longrightarrow 2CaO + 4NO_2 + O_2$

Molar mass of $Ca(NO_3)_2 = 40 + 2(14) + 6(16) = 164$

No. of moles of $Ca(NO_3)_3 = \frac{\text{Given weight}}{\text{Molecular weight}}$

$= \frac{8.2}{164} = 0.05$ mol. **(1)**

2 moles of $Ca(NO_3)_2$ gives 4 moles of NO_2.

0.05 moles of $Ca(NO_3)_2$ gives 0.1 moles of NO_2.

(i) ∴ Volume of NO_2 at STP

= No. of moles of NO_2 × molar volume in litres (at STP)

$= 0.1 \times 22.4 = 2.24$ L **(1)**

(ii) Molar mass of CaO = 40 + 16 = 56

328 grams of $Ca(NO_3)_2$ produces 112 grams of CaO.

1 gram of $Ca(NO_3)_2$ produces $\frac{112}{328}$ grams of CaO.

8.2 grams of $Ca(NO_3)_2$ produces $\frac{8.2 \times 112}{328}$ grams of CaO = 2.8 g of CaO formed. **(2)**

Q.10 Aluminium carbide reacts with water according to the following equation.

$$Al_4C_3 + 12H_2O \longrightarrow 4Al(OH)_3 + 3CH_4$$

(i) What mass of aluminium hydroxide is formed from 12 g of aluminium carbide?

(ii) What volume of methane at STP is obtained from 12 g of aluminium carbide?

(Relative molecular weight of Al_4C_3 = 144g, $Al(OH)_3$ = 78g) **(ICSE 2018)**

Ans. (i) $Al_4C_3 + 12H_2O \longrightarrow 4Al(OH)_3 + 3CH_4$

1 mol, 12 mol, 4 mol, 3 mol

144 g, 4 × 78 g

144 g of Al_4C_3 produced = 4 × 78 g of $Al(OH)_3$

∴ 12 g of Al_4C_3 produced $= \frac{4 \times 78}{144} \times 12$ of $Al(OH)_3$

= 26 g of $Al(OH)_3$ **(2)**

(ii) $Al_4C_3 + 12H_2O \longrightarrow 4Al(OH)_3 + 3CH_4$

1 mol, 12 mol, 4 mol, 3 mol

144 g, 3 × 22.4 L at STP

144 g of Al_4C_3 will produce = 3 × 22.4 L of CH_4

∴ 12 g of Al_4C_3 will produce $= \frac{22.4 \times 3 \times 12}{144} = 5.6$ L **(2)**

Q.11 Ethane burns in oxygen to form CO_2 and H_2O according to the equation,

$$2C_2H_6 + 7O_2 \longrightarrow 4CO_2 + 6H_2O$$

If 1250 cc of oxygen is burnt with 300 cc of ethane. Calculate

(i) the volume of CO_2 formed.

(ii) the volume of unused O_2. **(ICSE 2018)**

Ans. $2C_2H_6 + 7O_2 \longrightarrow 4CO_2 + 6H_2O$

2 mol, 7 mol, 4 mol

2 × 22400 cm³, 7 × 22400 cm³, 4 × 22400 cm³

2 × 22400 cm³ of C_2H_6 reacts with 7 × 22400 cm³ of O_2.

∴ 1 cm³ of C_2H_6 will reacts with $\frac{7 \times 22400}{2 \times 22400}$

= 3.5 cm³ of O_2

∴ 300 cm³ of C_2H_6 will react with

3.5 × 300 = 1050 cm³ of O_2 **(2)**

Thus, **C_2H_6 is the limiting reagent.**

(i) 2 × 22400 cm³ of C_2H_6 will produce 4 × 22400 cm³ of CO_2.

Thus, 300 cm³ of C_2H_6 will produce CO_2

$= \frac{4 \times 22400}{2 \times 22400} \times 300 = 600$ cm³ **(1)**

(ii) Volume of unused O_2 = (1250 – 1050) cm³

= 200 cm³ **(1)**

Q.12 (i) What is the volume (measured in dm^3 or litres) occupied by one mole of a gas at STP?

(ii) 112 cm^3 (at STP) of a gaseous fluoride of phosphorus has a mass of 0.63 g. Calculate the relative molecular mass of the fluoride. If the molecule of the fluoride contains only one atom of phosphorus, then determine the formula of the phosphorus fluoride [F = 19, P = 31].

Ans. (i) The volume occupied by one mole of a gas at STP is **22.4 L or 22.4 dm^3**. This volume is known as **molar volume**. **(1)**

(ii) Mass of 112 cm^3 of phosphorus fluoride = 0.63 g

Mass of 22400 cm^3 of phosphorus fluoride

$$= \frac{0.63}{112\ cm^3} \times 22400 = 126\ g$$

Relative molecular mass of fluoride = 126 g

Let the formula is PF_x, therefore,

$$PF_x = 126$$

$$31 + 19x = 126$$

$$19x = 126 - 31 = 95$$

$$\Rightarrow \quad x = \frac{95}{19} = 5$$

Hence, the formula is PF_5. **(3)**

Q.13 The equation for the burning of octane is

$$2C_8H_{18} + 25O_2 \longrightarrow 16CO_2 + 18H_2O$$

(i) How many moles of carbon dioxide are produced when one mole of octane burns?

(ii) What volume, at STP, is occupied by the number of moles determined in (i)?

(iii) If the relative molecular mass of carbon dioxide is 44, what is the mass of carbon dioxide produced by burning two moles of octane?

Ans. $\underset{\substack{2\ mol \\ 1\ mol}}{2C_8H_{18}} + 25O_2 \longrightarrow \underset{\substack{16\ mol \\ 8\ mol}}{16CO_2} + 18H_2O$

(i) One mole of octane forms 8 moles of CO_2 on burning. **(1)**

(ii) At STP one mole of gas occupies 22.4 L

$\therefore$ 8 moles of CO_2 will occupy = 22.4 × 8 = 179.2 L **(1)**

(iii) From equation we know that 2 moles of octane produces 16 moles of CO_2.

$\therefore$ Mass of CO_2 produced = 16 × 44 = 704 g **(2)**

Q.14 4.5 moles of calcium carbonate are reacted with dilute hydrochloric acid.

(i) Write the equation for the reaction and find the mass of 4.5 moles of calcium carbonate? (Relative molecular mass of calcium carbonate is 100).

(ii) What is the volume of carbon dioxide liberated at STP?

(iii) What mass of calcium chloride is formed? (Relative molecular mass of calcium chloride is 111).

(iv) How many moles of HCl are used in this reaction?

Ans. (i) Equation for the reaction is

$$CaCO_3 + 2HCl \longrightarrow CaCl_2 + H_2O + CO_2$$

Relative molecular mass of $CaCO_3$ = 100

If mass of 1 mole of $CaCO_3$ = 100 g

Then, mass of 4.5 moles of $CaCO_3 = \frac{100}{1} \times 4.5$

= 450 g **(1)**

(ii) According to the equation,

1 mole of $CaCO_3$ produces 1 mole of CO_2

$\therefore$ 4.5 moles of $CaCO_3$ will produce 4.5 moles of CO_2

$\because$ 1 mole of CO_2 occupies 22.4 L at STP.

$\therefore$ 4.5 moles of CO_2 will occupy = 4.5× 22.4 L

= 100.80 L **(1)**

(iii) Relative molecular mass of $CaCl_2$ = 111g

$\therefore$ 4.5 moles of $CaCl_2 = \frac{111}{1} \times 4.5 = 499.5$ g **(1)**

[$\because$ 1 moles of $CaCO_3$ gives 1 mole of $CaCl_2$

$\therefore$ 4.5 moles of $CaCO_3$ will give 4.5 moles of $CaCl_2$]

(iv) According to equation,

$$\underset{1\ mol}{CaCO_3} + \underset{2\ mol}{2HCl} \longrightarrow \underset{1\ mol}{CaCl_2} + H_2O + CO_2$$

1 mole of $CaCO_3$ uses 2 moles of HCl

$\therefore$ 4.5 moles of $CaCO_3$ will use

$= \frac{2}{1} \times 4.5 = 9$ moles of HCl **(1)**

Q.15 Concentrated nitric acid oxidises phosphorus to phosphoric acid according to the following equation,

$$P + 5HNO_3(conc.) \longrightarrow H_3PO_4 + H_2O + 5NO_2$$

If 9.3 g of phosphorus was used in the reaction, calculate

(i) number of moles of phosphorus taken.

(ii) the mass of phosphoric acid formed.

(iii) the volume of nitrogen dioxide produced at STP.

[H = 1, N = 14, P = 31, O = 16]

Ans. The given equation is

$$\underset{31\ g}{P} + \underset{(Conc.)}{5HNO_3} \longrightarrow \underset{\substack{3\times 1 + 31 + 16\times 4 \\ = 98\ g}}{H_3PO_4} + H_2O + \underset{\substack{5\times 22.4 \\ = 112\ L}}{5NO_2}$$ **(1)**

(i) 31 g of phosphorus = 1 mol

9.3 g of phosphorus $= \frac{1}{31} \times 9.3 = 0.3$ mol **(1)**

(ii) **Mass of H_3PO_4**

31 g of P produces 98 g of H_3PO_4.

Then, 9.3 g of P produces $= \frac{98}{31} \times 9.3$

= 29.4 g of H_3PO_4 **(1)**

(iii) **Volume of nitrogen dioxide at STP**

31 g of P releases 112 L of NO_2 at STP.

Then, 9.3 g of P releases $= \frac{112}{31} \times 9.3$

$= 33.6$ L of NO_2 at STP **(1)**

Q.16 When excess lead nitrate solution was added to a solution of sodium sulphate, 15.15 g of lead sulphate were precipitated.

What mass of sodium sulphate was present in the original solution?

$$Na_2SO_4 + Pb(NO_3)_2 \longrightarrow PbSO_4 + 2NaNO_3$$

[H = 1, C = 12, O = 16, Na = 23, S = 32, Pb = 207]

Ans. $Na_2SO_4 + Pb(NO_3)_2 \longrightarrow PbSO_4 + 2NaNO_3$

Molecular weight of $Na_2SO_4 = 2 \times 23 + 32 + 64$

$= 46 + 32 + 64 = 142$ g **(1)**

Molecular weight of $PbSO_4 = 207 + 32 + 64 = 303$ g **(1)**

303 g lead sulphate is precipitated by 142 g Na_2SO_4.

15.15 g lead sulphate is precipitated by $\frac{15.15 \times 142}{303}$

$= 7.1$g of sodium sulphate. **(2)**

Q.17 (i) **Propane burns in air according to the following equation:**

$$C_3H_8 + 5O_2 \longrightarrow 3CO_2 + 4H_2O$$

What volume of propane is consumed on using 1000 cm^3 of air, considering only 20% of air contains oxygen?

(ii) **The mass of 11.2 L of a certain gas at STP is 24 g. Find the gram molecular mass of the gas.** **(ICSE 2017)**

Ans. (i) Oxygen present in air $= \frac{20}{100} \times 1000 = 200$ cm^3

$$\underset{1\text{ vol}}{C_3H_8} + \underset{5\text{ vol}}{5O_2} \longrightarrow 3CO_2 + 4H_2O$$

5 volume of O_2 is required for 1 volume of C_3H_8.

$\therefore$ 200 cm^3 of O_2 is required

$= \frac{200}{5}$ cm^3 of C_3H_8

$= 40$ cm^3 of C_3H_8 **(2)**

(ii) The mass of 22.4 L of a gas at STP is equal to its gram molecular mass.

11.2 L of gas at STP weigh = 24 g

$\therefore$ 22.4 L of gas will weigh $= \frac{24}{11.2} \times 22.4 = 48$ g **(2)**

Q.18 A sample of ammonium nitrate when heated yields 8.96 L of steam (measured at STP).

$$NH_4NO_3 \longrightarrow N_2O + 2H_2O$$

(i) **What volume of dinitrogen oxide is produced at the same time as 8.96 L of steam?**

(ii) **What mass of ammonium nitrate should be heated to produce 8.96 L of steam? (Relative molecular mass of ammonium nitrate is 80).**

Ans. (i) $NH_4NO_3 \longrightarrow \underset{1\text{ vol}}{N_2O} + \underset{2\text{ vol}}{2H_2O}$

When 2 volumes of steam is produced, 1 volume of N_2O is formed.

$\therefore$ When steam produced is 8.96 L

$\therefore$ Volume of $N_2O = \frac{8.96}{2} = 4.48$ L **(2)**

(ii) $\underset{\substack{1\text{mol}\\80\text{ g}}}{NH_4NO_3} \longrightarrow N_2O + \underset{\substack{2\text{ mol}\\2\times22.4\text{ L at STP}\\44.8\text{ L}}}{2H_2O}$

$\because$ 44.8 L of steam is produced from 80 g of NH_4NO_3

$\therefore$ 8.96 L of steam will be produced from

$= \frac{80 \times 8.96}{44.8} = 16$ g of NH_4NO_3 **(2)**

Q.19 10 g of a mixture of barium chloride and anhydrous sodium sulphate is dissolved in water. An excess of barium chloride solution is added and 6.99g of barium sulphate is precipitated according to the equation given below.

$$Na_2SO_4 + BaCl_2 \longrightarrow BaSO_4 + 2NaCl$$

[O = 16, Na = 23, S = 32, Ba = 137]

Calculate the percentage of sodium sulphate in the original mixture.

Ans. $Na_2SO_4 + BaCl_2 \longrightarrow \underset{6.99\text{ g}}{BaSO_4} + 2NaCl$

Molecular weight of $BaSO_4 = 137 + 32 + 64 = 233$ g

Molecular weight of $Na_2SO_4 = 2 \times 23 + 32 + 64$

$= 142$ g **(2)**

233 g of $BaSO_4$ is obtained from 142 g of Na_2SO_4

6.99 g of $BaSO_4$ is obtained from $\frac{142}{233} \times 6.99 = 4.26$ g

$\therefore Na_2SO_4$ in 10 g of mixture $= \frac{4.26}{10} \times 100 = 42.6\%$ **(2)**

Q.20 Washing soda has the formula $Na_2CO_3 \cdot 10H_2O$. What mass of anhydrous sodium carbonate is left when all the water of crystallisation is expelled by heating 57.2 g of washing soda.

Ans. $Na_2CO_3 \cdot 10H_2O \longrightarrow Na_2CO_3 + 10H_2O$

Molecular weight of $Na_2CO_3 = 2 \times 23 + 12 + 48 = 106$ g

Molecular weight of $Na_2CO_3 \cdot 10H_2O$

$= 106 + 10(2 + 16)$

$= 106 + 180$

$= 286$ g **(2)**

$\because$ 286 g washing soda heated to produce 106 g anhydrous sodium carbonate.

$\therefore$ 57.2 g washing soda when heated will produce

$$= \frac{57.2 \times 106}{286} = 21.2 \text{ g}$$

$\therefore$ Mass of anhydrous Na_2CO_3 = 21.2 g **(2)**

Q.21 From the equation

$$C + 2H_2SO_4 \longrightarrow CO_2 + 2H_2O + 2SO_2$$

Calculate

(i) The mass of carbon oxidised by 49 g of sulphuric acid (C = 12, relative molecular mass of sulphuric acid = 98).

(ii) The volume of sulphur dioxide measured at STP liberated at the same time. (Volume occupied by 1 mole of a gas at STP is 22.4 dm^3).

Ans. (i) The equation is

$$\underset{12\text{ g}}{C} + \underset{2\times 98\text{ g}}{2H_2SO_4} \longrightarrow CO_2 + 2H_2O + \underset{2\times 22.4\text{ L}}{2SO_2}$$

From equation 2 × 98 g of sulphuric acid oxidises 12 g of C.

$$\therefore 49 \text{ g of sulphuric acid will oxidise} = \frac{12 \times 49}{2 \times 98}$$

$$= 3 \text{ g of C}$$ **(2)**

(ii) From equation 2 × 98 g of sulphuric acid liberates = 2 × 22.4 L of SO_2

$\therefore$ 49 g of sulphuric acid will liberate

$$= \frac{2 \times 22.4 \times 49}{2 \times 98} = 11.2 \text{ L of } SO_2$$ **(2)**

22. From the equation

$$(NH_4)_2Cr_2O_7 \longrightarrow Cr_2O_3 + 4H_2O + N_2$$

Calculate

(i) The volume of nitrogen at STP, evolved when 63g of ammonium dichromate is heated.

(ii) The mass of chromium (III) oxide (Cr_2O_3) formed at the same time.

[N= 14, H= 1, Cr= 52, O= 16]

Ans. (i)
$$\underset{252\text{ g}}{(NH_4)_2Cr_2O_7} \longrightarrow \underset{152\text{ g}}{Cr_2O_3} + 4H_2O + \underset{22.4\text{ L}}{N_2}$$

Molecular weight of Cr_2O_3 = 104 + 48
= 152 g

Molecular weight of $(NH_4)_2Cr_2O_7$
= 28 + 8 + 104 + 112
= 252 g

Volume of N_2 evolved at STP by decomposing

$$31.5 \text{ g } (NH_4)_2Cr_2O_7 = \frac{22.4}{252} \times 31.5 = 2.8 \text{ L}$$ **(3)**

(ii) Amount of Cr_2O_3 formed $= \frac{152}{252} \times 31.5 = 19.0$ g **(1)**

Q.23 (i) When gases react together, their reaction volume bears a simple ratio to each other under the same conditions of temperature and pressure. Who proposed this gas law?

(ii) What volume of oxygen would be required for the complete combustion of 100 L of ethane according to the following equation?

$$2C_2H_6 + 7O_2 \longrightarrow 4CO_2 + 6H_2O$$

(iii) The gases chlorine, nitrogen, ammonia and sulphur dioxide are collected under the same conditions of temperature and pressure. Copy the following table which gives the volumes of gases collected and the number of molecules (*X*) in 20 L of nitrogen. You are to complete the table giving the number of molecules in the other gases in terms of *X*.

Gas	Volume	Number of molecules
Chlorine	10	
Nitrogen	20	*X*
Ammonia	20	
Sulphur dioxide	5	

Ans. (i) **Gay Lussac** proposed this law. **(1)**

(ii) The given equation is

$$\underset{2\text{ vol}}{2C_2H_6} + \underset{7\text{ vol}}{7O_2} \longrightarrow 4CO_2 + 6H_2O$$

2 volumes of ethane requires 7 volumes of O_2

$\therefore$ 100 L of ethane requires

$$= \frac{7}{2} \times 100 \text{ L of } O_2 = 350 \text{ L of } O_2$$ **(2)**

(iii)

Gas	Volume (L)	Number of molecule
Chlorine	10	X/2
Nitrogen	20	X
Ammonia	20	X
Sulphur dioxide	5	X/4

(2)

Q.24 (i) A gas of mass 32 g has a volume of 20 L at STP. Calculate the gram molecular weight of the gas.

(ii) How much calcium oxide is formed, when 82 g of calcium nitrate is heated? Also, find the volume of nitrogen dioxide evolved.

$$2Ca(NO_3)_2 \xrightarrow{\Delta} 2CaO + 4NO_2 + O_2$$

(Atomic mass: Ca= 40, N= 14, O= 16) **(ICSE 2016)**

Ans. (i) Mass of the gas = 32 g

Volume of gas at STP = 20 L

20 L of gas at STP occupies 32 g.

$\therefore$ 1L of gas at STP occupies $\frac{32}{20}$ g = 1.6 g

22.4 L of gas at STP will occupy = 22.4 × 1.6 g = 35.84 g

Gram molecular wt. = 35.84 g **(2)**

(ii) The given equation is

$$\underset{\substack{2[40+2(14+3\times16)]\\=328\text{ g}}}{2Ca(NO_3)_2} \xrightarrow{\Delta} \underset{\substack{2[40+16]\\=112\text{ g}}}{2CaO} + \underset{\substack{4\times22.4\text{ L}\\=89.6\text{ L}}}{4NO_2} + O_2$$

328 g of $Ca(NO_3)_2$ produces 112 g of CaO.

Then, 82 g of $Ca(NO_3)_2$ produces

$= \frac{112}{328} \times 82 = 28$ g of CaO

Now, since 328 g of $Ca(NO_3)_2$ produces 89.6 L of NO_2 at STP.

Then, 82 g of $Ca(NO_3)_2$ releases

$= \frac{89.6}{328} \times 82 = 22.4$ L of NO_2 at STP **(3)**

Q.25 Complete the following calculations.

[Atomic masses: S = 32, Ca = 40]

(i) Calculate the mass of calcium that will contain the same number of atoms as are present in 3.2 g of sulphur.

(ii) If 6 L of hydrogen and 4 L of chlorine are mixed and exploded and if water is added to the gases formed, find the volume of the residual gas.

(iii) If the empirical formula of a compound is CH and it has a vapour density of 13, find the molecular formula of the compound. **(ICSE 2015)**

Ans. (i) **Number of atoms in 3.2 g of sulphur**

$N = \frac{3.2}{32} \times 6.02 \times 10^{23} = 6.02 \times 10^{22}$

= Number of atoms of Ca

Let mass of Ca be x g.

Molecular mass of Ca = 40

$\frac{x}{40} = \frac{6.02 \times 10^{22}}{6.02 \times 10^{23}}$

$\Rightarrow \quad x = 4$ g **(2)**

(ii) $H_2 + Cl_2 \longrightarrow 2HCl$

4 L of Cl_2 will need only 4 L of H_2.

$\because$ 6 L of H_2 is mixed with 4 L of Cl_2.

$\therefore$ (6 − 4) = 2 L of H_2 will remain unreacted. **(2)**

(iii) Empirical formula of a compound = CH

Empirical formula mass = 12 + 1 = 13 g

Molecular formula mass = 2 × V.D. = 2 × 13 = 26 g

$\Rightarrow \quad n = \frac{26}{13} = 2$

Molecular formula = (Empirical formula)$_n$

$\therefore$ Molecular formula = $(CH)_2 = C_2H_2$ **(1)**

Q.26 Calculate

(i) The amount of each reactant required to produce 750 mL of carbon dioxide, when two volumes of carbon monoxide combine with one volume of oxygen to produce two volumes of carbon dioxide.

$$2CO + O_2 \longrightarrow 2CO_2$$

(ii) The volume occupied by 80 g of carbon dioxide at STP.

(iii) Calculate the number of molecules in 4.4 g of CO_2.

[Atomic mass of C = 12, O = 16]

(iv) State the law associated in (i) above. **(ICSE 2020)**

Ans. (i) $2CO(g) + O_2(g) \longrightarrow 2CO_2(g)$

2 mol	1 mol	2 mol
1 mol	0.5 mol	1 mol

At STP, 22400 mL CO_2 production requires 1 mole of CO and 0.5 mole of O_2.

For 750 mL CO_2 production = $\frac{750}{22400} \times$ 1mol CO and $\frac{750}{22400} \times$ 0.5 mol oxygen is required

= 0.0334 mole of CO and 0.0167 mol O_2

$\Rightarrow$ 0.0334 × 28 = 0.935 g CO

$\Rightarrow$ 0.0167 × 32 = 0.534 g O_2 **(2)**

(ii) Volume occupied by 44 g (1 mol) of CO_2 at STP = 22400 mL

Volume occupied by 80 g of CO_2 at STP

$= \frac{22400}{44} \times 80 = 40727$ mL = 40.727 L **(1)**

(iii) Number of molecules in 44 g (1 mole) of CO_2 = 6.022×10^{23}

No. of molecules in 4.4 g of CO_2

$= \frac{6.022 \times 10^{23}}{44} \times 4.4 = 6.022 \times 10^{22}$ **(1)**

(iv) The law associated in (i) above is **Gay-Lussac's law.** **(1)**

Q.27 O_2 is evolved by heating $KClO_3$ using MnO_2 as a catalyst.

$$2KClO_3 \xrightarrow{MnO_2} 2KCl + 3O_2$$

(i) Calculate the mass of $KClO_3$ required to produce 6.72 L of O_2 at STP.

[Atomic masses of K = 39, Cl = 35.5, O = 16]

(ii) Calculate the number of moles of oxygen present in the above volume and also the number of molecules.

(iii) Calculate the volume occupied by 0.01 mole of CO_2 at STP.

Ans. $2KClO_3 \xrightarrow{MnO_2} 2KCl + 3O_2$

$2 \times (39 + 35.5 + 3 \times 16)$ $2 \times (39 + 35.5)$ 3×22.4 L

$2 \times 122.5 = 245.0$ g $2 \times 74.5 = 149$ g $= 67.2$ L

(i) 67.2 L of O_2 is produced by $KClO_3 = 245$ g

1 L of O_2 is produced by $KClO_3 = \frac{245}{67.2}$

6.72 L of O_2 is produced by $KClO_3$

$= \frac{245 \times 6.72}{67.2} = 24.5$ g **(2)**

(ii) 245 g of $KClO_3$ gives 3 moles of oxygen

24.5 g of $KClO_3$ gives $= \frac{3 \times 24.5}{245} = 0.3$ mol

Since, 1 mole of oxygen contain

$= 6.022 \times 10^{23}$ molecule

$\therefore$ 0.3 mole of oxygen contain $= 6.022 \times 10^{23} \times 0.3$

$= 1.8066 \times 10^{23}$ molecules **(2)**

(iii) Since, 1 mole of CO_2 occupied = 22.4 L

$\therefore$ 0.01 mole of CO_2 occupied

$= 22.4 \times 0.01 = 0.224$ L **(1)**

Q.28 Consider the following reaction and based on the reaction answer the questions that follow

$$(NH_4)_2Cr_2O_7 \xrightarrow{Heat} N_2(g) + 4H_2O(g) + Cr_2O_3$$

Calculate

(i) the quantity in moles of $(NH_4)_2Cr_2O_7$, if 63 g of $(NH_4)_2Cr_2O_7$ is heated.

(ii) the quantity in moles of nitrogen formed.

(iii) the volume in litres or dm^3 of N_2 evolved at STP.

(iv) the mass in grams of Cr_2O_3 formed at the same time.

[Atomic masses: H = 1, Cr = 52, N = 14] **(ICSE 2015)**

Ans. (i) $(NH_4)_2Cr_2O_7 \xrightarrow{Heat} N_2(g) + 4H_2O(g) + Cr_2O_3$

1 mol   1 mol

Molecular mass of $(NH_4)_2Cr_2O_7$

$= 28 + 8 + 104 + 112 = 252$ g $= 1$ mol

63 g of $(NH_4)_2Cr_2O_7 = \frac{63}{252} = 0.25$ mol **(2)**

(ii) According to equation,

1 mol of $(NH_4)_2Cr_2O_7$ gives = 1 mol N_2

So, 0.25 mol of $(NH_4)_2Cr_2O_7$ will give = 0.25 mol N_2 **(1)**

(iii) Moles of nitrogen = 0.25

So, volume = number of moles × 22.4 L

$= 0.25 \times 22.4$ L $= 5.6$ L **(1)**

(iv) 252 g of ammonium dichromate yield 152 g of Cr_2O_3. (Molecular mass of $Cr_2O_3 = 152$ g)

$\therefore$ 63 g will yield $= \frac{152}{252} \times 63 = 38$ g of Cr_2O_3

$\therefore$ Mass of chromium oxide = 38 g **(1)**

Q.29 (i) A compound has the following percentage composition by mass, carbon 14.4%, hydrogen 1.2% and chlorine 84.5%. Determine the empirical formula of this compound.

[H = 1, C = 12, Cl = 35.5]

(ii) The relative molecular mass of this compound is 168, so what is its relative molecular formula?

Ans. (i) Empirical formula $\rightarrow CHCl_2$ **(3)**

(ii) $n = \frac{\text{Molecular mass}}{\text{Empirical formula weight}}$

($\because$ wt. of $CHCl_2 = 12 + 1 + 71 = 84$)

$= \frac{168}{84} = 2$ **(1)**

Molecular formula = $n \times$ Empirical formula

$= 2 \times CHCl_2$

$= C_2H_2Cl_4$ **(1)**

Q.30 (i) The empirical formula of a hydrocarbon is C_2H_3. The hydrocarbon has a relative molecular mass of 54. (At wt: H = 1, C = 12)

(a) What is the molecular formula of the hydrocarbon?

(b) Draw the structural formula of the hydrocarbon.

(c) Give the general formula of the hydrocarbon.

(Competency Based Que.)

(ii) Pratik heated 11.2 grams of element '*M*' (atomic weight 56) with 4.8 grams of element '*N*' (atomic weight 16) to form a compound. Find the empirical formula of the compound obtained by Pratik.

(ICSE Specimen 2025)

Ans. (i) (a) C_4H_6

(b) $H_3C—CH_2—C \equiv CH$ or $H_3C—C \equiv C—CH_3$

(c) C_nH_{2n-2} **(1 × 3)**

(ii) No. of moles of $M = \frac{11.2}{56} = 0.2$

$\Rightarrow$ no. of moles of $N = \frac{4.8}{16} = 0.3$

Then, $\frac{\text{no. of moles of M}}{\text{no. of moles of N}} = \frac{0.2}{0.3}$

Empirical formula is M_2N_3. **(2)**

TYPE - 10   03 Marks

Case Based Questions

1. Amit found that 30 g of a gas occupied 1000 c.c at STP.

(i) What will be the gram molecular weight of this gas?

(ii) Calculate the vapour density of this gas.

(iii) How many molecules of this gas will be present in 44.8 L of it? **(Competency Based Que.)**

Ans. (i) At STP, 1 mole of any ideal gas occupies 22.4 L.

$$\text{Number of moles} = \frac{\text{Volume of gas}}{\text{Molar volume at STP}}$$

$$= \frac{1\text{ L}}{22.4\text{ L / mol}} = 0.04464 \text{ mol}$$

The molar mass (gram molecular weight) is the mass of the gas divided by the number of moles.

$$\text{Gram Molecular Weight } (M) = \frac{\text{Mass of gas}}{\text{Number of moles}}$$

$$= \frac{30\text{ g}}{0.04464\text{ mol}} = 672.04 \text{ g/mol}$$

Thus, the gram molecular weight of the gas is **672.04 g/mol.** **(1)**

(ii) The **vapour density (VD)** of a gas is defined as the ratio of the molar mass of the gas to the molar mass of hydrogen (H_2), which is approximately 2 g/mol.

$$\text{Vapour Density (VD)} = \frac{\text{Molar Mass of Gas}}{\text{Molar Mass of } H_2}$$

$$\text{Vapour Density (VD)} = \frac{672.04\text{ g/mol}}{2\text{ g/mol}} = 336.02$$

Thus, the vapour density of the gas is **336.02.** **(1)**

(iii) $\text{Number of moles in 44.8 L} = \frac{44.8\text{ L}}{22.4\text{ L / mol}} = 2 \text{ mol}$

$\text{Number of molecules} = 2 \times 6.022 \times 10^{23}$

$= 1.204 \times 10^{24}$ molecules

Thus, the number of molecules present in 44.8 L of the gas is $\mathbf{1.204 \times 10^{24}}$ **molecules**. **(1)**

2. Ram took 5 moles of carbon atoms in a container, and Krish took 5 moles of sodium atoms in another container of the same volume **(Competency Based Que.)**

(i) Whose container is heavier?

(ii) Which container has a larger number of atoms?

(iii) Which container has a higher density?

Ans. (i) The molar mass of carbon (C) is approximately 12 g/mol.

So, the mass of 5 moles of carbon

$= 5 \text{ mol} \times 12 \text{ g/mol} = 60 \text{ g}$

The molar mass of sodium (Na) is approximately 23 g/mol.

So, the mass of 5 moles of sodium

$= 5 \text{ mol} \times 23 \text{ g/mol}$

$= 115 \text{ g}$

The mass of 5 moles of sodium (Na) (115 g) is heavier than the mass of 5 moles of carbon (C) (60 g).

Therefore, **Krish's container is heavier than Ram's container**. **(1)**

(ii) Since, 1 mole of any substance contains 6.022 $\times 10^{23}$ atoms.

Number of atoms in 5 moles of C $= 5 \times 6.022 \times 10^{23}$

$= 3.011$ atoms

Similarly, number of atoms in 5 moles of Na $= 5 \times 6.022 \times 10^{23} = 3.011 \times 10^{24}$ atoms

The number of atoms in 5 moles of both carbon and sodium is the same.

Therefore, both containers have the same number of atoms (i.e., 3.011×10^{24} atoms). **(1)**

(iii) Density is given by

$$\text{Density} = \frac{\text{Mass}}{\text{Volume}}$$

Since both containers have the same volume, the container with greater mass will have a higher density.

Krish's container (with sodium) has a higher density because it has a greater mass (115 g) compared to Ram's container (60 g). **(1)**

3. Ravi heated 367.5 g of $KClO_3$, in a test tube. The decomposition of potassium chlorate took place according to the equation.

[Atomic masses of K = 39, Cl = 35.5, O = 16]

$$2KClO_3 \longrightarrow 2KCl + 3O_2$$

Find

(i) the volume of the colourless and odourless gas liberated during the experiment.

(ii) the weight of the residue left behind in the test tube. **(Competency Based Que.)**

Ans. (i) $\text{Moles of } KClO_3 = \frac{\text{Mass of } KClO_3}{\text{Molar mass of } KClO_3}$

$\text{Moles of } KClO_3 = \frac{367.5\text{ g}}{122.5\text{ g / mol}} = 3 \text{ mol}$

From the reaction, 2 moles of $KClO_3$ produces 3 moles of O_2. So, for 3 moles of $KClO_3$, the moles of O_2 produced are $= \frac{3}{2} \times 3 = 4.5$ mol

At STP, 1 mole of gas occupies 22.4 L. So, the volume of O_2 gas produced is $4.5 \times 22.4 = 100.8$ L

The volume of the colourless and odourless gas (O_2) liberated is **100.8 L.** **(2)**

(ii) From the balanced equation, 2 moles of $KClO_3$ produces 2 moles of KCl. Therefore, the moles of KCl produced from 3 moles of $KClO_3$ are 3.

Molar mass of KCl = 39 + 35.5 = 74.5 g/mol

Mass of KCl = Moles of KCl × Molar mass of KCl

Mass of KCl = 3 mol × 74.5 g/mol = 223.5 g **(1)**

06

ELECTROLYSIS

Electrolysis is defined as "a process of decomposition of a chemical compound by the passage of electricity through its aqueous solution or molten (fused) state".

Terms Related to Electrolysis

1. Conductors

The substances which have very high conductivity for the flow of electric current are known as **conductors**. e.g. Metals and their alloys, certain non-metals like carbon-black, graphite and some organic polymers are conducting in nature.

- Conductors are generally of two types, i.e. **metallic conductors** (e.g. Cu wire) and **electrolytic conductors** (e.g. $CuSO_4$ solution).
- The compounds which do not allow electricity to pass through them are called as **non-conductors (insulators)** of electricity. e.g. Non metals (sulphur, phosphorus, etc.)

2. Electrolytes

The compounds which conduct electricity, when dissolved in water or in the molten state are called **electrolytes**. Electrolytes are of two types, i.e. **strong electrolytes** and **weak electrolytes**.

Comparative Study of Strong and Weak Electrolytes

Strong electrolytes	Weak electrolytes
• These are **good conductors** of electricity and have **high conductance**.	• These are **poor conductors** of electricity and have **low conductance**.
• Strong electrolytes are **completely dissociated** in fused or aqueous solution state.	• Weak electrolytes are **partially/less dissociated** in fused state or in aqueous solution.
• These electrolytes contain **only free mobile ions**.	• These electrolytes contain **ions as well as molecules**.
e.g. **Acids** – Dil. HCl, H_2SO_4, etc. **Bases** – NaOH, KOH, etc. **Salts** – NaCl, KCl (aqueous solutions), etc.	e.g. **Acids** – Carbonic acid (H_2CO_3), acetic acid (CH_3COOH), etc. **Bases** – NH_4OH, $Ca(OH)_2$, etc. **Salts** – Na_2CO_3, $NaHCO_3$, etc.

3. Non-electrolytes

Chemical compounds which do not conduct electricity in the fused state or in aqueous solution are called **non-electrolytes**. e.g. Pure or distilled water, alcohol, kerosene, glucose, etc.

4. Electrolytic Cell

The device in which electrolysis is carried out is called **electrolytic cell** or **voltameter**. A typical electrolytic cell contains **electrodes** and the **electrolytic solution**. It converts electrical energy into chemical energy.

Note - Electrochemical cell is a device which is used to convert chemical energy into electrical energy.

5. Electrodes

These are two graphite (carbon) rods or metal plates immersed in the electrolyte through which the current enters and leaves the electrolytic cell. The electrodes of a cell can be differentiated into two types.

Difference between Cathode and Anode

Cathode	Anode
• The electrode connected to the negative terminal of the battery is called **cathode**.	• The electrode connected to the positive terminal of the battery is called **anode**.
• During electrolysis, cathode acquires a **negative** charge and hence, ions in a solution which are positively charged (i.e. cations) migrate towards the cathode.	• During electrolysis, anode acquires a **positive** charge and hence, ions in a solution which are negatively charged (i.e. anions) migrate towards the anode.
• It is a **reducing electrode**, i.e. reduction takes place at cathode.	• It is an **oxidising electrode,** i.e. oxidation takes place at anode.

6. Ions

Atoms or group of atoms which carry a positive or a negative charge are known as **ions**. The charge on an ion, positive or negative is equal to the valency of the atom or the ion. The two types of ions are:

(i) **Anions** These are **negatively charged ions.** Anions migrate to the anode during electrolysis. Anions donate or lose electrons to the anode (oxidation process) and get oxidised to neutral atom.

e.g. **At anode** $\underset{\text{Anion}}{Cl^-} \longrightarrow \underset{\text{Atom}}{Cl} + 1e^-$ (oxidation)

(ii) **Cations** These are **positively charged ions**. Cations migrate to the cathode during electrolysis. Cations accept or gain electrons from the cathode (reduction process) and get reduced to neutral atoms.

e.g. **At cathode** $\underset{\text{Cation}}{Na^+} + 1e^- \longrightarrow \underset{\text{Atom}}{Na}$ (reduction)

7. Oxidation

It is a process which involves the **loss of electron** or **addition of oxygen** or **removal of hydrogen.**

e.g.

$Na \longrightarrow Na^+ + 1e^-$ (loss of e^-)

$C + O_2 \longrightarrow CO_2$ (addition of oxygen)

$H_2S + Cl_2 \longrightarrow 2HCl + S\downarrow$ (removal of hydrogen from sulphur)

8. Reduction

It is a process which involves **gain of electrons** or **removal of oxygen** or **addition of hydrogen.**

e.g.

$Cu^{2+} + 2e^- \longrightarrow Cu$ (gain of e^-)

$ZnO + C \longrightarrow Zn + CO$ (removal of oxygen)

$3Cl_2 + 2NH_3 \longrightarrow N_2 + 6HCl$ (addition of hydrogen to chlorine)

Note • **Oxidising agent** carries out oxidation of another substance and itself gets reduced.

• **Reducing agent** carries out reduction of another substance and itself gets oxidised.

9. Electrolytic Dissociation

The process due to which an ionic compound in the molten state or in the aqueous solution state, dissociates into ions by the passage of electric current through it, is called **electrolytic dissociation.**

e.g. $\underset{\text{Ionic}}{PbBr_2} \rightleftharpoons Pb^{2+} + 2Br^-$

10. Ionisation

The process by which polar covalent compounds are converted into ions, when dissolved in water is called **ionisation**. These solutions conduct an electric current.

e.g. Ionisation of hydrogen chloride (when added to water).

$$H^{\delta+}—Cl^{\delta-} + \underset{\text{Water}}{\overset{\delta-}{O}(H^{\delta+})_2} \rightleftharpoons \underset{\text{Hydronium ion}}{H_3O^+} + \underset{\text{Chloride ion}}{Cl^-}$$

H^+ ions combine with water to form **hydronium ion** $[H_3O]^+$.

Electrochemical Series (Activity Series)

The series of metals in which metals are arranged on the basis of ease with which their atoms lose electrons to form positive ions is called **electrochemical series of metals** (activity series).

Electrochemical Series

Metal	Cation	Increasing ease of loosing electrons (↑) / Increasing ease of reduction (↓)
K	K^{+}	
Ca	Ca^{2+}	
Na	Na^{+}	
Mg	Mg^{2+}	
Al	Al^{3+}	
Zn	Zn^{2+}	
Fe	Fe^{3+}	
Ni	Ni^{2+}	
Sn	Sn^{4+}	
Pb	Pb^{2+}	
H	H^{+}	
Cu	Cu^{2+}	
Hg	Hg^{2+}	
Ag	Ag^{+}	
Au	Au^{3+}	
Pt	Pt^{4+}	

Preferential or Selective Discharge of Ions at Electrodes

It refers to the preferential discharge of one particular cation at cathode and one particular anion at anode when an electrolyte contains two or more anions or cations.

1. **The Relative Position of Ions in an Electrochemical Series** Lower the position of an ion in an electrochemical series, more easily it will get discharged at the respective electrode.
2. **Concentration of Ions in the Electrolyte** Higher the concentration of the ions, greater is the chance of them getting discharged at the respective electrode.
3. **Nature of the Electrodes** Electrodes used in the process of electrolysis are **either inert or active**. If electrodes are active like Cu, Ni, etc. they will take part in electrolysis. If electrodes are inert like graphite, platinum, etc. they will not take part in electrolysis.

Electrolysis of Molten Lead Bromide

Electrolytic cell Crucible (i.e. made of silica)

Electrolyte Molten lead bromide ($PbBr_2$)

Electrodes Cathode and anode, both are made up of graphite plates (inert electrodes).

Temperature Above 380°C

Ions present Pb^{2+} and Br^{-}

Electrode Reactions

At cathode

$$Pb^{2+} + 2e^{-} \longrightarrow Pb$$

At anode

$$Br^{-} \longrightarrow Br + 1e^{-}$$

$$Br + Br \longrightarrow Br_2$$

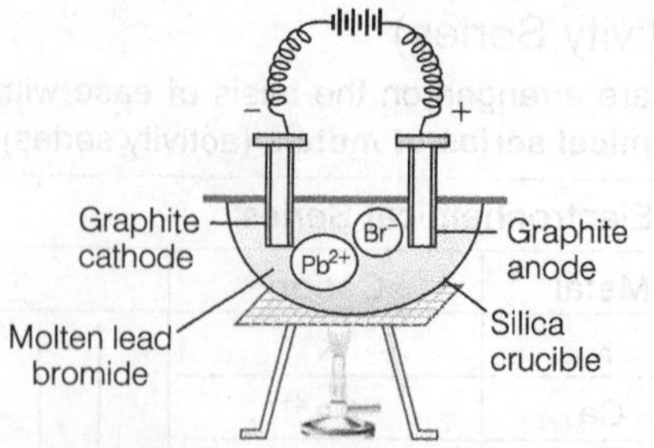

Electrolysis of molten lead bromide

Overall reaction $PbBr_2(l) \xrightarrow{380°C} Pb(s) + Br_2(g)$

Observation

- Dark reddish brown fumes of **bromine** evolve at the **anode.**
- Greyish white metal **lead** is formed at the **cathode.**

Note The electrolytic cell is made of silica because it is non-reactive, almost a non-conductor of heat and it can withstand high temperature. The silica crucible is heated slowly from outside to keep lead bromide in the molten state.

Electrolysis of Acidified Water Using Platinum Electrode

Electrolytic cell Hofmann's Voltameter

Electrolyte Acidified water (water + dil. H_2SO_4)

Electrodes Platinum foils (inert), connected by copper wires to the two terminals of a battery.

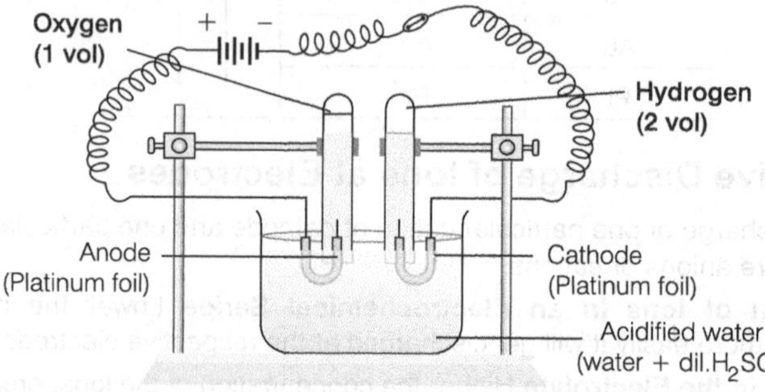

Electrolysis of acidified water using platinum electrodes

Ionisation of Acidified Water

Water is a non-conductor of electricity. It is a polar covalent compound and can form ions, when traces of dil. H_2SO_4 is added. Dil. H_2SO_4 catalyses this ionisation.

$$H_2O \rightleftharpoons H^+ + OH^-$$

$$H_2SO_4 \rightleftharpoons 2H^+ + SO_4^{2-}$$

Ions present H^+, OH^-, SO_4^{2-}

At cathode

$$H^+ + 1e^- \longrightarrow [H]$$

$$[H] + [H] \longrightarrow H_2 \uparrow$$

At anode

$$OH^- - e^- \longrightarrow OH$$

$$OH + OH \longrightarrow H_2O + O$$

$$O + O \longrightarrow O_2$$

(or) $$4OH \longrightarrow 2H_2O + O_2$$

Note The SO_4^{2-} and OH^- both migrate to the anode. OH^- being lower in the electrochemical series is discharged preferentially.

The electrolysis of acidified water can be summarised as

$$\underset{1\text{ vol}}{2H_2O} \xrightarrow[\text{Electric current}]{H_2SO_4} \underset{\substack{\text{(Cathode)}\\ 2\text{ vol}}}{2H_2(g)} + \underset{\substack{\text{(Anode)}\\ 1\text{ vol}}}{O_2(g)}$$

The ratio of hydrogen and oxygen liberated at the cathode and anode is in the ratio **2:1 by volume.**

Electrolysis of Copper Sulphate Solution Using Platinum Anode and Copper or Platinum Cathode

Electrolyte Saturated solution of copper (II) sulphate in distilled water (with traces of H_2SO_4)

Electrode Cathode Platinum

Anode Platinum

Dissociation of aqueous copper sulphate

$$CuSO_4 \rightleftharpoons Cu^{2+} + SO_4^{2-}$$

$$H_2O \rightleftharpoons H^+ + OH^-$$

Ions present Cu^{2+}, H^+, SO_4^{2-}, OH^-

At cathode The Cu^{2+} ions are below H^+ in the activity series, thus copper ions discharge in preference to H^+ ions, to neutral copper atoms.

$$Cu^{2+} + 2e^- \longrightarrow Cu$$

At Anode The SO_4^{2-} and OH^- ions both migrate to the anode. The OH^- ions, being lower in electrochemical series as compared to SO_4^{2-} ions, discharge to form neutral (OH) radical. The neutral (OH) radical rewrite to form water and oxygen.

$$4OH^- - 4e^- \longrightarrow 4OH$$

$$2OH + 2OH \longrightarrow 2H_2O + O_2$$

Product at anode Oxygen

Product at cathode Pink or reddish brown copper is deposited.

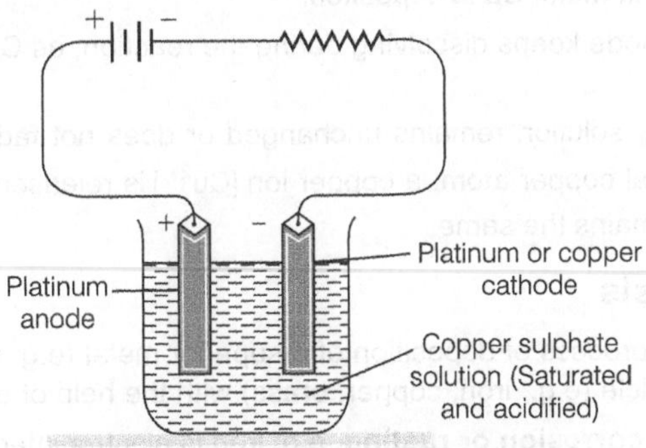

Electrolysis of copper sulphate solution using platinum as anode and copper or

Note The blue colour of Cu^{2+} ions in the electrolyte solution fades due to decrease in Cu^{2+} ions concentration and finally the solution becomes colourless as soon as Cu^{2+} ions are finished.

Electrolysis of Aqueous Copper Sulphate Using Copper Electrodes

Electrolytic cell Iron crucible/glass voltameter

Electrolyte Aqueous copper sulphate

Electrode Cathode:Copper, Anode:Copper

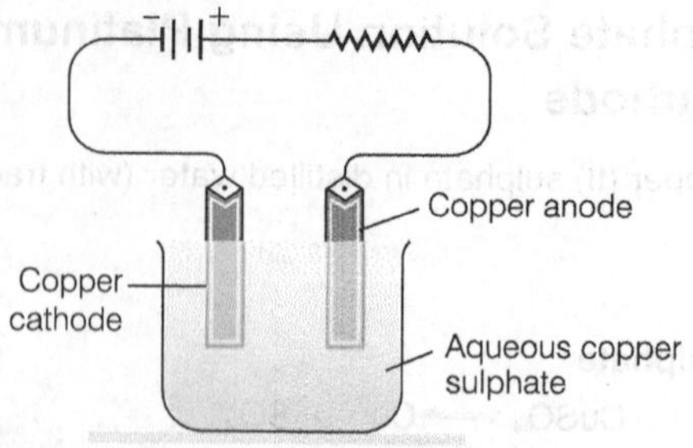

Electrolysis of aqueous copper sulphate using copper electrodes

- **Dissociation of copper sulphate** (*aq*)

$$\underset{\text{Copper sulphate}}{CuSO_4} \longrightarrow Cu^{2+} + SO_4^{2-}$$

$$H_2O \rightleftharpoons H^+ + OH^-$$

Ions present Cu^{2+}, H^+, SO_4^{2-}, OH^-

At Cathode $Cu^{2+} + 2e^- \longrightarrow Cu$ (Reduction reaction)

Both Cu^{2+} and H^+ ions migrate to the cathode, Cu^{2+} ions gets discharged as neutral copper atoms, by accepting electrons, as it is lower in the series.

At anode $Cu \longrightarrow Cu^{2+} + 2e^-$ (oxidation reaction)

SO_4^{2-} and OH^- ions migrate to the anode but neither of them are discharged due to the nature of the anode (active electrode). Thus, copper anode itself loses electrons to give Cu^{2+} ions.

- **Product at cathode** Brownish pink metal Cu is deposited.
- **Product at anode** Nil [Copper anode keeps dissolving during the reaction, as Cu^{2+} ions are formed, which will pass into the solution.]

Note The blue colour of *aq.* $CuSO_4$ solution remains unchanged or does not fade, as for every copper ion [Cu^{2+}] discharged at the cathode as neutral copper atom, a copper ion [Cu^{2+}] is released by the anode in the solution and hence total number of Cu^{2+} ions remains the same.

Applications of Electrolysis

- **Electroplating** is the electrolytic process of deposition of a superior metal (e.g. nickel, silver, chromium, gold) on the surface of a base metal or article (e.g., iron, copper, brass) with the help of electricity.
- Electroplating is done to **prevent corrosion or rusting**, e.g. iron is electroplated with nickel or chromium to protect against rusting. Electroplating is also done for **decoration purposes**, i.e. it makes the article attractive and gives it an expensive appearance. e.g. Brass metal plated with silver or gold.

Some Cases of Electrolysis

1. Electroplating with Silver

In order to get a perfect deposit of silver on brass spoon (article), the spoon is first cleaned and then washed with caustic soda, followed by hydrochloric acid and water.

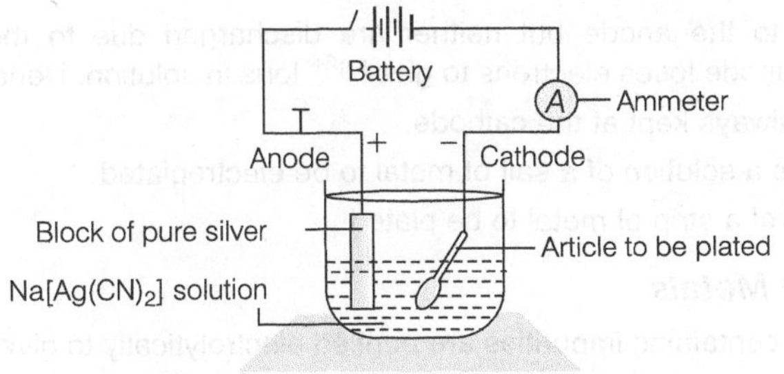

Electroplating an article (brass spoon) with silver

Electrolyte Aqueous solution of sodium silver cyanide i.e., sodium argentocyanide $Na[Ag(CN)_2]$ (or potassium silver cyanide, $K[Ag(CN)_2]$). It is prepared by adding sodium cyanide to a solution of silver nitrate till the precipitate is formed.

$$AgNO_3 + NaCN \longrightarrow AgCN\downarrow + NaNO_3$$

$$AgCN + NaCN \longrightarrow \underset{\text{(Sodium argentocyanide)}}{Na[Ag(CN)_2]}$$

Nature of Electrode

- **Cathode** Cleaned article to be electroplated.
- **Anode** Active electrode plate or block of pure silver metal.

Dissociation of aqueous sodium silver cyanide

$$Na[Ag(CN)_2] \rightleftharpoons Na^+ + Ag^+ + 2CN^-$$

$$H_2O \rightleftharpoons H^+ + OH^-$$

Reaction at cathode $$\underset{\text{(From electrolyte)}}{Ag^+} + 1e^- \longrightarrow \underset{\text{(Deposited)}}{Ag}$$

Ag^+ ions move towards the cathode and are discharged as neutral Ag atoms. Thus, silver is deposited on the spoon [cathode].

Reaction at anode $$\underset{\text{(from anode)}}{Ag} - 1e^- \longrightarrow \underset{\text{(goes into electrolyte)}}{Ag^+}$$

CN^- and OH^- ions migrate to the anode but neither gets discharged.

Silver anode loses electrons to give Ag^+ ions in solution due to the nature of the anode (active electrode). Hence, anode diminishes in mass.

2. Electroplating with Nickel

Iron article gets easily rusted when exposed to air. If they are coated with a metal like nickel, tin or zinc, rusting can be prevented.

Electrolyte Aqueous solution of nickel sulphate [$NiSO_4$] with few drops of dilute H_2SO_4.

Nature of Electrode

- **Cathode** Cleaned article to be electroplated.
- **Anode** Block of pure nickel metal.

Dissociation of aqueous nickel sulphate

$$NiSO_4 \rightleftharpoons Ni^{2+} + SO_4^{2-}$$

$$H_2O \rightleftharpoons H^+ + OH^-$$

Reaction at cathode $$Ni^{2+} + 2e^- \longrightarrow \underset{\text{[deposited]}}{Ni}$$

Ni^{2+} ions move towards the cathode and are discharged as neutral Ni atoms. Nickel is deposited on the article.

Reaction at anode $$Ni \longrightarrow Ni^{2+} + 2e^-$$

SO_4^{2-} and OH^- ions migrate to the anode but neither are discharged due to the nature of electrode (active electrode). Instead, the nickel anode loses electrons to give Ni^{2+} ions in solution. Hence, anode diminishes in mass.

Note
- Article to be plated is always kept at the cathode.
- The electrolyte must be a solution of a salt of metal to be electroplated.
- The anode is made up of a strip of metal to be plated.

3. *Electrolytic Refining of Metals*

It is a process by which metals containing impurities are purified electrolytically to give a pure metal.

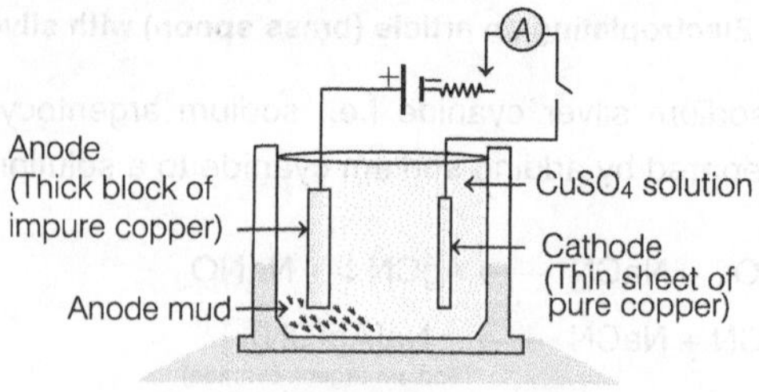

Electrorefining of copper

Electrolyte Aqueous copper sulphate solution [acidified with dil. H_2SO_4].

Nature of Electrode

- **Cathode** Pure thin sheet of copper.
- **Anode** Impure block of copper.

Dissociation of aqueous copper sulphate

$$CuSO_4 \longrightarrow Cu^{2+} + SO_4^{2-}$$

$$H_2O \rightleftharpoons H^+ + OH^-$$

Reaction at cathode $Cu^{2+} + 2e^- \longrightarrow Cu$

Cu^{2+} ions are discharged at the cathode. Thus, pure copper gets deposited on the thin sheet of pure copper placed at the cathode. [Cu – active electrode]

Reaction at anode $Cu - 2e^- \longrightarrow Cu^{2+}$

SO_4^{2-} and OH^- migrate to the anode but neither are discharged. Instead the copper at anode, loses electrons to give Cu^{2+} ions in solution. Hence, anode diminishes in mass.

Some impurities get dissolved in the acid while others, like silver and gold, remains insoluble and gets collected near the anode as **anode mud**, and are recovered later.

EXAM ORIENTED QUESTIONS

TYPE - 1   01 Mark

Multiple Choice Questions

Q.1 Which statement about conduction of electricity is correct? **(ICSE 2021-22, Sem-I)**

(a) Electricity is conducted in an aqueous solution by electrons.
(b) Electricity is conducted in a metal wire by ions.
(c) Electricity is conducted in a molten electrolyte by electrons.
(d) Electricity is conducted in an acidic solution by ions.

Ans. (d) Electricity is conducted in an acidic solution by ions.

Q.2 An electrolyte which completely dissociates into ions is **(ICSE 2019)**

(a) alcohol (b) carbonic acid
(c) sucrose (d) sodium hydroxide

Ans. (d) **Sodium hydroxide** is a strong electrolyte, therefore it dissociates completely into ions.

Q.3 The particles present in strong electrolytes are **(ICSE 2016)**

(a) Only molecules (b) mainly ions
(c) ions and molecules (d) Only atoms

Ans. (b) Greater the number of ions present in solution, stronger is the electrolyte.

Q.4 Identify the weak electrolyte from the following.

(a) Sodium chloride solution
(b) Dilute hydrochloric acid
(c) Dilute sulphuric acid
(d) Aqueous acetic acid

Ans. (d) **Aqueous acetic acid** is a weak electrolyte.

Q.5 A weak electrolyte is **(ICSE Specimen 2023)**

(a) alcohol (b) potassium hydroxide
(c) ammonium hydroxide (d) glucose

Ans. (c) **Ammonium hydroxide** is a weak electrolyte as it slightly ionises in water.

Q.6 Which of these will act as a non-electrolyte?

(a) Carbon disulphide
(b) Acetic acid
(c) Sodium hydroxide aqueous solution
(d) Potassium chloride aqueous solution

Ans. (a) **Carbon disulphide (CS_2)** will act as a non-electrolyte.

Q.7 The compound which is a non-electrolyte **(ICSE Specimen 2021-22, Sem-I)**

(a) KCl (*aq*)
(b) H_2SO_4 (dil.)
(c) CCl_4(*l*)
(d) CH_3COOH (*aq*)

Ans. (c) **CCl_4 is a non-electrolyte** because it is a non-polar molecule with covalent bonding. It does not contain ions.

Q.8 Two cells, *P* and *Q*, containing different liquids, were connected in series with a battery, a suitable lamp and inert electrodes, as shown in the diagram.

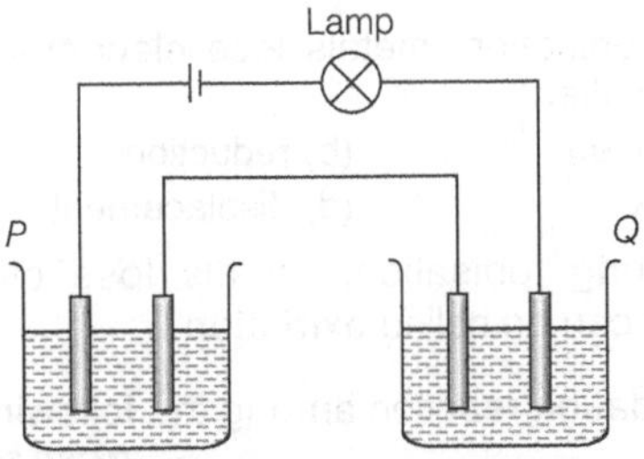

For which pair of liquids did the lamp light up?

	In *P*	In *Q*
(a)	concentrated sodium chloride solution	concentrated sugar solution
(b)	copper(II) sulphate solution	propanol
(c)	ethanol	molten lead(II) bromide
(d)	mercury	dilute hydrochloric acid

Ans. (d) **Mercury** being a metal helps to conduct electricity through free electrons. **Dil. HCl** have free ions i.e. H^+ and Cl^-, which helps to conduct electricity.

Q.9 Cathode is a reducing electrode because **(ICSE Specimen 2021-22, Sem-I)**

(a) it has less number of electrons.
(b) it has deficiency of electrons.
(c) cations gain electrons from cathode.
(d) anions lose electrons to cathode.

Ans. (c) During electrolysis, the **cathode can gain electrons** as it is positively charged. Moreover at cathode, reduction happens always.

Q.10 Which statement is not true for electrolysis? **(ICSE Specimen 2021-22, Sem-I)**

(a) Cations migrate towards cathode.
(b) Anions discharge at anode.
(c) Anions get reduced during electrolysis.
(d) Cations get reduced during electrolysis.

Ans. (c) During electrolysis, anions donate excess electrons and gets **oxidised** to neutral atoms.

Q.11 Which one of the following statement is not correct? **(ICSE Specimen 2021-22, Sem-I)**

(a) Pure water does not allow a current to flow through it.
(b) The electrolyte only conducts when in the molten state.
(c) Electrodes that react with the electrolytes are said to be 'active'.
(d) Ions must be present in the electrolyte in order that it conducts electricity.

Ans. (b) Electrolytes are those substances which conduct electricity in both **molten and aqueous solution**.

Q.12 During ionisation, metals lose electrons, this change can be called

(a) oxidation (b) reduction
(c) redox (d) displacement

Ans. (a) During ionisation, metals lose electrons, this change can be called **oxidation**.

Q.13 The oxidation reaction among the following is **(ICSE 2021-22, Sem-I)**

(a) $Fe^{3+} + 3e^- \longrightarrow Fe$ (b) $Fe^{2+} - e^- \longrightarrow Fe^{3+}$
(c) $Cl_2 + 2e^- \longrightarrow 2Cl^-$ (d) $Cu^{2+} + 2e^- \longrightarrow Cu$

Ans. (b) Among the given reactions, (b) is an example of oxidation reaction, as Fe^{2+} loses one electron to give Fe^{3+}.

Q.14 Solid sodium chloride does not conduct electricity as

(a) the strength of the bond is weak. **(ICSE 2021-22, Sem-I)**
(b) it contains free ions.
(c) it does not contain any free ion.
(d) it contains free ions as well as molecules.

Ans. (c) Solid sodium chloride does not conduct electricity as **it does not contain any free ions.**

Q.15 In a circuit below, the lamp lights up. **(ICSE 2021-22, Sem-I)**

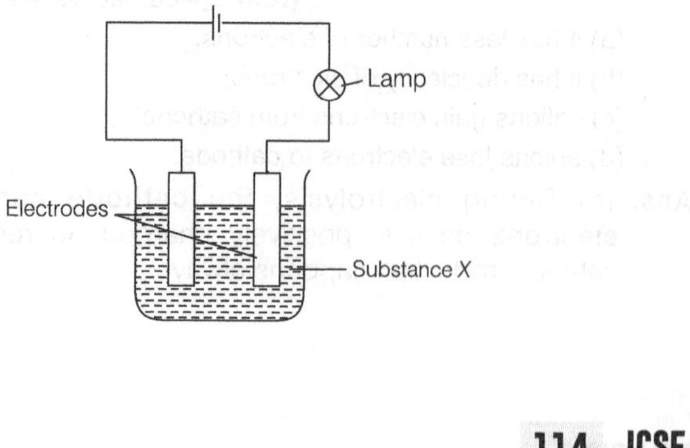

What could X be ?

(a) A solution of alcohol and water
(b) A solution of sodium chloride in water
(c) Sugar solution
(d) Solid potassium chloride

Ans. (b) X is a solution of **sodium chloride in water**.

Q.16 When a compound was electrolysed using inert electrodes, the gas released at the anode made a glowing splinter rekindle. The electrolyte that will not produce such gas observation at the anode is **(Competency Based Que.)**

(a) diluted solution of NaCl.
(b) concentrated solution of NaCl.
(c) dilute solution of copper sulphate.
(d) acidified water.

Ans. (b) Concentrated solution of NaCl.

Q.17 Hydronium ion is formed when a molecule of water combines with **(ICSE Specimen 2021-22, Sem-I)**

(a) hydrogen atom
(b) proton
(c) hydrogen molecule
(d) oxygen atom

Ans. (b) A molecule of water combines with **proton (H^+)** to form hydronium ion.

$$\underset{}{H_2O} + \underset{\text{Proton}}{H^+} \longrightarrow \underset{\text{Hydronium ion}}{H_3O^+}$$

Q.18 Select the ion that would get selectively discharged from the aqueous mixture of the ions listed below. **(ICSE Specimen 2021-22, Sem-I)**

(a) SO_4^{2-} (b) NO_3^-
(c) OH^- (d) Cl^-

Ans. (c) **OH^- ions** would get selectively discharged from the aqueous mixture due to **high discharge potential**.

Q.19 Three different beakers are set up as shown.

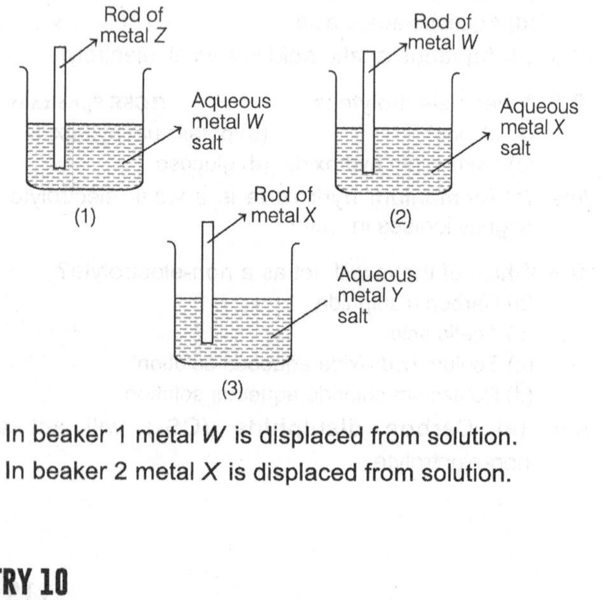

In beaker 1 metal W is displaced from solution.
In beaker 2 metal X is displaced from solution.

In beaker 3 metal *Y* is displaced from solution.

What is the order of decreasing reactivity of the four metals?

	Most reactive	→		Least reactive
(a)	*W*	*X*	*Y*	*Z*
(b)	*X*	*Y*	*W*	*Z*
(c)	*Z*	*W*	*X*	*Y*
(d)	*Z*	*X*	*W*	*Y*

Ans. (c) The lesser reactive metal will be displaced from it's solution by the higher reactive metal. Thus, the order of reactivity is $Z > W > X > Y$.

Q.20 The statements below show the results when three metal strips, P, Q and R, are placed in blue copper sulphate solution.

P. Solution turns green.

Q. Solution becomes colourless.

R. Solution remains blue.

Which of the following metals could be P, Q and R? **(Competency Based Que.)**

(a) P-Al, Q-Zn, R-Fe

(b) P-Zn, Q-Fe, R-Ag

(c) P-Fe, Q-Zn, R-Ag

(d) P- Zn, Q-Al, R-Fe

Ans. (c) Since Fe and Zn are more reactive than Cu so, Fe forms a greenish solution when reacting with $CuSO_4$, and Zn forms a colourless solution. Ag being less reactive, does not react with $CuSO_4$ and the solution remains blue.

Q.21 When electrolysis of molten lead bromide is carried out, the products formed at the respective electrodes are :

	At the positive electrode	At the negative electrode
(a)	Bromine	Lead
(b)	Bromine	Hydrogen
(c)	Lead	Bromine
(d)	Lead	Oxygen

Ans. (a) Dark reddish brown forms of Br_2 evolve at the anode. Whereas, greyish white metal lead is formed at the cathode.

Q.22 During the electrolysis of molten lead bromide, which of the following takes place?

(a) Bromine is released at the cathode

(b) Lead is deposited at the anode

(c) Bromine ions gain electrons

(d) Lead is deposited at the cathode

Ans. (d) Lead is deposited at the cathode.

Q.23 A compound which liberates reddish brown gas around the anode during electrolysis in its molten state is

(a) sodium chloride (b) copper (II) oxide

(c) copper (II) sulphate (d) lead (II) bromide

Ans. (d) Lead (II) bromide

Q.24 Identify one statement that holds true for electrolysis of molten lead bromide. **(ICSE 2021-22, Sem-I)**

(a) Silver grey metal deposits at the anode.

(b) Temperature is not maintained during electrolysis.

(c) Brown vapours of bromine are obtained at the anode.

(d) Electrolyte contains H^+ ions alongwith Pb^{2+} ions.

Ans. (c) Brown vapours of bromine are obtained at the anode.

Q.25 The picture given below shows an apparatus that a teacher used for demonstrating the properties of ionic substances. The teacher heats a sample of lead bromide in a crucible which contains two electrodes which are part of the circuit shown. The bulb does not light up. What is the best explanation for this?

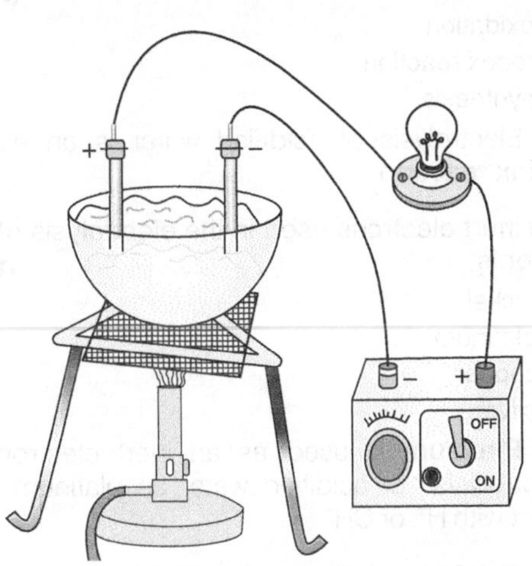

(Competency Based Que.)

(a) The circuit is complete.

(b) Molten lead bromide does not conduct electricity.

(c) The sample of lead bromide was not heated up to the melting point by the teacher.

(d) The DC power supply was set up correctly.

Ans. (c) The sample of lead bromide was not heated up to the melting point by the teacher.

Q.26 The electrolytic cell used for the electrolysis of molten lead bromide is made of silica.

Which of the following properties of silica that is the reason for it not having much significance in the process of electrolysis?

(a) Hard and strong
(b) Non-conductor of electricity
(c) Non- reactive.
(d) Withstands high temperature

Ans. (a) Silica is hard and strong, does not have much significance in the process of electrolysis.

Q.27 Which of the following statement(s) is/are correct regarding electrolysis of molten lead bromide?

I. Pb is oxidised to Pb^{2+}.
II. Pb^{2+} is reduced to Pb.
III. Pb^{2+} is attracted towards cathode.
IV. Pb is attracted towards anode.

(a) Both I and III
(b) Both II and III
(c) Both I and IV
(d) Only II

Ans. (b) During electrolysis of lead bromide, **Pb^{2+} is attracted towards cathode** and is **reduced to Pb** by gaining electrons.

Q.28 The electrolysis of acidified water is an example of **(ICSE 2018)**

(a) reduction
(b) oxidation
(c) redox reaction
(d) synthesis

Ans. (c) Electrolysis of acidified water is an example of **redox reaction**.

Q.29 The inert electrode used in the electrolysis of acidified water is **(ICSE 2020)**

(a) nickel
(b) platinum
(c) copper
(d) silver

Ans. (b) **Platinum** is used as an inert electrode in the electrolysis of acidified water as platinum does not react with H^+ or OH^-.

Q.30 Which of the following ions will readily discharge at the anode during the electrolysis of acidulated water? **(ICSE 2021-22, Sem-I)**

(a) OH^- (b) SO_4^{2-}
(c) Cl^- (d) H^+

Ans. (a) Among the given ions, **OH^-** will readily discharge at the anode during the electrolysis of acidulated water.

Q.31

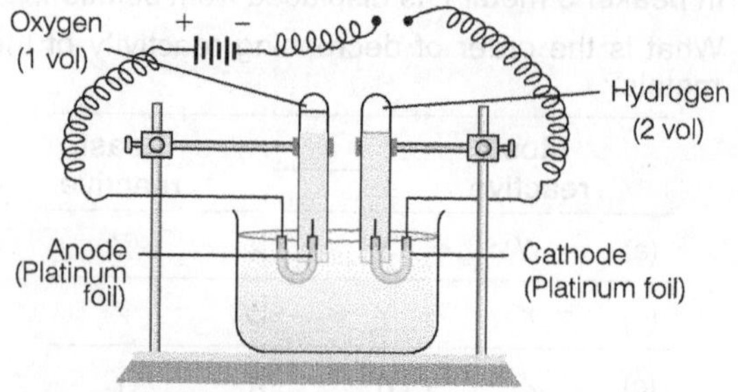

The above diagram represents the electrolysis of acidulated water. The reaction occurring at the anode is **(Competency Based Que.)**

(a) $H_2SO_4 \longrightarrow 2H^+ + SO_4^{2-}$
(b) $H_2O \longrightarrow H^+ + OH^-$
(c) $H^+ + e^- \longrightarrow H$, $2[H] + 2[H] \rightarrow H_2$
(d) $OH^- - e^- \longrightarrow OH$, $[4OH] \rightarrow 2H_2O + O_2$

Ans. (d) **At anode:**

$$OH^- - 1e^- \longrightarrow OH$$
$$2OH + 2OH \longrightarrow 2H_2O + O_2$$

Q.32 An aqueous solution of copper sulphate turns colourless on electrolysis. **(ICSE Specimen 2025, 2024)**

Which of the following could be the electrodes?

P. anode: copper; cathode: copper
Q. anode: platinum; cathode: copper
R. anode: copper; cathode: platinum

(a) Only P (b) Only Q
(c) Only R (d) Both Q and R

Ans. (b) Only Q. On electrolysis of copper sulphate solution with copper as cathode and platinum as anode, the solution turns colourless.

Q.33 Aqueous copper(II) sulphate is electrolysed using copper electrodes. The current is constant and the anode is weighed at regular time intervals.

Which graph is obtained when the mass of the anode is plotted against time?

(a)
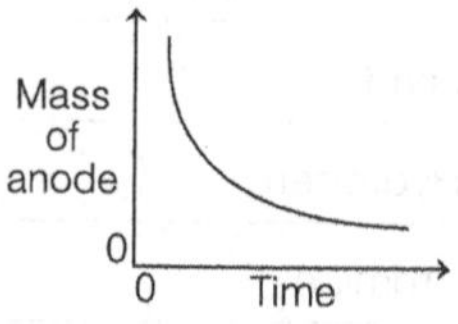

(b)
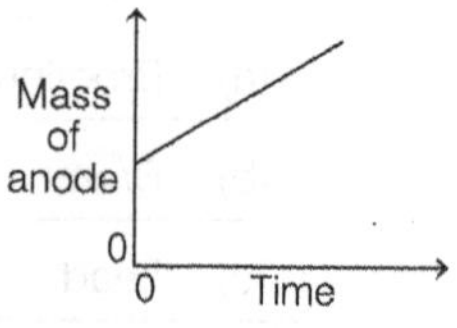

(c)
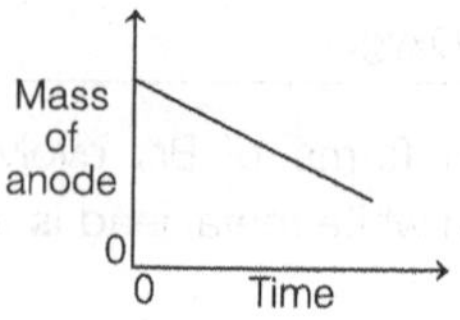

(d)
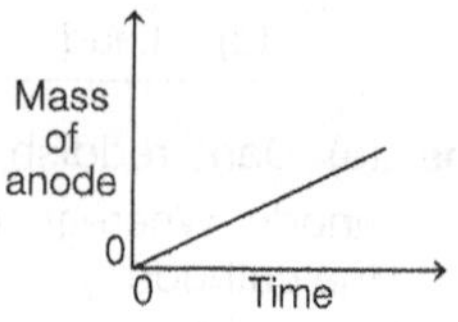

Ans. (c) When copper electrodes are used in the electrolysis of copper sulphate solution, the reactions at anode and cathode are

At anode

$$Cu \longrightarrow Cu^{2+} + 2e^-$$

(Copper dissolves from the electrode)

At cathode

$$Cu^{2+} + 2e^- \longrightarrow Cu$$

(Copper is deposited on the electrode)

Since, copper anode loses electrons to form Cu^{2+} ions. Thus, anode **diminishes in mass**

As the current is constant, the decrease in mass measured must be constant.

Q.34 The diagram shows the electrolysis of aqueous copper(II) sulphate using copper electrodes.

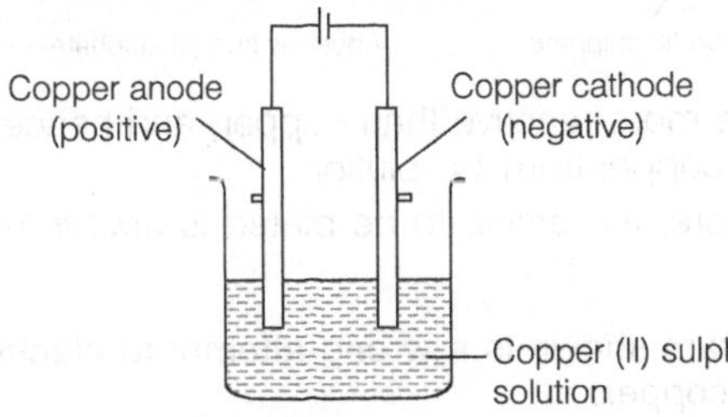

Which graph shows how the mass of the cathode changes during electrolysis?

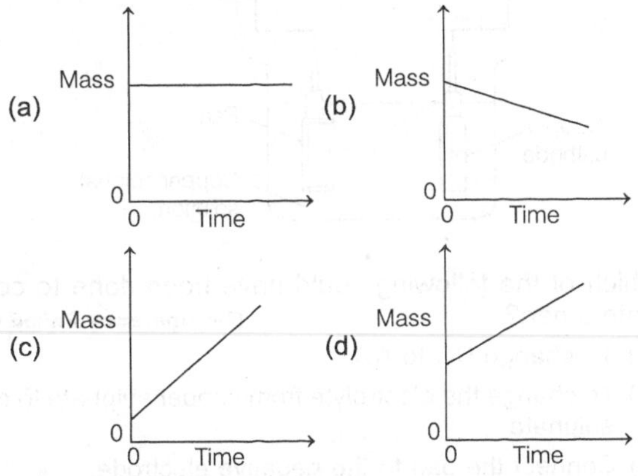

Ans. (d) Mass of cathode **increases** during electrolysis. At the start cathode must have certain mass, so that its mass can not be zero at the start of reaction.

Q.35 Aqueous copper (II) sulphate is electrolysed using copper electrodes.

Which statement about the electrolysis is not correct? **(ICSE 2025)**

(a) An oxidation reaction occurs at the positive electrode.
(b) The current is carried through the electrolyte by ions.
(c) The positive electrode loses mass.
(d) The number of copper (II) ions in the electrolyte decreases.

Ans. (d) The number of copper (II) ions does not decrease in the electrolyte, but it **remains the same**. This is because, for every copper ion discharged at the cathode to form copper metal, a Cu^{2+} ion is added to the solution by the anode.

Thus, the blue colour of the solution also does not fade during electrolysis.

Q.36 Thickness of metal coating during electroplating depends on **(ICSE Specimen 2021-22, Sem-I)**

(a) duration of current passage
(b) a low current
(c) nature of cathode
(d) purity of anode

Ans. (a) The thickness of the electroplating layer depends on time. **Longer the duration of current passage, thicker will be the plating.**

Q.37 Which of the following reactions takes place at the anode during the electroplating of an article with silver ? **(ICSE 2023)**

(a) $Ag - e^- \longrightarrow Ag^+$
(b) $Ag + 1e^+ \longrightarrow Ag^-$
(c) $Ag - 1e^- \longrightarrow Ag$
(d) None of the above

Ans. (a) $Ag - 1e^- \longrightarrow Ag^+$

Q.38 In which of the following electrolytic cells [*P*, *Q*, *R* or *S*] will silver plating be done on the spoon? **(ICSE Specimen 2024)**

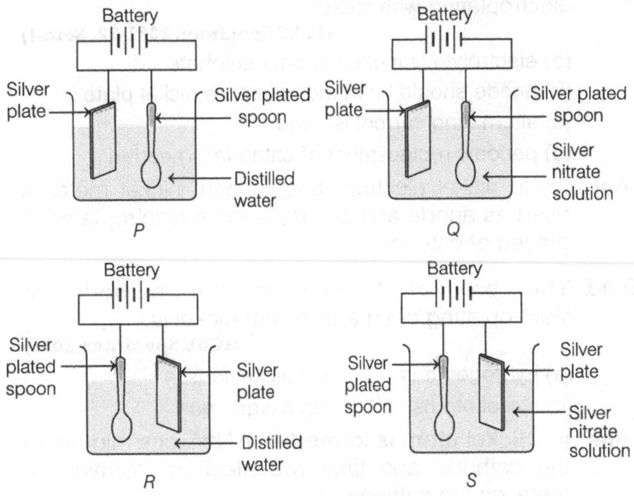

(a) *P* (b) *Q* (c) *R* (d) *S*

Ans. (b) The **anode is bar of silver metal** and the **electrolyte must contain Ag^+ ions** (i.e $AgNO_3$), so that when the direct current is passed through the cell, positive (Ag^+) ions move towards the **cathode (spoon)**. At cathode, Ag^+ ions gain electrons to form silver metal, which gets plated (or deposited) at the spoon.

Q.39 The diagram below shows a circuit used to electrolyse aqueous sodium argentocyanide. Which arrow indicates the movement of the silver ions in the electrolyte and of the electrons in the external circuit? **(Competency Based Que.)**

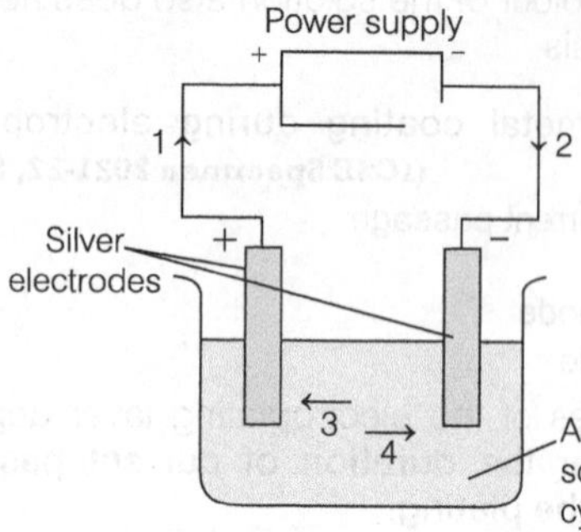

	Silver ions	Electrons
(a)	3	1
(b)	3	2
(c)	2	4
(d)	4	1

Ans. (d) Silver ions (Ag^+) are attracted to the cathode and the electrons move from the anode towards the cathode through the external circuit.

Q.40 The condition that is most appropriate for electroplating with nickel **(ICSE Specimen 2021-22, Sem-I)**

(a) electrolyte is molten copper sulphate
(b) anode should be made of impure nickel plate
(c) alternating current is used
(d) periodic replacement of cathode is needed

Ans. (b) In nickel electroplating, impure nickel metal is used as anode and an article to be electroplated is placed at cathode.

Q.41 The product formed at the cathode in electroplating of an article with nickel is **(ICSE Specimen 2023)**

(a) hydrogen gas (b) nickel ions
(c) nickel atoms (d) oxygen gas

Ans. (c) **Nickel atom is formed**. The Ni^{2+} ions migrate to the cathode and take two electrons forming Ni metal on the cathode.

Q.42 Which apparatus could electroplate an iron nail with copper? **(ICSE 2021, Sem-I)**

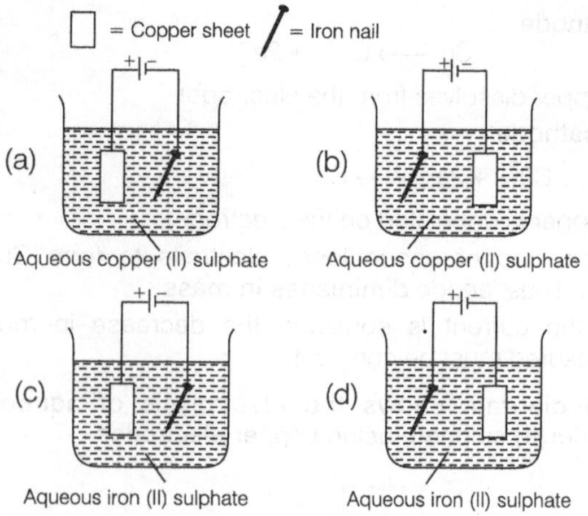

Ans. (a) Iron is more reactive than copper, and hence iron will displace copper from its solution.

Furthermore, the article to be plated is always made the cathode.

Q.43 The diagram shown is a wrong attempt to electroplate a pan with copper:

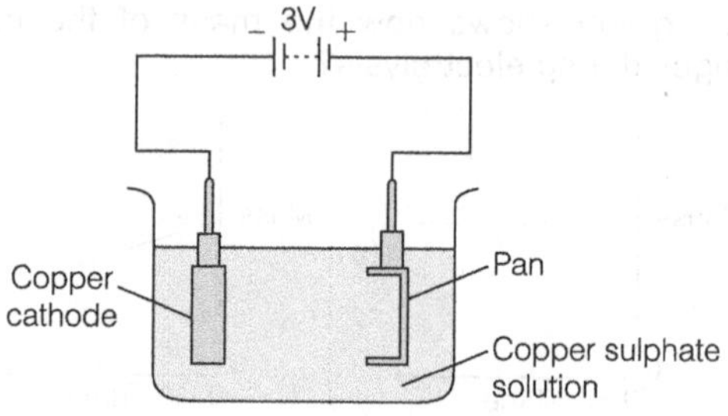

Which of the following could have been done to copper plate a pan? **(Competency Based Que.)**

(a) To change DC to AC.
(b) To change the electrolyte from copper sulphate to cobalt sulphate.
(c) Connect the pan to the negative electrode.
(d) To induce a higher current.

Ans. (c) The object to be electroplated is always placed at the cathode. So, connect the pan to the cathode (negative electrode).

Q.44 Identify one statement that does not hold true for electrorefining of copper. **(ICSE Specimen 2021-22, Sem-I)**

(a) Electrolyte is acidified $CuSO_4$ solution.

(b) Cathode is a thin strip of impure copper.

(c) Anode dissolves in the electrolyte.

(d) Cathode gets thicker.

Ans. (b) In electrorefining of copper, pure copper is obtained from impure copper and impure copper strip is used as anode and **pure copper strip is used as cathode**. Pure copper transfers from anode to cathode and deposits at cathode during the electrorefining process. **Deposition at cathode makes it thicker**.

TYPE - 2 — 01 Mark

Assertion-Reason Questions

Directions (Q. Nos. 1-5) In the following questions, a statement of Assertion (A) is followed by a statement of Reason (R). Choose the answer based on the codes given below.

(a) Both (A) and (R) are true and (R) in the correct explanation of (A)

(b) Both (A) and (R) are true but (R) is not the correct explanation of (A)

(c) (A) is true but (R) is false.

(d) (A) is false but (R) is true.

Q.1 Assertion (A) In an aqueous solution of salt, the ions present can carry electric charge.

Reason (R) The ions in the solution are free to move, allowing the solution to conduct electricity.

Ans. (a) In an aqueous solution, salts dissociate into ions, which are free to move and conduct electricity. This is why **salt solutions are electrolytes**. Thus, (A) and (R) are true and (R) is the correct explanation of (A).

Q.2 Assertion (A) Cations move towards the anode during electrolysis.

Reason (R) Cations are positively charged and are attracted to the negative electrode.

Ans. (d) **Cations**, being positively charged, **move towards the cathode (the negative electrode)**, not the anode. Thus, (A) is false but (R) is true

Q.3 Assertion (A) Hydrogen gas is not a common reducing agent in various redox reactions.

Reason (R) A reducing agent donates electrons to another substance, causing it to get reduced.

Ans. (d) (A) is false because hydrogen gas is a very common reducing agent in redox reactions, as it donates electrons to other substances, helping them to be reduced. (R) is true because a reducing agent donates electrons (not accepts them) to another substance, causing that substance to undergo reduction.Thus, (A) is false but (R) is true.

Q.4 Assertion (A) When an iron nail is added to blue copper sulphate solution, the solution turns colourless.

Reason (R) Iron is more reactive than copper so, it displaces copper from copper sulphate solution.

Ans. (a) Iron being more reactive than copper displaces copper from copper sulphate solution to form iron sulphate (colourless solution).

Thus, both (A) and (R) are true and (R) is the correct explanation of (A).

Q.5 Assertion (A) Electroplating is the process of using electrolysis to deposit a thin layer of metal onto another surface

Reason (R) Electroplating is only used to improve the mechanical strength of objects.

Ans. (c) (A) is true because electroplating uses electricity to coat a surface with metal. (R) is false because electroplating is mainly used to improve appearance, prevent corrosion and reduce friction, not just to strengthen objects.

Thus, (A) is true but (R) is false.

TYPE - 3 — 01 Mark

Fill in the Blanks

Q.1 Electrolysis is the passage of electricity through a liquid or a solution accompanied by a .... (physical/chemical) change.

Ans. chemical

Q.2 Cations are formed by ...... (loss/gain) of electrons and anions are formed by gain of electrons.

Ans. loss

Q.3 Metals are good .... (oxidising agents/reducing agents). **(ICSE 2023)**

Ans. reducing agents

Q.4 .... [Molten iron/Molten sodium chloride] conducts electricity by the movement of ions. **(ICSE 2025)**

Ans. Molten sodium chloride

Q.5 The ....(higher/lower) is the position of the cation in the electrochemical series, the greater the difficulty of it being discharged at the cathode. **(Competency Based Que.)**

Ans. higher

Q.6 The ion which could be discharged most readily during electrolysis is ... [Fe^{2+}/Cu^{2+}] **(ICSE 2023)**

Ans. Cu^{2+}

Q.7 Electrolysis of aqueous sodium chloride solution will form .... at the cathode. (hydrogen gas/sodium metal). **(ICSE 2018)**

Ans. hydrogen gas

Q.8 During electrolysis, the compound .... ($NaCl/PbBr_2$) in its molten state liberates reddish brown fumes at anode. **(ICSE 2023)**

Ans. $PbBr_2$

Q.9 An inert electrode used in electrolysis of acidified water is .... (iron/platinum). **(ICSE Specimen 2023)**

Ans. platinum

Q.10 During the electrolysis of copper sulphate solution, if .... is used as electrodes, the colour of the electrolytes does not fade. (copper/platinum)

Ans. copper **(ICSE 2024)**

Q.11 The reaction that takes place at the anode during the electrolysis of aqueous. Sodium argentocyanide with silver electrodes is ....

$[Ag \longrightarrow Ag^+ + e^- \ / \ Ag^+ + e^- \longrightarrow Ag]$ **(ICSE 2025)**

Ans. $Ag \longrightarrow Ag^+ + e^-$

Q.12 .... (Electrolysis/Electrolytic refining) is a process by which metals containing impurities are purified electrolytically to give a pure metal.

Ans. Electrolytic refining`

TYPE - 4 — 01 Mark

Correct the Incorrect Statement

Q.1 The ions in an electrolyte are free to move or carry charge only when the electrolyte is in solid state.

Ans. Ions in an electrolyte are free to move and carry charge only when the electrolyte is **molten or in aqueous solution**.

In the solid state, the ions are fixed in place and cannot move.

Q.2 Electrolysis does not occur in non-aqueous solution.

Ans. Electrolysis occurs in non-aqueous solution, if the compound is **molten**.

Q.3 Electrolysis is a reversible process. If we pass current in the reverse direction the products can be recombined into the original compound.

Ans. Electrolysis is **not a** reversible process. While electrolysis breaks a compound into its elements, simply reversing the current does not recombine the elements into the original compound.

Q.4 The process of electrolysis requires alternating current (AC).

Ans. The process of electrolysis requires **direct current** (DC).

Q.5 The electrolysis of copper sulphate using platinum electrodes produces copper at the cathode and sulphur at the anode.

Ans. The electrolysis of copper sulphate using platinum electrodes produces copper at the cathode (negative electrode), and **oxygen** at the anode (positive electrode).

Q.6 In electrolytic refining of copper, impure copper is taken as cathode.

Ans. In electrolytic refining of copper, impure copper is taken as **anode**.

TYPE - 5 — 01×05 = 05 Marks

Matching Type Question

Q.1 Match the Column I with Column II.

Column I	Column II
A. Copper	1. Electrolyte
B. Potassium	2. Metallic conductor
C. Sugar solution	3. Oxidising agent
D. Silver	4. Non-electrolyte
E. HCl solution	5. Reducing agent

Ans. A → 2, B → 5, C → 4, D → 3, E → 1

TYPE - 6 — 01 Mark

Identify the Following

Q.1 Name a substance that conducts electricity in molten or aqueous state. **(ICSE Specimen 2023)**

Ans. Electrolyte

Q.2 What type of electrolyte is an acidic solution which shows only partial ionisation of the solute molecules.

Ans. Weak electrolyte

Q.3 State the term used for two metal plates or wires through which the current enters and leave the electrolytic cell.

Ans. Electrode

Q.4 Name the process of formation of ions from molecules, which are not in ionic state.

Ans. Ionisation **(ICSE 2018, 2014)**

Q.5 Name a gas that is produced at the anode during the electrolysis of acidified water. **(ICSE 2018)**

Ans. Oxygen gas (O_2)

Q.6 Which gas is produced at cathode during the electrolysis of acidified water using platinum electrode.

Ans. Hydrogen gas (H_2)

Q.7 What ions must be present in a solution used for electroplating a particular metal?

Ans. Metal ions

Q.8 During silver plating of an article using potassium argentocyanide as an electrolyte, the anode material should be [Cu, Ag, Pt, Fe].

Ans. Silver (Ag)

Q.9 Name the electrolyte which is used for electroplating an article with silver. **(ICSE 2017)**

Ans. Sodium argentocyanide, $Na[Ag(CN)_2]$

Q.10 Name the metallic ions that should be present in the electrolyte, when an article made of copper is to be electroplated with silver. **(ICSE 2016)**

Ans. Ag^+ and Na^+

Q.11 Name the pink metal which deposits at the cathode, during the electrolysis of the solution of its salt.

Ans. Copper

Q.12 The electrode used as cathode in electrorefining of impure copper. **(ICSE 2020)**

Ans. Pure thin sheet of copper

TYPE - 7 02 Mark

Short Answer Type I Questions

Q.1 Differentiate between the terms, strong electrolyte and weak electrolyte. (Stating any two differences) **ICSE 2015**

Ans.

Strong electrolyte	Weak electrolyte
Electrolytes which allow a large amount of electricity to flow through them.	Electrolytes which allow a small amount of electricity to flow through them.
These are almost **completely dissociated** in fused or aqueous solution.	These are **partially dissociated** in fused or aqueous solution.
e.g. HCl, NaOH.	e.g. $CH_3COOH, Ca(OH)_2$.

(2)

Q.2 Give reasons, why?

(i) Although, copper is a good conductor of electricity, but it is a non-electrolyte. **(ICSE 2016)**

(ii) Why is carbon tetrachloride, which is a liquid, a non-electrolyte?

Ans. (i) Copper is a good conductor of electricity, but acts as a non-electrolyte, because copper metal is a solid element and does not have mobile ions to conduct electricity, i.e., it does not undergo chemical decomposition due to the flow of electric current through it. **(1)**

(ii) Carbon tetrachloride, being a **non-polar covalent** compound, does not have ions, so it does not conduct electricity and hence, called a non-electrolyte. **(1)**

Q.3 PQ_2 is a hard crystalline solid having high melting and boiling points. It is a good conductor of electricity in both molten and aqueous forms.

(i) The conductivity of PQ_2 is due to the presence of free .... (ions, molecules, electrons)

(ii) During electrolysis of aqueous PQ_2, if thickening of the cathode and thinning of the anode is observed, the anode material will be .... (graphite, metal P) **(Competency Based Que.)**

Ans. (a) ions (b) metal P **(1 × 2 = 2)**

Q.4 Explain how electrolysis is an example of redox reaction? Give an example.

Ans. Electrolysis is an example of redox reaction because it involves **both oxidation (at anode) and reduction (at cathode) reactions** at the electrodes. **(1)**

e.g. Dissociation of sodium chloride during electrolysis.

$$\underset{\text{(Aqueous)}}{NaCl} \rightleftharpoons Na^+ + Cl^-$$

At cathode: $Na^+ + e^- \longrightarrow Na$ (Reduction)

At anode: $Cl^- - e^- \longrightarrow Cl$ (Oxidation)

$Cl + Cl \longrightarrow Cl_2$

Overall reaction: $2NaCl \longrightarrow 2Na + Cl_2$ **(1)**

Q.5 Which electrode, anode or cathode is the oxidising electrode? Why? **(ICSE 2025, 2014)**

Ans. The **anode** is the oxidising electrode because it is the electrode where oxidation takes place. Oxidation means a substance loses electrons, and at the anode, these electrons are released and flow to the other electrode (the cathode). So, the anode is the electrode where substances give up electrons. **(2)**

Q.6 X : $HCl \rightleftharpoons H^{1+} + Cl^-$ (in solution state)

Y : $PbBr_2 \rightleftharpoons Pb^{2+} + 2Br^{-1}$ (in molten state)

From the above reactions X or Y, identify the reaction which exhibits

(i) electrolytic dissociation

(ii) ionisation **(ICSE 2024)**

Ans. (i) $PbBr_2 \rightleftharpoons Pb^{2+} + 2Br^-$ (in molten state)

Above reaction exhibits **electrolytic dissociation**. **(1)**

(ii) $HCl \rightleftharpoons H^+ + Cl^-$ (in solution state)

This reaction exhibits **ionisation**. **(1)**

Q.7 Select the ion in each case, that would get selectively discharged from the aqueous mixture of the ions listed below **(ICSE 2017)**

(i) SO_4^{2-}, NO_3^- and OH^- (ii) Pb^{2+}, Ag^+ and Cu^{2+}

Ans. (i) Based on the **tendency to lose electrons** and **getting discharged at the anode**, the anions have been arranged in **increasing order (on moving downward)** in electrochemical series. For given ions order is as follows

$$SO_4^{2-} < NO_3^- < OH^-$$ **(1)**

(ii) Based on the ease with which metal ions gain **electrons** to form metal atoms and get discharged, the metals are arranged in **increasing order (on moving downward)** in electrochemical series. For the given ions, order is :

$$Pb^{2+} < Cu^{2+} < Ag^+$$ **(1)**

Q.8 The diagram shows the electrolysis of a mixture of aqueous copper (II) nitrate, $Cu(NO_3)_2(aq)$ and aqueous silver nitrate, $AgNO_3(aq)$. Electrodes *X* and *Y* are inert.

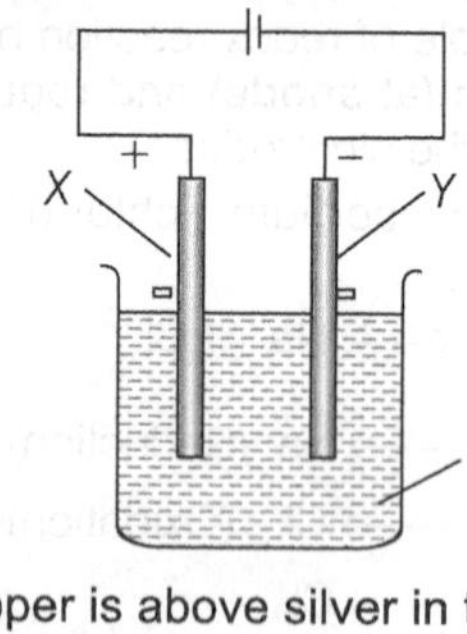

Copper is above silver in the reactivity series.

It can be deduced that ......1...... is initially deposited at electrode ......2...... .

which words correctly complete gaps 1 and 2?

Ans. Silver is lower than copper in the reactivity series which means it will be **reduced** and deposited at the **cathode** as the electrolysis starts. Thus, **1 is silver and 2 is *Y*.** **(2)**

Q.9 Give reason, why is the electrolysis of acidulated water considered to be an example of catalysis. Also, why dilute nitric acid or hydrochloric acid are not preferred during this electrolysis?

Ans. Water is a polar covalent compound. On addition of dilute sulphuric acid, it ionises into its ions. Acid **catalyses its ionisation** hence, electrolysis of acidulated water is considered as an example of catalysis.

Dilute sulphuric acid is preferred because it is **non-volatile** while, dilute nitric acid or hydrochloric acid are volatile acids. **(2)**

Q.10 State one observation for each of the following.

(i) Copper sulphate solution is electrolysed using copper electrodes.

(ii) Mg^{2+}, Cu^{2+}, Na^+, H^+ (In the order of preferential discharge at the cathode) **(ICSE 2019)**

Ans. (i) Copper sulphate solution is electrolysed using copper electrodes as:

Reaction at cathode

$$Cu^{2+} + 2e^- \longrightarrow \underset{\text{Reddish brown}}{Cu} \quad \text{(Reduction reaction)}$$

Reaction at anode

$$Cu \longrightarrow Cu^{2+} + 2e^- \quad \text{(Oxidation reaction)}$$ **(1)**

(ii) The order of preferential discharge at the cathode is as follows:

$$Na^+ < Mg^{2+} < H^+ < Cu^{2+}$$ **(1)**

Q.11 Define electroplating and give two reasons why an article is electroplated?

Ans. Electroplating is a process in which a thin film of a metal like gold, silver, nickel, chromium, etc., is deposited on another metallic article with the help of electricity. **(1)**

Two reasons for electroplating are:

(i) **Decorative purpose.**

(ii) To **protect from rusting and corrosion.** **(1)**

Q.12 Give reason for the following.

(i) An aqueous solution of sodium chloride conducts electricity.

(ii) In the electroplating of an article with silver, the electrolyte sodium argentocyanide solution is preferred over silver nitrate solution. **(ICSE 2016)**

Ans. (i) Aqueous solution of sodium chloride contains **mobile ions** like $Na^+, Cl^-, H^+, OH^-, H_3O^+$ ions, which are responsible for conduction of electricity. **(1)**

(ii) If silver nitrate solution is used directly instead of argentocyanide solution, the deposition of silver will be **very fast** and hence **not very smooth and uniform.** **(1)**

Q.13 For the electro-refining of copper,

(i) what is the cathode made up of?

(ii) write the reaction that takes place at the anode. **(ICSE 2018)**

Ans. For the electrolytic refining of copper:

(i) **Pure copper strip** is taken as cathode and Cu^{2+} ions are discharged at the cathode. Thus, pure copper gets deposited on the thin sheet of copper placed at a cathode. **(1)**

(ii) **Reaction at anode**, $Cu \longrightarrow Cu^{2+} + 2e^-$

Impure copper is taken as anode and acidified solution of copper sulphate ($CuSO_4$) acts as an electrolyte. **(1)**

TYPE - 8

03 Marks

Short Answer Type II Questions

Q.1 Define the following

(i) strong electrolyte

(ii) non-electrolyte

(iii) weak electrolyte **(ICSE 2019)**

Ans. (i) **Strong electrolyte** Those electrolytes which are **completely dissociated** in fused or aqueous solution state and are **good conductors of electricity** are called as strong electrolytes.

e.g., HCl, NaOH, $CuSO_4(aq)$, etc. **(1)**

(ii) **Non-electrolyte** Those electrolytes which **do not have ions** even in the solution and which neither in the solution nor in the molten state allows an electric current to pass through it are called as non-electrolytes.

e.g. alcohol, cane sugar, urea, etc. **(1)**

(iii) **Weak electrolyte** Those electrolytes which are **partially dissociated** in fused or aqueous solution state and are **poor conductors of electricity** are called as weak electrolytes.

e.g. carbonic acid, oxalic acid, etc. **(1)**

Q.2 Name the particles present in

(i) strong electrolyte

(ii) weak electrolyte

(iii) non-electrolyte **(ICSE Specimen 2023, 2019)**

Ans. (i) **Only ions** are present in strong electrolyte. **(1)**

(ii) **Both molecules and ions** are present in weak electrolyte. **(1)**

(iii) **Only molecules** are present in non-electrolyte. **(1)**

Q.3 Name the kind of particles present in

(i) sodium hydroxide solution

(ii) carbonic acid

(iii) sugar solution **(ICSE 2014)**

Ans. (i) Sodium hydroxide solution is a **strong electrolyte**.

Particles present in sodium hydroxide solution are **ions only**, i.e.,

$$NaOH \longrightarrow Na^+ + OH^-$$ **(1)**

(ii) Carbonic acid is a **weak electrolyte**, so particles present in weak electrolytes are **ions and unionised molecules**. **(1)**

(iii) Particles present in sugar solution (a **non-electrolyte**) are **molecules only**. **(1)**

Q.4 Three different electrolytic cells *A*, *B* and *C* are connected in separate circuits. Electrolytic cell *A* contains sodium chloride solution. When the circuit is completed, a bulb in the circuit glows brightly. Electrolytic cell *B* contains acetic acid solution and in this case, the bulb in the circuit glows dimly. The electrolytic cell *C* contains sugar solution and the bulb does not glow. Give a reason for each of these observations.

Ans. *A* contains sodium chloride solution, which is a **strong electrolyte**. Thus, contains only ions. So, **more electricity is conducted** and bulb glows brightly.

B contains acetic acid, which is a **weak electrolyte** and contains both ions and molecules. So, acetic acid has **less number of ions**. So, **less electricity is conducted** and bulb glows dimly.

C contains sugar solution, which is a **non-electrolyte** and a **covalent compound**. It **does not contain ions** in the solution. So, **electricity is not conducted** and bulb does not glow. **(3)**

Q.5 Electrons are getting added to an element *Y*.

(i) Is *Y* getting oxidised or reduced?

(ii) What charge will *Y* have after the addition of electrons?

(iii) Which electrode will *Y* migrate to, during the process of electrolysis?

Ans. (i) Electrons are getting added to an element *Y*.

So, *Y* is getting **reduced**. **(1)**

(ii) After the addition of electrons, *Y* will have **negative charge**. **(1)**

(iii) *Y* will migrate to **anode**, during the process of electrolysis. **(1)**

Q.6 Identify the following reactions as either oxidation or reduction.

(i) $O + 2e^- \longrightarrow O^{2-}$ (ii) $K \longrightarrow K^+ + e^-$

(iii) $Fe^{3+} + e^- \longrightarrow Fe^{2+}$

Ans. (i) **Reduction**

∵ Gain of electrons is taking place. **(1)**

(ii) **Oxidation**

∵ Loss of electrons is taking place. **(1)**

(iii) **Reduction**

∵ Gain of electrons is taking place. **(1)**

Q.7 State one relevant reason for the following.

(i) Graphite anode is preferred to platinum in the electrolysis of molten lead bromide. **(ICSE 2025, 2020, 2015)**

(ii) Electrolysis of molten lead bromide is considered to be a redox reaction. **(ICSE 2015)**

Ans. (i) Graphite anode is preferred to platinum in electrolysis of molten lead bromide as graphite is an **inert electrode** which **does not react with bromine liberated at anode**, while platinum may react with bromine. **(1)**

(ii) **Electrode reaction**

At cathode

$$Pb^{2+} + 2e^- \longrightarrow Pb \text{ (Reduction)}$$

At anode

$$Br^- - e^- \longrightarrow Br \text{ (Oxidation)}$$

$$Br + Br \longrightarrow Br_2$$

Since, **both oxidation and reduction** takes place at electrodes therefore, it is a **redox reaction**. **(2)**

Q.8 Acidulated water is electrolysed using platinum electrodes.

Answer the following questions:

(i) Why is dilute sulphuric acid added to water?

(ii) Write the reaction taking place at the cathode.

(iii) What is the observation at the anode? **(ICSE 2025)**

Ans. (i) Dilute sulphuric acid **catalyses** the ionisation of water. **(1)**

(ii) **At cathode** $H^+ + e^- \longrightarrow H$

$$H + H \longrightarrow H_2$$ **(1)**

(iii) **At anode, oxygen gas** is liberated with the formation of **water**.

$$OH^- \longrightarrow OH + e^-$$

$$OH + OH \longrightarrow H_2O + O$$

$$O + O \longrightarrow O_2$$ **(1)**

Q.9 During the electrolysis of copper (II) sulphate solution using platinum as cathode and graphite as anode.

(i) State what you observe at the cathode?

(ii) State the change noticed in the electrolyte.

(iii) Write the reaction at the cathode.

(ICSE Specimen 2023)

Ans. (i) During the electrolysis of copper (II) sulphate solution, the observation is that **red metal copper deposits** at the cathode. **(1)**

(ii) The change noticed in the electrolyte is that the **blue colour of copper sulphate solution fades very soon**. **(1)**

(iii) The reaction involve at the cathode is:

$$Cu^{2+} + 2e^- \longrightarrow Cu$$ **(1)**

Q.10 Rohan wants to electroplate a spoon with nickel. **(Competency Based Que.)**

(i) To which electrode should he connect the article to be electroplated?

(ii) Write the equation for the reaction that will occur at the cathode.

(iii) What should the anode be made up of?

Ans. (i) Cathode

(ii) At cathode, $Ni^{2+} + 2e^- \longrightarrow Ni$ (Reduction)

(iii) The anode should be a block of nickel. **(1 × 3 = 3)**

Q.11 (i) Copy and complete the following table : **ICSE 2015**

	Anode	Electrolyte
Purification of copper		

(ii) Write the equation taking place at the anode.

Ans. (i)

	Anode	**Electrolyte**
Purification of copper	Impure copper metal	Aqueous copper sulphate with traces of H_2SO_4.

(2)

(ii) Equation taking place at the anode is

$$\underset{\text{Metal}}{Cu} \longrightarrow Cu^{2+} + 2e^-$$ **(1)**

Q.12 Differentiate between electrical conductivity of copper sulphate solution and copper metal.

Ans. Copper (II) sulphate is an **electrolyte**. During electrolysis of copper (II) sulphate solution, the $CuSO_4$ solution splits into Cu^{2+} and SO_4^{2-} ions. The Cu^{2+} ions are discharged at the cathode as copper metal.

Copper metal only conducts electricity, but is a **non-electrolyte**, since it does not undergo any change due to flow of electric current through it. **(3)**

Q.13

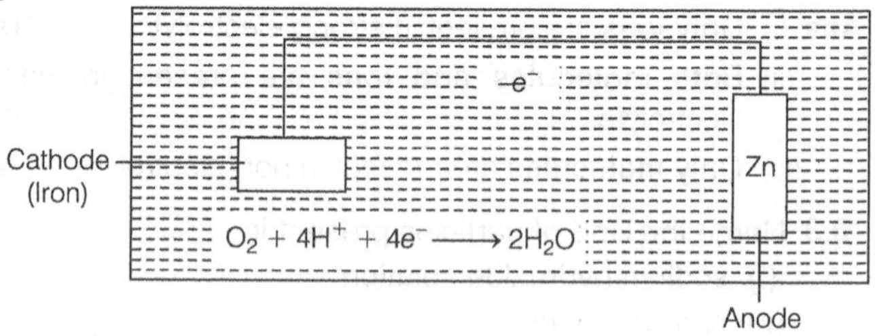

$$2Zn \longrightarrow 2Zn^{2+} + 4e^-$$

Study the given figure and answer the given questions.

(i) Identify the application of electrolysis demonstrated above.

(ii) Which metal is protected in the above process?

(iii) Why should the metal be protected?

(Competency Based Que.)

Ans. (i) **Electroplating** process is demonstrated in the figure.

(ii) **Iron** is protected by **electroplating with zinc**.

(iii) The metal is protected by electroplating to **prevent it from rusting**. **(1 × 3 = 3)**

TYPE - 9 04/05 Marks

Long Answer Type Questions

Q.1 Choose the correct word which refers to the process of electrolysis from *A* to *E*, to match the description (i) to (iv):

A : Oxidation, B : Cathode, C : Anode,
D : An electrolyte, E : Reduction

(i) Conducts electricity in aqueous or in molten state.
(ii) Loss of electron takes place at anode.
(iii) A reducing electrode.
(iv) Electrode connected to the positive end or terminal of the battery. **(ICSE 2020)**

Ans. (i) D : An electrolyte (ii) A : Oxidation
(iii) B : Cathode (iv) C : Anode **(1 × 4 = 4)**

Q.2 Copy and complete the following table which refers to the conversion of ions to neutral particles. **(ICSE 2018)**

Conversion	Ionic equation	Oxidation/Reduction
Chloride ion to chlorine molecule	(i)	(ii) ....
Lead (II) ion to lead atom	(iii)	(iv) ....

Ans.

Conversion	Ionic equation	Oxidation/ Reduction
Chloride ion to chlorine molecule	(i) $2Cl^- \longrightarrow \overset{0}{Cl_2} + 2e^-$	(ii) Oxidation (Loss of electrons)
Lead (II) ion to lead atom	(iii) $Pb^{2+} + 2e^- \longrightarrow \overset{0}{Pb}$	(iv) Reduction (Gain of electrons)

(2 × 2 = 4)

Q.3 (i) At which electrode (anode or cathode) would following reaction take place? Is this an example of oxidation or reduction?

$$Cu \longrightarrow Cu^{2+} + 2e^-$$

(ii) A solution contains magnesium ions (Mg^{2+}), iron (II) ions (Fe^{2+}), and copper ions (Cu^{2+}). On passing an electric current through this solution, which ions will be the first to be discharged at the cathode? Write the equation for the cathode reaction.

Ans. (i) This reaction will take place at **anode**, because **oxidation** takes place at anode. It is an example of oxidation, oxidation involves the **loss of electron(s)**. **(2)**

(ii) Cu^{2+} **ions** will be discharged first.

∵ Based on the ease with which ions of metals will **gain electrons** to form atoms, the ions are arranged in **increasing order (on moving downward)** to undergo **reduction**, $Mg^{2+} < Fe^{2+} < Cu^{2+}$

$$Cu^{2+} + 2e^- \longrightarrow Cu \quad \text{(At cathode)}$$ **(2)**

Q.4 Select the correct answer from the list given in brackets. **(ICSE 2014)**

(i) An aqueous electrolyte consists of the ions mentioned in the list, the ion which could be discharged most readily during electrolysis.
[Fe^{2+}, Cu^{2+}, Pb^{2+}, H^+]

(ii) The metallic electrode which does not take part in an electrolytic reaction.
[Cu, Ag, Pt, Ni]

(iii) The ion which is discharged at the anode during the electrolysis of copper sulphate solution using copper electrodes as anode and cathode.
[Cu^{2+}, OH^-, SO_4^{2-}, H^+]

(iv) When dilute sodium chloride is electrolysed using graphite electrodes, the cation which is discharged at the cathode most readily.
[Na^+, OH^-, H^+, Cl^-]

Ans. (i) Cu^{2+} (ii) Pt
(iii) Cu^{2+} (iv) H^+ **(1 × 4 = 4)**

Q.5 Write equations for the reactions taking place at the two electrodes (mentioning clearly the name of the electrode) during the electrolysis of **(ICSE 2016)**

(i) acidified copper sulphate solution with copper electrodes.
(ii) molten lead bromide with inert electrodes.

Ans. (i) **At anode** Electrode is that of copper metal.

$$Cu \longrightarrow Cu^{2+} + 2e^-$$

At cathode Electrode is that of copper metal.

$$Cu^{2+} + 2e^- \longrightarrow Cu$$ **(2)**

(ii) **At anode** Electrode is that of graphite.

$$Br^- \longrightarrow Br + e^-$$
$$Br + Br \longrightarrow Br_2$$

At cathode Electrode is that of graphite.

$$Pb^{2+} + 2e^- \longrightarrow Pb$$ **(2)**

Q.6 State the observations at the anode and at the cathode during the electrolysis of **(ICSE 2017)**

(i) fused lead bromide using graphite electrodes.

(ii) copper sulphate solution using copper electrodes.

Ans. Electrode reactions

(i) **At anode** Dark reddish brown fumes of bromine evolve at the anode.

$$Br^- \longrightarrow Br + e^- \text{(Oxidation)}$$

$$Br + Br \longrightarrow Br_2$$

At cathode Greyish white metal lead is formed at the cathode.

$$Pb^{2+} + 2e^- \longrightarrow Pb \text{ (Reduction)}$$ **(2)**

(ii) **At cathode** Cu^{2+} ions and H^+ ions migrate towards the cathode but Cu^{2+} ions are discharged in preference to H^+.

$$Cu^{2+} + 2e^- \longrightarrow Cu \quad \text{(Oxidation)}$$

At anode $Cu \longrightarrow Cu^{2+} + 2e^-$ (Reduction)

SO_4^{2-} and OH^- ions migrate to anode, but neither of them are discharged, due to nature of the anode. Copper loses electrons more easily than SO_4^{2-} and OH^- because copper anode itself ionises to give Cu^{2+} ions. **(2)**

Q.7 During the electrolysis of copper (II) sulphate solution using platinum as cathode and carbon as anode.

(i) What do you observe at the cathode and at the anode?

(ii) What changes is noticed in the electrolyte?

(iii) Write the reactions at the cathode and at the anode.

Ans. (i) Copper metal deposits at cathode, while colourless and odourless oxygen gas is liberated at anode. **(1)**

(ii) The blue colour of copper sulphate solution soon fades. **(1)**

(iii) **At cathode** $Cu^{2+} + 2e^- \longrightarrow Cu$

At anode $4OH^- - 4e^- \longrightarrow 4OH$

$$2OH + 2OH \longrightarrow 2H_2O + O_2$$ **(2)**

Q.8 Give any four conditions required for electroplating.

Ans. 1. The article to be electroplated is always placed at the cathode.

2. The metal to be plated on the article is always made the anode.

3. The electrolyte must contain ions of the metal which is to be plated on the article [i.e., it should be a suitable salt of the plating metal].

4. A low current for a longer time should be used.

(1 × 4 = 4)

Q.9

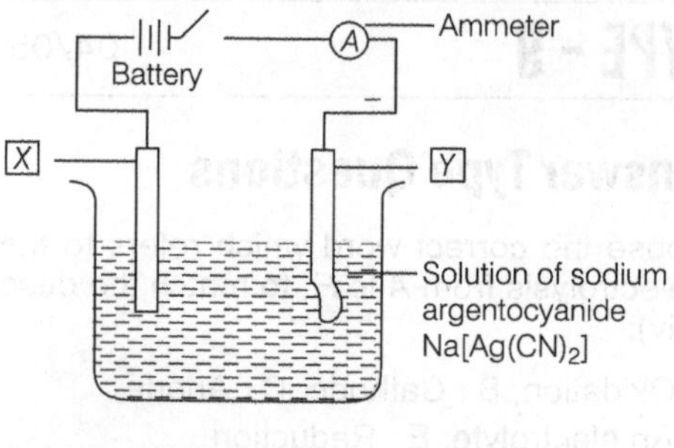

Electroplating of a brass spoon with silver is shown in the above diagram.

(i) Identify *X* and *Y*.

(ii) How will you prepare the electrolyte used in the above process?

(iii) Give the reaction taking place at cathode.

(iv) What reaction will take place at anode?

Ans. (i) *X* = Block of pure silver (anode)

Y = Article to be electroplated of brass spoon (cathode) **(1)**

(ii) The electrolyte, sodium argentocyanide ($Na[Ag(CN)_2]$) can be prepared by adding sodium cyanide to a solution of silver nitrate until the precipitate formed just dissolves.

$$AgNO_3 + NaCN \longrightarrow AgCN\downarrow + NaNO_3$$

$$AgCN + NaCN \longrightarrow \underset{\text{Sodium argentocyanide}}{Na[Ag(CN)_2]}$$ **(1)**

(iii) **At cathode** $\underset{\text{(From electrolyte)}}{Ag^+} + e^- \longrightarrow \underset{\text{(Deposited)}}{Ag}$ **(1)**

(iv) **At anode** $\underset{\text{(From anode)}}{Ag} - e^- \longrightarrow \underset{\text{(Goes into electrolyte)}}{Ag^+}$ **(1)**

Q.10 An aqueous solution of nickel (II) sulphate was electrolysed using nickel electrodes. Observe the diagram and answer the questions that follows: **(ICSE 2020)**

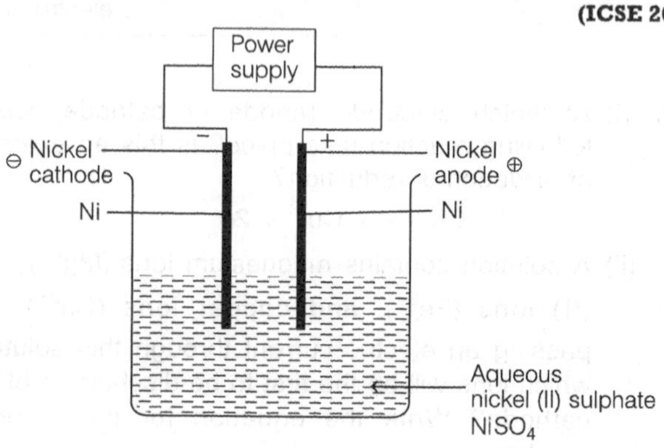

(i) What do you observe at the cathode and anode respectively?

(ii) Name the cation that remains as a spectator ion in the solution.

(iii) Which equation for the reaction at the anode is correct?

(a) $Ni \longrightarrow Ni^{2+} + 2e^-$ (b) $Ni + 2e^- \longrightarrow Ni^{2+}$

(c) $Ni^{2+} \longrightarrow Ni + 2e^-$ (d) $Ni^{2+} + 2e^- \longrightarrow Ni$

Ans. (i) **At anode**, oxidation or loss of e^- takes place.
At cathode, reduction or gain of e^- takes place. **(2)**

(ii) H^+ **(1)**

(iii) (a) $Ni \longrightarrow Ni^{2+} + 2e^-$ **(1)**

Q.11 **Choose A, B, C or D to match the description (a) to (e) below. Some alphabets may be repeated**

A. non-electrolyte B. strong electrolyte

C. weak electrolyte D. metallic conductor

(a) Molten ionic compound

(b) Carbon tetrachloride

(c) An aluminium wire

(d) A solution containing solvent molecules, solute molecules and ions formed by the dissociation of solute molecules.

(e) A sugar solution with sugar molecules and water molecules.

Ans.

a. Molten ionic compound	B. Strong electrolyte
b. Carbon tetrachloride	A. Non-electrolyte
c. An aluminium wire	D. Metallic conductor
d. Solution containing solvent, solute and ions	C. Weak electrolyte
e. Sugar solution	A. Non-electrolyte

(1 × 5 = 5)

Q.12 **(i) Study the diagram and answer the questions given below**

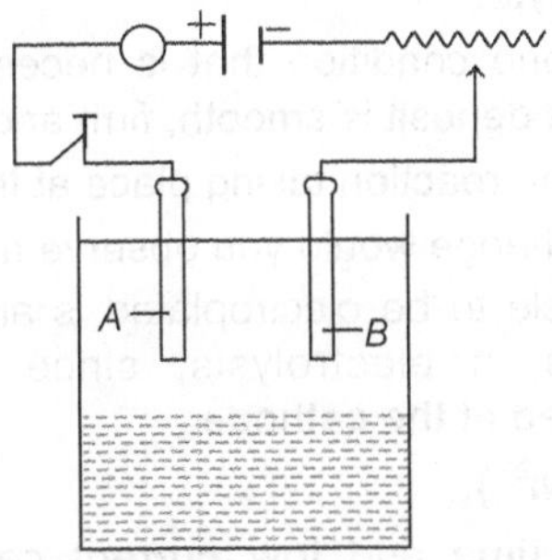

(a) Give the names of the electrodes *A* and *B*.

(b) Which electrode is the oxidising electrode?

(ii) A strip of copper is placed in three different colourless salt solutions. They are $AgNO_3$, KNO_3, and $Zn(NO_3)_2$. Which one of the solution will finally turn blue?

(iii) Write the equations of the reactions which take place at the cathode and anode when acidified water is electrolysed.

Ans. (i) (a) A-Anode; B-Cathode

(b) **Anode A** is the oxidising electrode. **(2)**

(ii) **$AgNO_3$ solution.**

Copper can displace a metal from its salt to form blue salt solution only when the **metal is less reactive than copper.** **(1)**

(iii) **At cathode** $H^+ + e^- \longrightarrow H$

$H + H \longrightarrow H_2$

At anode $OH^- \longrightarrow OH + e^-$

$OH + OH \longrightarrow H_2O + O$

$O + O \longrightarrow O_2$ **(2)**

Q.13 **Copper sulphate solution is electrolysed using copper electrodes.**

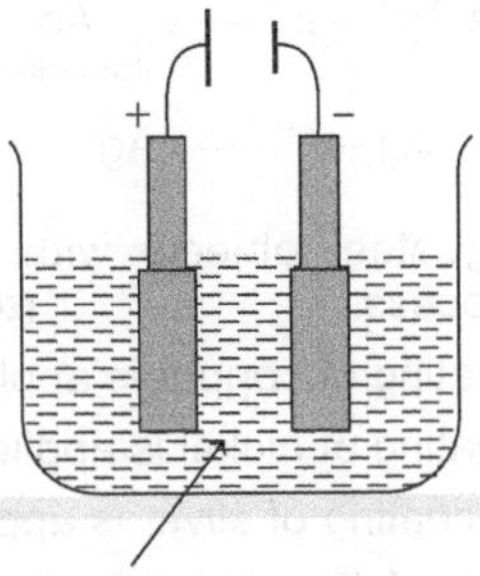

Study the given diagram and answer the questions that follows

(i) Which electrode to your left or right is known as the oxidising electrode and why?

(ii) Write the equations representing the reactions that occurs at cathode and anode.

(ICSE specimen 2025)

(iii) State two appropriate observations for the above electrolysis reactions.

Ans. (i) **Left** is oxidising electrode, as **oxidation** (loss of electrons) take place at this electrode. **(1)**

(ii) **At anode** $Cu - 2e^- \longrightarrow Cu^{2+}$ (Oxidation)

At cathode $Cu^{2+} + 2e^- \longrightarrow Cu$ (Reduction) **(2)**

(iii) (a) Reddish brown copper is deposited at cathode.

(b) Blue colour of electrolytic solution, i.e., $CuSO_4$ **does not fade** during the process due to the copper electrodes. **(2)**

Q.14 A metal article is to be electroplated with silver. The electrolyte selected is sodium argentocyanide.

(i) What kind of salt is sodium argentocyanide?

(ii) Why is it preferred to silver nitrate as an electrolyte?

(iii) State one condition to ensure that the deposit is smooth, firm and long lasting.

(iv) Write the reaction taking place at the cathode.

(v) Write the reaction taking place at the anode.

Ans. (i) Sodium argentocyanide is a **complex salt**.

(ii) Sodium argentocyanide is preferred over silver nitrate for electroplating an article with silver because it **dissociates slowly** in comparison to silver nitrate which makes the **deposition of silver ions slow and smooth** and resulting in **more smooth coating**.

(iii) **Less amount of current should be supplied for longer time** and only **direct current** is to be used for electroplating, otherwise no effective coating takes place on cathode.

(iv) **At cathode** $Ag^+ + e^- \longrightarrow \underset{\text{(Deposited)}}{Ag}$

(v) **At anode** $Ag - e^- \longrightarrow Ag^+$ **(1 × 5 = 5)**

Q.15 Electroplating steel objects with silver involves a three-step process. **(ICSE Specimen 2025)**

Step 1 : A coating of copper is applied to the object.

Step 2 : A coating of nickel is applied to the object.

Step 3 : The coating of silver is applied to the object.

(i) A diagram of the apparatus used for step 1 is shown.

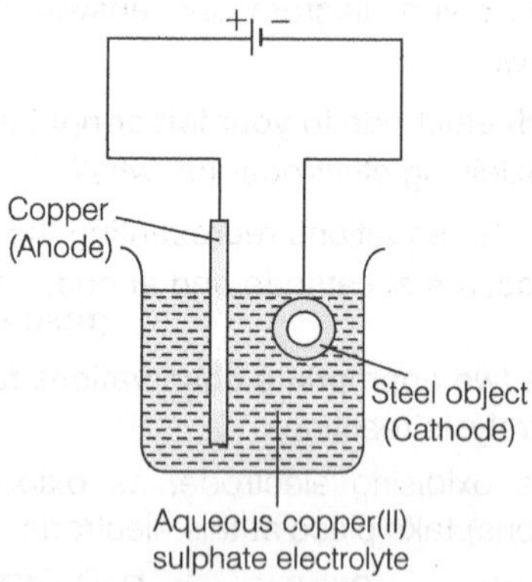

(a) The chemical process taking place on the surface of the object is

$$Cu^{2+}(aq) + 2e^- \longrightarrow Cu(s)$$

What is the observation seen on the surface of the object?

(b) Explain why the concentration of copper ions in the electrolyte remains constant throughout step 1?

(ii) Give two changes which would be needed in order to coat nickel onto the object in step 2.

(iii) Write down the reaction taking place at the positive electrode during step 3.

Ans. (i) (a) On the surface of the object, **pink or reddish brown deposit of copper** takes place. **(1)**

(b) As anode releases copper ions into the electrolyte, the concentration of copper ions does not decrease. **(1)**

(ii) Anode should be made up of nickel so that, reaction at anode is

$$Ni - 2e^- \longrightarrow Ni^{2+}$$

The electrolyte nickel sulphate solution or any salt solution of nickel should be used.

$$NiSO_4 \longrightarrow Ni^{2+} + SO_4^{2-}$$

(Dissociation of electrolyte) **(2)**

(iii) At anode, $Ag \longrightarrow Ag^+ + e^-$

Here, anode is a plate of pure silver. **(1)**

Q.16 The following sketch represents the electroplating of an iron cup with nickel metal. Study the diagram and answer the following questions. **(ICSE 2024)**

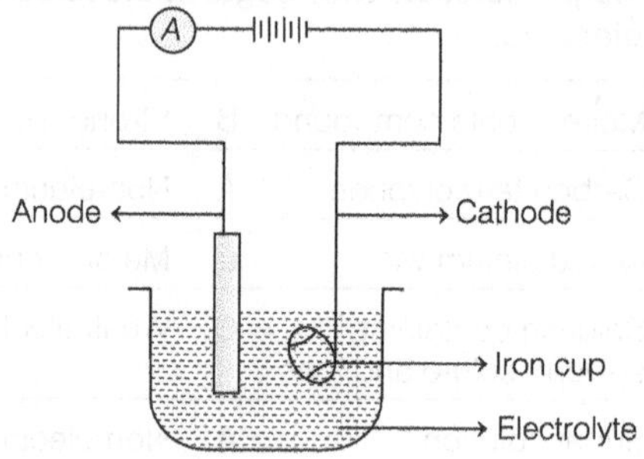

(i) During electroplating the iron cup is placed at the cathode. Why?

(ii) Name the ion that must be present in the electrolyte.

(iii) State one condition that is necessary to ensure that the deposit is smooth, firm and even.

(iv) Write the reaction taking place at the cathode.

(v) What change would you observe at the anode?

Ans. (i) The article to be electroplated is always made the cathode in electrolysis, since the **metal is deposited at the cathode**.

(ii) **Ni ion (Ni^{2+})**.

(iii) **Longer time** and **low current** causes a thicker uniform deposition of metal.

(iv) Reaction of cathode:

$$\underset{\text{(From electrolyte)}}{Ni^{2+}} + 2e^- \longrightarrow \underset{\text{(Deposited)}}{Ni}$$

(v) Anode diminishes in mass because anode (nickel) loses electrons to give Ni^{2+} ions in solution.

$$Ni \longrightarrow Ni^{2+} + 2e^-$$ **(1 × 5 = 5)**

Q.17 **Copy and complete the following table which refers to two practical applications of electrolysis**

	Anode	Electrolyte	Cathode
Silver plating a spoon	......	Solution of potassium argentocyanide	......
Purification of copper	......	......	......

Ans.

	Anode	Electrolyte	Cathode
Silver plating a spoon	Pure silver	Solution of potassium argentocyanide	Spoon
Purification of copper	Impure block of copper	Copper sulphate solution	Pure strip of copper

(1 × 5 = 5)

TYPE - 10

03 Marks

Case Based Questions

Q.1 **Ramesh is studying the process of electrolytic refining of copper, which is an essential method used to purify copper metal. This process helps in obtaining pure copper from impure copper by using the process of electrolysis. He drew the diagram given below.**

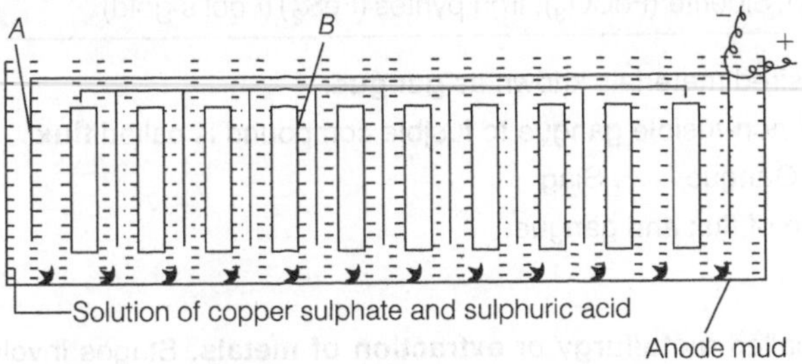

(i) Identify *A* and *B*.

(ii) Which among *A* and *B* are cathode and anode?

(iii) What is anode mud?

Ans. (i) A = Thin strips of pure copper

B = Slabs of impure copper **(1)**

(ii) *A* is cathode and *B* is anode. **(1)**

(iii) Some impurities like gold and silver, which are insoluble, gets collected near the anode and are called as **anode mud**. **(1)**

Q.2 **Tripti was conducting an experiment in which she used sodium chloride in two states. She observed that sodium chloride in state-1 does not conduct electricity, while NaCl in state-2, conducts electricity.**

(i) Which diagrams given below shows state-1 and state-2 respectively?

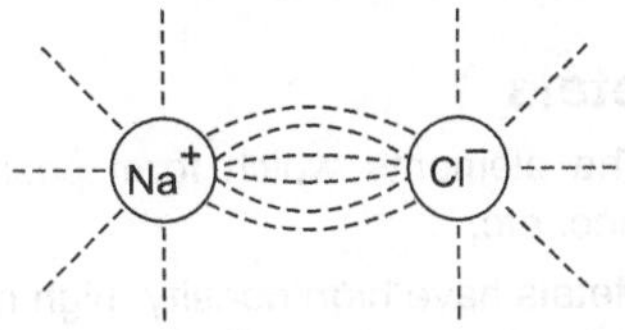

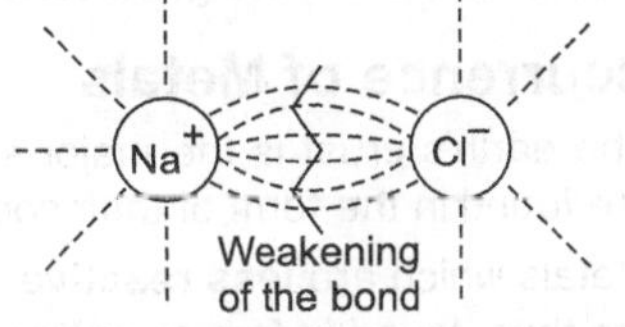

(ii) Why state-1 does not conduct electricity?

(iii) Give reason, why state-2 conducts electricity?

Ans. (i) The correct diagrams for state-1 and state-2 are

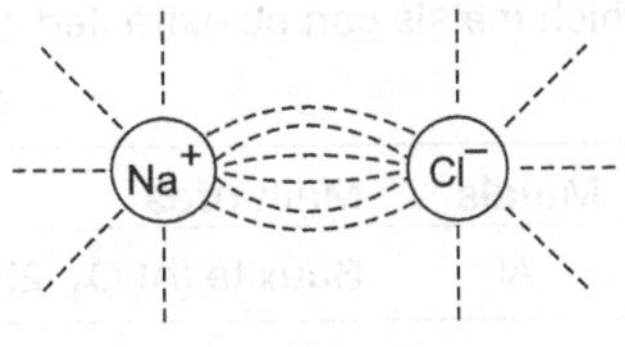

State-1(Solid state)

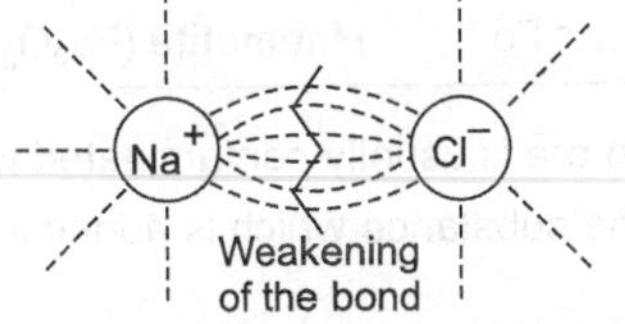

State-2 (Aqueous or molten state) **(1)**

(ii) In **solid state**, sodium and chloride ions are not free but are held together by a **strong electrostatic force of attraction**, so there are **no free ions present**, hence it does not conduct electricity. **(1)**

(iii) In **aqueous or molten state**, the ionic bond between sodium and chloride ions is **weakened**, so the force of attraction between them is lost and **ions are free to move** about and hence, it conducts electricity. **(1)**

METALLURGY

Metals

- The elements which form positive ions by losing electrons are called **metals**. e.g. Copper, silver, aluminium, zinc, etc.
- Metals have high density, high melting points and high tensile strength.
- Almost all metals are good conductors of heat and electricity.

Occurrence of Metals

- The earth's crust is the major source of metals. Some metals are found in earth's crust in free state while some are found in the form of their compounds.
- Metals which are **less reactive**, do not react with oxygen, water, carbon dioxide, etc., under normal conditions and are thus, found in free or **native state.** e.g. Gold and platinum.
- Most of the metals are **reactive**, so they occur in **combined state** in the form of their chlorides, oxides, carbonates, sulphides, etc. Sodium and potassium occur mainly as their chlorides, calcium and magnesium as carbonates and aluminium as its oxide. While, zinc, lead, copper, mercury and silver are found as their sulphides.
- The elements or compounds, which occur naturally in earth's crust are called **minerals**. Those minerals from which metals can be extracted conveniently and economically are called **ores**.

Common Ores of Aluminium, Iron and Zinc

Metals	Main ores
Al	**Bauxite ($Al_2O_3 \cdot 2H_2O$)**, Cryolite (Na_3AlF_6), Feldspar ($KAlSi_3O_8$), Corundum (Al_2O_3)
Zn	**Zinc blende (ZnS)**, Calamine ($ZnCO_3$), Zincite (ZnO), Willemite (Zn_2SiO_4)
Fe	**Haematite (Fe_2O_3)**, Magnetite (Fe_3O_4), Siderite ($FeCO_3$), Iron pyrites (FeS_2) (Fool's gold)

- An ore is usually contaminated with earthly or undesired materials known as **gangue.**
- The substance which is added in the ore, to convert non-fusible gangue to fusible compound is called **flux.**

$$\text{Flux} + \text{Gangue} \longrightarrow \text{Slag}$$

- **Slag** is the fusible compound formed by combination of flux and gangue.

Extraction of Metals

The process of obtaining pure metal from its ore is called **metallurgy** or **extraction of metals**. Stages involved in extraction of metals are

I. Crushing and grinding of the ore.
II. Concentration or dressing or benefaction of the ore.
III. Conversion of concentrated ore to oxide by roasting or calcination.
IV. Reduction of metallic oxides (smelting).
V. Refining or purification of metals.

I. Crushing and Grinding of Ores

Ores are crushed into a fine powder in big jaw crushers and ball mills. This process is called **pulverisation**.

II. Concentration or Dressing of Ores

The process of removing gangue present in an ore, is called **concentration of an ore or ore dressing** and the purified ore is called **concentrated ore**.

1. Hydraulic Washing or Gravity Separation

- In this process, powdered ore is washed with the upward stream of running water. The heavier ore particles settle down whereas, lighter impurities are washed away. This method is used for oxide and carbonate ores. e.g. Haematite.
- This method is based upon the **differences in densities (or gravities)** of ores and the gangue particles. Therefore, it is also known as **gravity separation** or **levigation**.

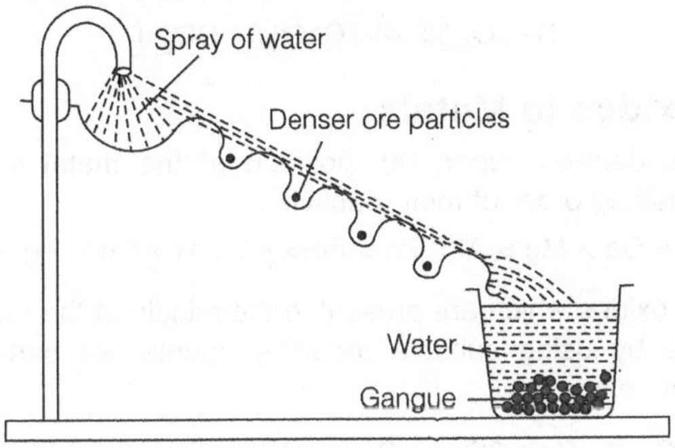

2. Magnetic Separation

- In this method, the powdered ore is placed on the conveyer belt moving on two rollers, one of which is a strong magnet. The particles which are magnetic in nature are attracted by the magnet and fall closer to the roller, while non-magnetic particles fall away from the roller.
- This method is based upon the **differences in the magnetic properties of the ore components**.

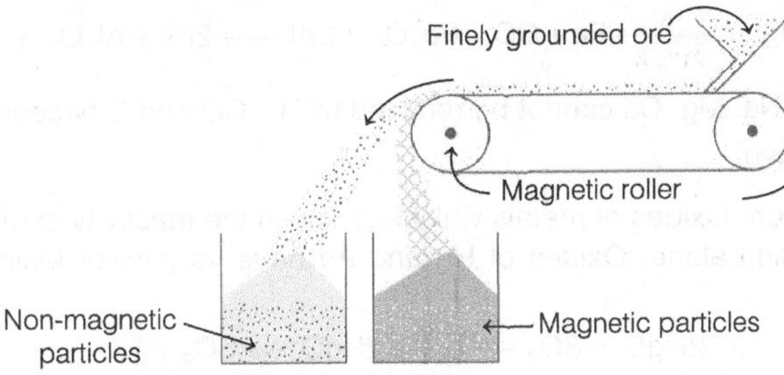

3. Froth Floatation

- In this process, powdered ore is mixed with water containing collectors and froth stabilisers like cresols, aniline, etc.
- This method is based upon the **preferential wetting properties with frothing agent and water**.

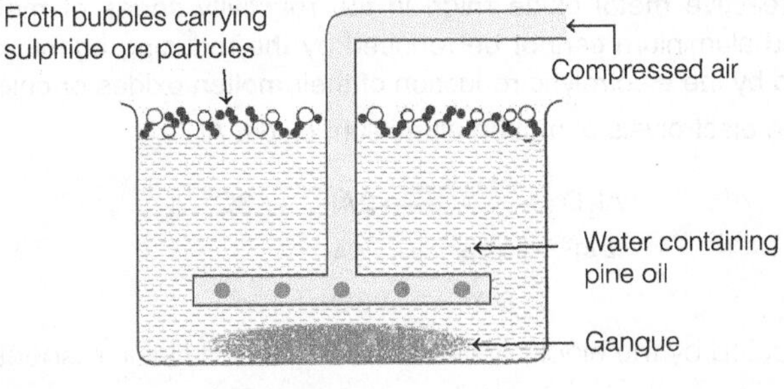

- The mineral particles become wet with oil, while the gangue particles by water. A stream of hot compressed air is passed which agitates the mixture and produces froth. This **froth carries mineral particles**.
- Afterwards, the light froth is skimmed off. It is then dried for recovery of ore particles. Water wets the gangue particles which sink to bottom.

III. Conversion of Concentrated Ore to its Oxide

Concentrated ore is converted to its oxide because oxides are easier to reduce into metals. Depending upon the nature of the ores, two methods are used to convert the ore into its oxide, (i) roasting and (ii) calcination.

(i) **Roasting** In roasting, the ore is heated in a **regular supply** of air in a furnace at a temperature below the melting point of the metal. Generally, **sulphide ores** are roasted and thus, SO_2 is produced.

e.g. $2ZnS + 3O_2 \xrightarrow{\Delta} 2ZnO + 2SO_2 \uparrow$ $\quad 2PbS + 3O_2 \xrightarrow{\Delta} 2PbO + 2SO_2 \uparrow$

(ii) **Calcination** The process of heating the concentrated ore in the **absence or limited supply** of air at a temperature not sufficient to melt the ore is called calcination. **Carbonate ores** are calcined and hence, **carbon dioxide** is produced. e.g.

$$CaCO_3(s) \xrightarrow{\Delta} CaO(s) + CO_2 \uparrow$$

IV. Reduction of Metal Oxides to Metals

The selection of reducing agents depends upon the position of the metal in the **reactivity series**. It is the arrangement of metals in the decreasing order of their reactivity.

$$K > Na > Ca > Mg > Al > Zn > Fe > Pb > H > Cu > Hg > Ag > Au$$

(i) **By reducing agents** Metal oxides which are present in the middle of the reactivity series like Zn, Fe, Pb, etc., are reduced to free metals by using suitable reducing agents like carbon, carbon monoxide, hydrogen, aluminium, sodium or calcium. e.g.

(a) **Copper oxide** $CuO + C \xrightarrow{\Delta} Cu + CO$, $\quad CuO + CO \xrightarrow[250\text{-}450°C]{\Delta} Cu + CO_2$, $\quad CuO + H_2 \xrightarrow{\Delta} Cu + H_2O$

(b) **Lead (II) oxide** $PbO + C \xrightarrow{\Delta} Pb + CO$, $\quad PbO + CO \xrightarrow[1200°C]{\Delta} Pb + CO_2$, $\quad PbO + H_2 \xrightarrow[200\text{-}250°C]{\Delta} Pb + H_2O$

(c) **Zinc oxide** $ZnO + C \xrightarrow[1673\text{ K}]{\Delta} Zn + CO$

(d) **Iron oxide** $FeO + C \xrightarrow[2170\text{ K}]{\Delta} Fe + CO$, $\quad Fe_2O_3 + 2Al \longrightarrow 2Fe + Al_2O_3 + \text{Heat}$

Note Oxides of metals K, Na, Mg, Ca cannot be reduced by H_2, CO and C because these metals have great affinity towards oxygen.

(ii) **By thermal decomposition** Oxides of metals which are low in the reactivity series are least stable and can be reduced to metal by heating alone. Oxides of Hg and Ag have very weak ionic bonds which can broken by direct heating.

$$2HgS + 3O_2 \xrightarrow{\text{Roasting}} 2HgO + 2SO_2$$

$$2HgO \xrightarrow[\text{Reduction}]{\text{Heat}} 2Hg + O_2$$

$$2Ag_2O \xrightarrow{\Delta} 4Ag + O_2$$

(iii) **By electrolysis** Most reactive metal oxide (high in the reactivity series of metals) like sodium, potassium, magnesium, calcium and aluminium cannot be reduced by the reducing agents or by thermal decomposition, hence they are extracted by the electrolytic reduction of their molten oxides or chlorides.

e.g. Al is extracted by the electrolysis of molten aluminium oxide, Al_2O_3.

$$Al_2O_3 \xrightarrow{\text{Electrolysis}} 2Al^{3+} + 3O^{2-}$$

At cathode $\quad 4Al^{3+} + 12e^- \longrightarrow 4Al$

At anode $\quad 6O^{2-} \longrightarrow 3O_2 + 12e^-$

- K and Na are extracted by the electrolysis of fused KBr and NaCl, respectively.

e.g. $\quad KBr \rightleftharpoons K^+ + Br^-$

At cathode $\quad K^+ + e^- \longrightarrow K$

At anode $\quad Br^- \longrightarrow Br + 1e^-$

$$Br + Br \longrightarrow Br_2$$

e.g.
$$NaCl \rightleftharpoons Na^+ + Cl^-$$

At cathode
$$Na^+ + e^- \longrightarrow Na$$

At anode
$$Cl^- \longrightarrow Cl + 1e^-$$
$$Cl + Cl \longrightarrow Cl_2$$

V. Refining of Impure Metal

The process of removal of impurities to get more pure metal is called **refining**. Depending upon the nature of metals and associated impurities, and the purpose for which the metal is to be used, the methods employed to purify metals are as follows.

(i) **Distillation** This method is used for refining volatile metals and low boiling metals, e.g. Zn, Hg.
On heating, metal vaporises and is condensed. Pure metal is collected, while non-volatile impurities remain behind.

(ii) **Liquation** It is used for refining metals with low melting point, e.g. Pb, Sn.
On heating, pure metal liquefies and flows down the sloping furnace, whereas non-volatile impurities are infusible and remains behind.

(iii) **Oxidative refining** It is employed for refining metals by oxidation from their impurities. e.g. Fe.
On oxidation, pure metal remains behind in molten form and impurities are oxidised by air to their respective oxides.

(iv) **Electrolytic refining** This method is used for refining impure metal by electrolysis, e.g. Cu, Al, Pb. Impure metal is used as anode, a thin strip of pure metal is used as cathode and a soluble salt of metal is used as an electrolyte. On passing electric current, pure metal is deposited at the cathode and impurities settle down forming anode mud.

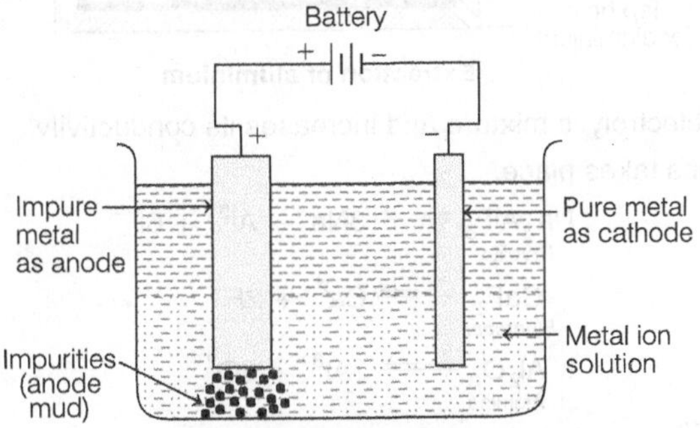

Experimental set up for the electrolytic refining of a metal

At anode
$$M \longrightarrow M^{n+} + ne^-$$

At cathode
$$M^{n+} + ne^- \longrightarrow M \qquad [M \text{ is a metal}]$$

Extraction of Aluminium

Aluminium is the most abundant metal in the earth's crust. It is a reactive metal and so does not occur in free state in nature. The most common ore of aluminium is **bauxite**, $Al_2O_3 \cdot 2H_2O$.

1. Purification of Bauxite Ore (Baeyer's Process)

Bauxite ore is purified by Baeyer's process. This method makes use of difference between the chemical properties of the ore and the gangue. Bauxite ore contains iron(III) oxide (Fe_2O_3) and silica (SiO_2) as the main impurities.

(i) **Conversion of impure bauxite to sodium aluminate**

$$\underset{\text{Impure bauxite}}{Al_2O_3 \cdot 2H_2O} + \underset{\text{Conc. solution}}{2NaOH} \xrightarrow{140\text{-}150^\circ C} \underset{\text{Sodium } meta \text{ aluminate}}{2NaAlO_2} + 3H_2O$$

(ii) **Conversion of sodium *meta* aluminate to aluminium hydroxide**

$$\underset{\text{Sodium } meta \text{ aluminate}}{NaAlO_2} + 2H_2O \xrightarrow{50\text{-}60°C} \underset{\text{Sodium hydroxide}}{NaOH} + \underset{\text{Aluminium hydroxide}}{Al(OH)_3} \downarrow$$

(iii) **Conversion of aluminium hydroxide to pure alumina**

$$\underset{\text{Aluminium hydroxide}}{2Al(OH)_3} \xrightarrow[1000°C]{\Delta} \underset{\text{Pure alumina}}{Al_2O_3} + 3H_2O$$

2. *Electrolytic Reduction of Fused Alumina (Hall-Herault's Process)*

The electrolytic reduction of fused alumina takes place in **electrolytic cell**. The tank is lined with carbon, which acts as the cathode. The anode of the cell is made up of carbon (graphite). **Powdered coke** is sprinkled over the surface of the electrolyte. It reduces heat loses by the radiation and prevents the burning of anode.

Electrolyte It is a mixture of 20% molten alumina, 60% cryolite and 20% fluorspar.

Cryolite is added in the electrolyte to lower the fusion temperature from 2050°C to 950°C and increases the conductivity.

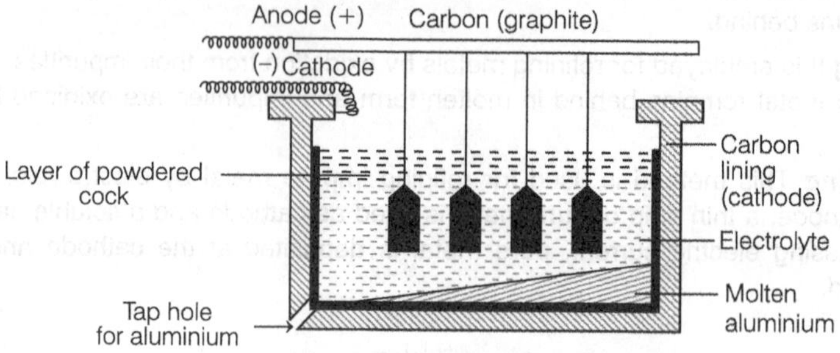

Extraction of aluminium

Fluorspar acts as a solvent for electrolytic mixture and increases its conductivity.

Reactions The following reactions takes place.

$$\underset{\text{Cryolite}}{Na_3AlF_6} \rightleftharpoons 3Na^+ + Al^{3+} + 6F^-$$

$$\underset{\text{Fluorspar}}{CaF_2} \rightleftharpoons Ca^{2+} + 2F^-$$

$$\underset{\text{Alumina}}{Al_2O_3} \rightleftharpoons 2Al^{3+} + 3O^{2-}$$

Cathode Carbon lining of the cell.

$$4Al^{3+} + 12e^- \longrightarrow 4Al$$

Anode Thick rods of graphite are suspended into the fused electrolyte.

$$6O^{2-} \longrightarrow 6[O] + 12e^-$$

$$6[O] \longrightarrow 3O_2$$

Anode oxidises carbon to carbon monoxide and then to carbon dioxide.

$$2C + O_2 \longrightarrow 2CO$$

$$2CO + O_2 \longrightarrow 2CO_2$$

The oxygen evolved at the anode escapes as a gas and reacts with carbon anode to form CO_2 gas, thus the anode needs to be replaced regularly.

3. *Refining of Aluminium*

It is done by **Hoope's electrolytic process**. The process involves an electrolytic tank which contains three immiscible layers of molten substances of different specific gravity.

- **Upper layer** consist of pure molten Al with carbon electrodes, which serve as cathode.
- **Middle layer** consist of a mixture of fluorides of Na, Ba and Al.
- **Lower layer** consist of impure Al along with carbon lining which serves as anode.

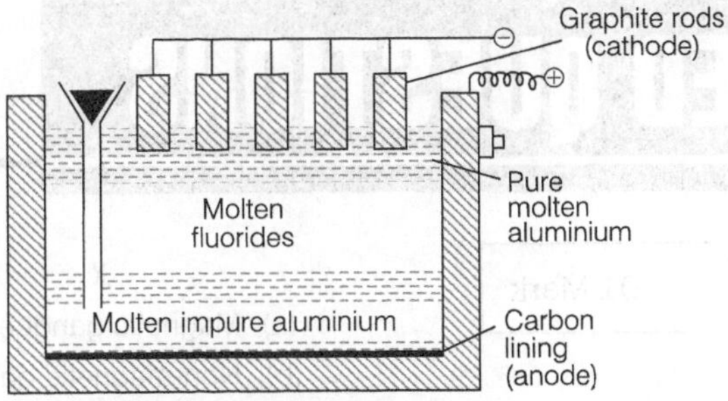

Refining of aluminium

When the current is passed, aluminium moves from the middle layer to the top layer and simultaneously, equivalent amount is shifted from lower layer to middle layer. By this method, pure aluminium can be easily obtained.

Anode $\underset{\text{(Impure)}}{Al} \longrightarrow Al^{3+} + 3e^-$ **Cathode** $Al^{3+} + 3e^- \longrightarrow \underset{\text{(Pure)}}{Al}$

Note Aluminium mixed with haematite is used for thermit welding process.

Alloys

An **alloy** is a homogeneous mixture of two or more metals or a metal and a non-metal. It is prepared by mixing the metals in molten state and then cooling the mixture. The electrical conductivity and melting point of an alloy is less than that of pure metals. e.g. Brass, an alloy of copper and tin (Cu and Sn) is not the good conductor of electricity whereas, copper is used for making electrical circuits.

Composition, Properties and Uses of Alloys

Principal metal	Alloy's name	Composition	Properties	Used for making
Aluminium	Duralumin	95% Al, 4% Cu 0.5% Mg 0.5% Mn	1. Light but as strong as steel. 2. Hard and resistant to corrosion. 3. Highly ductile.	1. Bodies of aircraft, buses and tube trains. 2. Light tools. 3. Pressure cookers.
Iron	Stainless steel	73% Fe, 18% Cr, 8% Ni, 1% C	1. Resists corrosion. 2. Lustrous and hard. 3. Resistant to acids and alkalis.	1. Utensils 2. Cutlery 3. Ornamental pieces. 4. Surgical instruments.
Copper	Brass	60-80% Cu 40-20% Zn	1. Malleable and ductile. 2. Can be easily cast. 3. Resists corrosion. 4. Yellow/silvery in colour.	1. Decorative hardware, utensils. 2. Screws and handles. 3. Cartridge and containers. 4. Parts of watches. 5. Musical instruments. 6. Electrical goods.
Copper	Bronze	80% Cu 18% Sn 2% Zn	1. Hard and easy to cast. 2. Can take up polish. 3. Resists corrosion.	1. Medals and statues. 2. Utensils. 3. Bearings and coins.
Lead	Solder or Fuse metal	50% Pb 50% Sn	1. Low melting point, high tensile strength.	1. Welding. 2. Electrical fuse.
Aluminium	Magnalium	90-95% Al 10-5% Mg	1. Great strength, high corrosion resistance 2. Lower density	1. Used in aircraft automobiles parts. 2. Used in making metal mirrors. 3. Used in making of light tools and scientific instruments.

EXAM ORIENTED QUESTIONS

TYPE - 1   01 Mark

Multiple Choice Questions

Q.1 Which of the following metal is found in its free state in nature?
(a) Iron (b) Gold
(c) Copper (d) Zinc

Ans. (b) **Gold** is found in its free state because it is a **chemically inert** element.

Q.2 The substance formed when flux reacts with impurities in the ore is called
(a) alloy (b) slag
(c) molten metal (d) gangue

Ans. (b) **Slag** (flux + gangue $\longrightarrow$ slag),
e.g. $\underset{\text{(Flux)}}{CaO} + \underset{\text{(Gangue)}}{SiO_2} \longrightarrow CaSiO_3$.

Q.3 Which method is used to concentrate ores based on their differences in density?
(a) Froth-floatation
(b) Hydraulic washing
(c) Magnetic separation
(d) Leaching

Ans. (b) **Hydraulic washing** separates heavier ore particles from lighter impurities using water.

Q.4 The ore that can be concentrated by using magnetic separation.
(a) corundum (b) haematite
(c) calamine (d) bauxite

Ans. (b) **Haematite** can be concentrated by using magnetic separation as it is magnetic in nature and it can be separated from the non-magnetic gangue particles.

Q.5 The diagram of magnetic separation is given below. Identify *X* and *Y*.

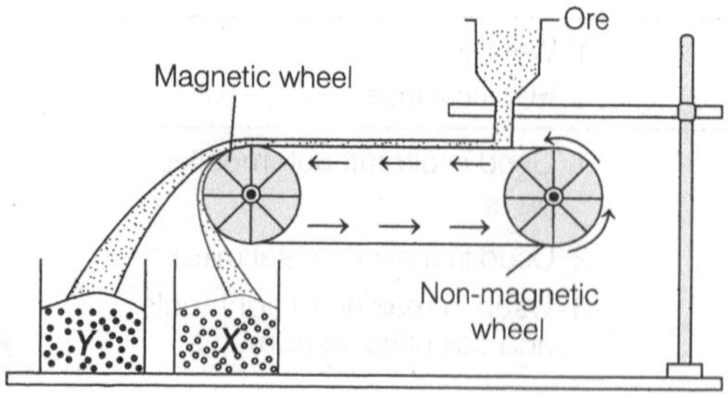

	X	Y
(a)	Magnetic gangue	Magnetic ore
(b)	Non-magnetic gangue	Magnetic ore
(c)	Non-magnetic ore	Magnetic gangue
(d)	Magnetic ore	Non-magnetic gangue

Ans. (d) *X* = Magnetic ore
Y = Non-magnetic gangue

Q.6 The method used to concentrate sulphide ores is
(a) froth floatation
(b) magnetic separation
(c) hydraulic washing
(d) leaching

Ans. (a) Sulphide ores are concentrated using **froth floatation**, where the ore particles attach to froth and are separated.

Q.7 Which gas is commonly released during roasting of sulphide ores?
(a) Oxygen (b) Carbon dioxide
(c) Sulphur dioxide (d) Hydrogen

Ans. (c) **Sulphur dioxide** (SO_2) is released as a by product when sulphide ores are roasted.
e.g. $2ZnS + 3O_2 \xrightarrow[\text{800-900°C}]{\text{Roasting}} 2ZnO + 2SO_2 \uparrow$

Q.8 Calcination is the process of
(a) heating ores in absence of air.
(b) heating ores in the presence of air.
(c) adding flux to the ore.
(d) electrolysis of molten ore.

Ans. (a) Calcination is the process of **heating ores in absence of air**. Calcination removes water and volatile impurities from carbonate ores.
e.g. $ZnCO_3 \xrightarrow{\Delta} ZnO + CO_2(g) \uparrow$

Q.9 The metal whose oxide can be reduced by common reducing agents. **(ICSE 2025)**
(a) Copper (b) Sodium
(c) Aluminium (d) Potassium

Ans. (a) **Copper** can be obtained by the reduction of copper oxide with common reducing agents like carbon, carbon monoxide, hydrogen, etc.
Sodium, potassium and aluminium are highly active metals and have great affinity for oxygen, so, their oxides cannot be reduced by common reducing agents.

Q.10 Which impurity floats as anode mud during electrolytic refining?
(a) Non-metallic impurities
(b) More reactive metals
(c) Less reactive metals
(d) Volatile impurities

Ans. (c) **Less reactive metals** like silver and gold settle as anode mud during electrolytic refining.

Q.11 In the refining of metals, the process in which molten metal is cooled to remove impurities is called
(a) electrolysis (b) distillation
(c) liquation (d) leaching

Ans. (c) **Liquation** is the process in which metals with lower melting points are separated from the impurities by cooling the molten mixture.

Q.12 The ore of aluminium is **(ICSE 2021-22, Sem-II)**
(a) calamine (b) haematite (c) magnetite (d) cryolite

Ans. (d) The ore of aluminium is **cryolite** (Na_3AlF_6).

Q.13 The compound that is not an ore of aluminium.
(a) Cryolite (b) Corundum **(ICSE 2023)**
(c) Fluorspar (d) Bauxite

Ans. (c) **Fluorspar** (CaF_2) is not an ore of aluminium.

Q.14 The compound that is not a constituent of the electrolytic mixture used in the Hall-Herault's process is **(ICSE 2024)**
(a) Al_2O_3 (b) $NaAlO_2$ (c) Na_3AlF_6 (d) CaF_2

Ans. (b) **Al_2O_3** The electrolytic reduction of fused alumina (Al_2O_3) takes place in electrolytic cell.
Na_3AlF_6 (cryolite) It is added to alumina (electrolyte) to lower the fusion temperature from 2050°C to 950°C and increases the conductivity.
CaF_2 (fluorspar) It acts as a solvent for electrolytic mixture and also increases the conductivity.

Q.15 Given below in Column I is a schematic diagram of the electrolytic reduction of alumina. Identify the parts labelled as *A*, *B* and *C* with the correct options from the Column II. **(ICSE Specimen 2025)**

Column I	Column II
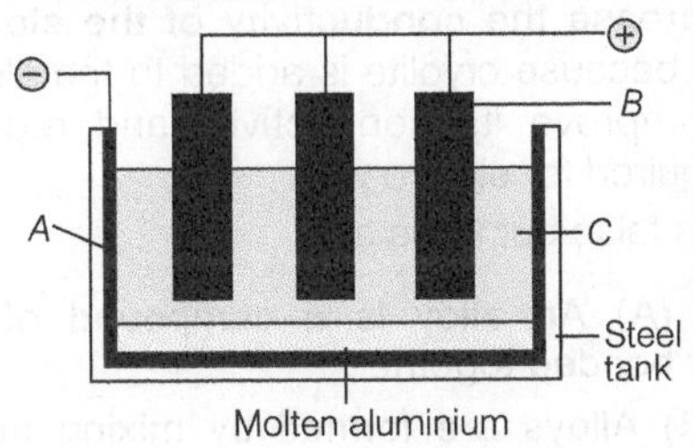	1. Platinum
	2. Anode
	3. Cathode
	4. Electrolyte mixture
	5. Bauxite

(a) A→ 3, B→ 2, C→ 5 (b) A→ 2, B→ 3, C→ 4
(c) A→ 3, B→ 2, C→ 4 (d) A→ 1, B→ 2, C→ 5

Ans. (c) A→ 3, B→ 2, C→ 4.

Q.16 During the extraction of aluminium by Hall Herault's process, the carbon rods are replaced continuously. This is because **(Competency Based Que.)**
(a) it minimises heat loss by radiation.
(b) it enhances the mobility of ions.
(c) the carbon anode is consumed.
(d) it lowers the fusion point.

Ans. (c) During electrolytic reduction of fused alumina (Hall-Heroult's process), carbon is oxidised to carbon monoxide at anode and then it is oxidised to carbon dioxide.

$$2C + O_2 \longrightarrow 2CO$$
$$2CO + O_2 \longrightarrow 2CO_2$$

The **carbon anode is oxidised** and thus is **consumed** during the process.

Q.17 Fused alumina is reduced to aluminium by electrolytic reduction, since **(ICSE Specimen 2021-22, Sem-I)**
(a) alumina is highly stable.
(b) alumina is least stable.
(c) alumina is not reduced by drying agents.
(d) alumina is not reduced by reducing agents.

Ans. (d) Fused alumina is **highly stable**. It has **very high enthalpy of formation**.
Therefore, reducing agents cannot be used to reduce it to aluminium. Hence, it is reduced by electrolytic reduction only.

Q.18 The reason for using aluminium in the alloy duralumin is **(ICSE 2019)**
(a) aluminium is brittle.
(b) aluminium gives strength.
(c) aluminium brings lightness.
(d) aluminium lowers melting point.

Ans. (b) Duralumin is an alloy in which, aluminium is one of its component and it gives **strength** to the alloy.

Q.19 Copper, zinc and tin are the metals alloyed to form
(a) duralumin (b) brass **(ICSE 2024)**
(c) bronze (d) solder

Ans. (c) **Bronze** (It has 80% Cu, 18% Sn and 2% Zn).

Q.20 The two main metals present in bronze are **(ICSE 2016)**
(a) copper and zinc (b) copper and lead
(c) copper and nickel (d) copper and tin

Ans. (d) Bronze is an alloy of **copper and tin.**

Q.21 This is not an alloy of copper. **(ICSE 2015)**
(a) Brass (b) Bronze
(c) Solder (d) Duralumin

Ans. (c) **Solder** is not an alloy of copper.

Q.22 Brass is an alloy of
(a) copper and tin (b) copper and zinc
(c) zinc and lead (d) lead and tin

Ans. (b) Brass is an alloy of **copper and zinc**.

Q.23 Nikita wanted to gift her friend a decorative piece that is quite hard and strong, does not get corroded and can be polished. She selected a statue that matched her criteria as it was made of an alloy whose main constituent was .... **(Competency Based Que.)**

(a) Cu (b) Al (c) Fe (d) Zn

Ans. (a) **Copper (Cu)** is a metal that is hard and strong, resistant to corrosion, and can be polished.

Q.24 Thermit mixture is used to weld the broken ends of the iron girders. This mixture consists of ferric oxide and aluminium powder, which when heated, produces molten iron. In this reaction, the aluminium powder acts as a/an .... agent. **(Competency Based Que.)**

(a) oxidising (b) reducing
(c) dehydrating (d) corroding

Ans. (b) In the thermit reaction, aluminium powder acts as a **reducing agent**. It **reduces ferric oxide (Fe_2O_3) to iron (Fe)** by donating electrons, while itself being oxidised to form aluminium oxide (Al_2O_3).

TYPE - 2

01 Mark

Assertion-Reason Questions

Directions (Q. Nos. 1-6) In the following questions, a statement of Assertion (A) is followed by a statement of Reason (R). Choose the answer based on the codes given below.

(a) Both (A) and (R) are true and (R) is the correct explanation of (A).
(b) Both (A) and (R) are true but (R) is not the correct explanation of (A).
(c) (A) is true but (R) is false.
(d) (A) is false but (R) is true.

Q.1 Assertion (A) Metals are extracted from their ores through chemical processes such as reduction.

Reason (R) Ores are naturally occurring compounds of metals mixed with impurities, and metals are often found in a combined state due to their reactivity.

Ans. (a) Metals are extracted from their ores through chemical processes like reduction, which removes oxygen and separates the metal. This is necessary because most metals are found in combined forms, such as oxides or sulphides, due to their reactivity. Thus, (A) and (R) are true and (R) is the correct explanation of (A).

Q.2 Assertion (A) Gangue is removed from ore during the process of froth flotation.

Reason (R) Froth floatation is a process that separates hydrophobic materials from hydrophilic materials.

Ans. (a) **Froth floatation** is a method used to remove gangue (unwanted impurities) from ores, especially in the case of **sulphide ores**.

In this process, the ore particles are made hydrophobic by adding collectors, allowing them to attach to air bubbles and float to the surface. Gangue, being hydrophilic, remains in the water and is discarded. Thus, the (A) is true.

(R) is also true because froth floatation works by using the **difference between hydrophobic and hydrophilic properties of materials**.

Since, the (R) explains why gangue is removed during froth flaotation, both statements are true, and the (R) correctly explains the (A).

Q.3 Assertion (A) Roasting is a process used for sulphide ores.

Reason (R) In roasting, sulphide ores are heated in the absence of air to convert them into oxides.

Ans. (c) In roasting, sulphide ores are heated in the **presence of air** (not in the absence of air) to convert them into metal oxides, releasing sulphur dioxide gas. Thus, the (A) is true but the (R) is false.

Q.4 Assertion (A) The electrolytic refining process is used to extract iron from its ore.

Reason (R) Iron is extracted by reducing iron ore in a blast furnace.

Ans. (d) (A) is false because the electrolytic refining process is not used to extract iron from its ore. Electrolysis is typically used for refining metals like copper. (R) is true because iron is extracted from its ore (mainly haematite) by reducing it in a blast furnace, using **carbon monoxide as a reducing agent**. Electrolysis is not involved in the extraction of iron.

Thus, (A) is false but (R) is true.

Q.5 Assertion (A) Cryolite is used in the Hall-Heroult's process as a catalyst.

Reason (R) Cryolite improves the conductivity of the electrolyte in aluminium extraction.

Ans. (d) (A) is false because cryolite is not used as a catalyst in the Hall-Heroult's process. It is used to **lower the melting point of aluminium oxide** (Al_2O_3) and to **increase the conductivity of the electrolyte**. (R) is true because cryolite is added to the aluminium oxide to improve its conductivity and reduce the energy required for electrolysis.

Thus, (A) is false but (R) is true.

Q.6 Assertion (A) An alloy is a compound of metals chemically bonded together.

Reason (R) Alloys are formed by mixing metals to improve their properties.

Ans. (d) (A) is false because an alloy is not a compound, it is a mixture of metals (or metals and non-metals), where the components are **not chemically bonded**. The metals retain their individual properties to some extent.

(R) is true because alloys are formed by mixing metals (or a metal with a non-metal) to **enhance or improve their physical properties**, such as strength, corrosion resistance or conductivity.

Thus, (A) is false but (R) is true.

TYPE - 3 — 01 Mark

Fill in the Blanks

Q.1 A mineral from which the metal can be extracted economically and conveniently is known as ...... (ore/gangue).

Ans. ore

Q.2 The most common ore of iron is .... (calamine/ haematite) **(ICSE 2018)**

Ans. haematite

Q.3 The ore which can be concentrated by magnetic separation is .... (zinc blende/haematite)

Ans. haematite

Q.4 The process of heating the concentrated ore in a limited supply or absence of air is .... (roasting/ calcination). **(ICSE 2024)**

Ans. calcination

Q.5 Zinc blende is converted to zinc oxide by ...... (calcination/roasting) **(ICSE 2025)**

Ans. roasting

Q.6 The metallic oxide which can be reduced by using common reducing agents is .... (Fe_2O_3 / Al_2O_3) **(ICSE 2024)**

Ans. Fe_2O_3

Q.7 Metals are good ......(oxidising agents/reducing agents) **(ICSE 2023)**

Ans. Reducing agents

Q.8 In electrolysis of fused Alumina, the anode is made of .... (gas carbon/graphite). **(ICSE 2022)**

Ans. graphite

Q.9 The product formed at cathode during electrolysis of fused alumina is ...... (oxygen/aluminium). **(ICSE 2021)**

Ans. aluminium

Q.10 An alloy used to make statues is ...... (bronze/brass) **(ICSE 2020)**

Ans. bronze

TYPE - 4 — 01 Mark

Correct the Incorrect Statement

Q.1 Ores are the naturally occuring compounds of metals which are generally mixed with other substances.

Ans. **Minerals** are the naturally occuring compounds of metals which are generally mixed with other substances.

Q.2 In the extraction of metals, the first stage is generally concentration of the ore.

Ans. In the extraction of metals, the first stage is generally **pulverisation** of the ore.

Q.3 Calcination is a process of heating the concentrated sulphide ore to a high temperature below its melting point in the presence of excess air.

Ans. **Roasting** is a process of heating the concentrated sulphide ore to a high temperature below its melting point in the presence of excess air.

Q.4 The Hall-Heroult's process is used to extract iron from its ore.

Ans. The Hall-Heroult's process is an electrolytic method used to extract **aluminium** from is ore (bauxite).

Q.5 Alloys are always formed by chemically bonding metals together.

Ans. Alloys are mixtures of metals (or a metal and non-metal), where the components are **not** chemically bonded.

Q.6 Amalgam is an alloy of copper with a number of metals such as sodium, zinc, gold and silver.

Ans. Amalgam is an alloy of **mercury** with a number of metals such as sodium, zinc, gold and silver.

TYPE - 5 — 01 × 05 = 05 Marks

Matching Type Questions

Q.1 Match the Column I with Column II.

	Column I		Column II
A.	Element with atomic no. 19	1.	Acid salt
B.	Element with atomic no. 9	2.	Non-metal
C.	Sodium aluminate	3.	Metal
D.	Sodium bisulphite	4.	Hall-Heroult's process
E.	Calcium fluoride	5.	Baeyer's process

Ans. A → (3), B → (2), C → (5), D → (1), E → (4).

Q.2 Match the properties and uses of alloys in Column I with the appropriate answer from Column II.

Column I	Column II
A. The alloy contains Cu and Zn, is hard, silvery and is used in decorative articles.	1. Duralumin
B. It is stronger than aluminium, light and is used in making light tools.	2. Brass
C. It is lustrous, hard, corrosion resistant and is used in surgical instruments.	3. Bronze
D. Tin lowers the melting point of the alloy and is used for soldering purpose.	4. Stainless steel
E. The alloy is hard, brittle, takes up polish and is used for making statues.	5. Solder

Ans. A→ (2), B → (1), C → (4), D → (5), E → (3).

Q.3 Match the alloys given in Column I to the uses given in Column II. **(ICSE 2019)**

	Column I		Column II
A.	Duralumin	1.	Electrical fuse
B.	Solder	2.	Surgical instruments
C.	Brass	3.	Aircraft body
D.	Stainless steel	4.	Decorative articles
E.	German silver	5.	Resistors

Ans. A → (3), B → (1), C → (4), D → (2), E → (5).

TYPE - 6 — 01 Mark

Identify the Following

Q.1 Name the following.

An ore of zinc containing sulphide. **(ICSE specimen 2024, 2017)**

Ans. Zinc blende [ZnS]

Q.2 Calcite ($CaCO_3$), a sedimentary rock, is found most abundantly in many geological environments. It has a perfect cleavage in 3 directions, which makes it the most difficult rock to cut, and moreover, the labour of cutting calcite is also very high.

What term related to metallurgy will suitably describe calcite in the context of extracting calcium from calcite? **(Competency Based Que.)**

Ans. Mineral

Q.3 Name the following.

A black powdery substance used for the reduction of zinc oxide during its extraction.

Ans. Coke

Q.4 Which metal present in cryolite other than sodium?

Ans. Aluminium

Q.5 Name the compound formed when bauxite reacts with sodium hydroxide. **(ICSE Specimen 2021-22, Sem-I)**

Ans. Sodium meta aluminate.

$$\underset{\text{Bauxite}}{Al_2O_3} + \underset{\text{Sodium hydroxide}}{2NaOH} \longrightarrow \underset{\text{Sodium } meta\text{-aluminate}}{2NaAlO_2} + \underset{\text{Water}}{H_2O}$$

Q.6 The name of the process by which the bauxite ore is concentrated. **(ICSE 2025, Specimen 2023)**

Ans. Baeyer's process

Q.7 What is the chief ore of aluminium?

Or

Name the most commonly used oxide ore of aluminium. **(ICSE specimen 2024)**

Ans. Bauxite

Q.8 Which process is used to purify alumina by electrolytic reduction? **(ICSE 2021-22, Sem-II)**

Ans. Hoope's process

Q.9 Name a homogenous mixture of two or more metals or a metal and a non-metal in a definite proportion in their molten state. **(ICSE Specimen 2025, 2024)**

Ans. An alloy

Q.10 Give the name of an alloy of lead and tin, that is used in electrical circuits. **(ICSE 2017)**

Ans. Solder

TYPE - 7 — 02 Marks

Short Answer Type I Questions

Q.1

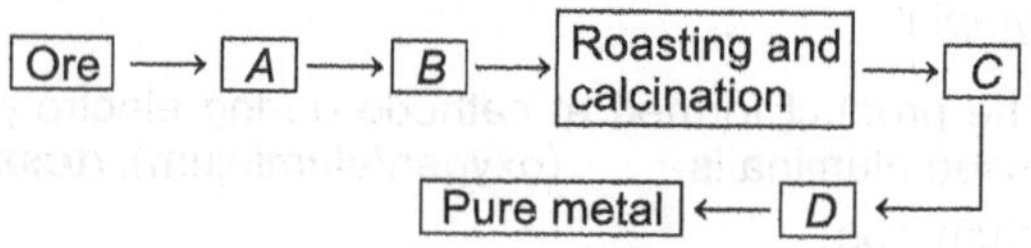

The above flowchart represents the steps involved in the extraction of metals. Identify *A*, *B*, *C* and *D* and complete the flowchart.

Ans.

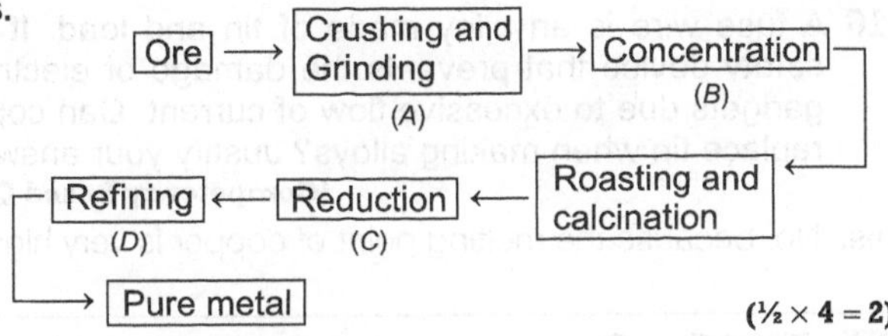

(½ × 4 = 2)

Q.2 Answer the following questions with reference to electrorefining of copper. **(ICSE 2023)**

(i) What do you observe at the cathode?

(ii) Write the reaction taking place at the cathode.

Ans. (i) At the cathode, the **copper is deposited** due to which it becomes **thicker** with time when electrorefining is done. **(1)**

(ii) At cathode, $Cu^{2+}(aq) + 2e^{-} \longrightarrow Cu(s)$ **(1)**

Q.3 Write the balanced chemical equation to show the concentration of ore in Baeyer's process.

(i) Sodium aluminate to aluminium hydroxide. **(ICSE 2020)**

(ii) Aluminium hydroxide to alumina. **(ICSE 2025)**

Ans. (i) Sodium aluminate reacts with water to form sodium hydroxide and aluminium hydroxide.

$$\underset{\text{Sodium aluminate}}{NaAlO_2} + \underset{\text{Water}}{2H_2O} \longrightarrow \underset{\text{Sodium hydroxide}}{NaOH} + \underset{\text{Aluminium hydroxide}}{Al(OH)_3\downarrow}$$ **(1)**

(ii) The precipitate of aluminium hydroxide is filtered, washed, dried and ignited at 1000°C to get alumina (Al_2O_3).

$$2Al(OH)_3 \xrightarrow[1000^\circ C]{\text{Heat}} \underset{\text{Alumina}}{Al_2O_3} + 3H_2O$$ **(1)**

Q.4 State the relevant reason for the following.

(i) Concentrated alkali is used for the concentration of bauxite ore.

(ii) Fused alumina is reduced to aluminium by electrolysis. **(ICSE 2021-22, Sem-II)**

Ans. (i) Concentrated alkali is used for the concentration of bauxite ore because **bauxite is soluble only in hot concentrated alkali** (like NaOH), while **impurities are insoluble** so, they can be easily filtered. **(1)**

(ii) Fused alumina is reduced to aluminium by electrolysis, since alumina is **highly stable** and it is not reduced by reducing agents. **(1)**

Q.5 State the relevant reason for the following.
(ICSE Specimen 2023, 2021-22, Sem-II)

(i) A layer of powdered coke is used over the electrolytic mixture in Hall-Heroult's process. **(ICSE 2019, 2017)**

(ii) Graphite anodes are continuously replaced during the electrolysis of alumina.

Ans. (i) A layer of powdered coke is sprinkled over the surface of the electrolytic mixture in Hall-Heroult's process because

- it reduces heat loss by radiation.
- it prevents the burning of anode. **(1)**

(ii) The graphite anode is continuously replaced time to time during the electrolysis of alumina, as it gets **oxidised by the oxygen evolved at the anode.** **(1)**

Q.6 Name the following. **(ICSE 2020, 2014)**

(i) A compound added to lower the fusion temperature of electrolytic bath, in the extraction of aluminium.

(ii) The ore of zinc containing its sulphide.

Ans. (i) Cryolite (Na_3AlF_6) **(1)**

(ii) Zinc blende (ZnS). **(1)**

Q.7 For each of the substances given below, what is the role played in the extraction of aluminium? **(ICSE Specimen 2023)**

(i) Cryolite **(ICSE 2019)**

(ii) Graphite

Ans. (i) Cryolite **increases the conductivity** of the mixture. This helps in **saving electric energy**. It also **lowers the fusion temperature** from 2050°C to 950°C **(1)**

(ii) Graphite is used as a cathode. It is a **good conductor of electricity** and is **not attacked by chemicals**. **(1)**

Q.8 The following questions relate to the extraction of aluminium by electrolysis.
(ICSE Specimen 2025, Specimen 2024)

(i) Name the other aluminium containing compound added to alumina.

(ii) Give a balanced equation for the reaction that takes place at the cathode.

Ans. (i) The other aluminium containing compound added to alumina is **cryolite**. **(1)**

(ii) The reaction that takes place at the cathode is,

$$Al^{3+} + 3e^{-} \longrightarrow Al$$ **(1)**

Q.9 Name the alloy which is made up of.
(i) Copper, zinc and tin
(ii) Lead and tin **(ICSE Specimen 2025, Specimen 2024)**

Ans. (i) **Bronze** is an alloy which is made up of copper, zinc and tin. **(1)**
(ii) **Solder** is an alloy of lead and tin. **(1)**

Q.10 Name the main component of the following alloys.
(i) Brass (ii) Duralumin **(ICSE 2018, 2014)**

Ans. The main components of alloys brass and duralumin with their composition are as follows:
(i) Brass – Cu (60-80%) and Zn (40-20%). **(1)**
(ii) Duralumin – Al (95%), Cu (4%), Mg (0.5%) and Mn (0.5%). **(1)**

Q.11 Identify alloy in each case from the given composition.
(i) Aluminium, magnesium, mangnese, copper.
(ii) Iron, nickel, chromium, carbon. **(ICSE 2023)**

Ans. (i) Duralumin. **(1)**
(ii) Stainless steel. **(1)**

Q.12 Name the alloys for the given composition.
(i) Magnesium and aluminium
(ii) Magnesium + Manganese + Aluminium + Copper
Also give one property of each alloy. **(ICSE 2019)**

Ans. (i) **Magnalium** alloy consist of aluminium (90-95%) and magnesium (10-5%). It is light and **strong**, as well as **corrosion resistant**. **(1)**
(ii) **Duralumin** is an alloy which consist of 95% aluminium, 4% copper, 0.5%, magnesium and 0.5% manganese. It is **highly ductile**. **(1)**

Q.13 Write one use of the following alloys. **(ICSE 2023)**
(i) Bronze
(ii) Fuse metal

Ans. (i) Bronze is used in **making coins**.
(ii) Fuse metal is used for **welding**. **(1 × 2 = 2)**

Q.14 State one use of the given alloys. **(ICSE 2021-22, Sem-II)**
(i) Magnalium
(ii) Duralumin

Ans. (i) **Use of magnalium** Used in aircraft and automobile parts. **(1)**
(ii) **Use of duralumin** Used in pressure cookers. **(1)**

Q.15 For construction work the alloy of aluminium, i.e., duralumin is used rather than pure aluminium. Give two valid reasons. **(Competency Based Que.)**

Ans. Duralumin is **light and strong**, while aluminium is light and weak. It is also **unaffected by moist air**.
It is **corrosion resistant** and has **high tensile strength**. **(2)**

Q.16 A fuse wire is an alloy made of tin and lead. It is a safety device that prevents the damage of electronic gadgets due to excessive flow of current. Can copper replace tin when making alloys? Justify your answer. **(Competency Based Que.)**

Ans. No, because the melting point of copper is very high. **(2)**

TYPE - 8

03 Marks

Short Answer Type II Questions

Q.1 Giving examples, differentiate between roasting and calcination.

Ans. Differences between roasting and calcination are:

Roasting	Calcination
Sulphide ore is heated in the **excess of air**.	**Carbonate ore** is heated in the **absence or limited supply of air.**
This is used for **sulphide ores**.	This is used for **carbonate ores**.
SO_2 is produced along with metal oxide.	CO_2 is produced along with metal oxide.
e.g. $2ZnS + 3O_2 \xrightarrow{\Delta} 2ZnO + 2SO_2$	e.g. $ZnCO_3 \xrightarrow{\Delta} ZnO + CO_2$

(3)

Q.2 Complete the following reactions :
(i) $FeS + O_2 \longrightarrow$ .... + ...
(ii) $CuO + H_2 \xrightarrow{\Delta}$ .... + ...
(iii) $Cu_2O + Cu_2S \xrightarrow{\Delta}$ .... + ...
Also, balance the given equations.

Ans. (i) $4FeS + 7O_2 \longrightarrow 2Fe_2O_3 + 4SO_2$ **(1)**
(ii) $CuO + H_2 \xrightarrow{\Delta} Cu + H_2O$ **(1)**
(iii) $2Cu_2O + Cu_2S \xrightarrow{\Delta} 6Cu + SO_2$ **(1)**

Q.3 (i) What is the main principle behind the hydraulic washing method of concentrating ores?
(ii) What happens when an impure metal is refined by the process of oxidation refining?
(iii) What is the basic difference between distillation refining and liquation refining?

Ans. (i) The main principle of hydraulic washing is the **difference in density between the ore and the gangue**.

The gangue, being lighter, is washed away by water, while the heavier ore particles sink and are collected at the bottom. **(1)**

(ii) On oxidation of an impure metal, pure metal remains behind in molten form and **impurities are oxidised by air** to form their respective oxides. **(1)**

(iii) **Distillation** Separation based on boiling points (used for volatile metals).

Liquation Separation based on melting points (used for low melting point metals). **(1)**

Q.4 (i) **Explain why the anode gradually decreases in size and the cathode increases in size?**

(ii) **Label *A, B, C* and *D* correctly.**

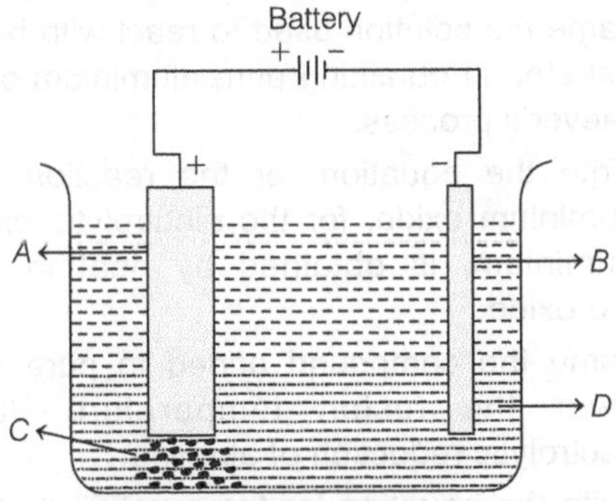

Experimental set up for the electrolytic refining of copper

Ans. (i) The anode decreases in size because metal ions are released into the electrolyte during oxidation. The cathode increases in size as metal ions are reduced and deposited onto the cathode during the refining process. **(1)**

(ii) *A*—Impure copper metal (anode)

B—Pure copper metal (cathode)

C—Anode mud

D—$CuSO_4$ electrolyte solution **(2)**

Q.5 **Give the chemical formula of** **(ICSE 2019)**

(i) **bauxite**

(ii) **cryolite**

(iii) **sodium aluminate**

Ans. (i) $Al_2O_3 \cdot 2H_2O$

(ii) Na_3AlF_6

(iii) $NaAlO_2$ **(1 × 3 = 3)**

Q.6 (i) **Name the chief ore of aluminium and the process of concentration of the ore.**

(ii) **Write balanced equations for the conversion of the above ore of aluminium to pure alumina.** **(ICSE 2020)**

(iii) **Name one alloy of aluminium.** **(ICSE Specimen 2023)**

Ans. (i) Chief ore of aluminium is **bauxite**. The ore is first purified and the metal is extracted from it by **Baeyer's process**. **(1)**

(ii) Balanced chemical equations for the conversion of bauxite ore to alumina are as follows.

$$\underset{\text{Impure bauxite}}{Al_2O_3 \cdot 2H_2O} + \underset{\text{Conc. solution}}{2NaOH} \xrightarrow{140\text{-}150°C} \underset{\text{Sodium meta aluminate}}{2NaAlO_2} + 3H_2O$$

$$\underset{\text{Sodium meta aluminate}}{NaAlO_2} + 2H_2O \xrightarrow{50-60°C} \underset{\text{Sodium hydroxide}}{NaOH} + \underset{\text{Aluminium hydroxide}}{Al(OH)_3 \downarrow}$$

$$\underset{\text{Aluminium hydroxide}}{2Al(OH)_3} \xrightarrow{1000°C} \underset{\text{Pure alumina}}{Al_2O_3} + 3H_2O$$ **(1)**

(iii) **Magnalium** is an alloy of aluminium. It consists of 90-95% Al and 10-5 % Mg. **(1)**

Q.7 **Compound *X* and aluminium are used to join railway tracks.**

(i) **Identify the compound *X*.**

(ii) **The metal of *X* is present in which part of reactivity series.**

(iii) **Write down its reaction.**

Ans. (i) Compound *X* is **iron (III) oxide**, Fe_2O_3. **(1)**

(ii) **Middle** of the reactivity series. **(1)**

(iii) The reaction that takes place is as follows

$$\underset{\substack{\text{Iron (III) oxide} \\ (X)}}{Fe_2O_3(s)} + \underset{\substack{\text{Aluminium powder} \\ \text{(reducing agent)}}}{2Al(s)} \xrightarrow{\Delta} \underset{\substack{\text{Iron metal} \\ \text{(molten state)}}}{2Fe(l)} + \underset{\substack{\text{Aluminium} \\ \text{oxide}}}{Al_2O_3(s)} + \text{Heat}$$ **(1)**

Q.8 **In order to obtain 1 tonne of aluminium, the following inputs are required 4 tonnes of bauxite, 150 kg of sodium hydroxide and 600 kg of graphite. The aluminium compound in bauxite is aluminium oxide and the main impurity is iron (III) oxide. Aluminium is obtained by the electrolysis of aluminium oxide dissolved in cryolite.**

(i) **When bauxite is treated with sodium hydroxide solution what happens to**

(a) **the aluminium oxide?**

(b) **the iron (III) oxide?**

(ii) (a) **Name the process used for the purification of bauxite.**

(b) **Write the equation for the action of heat on aluminium hydroxide.**

Ans. (i) (a) Aluminium oxide being an **amphoteric oxide**, reacts with sodium hydroxide solution to form **soluble sodium meta aluminate**. **(1)**

(b) Iron (III) oxide remains in sodium hydroxide undissolved. **(1)**

(ii) (a) **Baeyer's process** is used for the purification of bauxite ore. **(½)**

(b) $2Al(OH)_3 \xrightarrow{\Delta} Al_2O_3 + 3H_2O$ **(½)**

Q.9

Alloy	Composition	Uses
X	Pb and Sn	Fuse
German silver	*Y*, Zn and Ni	Resistors and electric heaters
Bronze	Cu, Sn and Zn	*Z*

Complete the given table by identifying *X*, *Y* and *Z*.

Ans. *X* = Solder, *Y* = Cu, *Z* = Medals **(1 × 3 = 3)**

Q.10 Choose the major metals from the list given above to make the following alloys.

Calcium, Copper, Lead, Aluminium, Zinc, Chromium, Magnesium, Iron, Tin

(i) Stainless steel (ii) Brass (iii) Bronze

Ans. (i) **Iron** and **chromium** are used to make stainless steel.

(ii) **Copper** and **zinc** are used to make brass.

(iii) **Copper** and **tin** are used to make bronze. **(1 × 3 = 3)**

TYPE - 9 04/05 Marks

Long Answer Type Questions

Q.1 (i) Name the ore of zinc containing its carbonate.

(ii) In the process of extracting zinc, the above named ore is calcinated. Write the equation for the reaction which takes place, when the carbonate ore is calcinated.

(iii) 'Iron is removed from a blast furnace as a liquid'. State how zinc leaves a furnace?

(iv) Are liquid zinc and liquid lead miscible or immiscible?

Ans. (i) Zinc carbonate ($ZnCO_3$) **(1)**

(ii) When zinc carbonate is calcinated, the reaction is given by:

$$ZnCO_3 \xrightarrow{\Delta} ZnO + CO_2 \uparrow$$ **(1)**

(iii) Zinc leaves a furnace in the **vapour form**. **(1)**

(iv) **Immiscible** liquids. Zinc is lighter than lead. **(1)**

Q.2 (i) Name the most common ore of the metal aluminium from which the metal is extracted. Write the chemical formula of the ore.

(ii) Name the process by which impure ore of aluminium gets purified by using concentrated solution of an alkali. (Give reactions involved also)

(iii) Write the equation for the formation of aluminium at the cathode, during the electrolysis of alumina. **(ICSE 2018)**

Ans. (i) The most common ore of the metal aluminium is **bauxite** having chemical formula, $Al_2O_3 \cdot 2H_2O$. **(1)**

(ii) **Baeyer's process** is used to obtain pure aluminium oxide from bauxite ore.

In this method of chemical purification, the finely powdered ore is treated with hot sodium hydroxide solution. i.e.

$$\underset{\text{Impure bauxite}}{Al_2O_3 \cdot 2H_2O} + \underset{\text{Conc. solution}}{2NaOH} \xrightarrow{140\text{-}150°C} \underset{\text{Sodium meta-aluminate}}{2NaAlO_2} + 3H_2O$$

$$\underset{\text{Sodium meta-aluminate}}{NaAlO_2} + 2H_2O \xrightarrow{50\text{-}60°C} \underset{\text{Sodium hydroxide}}{NaOH} + \underset{\text{Aluminium hydroxide}}{Al(OH)_3 \downarrow}$$

$$\underset{\text{Aluminium hydroxide}}{2Al(OH)_3} \xrightarrow{1000°C} \underset{\text{Pure alumina}}{Al_2O_3} + 3H_2O$$ **(2)**

(iii) During electrolysis of alumina, the reaction which occurs at cathode is $Al^{3+} + 3e^- \longrightarrow Al$. **(1)**

Q.3 Answer the following questions.

(i) Name the solution used to react with bauxite as a first step in obtaining pure aluminium oxide in the Baeyer's process.

(ii) Write the equation for the reaction where the aluminium oxide, for the electrolytic extraction of aluminium, is obtained by heating aluminium hydroxide.

(iii) Name the compound added to pure alumina to lower the fusion temperature during the electrolytic reduction of alumina.

(iv) Write the equation for the reaction that occurs at the cathode during the extraction of aluminium by electrolysis. **(ICSE 2016)**

Ans. (i) **Hot sodium hydroxide solution** is used to react with bauxite as a first step in obtaining pure aluminium oxide in the Baeyer's process. **(1)**

(ii) $$\underset{\text{(Aluminium hydroxide)}}{2Al(OH)_3} \xrightarrow[\Delta]{1000°C} \underset{\text{(Pure alumina)}}{Al_2O_3} + 2H_2O$$ **(1)**

(iii) Cryolite (Na_3AlF_6) **(1)**

(iv) Reaction at cathode, $4Al^{3+} + 12e^- \longrightarrow 4Al$ **(1)**

Q.4 Following is the sketch of eletrolytic cell used in the extraction of aluminium.

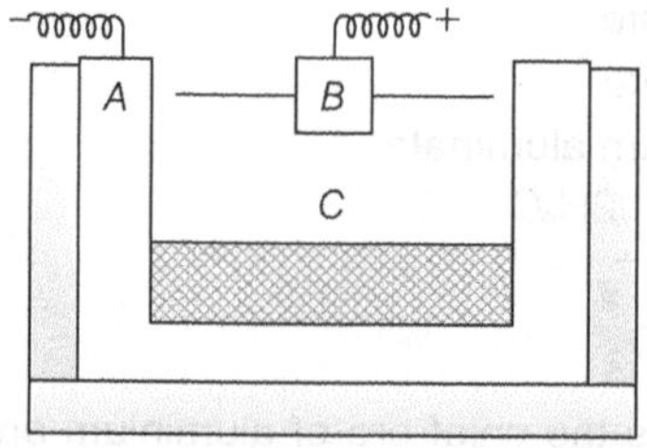

(i) What is the substance, of which the electrodes *A* and *B* are made of?

(ii) At which electrode (*A* or *B*) the aluminium is formed?

(iii) What are the two aluminium compounds in the electrolyte *C*?

(iv) Why is it necessary for electrode *B* to be continuously replaced ?

Ans. (i) Electrodes *A* and *B* are made up of **graphite or carbon**. **(1)**

(ii) Aluminium is formed at **electrode *A***. **(1)**

(iii) **Alumina** (aluminium oxide, Al_2O_3) and **cryolite** (sodium aluminium fluoride, Na_3AlF_6). **(1)**

(iv) It is necessary for electrode *B* to be continuously replaced, because electrode *B* gets **oxidised by oxygen** produced at anode, to release CO_2 gas. **(1)**

Q.5 **Zinc is extracted from zinc blende. The zinc blende is roasted. The solid product is mixed with coke in a blast furnace, from which zinc vapour emerges.**

(i) Write the equation for the roasting of zinc blende?

(ii) What is the purpose of using coke?

(iii) What is the reducing agent in this extraction?

(iv) How are the zinc vapours condensed to liquid?

Ans. (i) $2ZnS + 3O_2 \longrightarrow 2ZnO + 2SO_2$

(ii) Coke is used for the **reduction of oxide**.

(iii) **Coke** is the reducing agent.

(iv) Zinc vapours are sent into **condenser**, containing lead droplets. Zinc vapours are absorbed into these droplets and on cooling these droplets from 560°C to 430°C, zinc comes as solution and **floats on the surface**. **(1 × 4 = 4)**

Q.6 **The following sketch illustrates the process of conversion of alumina to aluminium. Study the diagram and answer the following.** **(ICSE 2023)**

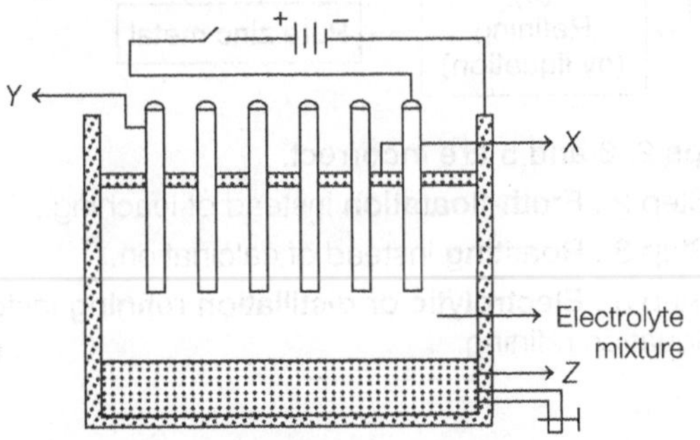

(i) Name the constituent of the electrolyte mixture which has a divalent metal in it.

(ii) Name the powdered substance 'X' sprinkled on the surface of the electrolyte mixture.

(iii) What is the name of the process?

(iv) Write the reactions taking place at the electrodes 'Y' (anode) and 'Z' (cathode) respectively.

Ans. (i) The electrolyte are mixture of molten alumina, cryolite and fluorspar (CaF_2). **CaF_2 has Ca^{2+}** in it (divalent metal). **(1)**

(ii) *X* is **coke**, which is sprinkled on the surface of electrolyte. **(1)**

(iii) Hall-Heroult's process. **(1)**

(iv) Reactions taking place are

At cathode (*Z*), $4Al^{3+} + 12e^- \longrightarrow 4Al$

At anode (*Y*), $6O^{2-} \longrightarrow 6[O] + 12e^-$

$3O + 3O \longrightarrow 3O_2$ **(2)**

Q.7 **(A) to (F) given below relate to the source and extraction of either zinc or aluminium.**

(A) Bauxite **(B) Coke**

(C) Cryolite **(D) Froth-floatation**

(E) Sodium hydroxide solution **(F) Zinc blende.**

(i) Write down the three letters each from the above list which are relevant to

(a) Zinc **(b) Aluminium**

(ii) Fill in the blanks using the most appropriate words from (a) to (b).

(a) The ore, from which aluminium is extracted, must first be treated with .... so, that pure aluminium oxide can be obtained.

(b) Pure aluminium oxide is dissolved in ...... to make a conducting solution.

(iii) Write the formula of cryolite.

Ans. (i) (a) For zinc

(B) Coke (D) Froth-floatation

(F) Zinc blende **(1)**

(b) For aluminium

(A) Bauxite (C) Cryolite

(E) Sodium hydroxide solution **(1)**

(ii) (a) sodium hydroxide (b) cryolite **(2)**

(iii) Cryolite, Na_3AlF_6 (sodium aluminium fluoride) **(1)**

TYPE - 10 — 03 Marks

Case Based Questions

Q.1 **A student is studying the processes involved in the extraction of metals and learns about the concentration of ores. The student discovers that before extracting metal from its ore, it is essential to concentrate the ore to remove impurities. The student reads about two methods of concentration; the froth flotation process, used for concentrating copper ore, and magnetic separation, used for concentrating iron ore.**

(i) What is the main purpose of concentrating ores before metal extraction?

(ii) What property of the ore is used in the froth flotation process for copper ore concentration?

(iii) Why is magnetic separation particularly useful for iron ore concentration?

Ans. (i) The main purpose is to **remove impurities (gangue)** and **increase the metal content** in the ore for **efficient extraction.** **(1)**

(ii) The froth floatation process is based on the **difference in how water and oil wet ore and gangue particles**. It is commonly used for sulphide ores of copper.

In this process, the ore is mixed with water, and chemicals are added to make the valuable mineral particles hydrophobic (repel water) while the gangue particles remain hydrophilic (attract water).

Air is passed through the mixture, causing the hydrophobic minerals to attach to air bubbles, which rise to the surface, forming a froth. The froth is removed, leaving the gangue behind. **(1)**

(iii) Magnetic separation is useful because iron ore contains **magnetic materials** (such as **magnetite**), which can be easily separated from non-magnetic impurities. **(1)**

Q.2 **A metal extraction factory is processing zinc and calcium ores using two different methods. For zinc extraction, the factory uses the roasting process, where zinc sulphide (ZnS) is heated in the presence of air. On the other hand, calcium carbonate ($CaCO_3$) is being heated in the factory's calcination furnace for the extraction of calcium.**

(i) What gases are evolved during the roasting of zinc sulphide (ZnS) and calcination of calcium carbonate ($CaCO_3$)?

(ii) Write the chemical equations for the roasting of zinc sulphide (ZnS) and calcination of calcium carbonate ($CaCO_3$).

(iii) Why is air needed for roasting, but not for calcination?

Ans. (i) During the roasting of zinc sulphide (ZnS), **sulphur dioxide** (SO_2) gas is evolved. During the calcination of calcium carbonate ($CaCO_3$), **carbon dioxide** (CO_2) gas is evolved. **(1)**

(ii) The chemical equation for the roasting of zinc sulphide (ZnS) is

$$2ZnS + 3O_2 \xrightarrow{\Delta} 2ZnO + 2SO_2\uparrow$$

The chemical equation for the calcination of calcium carbonate ($CaCO_3$) is

$$CaCO_3 \xrightarrow{\Delta} CaO + CO_2\uparrow$$ **(1)**

(iii) Air is needed for roasting because oxygen in the air is required to oxidise the zinc sulphide into zinc oxide, and the sulphur is released as sulphur dioxide (SO_2).

In calcination, no air is needed because the process involves heating the calcium carbonate in the absence of air, which leads to its **decomposition** into calcium oxide and carbon dioxide gas. **(1)**

Q.3 **A student was asked to draw the flowchart for the extraction of zinc from zinc blende based on the principles of metallurgy. What he drew is given below. 3 steps out of the 5 were incorrect. Identify and correct them.**

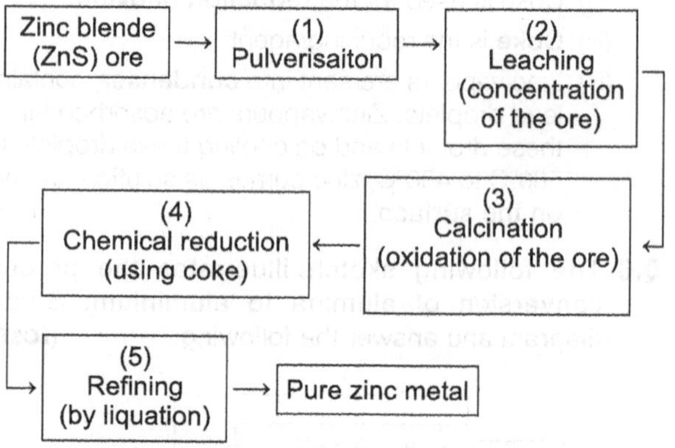

Ans. Steps 2, 3 and 5 are incorrect.

(a) Step 2 : **Froth-floatation** instead of leaching.

(b) Step 3 : **Roasting** instead of calcination.

(c) Step 5 : **Electrolytic or distillation refining** instead of liquation refining. **(1 × 3 = 3)**

08

STUDY OF COMPOUNDS

Compound I : Hydrogen Chloride

Molecular formula : HCl

Molecular mass : 36.5 u

Bond : Polar Covalent

Structure :

H $\overset{\times}{\bullet}$ $\ddot{\underset{\cdot\cdot}{Cl}}$: or H—Cl

Lewis structure

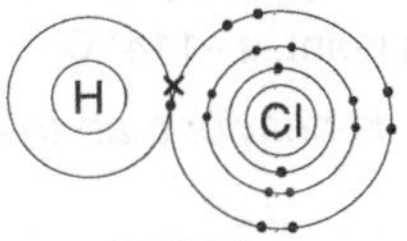

Orbital diagram

Laboratory Preparation of Hydrogen Chloride Gas

Hydrogen chloride gas is prepared in the laboratory, by the reaction of metallic chloride (NaCl) with conc. H_2SO_4.

$$\underset{}{NaCl} + \underset{\text{(conc.)}}{H_2SO_4} \xrightarrow[200°C]{\text{Below}} \underset{\substack{\text{Sodium}\\ \text{bisulphate}}}{NaHSO_4} + \underset{\substack{\text{Hydrogen}\\ \text{chloride gas}}}{HCl \uparrow}$$

$$2NaCl + \underset{\text{(conc.)}}{H_2SO_4} \xrightarrow[200°C]{\text{Above}} Na_2SO_4 + 2HCl \uparrow$$

Note Concentrated HNO_3 is not used during the preparation of HCl, because it is volatile and may volatilise out alongwith HCl gas.

- **Procedure** Common salt is taken in a flask and conc. H_2SO_4 is added through the thistle funnel. On heating the mixture gently, there is effervescence and HCl gas is evolved.

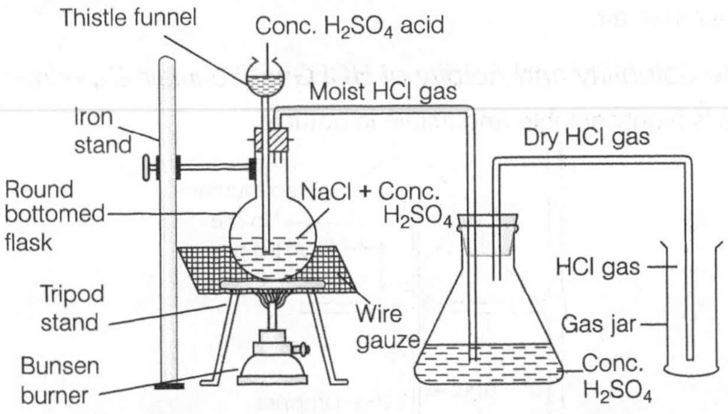

Laboratory preparation of dry hydrogen chloride gas

- **Observation** The HCl gas formed in the flask passes through conc. sulphuric acid and is collected in the jar as dry HCl.
- **Purification of HCl gas** It is dried by passing through **conc. H_2SO_4**. Drying agents like phosphorus pentoxide (P_2O_5) and quicklime (CaO) cannot be used, since they react with HCl.

$$2P_2O_5 + 3HCl \longrightarrow POCl_3 + 3HPO_3$$

$$CaO + 2HCl \longrightarrow CaCl_2 + H_2O$$

- **Collection** The gas is collected by **upward displacement of air** in a gas jar. It is not collected over water, since it is highly soluble in water.
- **Identification** In order to know if the gas jar is full, a glass rod dipped in NH_3 (ammonia) solution or ammonium hydroxide, is brought near the mouth of gas jar containing HCl gas. Dense white fumes of ammonium chloride are formed, proving that jar is full of HCl gas.

$$NH_4OH + HCl \longrightarrow NH_4Cl + H_2O$$

- **Precautions**
  (i) The lower end of the thistle funnel should dip below the acid in flask, otherwise the HCl gas obtained will escape out from the thistle funnel.
  (ii) Temperature is maintained at 200°C, otherwise sodium sulphate is formed which forms a hard crust, that sticks to the glass and is difficult to remove.

Physical Properties

- Colourless, pungent choking odour and slightly sour in taste.
- It is 1.28 times heavier than water and highly soluble in water.
- Liquefies at about 10°C and 40 atmospheric pressure.
- Boiling point is –85°C and melting point is –114°C.

Experiment (To show that HCl gas is heavier than air)

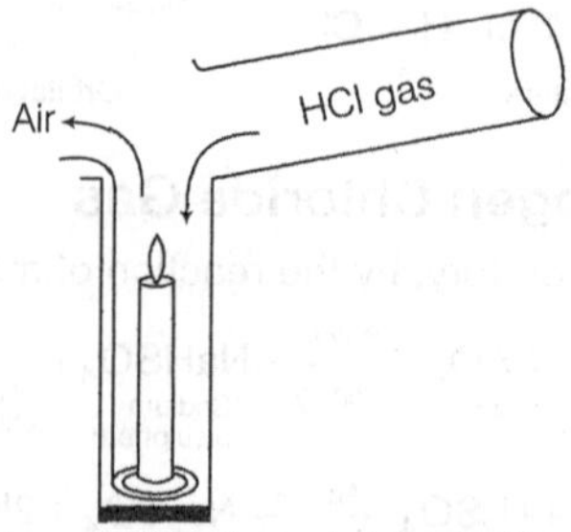

To show that HCl gas is heavier than air

- **Apparatus** A dry gas jar filled with dry HCl gas and an empty gas jar, in which a burning candle is placed.
- **Procedure** HCl gas from the dry gas jar is poured into the lower jar containing the burning candle.
- **Observation** The burning candle gets extinguished, because HCl gas being heavier than air, displaces the air from the lower jar and forces the air out of it.
- **Inference** HCl gas is heavier than air.

Experiment to Demonstrate Solubility and Acidity of HCl Gas (Fountain Experiment)

- **Aim** To show that HCl gas is highly soluble and acidic in nature.

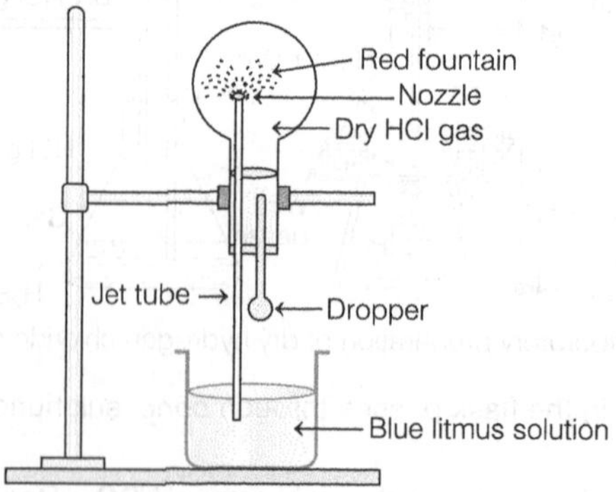

Fountain experiment

- **Apparatus** Dry round bottom flask with dry HCl gas, a rubber stopper with two holes, blue litmus solution.
- **Procedure** Set the apparatus as shown in the figure. The dropper containing water is squeezed and the water enters the flask.

REVISION NOTES

- **Observation** As HCl gas present in the flask dissolves in water due to its high solubility, thereby lowering the pressure inside. The outside pressure being higher pushes the blue litmus solution inside through the jet tube, which emerges out at the end of the tube as a red fountain.
- **Inference** HCl gas is highly soluble in water and acidic in nature.

Hydrochloric Acid

Hydrochloric acid is prepared by dissolving hydrogen chloride gas in water using a special funnel arrangement because direct absorption of HCl gas in water using a delivery tube causes back suction.

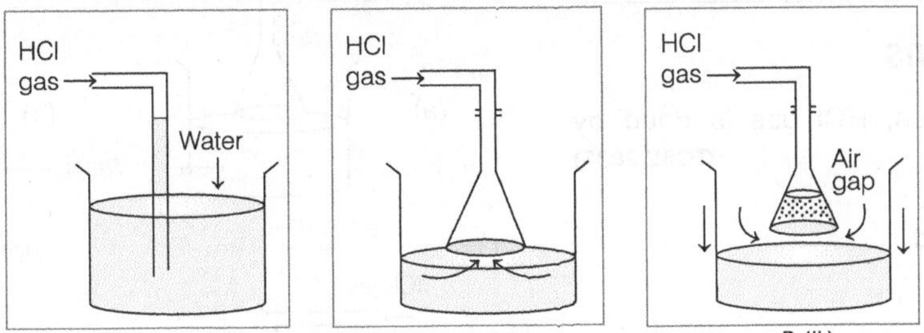

A B (i) B (ii)

Funnel arrangement

Physical Properties

- Colourless and slightly pungent smell with sharp sour taste.
- Corrosive in nature and causes blisters on the skin.
- Density is 1.2 gm/cc with boiling point of 110°C.

Chemical Properties

1. **Nature** Aqueous solution is **strongly acidic** and shows all properties of acids. It changes, moist litmus → blue to red; Methyl orange → orange to pink and phenolphthalein → colourless to colourless (no change).
2. **Action on metals** Hydrochloric acid reacts with metals, which are above hydrogen in the activity series, and form **metal chlorides** and **hydrogen gas.**

$$Mg + 2HCl \longrightarrow MgCl_2 + H_2\uparrow$$

3. **Action on oxides and hydroxides** Hydrochloric acid reacts with oxides and hydroxides to form **salt** and **water** only.

$$ZnO + 2HCl \longrightarrow ZnCl_2 + H_2O$$
$$Zn(OH)_2 + 2HCl \longrightarrow ZnCl_2 + 2H_2O$$

4. **Decomposition of carbonates, hydrogen carbonates, sulphides and sulphites** HCl acid decomposes salts of weaker acids, e.g. carbonates, bicarbonates, sulphites and sulphides.

$$Na_2CO_3 + 2HCl \longrightarrow 2NaCl + H_2O + CO_2\uparrow$$
$$NaHCO_3 + HCl \longrightarrow NaCl + H_2O + CO_2\uparrow$$
$$Na_2SO_3 + 2HCl \longrightarrow 2NaCl + H_2O + SO_2\uparrow$$
$$MgSO_3 + 2HCl \longrightarrow MgCl_2 + H_2O + SO_2\uparrow$$
$$FeS + 2HCl \longrightarrow FeCl_2 + H_2S\uparrow$$

5. **Precipitation reaction (Reaction with nitrates)** Lead nitrate and mercury (I) nitrate react with hydrochloric acid, to give **white precipitate** of lead chloride and mercury (I) chloride (which are soluble in hot water).

$$Pb(NO_3)_2 + 2HCl \longrightarrow PbCl_2\downarrow + 2HNO_3$$

Silver nitrate gives **thick curdy white precipitate** of silver chloride.

$$AgNO_3 + HCl \longrightarrow AgCl\downarrow + HNO_3$$

6. **Reaction with ammonia** Hydrogen chloride gas reacts with ammonia to form dense white fumes of **ammonium chloride.**

$$NH_3 + HCl \longrightarrow \underset{\text{Dense white fumes}}{NH_4Cl}$$

EXAM ORIENTED QUESTIONS

TYPE - 1 01 Mark

Multiple Choice Questions

Q.1 In the laboratory preparation, HCl gas is dried by passing through **(ICSE 2023)**

(a) dilute nitric acid

(b) concentrated sulphuric acid

(c) dilute sulphuric acid

(d) acidified water

Ans. (b) HCl gas is passed through a drying agent to remove the moisture, so here **concentrated sulphuric acid** acts as dehydrating agent.

Q.2 Hydrogen chloride gas is not collected over water, as **(ICSE 2021-22, Sem-II)**

(a) it is highly soluble in water

(b) it is less soluble in water

(c) it is lighter than air

(d) it is heavier than air

Ans. (a) Hydrogen chloride is not collected over water, as it is **highly soluble** in water.

Q.3 Hydrogen chloride gas being highly soluble in water is dried by

(a) anhydrous calcium chloride

(b) phosphorus pentoxide

(c) quicklime

(d) concentrated sulphuric acid

Ans. (d) Concentrated sulphuric acid

Q.4 The aim of the fountain experiment is to prove that **(ICSE 2016)**

(a) HCl turns blue litmus red

(b) HCl is denser than air

(c) HCl is highly soluble in water

(d) HCl fumes in moist air

Ans. (c) Fountain experiment is used to show **high solubility** of HCl in water.

Q.5 Given below are four different illustrations of preparing hydrochloric acid drawn by students. Which of these is the correct? **(Competency Based Que.)**

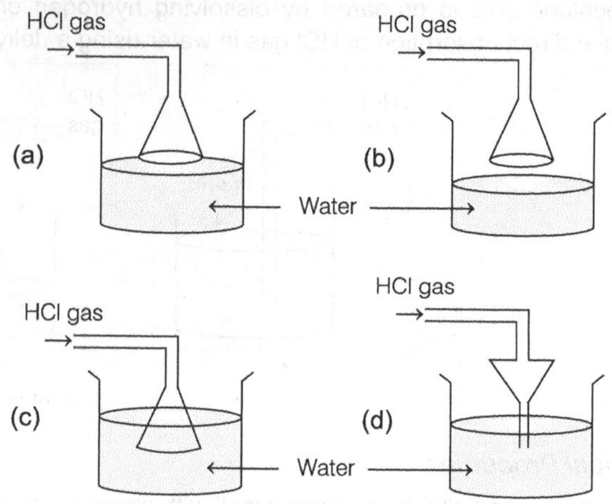

Ans. (a)

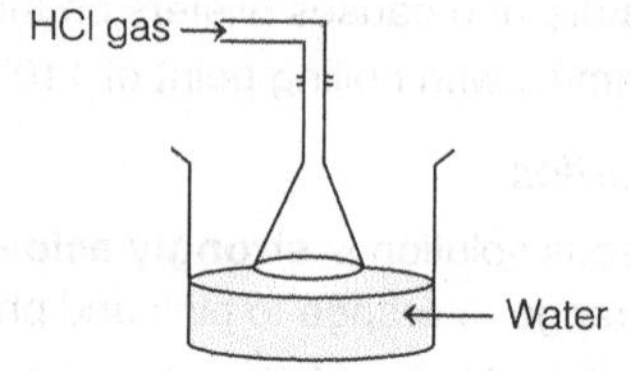

Q.6 Which metal does not react with HCl to form a colourless, odourless gas which burns with a pop sound? **(Competency Based Que.)**

(a) Ca (b) Mg

(c) Cu (d) Zn

Ans. (c) **Cu**; Copper lies below hydrogen in the activity series.

Q.7 The diagram shows the apparatus used in an experiment to reduce substance *Q* with the gas generated in the flask.

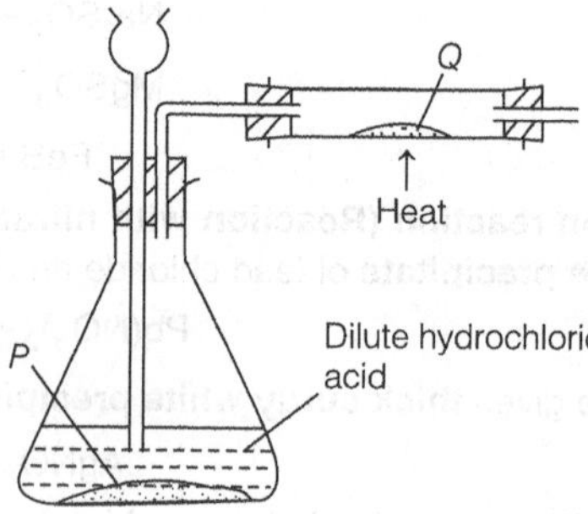

What are substances *P* and *Q* ?

	P	*Q*
(a)	Copper	Copper(II) oxide
(b)	Lead	Lead(II) oxide
(c)	Magnesium	Zinc oxide
(d)	Zinc	Copper(II) oxide

Ans. (d) Dilute HCl will react with **zinc** metal to produce hydrogen gas which acts as a reducing agent to **reduce CuO to Cu**.

Q.8 Which of the following is not used to detect hydrochloric acid?
(a) NH_3
(b) H_2SO_4
(c) $AgNO_3$
(d) MnO_2

Ans. (b) H_2SO_4

Q.9 Rotten egg smell is due to the liberation of **(ICSE 2024)**
(a) HCl gas
(b) H_2S gas
(c) Cl_2 gas
(d) SO_2 gas

Ans. (b) **H_2S gas** (rotten egg smell gas).

TYPE - 2 — 01 Mark

Assertion-Reason Questions

Directions (Q. Nos. 1-2) In the following questions, a statement of Assertion (A) is followed by a statement of Reason (R). Choose the answer based on the codes given below.

(a) Both (A) and (R) are true and (R) is the correct explanation of (A).
(b) Both (A) and (R) are true but (R) is not the correct explanation of (A).
(c) (A) is true but (R) is false.
(d) (A) is false but (R) is true.

Q.1 Assertion (A) Dry hydrogen chloride gas is collected by the upward displacement of air. **(ICSE Specimen 2025)**

Reason (R) Hydrogen chloride gas is lighter than air.

Ans. (c) Dry hydrogen chloride (HCl) gas is collected by the upward displacement of air, as it is 1.28 times heavier than air.

Thus, (A) is true but (R) is false.

Q.2 Assertion (A) Hydrogen chloride gas gives white fumes when exposed to air.

Reason (R) Hydrogen chloride gas reacts with atmospheric water vapour to form hydrochloric acid.

Ans. (a) When hydrogen chloride gas is exposed to air, it gives white fumes due to the formation of hydrochloric acid on dissolving in atmospheric water vapour.

Thus, both (A) and (R) are true and (R) is the correct explanation of (A).

TYPE - 3 — 01 Mark

Fill in the Blanks

Q.1 Hydrogen chloride gas is a .... compound. (non-polar/polar)

Ans. polar

Q.2 When sodium chloride is heated with concentrated sulphuric acid below 200°C, one of the products formed is .... (sodium hydrogen sulphate /sodium sulphate) **(ICSE 2014)**

Ans. sodium hydrogen sulphate.

Q.3 Quicklime is not used to dry HCl gas because .... (CaO is alkaline/CaO is acidic) **(ICSE 2014)**

Ans. CaO is alkaline

Q.4 Dry hydrogen chloride gas can be collected by .... displacement of air (downward/upward). **(ICSE 2018)**

Ans. upward

Q.5 .... gas is heavier than air. (NH_3/HCl)

Ans. HCl

Q.6 The indicator which does not change colour on passage of HCl gas is .... (methyl orange/ phenolphthalein)

Ans. phenolphthalein

Q.7 Potassium sulphite on reacting with hydrochloric acid releases .... gas. (Cl_2/SO_2)

Ans. SO_2

TYPE - 4 — 01 Mark

Correct the Incorrect Statement

Q.1 Dry hydrogen gas combines with chlorine in the presence of diffused sunlight to form hydrogen chloride gas.

Ans. Moist hydrogen gas combines with chlorine in the presence of diffused sunlight to form hydrogen chloride gas.

Q.2 Hydrogen chloride gas is collected by the upward displacement of air as it is 1.28 times lighter than air.

Ans. Hydrogen chloride gas is collected by the upward displacement of air as it is 1.28 times **heavier** than air.

TYPE - 5 01 Mark

Identify the Following

Q.1 Identify the underlined substance in the following question.

A gas which does not conduct electricity in the liquid state, but conducts electricity when dissolved in water.

Ans. Hydrogen chloride

Q.2 Name the gas evolved when dilute hydrochloric acid reacts with sodium sulphide. **(ICSE 2018)**

Ans. Hydrogen sulphide (H_2S) gas

$$\underset{\text{Sodium sulphide}}{Na_2S} + \underset{(\text{Dil.})}{2HCl} \longrightarrow \underset{\text{Sodium chloride}}{2NaCl} + H_2S\uparrow$$

Q.3 Name the gas produced when ferrous sulphide reacts with dilute hydrochloric acid. **(ICSE 2025)**

Ans. Hydrogen sulphide (H_2S) gas

$$FeS + \underset{(\text{Dil.})}{2HCl} \longrightarrow FeCl_2 + H_2S\uparrow$$

Q.4 Name the acid which on mixing with silver nitrate solution produces a white precipitate, which is soluble in excess ammonium hydroxide. **(ICSE 2015)**

Ans. Hydrochloric acid

Q.5 Name the gas evolved when MnO_2 reacts with concentrated HCl. **(ICSE 2024)**

Ans. Cl_2 (greenish yellow gas)

$$MnO_2 + 4HCl \longrightarrow MnCl_2 + 2H_2O + Cl_2\uparrow$$

TYPE - 6 02 Marks

Short Answer Type I Questions

Q.1 Give one relevant reason for the following statements.

(i) Hydrogen chloride gas fumes in moist air. **(ICSE 2019, Competency Based Que.)**

(ii) Hydrogen chloride gas cannot be dried over quicklime.

Ans. (i) Hydrogen chloride gas fumes in moist air because it has **high solubility** in water. It forms a mist of droplets of hydrogen chloride. **(1)**

(ii) Because quicklime is **alkaline** in nature and it reacts with HCl gas to form a **salt**. **(1)**

Q.2 Certain blank spaces are left in the following table and these are labelled as *A*, *B*. Identify each of them. **(ICSE 2017)**

Lab preparation	Reactants used	Products formed	Drying agent	Method of collection
HCl gas	NaCl+ H_2SO_4	*A*	Conc. H_2SO_4	*B*

Ans. $A - \underset{\text{Sodium bisulphate}}{NaHSO_4} + \underset{\text{Hydrogen chloride}}{HCl\uparrow}$ **(1)**

B – Upward displacement of air. **(1)**

Q.3 (i) Of the two gases, ammonia and hydrogen chloride, which is more dense? Name the method of collection of this gas.

(ii) Give one example of a reaction between the above two gases, which produces a solid compound?

Ans. (i) **Hydrogen chloride** is more dense. It is collected by the upward displacement of air. **(1)**

(ii) Hydrogen chloride and ammonia gas react together to give **solid ammonium chloride.**

$$NH_3(g) + HCl(g) \longrightarrow NH_4Cl(s) \quad \textbf{(1)}$$

Q.4 For the preparation of hydrochloric acid in the laboratory.

(i) Why is direct absorption of hydrogen chloride gas in water not feasible?

(ii) What arrangement is done to dissolve hydrogen chloride gas in water ? **(ICSE 2018)**

Ans. (i) Hydrogen chloride gas is **highly soluble in water**. If delivery tube, through which HCl gas is passed, is directly immersed in water, then the partial vacuum is created in the tube because rate of absorption of HCl gas is high. The pressure outside being higher, causes the water to be pushed up into the delivery tube **(back-suction)**.

Thus, the direct absorption of hydrogen chloride gas in water is not feasible. **(1)**

(ii) To dissolve hydrogen chloride gas in water, a special funnel arrangement is used.

The funnel arrangement prevents or minimise **back-suction** of water and it also provides a large surface area for the absorption of gas. **(1)**

Q.5 What is the difference between the chemical nature of an aqueous solution of hydrogen chloride and an aqueous solution of ammonia?

Ans. Aqueous solution of HCl is **acidic** and neutralises bases or alkalies and **turns blue litmus red**. Aqueous solution of ammonia is **alkaline** and **turns red litmus blue**. **(2)**

Q.6 Identify the gas evolved and give the chemical test in each of the following cases and justify your answer.

(i) Dilute hydrochloric acid reacts with sodium sulphite.

(ii) Dilute hydrochloric acid reacts with iron (II) sulphide. **(ICSE 2016)**

Ans. (i) SO_2 **gas** is evolved.

Test To the solution of hydrogen chloride, sodium sulphite is added, **suffocating odour gas** (SO_2) is evolved.

$$Na_2SO_3 + 2HCl \longrightarrow 2NaCl + H_2O + SO_2\uparrow \quad \textbf{(1)}$$

(ii) **H_2S gas** is evolved.

Test To the solution of hydrogen chloride, iron (II) sulphide is added, **rotten egg smelling gas** (H_2S) is evolved.

$$FeS + 2HCl \longrightarrow FeCl_2 + H_2S\uparrow \quad \textbf{(1)}$$

TYPE - 7 — 03 Marks

Short Answer Type II Questions

Q.1 (i) **Name the acid used for the preparation of hydrogen chloride gas in the laboratory. Why is this particular acid preferred to other acids?**

(ii) **Write the balanced chemical equation for the laboratory preparation of hydrogen chloride gas.** **(ICSE 2024, 2018)**

Ans. (i) Hydrogen chloride gas is prepared in the laboratory by the reaction of sodium chloride (common salt) with concentrated sulphuric acid. It is preferred over other acids, because of its **oxidising and dehydrating property**. **(1)**

(ii) Balanced chemical equations for the preparation of HCl gas in laboratory are as follows:

$$\underset{\text{Sodium chloride}}{NaCl} + \underset{\text{Conc. sulphuric acid}}{H_2SO_4} \xrightarrow[200°C]{\text{Below}} \underset{\text{Sodium bisulphate}}{NaHSO_4} + \underset{\text{Hydrogen chloride gas}}{HCl\uparrow}$$

$$2NaCl + \underset{\text{(Conc.)}}{H_2SO_4} \xrightarrow[200°C]{\text{Above}} \underset{\text{Sodium sulphate}}{Na_2SO_4} + 2HCl\uparrow \quad \textbf{(2)}$$

Q.2 The following questions are pertaining to the laboratory preparation of hydrogen chloride gas. **(ICSE Specimen 2023)**

(i) **Why is concentrated nitric acid not used in the preparation of hydrogen chloride gas?**

(ii) **How is hydrogen chloride gas collected?** **(ICSE 2024)**

(iii) **What is the property of sulphuric acid that makes it a suitable reagent for the reaction?**

Ans. (i) Concentrated nitric acid is not used in the preparation of hydrogen chloride gas because it is a **strong oxidising agent**. **(1)**

(ii) Hydrogen chloride gas is collected by **upward displacement of air** as it is 1.28 times heavier than air. **(1)**

(iii) Concentrated sulphuric acid is a **non-volatile acid**, so it is used in this preparation. It is also used as a **drying agent** to obtain dry HCl gas. **(1)**

Q.3 Study the figure given below and answer the questions that follow.

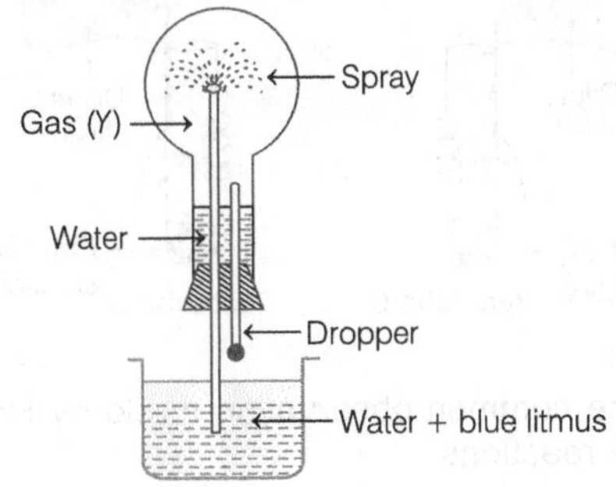

(i) **Identify the gas Y.**

(ii) **What property of gas Y does this experiment demonstrate?**

(iii) **Name another gas which has the same property and can be demonstrated through this experiment.** **(ICSE 2014)**

Ans. (i) Hydrogen chloride gas (HCl). **(1)**

(ii) Gas Y, i.e. HCl gas is **highly soluble in water** and **acidic** in nature. **(1)**

(iii) Ammonia gas. **(1)**

Q.4

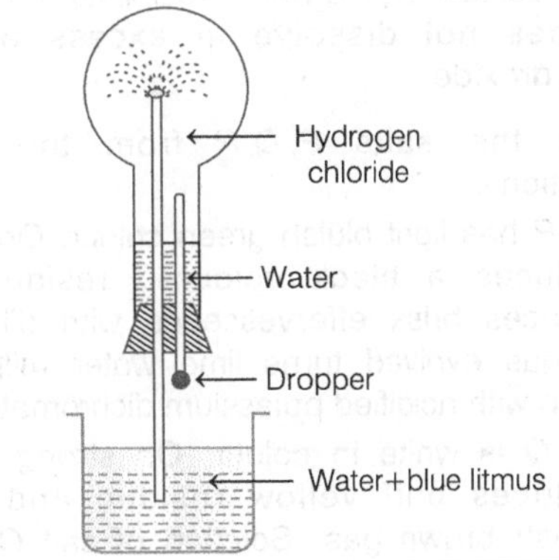

(i) **Name the experiment illustrated above.**

(ii) **State the colour of the water that has entered the round-bottomed flask. Explain.**

Ans. (i) Fountain experiment. **(1)**

(ii) Blue litmus solution enters the jet tube (round-bottomed flask) with a great force, forming a red fountain. The **blue litmus solution turns red** due to the **acidic nature** of hydrogen chloride gas. **(2)**

Q.5 **Rohit took two different salt solutions in test tubes C and D as shown in the figure below. He added dilute HCl to each of the two test tubes. The products formed in the test tubes C and D are silver chloride and lead chloride respectively,**

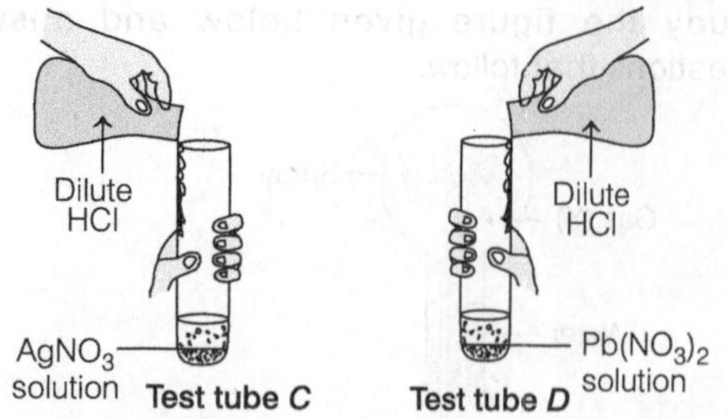

State:

(i) One common observation made by Rohit in both the reactions.

(ii) The observations made by him on addition of excess of ammonium hydroxide to the products formed in:

(a) test tube *C* (b) test tube *D* **(ICSE 2025)**

Ans. (i) In both the test tubes a **white precipitate** is formed. **(1)**

(ii) (a) In test tube *C*, the white precipitate of silver chloride **dissolves in excess ammonium hydroxide** and forms a complex salt called diammine silver (I) chloride.

$$AgCl + 2NH_4OH \longrightarrow [Ag(NH_3)_2]^+Cl^- + 2H_2O$$

(b) In test tube *D*, the white precipitate of lead chloride **does not dissolve in excess ammonium hydroxide.** **(2)**

Q.6 Identify the salts *P*, *Q*, *R* from the following observations.

(i) Salt *P* has light bluish green colour. On heating, it produces a black coloured residue. Salt *P* produces brisk effervescence with dil. HCl and the gas evolved turns lime water milky, but no action with acidified potassium dichromate solution.

(ii) Salt *Q* is white in colour. On strong heating, it produces buff yellow residue and liberates reddish brown gas. Solution of salt *Q* produces chalky white insoluble precipitate with excess of ammonium hydroxide.

(iii) Salt *R* is black in colour. On reacting with concentrated HCl, it liberates a pungent greenish yellow gas which turns moist starch iodide paper blue black. **(ICSE 2020)**

Ans. (i) The reactions involved are following:

***P* = Copper carbonate**

$$\underset{\substack{(P)\\(\text{Bluish green colour})}}{CuCO_3} \xrightarrow{\Delta} \underset{\substack{(\text{Black coloured}\\\text{residue})}}{CuO} + CO_2$$

$\downarrow$ Dil. HCl

$$CuCl_2 + H_2O + \underset{\substack{\text{Brisk}\\\text{effervescence}}}{CO_2\uparrow} \longrightarrow \text{Turns lime water milky}$$

$\downarrow$ Passed through acidified $K_2Cr_2O_7$

No reaction **(1)**

(ii) The reactions involved are following:

***Q* = Lead nitrate**

$$\underset{\substack{(Q)\\(\text{White})}}{2Pb(NO_3)_2\downarrow} \xrightarrow{\Delta} \underset{\substack{(\text{Buff yellow}\\\text{residue})}}{2PbO} + \underset{\substack{(\text{Reddish}\\\text{brown gas})}}{4NO_2\uparrow} + O_2\uparrow$$

$\downarrow$ $4NH_4OH$

$$\underset{(\text{Chalky white ppt.})}{2Pb(OH)_2\downarrow} + 4NH_4NO_3$$ **(1)**

(iii) The reactions involved are following:

***R* = Manganese dioxide**

$$\underset{(\text{Black})}{MnO_2} + \underset{(\text{conc.})}{4HCl} \longrightarrow \underset{\substack{(\text{Greenish}\\\text{yellow gas})}}{Cl_2} + MnCl_2 + 2H_2O$$

$\downarrow$

Turns moist starch iodide paper blue black **(1)**

TYPE - 8 04/05 Marks

Long Answer Type Questions

Q.1 Answer the following questions pertaining to the laboratory preparation of hydrogen chloride gas.

(i) Write an equation for the laboratory preparation of hydrogen chloride. **(ICSE Specimen 2019)**

(ii) Name the drying agent used and justify your choice.

(iii) State a safety precaution you would take during the preparation of hydrochloric acid. **(ICSE 2015)**

Ans. (i) Common salt is added to conc. H_2SO_4, this mixture on heating liberates HCl gas.

$$NaCl + \underset{(\text{Conc.})}{H_2SO_4} \xrightarrow[200^\circ C]{\text{Below}} \underset{\substack{\text{Sodium}\\\text{bisulphate}}}{NaHSO_4} + \underset{\substack{\text{Hydrogen}\\\text{chloride (gas)}}}{HCl}$$

$$2NaCl + \underset{(\text{Conc.})}{H_2SO_4} \xrightarrow{\text{Above } 200^\circ C} \underset{\substack{\text{Sodium}\\\text{sulphate}}}{Na_2SO_4} + 2HCl\uparrow$$ **(1)**

(ii) It is dried by passing through **conc. sulphuric acid.** The other drying agents like phosphorus pentaoxide (P_2O_5) and quicklime (CaO) cannot be used, since they react with hydrogen chloride.

$$2P_2O_5 + 3HCl \longrightarrow POCl_3 + 3HPO_3$$

$$CaO + 2HCl \longrightarrow CaCl_2 + H_2O$$ **(2)**

(iii) Temperature is maintained **at nearly 200°C.** **(1)**

Q.2 The diagram shows an apparatus for the laboratory preparation of hydrogen chloride.

(i) Identify *A* and *B*.

(ii) Write the equation for the reaction.

(iii) How would you check, whether or not the gas jar is filled with hydrogen chloride?

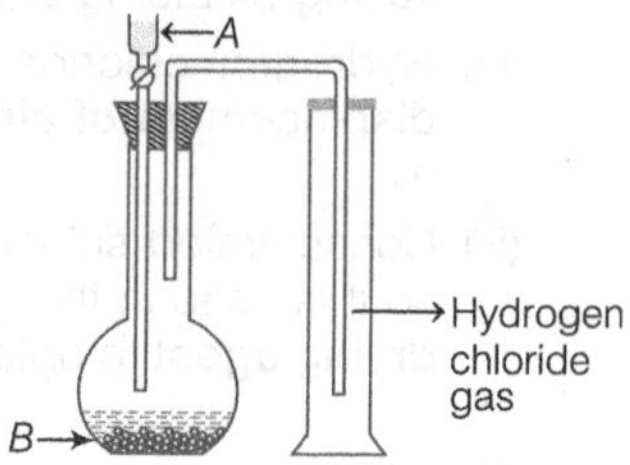

(iv) What does the method of collection tell you about the density of hydrogen chloride?

Ans. (i) *A* is **concentrated sulphuric acid**. *B* is **sodium chloride**. **(1)**

(ii) $\underset{\text{Sodium chloride}}{NaCl} + \underset{\text{Conc. sulphuric acid}}{H_2SO_4} \xrightarrow{< 200°C} \underset{\text{Sodium hydrogen sulphate}}{NaHSO_4} + \underset{\text{Hydrogen chloride gas}}{HCl\uparrow}$ **(1)**

(iii) A glass rod dipped in NH_4OH solution if brought near the mouth of the gas jar, it evolves **dense white fumes.** It shows that the jar is full of HCl gas. **(1)**

(iv) Since, the gas is collected by the **upward displacement** of air, it means it is **heavier than air**. **(1)**

Q.3 Write balanced chemical equation for the following:

(i) Action of dilute hydrochloric acid on magnesium sulphite. **(ICSE 2018)**

(ii) Action of hydrochloric acid on sodium bicarbonate. **(ICSE 2016)**

(iii) Action of dilute hydrochloric acid on sodium sulphide. **(ICSE 2014)**

(iv) Action of dilute hydrochloric acid on ammonium carbonate. **(ICSE 2025)**

Ans. (i) $\underset{\text{Magnesium sulphite}}{MgSO_3} + \underset{\text{(Dil.)}}{2HCl} \longrightarrow \underset{\text{Magnesium chloride}}{MgCl_2} + H_2O + SO_2\uparrow$

(ii) $\underset{\text{Sodium bicarbonate}}{NaHCO_3} + \underset{\text{(Dil.)}}{HCl} \longrightarrow \underset{\text{Sodium chloride}}{NaCl} + H_2O + CO_2\uparrow$

(iii) $Na_2S + 2HCl \longrightarrow 2NaCl + H_2S\uparrow$

(iv) $(NH_4)_2CO_3 + \underset{\text{(Dil.)}}{2HCl} \longrightarrow 2NH_4Cl + H_2O + CO_2\uparrow$

(1 × 4 = 4)

Q.4 State one relevant observation for the following statements.

(i) Lead nitrate solution is mixed with dilute hydrochloric acid and heated. **(ICSE 2018)**

(ii) Action of dilute hydrochloric acid on iron (II) sulphide. **(ICSE 2017)**

(iii) When dilute hydrochloric acid is added to copper carbonate. **(ICSE 2016)**

(iv) Glass rod dipped in ammonia is brought near the mouth of the concentrated hydrochloric acid bottle.

Ans. (i) Lead nitrate reacts with dilute hydrochloric acid to give **white precipitate of lead chloride**.

$Pb(NO_3)_2 + 2HCl\ (\text{dil.}) \xrightarrow{\Delta} PbCl_2\downarrow + 2HNO_3$ **(1)**

(ii) Hydrochloric acid decomposes salts of weaker acids (like carbonates, bicarbonates, sulphates, sulphides) into metal chloride.

$FeS + 2HCl \longrightarrow FeCl_2 + H_2S\uparrow$ **(1)**

Rotten egg smelling, H_2S gas is evolved during this reaction.

(iii) Copper carbonate reacts with dilute hydrochloric acid to produce the copper chloride salt, water and carbon dioxide.

$\underset{\text{Copper carbonate}}{CuCO_3} + 2HCl \longrightarrow \underset{\text{Copper chloride}}{CuCl_2} + H_2O + CO_2\uparrow$ **(1)**

(iv) **Dense white fumes** of ammonium chloride (NH_4Cl) are formed. **(1)**

$NH_3 + HCl \longrightarrow NH_4Cl$

Q.5 Refer to the flowchart diagram given and give balanced equations (with conditions, if any) for the given conversions *A* to *E*.

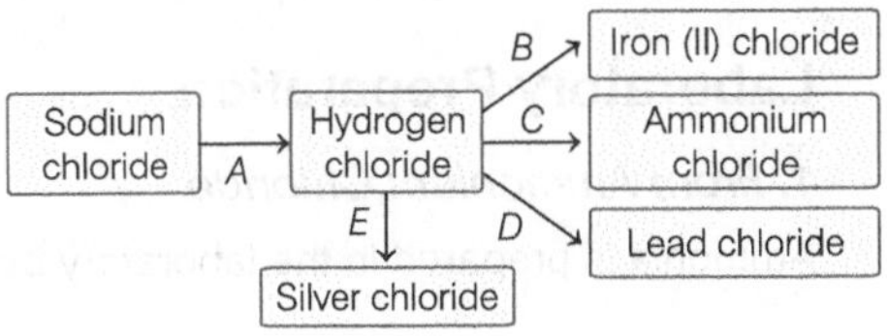

Ans. (*A*) $NaCl + H_2SO_4 \xrightarrow{< 200°C} NaHSO_4 + HCl\uparrow$

(*B*) $Fe + 2HCl \longrightarrow FeCl_2 + H_2\uparrow$

(*C*) $NH_3 + HCl \longrightarrow NH_4Cl$

(*D*) $PbO_2 + \underset{\text{(Conc.)}}{4HCl} \longrightarrow PbCl_2 + 2H_2O + Cl_2\uparrow$

(*E*) $AgNO_3 + HCl \longrightarrow AgCl\downarrow + HNO_3$ **(1 × 5 = 5)**

TYPE - 9

03 Marks

Case-Based Question

Q.1 A student is preparing hydrogen chloride gas in the laboratory by reacting sodium chloride (NaCl) with concentrated sulphuric acid (H_2SO_4). The reaction proceeds smoothly, producing hydrogen chloride gas. However, the student is also considering using concentrated nitric acid (HNO_3) for the same purpose. But it was seen that it is less efficient and it makes H_2SO_4 a preferred choice for the preparation of hydrogen chloride gas.

(i) Why conc. HNO_3 is not used for the preparation of HCl?

(ii) What is the chemical equation when NaCl reacts with sulphuric acid?

(iii) Why only NaCl is preferred for the preparation of HCl over other metal chlorides?

Ans. (i) Conc. HNO_3, is **volatile** and it may volatilize out alongwith hydrogen chloride, therefore, it cannot be used for the preparation of HCl. **(1)**

(ii) The chemical reaction when NaCl reacts with sulphuric acid is

$NaCl + H_2SO_4 \xrightarrow{< 200°C} NaHSO_4 + HCl\uparrow$ **(1)**

(iii) Sodium chloride is **cheap** and therefore, it is preferred for the preparation of HCl over other metal chlorides. **(1)**

Compound II : Ammonia

Molecular formula : NH_3

Molecular mass : 17 u

Bond : Polar covalent

Structure :

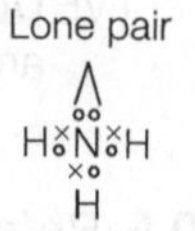

Lewis diagram or dot structure

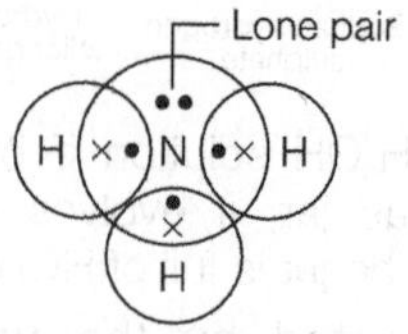

Lewis diagram

Laboratory Preparation

1. From Ammonium Chloride

Ammonia is prepared in the laboratory by heating a mixture of **ammonium salt (NH_4Cl)** with an **alkali [$Ca(OH)_2$]**.

$$2NH_4Cl + Ca(OH)_2 \xrightarrow{\Delta} CaCl_2 + 2H_2O + 2NH_3\uparrow$$

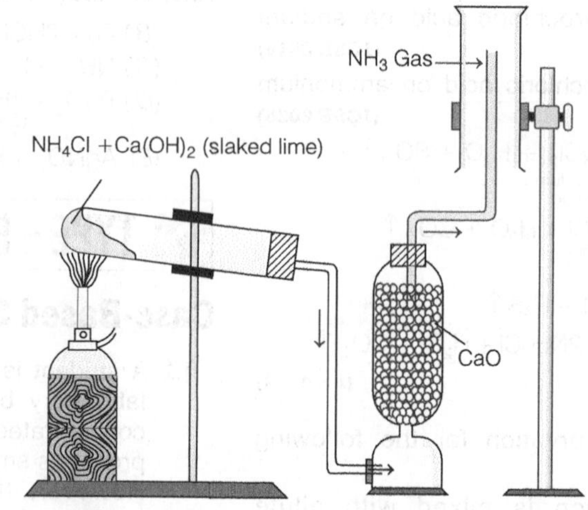

Laboratory preparation of ammonia from ammonium chloride

- **Procedure** The reactants, i.e. ammonium chloride and calcium hydroxide are grinded together and heated slowly in a test tube with its neck sloping downward.
- **Observation** The ammonia gas obtained in test tube passes through a delivery tube into a drying tower and is collected in an inverted gas jar.
- **Drying agent** Quicklime (CaO) in a drying tower.
- **Collection** Ammonia gas is collected by the **downward displacement of air**. It is lighter than air. It is highly soluble in water, hence not collected over water.

2. Preparation of Ammonia from Metal Nitrides

Ammonia can also be prepared by the action of warm water on magnesium or aluminium nitride.

$$Mg_3N_2 + 6H_2O \longrightarrow 3Mg(OH)_2 + 2NH_3\uparrow$$
$$AlN + 3H_2O \longrightarrow Al(OH)_3 + NH_3\uparrow$$

Note Ammonia gas cannot be dried by passing it through concentrated sulphuric acid because ammonia, being a basic gas, reacts with acid to form ammonium sulphate, i.e.

$$2NH_3 + H_2SO_4 \longrightarrow (NH_4)_2SO_4$$

3. Manufacture of Ammonia (Haber's Process)

Ammonia is manufactured by Haber's process which involves direct combination of nitrogen and hydrogen in the ratio of 1:3 by volume.

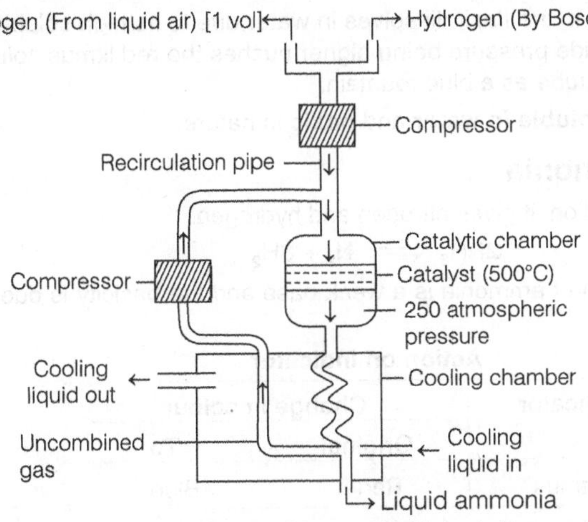

Manufacture of Ammonia (Haber's Process)

Nitrogen reacts with hydrogen under specific conditions liberating ammonia

$$\underset{[1\text{ vol}]}{N_2} + \underset{[3\text{ vol}]}{3H_2} \underset{\substack{\text{above 200 atm} \\ \text{(Fe and Mo)}}}{\overset{450°\text{C-}500°\text{C}}{\rightleftharpoons}} \underset{[2\text{ vol}]}{2NH_3} + \text{Heat}$$

- **Conditions** Reaction is reversible and exothermic, therefore low temperature and high pressure favours the forward reaction.

Temperature	:	Optimum temperature is 450-500°C.
Pressure	:	Above 200 atm.
Catalyst	:	Finely divided iron.
Promoter	:	Traces of molybdenum or Al_2O_3.

- **Recovery of ammonia** The ammonia is separated and recovered from the unreacted nitrogen and hydrogen by **liquefaction** or by **absorbing in water.**

Physical Properties of Ammonia

- It has strong and pungent **choking smell**. It is colourless and non-poisonous gas.
- It is **alkaline** in nature and is **easily liquefied by compressing.**
- It is **highly soluble in water** and has vapour density of 8.5 thus **lighter than air.**

Basicity and Solubility of Ammonia (Fountain Experiment)

- **Aim** To demonstrate the basicity of NH_3 gas and its high solubility in water.

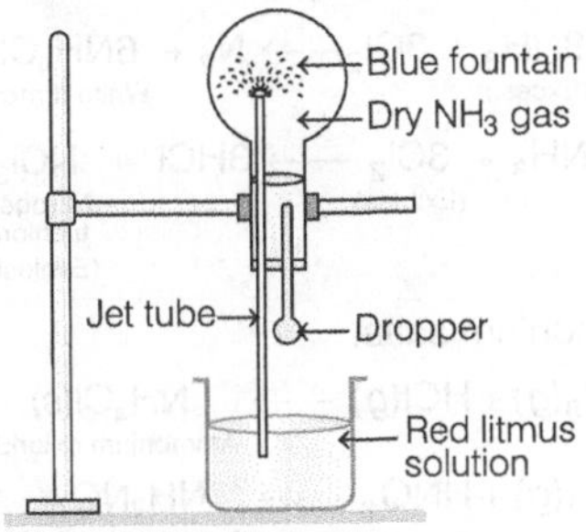

Fountain experiment

- **Apparatus** Dry round bottom flask filled with ammonia gas. Mouth of the flask has a rubber stopper with two holes for, (a) jet tube (b) dropper containing water. Red litmus solution is placed in the trough below.
- **Procedure** The dropper containing water is squeezed and the water enters into the flask.
- **Observation** Ammonia gas present in the flask dissolves in water due to its high solubility, thereby creating a partial vacuum in the flask. The outside pressure being higher pushes the red litmus solution up the jet tube, which emerges out at the end of the tube as a blue fountain.
- **Inference** Ammonia gas is **highly soluble in water** and **basic** in nature.

Chemical Properties of Ammonia

1. **Thermal dissociation** On dissociation, it gives nitrogen and hydrogen.

$$2NH_3 \rightleftharpoons N_2 + 3H_2$$

2. **Basic properties** Aqueous solution of ammonia is a weak base and the basicity is due to a lone pair of electrons on its nitrogen atom.

Action on Indicator

Indicator	Change in colour	
	Original	To
Moist litmus	Red	Blue
Methyl orange	Orange	Yellow
Phenolphthalein	Colourless	Pink

3. **Burning of ammonia in oxygen** Ammonia is not a supporter of combustion. It extinguishes a burning splint and does not burn in air. It burns in oxygen with **greenish yellow flame**.

$$4NH_3 + 3O_2 \longrightarrow 2N_2 + 6H_2O$$

4. **Catalytic oxidation of ammonia** Ammonia reacts with oxygen in the presence of platinum at 800°C to give nitric oxide and water vapour.

$$4NH_3 + 5O_2 \xrightarrow{\text{Pt, 800°C}} 6H_2O + \underset{\text{Colourless}}{4NO} \uparrow + \text{Heat}$$

$$\underset{\text{(Colourless)}}{2NO} + O_2 \longrightarrow \underset{\text{(Reddish brown gas)}}{2NO_2}$$

Note The platinum continues to glow even after the heating is discontinued.

5. **Ammonia as a reducing agent**

(i) **Reduction of metallic oxides** Ammonia reduces heated metallic oxides to give metals, water vapour and nitrogen.

e.g. Reaction of ammonia with hot copper (II) oxide.

$$2NH_3 + \underset{\text{Black solid}}{3CuO} \longrightarrow \underset{\text{Reddish brown solid}}{3Cu} + 3H_2O + \underset{\text{Gas}}{N_2}\uparrow$$

The black copper oxide is reduced to reddish brown copper.

(ii) **Reduction of chlorine to hydrogen chloride** Chlorine reacts with ammonia to give HCl, which further combines with excess of ammonia and forms NH_4Cl.

- When ammonia is in excess, $\underset{\text{(Excess)}}{8NH_3} + 3Cl_2 \longrightarrow N_2 + \underset{\text{White fumes}}{6NH_4Cl}$
- When chlorine is in excess, $NH_3 + \underset{\text{(Excess)}}{3Cl_2} \longrightarrow 3HCl + \underset{\text{Nitrogen trichloride (Explosive)}}{NCl_3}$

6. **Reaction with acids**

Ammonia reacts with acids to form ammonium salts.

$$NH_3(g) + HCl(g) \longrightarrow \underset{\text{Ammonium chloride}}{NH_4Cl(s)}$$

$$NH_3(g) + HNO_3 \longrightarrow \underset{\text{Ammonium nitrate}}{NH_4NO_3}$$

$$2NH_3(g) + H_2SO_4 \longrightarrow \underset{\text{Ammonium sulphate}}{(NH_4)_2SO_4}$$

Aqueous solution of ammonia

An aqueous solution of **ammonia (NH_4OH)** is a **weak base**. It dissociates partially to give hydroxyl ions. The alkaline behaviour of NH_4OH is due to the hydroxyl ions.

$$NH_3 + H_2O \longrightarrow NH_4OH$$

It undergoes following reactions:

(i) **Reaction with acids** (Sulphuric acid, nitric acid and hydrochloric acid)

(aq) Ammonia +	Acid	$\longrightarrow$	Ammonia salt +	Water
NH_4OH +	HCl	$\longrightarrow$	NH_4Cl +	H_2O
NH_4OH +	HNO_3	$\longrightarrow$	NH_4NO_3 +	H_2O
$2NH_4OH$ +	H_2SO_4	$\longrightarrow$	$(NH_4)_2SO_4$ +	$2H_2O$

(ii) **Reaction with metal salts** Ammonium hydroxide (NH_4OH) reacts with soluble salts of metals to give insoluble precipitates of their respective metallic hydroxide **(except Na and K)**.

Metallic salt solution	Ammonium hydroxide	Ammonium salt	Metallic hydroxide [ppt.]	Colour of precipitate	Solubility in excess of NH_4OH
$FeSO_4$ +	$2NH_4OH \longrightarrow$	$(NH_4)_2SO_4$ +	$Fe(OH)_2 \downarrow$	Dirty green	Insoluble
$FeCl_3$ +	$3NH_4OH \longrightarrow$	$3NH_4Cl$ +	$Fe(OH)_3 \downarrow$	Reddish brown	Insoluble
$Pb(NO_3)_2$ +	$2NH_4OH \longrightarrow$	$2NH_4NO_3$ +	$Pb(OH)_2 \downarrow$	White	Insoluble
$Zn(NO_3)_2$ +	$2NH_4OH \longrightarrow$	$2NH_4NO_3$ +	$Zn(OH)_2 \downarrow$	White gelatinous	Soluble
$CuSO_4$ +	$2NH_4OH \longrightarrow$	$(NH_4)_2SO_4$ +	$Cu(OH)_2 \downarrow$	Pale blue	Soluble

Uses of Ammonia

(i) **Nitrogenous fertilizers** Ammonium sulphate $(NH_4)_2SO_4$, ammonium nitrate (NH_4NO_3), and urea (NH_2CONH_2).

(ii) **Explosives** Ammonium nitrate (NH_4NO_3) decomposes explosively, leaving no residue behind.

$$NH_4NO_3 \xrightarrow{\Delta} \underset{\text{Nitrous oxide}}{N_2O(g)} + 2H_2O\ (vap.)$$

(iii) Other ammonium salts such as ammonium carbonate, ammonium chloride are used in dry cell and in the preparation of nitrogen gas.

$$\underset{\text{Sodium nitrite}}{NaNO_2} + NH_4Cl(aq) \longrightarrow NaCl(aq) + NH_4NO_2$$

$$\underset{\text{Ammonium nitrite}}{NH_4NO_2\ (aq)} \xrightarrow{\Delta} N_2(g) + 2H_2O(g)$$

(iv) **Liquid ammonia** is used as a **refrigerant** in ice plants. Ammonia is a good refrigerant because anhydrous ammonia is a clear, colourless liquid under pressure. It evaporates rapidly and produce cooling effect. Main refrigerants used are freons, chlorofluorocarbons (CFCs). They cause ozone depletion and also contribute to global warming.

$$CF_2Cl_2(g) \xrightarrow[\text{(Ultraviolet)}]{\text{Decompose}} CF_2Cl^\bullet(g) + Cl^\bullet(g)$$

$$Cl^\bullet(g) + \underset{\text{Ozone gas}}{O_3(g)} \longrightarrow ClO(g) + O_2(g)$$

This free radical [$Cl^\bullet$] destroys ozone and the process continues, thereby giving rise to ozone depletion.

(v) Liquid ammonia can be used as **cleansing agent** for removing oil (as it is a good emulsifier).

(vi) Ammonia is used in the **manufacturing of nitric acid** through Ostwald's process.

EXAM ORIENTED QUESTIONS

TYPE - 1

01 Mark

Multiple Choice Questions

Q.1 Nitrogen gas can be obtained by heating

(a) ammonium nitrate (b) ammonium nitrite
(c) magnesium nitride (d) ammonium chloride

Ans. (b) Ammonium nitrite

Q.2 Ammonia can be obtained by adding water to

(a) ammonium chloride (b) ammonium nitride
(c) magnesium nitride (d) magnesium nitrate

Ans. (c) Magnesium nitride.

Q.3 Prateek added warm water to magnesium nitride, and a colourless gas evolved, which when tested with phenolphthalein, turned it pink. The gas evolved is **(Competency Based Que.)**

(a) carbon dioxide (b) ammonia
(c) nitrogen (d) hydrogen chloride

Ans. (b) Ammonia

Q.4 Ammonia gas is collected by downward displacement of air since ammonia is **(ICSE 2024)**

(a) very slightly soluble in water
(b) heavier than air
(c) lighter than air
(d) insoluble in water

Ans. (c) lighter than air

Q.5 The drying agent used to dry NH_3 gas is

(a) P_2O_5 (b) conc. H_2SO_4
(c) $CaCl_2$ (d) CaO

Ans. (d) CaO

Q.6 The catalyst used in the Haber's process is **(ICSE Specimen 2023)**

(a) molybdenum (b) platinum
(c) nickel (d) finely divided iron

Ans. (d) **Finely divided iron** is used as a catalyst in Haber's process.

Q.7 The temperature which is suitable for catalytic oxidation of ammonia is

(a) 800°C (b) 900°C
(c) 1200°C (d) 600°C

Ans. (a) 800°C

Q.8 In the Haber process, nitrogen and hydrogen react to form ammonia.

$$N_2(g) + 3H_2(g) \rightleftharpoons 2NH_3(g) \quad \Delta H = -92 \text{ kJ}$$

Which factor increases both the speed of reaction and the amount of ammonia produced?

(a) Addition of a catalyst
(b) Decreasing the temperature
(c) Increasing the pressure
(d) Increasing the temperature

Ans. (c) By increasing pressure, intermolecular collision increases, therefore, speed of reaction increases. Increase in pressure shifts equilibrium to right side, increasing the amount of product.

Q.9 Ammonia can be produced industrially from nitrogen and hydrogen.

$$N_2(g) + 3H_2(g) \rightleftharpoons 2NH_3(g)$$

The forward reaction is exothermic.
Which change would not alter the yield of ammonia?

(a) Adding a catalyst
(b) Decreasing the pressure
(c) Decreasing the temperature
(d) Removing some ammonia during the reaction

Ans. (a) Catalyst increases the rate of both forward and backward reaction simultaneously, therefore percentage yield is not affected by the catalyst.

Q.10 On passing ammonia gas over heated copper oxide for some time, a reddish-brown residue is left behind. What property is demonstrated here? **(ICSE 2024)**

(a) Basic property (b) Oxidising property
(c) Reducing property (d) Acidic property

Ans. (c) Reducing property

$$2NH_3 + \underset{\text{Black solid}}{3CuO} \longrightarrow \underset{\text{Reddish brown solid}}{3Cu\downarrow} + 3H_2O + \underset{\text{Gas}}{N_2\uparrow}$$

Q.11 Which among the following is Nessler's reagent?

(a) $KHgI_4$ (b) K_2HgI_4 (c) K_2HgI_2 (d) $KHgI_2$

Ans. (b) K_2HgI_4

Q.12 The chemical which is used in preparing explosives is

(a) sodium carbonate
(b) ammonium nitrate
(c) sodium hydrogen carbonate
(d) ammonia

Ans. (b) Ammonium nitrate

TYPE - 2 01 Mark

Assertion-Reason Questions

Directions (Q. Nos. 1-2) In the following questions, a statement of Assertion (A) is followed by a statement of Reason (R). Choose the answer based on the codes given below.

(a) Both (A) and (R) are true and (R) is the correct explanation of (A).
(b) Both (A) and (R) are true but (R) is not the correct explanation of (A).
(c) (A) is true but (R) is false.
(d) (A) is false but (R) is true.

Q.1 Assertion (A) Haber's process is used to manufacture hydrochloric acid.

Reason (R) The catalyst used in this process is finely divided iron.

Ans. (d) Haber's process is used to manufacture **ammonia** not hydrochloric acid. And the catalyst used in Haber's process is finely divided iron.

Thus, (A) is false but (R) is true.

Q.2 Assertion (A) In the preparation of ammonia, hydrogen is obtained by Bosch process.

Reason (R) Hydrogen and nitrogen are used in the ratio 3:1 by volume.

Ans. (b) In the preparation of ammonia, the hydrogen gas is obtained from water gas (Bosch process) and the hydrogen and nitrogen are taken in 3:1 by volume.

Thus, both (A) and (R) are true but (R) is not the correct explanation of (A).

TYPE - 3 01 Mark

Fill in the Blanks

Q.1 Ammonia gas is collected by .... (a downward displacement of water /a downward displacement of air). **(ICSE 2014)**

Ans. a downward displacement of air

Q.2 Ammonia can be obtained by adding water to .... (iron oxide/magnesium nitride)

Ans. magnesium nitride

Q.3 Ammonia is soluble in water because it is an...... molecule. (acidic/alkaline)

Ans. alkaline

Q.4 Dry ammonia ....the colour of moist red litmus paper. (change/disappear)

Ans. change

Q.5 Ammonia can convert heated copper oxide to copper. This shows that ammonia is a ....(reducing agent/oxidising agent). **(Competency Based Que.)**

Ans. reducing agent

Q.6 Ammonia reacts with excess chlorine to form .... (nitrogen trichloride/ammonium chloride

Ans. nitrogen trichloride

TYPE - 4 01 Mark

Correct the Incorrect Statement

Q.1 The promoter used in Haber's process is traces of molybdenum or Fe_2O_3.

Ans. The promoter used in Haber's process is traces of molybdenum or $\mathbf{Al_2O_3}$.

Q.2 The ammonia have strong, suffocating smell.

Ans. The ammonia have strong, **pungent choking** smell.

Q.3 Ammonia is acidic in nature.

Ans. Ammonia is **alkaline** in nature.

TYPE - 5 01 Mark

Identify the Following

Q.1 Name the process by which ammonia is manufactured on a large scale. **(ICSE 2023)**

Ans. Haber's process

Q.2 Which gas is used as a reducing agent in reducing copper oxide to copper? **(ICSE 2015)**

Ans. Ammonia

Q.3 Name the gas evolved when ammonia reacts with heated copper oxide. **(ICSE 2019)**

Ans. Nitrogen (N_2) gas

When ammonia reacts with heated copper oxide (CuO), it gives copper (Cu), $N_2(g)$ and H_2O vapour.

$$2NH_3 + 3CuO \xrightarrow{\Delta} N_2\uparrow + 3Cu + 3H_2O$$

Q.4 A compound formed when excess ammonia gas reacts with chlorine. **(ICSE 2021-22, Sem-II)**

Ans. NH_4Cl (ammonium chloride)

Q.5 Name a nitrogen containing product formed when ammonium nitrate is heated.

Ans. Nitrous oxide (N_2O) gas

TYPE - 6 — 02 Marks

Short Answer Type I Questions

Q.1 Certain blank spaces are left in the following table and these are labelled as *C*, *D* and *E*. Identify each of them. **(ICSE 2017)**

Lab preparation	Reactants used	Products formed	Drying agent	Method of collection
NH_3 gas	*C*	$Mg(OH)_2 + NH_3$	*D*	*E*

Ans. *C* – $\underset{\text{Magnesium nitride}}{Mg_3N_2} + \underset{\text{Water}}{H_2O}$, *D* – $\underset{\text{Quicklime}}{CaO}$ **(1)**

E – Downward displacement of air. **(1)**

Q.2 Give reason for the following statements.

(i) Concentrated sulphuric acid is not used for drying ammonia gas.

(ii) Ammonia gas is not collected over water. **(ICSE 2018)**

Ans. (i) Ammonia gas cannot be dried by passing it through concentrated sulphuric acid because ammonia being a **basic gas** reacts with conc. H_2SO_4 to form ammonium sulphate.

$$2NH_3 + H_2SO_4 \longrightarrow (NH_4)_2SO_4$$ **(1)**

(ii) Ammonia gas is not collected over water, because it is **highly soluble in water.** **(1)**

Q.3 Write the equations for the following reactions, which result in the formation of ammonia.

(i) A mixture of ammonium chloride and slaked lime is heated.

(ii) Aluminium nitride and water.

Ans. (i) $2NH_4Cl + Ca(OH)_2 \xrightarrow{\Delta} CaCl_2 + 2H_2O + 2NH_3 \uparrow$ **(1)**

(ii) $AlN + 3H_2O \longrightarrow Al(OH)_3 + NH_3 \uparrow$ **(1)**

Q.4 Name the gas evolved, when the following mixtures are heated.

(i) Calcium hydroxide and ammonium sulphate.

(ii) Sodium nitrite and ammonium chloride. **(ICSE 2016)**

Ans. (i) When mixture of calcium hydroxide and ammonium sulphate are heated, **ammonia (NH_3) gas** is evolved.

The following reaction takes place:

$$Ca(OH)_2 + (NH_4)_2SO_4 \xrightarrow{\Delta} CaSO_4 + 2NH_3 \uparrow + 2H_2O$$ **(1)**

(ii) When mixture of sodium nitrite and ammonium chloride are heated, **nitrogen (N_2) gas** is evolved.

The following reaction takes place:

$$NaNO_2 + NH_4Cl \longrightarrow NaCl + N_2 \uparrow + 2H_2O$$ **(1)**

Q.5 Ammonia gas is passed into water as shown below.

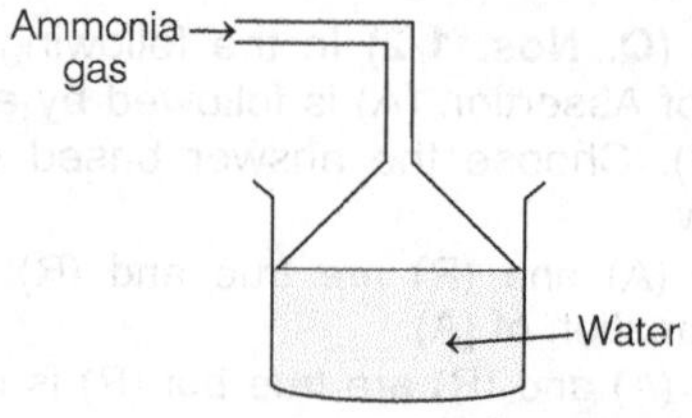

(Competency Based Que.)

(i) When a red litmus paper was dropped into the resulting solution, it turned blue. Which ions in the solution would have resulted for the colour change in the litmus paper?

(ii) Why is the funnel kept in an inverted position?

Ans. (i) OH^- ions/hydroxyl ions **(1)**

(ii) To **prevent back suction of water** or to increase area of absorption, the funnel is kept in an inverted position. **(1)**

Q.6 Copy and complete the following table relating to important industrial processes output refers to the product of the process not the intermediate steps. **(ICSE 2024)**

Name of process	Inputs	Catalyst	Equation for catalysed reaction	Output
Haber's process	Hydrogen + Nitrogen			Ammonia

Ans.

Name of process	Inputs	Catalyst	Equation for catalysed reaction	Output
Haber's process	Hydrogen + Nitrogen	Finely divided iron	$N_2 + 3H_2 \longrightarrow 2NH_3$	Ammonia

(2)

Q.7 (i) Write the equation for the reaction in the Haber's process that forms ammonia.

(ii) State the purpose of liquefying the ammonia produced in the process.

Ans. (i) $N_2 + 3H_2 \underset{\text{Above 200 atm, Fe and Mo}}{\overset{450°C - 500°C}{\rightleftharpoons}} 2NH_3 + \text{Heat}$ **(1)**

(ii) Ammonia is separated from the unreacted nitrogen and hydrogen by **liquefaction**, as ammonia, compared to N_2 and H_2 is **easily liquefiable.** **(1)**

Q.8 In the Haber's process, the optimum yield of ammonia is obtained when a temperature of 450°C – 500°C, a pressure of 200 atmospheres, an iron catalyst and promoter molybdenum are used.

$$N_2 + 3H_2 \rightleftharpoons 2NH_3 + \text{heat}$$

How and why would the yield of ammonia be affected if the temperature was raised to 600°C?

Ans. Since, the forward reaction is exothermic then increasing the temperature will favour the reaction to proceed in backward direction and thereby **decreasing the yield of ammonia.** **(2)**

Q.9 Name the other ion formed when ammonia dissolves in water. Give one test that can be used to detect the presence of the ion produced. **(ICSE 2014)**

Ans. **Hydroxyl ion** $[OH^-]$ is formed other than ammonium ion. **(1)**

Test for detection of hydroxyl ion

Red litmus turns blue or phenolphthalein indicator turns pink in this solution.

Phenolphthalein is a colourless, weak acid that is used as an indicator in titration experiments. It changes colour depending on whether it contacts an acid or base, colourless ⟶ Acid; Pink ⟶ Base **(1)**

Q.10 Ammonia gas is passed over heated copper (II) oxide in a combustion tube: **(ICSE 2025)**

(i) Name the gas evolved.

(ii) What will the colour of the residue that is left in the combustion tube at the end of the reaction?

Ans. (i) $\underset{\text{}}{2NH_3} + \underset{\text{Black solid}}{3CuO} \longrightarrow \underset{\text{Reddish brown solid}}{3Cu} + 3H_2O + \underset{\text{Gas}}{N_2\uparrow}$

Nitrogen gas and **water vapour** are evolved. **(1)**

(ii) **Reddish-brown residue of copper** is left in the combustion tube at the end of the reaction. **(1)**

Q.11 (i) Ranjana wants to prove that ammonia is a reducing agent. To demonstrate this, she passes ammonia gas over heated copper oxide. What will she observe?

(ii) Write a balanced chemical equation for the above reaction. **(ICSE specimen 2025, Specimen 2024)**

Ans. (i) When ammonia is passed over heated copper oxide, the black colour copper oxide will change to reddish brown copper. It shows that ammonia is a reducing agent as it reduces cupric oxide to copper metal. **(1)**

(ii) The reaction is as follows

$$\underset{\text{Black solid}}{3CuO} + 2NH_3 \longrightarrow \underset{\text{Reddish brown solid}}{3Cu} + N_2\uparrow + 3H_2O$$ **(1)**

TYPE - 7

03 Marks

Short Answer Type II Questions

Q.1 Complete the table given below which refers to the laboratory preparation of ammonia gas.

Laboratory preparation	Reactants used	Products formed	Drying agent	Method of collection
Ammonia gas	(i) ______	Calcium chloride + water + ammonia	(ii) ______	(iii) ______

(ICSE 2022, Sem-II)

Ans. (i) **Reactants used** A mixture of ammonium chloride (NH_4Cl) and calcium hydroxide $[Ca(OH)_2]$ **(1)**

(ii) **Drying agent** Quicklime (CaO)

NH_3 is basic in nature, so quicklime (CaO) is used as a drying agent. Sulphuric acid or phosphorus pentoxide cannot be used for drying ammonia as these are acidic in nature and form salts with NH_3. **(1)**

(iii) **Method of collection** Ammonia gas is collected by the downward displacement of air. It is lighter than air. It is highly soluble in water, hence not collected over water. **(1)**

Q.2 The following question are pertaining to the laboratory preparation of ammonia gas from magnesium nitride. **(ICSE 2023)**

(i) Write a balanced chemical equation for preparation.

(ii) Why is this method seldom used?

(iii) How do you identify the gas formed?

Ans. (i) $Mg_3N_2 + 6H_2O \longrightarrow 3Mg(OH)_2 + 2NH_3\uparrow$ **(1)**

(ii) This method is **costly**. **(1)**

(iii) Ammonia (NH_3) gas is basic in nature. So, we can identify this gas by **litmus test**. Basic solution turns red litmus into blue. **(1)**

Q.3 Study the flowchart given and give balanced equations to represent the reactions *A*, *B* and *C*.

$$\boxed{Mg_3N_2} \xrightarrow{A} \boxed{NH_3} \underset{C}{\overset{B}{\rightleftharpoons}} \boxed{NH_4Cl}$$ **(ICSE 2019)**

Ans. $Mg_3N_2 \xrightarrow{(A)} NH_3 \underset{(C)}{\overset{(B)}{\rightleftharpoons}} NH_4Cl$

In above reaction,

(*A*) is H_2O.

$\because \quad Mg_3N_2 + \underset{(A)}{6H_2O} \xrightarrow[-3Mg(OH)_2]{} 2NH_3$ **(1)**

and (*B*) is HCl

$\because \quad NH_3 + \underset{(B)}{HCl} \longrightarrow NH_4Cl$ **(1)**

and (*C*) is $Ca(OH)_2$

$\because \; 2NH_4Cl + Ca(OH)_2 \xrightarrow{\Delta} CaCl_2 + 2H_2O + 2NH_3\uparrow$ **(1)**

Q.4 **Copy and complete the following table relating to important industrial process.**

Name of the process	Temperature	Catalyst	Equation for the catalysed reaction
Haber's process			

Ans.

Name of the process	Temperature	Catalyst	Equation for catalysed reaction
Haber's process	450°C-500°C	Finely divided iron, Mo as promoter	$N_2 + 3H_2 \rightleftharpoons 2NH_3$

(1 × 3 = 3)

Q.5

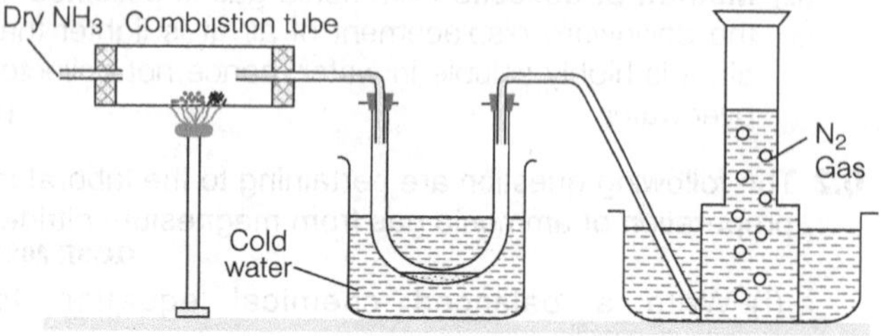

Study the above diagram and choose the correct option related to the content given below.

Compound *X* reacts with ammonia in the combustion tube, which leaves a residue *Y*. Identify *X* and *Y*, as well as the property *Z* of ammonia demonstrated in this particular reaction. **(Competency Based Que.)**

Ans. *X* = CuO, *Y* = copper, *Z* = Reducing property **(1 × 3 = 3)**

Q.6 **(i) Which feature of the ammonia molecules leads to the formation of the ammonium ion when ammonia dissolves in water?**

(ii) Name the other ion formed when ammonia dissolves in water.

(iii) Give one test that can be used to detect the presence of the ion produced in (ii).

Ans. (i) In ammonia molecule, there is one lone pair of electrons available on nitrogen atom. This lone pair of electron leads to the formation of ammonium ion.

(ii) Hydroxyl ion (OH^-)

(iii) It will give reddish brown precipitate with aqueous $FeCl_3$. **(1 × 3 = 3)**

TYPE - 8

04/05 Marks

Long Answer Type Questions

Q.1 **The following questions are based on the preparation of ammonia gas in the laboratory.**

(i) Explain why ammonium nitrate is not used in the preparation of ammonia?

(ii) Name the compound normally used as a drying agent during the process.

(iii) How is ammonia gas collected?

(iv) Explain why it is not collected over water?

Ans. (i) Because ammonium nitrate is a highly explosive substance and cannot be heated and it may itself decomposes to form nitrous oxide and water vapour.

(ii) Quicklime (CaO)

(iii) By downward displacement of air, as it is lighter than air.

(iv) Ammonia is highly soluble in water, so it cannot be collected over water. **(1 × 4 = 4)**

Q.2 **Write the balance chemical equations for the following**

(i) Reaction of ammonia with heated copper oxide. **(ICSE 2017)**

(ii) Laboratory preparation of ammonia from ammonium chloride. **(ICSE 2017)**

(iii) Action of warm water on AlN. **(ICSE 2016)**

(iv) Action of warm water on magnesium nitride. **(ICSE 2014)**

Ans. (i) When ammonia reacts with heated copper oxide (CuO), it gives copper (Cu), $N_2(g)$ and H_2O vapour.

$$2NH_3 + 3CuO \xrightarrow{\Delta} N_2\uparrow + 3Cu + 3H_2O$$

(ii) In laboratory, ammonia is prepared by reaction of ammonium chloride and calcium hydroxide.

$$\underset{\text{Ammonium chloride}}{2NH_4Cl} + \underset{\text{Calcium hydroxide}}{Ca(OH)_2} \longrightarrow \underset{\text{Calcium chloride}}{CaCl_2} + 2H_2O + \underset{\text{Ammonia gas}}{2NH_3\uparrow}$$

(iii) $$\underset{\text{Aluminium nitride}}{AlN} + \underset{\text{Water}}{3H_2O} \longrightarrow \underset{\text{Aluminium hydroxide}}{Al(OH)_3} + \underset{\text{Ammonia}}{NH_3\uparrow}$$

(iv) $Mg_3N_2 + 6H_2O \longrightarrow 3Mg(OH)_2 + 2NH_3\uparrow$ **(1 × 4 = 4)**

Q.3 **The diagram shows an experiment set up for the laboratory preparation of a pungent smelling gas. The gas is alkaline in nature.** **(ICSE Specimen 2023)**

(i) Name the gas collected in the gas jar.

(ii) Write a balanced chemical equation for the above preparation.

(iii) How is the gas being collected?

(iv) What is the purpose of using *Y*?

(v) How will you find that the jar is full of gas?

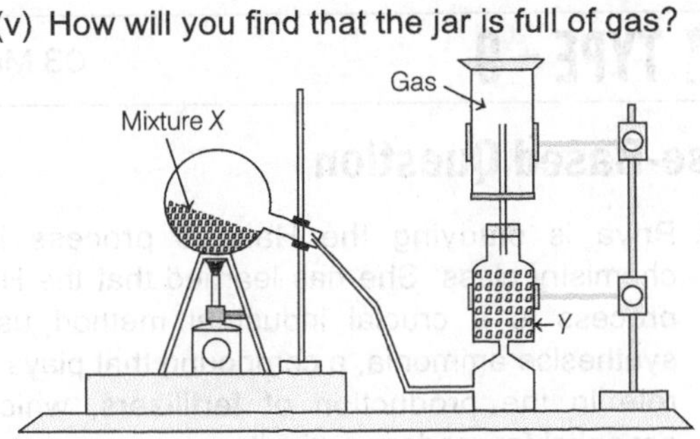

Ans. (i) The gas collected in the gas jar is **ammonia**.

(ii) The balanced chemical equation is

$$\underset{\text{Ammonium chloride}}{2NH_4Cl} + \underset{\text{Calcium hydroxide}}{Ca(OH)_2} \xrightarrow{\Delta} \underset{\text{Calcium chloride}}{CaCl_2} + \underset{\text{Water}}{2H_2O} + \underset{\text{Ammonia gas}}{2NH_3} \uparrow$$

(iii) The gas is collected by the **downward displacement of air**.

(iv) *Y* is **quicklime** (CaO). The ammonia gas containing water vapour is passed through a drier containing quicklime. The water vapour reacts chemically with quicklime and is removed, thereby drying the ammonia gas.

(v) When the jar is full of ammonia, small amounts of gas emerge from the jar and a strong smell of ammonia is detected. **(1 × 5 = 5)**

Q.4 A student was instructed by the teacher to prepare and collect ammonia gas in the laboratory by using aluminium nitride. The student had set up the apparatus as shown in the diagram below. Study the given diagram and answer the following questions:

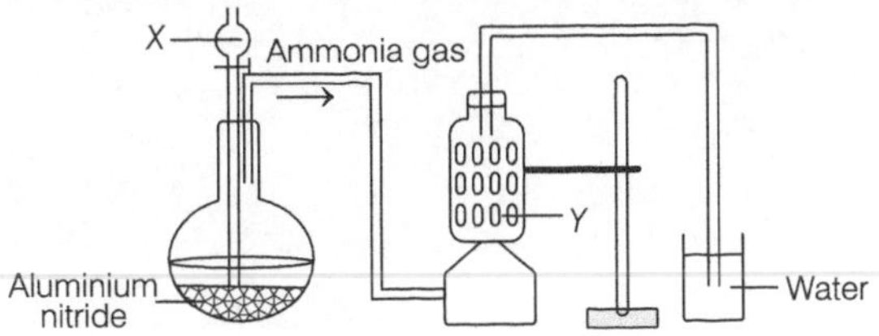

(i) Name the substance *X* added through the thistle funnel by the student.

(ii) Write a balanced equation for the reaction occurring between aluminium nitride and substance *X*.

(iii) Identify the substance *Y*.

(iv) State the function of *Y*.

(v) Why could the student not collect ammonia gas at the end of the experiment? **(ICSE 2025)**

Ans. (i) Substance *X* added through thistle funnel by the student is **water**.

(ii) $AlN + 3H_2O \longrightarrow Al(OH)_3 + NH_3\uparrow$

(iii) The substance *Y* is **quicklime (CaO)**

(iv) *Y*(CaO) acts as the **drying agent**.

(v) The student could not collect ammonia gas at the end of the experiment because it is **highly soluble** in **water** and cannot be collected. **(1 × 5 = 5)**

Q.5 The questions given below are related to the manufacturing of ammonia from hydrogen and nitrogen gas.

(i) Name the process.

(ii) In what ratio must the reactants be taken?

(iii) Name the catalyst used.

(iv) Give the equation for the manufacturing of ammonia.

(v) Ammonia can act as a reducing agent, write a relevant equation for such a reaction.

Ans. (i) Haber's process.

(ii) 1 part of nitrogen gas and 3 parts of hydrogen gas.

(iii) Finely divided iron.

(iv) $N_2 + 3H_2 \underset{\substack{\text{Above 200 atm} \\ \text{Fe as catalyst} \\ \text{Mo as promoter}}}{\overset{450°C-500°C}{\rightleftharpoons}} 2NH_3 + \text{Heat}$

(v) $\underset{\text{(Yellow)}}{3PbO} + 2NH_3 \xrightarrow{\Delta} \underset{\text{(Greyish)}}{3Pb} + N_2\uparrow + 3H_2O$ **(1 × 5 = 5)**

Q.6 From the list given below, select the word(s) required to correctly complete the blanks (i) to (v) in the following passage.

Note • Words choosen from the list are to be used only once. Write only the answers.

• Do not copy the passage.

[Reddish brown, ammonium, nitrogen dioxide, hydroxyl, dirty green , ammonia, acidic, alkaline]

Nitrogen and hydrogen combine in the presence of a catalyst to give (i) ....gas.

When the above mentioned gas is passed through water it forms a solution which will be (ii) ....in nature and the solution contains (iii) ....ions and (iv) .... ions.

The above solution when added to iron sulphate solution, gives a (v) .... coloured precipitate of iron hydroxide.

Ans. (i) ammonia (ii) alkaline (iii) ammonium (iv) hydroxyl (v) dirty green **(1 × 5 = 5)**

Q.7 State the observation for the following:

(i) (a) Dry ammonia gas reacts with oxygen in the presence of a catalyst.

(b) Excess chlorine gas reacts with ammonia gas. **(ICSE 2021-22, Sem-II)**

(c) To the copper nitrate solution initially few drops of sodium hydroxide solution is added and then added in excess. **(ICSE 2023)**

(ii) Name the gas produced during each of the following reaction.

(a) Burning of ammonia in excess of oxygen. **(ICSE 2025)**

(b) Dry ammonia gas is passed over heated PbO.

Ans. (i) (a) Dry ammonia gas reacts with oxygen in the presence of a catalyst to give nitric oxide and water vapour. The reaction involve is as follows:

$$\underset{\text{Ammonia}}{4NH_3} + \underset{\text{Oxygen}}{5O_2} \xrightarrow{\text{Pt, 800°C}} \underset{\text{Colourless}}{4NO} + \underset{\text{Water}}{6H_2O} + \text{Heat}$$ **(1)**

(b) When excess chlorine gas reacts with ammonia gas, hydrogen chloride and yellow coloured highly explosive liquid nitrogen trichloride are formed.

$$NH_3 + \underset{\text{(Excess)}}{3Cl_2} \longrightarrow NCl_3 + 3HCl$$ **(1)**

(c) When few drops of sodium hydroxide solution is added to the copper nitrate solution, copper hydroxide is formed which is light blue in colour and insoluble with excess NaOH. **(1)**

(ii) (a) Combustion of ammonia, produces nitrogen and water vapour.

$$4NH_3 + 3O_2 \longrightarrow 2N_2 + 6H_2O$$ **(1)**

(b) When dry ammonia gas is passed over heated PbO, it produces nitrogen gas and greyish metallic lead.

$$3PbO + 2NH_3 \longrightarrow 3Pb + N_2\uparrow + 3H_2O$$ **(1)**

TYPE - 9

03 Marks

Case-Based Question

Q.1 Priya is studying the Haber's process in her chemistry class. She has learned that the Haber's process is a crucial industrial method used to synthesise ammonia, a compound that plays a vital role in the production of fertilizers, which are essential for modern agriculture.

(i) What are the raw materials used in the Haber's process?

(ii) Why is the temperature maintained at around 450°C in the Haber's process?

(iii) What is the role of the iron catalyst in the Haber's process?

Ans. (i) The raw materials used are **nitrogen (N_2) and hydrogen (H_2) gases.** **(1)**

(ii) The temperature is maintained at around 450°C to **increase the rate of reaction** while maintaining a reasonable yield of ammonia. **(1)**

(iii) The iron catalyst **speeds up the reaction** without being consumed, allowing ammonia to be produced more efficiently. **(1)**

Compound III : Nitric Acid

Molecular formula : HNO_3

Molecular mass : 63 u

Structure :

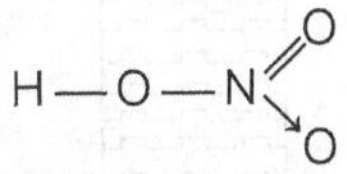

Laboratory Preparation of Nitric Acid

1. From Potassium Nitrate or Sodium Nitrate

Nitric acid is prepared by distilling a mixture of potassium or sodium nitrate with conc. sulphuric acid.

$$\underset{\text{(Nitre)}}{KNO_3} + \underset{\text{(conc.)}}{H_2SO_4} \xrightarrow{<200°C} \underset{\substack{\text{Potassium}\\\text{bisulphate}}}{KHSO_4} + HNO_3; \quad \underset{\text{(Chile saltpetre)}}{NaNO_3} + \underset{\text{(conc.)}}{H_2SO_4} \xrightarrow{<200°C} \underset{\substack{\text{Sodium}\\\text{bisulphate}}}{NaHSO_4} + HNO_3$$

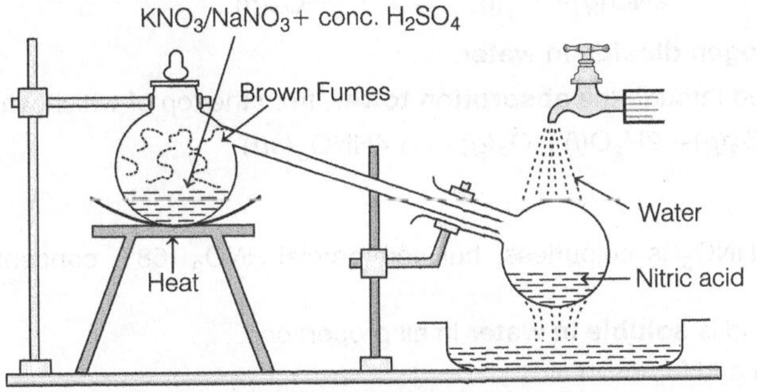

Laboratory preparation of nitric acid

The vapour of nitric acid are condensed to a **light yellow liquid.** The yellow colour is due to the presence of lower oxides of nitrogen, like NO_2. It turns colourless when it is diluted because NO_2 absorbs in water to give nitric acid. The yellow colour of the acid is removed by passing dry air or CO_2 in it.

Precautions to be followed while preparing HNO_3 in labs

- All glass apparatus should be used as HNO_3 vapours attack rubber and cork.
- Conc. HCl, should not be used in place of conc. H_2SO_4 as HCl is volatile and hence, HNO_3 vapours will carry HCl vapours.
- The temperature of the reaction should not exceed 200°C, as it may damage the glass apparatus and cause decomposition of HNO_3.

2. Manufacture of Nitric Acid by Ostwald Process

This process involves catalytic oxidation of ammonia to prepare nitric acid. The whole process is explained in three steps :

***Step* I : Catalytic oxidation of ammonia**

Mixture of dry air and dry ammonia in the ratio 1:10 by volume, is first compressed and then passed into the **catalytic chamber** containing platinum gauze as catalyst at about 800°C.

Oxidation of ammonia into nitrogen monoxide (nitric oxide) takes place.

$$4NH_3 + 5O_2 \xrightarrow[800°C]{Pt} 4NO + 6H_2O + Heat$$

Hot gases are passed through a heat exchanger, mixed with air and passed into another cooling chamber called **oxidising chamber**.

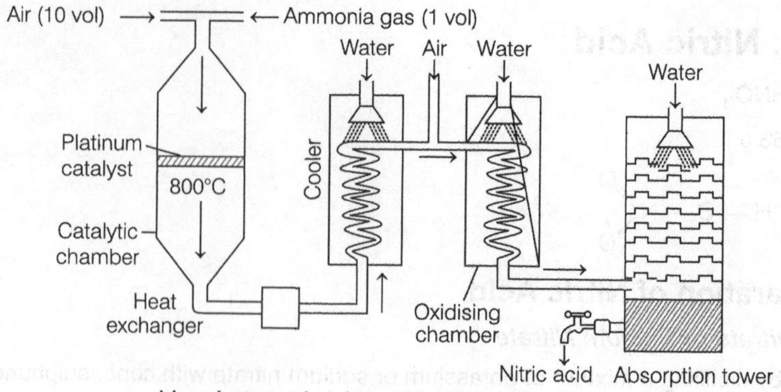

Manufacture of nitric acid by Ostwald process

***Step* II : Oxidation of nitric oxide in oxidation chamber.**

$$2NO(g) + O_2(g) \xrightarrow{50^\circ C} 2NO_2(g)$$

***Step* III : Absorption of nitrogen dioxide in water.**

The nitrogen dioxide is passed through the **absorption tower**, from the top of which warm water trickles.

$$4NO_2(g) + 2H_2O(l) + O_2(g) \longrightarrow 4HNO_3(aq)$$

Physical Properties

- Pure (98% concentrated) HNO_3 is colourless, but commercial HNO_3 (68% concentrated) is yellowish brown in colour.
- It has **suffocating smell** and is **soluble in water** in all proportions.
- It is **hygroscopic** in nature and fumes in air.
- It is **non-poisnous** and **acidic** in nature.

Note Pure nitric acid is colourless and unstable, and decomposes slightly even at ordinary temperature and in the presence of sunlight.

$$4HNO_3 \xrightarrow[\text{Sunlight}]{\Delta} \underset{\text{Brown colour}}{4NO_2} + 2H_2O + O_2$$

Oxidising Properties

Oxidising properties are due to **nascent oxygen** which it gives on decomposition.

$$2HNO_3(\text{conc.}) \longrightarrow 2NO_2 + H_2O + [O]$$

$$2HNO_3(\text{dil.}) \longrightarrow 2NO + H_2O + 3[O]$$

(i) **Action on non-metals**

$$\underset{\text{Carbon}}{C} + \underset{\text{(Conc.)}}{4HNO_3} \longrightarrow CO_2 + 2H_2O + 4NO_2$$

$$\underset{\text{Sulphur}}{S} + \underset{\text{(Conc.)}}{6HNO_3} \longrightarrow H_2SO_4 + 2H_2O + 6NO_2$$

(ii) **Action on metals** Nitric acid reacts with all metals except gold and platinum.

(a) **Cold and dilute nitric acid** oxidises metal to their nitrates and liberate nitric oxide.

$$\underset{\text{Copper}}{3Cu} + \underset{\text{(Dil.)}}{8HNO_3} \longrightarrow 3Cu(NO_3)_2 + 4H_2O + 2NO\uparrow$$

(b) **Hot and concentrated nitric acid** oxidises metal to their nitrates and liberates nitrogen dioxide.

$$Cu + \underset{\text{(Conc.)}}{4HNO_3} \longrightarrow Cu(NO_3)_2 + 2H_2O + 2NO_2\uparrow$$

$$Zn + 4HNO_3 \longrightarrow Zn(NO_3)_2 + 2H_2O + 2NO_2$$

Note Dilute nitric acid generally does not liberate hydrogen gas on reacting with metals. This is a powerful oxidising agent and the nascent oxygen formed oxidises the hydrogen to water is :

But very dilute nitric acid reacts with magnesium and manganese metals as follows

$$Mg + 2HNO_3 \longrightarrow Mg(NO_3)_2 + H_2$$

$$Mn + 2HNO_3 \longrightarrow Mn(NO_3)_2 + H_2$$

EXAM ORIENTED QUESTIONS

TYPE - 1

01 Mark

Multiple Choice Questions

Q.1 The formula of chile saltpetre is

(a) KNO_3 (b) $NaNO_3$

(c) HNO_3 (d) None of these

Ans. (b) $NaNO_3$

Q.2 Which process is used for the preparation of nitric acid?

(a) Ostwald's process (b) Contact process

(c) Haber's process (d) Fountain process

Ans. (a) Ostwald's process

Q.3 The ratio of ammonia and air taken in Ostwald's process is

(a) 1 : 10 (b) 10 : 1

(c) 1 : 3 (d) 3 : 1

Ans. (a) 1 : 10

Q.4 Name the oxidising agent used in Ostwald's process.

(a) NO (b) NO_2 (c) CO (d) O_2

Ans. (d) O_2

Q.5 In the preparation of nitric acid during catalytic oxidation of ammonia a mixture of dry air is free from

(i) Carbon dioxide (ii) Ammonia

(iii) Dust particle (iv) Platinum gauze

(a) (i) and (iii) (b) (i) and (ii)

(c) (iii) and (iv) (d) (i) and (iv)

Ans. (a) (i) and (iii)

Q.6 Which of the following is not true with respect to nitric acid? **(ICSE Specimen 2024)**

(a) It is a strong reducing agent.

(b) It is a strong oxidising agent.

(c) It is unstable to heat.

(d) It liberates sulphur dioxide gas when treated with potassium sulphite.

Ans. (a) Nitric acid is a **strong oxidising agent**.

Q.7 *Aqua-regia* is a mixture of

(a) conc. hydrochloric acid (3 parts) and conc. nitric acid (1 part)

(b) conc. HCl (1 part) and conc. nitric acid (3 parts)

(c) dil. hydrochloric acid and conc. nitric acid

(d) conc. hydrochloric acid and dil. nitric acid

Ans. (a) *Aqua-regia* is a mixture of conc. hydrochloric acid (3 parts) and conc. nitric acid (1 part).

Q.8 A student reacts copper turnings with cold dilute nitric acid in a test tube. He tests the gas given off with moist red and blue litmus paper.

What is the name of the gas that evolved and what is the final colour of the litmus paper? **(Competency Based Que.)**

	Gas	Final colour of the litmus paper
(a)	NO	No change in blue and red litmus paper
(b)	NO_2	Blue litmus turns red and no change in red litmus
(c)	N_2	No change in blue and red litmus paper
(d)	N_2O	No change in blue and red litmus paper

Ans. (a) NO, no change in blue and red litmus paper.

Q.9 The brown ring test is used for the detection of

(a) CO_3^{2-} (b) NO_3^-

(c) SO_3^{2-} (d) Cl^-

Ans. (b) NO_3^-

Q.10 The nitrate which on thermal decomposition leaves behind a residue which is yellow when hot and white when cold **(ICSE 2023)**

(a) lead nitrate

(b) ammonium nitrate

(c) copper nitrate

(d) zinc nitrate

Ans. (d) zinc nitrate

Chemical reaction occurs as

$$2Zn(NO_3)_2 \xrightarrow{\Delta} 2ZnO + 4NO_2 + O_2$$

Here, ZnO appears yellow when it is hot and white when it is cold.

Q.11 The correct order of increasing volatility of the acids is **(Competency Based Que.)**

(a) $HCl < CH_3COOH < HNO_3$

(b) $CH_3COOH < HCl < HNO_3$

(c) $HNO_3 < HCl < CH_3COOH$

(d) $HCl < HNO_3 < CH_3COOH$

Ans. (d) $HCl < HNO_3 < CH_3COOH$.

TYPE - 2 01 Mark

Assertion-Reason Questions

Directions (Q. Nos. 1-2) In the following questions, a statement of Assertion (A) is followed by a statement of Reason (R). Choose the answer based on the codes given below.

(a) Both (A) and (R) are true and (R) is the correct explanation of (A).

(b) Both (A) and (R) are true but (R) is not the correct explanation of (A).

(c) (A) is true but (R) is false.

(d) (A) is false but (R) is true.

Q.1 Assertion (A) Pure nitric acid is very stable.

Reason (R) Pure nitric acid decomposes slightly even at ordinary temperature and in the presence of sunlight.

Ans. (d) Pure nitric acid is unstable and decomposes slightly even at ordinary temperature and in the presence of sunlight.

$$4HNO_3 \xrightarrow[\text{Sunlight}]{\Delta} \underset{\text{(Brown colour)}}{4NO_2} + 2H_2O + O_2$$

Thus, (A) is false but (R) is true.

Q.2 Assertion (A) Nitric acid is used to purify gold ornaments.

Reason (R) The impurities present in gold dissolve in nitric acid.

Ans. (a) Nitric acid is used to purify gold ornaments. because, gold may contain Cu, Ag, Zn, Pb, etc, as impurities which dissolves in nitric acid.

Thus, both (A) and (R) are true and (R) is the correct explanation of (A).

TYPE - 3 01 Mark

Fill in the Blanks

Q.1 Commercial sample of nitric acid is pale yellow in colour due to the presence of dissolved .... (nitrogen dioxide/nitrogen trioxide)

Ans. nitrogen dioxide

Q.2 Nitric acid on heating gives ...., O_2 and H_2O (NO_3/NO_2).

Ans. NO_2 (Nitrogen dioxide)

Q.3 Cold, dilute nitric acid reacts with copper to give .... (nitric oxide / nitrogen dioxide) **(ICSE 2014)**

Ans. nitric oxide

Q.4 Hot, concentrated nitric acid reacts with sulphur to form.......... . (nitrogen dioxide/nitric oxide) **(ICSE 2016)**

Ans. nitrogen dioxide

Q.5 .... acid does not liberate hydrogen on reacting with metal. (Nitric/hydrochloric)

Ans. Nitric

Q.6 The metal nitrate which on thermal decomposition forms a black residue is .... [zinc nitrate/copper nitrate]

Ans. Copper nitrate

$$\underset{\text{Blue, crystalline}}{2Cu(NO_3)_2} \xrightarrow{\Delta} \underset{\text{Black}}{2CuO} + 4NO_2 + O_2$$

TYPE - 4 01 Mark

Correct the Incorrect Statement

Q.1 The bottle containing nitric acid should always be stoppered as it is deliquescent in nature.

Ans. The bottle containing nitric acid should always be stoppered as it is **hygroscopic** in nature.

Q.2 Cold and concentrated nitric acid oxidises metal to their nitrates and liberates nitric oxide.

Ans. Cold and **dilute** nitric acid oxidises metal to their nitrates and liberates nitric oxide.

TYPE - 5 01 Mark

Identify the Following

Q.1 Name an acid which is prepared by catalytic oxidation of ammonia. **(ICSE 2015)**

Ans. Nitric acid

Q.2 What is the temperature required in the manufacture of nitric acid by Ostwald's process?

Ans. 800°C

Q.3 Identify the underlined substance in the following question.

The catalyst used to oxidise ammonia into nitric oxide. **(ICSE 2020)**

Ans. Platinum (Pt).

Q.4. Identify the underlined substance in the following question.

The dilute acid which is an oxidising agent. **(ICSE 2019)**

Ans. dil. HNO_3

Q.5. Name the gas produced when copper is treated with hot concentrated nitric acid. **(ICSE 2025)**

Ans. Nitrogen dioxide (NO_2) gas

TYPE - 6 — 02 Marks

Short Answer Type I Questions

Q.1 (i) What is the type of salt formed when the reactants are heated at a suitable temperature for the preparation of nitric acid?

(ii) Write a chemical equation to illustrate the acidic nature of nitric acid.

Ans. (i) During the preparation of nitric acid at suitable temperature, (< 200°C), **sodium and potassium bisulphates** are formed.

$$\underset{\text{Conc.}}{KNO_3 + H_2SO_4} \xrightarrow{< 200°C} \underset{\text{Potassium bisulphate}}{KHSO_4} + \underset{\text{Nitric acid}}{HNO_3}$$

$$\underset{\text{Conc.}}{NaNO_3 + H_2SO_4} \xrightarrow{< 200°C} \underset{\text{Sodium bisulphate}}{NaHSO_4} + \underset{\text{Nitric acid}}{HNO_3}$$ **(1)**

(ii) $CaCO_3 + \underset{\text{Dil.}}{2HNO_3} \longrightarrow Ca(NO_3)_2 + H_2O + CO_2\uparrow$ **(1)**

Q.2 Platinum catalyst is used in the catalytic oxidation of ammonia. **(Competency Based Que.)**

(i) Write an equation for the reaction that occurs in the above case.

(ii) Why does the platinum continue to glow even after the heating is discontinued?

Ans. (i) $4NH_3 + 5O_2 \xrightarrow[800°C]{Pt} 4NO + 6H_2O + \text{Heat}$ **(1)**

(ii) The platinum continues to glow even after the heating is discontinued because the reaction is **exothermic**. **(1)**

Q.3 (i) What is the special feature of the apparatus that is used in the laboratory preparation of nitric acid?

(ii) Why should the temperature of the reaction mixture of nitric acid not be allowed to rise above 200°C?

Ans. (i) Entire apparatus should be made up of glass because nitric acid is highly corrosive in nature and will damage wood, metal, rubber, plastic, etc. **(1)**

(ii) Above 200° C, the nitric acid decomposes into H_2O, NO_2 and O_2, as it is very unstable to heat.

The higher temperature may also damage the glass apparatus. **(1)**

Q.4 Identify the reactant and write the balanced equation for the following:

Nitric acid reacts with compound *Q* to give a salt $Ca(NO_3)_2$, water and carbon dioxide. **(ICSE Specimen 2025)**

Ans. ***Q*** **is calcium carbonate/calcium bicarbonate**

$$CaCO_3 + 2HNO_3 \longrightarrow Ca(NO_3)_2 + H_2O + CO_2\uparrow$$

Or $Ca(HCO_3)_2 + 2HNO_3 \longrightarrow Ca(NO_3)_2 + 2H_2O + 2CO_2\uparrow$ **(2)**

Q.5 Seema added a few pieces of copper turnings to a test tube containing concentrated acid *P* and she noticed that a reddish-brown gas evolved. **(ICSE 2025)**

(i) Name the acid *P* used by Seema.

(ii) Write a balance chemical equation for the reaction that took place.

Ans. (i) The acid *P* is **nitric acid.** When a few pieces of copper turnings are added to a test tube containing conc. HNO_3, reddish-brown gas of nitrogen dioxide is evolved. **(1)**

(ii) $Cu + \underset{\text{(conc.)}}{4HNO_3} \longrightarrow Cu(NO_3)_2 + 2H_2O + \underset{\text{(Reddish-brown gas)}}{2NO_2\uparrow}$ **(1)**

Q.6 Give reason for the following statements.

(i) Concentrated nitric acid appears yellow, when it is left for a while in a glass bottle. **(ICSE 2019)**

(ii) Iron is rendered passive with fuming nitric acid.

Ans. (i) Conc. nitric acid appears yellow, when left for a while in glass bottles, because concentrated nitric acid undergose **decomposition** as it it very unstable to heat.

On decomposition, they form reddish brown nitrogen dioxide gas which when dissolved in the acid appears yellow in colour.

$$4HNO_3 \xrightarrow[\text{Sunlight}]{\Delta} 4NO_2 + 2H_2O + O_2$$ **(1)**

(ii) Iron forms a thin layer of unsoluble metallic oxide which stops further reaction. **(1)**

Q.7 Brown ring test is used for the identification of nitrate ions.

(i) Why is freshly prepared ferrous sulphate solution is used in the above test? **(Competency Based Que.)**

(ii) What is the chemical name of the brown ring?

Ans. (i) If ferrous sulphate is left exposed to air for some time, then it will be **oxidised to ferric sulphate** and it will not respond to the test. **(1)**

(ii) Nitroso ferrous sulphate. **(1)**

TYPE - 7 — 03 Marks

Short Answer Type II Questions

Q.1 When two dry gases, oxygen and *X*, are passed over heated platinum, reddish-brown fumes are seen in the receiving flask. **(Competency Based Que.)**

(i) Name the gas *X*.

(ii) Give equation(s) for the reaction(s) that resulted in the formation of brown fumes.

Ans. (i) NH_3 **(1)**

(ii) $4NH_3 + 5O_2 \xrightarrow[800°C]{Pt} 6H_2O + 4NO + \text{Heat}$

$$2NO(g) + O_2(g) \xrightarrow{50°C} 2NO_2(g)$$ **(2)**

Q.2 The diagram given below is a representation of the industrial preparation of nitric acid by Ostwald's process. With respect to the process answer the following questions. **(Competency Based Que.)**

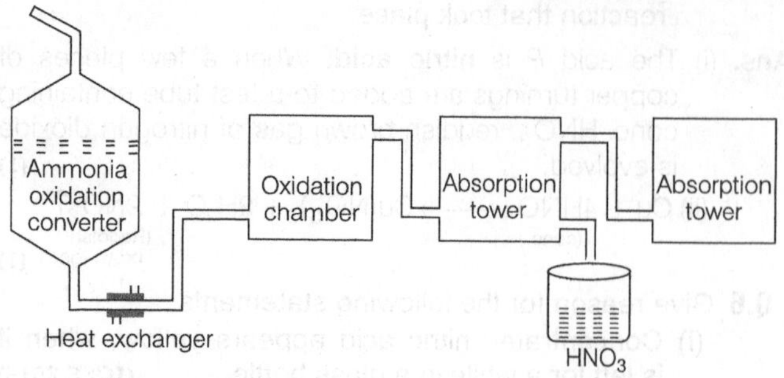

(i) Write the temperature and the catalyst during the catalytic oxidation of ammonia.

(ii) Give balanced chemical equation for the reaction occurring during the conversion of nitrogen dioxide to nitric acid. **(ICSE Specimen 2025)**

Ans. (i) $4NH_3 + 5O_2 \xrightarrow[800°C]{Pt} 4NO + 6H_2O + \text{Heat}$

Temperature required is **800°C** and the catalyst required is **platinum**. **(2)**

(ii) Balanced chemical equation for the conversion of NO_2 to HNO_3 is

$$\underset{\text{Nitrogen dioxide}}{4NO_2(g)} + 2H_2O(l) + O_2(g) \longrightarrow \underset{\text{Nitric acid}}{4HNO_3(aq.)}$$ **(1)**

Q.3 (i) Dilute nitric acid is generally considered a typical acid except for its reaction with metals.

In what way is dilute nitric acid different from other acids when it reacts with metals?

(ii) Write the equation for the reaction of dilute nitric acid with copper.

(iii) Give a balanced equation for oxidation of carbon with conc. HNO_3. **(ICSE specimen 2025)**

Ans. (i) Dilute nitric acid is generally considered a typical acid except for its reaction with metals since, it does not liberate hydrogen. It is a **powerful oxidising agent** and the nascent oxygen formed oxidises the hydrogen to water.

(ii) $3Cu + \underset{\text{(Dil.)}}{8HNO_3} \longrightarrow 3Cu(NO_3)_2 + 4H_2O + 2NO$

(iii) $C + \underset{\text{(conc.)}}{4HNO_3} \longrightarrow CO_2 + 2H_2O + 4NO_2$ **(1 × 3 = 3)**

Q.4 Abhishek was given a salt '*X*' which was white in colour for analysis. On strong heating it produced a yellow residue, a colourless gas and also a reddish-brown gas. The solution of the salt '*X*' when tested with excess of ammonium hydroxide produced a chalky white insoluble precipitate.

(i) Name the coloured gas evolved when Abhishek heated the salt strongly.

(ii) Which cation was present in the sample given to Abhishek?

(iii) Identify the salt given to Abhishek for analysis. **(ICSE Specimen 2025)**

Ans. (i) Nitrogen dioxide (NO_2) gas

(ii) Lead ions

(iii) Lead nitrate

$$\underset{\text{(White)}}{Pb(NO_3)_2} \xrightarrow{\Delta} \underset{\text{(Yellow residue)}}{2PbO} + \underset{\text{(Reddish-brown gas)}}{4NO_2\uparrow} + \underset{\text{(Colourless gas)}}{O_2}$$ **(1 × 3 = 3)**

TYPE - 8

04/05 Marks

Long Answer Type Questions

Q.1 Write balanced chemical equations for the following.

(i) Copper reacts with concentrated nitric acid.

(ii) Aluminium nitride is treated with warm water. **(ICSE Specimen 2025, ICSE 2024)**

(iii) Oxidation of sulphur with hot concentrated nitric acid **(ICSE 2025)**

(iv) Laboratory preparation of nitric acid. **(ICSE Specimen 2025, 2017)**

Ans. (i) $Cu + \underset{\text{(Conc.)}}{4HNO_3} \longrightarrow Cu(NO_3)_2 + 2H_2O + \underset{\text{Nitrogen dioxide gas}}{2NO_2\uparrow}$

(ii) $\underset{\text{Aluminium nitride}}{AlN} + 3H_2O \longrightarrow Al(OH)_3 + \underset{\text{Ammonia gas}}{NH_3\uparrow}$

(iii) $\underset{\text{Sulphur}}{S} + \underset{\text{Conc. nitric acid}}{6HNO_3} \longrightarrow \underset{\text{Sulphuric acid}}{H_2SO_4} + 2H_2O + 6NO_2\uparrow$

(iv) $\underset{\text{Potassium nitrate}}{KNO_3} + \underset{\text{Conc. Sulphuric acid}}{H_2SO_4} \xrightarrow{< 200°C} \underset{\text{Potassium bisulphate}}{KHSO_4} + \underset{\text{Nitric acid}}{HNO_3}$

Or

$\underset{\text{Sodium nitrate}}{NaNO_3} + \underset{\text{Conc. Sulphuric acid}}{H_2SO_4} \xrightarrow{< 200°C} \underset{\text{Sodium bisulphate}}{NaHSO_4} + \underset{\text{Nitric acid}}{HNO_3}$ **(1 × 4 = 4)**

Q.2 Write balanced chemical equations for each of the following.

(i) (a) Catalytic oxidation of ammonia.

(b) Reaction of ammonia with nitric acid. **(ICSE 2017)**

(ii) (a) Laboratory preparation of ammonia using an ammonium salt.

(b) Reaction of ammonia with excess chlorine.

(c) Reaction of ammonia with sulphuric acid. **(ICSE 2015)**

Ans. (i)(a) Catalytic oxidation of ammonia gives **nitric oxide**, which on further oxidation gives **brown fumes of nitrogen dioxide**.

$4NH_3 + 5O_2 \xrightarrow{Pt,\ 800°C} 6H_2O + 4NO\uparrow + \text{Heat}$

$$2NO + O_2 \xrightarrow{50°C} \underset{\text{(Brown gas)}}{2NO_2}$$ **(1)**

(b) Ammonia on reaction with nitric acid gives **ammonium nitrate**.

$$\underset{\text{Ammonia}}{NH_3} + \underset{\text{Nitric acid}}{HNO_3} \longrightarrow \underset{\text{Ammonium nitrate}}{NH_4NO_3}$$ **(1)**

(ii) (a) $$\underset{\text{Ammonium chloride}}{2NH_4Cl} + \underset{\text{Calcium hydroxide}}{Ca(OH)_2} \longrightarrow CaCl_2 + 2H_2O + \underset{\text{Ammonia}}{2NH_3}$$ **(1)**

(b) $$NH_3 + \underset{\text{Chlorine (Excess)}}{3Cl_2} \longrightarrow \underset{\text{Hydrogen chloride}}{3HCl} + \underset{\text{Nitrogen trichloride (Yellow)}}{NCl_3}$$ **(1)**

(c) $$\underset{\text{Ammonia gas}}{2NH_3} + H_2SO_4 \longrightarrow \underset{\text{Ammonium sulphate}}{(NH_4)_2SO_4}$$ **(1)**

Q.3 The figure given below illustrates the apparatus used in the laboratory preparation of nitric acid.

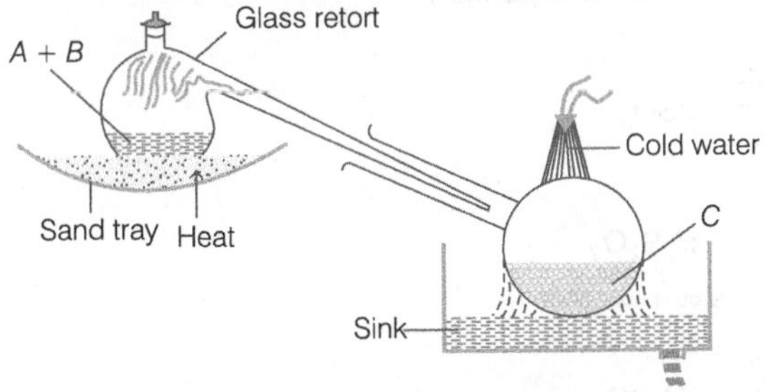

(i) Name *A* (a liquid), *B* (a solid) and *C* (a liquid). (Do not give the formulae)

(ii) Write an equation to show how nitric acid undergoes decomposition?

(iii) Write the equation for the reaction in which copper is oxidised by concentrated nitric acid.

Ans. (i) *A*–Conc. sulphuric acid, *B*–Potassium nitrate
C –Nitric acid **(1 × 3 = 3)**

(ii) $$4HNO_3 \longrightarrow 2H_2O + 4NO_2 + O_2$$ **(1)**

(iii) $$Cu + \underset{\text{(conc.)}}{4HNO_3} \longrightarrow Cu(NO_3)_2 + 2H_2O + 2NO_2 \uparrow$$ **(1)**

TYPE - 9 03 Marks

Case-Based Question

Q.1 A student is studying the Ostwald process used for the industrial production of nitric acid (HNO_3) and is asked to understand the sequence of reactions and the role of catalysts. In this process, ammonia gas (NH_3) is oxidised to form nitrogen dioxide (NO_2), which then reacts with water to form nitric acid. The process involves the use of a platinum catalyst.

(i) What is the first step in the Ostwald process for the production of nitric acid?

(ii) What is the role of the catalyst in the Ostwald process?

(iii) What is the final product obtained in the Ostwald process and write the reaction involved?

Ans. (i) The first step is the **catalytic oxidation of ammonia (NH_3) to form nitric oxide (NO)**, which is done by reacting ammonia with oxygen in the presence of a Pt as catalyst.

$$4NH_3 + 5O_2 \xrightarrow[800°C]{Pt} 4NO + 6H_2O + \text{Heat}$$ **(1)**

(ii) The catalyst, usually platinum (Pt), **speeds up the reaction** between ammonia and oxygen without being consumed in the process. It provides a surface for the reaction to occur, **lowering the activation energy** required for the reaction. **(1)**

(iii) In the last step, nitrogen dioxide and oxygen present in the air react with water to form **nitric acid**.

$$4NO_2(g) + 2H_2O(l) + O_2(g) \longrightarrow 4HNO_3(aq)$$ **(1)**

Compound IV : Sulphuric Acid

Molecular formula : H_2SO_4

Molecular mass : 98 u

Structure :

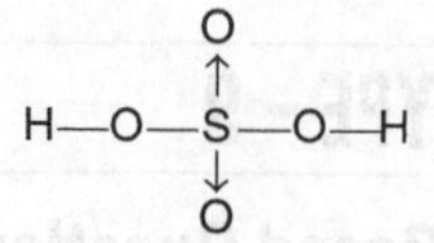

Manufacture of Sulphuric Acid (Contact Process)

The various steps in the contact process are as follows:

(i) **Production of sulphur dioxide**

$$S + O_2 \longrightarrow SO_2$$

or

$$\underset{\text{Iron pyrites}}{FeS_2} + 11O_2 \longrightarrow 2Fe_2O_3 + 8SO_2$$

(ii) **Purification of gases** The mixture of sulphur dioxide and air contains various impurities which must be removed, otherwise the catalyst loses its efficiency.

The mixture is passed through a purifier, scrubber and then arsenic purifier.

(iii) **Catalytic oxidation of sulphur dioxide**

$$2SO_2 + O_2 \underset{450°C}{\overset{V_2O_5}{\rightleftharpoons}} 2SO_3$$

(iv) **Absorption of sulphur trioxide in sulphuric acid**

$$SO_3 + H_2SO_4 \longrightarrow \underset{\substack{\text{Oleum} \\ \text{(Pyrosulphuric acid)}}}{H_2S_2O_7}$$

(v) **Dilution of oleum to obtain sulphuric acid**

$$H_2S_2O_7 + H_2O \longrightarrow 2H_2SO_4$$

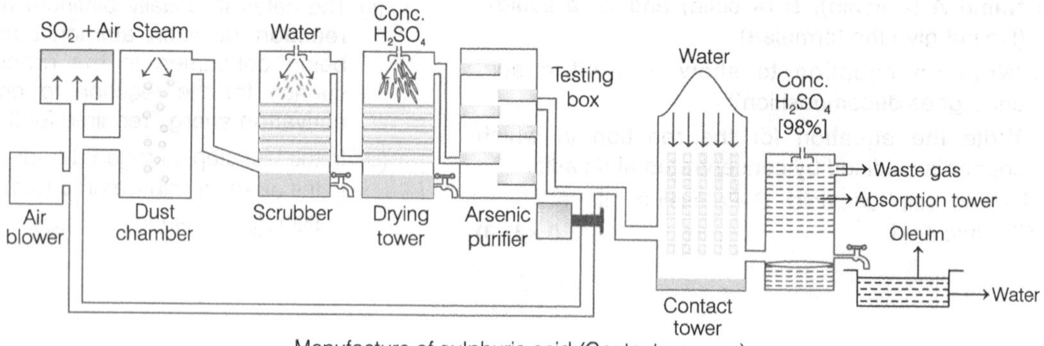

Manufacture of sulphuric acid (Contact process)

Favourable Conditions for $SO_2 \longrightarrow SO_3$ conversion in contact process

(i) **Exothermic reactions** are favoured at low temperature (410-450°C).

(ii) **High pressure** of 1-2 atmosphere is used because high pressure favours the reaction.

(iii) **Excess of oxygen increases** the production of sulphur trioxide.

(iv) **A suitable catalyst**, vanadium pentoxide (V_2O_5) is used as a catalyst.

Physical Properties

- It is colourless, odourless and sour in taste.
- It is highly dense, oily and hygroscopic liquid in nature.
- Pure acid is almost a non-conductor of electricity and is highly corrosive in nature whereas the dilute acid is a good conductor of electricity.

I. Properties of Dilute Sulphuric Acid

Acidic property (Typical properties of dilute acid)

1. Dilute sulphuric acid reacts **with metals, which are above hydrogen** in the activity series to form metallic sulphate and hydrogen at ordinary temperature.

Active metal	+	**Acid** (dil.)	⟶	**Metal sulphate**	+	**Hydrogen**
Mg	+	H_2SO_4	⟶	$MgSO_4$	+	$H_2\uparrow$

2. It **neutralises** bases (metal oxides and metal hydroxides) to form salts and water.

Base / Alkali	+	**Acid** (dil.)	⟶	**Salt**	+	**Water**
CuO	+	H_2SO_4	⟶	$CuSO_4$	+	H_2O
2NaOH	+	H_2SO_4	⟶	Na_2SO_4	+	$2H_2O$

3. It liberates **carbon dioxide** from **metallic carbonates** and **bicarbonates**.

Carbonate / bicarbonate	+	**Acid** (dil.)	⟶	**Salt**	+	**Water**	+	**Carbon dioxide**
Na_2CO_3	+	H_2SO_4	⟶	Na_2SO_4	+	H_2O	+	$CO_2\uparrow$
$2NaHCO_3$	+	H_2SO_4	⟶	Na_2SO_4	+	$2H_2O$	+	$2CO_2\uparrow$

4. It evolves **hydrogen sulphide** from metal **sulphides**.

Metal sulphide	+	**Acid** (dil.)	⟶	**Salt**	+	**Hydrogen sulphide**
Na_2S	+	H_2SO_4	⟶	Na_2SO_4	+	$H_2S\uparrow$

5. It evolves **sulphur dioxide** from **sulphites** and **hydrogen sulphites** (bisulphites).

Sulphite / bisulphites	+	**Acid** (dil.)	⟶	**Salt**	+	**Water**	+	**Sulphur dioxide**
Na_2SO_3	+	H_2SO_4	⟶	Na_2SO_4	+	H_2O	+	$SO_2\uparrow$
$2NaHSO_3$	+	H_2SO_4	⟶	Na_2SO_4	+	$2H_2O$	+	$2SO_2\uparrow$

Note Sulphur dioxide gas is oxidising as well as reducing agent. It also shows temporary bleaching property due to its reducing nature in presence of moisture.

$$SO_2 + 2H_2O \longrightarrow H_2SO_4 + \underset{\text{Nascent hydrogen}}{2[H]}$$

$$\text{Coloured material} + \underset{\text{Nascent hydrogen}}{[H]} \longrightarrow \text{Colourless product}$$

II. Properties of Concentrated Sulphuric Acid

1. Non-volatile nature

Concentrated sulphuric acid is a non-volatile acid. Therefore, it is used for preparing volatile acids like HCl, HNO_3 and CH_3COOH from their salts by double decomposition.

Salt of volatile acid	+	**Acid** (conc.)	⟶	**Acid salt**	+	**Volatile acid**
NaCl	+	H_2SO_4	⟶	$NaHSO_4$	+	HCl
KNO_3	+	H_2SO_4	⟶	$KHSO_4$	+	HNO_3
KCl	+	H_2SO_4	⟶	$KHSO_4$	+	HCl
$NaNO_3$	+	H_2SO_4	⟶	$NaHSO_4$	+	HNO_3

2. As an Oxidising Agent

The oxidising property of concentrated sulphuric acid is due to the fact that on thermal decomposition, it yields nascent oxygen [O]

$$H_2SO_4 \longrightarrow H_2O + SO_2 + [O]$$

Nascent oxygen oxidises non-metals, metals and inorganic compounds.

(i) Non-metals

1. **Carbon** $C + 2H_2SO_4(conc.) \longrightarrow CO_2 + 2H_2O + 2SO_2 \uparrow$
2. **Sulphur** $S + 2H_2SO_4(conc.) \longrightarrow 3SO_2 + 2H_2O$

(ii) Metals

1. **Copper** $Cu + 2H_2SO_4(conc.) \longrightarrow CuSO_4 + 2H_2O + SO_2 \uparrow$
2. **Zinc** $Zn + 2H_2SO_4(conc.) \longrightarrow ZnSO_4 + 2H_2O + SO_2 \uparrow$

3. As a Dehydrating Agent

H_2SO_4 has a great affinity for water. It readily removes chemically combined water molecules i.e., elements of water from other compounds thus it acts as a **dehydrating agent**.

(i) **Conc. H_2SO_4 removes water of crystallisation from salts**

For example, blue copper (II) sulphate ($CuSO_4 \cdot 5H_2O$) taken in a test tube becomes white (anhydrous copper sulphate), when a few drops of conc. sulphuric acid are added.

$$\underset{\text{Blue}}{CuSO_4 \cdot 5H_2O} \xrightarrow{\text{Conc.}H_2SO_4} \underset{\substack{\text{Dirty}\\\text{white}}}{CuSO_4(s)} + \underset{\substack{\text{(Removed}\\\text{by acid)}}}{5H_2O}$$

(ii) All **carbohydrates** such as glucose, sugar, and cellulose (paper, cotton, wood, etc.) react immediately to give a **black spongy mass of carbon** which rises up. Steam is given off and the whole mass gets heated due to an exothermic reaction. They are said to get **charred**.

$$\underset{\text{Glucose}}{C_6H_{12}O_6} \xrightarrow{\text{Conc. } H_2SO_4} 6C + 6H_2O$$

$$\underset{\text{Cane Sugar}}{C_{12}H_{22}O_{11}(s)} \xrightarrow{\text{Conc. } H_2SO_4} \underset{\substack{\text{Sugar}\\\text{charcoal}}}{12C(s)} + 11H_2O$$

Carbon obtained in this reaction is very pure and is called **sugar charcoal**.

REVISION NOTES

EXAM ORIENTED QUESTIONS

TYPE - 1 01 Mark

Multiple Choice Questions

Q.1 The catalyst preferred in the conversion of sulphur dioxide to sulphur trioxide is

(a) finely divided iron **(ICSE Specimen 2022, Sem-I)**
(b) graphite
(c) vanadium pentoxide
(d) platinum

Ans. (c) The catalyst which helps in the conversion of sulphur dioxide to sulphur trioxide is **vanadium pentoxide**.

$$2SO_2(g) + O_2(g) \underset{450°C}{\overset{V_2O_5}{\rightleftharpoons}} 2SO_3(g)$$

Q.2 These reactions are used in the manufacture of sulphuric acid.

(P) $S + O_2 \longrightarrow SO_2$
(Q) $2SO_2 + O_2 \rightleftharpoons 2SO_3$
(R) $SO_3 + H_2O \longrightarrow H_2SO_4$

Which reactions are speeded up by using a catalyst?

(a) Only *P* (b) Only *Q*
(c) Only *R* (d) *Q* and *R*

Ans. (b) A catalyst (V_2O_5) is needed to convert SO_2 to SO_3 which is **reaction *Q***.

Q.3 The following scheme shows four stages in the conversion of sulphur to sulphuric acid.
In which stage is a catalyst used?

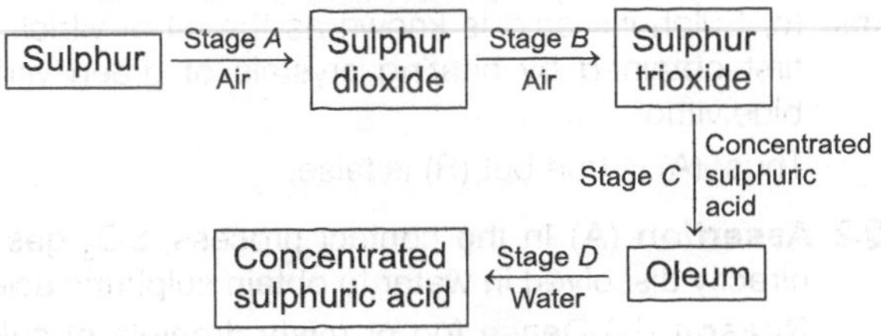

(a) Stage *A* (b) Stage *D*
(c) Stage *B* (d) Stage *C*

Ans. (c) V_2O_5 catalyses the reaction of SO_2 and O_2 to produce SO_3, in the manufacture of sulphuric acid.

$$2SO_2(g) + O_2(g) \xrightarrow[V_2O_5 \text{ catalyst}]{450°C,\ 1\text{-}2 \text{ atm}} 2SO_3(g)$$

Q.4 In the contact process for making sulphuric acid, one step involves the oxidation of sulphur dioxide as shown below.

$$2SO_2(g) + O_2(g) \rightleftharpoons 2SO_3(g)$$

The forward reaction is exothermic.
Which change would increase the amount of sulphur trioxide produced at equilibrium?

(a) Increasing the temperature
(b) Decreasing the temperature
(c) Decreasing the pressure
(d) Adding a catalyst

Ans. (b) By increasing the temperature, the equilibrium is shifted in the backward direction and *vice-versa*. The greater pressure favours the side with lesser number of gaseous moles and *vice-versa*. A catalyst increases forward and bakward reactions nearly to the same extent.

Q.5 The diagram represents the manufacture of sulphuric acid by the contact process.

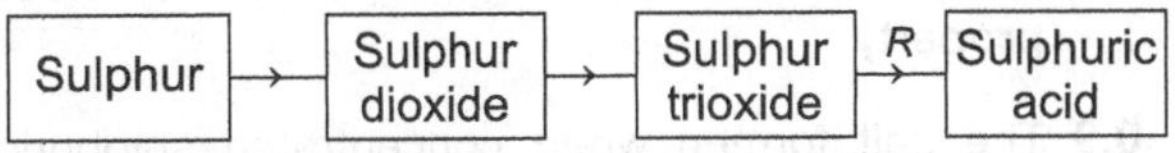

What is used in step *R*?

(a) vanadium(V) oxide
(b) Only water
(c) water followed by concentrated sulphuric acid
(d) concentrated sulphuric acid followed by water

Ans. (d) $SO_3 + H_2SO_4 \longrightarrow H_2S_2O_7$

$H_2S_2O_7 + H_2O \longrightarrow 2H_2SO_4$

SO_3 is dissolved in concentrated H_2SO_4 to form oleum ($H_2S_2O_7$), which reacts with water to produce H_2SO_4.

Q.6 The equation below shows the reaction between element '*X*' and dilute sulphuric acid.

$$X(s) + H_2SO_4(aq) \longrightarrow XSO_4(aq) + H_2(g)$$

Which particles are responsible for conducting electricity in dilute sulphuric acid and compound XSO_4? **(ICSE Specimen 2025)**

(a) Electrons
(b) Only positive ions
(c) Only negative ions
(d) Both positive and negative ions

Ans. (d) Both positive and negative ions.

Q.7 Which gas decolourises potassium permanganate ($KMnO_4$) solution? **(ICSE 2025)**

(a) Sulphur dioxide (b) Ammonia
(c) Hydrogen chloride (d) Carbon dioxide

Ans. (a) **Sulphur dioxide** decolourises pink potassium permanganate ($KMnO_4$) solution.

$$\underset{\text{(Pink)}}{2KMnO_4} + 5SO_2 + 2H_2O \longrightarrow \underset{\text{(Colourless)}}{K_2SO_4} + 2MnSO_4 + 2H_2SO_4$$

In this reaction, $KMnO_4$ is reduced and the pink colour of the solution changes to colourless.

Q.8 The property exhibited by concentrated sulphuric acid when it is used to prepare hydrogen chloride gas from potassium chloride. **(ICSE 2023)**

(a) Dehydrating property
(b) Drying property
(c) Oxidising property
(d) Non-volatile acid property

Ans. (d) H_2SO_4 reacts with KCl or NaCl to form volatile HCl and potassium or sodium hydrogen sulphate.

So, the property of sulphuric acid used in production of volatile hydrogen chloride gas when it reacts with potassium chloride (or sodium chloride) is **non-volatile property**.

Q.9 The salt formed when concentrated sulphuric acid reacts with KNO_3 above 200° C.

(a) K_2SO_4 (b) K_2SO_3
(c) $KHSO_4$ (d) $KHSO_3$

Ans. (c) $KHSO_4$

Q.10 In the reaction given below sulphuric acid acts as a/an **(ICSE 2025)**

$$S + 2H_2SO_4 \longrightarrow 3SO_2 + 2H_2O$$

(a) Non-volatile acid (b) Dibasic acid
(c) Oxidising agent (d) Reducing agent

Ans. (c) In the given reaction, sulphuric acid acts as an **oxidising agent** as it oxidises sulphur to sulphur dioxide.

Q.11 The oxidising agent in the equation $S + 2H_2SO_4 \longrightarrow 3SO_2 + 2H_2O$ is **(ICSE 2024)**

(a) sulphur (b) sulphuric acid
(c) sulphur dioxide (d) water

Ans. (b) Sulphuric acid.

On thermal decomposition sulphuric acid gives nascent oxygen, which oxidises metal, non-metal and inorganic compounds.

$$H_2SO_4 \longrightarrow H_2O + SO_2 + \underset{\text{Nascent oxygen}}{[O]}$$

Q.12 The acid which can produce carbon from cane sugar is

(a) concentrated hydrochloric acid
(b) concentrated nitric acid
(c) concentrated sulphuric acid
(d) concentrated acetic acid

Ans. (c) concentrated sulphuric acid.

Q.13 When $BaCl_2$ reacts with H_2SO_4,

(a) white precipitate of $BaSO_4$ is formed.
(b) white precipitate of Ba_2SO_4 is formed.
(c) black precipitate of $BaSO_4$ is formed.
(d) black precipitate of Ba_2SO_4 is formed.

Ans. (a) White precipitate of $BaSO_4$ is formed.

$$BaCl_2 + H_2SO_4 \longrightarrow \underset{\text{(White ppt.)}}{BaSO_4\downarrow} + 2HCl$$

TYPE - 2

01 Mark

Assertion-Reason Questions

Directions (Q. Nos. 1-3) In the following questions, a statement of Assertion (A) is followed by a statement of Reason (R). Choose the answer based on the codes given below.

(a) Both (A) and (R) are true and (R) is the correct explanation of (A).
(b) Both (A) and (R) are true but (R) is not the correct explanation of (A).
(c) (A) is true but (R) is false.
(d) (A) is false but (R) is true.

Q.1 Assertion (A) Sulphuric acid is known as the oil of vitriol.

Reason (R) Sulphuric acid was first obtained by heating crystals of blue vitriol.

Ans. (c) Sulphuric acid is known as the oil of vitriol. It was first obtained by heating crystals of green vitriol not blue vitriol.

Thus, (A) is true but (R) is false.

Q.2 Assertion (A) In the contact process, SO_3 gas is not directly dissolved in water to obtain sulphuric acid.

Reason (R) Dense fog or misty droplets of sulphuric acid are formed which is difficult to condense. **(ICSE 2025)**

Ans. (a) In contact process, SO_3 gas is not directly dissolved in water as it gives a **lot of heat** on dissolution and forms misty droplets of sulphuric acid, which are difficult to condense.

Thus, both (A) and (R) are true and (R) is the correct explanation of (A).

Q.3 Assertion (A) Few drops of dilute acid is added to a solution of zinc sulphide, a colourless gas is formed with a rotten egg odour.

Reason (R) Gas formed does not turn moist lead acetate paper silvery black. **(Competency Based Que.)**

Ans. (b) Few drops dilute acid is added to a solution of zinc sulphide, a colourless gas of H_2S is formed with a rotten egg odour. The gas formed does not turn moist lead acetate paper silvery black.

Thus, both (A) and (R) are true but (R) is not the correct explanation of (A).

TYPE - 3 — 01 Mark

Fill in the Blanks

Q.1 Sulphuric acid is called .... (oil of vitriol/blue vitriol)

Ans. oil of vitriol

Q.2 SO_2 and ...... gas are produced during contact process. (SO_3/NO_2)

Ans. SO_3 (Sulphur trioxide)

Q.3 When sodium chloride is heated with concentrated sulphuric acid below 200°C, one of the products formed is .... (sodium hydrogen sulphate / sodium sulphate).

Ans. sodium hydrogen sulphate

Q.4 .... property is shown by sulphuric acid when it is treated with metals like Zn, Mg, etc. Oxidising/ Dehydrating)

Ans. Oxidising

Q.5 Blue copper (II) sulphate turns .... (black/white), when it is treated with conc. H_2SO_4.

Ans. white

TYPE - 4 — 01 Mark

Correct the Incorrect Statement

Q.1 The molecular formula of oleum is $H_2S_2O_8$.

Ans. The molecular formula of oleum is $\mathbf{H_2S_2O_7}$.

Q.2 Sulphuric acid when dissolved in water form hydroxyl ion, thus shows acidic properties.

Ans. Sulphuric acid when dissolved in water form **hydronium ion**, thus shows acidic properties.

TYPE - 5 — 01×05 = 05 Marks

Matching Type Questions

Q.1 Match the following columns. **(Competency Based Que.)**

Column I	Column II
A. Calamine	1. Ammonium nitrate
B. Funnel arrangement	2. Nitrate radical
C. An explosive	3. Sulphuric acid
D. Brown ring test	4. Hydrochloric acid
E. Non-volatile acid	5. Zinc carbonate

Ans. (A) → (5), (B) → (4), (C) → (1), (D) → (2), (E) → (3).

Q.2 Match the following columns.

Column I (Compound)	Column II (Formula)
A. Fertilizers	1. NH_4NO_2
B. Production of N_2	2. NH_4NO_3
C. Dry cell	3. $H_2S_2O_7$
D. Oleum	4. NH_4Cl
E. Chile salt petre	5. $NaNO_3$

Ans. (A) → (2), (B) → (1), (C) → (4), (D) → (3), (E) → (5).

Q.3 Match the following columns.

Column I (Reactions)	Column II (Property of sulphuric acid)
A. Conc. sulphuric acid reacts with zinc to liberate sulphur dioxide.	1. Least volatile acid
B. Action of dil. sulphuric acid on active metals to give hydrogen.	2. Dehydrating agent
C. Reaction of conc. sulphuric acid with formic acid to give carbon monoxide.	3. Typical acid
D. Action of conc. sulphuric acid on rock salt (preparation of HCl).	4. Reducing agent
E. Bleaching action of SO_2 in the presence of moisture of H_2O	5. Oxidising agent

Ans. (A) → (5), (B) → (3), (C) → (2), (D) → (1), (E) → (4).

Q.4 Match the following columns.

Column I (Reactions)	Column II (Chemicals)
A. Reactants of Ostwald's process.	1. Nitric oxide
B. Action of nitric acid on sulphur.	2. Nitrogen and hydrogen
C. Gas that exits the catalytic chamber during Ostwald's process.	3. Ammonia and oxygen
D. Nitric acid comes in contact with air.	4. Sulphuric acid
E. Reactants of Haber's process	5. Nitrogen dioxide

Ans. (A) → (3), (B) → (4), (C) → (1), (D) → (5), (E) → (2).

Q.5 Match the following columns. **(ICSE 2025)**

Column I	Column II
A. $N_2 + 3H_2 \rightleftharpoons 2NH_3$	1. Vanadium pentoxide
B. $4NH_3 + 5O_2 \longrightarrow 4NO + 6H_2O$	2. Nickel
C. $2SO_2 + O_2 \rightleftharpoons 2SO_3$	3. Iron
D. $C_2H_4 + H_2 \rightarrow C_2H_6$	4. Concentrated sulphuric acid
E. $CuSO_4 \cdot 5H_2O \rightarrow CuSO_4 + 5H_2O$	5. Platinum

Ans. (A) → (3), (B) → (5), (C) → (1), (D) → (2), (E) → (4).

TYPE - 6 — 01 Mark

Identify the Following

Q.1 What is a substance which is added to water, to manufacture sulphuric acid in contact process. **(ICSE 2021- 2022, Sem-II)**

Ans. Oleum ($H_2S_2O_7$) dissolves in water to give sulphuric acid.

Q.2 Name the chemical property of sulphuric acid to form two types of salts with an alkali. **(ICSE 2021-2022, Sem-II)**

Ans. Sulphuric acid is a **dibasic acid**, thus it form two types of salts when reacts with alkali (NaOH).

Q.3 Identify the underlined substance in the following question.

The acid that is dehydrating as well as a drying agent. **(ICSE 2020)**

Ans. Concentrated sulphuric acid.

Q.4 Name the acid used to remove water of crystallisation from salts.

Ans. Conc. H_2SO_4.

Q.5 Name the acid which precipitates the insoluble sulphates of lead, barium and calcium from the solutions of their salts.

Ans. Sulphuric acid.

TYPE - 7 — 02 Marks

Short Answer Type I Questions

Q.1 In the preparation of H_2SO_4 by contact process, why is SO_3 not absorbed directly in water to form H_2SO_4 ?

Ans. In contact process, SO_3 is not absorbed directly in water to form H_2SO_4 because the reaction is **highly exothermic**. This forces the sulphuric acid to form a mist of tiny droplets. These are highly corrosive, which can even attack and corrode the lead pipelines which cover the tower in contact process. Hence, the reaction becomes difficult to handle. **(2)**

Q.2 (i) Name the acid formed when sulphur dioxide dissolves in water.

(ii) Name the gas released when sodium carbonate is added to a solution of sulphuric acid.

Ans. (i) Sulphur dioxide dissolves in water to give **sulphurous acid**.

$$SO_2 + H_2O \longrightarrow H_2SO_3 \quad \textbf{(1)}$$

(ii) Gas released is **carbon dioxide**.

$$Na_2CO_3 + H_2SO_4 \longrightarrow Na_2SO_4 + H_2O + CO_2\uparrow \quad \textbf{(1)}$$

Q.3 How will you distinguish between dilute hydrochloric acid and dilute sulphuric acid using lead nitrate solution?

Ans. Sulphuric acid gives white insoluble precipitate of lead sulphate, which remains insoluble on heating.

$$\underset{\text{Lead nitrate}}{Pb(NO_3)_2} + \underset{\text{Sulphuric acid}}{H_2SO_4} \longrightarrow PbSO_4\downarrow + \underset{\text{Nitric acid}}{2HNO_3}$$

Lead nitrate react with HCl to give white ppt.

$$\underset{\text{Lead nitrate}}{Pb(NO_3)_2} + \underset{\text{Hydrochloric acid}}{2HCl} \longrightarrow \underset{\text{Lead chloride (white ppt.)}}{PbCl_2\downarrow} + \underset{\text{Nitric acid}}{2HNO_3}$$

The ppt. of $PbCl_2$ gets redissolved on heating.

By this method we can distinguish between dilute hydrochloric acid and dilute sulphuric acid using lead nitrate solution. **(2)**

Q.4 Which property of sulphuric acid is shown by the reaction of concentrated sulphuric acid with
(i) ethanol (ii) carbon **(ICSE 2018)**

Ans. (i) Concentrated sulphuric acid acts as a **dehydrating agent**. It dehydrates ethanol to form ethene.

$$\underset{\text{Ethanol}}{C_2H_5OH} \xrightarrow[170°C]{\text{Conc. } H_2SO_4} \underset{\text{Ethene}}{CH_2{=}CH_2} + H_2O$$ **(1)**

(ii) Concentrated sulphuric acid acts as an **oxidising agent**, when it reacts with carbon.

Due to presence of nascent oxygen, it oxidises carbon to carbon dioxide.

$$\underset{\text{Carbon}}{C} + \underset{\text{Conc. sulphuric acid}}{2H_2SO_4} \longrightarrow CO_2 + 2H_2O + 2SO_2\uparrow$$ **(1)**

Q.5 What property of sulphuric acid is exhibited in each of the following cases: **(ICSE Specimen 2025, Specimen 2024)**
(i) In the preparation of HCl gas when it reacts with sodium chloride.
(ii) When conc. sulphuric acid reacts with copper to produce sulphur dioxide gas.

Ans. (i) The property of sulphuric acid used in the preparation of HCl gas when it reacts with sodium chloride is its **non-volatile nature**.

$$NaCl + H_2SO_4 \longrightarrow NaHSO_4 + HCl$$ **(1)**

(ii) **Oxidising property** of concentrated sulphuric acid is used in the preparation of sulphur dioxide by warming a mixture of conc. sulphuric acid and copper.

$$Cu + 2H_2SO_4 \longrightarrow CuSO_4 + 2H_2O + SO_2\uparrow$$ **(1)**

Q.6 Write the following statements by adding the correct word as shown in the example. **(ICSE 2024)**
Example:
Given Statement : Ammonia changes moist red litmus to blue.
Correct Statement : Aqueous ammonia changes moist red litmus to blue.
(i) Sulphuric acid acts as a dehydrating agent.
(ii) Ammonia reacts with chlorine to give ammonium chloride and nitrogen.

Ans. (i) **Concentrated sulphuric acid** acts as a dehydrating agent. **(1)**

(ii) **Ammonia in excess** reacts with chlorine to give ammonium chloride and nitrogen. **(1)**

Q.7 Differentiate between the following pairs based on the criteria given in the brackets. **(ICSE 2023)**
(i) Cane sugar and hydrated copper sulphate [using concentrated H_2SO_4]
(ii) Sulphuric acid and hydrochloric acid [type of salts formed]

Ans. (i) $C_{12}H_{22}O_{11} + \text{Conc.}H_2SO_4 \longrightarrow 12C + 11H_2O$

Here, conc. H_2SO_4 acts as **dehydrating agent**.

$$\underset{\text{Blue}}{CuSO_4\cdot 5H_2O(s)} \xrightarrow{\text{Conc. } H_2SO_4} \underset{\text{White}}{CuSO_4} + 5H_2O$$

Here, also act as **dehydrating agent.** **(1)**

(ii) The salts of sulphuric acid are **sulphates** (Na_2SO_4) **and bisulphates** ($NaHSO_4$), while the salts of hydrochloric acid are **chlorides** like KCl. **(1)**

Q.8 With reference to the reaction occurring in the given figure **(Competency Based Que.)**

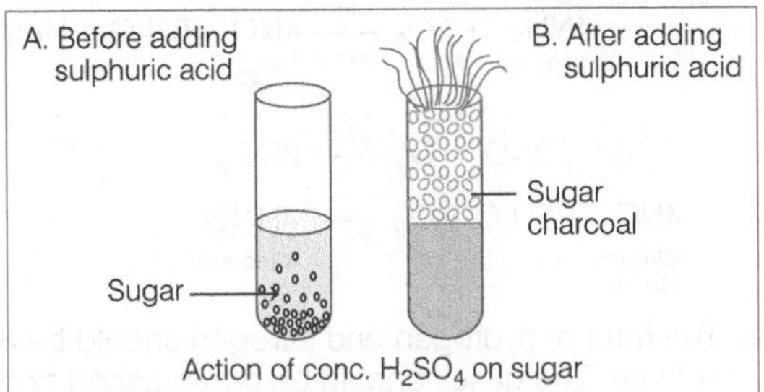

Action of conc. H_2SO_4 on sugar

(i) Write an equation for the reaction.
(ii) State the property of sulphuric acid exhibited in the above case.

Ans. (i) $C_{12}H_{22}O_{11} \xrightarrow{\text{Conc. } H_2SO_4} 12C + 11H_2O$ **(1)**

(ii) Conc. H_2SO_4 act as a **dehydrating agent**. **(1)**

Q.9 To the acid prepared by the contact process, barium chloride solution is added. State one observation and write an equation for the reaction that occurs. **(Competency Based Que.)**

Ans. Observation A white ppt. is formed **(1)**

Reaction $H_2SO_4 + BaCl_2 \longrightarrow BaSO_4\downarrow + 2HCl$ **(1)**

TYPE - 8

03 Marks

Short Answer Type II Questions

Q.1 State the conditions required for the following reactions with suitable explanation. **(ICSE Specimen 2023)**
(i) Conversion of sulphur dioxide to sulphur trioxide.
(ii) Conversion of ammonia to nitric acid.
(iii) Conversion of nitrogen to ammonia.

Ans. (i) Conversion of sulphur dioxide to sulphur trioxide:

A pure and dry mixture of two parts of sulphur dioxide gas and one part of oxygen by volume is passed over heated platinised asbestos or vanadium pentoxide (V_2O_5) maintained at 450°C, to get sulphur trioxide gas.

$$\underset{\text{Sulphur dioxide}}{2SO_2(g)} + \underset{\text{Oxygen}}{O_2(g)} \underset{450°C}{\overset{V_2O_5}{\rightleftharpoons}} \underset{\text{Sulphur trioxide}}{2SO_3(g)}$$ **(1)**

(ii) A mixture of dry air and dry ammonia in the ratio of 10:1 by volume is first compressed and then passed into the catalytic chamber containing platinum as catalyst at about 800° C.

Nitric oxide gas obtained by oxidation of ammonia is very hot. In order to reduce its temperature upto 50°C, it is passed through a heat exchanger, and it is oxidised to nitrogen dioxide.

Nitrogen dioxide gas is passed through the tower and water is showered over it. Thus, nitric acid is obtained.

$$\underset{\text{Ammonia}}{4NH_3} + 5O_2 \xrightarrow[800^{\circ}C]{Pt} \underset{\text{Nitric oxide}}{4NO} + 6H_2O + \text{Heat}$$

$$2NO + O_2 \xrightarrow{50^{\circ}C} 2NO_2$$

$$\underset{\text{Nitrogen dioxide}}{4NO_2} + 2H_2O + O_2 \longrightarrow \underset{\text{Nitric acid}}{4HNO_3}$$

(1)

(iii) The ratio of hydrogen and nitrogen should be 3:1 by volume. The gases should be compressed from 200 atm to 900 atm pressure and then passed over heated catalyst maintained at a temperature between 450°C to 500°C.

$$\underset{\text{Nitrogen}}{N_2} + \underset{\text{Hydrogen}}{3H_2} \xrightarrow[\substack{450^{\circ}C\text{-}500^{\circ}C \\ \text{above 200 atm}}]{\text{Te and Mo}} \underset{\text{Ammonia}}{2NH_3}$$

(1)

Q.2 Copy and complete the following table relating to important industrial processes output refers to the product of the process not the intermediate steps.

Name of process	Inputs	Catalyst	Equation for catalysed reaction	Output
Contact process	Sulphur dioxide + Oxygen			

Ans.

Name of process	Inputs	Catalyst	Equation for catalysed reaction	Output
Contact process	Sulphur dioxide + Oxygen	Vanadium pentoxide	$2SO_2 + O_2 \longrightarrow 2SO_3$	Sulphuric acid

(3)

Q.3 Choose the role played by concentrated sulphuric acid as *A*, *B*, *C* which is responsible for the reactions 1 to 3. **(ICSE Specimen 2023)**

(*A*) Oxidising agent

(*B*) Non-volatile acid

(*C*) Dehydrating agent

1. $NaNO_3 + H_2SO_4 \xrightarrow{< 200^{\circ}C} NaHSO_4 + HNO_3$

2. $CuSO_4 \cdot 5H_2O \xrightarrow{\text{conc.} H_2SO_4} CuSO_4 + 5H_2O$

3. $S + 2H_2SO_4 \text{ (conc.)} \longrightarrow 3SO_2 + 2H_2O$

Ans. 1. (*B*) Non-volatile acid 2. (*C*) Dehydrating agent

3. (*A*) Oxidising agent **(1 × 3 = 3)**

Q.4 *A*, *B*, *C* and *D* summarise the properties of sulphuric acid depending on whether it is dilute or concentrated.

A **= Typical acidic property**

B **= Non-volatile acid**

C **= Oxidising agent**

D **= Dehydrating agent**

Choose the property (*A*, *B*, *C* and *D*) depending on which is relevant to each of the following.

(i) Preparation of hydrogen chloride gas.

(ii) Preparation of copper sulphate from copper oxide.

(iii) Action of conc. sulphuric acid on carbon. **(ICSE 2016)**

Ans. (i) Preparation of hydrogen chloride gas from conc. H_2SO_4 depicts its **non-volatile nature (*B*)**.

$$\underset{\text{(Salt of volatile acid)}}{NaCl} + \underset{\text{(Non-volatile acid)}}{H_2SO_4\text{(conc)}} \longrightarrow \underset{\text{(Acid salt)}}{NaHSO_4} + \underset{\text{(Volatile acid)}}{HCl}$$

(1)

(ii) Preparation of copper sulphate from copper oxide is the property of dil. H_2SO_4 and depicts its **acidic property (*A*)**.

$$\underset{\text{(Copper oxide alkali)}}{CuO} + \underset{\text{(Sulphuric acid)}}{H_2SO_4} \longrightarrow \underset{\text{(Copper sulphate salt)}}{CuSO_4} + \underset{\text{(Water)}}{H_2O}$$

(1)

(iii) Action of conc. sulphuric acid on carbon depicts its **oxidising nature (C)**.

$$C + \underset{\text{(conc.)}}{2H_2SO_4} \longrightarrow CO_2 + 2H_2O + 2SO_2\uparrow$$

(1)

Q.5 Give one significant observation when

(i) a solution of barium chloride is added to zinc sulphate solution.

(ii) lead nitrate is heated in a test tube.

(iii) chlorine gas is passed over moist starch iodide paper. **(ICSE 2025)**

Ans. (i) When a solution of barium chloride is added to zinc sulphate solution, a **white precipitate** of barium sulphate is formed.

$$BaCl_2(aq) + ZnSO_4(aq) \rightarrow ZnCl_2(aq) + \underset{\text{(white ppt.)}}{BaSO_4(s)\downarrow}$$

(1)

(ii) When lead nitrate is heated in a test tube, the formation of **yellow lead oxide** and the release of **reddish brown fumes of nitrogen dioxide gas** takes place.

$$2Pb(NO_3)_2(s) \longrightarrow \underset{\text{(Yellow residue)}}{2PbO(s)} + \underset{\text{(Reddish-brown fumes)}}{4NO_2(g)} + O_2(g)$$

(1)

(iii) When chlorine gas is passed over moist starch iodide paper, the paper turns **blue-black**. This is because chlorine **oxidises iodide ions to iodine**, and then iodine reacts with starch to form a blue-black complex. **(1)**

Q.6 Write complete and balanced equations for the reactions occurring in the following cases **(Competency Based Que.)**

(i) Passing dry ammonia gas over heated lead oxide placed in a combustion tube to produce a silvery grey metal.

(ii) When concentrated nitric acid is reacted with zinc to produce a reddish-brown gas.

(iii) When concentrated sulphuric acid oxidises sulphur to produce a gas which turns acidified potassium dichromate paper green.

Ans. (i) $\underset{\text{(Yellow)}}{3PbO} + 2NH_3 \longrightarrow \underset{\text{(Greyish)}}{3Pb} + 3H_2O + N_2\uparrow$

(ii) $Zn + 4HNO_3 \longrightarrow Zn(NO_3)_2 + 2H_2O + \underset{\text{(Reddish-brown gas)}}{2NO_2\uparrow}$

(iii) $2H_2SO_4 + S \longrightarrow 3SO_2\uparrow + 2H_2O$ **(3)**

Q.7 You are provided with some compound in the box.

PbO	CH_4	PbO_2	CO_2
HCl	NCl_3	SO_2	

Choose the most appropriate compound which fits the descriptions (a) to (c) given below

(i) A colourless gas which turns acidic fied $K_2Cr_2O_7$ from orange to green.

(ii) A yelow explosive oily liquid formed when excess chlorine gas reacts with ammonia gas.

(iii) A yellow metallic oxide formed on thermal decomposition of $PbCO_3$. **(ICSE 2025)**

Ans. (i) SO_2

$$\underset{\text{(Orange)}}{K_2Cr_2O_7} + H_2SO_4 + 3SO_2 \longrightarrow \underset{\text{(Green)}}{Cr_2(SO_4)_3} + K_2SO_4 + H_2O$$ **(1)**

(ii) NCl_3

$$NH_3 + \underset{\text{(Excess)}}{3Cl_2} \longrightarrow 3HCl + NCl_3$$ **(1)**

(iii) **PbO**

$$PbCO_3 \xrightarrow{\Delta} \underset{\text{(Yellow)}}{PbO} + CO_2\uparrow$$ **(1)**

TYPE - 9 04/05 Marks

Long Answer Type Questions

Q.1 Write the balanced chemical equations for the following.

(i) Reaction of concentrated sulphuric acid with carbon. **(ICSE 2025, 2018, 2014)**

(ii) Action of concentrated sulphuric acid on sulphur. **(ICSE 2017)**

(iii) Action of dilute sulphuric acid on sodium sulphite. **(ICSE 2016)**

(iv) Dehydration of sugar with concentrated sulphuric acid crystals. **(ICSE 2016)**

Ans. (i) $C + \underset{\text{Conc. sulphuric acid}}{2H_2SO_4} \longrightarrow \underset{\text{Carbon dioxide}}{CO_2} + 2H_2O + \underset{\text{Sulphur dioxide}}{2SO_2\uparrow}$

(ii) Concentrated sulphuric acid on reaction with sulphur gives sulphur dioxide as major product.

$$\underset{\text{Sulphur}}{S} + \underset{\text{Conc. sulphuric acid}}{2H_2SO_4} \longrightarrow \underset{\text{Sulphur dioxide}}{3SO_2} + 2H_2O$$

(iii) $\underset{\text{Sodium sulphite}}{Na_2SO_3} + \underset{\text{(Dil.)}}{H_2SO_4} \longrightarrow \underset{\text{Sodium sulphate}}{Na_2SO_4} + H_2O + \underset{\text{Sulphur dioxide}}{SO_2\uparrow}$

(iv) $\underset{\text{Cane sugar}}{C_{12}H_{22}O_{11}} \xrightarrow{\text{Conc. } H_2SO_4} \underset{\text{Sugar charcoal}}{12C} + 11H_2O$ **(1 × 4 = 4)**

Q.2 (i) Name the process used for the large scale manufacturing of sulphuric acid.

(ii) Which property of sulphuric acid accounts for its use as a dehydrating agent?

(iii) Concentrated sulphuric acid acts as both an oxidising agent and a non-volatile acid. Write one equation each to illustrate the above mentioned properties of sulphuric acid.

Ans. (i) **Contact process** is used for the large scale manufacturing of sulphuric acid. **(1)**

(ii) Sulphuric acid has a great affinity for water. It readily removes molecules of water from other compounds, i.e. it acts as a dehydrating agent. **(1)**

(iii) As an **oxidising agent.**

$$S + \underset{\text{(Conc.)}}{2H_2SO_4} \longrightarrow 3SO_2 + 2H_2O$$

As a **non-volatile acid.**

$$NaNO_3 + \underset{\text{(conc.)}}{H_2SO_4} \longrightarrow NaHSO_4 + HNO_3$$ **(2)**

Q.3 (i) Give balanced chemical equations for the action of sulphuric acid on each of the following

(a) Potassium hydrogen carbonate

(b) Sulphur

(ii) In the contact process for the manufacture of sulphuric acid, give the equations for the conversion of sulphur trioxide to sulphuric acid. **(ICSE 2015)**

Ans. (i) (a) $\underset{\text{Potassium hydrogen carbonate}}{2KHCO_3} + \underset{\text{(Dil.)}}{H_2SO_4} \longrightarrow \underset{\text{Potassium sulphate}}{K_2SO_4} + \underset{\text{Carbon dioxide}}{2CO_2\uparrow} + 2H_2O$ **(1)**

(b) $\underset{\text{Sulphur}}{S} + \underset{\text{(Conc.)}}{2H_2SO_4} \longrightarrow \underset{\text{Sulphur dioxide}}{3SO_2} + 2H_2O$ **(1)**

(ii) (a) **Conversion of sulphur trioxide into oleum**

$$SO_3 + H_2SO_4 \longrightarrow \underset{\text{Oleum or pyrosulphuric acid}}{H_2S_2O_7}$$ **(1)**

(b) **Dilution of oleum**

$$H_2S_2O_7 + H_2O \longrightarrow \underset{\text{Sulphuric acid}}{2H_2SO_4}$$ **(1)**

Q.4 **Write balanced chemical equations to show**

(i) The oxidising action of conc. sulphuric acid on carbon.

(ii) The behaviour of H_2SO_4 as an acid when it reacts with magnesium.

(iii) The dehydrating property of conc. sulphuric acid with sugar. **(ICSE 2017)**

Ans. (i) Carbon on reaction with conc. H_2SO_4 gives CO_2, SO_2 and water.

$$\underset{\text{Carbon}}{C} + \underset{\text{Conc. sulphuric acid}}{2H_2SO_4} \longrightarrow \underset{\text{Carbon dioxide}}{CO_2} + 2H_2O + \underset{\text{Sulphur dioxide}}{2SO_2\uparrow}$$ **(1)**

(ii) Dilute sulphuric acid reacts with metals, which are present above hydrogen in the activity series to form metallic sulphate ($MgSO_4$) and hydrogen gas at ordinary temperature.

$$\underset{\text{Magnesium}}{Mg} + H_2SO_4 \longrightarrow MgSO_4 + H_2\uparrow$$ **(2)**

(iii) Carbohydrates (like sugar) are dehydrated by conc. H_2SO_4.

$$\underset{\text{Cane sugar}}{C_{12}H_{22}O_{11}(s)} \xrightarrow{\text{Conc. } H_2SO_4} \underset{\text{Charcoal}}{12C(s)} + 11H_2O$$ **(1)**

Q.5 (i) **Name the catalyst which helps in the conversion of sulphur dioxide to sulphur trioxide.**

(ii) In the contact process for the manufacturing of sulphuric acid, sulphur trioxide is not converted to sulphuric acid by reacting it with water. Instead a two steps procedure is used. Write the equations for these two steps involved.

(iii) What type of substance will liberate sulphur dioxide from sodium sulphite?

(iv) Write the equation for the reaction by which sulphur dioxide is converted to sodium sulphite.

Ans. (i) Vanadium pentoxide (V_2O_5) **(1)**

(ii) $H_2SO_4 + SO_3 \longrightarrow \underset{\text{Oleum}}{H_2S_2O_7}$

$H_2S_2O_7 + H_2O \longrightarrow 2H_2SO_4$ **(2)**

(iii) Dilute acid like H_2SO_4

$Na_2SO_3 + H_2SO_4 \longrightarrow Na_2SO_4 + H_2O + SO_2\uparrow$ **(1)**

(iv) $SO_2 + 2NaOH \longrightarrow Na_2SO_3 + H_2O$ **(1)**

Q.6 (i) **With the help of equations, give an outline for the manufacturing of sulphuric acid by the contact process.**

(ii) What property of sulphuric acid is shown by the reaction of concentrated sulphuric acid? When heated with

(a) potassium nitrate **(b) carbon**

Ans. (i) $S + O_2 \longrightarrow SO_2$

$$2SO_2 + O_2 \underset{450°C}{\overset{V_2O_5}{\rightleftharpoons}} 2SO_3$$

$$SO_3 + H_2SO_4 \longrightarrow \underset{\text{Oleum}}{H_2S_2O_7}$$

$$H_2S_2O_7 + H_2O \longrightarrow 2H_2SO_4$$ **(3)**

(ii) (a) **Non-volatile nature**

$$KNO_3 + H_2SO_4 \longrightarrow KHSO_4 + HNO_3$$

(b) **Oxidising nature**

$$C + 2H_2SO_4 \longrightarrow CO_2 + 2H_2O + 2SO_2\uparrow$$ **(2)**

Q.7 **Write balanced chemical equations for the following.**

(i) (a) Action of warm water on aluminium nitride.

(b) Oxidation of carbon with conc. nitric acid.

(c) Dehydration of ethanol by conc. sulphuric acid at a temperature of 170°C. **(ICSE Specimen 2024)**

(ii) (a) Carbon from cane sugar and concentrated sulphuric acid.

(b) Ammonium sulphate from ammonium hydroxide and sulphuric acid.

(ICSE 2021-2022, Sem-II)

Ans. (i) (a) The given reaction is represented as:

$$\underset{\text{Aluminium nitride}}{AlN} + \underset{\text{Water}}{3H_2O} \longrightarrow \underset{\text{Aluminium hydroxide}}{Al(OH)_3} + \underset{\text{Ammonia}}{NH_3}$$

(b) $C + \underset{\text{(Conc.)}}{4HNO_3} \longrightarrow CO_2 + 4NO_2 + 2H_2O$

(c) $\underset{\text{Ethanol}}{CH_3CH_2OH} \xrightarrow[170°C]{\text{Conc. } H_2SO_4} \underset{\text{Ethene}}{CH_2{=}CH_2} + H_2O$ **(3)**

(ii) (a) Sugar reacts with concentrated sulphuric acid to give sugar charcoal and water.

$$C_{12}H_{22}O_{11}(s) \xrightarrow{\text{Conc. } H_2SO_4} \underset{\text{Sugar charcoal}}{12C(s)} + 11H_2O$$ **(1)**

(b) Ammonium hydroxide reacts with sulphuric acid to form ammonium sulphate and water.

$$\underset{\text{Ammonium hydroxide}}{2NH_4OH} + \underset{\text{Sulphuric acid}}{H_2SO_4} \longrightarrow \underset{\text{Ammonium sulphate}}{(NH_4)_2SO_4} + \underset{\text{Water}}{2H_2O}$$ **(1)**

Q.8 (i) **State your observations for the following cases.**

(a) Moist blue litmus is introduced into a gas jar of sulphur dioxide.

(b) Dry red rose petals are placed in the jar of sulphur dioxide.

(c) Paper soaked in potassium permanganate solution is introduced into a gas jar of sulphur dioxide.

(d) Action of concentrated sulphuric acid on hydrated copper sulphate. **(ICSE 2017)**

(ii) Differentiate between the following pairs based on the criteria given **(ICSE 2024)**
Sulphuric acid and nitric acid (using barium chloride solution)

Ans. (i) (a) Moist blue litmus paper **turns red**. **(1)**

(b) Dry sulphur dioxide gas has **no effect** on dry red rose petals, because there is absence of moisture or water. **(1)**

(c) It reduces the pink colour of potassium permanganate to **colourless**. **(1)**

(d) Concentrated sulphuric acid removes water of crystallisation from salts. Due to which, blue coloured salt changes into **white colour**.

$$\underset{\text{Blue}}{CuSO_4 \cdot 5H_2O} \xrightarrow{\text{Conc. } H_2SO_4} \underset{\text{Dirty white}}{CuSO_4(s)} + 5H_2O$$ **(1)**

(ii) Sulphuric acid gives white precipitate of barium sulphate when $BaCl_2$ solution is added to it.

$$BaCl_2 + H_2SO_4 \longrightarrow \underset{\text{White ppt.}}{BaSO_4\downarrow} + 2HCl$$

Nitric acid will not give any precipitate with barium chloride solution. **(1)**

Q.9 Some properties of sulphuric acid are listed below. Choose the role played by sulphuric acid as *A*, *B*, *C* or *D*, which is responsible for the reactions (i) to (v). Some role/s may be repeated.

(*A*) Dilute acid (*B*) Dehydrating agent
(*C*) Non-volatile acid (*D*) Oxidising agent

(i) $CuSO_4 \cdot 5H_2O \xrightarrow{\text{Conc. } H_2SO_4} CuSO_4 + 5H_2O$

(ii) $S + \underset{\text{(Conc.)}}{2H_2SO_4} \longrightarrow 3SO_2 + 2H_2O$

(iii) $NaNO_3 + \underset{\text{(Conc.)}}{H_2SO_4} \xrightarrow{<200°C} NaHSO_4 + HNO_3$

(iv) $MgO + H_2SO_4 \longrightarrow MgSO_4 + H_2O$

(v) $Zn + \underset{\text{(Conc.)}}{2H_2SO_4} \longrightarrow ZnSO_4 + SO_2\uparrow + 2H_2O$

Ans. (i) (*B*) Dehydrating agent (ii) (*D*) Oxidising agent
(iii) (*C*) Non-volatile acid (iv) (*A*) Dilute acid
(v) (*D*) Oxidising agent **(1 × 5 = 5)**

Q.10 Some properties of sulphuric acid are listed below. Choose the property *A*, *B*, *C* or *D* which is responsible for the reactions (i) to (v). Some properties may be repeated

(*A*) Acid (*B*) Dehydrating agent
(*C*) Non-volatile acid (*D*) Oxidising agent

(i) $C_{12}H_{22}O_{11} \xrightarrow{\text{Conc.} H_2SO_4} 12C + 11H_2O$

(ii) $Cu + \underset{\text{(Conc.)}}{2H_2SO_4} \longrightarrow CuSO_4 + 2H_2O + SO_2\uparrow$

(iii) $NaCl + H_2SO_4 \longrightarrow NaHSO_4 + HCl$

(iv) $CuO + H_2SO_4 \longrightarrow CuSO_4 + H_2O$

(v) $Na_2CO_3 + H_2SO_4 \longrightarrow Na_2SO_4 + H_2O + CO_2\uparrow$

Ans. (i) (*B*) Dehydrating agent (ii) (*D*) Oxidising agent
(iii) (*C*) Non-volatile acid (iv) (*A*) Acid
(v) (*A*) Acid **(1 × 5 = 5)**

TYPE - 10
03 Marks

Case-Based Question

Q.1 A student is studying the industrial production of sulphuric acid (H_2SO_4), which is one of the most important industrial chemical. Sulphuric acid is widely used in manufacturing fertilizers, petroleum refining, chemical synthesis and other applications.
The student learns that sulphuric acid is produced in large quantities through the Contact process. This process involves the oxidation of sulphur dioxide (SO_2) to sulphur trioxide (SO_3), which then forms sulphuric acid

(i) What is the first step in the Contact process for the production of sulphuric acid?
(ii) Which catalyst is used in the Contact process?
(iii) What is the last step in the Contact process?

Ans. (i) The first step in the Contact process is the **production of sulphur dioxide (SO_2)** which is typically obtained by roasting metal sulphides (like zinc blende or iron pyrites) or by burning Louisiana sulphur (99.5% pure) in purified air.

$$\underset{\text{(Iron pyrites)}}{4FeS_2} + 11O_2 \longrightarrow 2Fe_2O_3 + 8SO_2$$

or $$S + O_2 \longrightarrow SO_2$$ **(1)**

(ii) The catalyst used in the Contact process is **vanadium pentoxide (V_2O_5)**. It speeds up the oxidation of sulphur dioxide (SO_2) to sulphur trioxide (SO_3) without being consumed in process.

$$2SO_2 + O_2 \underset{450°C}{\overset{V_2O_5}{\rightleftharpoons}} 2SO_3$$ **(1)**

(iii) The last step involves the dissolution of sulphur trioxide (SO_3) to water to produce sulphuric acid (H_2SO_4). However, due to the violent reaction of SO_3 with water, it is first dissolved in concentrated sulphuric acid to form oleum, which is then diluted with water to produce sulphuric acid.

$$SO_3 + H_2SO_4 \longrightarrow \underset{\text{(Oleum or pyrosulphuric acid)}}{H_2S_2O_7}$$

$$H_2S_2O_7 + H_2O \longrightarrow 2H_2SO_4$$ **(1)**

09

ORGANIC CHEMISTRY

- The compounds of carbon except oxides, carbonate and carbides are called **organic compounds**. The chemistry dealing with them is called **organic chemistry**.
- **Friedrich Wohler** prepared first organic compound urea in laboratory from ammonium cyanate.

$$\underset{\text{(Inorganic compound)}}{\underset{\text{Ammonium cyanate}}{NH_4CNO}} \longrightarrow \underset{\text{(Organic compound)}}{\underset{\text{Urea}}{NH_2CONH_2}}$$

Versatile Nature of Carbon

Carbon forms a large number of organic compounds due to its unique properties.

Tetravalency of Carbon

Carbon atom has 4 electrons in its outermost shell, its valency is 4, i.e. it is capable of bonding or pairing with four other carbon atoms or with the atoms of some other monovalent elements like hydrogen, halogen (chlorine, bromine), etc.

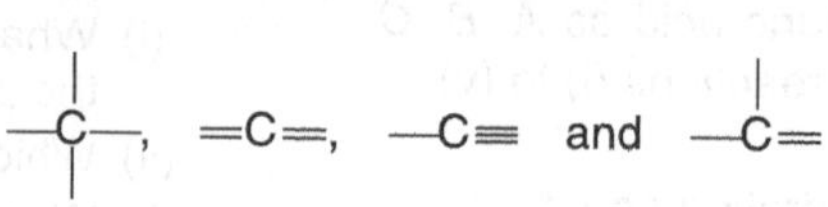

Catenation

- The property of self linking of elements, mainly C-atoms through covalent bonds to form long, straight or branched chains and rings of different sizes is called **catenation**.
- **Carbon** shows maximum catenation in the periodic table due to its **small size**. This enables the nucleus to hold on to the shared pairs of electrons strongly and C — C bond becomes strong.

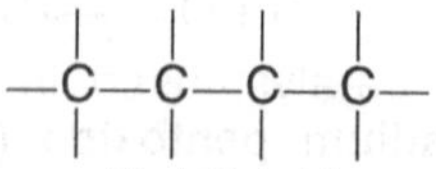
(Straight chain)

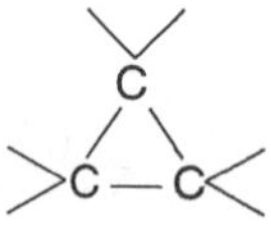
(Cyclic ring)

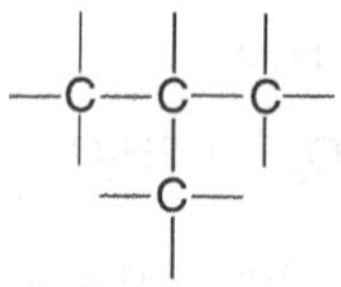
(Branched chain)

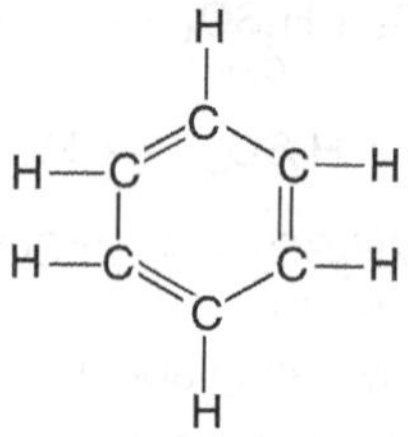
Cyclic compound (Benzene)

Tendency to form Multiple Bonds

Catenation and tetravalency also results in the formation of multiple bonds (double and triple bonds).

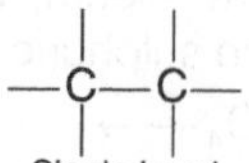
Single bond

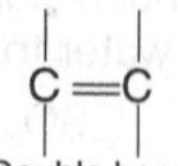
Double bond

Triple bond

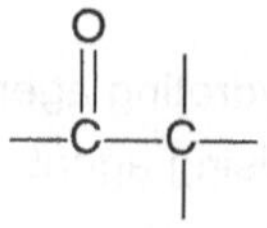
(Double bond with oxygen)

(Triple bond with N-atom)

REVISION NOTES

Structural Formula

A formula which shows the arrangement of atoms in the molecule of a compound is called **structural formula.**

e.g. Pentane (C_5H_{12}) can be represented as

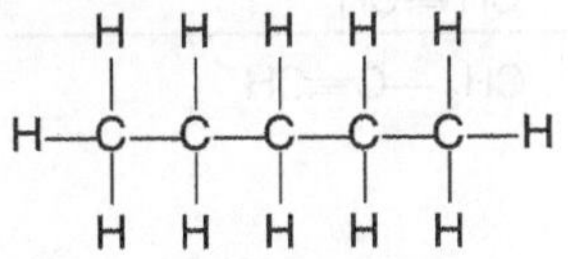

(Structural formula)

Similarly, it can also be written as $CH_3—CH_2—CH_2—CH_2—CH_3$ (Condensed formula).

Structural Formulae of Alkanes (Upto Five Carbon Atoms)

Name	Molecular formula	Structural formula
Methane	CH_4	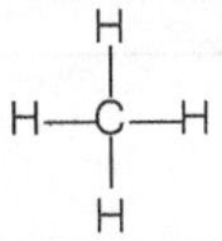
Ethane	C_2H_6	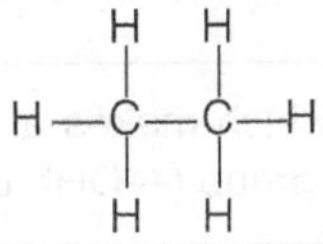
Propane	C_3H_8	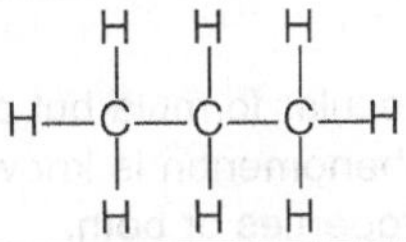
Butane	C_4H_{10}	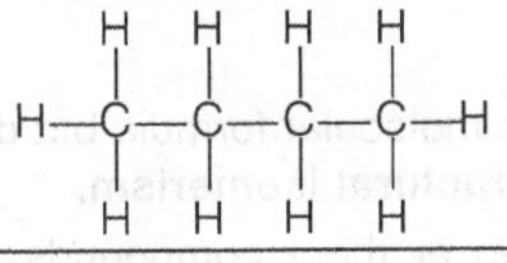
Pentane	C_5H_{12}	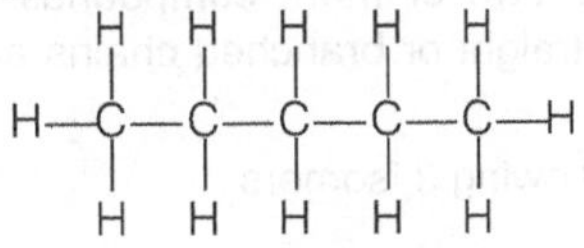

Structural Formulae of Alkenes (Upto Five Carbon Atoms)

Name	Molecular formula	Condensed formula	Structural formula
Ethene	C_2H_4	$CH_2=CH_2$	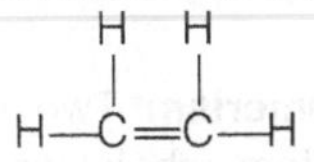
Propene	C_3H_6	$CH_3—CH=CH_2$	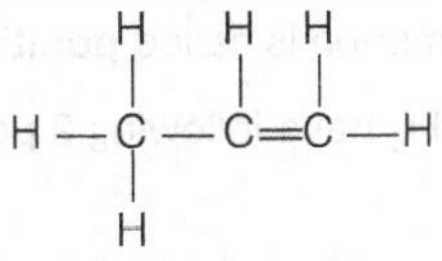
Butene	C_4H_8	$CH_3—CH_2—CH=CH_2$	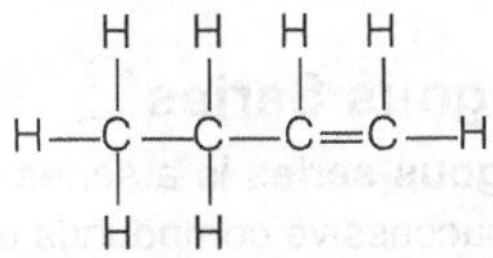
Pentene	C_5H_{10}	$CH_3—CH_2—CH_2—CH=CH_2$	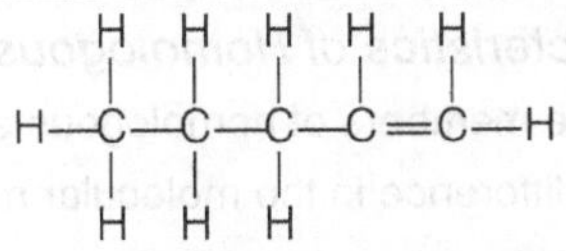

Structural Formulae of Alkynes (Upto Five Carbon Atoms)

Name	Molecular formula	Condensed formula	Structural formula
Ethyne	C_2H_2	$CH\equiv CH$	$H-C\equiv C-H$
Propyne	C_3H_4	$CH_3-C\equiv CH$	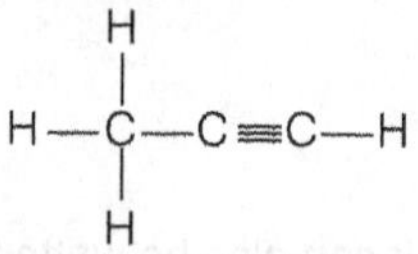
Butyne	C_4H_6	$CH_3-CH_2C\equiv CH$	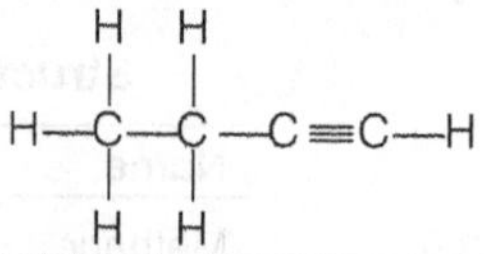
Pentyne	C_5H_8	$CH_3-CH_2-CH_2-C\equiv CH$	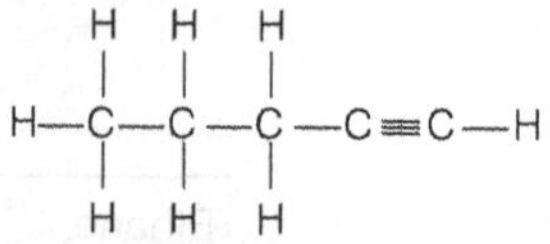

Note An atom or a group of atoms which makes a carbon compound reactive and decide its properties is called a **functional group**. e.g. Alcohol group (—OH), carbonyl group (—COOH), etc.

Isomerism

Compounds having the same molecular formula but different properties due to difference in structure or arrangement are known as **isomers** and the phenomenon is known as **isomerism** (*iso* = same, *meros* = parts). Isomers differ in physical properties or chemical properties or both.

Structural Isomerism

Compounds having the same molecular formula but different structural formula are called **structural isomers** and this phenomenon is called **structural isomerism.**

(i) **Chain isomerism** Two or more compounds having similar molecular formula but different arrangement of carbon atoms in straight or branched chains are known as **chain isomers** and the phenomenon is termed as **chain isomerism.**

e.g. C_5H_{12} have following 3 isomers

$CH_3CH_2CH_2CH_2CH_3$,
Pentane

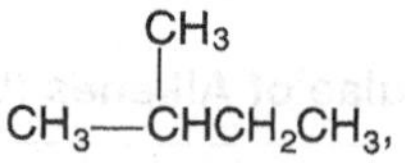
2-methylbutane

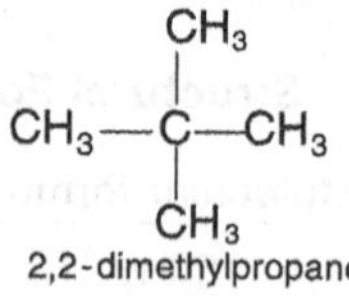
2,2-dimethylpropane

(ii) **Position isomerism** Two or more compounds having similar molecular formula but different position of substituent atom (chain) or functional group on the carbon atom are known as **position isomers** and the phenomenon is called **position isomerism.**

e.g. C_4H_6 have following 2 position isomers.

$\overset{4}{CH_3}-\overset{3}{C}\equiv\overset{2}{C}-\overset{1}{CH_3}$, $\overset{4}{CH_3}-\overset{3}{CH_2}-\overset{2}{C}\equiv\overset{1}{C}-H$

But-2-yne　　But-1-yne

Homologous Series

A **homologous series** is a series of organic compounds having similar structure and similar chemical properties in which the successive compounds differ by **—CH_2 units.**

Characteristics of Homologous Series

- All the members of homologous series can be represented by the **same general formula.**
- The difference in the molecular mass of any two adjacent homologous is **14 u** as they differ by —CH_2 group.
- All the compounds of homologous series show more or less **similar chemical properties.**

- The members of homologous series show a **gradual change in their physical properties** such as melting point, etc., with increase in molecular mass.
  E.g. melting point, boiling point and the density of the successive members of the homologous series increases with the increase in molecular mass.
- All the members of homologous series can be **prepared by the similar methods**.

Examples of Homologous Series

1. Alkanes

General formula for alkanes is C_nH_{2n+2}.

	Value of *n* in general formula, C_nH_{2n+2}	Molecular formula	IUPAC name	Molecular mass
	$n = 1$	CH_4	Methane	16
Alkanes	$n = 2$	C_2H_6	Ethane	30
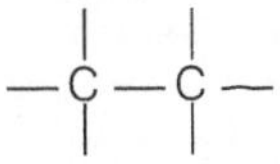	$n = 3$	C_3H_8	Propane	44
	$n = 4$	C_4H_{10}	Butane	58
	$n = 5$	C_5H_{12}	Pentane	72

2. Alkenes

General formula for alkenes is C_nH_{2n}.

	Value of *n* in general formula, C_nH_{2n}	Molecular formula	IUPAC name	Molecular mass
	$n = 1$	–	–	–
Alkenes	$n = 2$	C_2H_4	Ethene	28
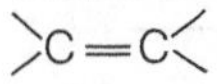	$n = 3$	C_3H_6	Propene	42
	$n = 4$	C_4H_8	Butene	56
	$n = 5$	C_5H_{10}	Pentene	70

3. Alkynes

General formula for alkynes is C_nH_{2n-2}.

	Value of *n* in general formula, C_nH_{2n-2}	Molecular formula	IUPAC name	Molecular mass
	$n = 1$	–	–	–
Alkynes	$n = 2$	C_2H_2	Ethyne	26
	$n = 3$	C_3H_4	Propyne	40
	$n = 4$	C_4H_6	Butyne	54
	$n = 5$	C_5H_8	Pentyne	68

Significance of the Homologous Series

(i) The nature of any member of that family of compounds can be found.

(ii) It helps to predict the properties of even those members of the series that are yet to be prepared.

(iii) It saves learning time as it is useful for the systematic study of organic chemistry.

Nomenclature of Organic Compounds

The **IUPAC names** have been adopted by the International Union of Pure and Applied Chemistry and are based on certain rules.

According to this system, the name of an organic compound consist of three parts :

(i) Root word (ii) Suffix (iii) Prefix

- **Root word** It indicates the number of carbon atoms present in a hydrocarbon (or any other organic compound). Some of the root words are tabulated below.

Number of carbon atoms	Root word
One carbon atom (C_1)	Meth
Two carbon atoms (C_2)	Eth
Three carbon atoms (C_3)	Prop
Four carbon atoms (C_4)	But
Five carbon atoms (C_5)	Pent
Six carbon atoms (C_6)	Hex
Seven carbon atoms (C_7)	Hept
Eight carbon atoms (C_8)	Oct
Nine carbon atoms (C_9)	Non
Ten carbon atoms (C_{10})	Dec

- **Suffix** It is always added to the root word usually to indicate the functional groups present in the molecule.

Types of carbon chain	Suffix	General name
C—C (Single bond)	– ane	Alkane
C═C (Double bond)	– ene	Alkene
C≡C (Triple bond)	– yne	Alkyne

- **Prefix** It denotes the substituent, alkyl or functional group and its position in the carbon chain.

e.g.

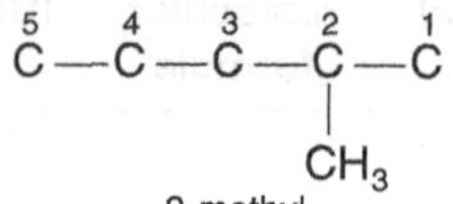

2-methyl
(Methyl group is attached to second C-atom)

Di, tri, tetra are used for two, three and four groups of the same type, respectively.

An **alkyl group** is obtained by removing one atom of hydrogen from an alkane molecule.

$$\underset{\text{Alkane}}{C_nH_{2n+2}} \xrightarrow{-H} \underset{\text{Alkyl}}{—C_nH_{2n+1}}$$

Thus, general formula of alkyl is $—C_nH_{2n+1}$.

IUPAC Rules for Naming an Organic Compound

- While writing the IUPAC name, first of all the longest continuous chain of 'C' atoms, known as **parent chain**, is selected. Remember, the longest chain is not always necessarily straight.

e.g.

$$\overset{1}{C}—\overset{2}{C}—\overset{3}{C}—\overset{4}{C}—\overset{5}{C}$$

Longest chain have 5 carbon atoms, so root word is 'pent'.

- The carbon atoms of the longest carbon chain are numbered in such a way that the alkyl groups (substituents) get the **lowest possible number**.

e.g.

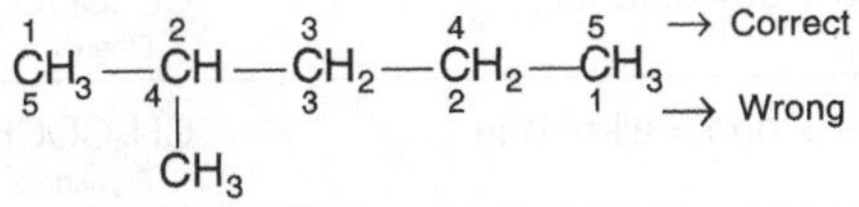

2-methylpentane

- Branch chains are also considered as substituents and their positions are indicated by the number of carbon atom to which they are attached like methyl (—CH_3) or ethyl (—C_2H_5) group.

e.g.

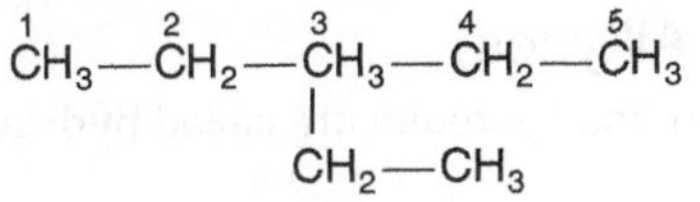

3-ethylpentane

- The IUPAC name of the compound is obtained by writing the position and name of alkyl group just before the name of parent 'hydrocarbon'.

e.g.

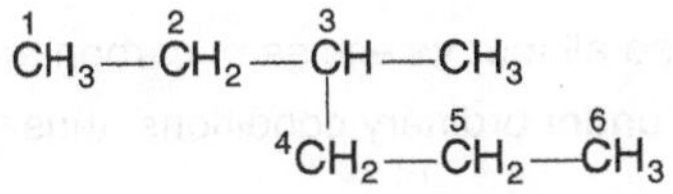

3-methylhexane

- Multiple alkyl groups are labelled as di for two, tri for three and tetra for four. If the two alkyl groups are on the same carbon atom, the **numeral is repeated**.

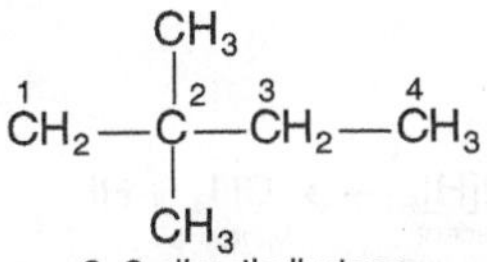

2, 2-dimethylbutane

- If the functional group is also present in the chain, then carbon atoms are numbered in such a way that the functional group gets the smallest possible number.

e.g.

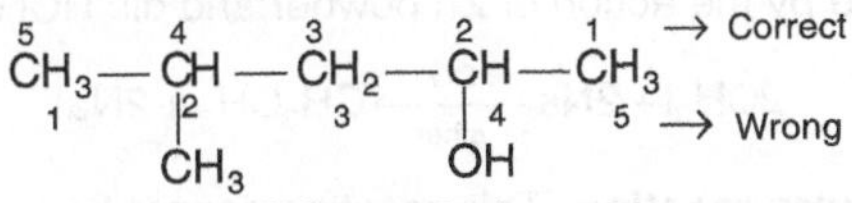

4-methylpentan-2-ol

- If different types of substituents are attached in the chain, they are preferred **alphabetically**.

e.g.

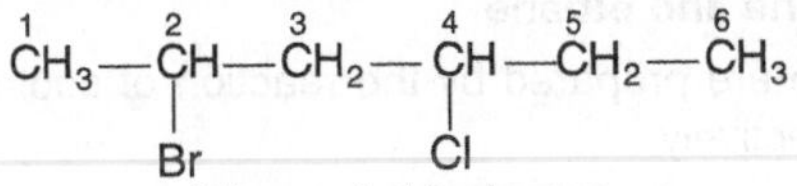

2-bromo-4-chlorohexane

Functional Groupwise Nomenclature

Functional group	General representation	Example
Alkane	Rootword + ane = alkane	$CH_3CH_2CH_2CH_3$ *n*-butane
Alkene	Alkane – ane + ene = alkene	$CH_2{=}CH{-}CH_2{-}CH_3$ But-1-ene
Alkyne	Alkane – ane + yne = alkyne	$CH_3{-}C{\equiv}C{-}CH_3$ But-2-yne
Alcohol	Alkane – e + ol = alkanol	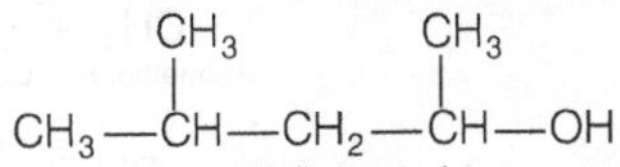 4-methylbutan-2-ol

Functional group	General representation	Example
Aldehyde	Alkane – e + al = alkanal	CH_3CHO Ethanal
Ketone	Alkane – e + one = alkanone	CH_3COCH_3 Propanone
Carboxylic group	Alkane – e + oic acid = alkanoic acid	CH_3CH_2COOH Propanoic acid

Hydrocarbons (Alkanes, Alkenes, Alkynes)

The organic compounds containing only carbon and hydrogen are called **hydrocarbons**. e.g. CH_4, C_2H_6, C_2H_4, etc.

Alkanes

- An alkane is a hydrocarbon in which all the linkages between the carbon atoms are **single covalent bonds**.
- General formula of alkanes is C_nH_{2n+2}.
- Alkanes are **saturated hydrocarbons** because all four valencies of carbon are fully satisfied with single bonds.
- These hydrocarbons are relatively unreactive under ordinary conditions, thus, they are also known as **paraffins**.

I. Methane and Ethane

The chemical formula of methane and ethane are CH_4 and C_2H_6 respectively. Methane is known as both **marsh gas** and **greenhouse gas**.

Preparation

(i) **From iodomethane and bromoethane**

(a)

$$\underset{}{CH_3I} + \underset{\text{Nascent hydrogen}}{2[H]} \longrightarrow \underset{\text{Methane}}{CH_4} + HI$$

$$C_2H_5Br + 2[H] \longrightarrow \underset{\text{Ethane}}{C_2H_6} + HBr$$

Nascent hydrogen [H] is prepared by the action of Zn powder and dil. HCl or Zn/Cu couple in alcohol.

(b)

$$2CH_3I + 2Na \xrightarrow[\text{ether}]{\text{Dry}} CH_3CH_3 + 2NaI$$

This reaction is referred to as **Wurtz reaction**. This reaction cannot be used to prepare methane. It is also not suitable for the preparation of alkanes with odd number of carbon atoms.

(ii) **Laboratory preparation of methane and ethane**

In laboratory, methane and ethane are prepared by the reaction of sodium ethanoate and sodium propionate with soda lime (NaOH + CaO) respectively.

$$CH_3COO^-Na^+ + NaOH \xrightarrow[300°C]{\text{Heat/CaO}} Na_2CO_3 + \underset{\text{Methane}}{CH_4} \uparrow$$

$$C_2H_6COO^-Na^+ + NaOH \xrightarrow[300°C]{\text{Heat/CaO}} Na_2CO_3 + \underset{\text{Ethane}}{C_2H_6} \uparrow$$

Physical Properties

- They both are colourless and odourless gas.
- They are insoluble or sparingly soluble in water but soluble in organic solvents.

Chemical Properties

(i) **Reaction with halogens (Substitution reaction)**

Alkanes react with chlorine, bromine or iodine in the presence of sunlight to give substituted products.

(a)

$$\underset{\text{Methane}}{CH_4} + \underset{\text{Chlorine}}{Cl_2} \xrightarrow[\text{or 600 K}]{\text{Sunlight}} \underset{\text{Chloromethane}}{CH_3Cl} + \underset{\text{Hydrogen chloride}}{HCl}$$

$$CH_3Cl + Cl_2 \xrightarrow{\text{Sunlight}} \underset{\text{Dichloromethane}}{CH_2Cl_2} + HCl$$

REVISION NOTES

$$CH_2Cl_2 + Cl_2 \xrightarrow{\text{Sunlight}} \underset{\substack{\text{Trichloromethane}\\\text{(Chloroform)}}}{CHCl_3} + HCl$$

$$CHCl_3 + Cl_2 \xrightarrow{\text{Sunlight}} \underset{\text{Tetrachloromethane}}{CCl_4} + HCl$$

(b)

$$\underset{\text{Ethane}}{C_2H_6} + Cl_2 \xrightarrow{\text{Sunlight}} \underset{\text{Monochloroethane}}{C_2H_5Cl} + HCl$$

$$\underset{\text{Chloroethane}}{C_2H_5Cl} + Cl_2 \xrightarrow{\text{Sunlight}} \underset{\text{Dichloroethane}}{C_2H_4Cl_2} + HCl$$

$$\underset{\text{Dichloroethane}}{C_2H_4Cl_2} + Cl_2 \xrightarrow{\text{Sunlight}} \underset{\text{Trichloroethane}}{C_2H_3Cl_3} + HCl$$

$$\underset{\text{Trichloroethane}}{C_2H_3Cl_3} + Cl_2 \xrightarrow{\text{Sunlight}} \underset{\text{Tetrachloroethane}}{C_2H_2Cl_4} + HCl$$

$$\underset{\text{Tetrachloroethane}}{C_2H_2Cl_4} + Cl_2 \xrightarrow{\text{Sunlight}} \underset{\text{Pentachloroethane}}{C_2HCl_5} + HCl$$

$$\underset{\text{Pentachloroethane}}{C_2HCl_5} + Cl_2 \xrightarrow{\text{Sunlight}} \underset{\text{Hexachloroethane}}{C_2Cl_6} + HCl$$

(ii) **Reaction with oxygen (Combustion reaction)**

Methane and ethane burn in air with a **bluish non-sooty flame** to produce carbon dioxide and water vapour with a large amount of heat.

$$CH_4 + 2O_2 \longrightarrow CO_2 + 2H_2O + \text{Heat}$$

$$2C_2H_6 + 7O_2 \longrightarrow 4CO_2 + 6H_2O + \text{Heat}$$

$$2CH_4 + 3O_2 \longrightarrow 2CO + 4H_2O \quad \text{(In limited supply of air)}$$

$$CH_4 + O_2 \longrightarrow \underset{\text{(Soot)}}{C} + 2H_2O \quad \text{(In very low supply of air)}$$

Soot is used in the manufacture of printing inks and tyres.

Uses of Methane and Ethane

- **Methane** is a source of carbon monoxide and hydrogen. It is also used as a domestic fuel and in preparation of ethyne, methanol, methanal, carbon tetrachloride, etc.
- **Ethane** is used in the preparation of ethene, ethanol, ethanal and ethanoic acid. It is a good fuel. It forms ethyl chloride, which is used to make tetraethyl lead (anti-knocking agent). 1, 1, 1-trichloroethane is one solvent that is used in dry cleaning.

Alkenes

- Alkenes are **unsaturated hydrocarbons** containing at least one carbon-carbon double bond (—C=C—). Their general formula is C_nH_{2n}.
- The lower members of alkenes form oily products when they are treated with chlorine or bromine, so they are also called **olefins** (oil-forming).

Ethene (Ethylene)

It is the first member of alkene series. It is present in natural gas and in plants. It occurs as a plant hormone responsible for the **ripening of fruits**.

Preparation

1. Laboratory Preparation

Ethene is prepared by **dehydration** of ethyl alcohol with concentrated sulphuric acid at 170°C.

e.g. $$\underset{\text{Ethanol}}{C_2H_5OH} \xrightarrow[\text{170°C}]{\text{Conc. } H_2SO_4} \underset{\text{Ethene}}{C_2H_4} + H_2O$$

REVISION NOTES

2. By dehydrohalogenation

Ethene is also prepared by **dehydrohalogenation** of ethyl halide by using alcoholic potassium hydroxide.

$$\underset{\text{Ethyl halide}}{C_2H_5X} + \underset{\text{(Alcoholic, hot and conc.)}}{KOH} \xrightarrow{\Delta} \underset{\text{Ethene}}{C_2H_4} + KX + H_2O \qquad (X = Cl,\ Br \text{ or } I)$$

Physical Properties

- It is a colourless and inflammable gas with a pleasant odour.
- It is slightly soluble in water and highly soluble in organic solvents like alcohol, ether and chloroform.
- It is slightly less denser than air.

Chemical Properties

(i) **Addition of hydrogen** (Hydrogenation)

$$\underset{\text{Ethene}}{C_2H_4} + H_2 \xrightarrow[\text{Ni}]{200°C} \underset{\text{Ethane}}{C_2H_6}$$

(ii) **Addition of halogens** (Halogenation)

$$\underset{\text{Ethene}}{CH_2{=}CH_2} + \underset{\text{Chlorine}}{Cl_2} \longrightarrow \underset{\text{1,2-dichloroethane}}{CH_2Cl{-}CH_2Cl}$$

$$\underset{\text{Ethene}}{CH_2{=}CH_2} + \underset{\text{Bromine}}{Br_2} \xrightarrow{CCl_4} \underset{\text{1, 2-dibromomethane}}{CH_2Br{-}CH_2Br}$$

$$\underset{\text{Ethene}}{CH_2{=}CH_2} + \underset{\text{Iodine}}{I_2} \longrightarrow \underset{\text{1, 2-diiodoethane}}{CH_2I{-}CH_2I}$$

Uses of Ethene

It is used in the production of oxy-ethylene torch for **welding** and **cutting metals**, for **artificial ripening** and **preservation of fruits**. It is used in manufacture of polythene, hardening of oils and in manufacture of synthetic chemicals.

Alkynes

Alkynes are **unsaturated hydrocarbons** containing a carbon-carbon triple bond (—C≡C—). Their general formula is C_nH_{2n-2}.

Ethyne (*Acetylene*)

Its molecular formula is C_2H_2. It is the first member of the alkyne series. It is not found in free state, as it is an unsaturated hydrocarbon and is **highly reactive**.

Preparation

1. Laboratory Preparation of Ethyne

$$\underset{\text{Calcium carbide}}{CaC_2} + 2H_2O \longrightarrow \underset{\text{Calcium hydroxide}}{Ca(OH)_2} + \underset{\text{Acetylene}}{C_2H_2\uparrow}$$

This is an **exothermic reaction.**

2. Preparation from 1, 2-dibromoethane (Ethylene Dibromide)

$$\begin{matrix} CH_2Br \\ | \\ CH_2Br \end{matrix} + \underset{\text{(Alc.)}}{2KOH} \xrightarrow[200°C]{\text{Boiling}} \underset{\text{Ethyne}}{CH{\equiv}CH} + 2KBr + 2H_2O$$

Physical Properties

- It is a gas at ordinary temperature. It is slightly lighter than air.
- It is colourless and has ether-like sweet odour when it is pure, or it has garlic like odour when prepared from calcium carbide.
- It is slightly soluble in water but highly soluble in organic solvents like acetone and alcohol.

Chemical Properties

Due to the presence of triple bond between two carbon atoms, ethyne is highly reactive and give following addition reactions.

(i) **Addition of hydrogen (Catalytic hydrogenation)** Ethyne reacts with hydrogen gas in the presence of nickel catalyst to form ethene, which on further hydrogenation, finally forms ethane.

$$\underset{\text{Ethyne}}{CH \equiv CH} \xrightarrow[Ni]{+H_2} \underset{\text{Ethene}}{CH_2{=}CH_2} \xrightarrow[Ni]{+H_2} \underset{\text{Ethane}}{CH_3{-}CH_3}$$

(ii) **Addition of halogens** If one molecule of halogen (chlorine, bromine, iodine, etc.) is added to ethyne it gives dihaloethene, which on further addition of one molecule of halogen forms saturated tetrahaloethane.

$$\underset{\text{Ethyne}}{H{-}C{\equiv}C{-}H} + X_2 \longrightarrow \underset{\text{1, 2-dihaloethane}}{H{-}\overset{X}{\overset{|}{C}}{=}\overset{X}{\overset{|}{C}}{-}H} \xrightarrow{+X_2} \underset{\text{1,1,2,2-tetrahaloethane}}{H{-}\underset{X}{\underset{|}{\overset{X}{\overset{|}{C}}}}{-}\underset{X}{\underset{|}{\overset{X}{\overset{|}{C}}}}{-}H} \quad \text{(where, } X_2 = Cl_2, Br_2, I_2\text{)}$$

Uses of Ethyne

It is used for **welding** at very high temperature. Its mixture with oxygen is called **oxy-acetylene**. It is also used as an **illuminant** in oxy-acetylene lamp and for **artificial ripening** and **preservation of food**.

Chemical Tests to Distinguish between Alkanes, Alkenes and Alkynes

Test	Alkanes (Methane and ethane) Saturated compounds	Alkenes (Ethylene) Unsaturated compounds	Alkynes (Acetylene) Unsaturated compounds
On adding a few drops of bromine solution in carbon tetrachloride, to the hydrocarbon.	No change is observed.	The reddish brown colour of bromine solution gets decolourised.	The reddish brown colour gets decolourised.
On adding a few drops of alkaline potassium permanganate (purple colour) to the hydrocarbon.	No change is observed.	The purple colour fades.	The purple colour fades. **(Baeyer's test)** $\underset{\text{(Ethyne)}}{CH \equiv CH} + 4[O] \xrightarrow[\text{potassium permanganate}]{\text{Alkaline}} \underset{\text{(Oxalic acid)}}{COOH{-}COOH}$
On adding a few drops of ammoniacal cuprous chloride to hydrocarbon.	No change is observed.	No change is observed.	Red precipitate of copper acetylide is formed.
On adding ammoniacal silver nitrate	No change is observed.	No change is observed.	White precipitate of silver acetylide is formed.

Examiner's Favourite Top 10 Equations

1. $CH_3{-}CH_2{-}I + KOH(alc.) \longrightarrow CH_2{=}CH_2 + KI + H_2O$
2. $C_2H_5OH \xrightarrow[170°C]{\text{conc. } H_2SO_4} CH_2{=}CH_2 + H_2O$
3. $CH_4 + 4Cl_2 \xrightarrow{\text{Sunlight}} CCl_4 + 4HCl$
4. $\underset{Br}{\underset{|}{CH_2}}{-}\underset{Br}{\underset{|}{CH_2}} + 2KOH\ (alc.) \xrightarrow[\text{Boiling}]{200°C} H{-}C{\equiv}C{-}H + 2KBr + 2H_2O$
5. $C_2H_5COONa + NaOH \xrightarrow[CaO]{300°C} C_2H_6 + Na_2CO_3$
6. $C_2H_4 + H_2 \xrightarrow[200°C]{Ni} C_2H_6$
7. $2C_2H_6 + 7O_2 \longrightarrow 4CO_2 + 6H_2O$
8. $C_2H_4 + Cl_2 \longrightarrow \underset{Cl}{\underset{|}{H_2C}}{-}\underset{Cl}{\underset{|}{CH_2}}$
9. $CH_3I + 2[H] \xrightarrow[\text{Alcohol}]{\text{Zu/Cu Couple}} CH_4 + HI$
10. $CaC_2 + 2H_2O \longrightarrow Ca(OH)_2 + C_2H_2 \uparrow$

EXAM ORIENTED QUESTIONS

TYPE - 1   01 Mark

Multiple Choice Questions

Q.1 The number of C—H bonds in ethane molecule are

(a) four (b) six (c) eight (d) ten

Ans. (b) Ethane (C_2H_6)

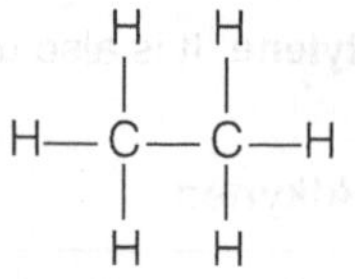

Number of C—H bonds in ethane is 6.

Q.2 An example of a cyclic organic compound is **(ICSE 2023)**

(a) propene (b) pentene
(c) butene (d) benzene

Ans. (d) Benzene

Q.3 The structures of four hydrocarbons are shown below **(ICSE Specimen 2025)**

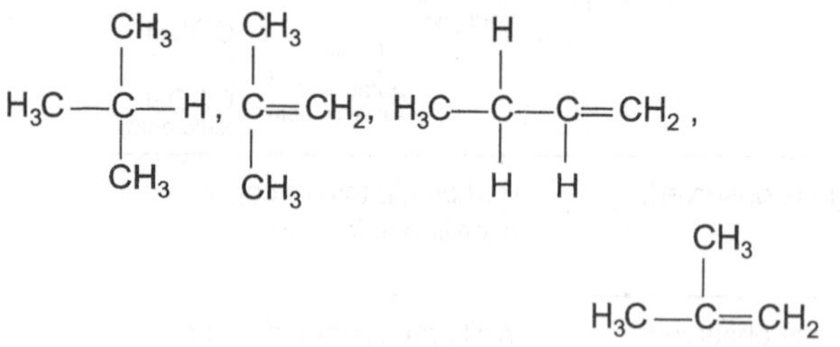

How many isomers of butene are there?

(a) 1 (b) 2 (c) 3 (d) 4

Ans. (c) 3

The molecular formula of butene is C_4H_{10}, thus isomers of butene are

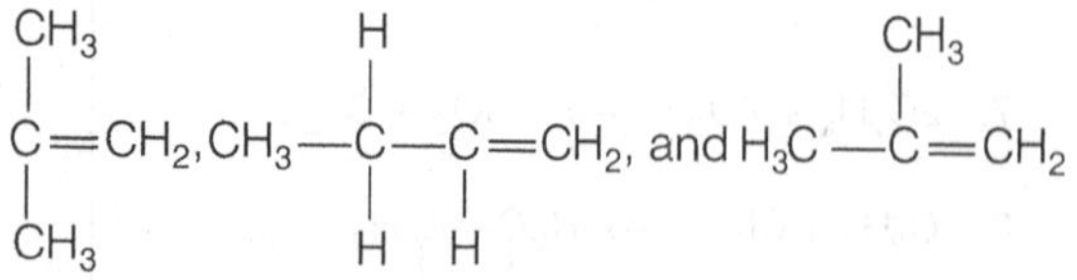

Q.4 Isomerism shown by pent-1-yne and 3-methylbut-1-yne is

(a) chain isomerism (b) position isomerism
(c) functional isomerism (d) stereoisomerism

Ans. (a) Chain isomerism

Q.5 The following are the structural diagrams of certain hydrocarbons **(Competency Based Que.)**

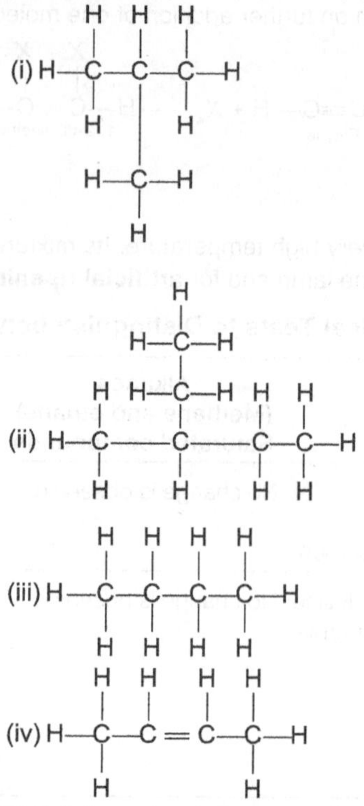

Which two structures are related to each other?

(a) (i) and (ii) (b) (ii) and (iii)
(c) (iii) and (iv) (d) (i) and (iii)

Ans. (d) (i) and (iii)

Q.6 The general formula of hydrocarbons with single covalent bonds is **(ICSE 2023)**

(a) C_nH_{2n+2} (b) C_nH_{2n}
(c) C_nH_{2n-2} (d) C_nH_{2n-6}

Ans. (a) C_nH_{2n+2}

Q.7 The structure of three hydrocarbons from the same homologous series are shown.

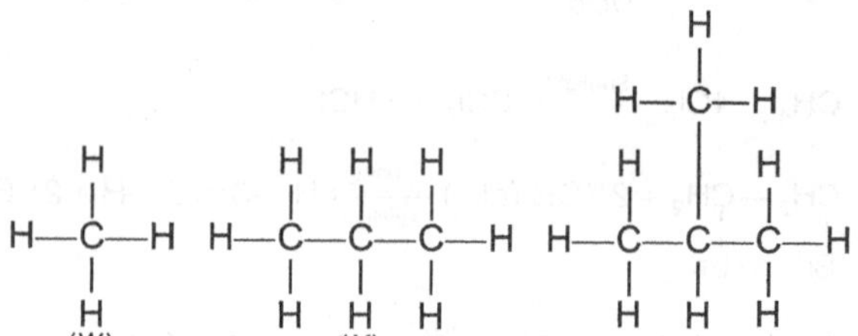

(W) (X) (Y)

Which statement is correct?

(a) All three molecules are unsaturated hydrocarbons.

(b) All three molecules have the same empirical formula.

(c) *W* has the lowest boiling point.

(d) *X* is an isomer of *Y*.

Ans. (c) *X*, *Y* and *Z* belong to the same homologous series of alkanes. The **boiling point of alkanes increases with the increase in the number of carbon atoms** in the alkane. All three molecules have different empirical formula and are saturated hydrocarbons. Also, *X* is not an isomer of *Y* as both of them have different molecular formula.

Q.8 Which of the following options has all the compounds which are members of the same homologous series? **(ICSE 2025)**

(a) CH_4, C_2H_6, C_3H_8

(b) CH_4, C_2H_6, C_3H_6

(c) C_3H_4, C_3H_6, C_3H_8

(d) C_2H_4, C_3H_6, C_4H_{10}

Ans. (a) The successive members of a homologous series differ by *a* **—CH_2 group**. Thus, CH_4, C_2H_6, C_3H_8 belong to the same homologous series.

Q.9 In the molecular formula of an organic compound is $C_{10}H_{18}$, it is **(ICSE 2017)**

(a) alkene (b) alkane

(c) alkyne (d) not a hydrocarbon

Ans. (c) alkyne

Q.10 The organic compound having a triple carbon-carbon covalent bond is **(ICSE 2020)**

(a) C_3H_4 (b) C_3H_6

(c) C_3H_8 (d) C_4H_{10}

Ans. (a) C_3H_4

Q.11 The IUPAC name of ethylene is **(ICSE Specimen 2023)**

(a) propane (b) propyne

(c) ethene (d) ethyne

Ans. (c) ethene

Q.12 The IUPAC name of acetylene is **(ICSE 2014)**

(a) propane (b) propyne

(c) ethene (d) ethyne

Ans. (d) ethyne

Q.13 The IUPAC name of methyl acetylene is

(a) propyne (b) ethene **(ICSE Specimen 2023)**

(c) propane (d) ethyne

Ans. (a) Propyne

Q.14 The IUPAC name of dimethyl ether is **(ICSE 2018)**

(a) ethoxy methane (b) methoxy methane

(c) methoxy ethane (d) ethoxy ethane

Ans. (b) methoxy methane

Q.15 Which formula represents a saturated hydrocarbon?

(a) C_4H_8 (b) C_5H_{12} **(ICSE 2025)**

(c) C_4H_6 (d) C_5H_{10}

Ans. (b) C_5H_{12} represents a saturated hydrocarbon as they are represented by the general formula C_nH_{2n+2}.

Q.16 A gas, which is also known as marsh gas

(a) ethane (b) methane

(c) ethene (d) None of these

Ans. (b) methane

Q.17 A hydrocarbon which is a greenhouse gas is

(a) acetylene (b) ethylene **(ICSE 2019)**

(c) ethane (d) methane

Ans. (d) methane

Q.18 The hydrocarbon formed when sodium propanoate and soda lime are heated together. **(ICSE 2023)**

(a) Methane (b) Ethane

(c) Ethene (d) Propane

Ans. (b) Ethane

Q.19 Substitution reaction is a characteristic property of **(ICSE Specimen 2021-22, Sem-I)**

(a) alcohols (b) alkanes

(c) alkenes (d) alkynes

Ans. (b) alkanes

Q.20 The organic compound which undergoes substitution reaction is **(ICSE 2018)**

(a) C_2H_2 (b) C_2H_4

(c) $C_{10}H_{18}$ (d) C_2H_6

Ans. (d) **C_2H_6 (ethane)** undergoes substitution reaction because it is a **saturated hydrocarbon**.

The rest of the options contains unsaturated hydrocarbons which undergoes addition reactions.

Q.21 Propane undergoes substitution reactions when mixed with chlorine gas in the presence of ultraviolet light.

Which compound could be formed when propane and chlorine are mixed in the presence of ultraviolet light?

(a) $CH_3CCl_2CH_3$ (b) CH_2ClCH_2Cl

(c) $CH_3CH_2CH_3Cl$ (d) $CH_3CHClCH_2CH_3$

Ans. (a) In the presence of chlorine gas, the hydrogen atoms in propane (C_3H_8) are substituted by chlorine atoms. It is possible for propane to form compounds where up to 8 hydrogen atoms are replaced by chlorine atoms.

Q.22 The hydrocarbon CH_3CHCH_2 will undergo a number of chemical reactions.

In which reaction will the carbon to carbon single bond be broken?

(a) Combustion with oxygen

(b) Hydrogenation

(c) Polymerisation

(d) Reaction with steam

Ans. (a) Combustion of hydrocarbons forms carbon dioxide and water. In the other three reactions, the C=C breaks and new atoms are added to the carbon atom.

Q.23 A 10 cm^3 sample of a gaseous hydrocarbon is completely burnt in oxygen. The total volume of the products is 70 cm^3.

Which equation represents the combustion of the hydrocarbon?

(a) $CH_4(g)+2O_2(g) \longrightarrow CO_2(g)+2H_2O(g)$

(b) $C_2H_4(g)+3O_2(g) \longrightarrow 2CO_2(g)+2H_2O(g)$

(c) $C_3H_8(g)+5O_2(g) \longrightarrow 3CO_2(g)+4H_2O(g)$

(d) $2C_2H_6(g)+7O_2(g) \longrightarrow 4CO_2(g)+6H_2O(g)$

Ans. (c) In gaseous chemical reactions, volume ratio is same as the mole ratio. In option (c), one mole of hydrocarbon gives seven moles of gaseous products, i.e. 30 cm^3 of CO_2 + 40 cm^3 of H_2O are produced as shown in equation.

Q.24 Identify the statement that is incorrect about alkanes.

(a) They are hydrocarbons.

(b) There is a single covalent bond between carbon and hydrogen.

(c) They can undergo both substitution as well as addition reactions.

(d) On complete combustion, they produce carbon dioxide and water.

Ans. (c) They can undergo only substitution reactions.

Q.25 Which of the following statements about ethane is false?

(a) It is a saturated hydrocarbon.

(b) It undergoes a substitution reaction.

(c) It is a gas at ordinary temperatures.

(d) It has a triple bond between the carbon atoms.

Ans. (d) Ethane has a single bond between the carbon atoms.

Q.26 Carbon to carbon double bond is found in **(ICSE Specimen 2021-22, Sem-I)**

(a) 2-butylene

(b) acetaldehyde

(c) acetic acid

(d) ethyl alcohol

Ans. (a) 2-butylene

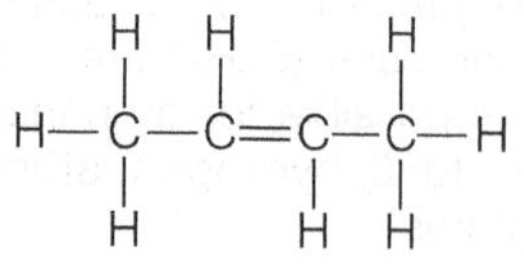

Q.27 Conversion of ethanol to ethene by the action of concentrated sulphuric acid involves **(ICSE 2024)**

(a) dehydration

(b) dehydrogenation

(c) dehydrohalogenation

(d) hydrolysis

Ans. (a) Dehydration

$$\underset{\text{Ethanol}}{C_2H_5OH} \xrightarrow{\text{Conc. } H_2SO_4,\ 170^\circ C} \underset{\text{Ethene}}{CH_2{=}CH_2} + H_2O$$

Q.28 Unsaturated hydrocarbons undergo **(ICSE 2024)**

(a) addition reaction (b) substitution reaction

(c) oxidation reaction (d) redox reaction

Ans. (a) Addition reaction

Q.29 A student investigated the reaction of different vegetable oils with hydrogen. 100 cm^3 of hydrogen was passed through 1 g samples of vegetable oils containing a suitable catalyst.

The volume of hydrogen remaining after each reaction was recorded.

Vegetable oil	Volume of hydrogen remaining/cm^3
P	100
Q	87
R	63
S	0

Which vegetable oils are unsaturated?

(a) Only *P*

(b) Only *Q* and *R*

(c) Only *Q*, *R* and *S*

(d) Only *S*

Ans. (c) Unsaturated compounds contain carbon to carbon multiple bonds, across which hydrogen can be added by breaking of the multiple bond. **Any change in volume of hydrogen shows unsaturation.**

Q.30 The formation of 1, 2-dibromoethane from ethene and bromine is an example of

(a) substitution reaction

(b) dehydration reaction

(c) dehydrohalogenation

(d) addition reaction

Ans. (d) The formation of 1, 2-dibromoethane from ethene and bromine is an example of **addition reaction**.

Q.31 Identify the statement which does not describe the property of alkenes. **(ICSE 2015)**

(a) They are unsaturated hydrocarbons.

(b) They decolourise bromine water.

(c) They can undergo addition as well as substitution reaction.

(d) They undergo combustion with oxygen forming carbon dioxide and water.

Ans. (c) They undergo addition reactions and not substitution reaction.

Q.32 The diagram shows the breakdown of an alkane to ethene.

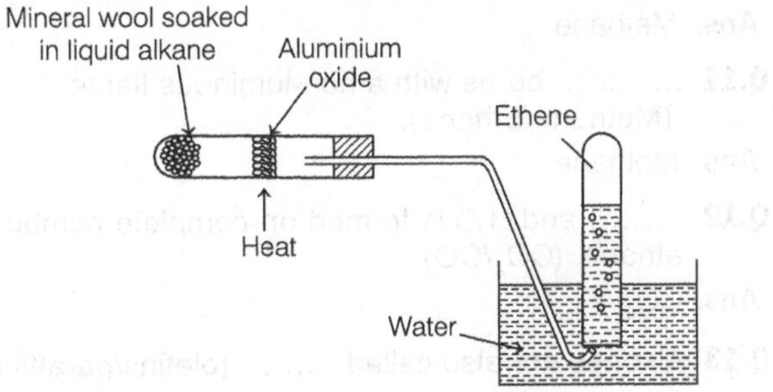

The ethene is then tested with aqueous bromine. Which information about ethene is correct?

	Solubility of ethene gas	Action on aqueous bromine
(a)	Insoluble	decolourised
(b)	Insoluble	no reaction
(c)	Soluble	decolourised
(d)	Soluble	no reaction

Ans. (a) Ethene being a non-polar hydrocarbon is **insoluble in water**, that is why it is collected over water. It being unsaturated hydrocarbon will decolourise aqueous bromine.

Q.33 Which of the following chains of hydrocarbons undergoes two steps of reactions to become saturated? **(Competency Based Que.)**

(a) 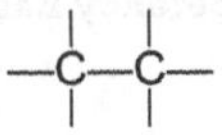

(b) 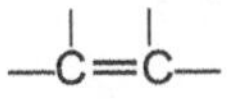

(c) 

(d) 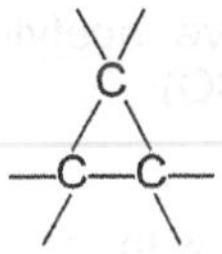

Ans. (c) 

Q.34 An organic compound undergoes addition reactions and gives a red colour precipitate with ammoniacal cuprous chloride. Therefore, the organic compound could be

(a) ethane
(b) ethene
(c) ethyne
(d) ethanol

Ans. (c) Ethyne

TYPE - 2 01 Mark

Assertion-Reasons Questions

Direction (Q. Nos. 1-5) In the following questions, a statement of Assertion (A) is followed by a statement of Reason (R). Choose the answer based on the codes given below.

(a) Both (A) and (R) are true and (R) is the correct explanation of (A).
(b) Both (A) and (R) are true but (R) is not the correct explanation of (A).
(c) (A) is true but (R) is false.
(d) (A) is false but (R) is true.

Q.1 Assertion (A) Carbon shows maximum catenation property in the periodic table.

Reason (R) Carbon has a small size and thus, forms strong C—C bond.

Ans. (a) Carbon shows **maximum catenation** property in the periodic table due to its **small size**. This enables the nucleus to hold on to the shared pairs of electrons strongly and C—C bond becomes strong.

Thus, both (A) and (R) are true and (R) is the correct explanation fo (A).

Q.2 Assertion (A) Alkenes, alkynes and alkanes are examples of homologous series.

Reason (R) Organic compounds of the homologous series have similar structures but different chemical properties. **(Competency Based Que.)**

Ans. (c) Alkanes, alkenes, alkynes are example of homologous series.

Organic compounds of the homologous series have **same chemical properties**.

Thus, (A) is true but (R) is false.

Q.3 Assertion (A) Alkanes are called paraffins.

Reason (R) Alkanes are relatively unreactive under ordinary conditions.

Ans. (a) Alkanes are called **paraffins** because they are **relatively unreactive** under ordinary conditions.

Thus, both (A) and (R) are true and (R) is the correct explanation of (A).

Q.4 Assertion (A) Propane can be prepared by reaction of sodium butanoate with soda lime.

Reason (R) Wurtz reaction is specifically used to prepare methane.

Ans. (c) Propane can be prepared by the decarboxylation of sodium butanoate.

Wurtz reaction is not used to prepare methane.

Thus, (A) is true but (R) is false.

Q.5 Assertion (A) Methane and ethane burn with a sooty flame.

Reason (R) Alkanes burn in an insufficient supply of air to form carbon monoxide and water.

Ans. (d) Methane and ethane burn with a **bluish, non-sooty flame.**

Alkanes burn in an insufficient supply of air to form carbon monoxide and water.

Thus, (A) is false but (R) is true.

TYPE - 3

01 Mark

Fill in the Blanks

Q.1 .... was the first organic compound prepared in laboratory. (Urea/Ethyne)

Ans. Urea

Q.2 Organic compounds are generally insoluble in .... (water/organic solvents). **(ICSE Specimen 2023)**

Ans. water

Q.3 The property of carbon to form chains and rings is called .... (catenation/polymerisation)

Ans. catenation

Q.4 .... is a cyclic hydrocarbon. (Cyclopentane/Cycloethane)

Ans. Cyclopentane

Q.5 When two or more compounds have .... molecular formula but different structural formula, then the compounds are called isomers. (same/different).

Ans. same

Q.6 The number of chain isomers possible for an alkane with 5 carbon atoms are .... (3/4). **(Competency Based Que.)**

Ans. 3

Q.7 One carbon atom in a hydrocarbon contain the root word as .... (meth/eth)

Ans. meth

Q.8 A .... is always added to the root word to indicate whether a carbon chain is single bonded, double or triple bonded. (suffix/prefix)

Ans. suffix

Q.9 Alkene contains .... bonds. (single with double /single with triple)

Ans. single with double

Q.10 .... forms chloroform on halogenation in the presence of sunlight. (Methane/Ethane)

Ans. Methane

Q.11 .... burns with a non-luminous flame. (Methane/Ethene).

Ans. Methane

Q.12 .... and H_2O is formed on complete combustion of ethane. (CO_2/CO)

Ans. CO_2

Q.13 Alkenes are also called .... (olefins/paraffins).

Ans. olefins

Q.14 .... can be used for ripening of many raw fruits. (Ethene/Butene)

Ans. Ethene

Q.15 The melting point of alkenes increases with .... in molecular weight. (increase/decrease).

Ans. increase

Q.16 Conversion of ethene to ethane is an example of .... (hydration/hydrogenation). **(ICSE 2023)**

Ans. hydrogenation

Q.17 The compound formed when ethene reacts with hydrogen is .... (CH_4 /C_2H_6) **(ICSE 2017)**

Ans. C_2H_6

Q.18 The catalyst used for conversion of ethene to ethane is commonly ...... (nickel/cobalt).

Ans. nickel

Q.19 If a hydrocarbon has the formula of $C_{50}H_{98}$, then it is likely to undergo .... (addition/substitution) reaction. **(Competency Based Que.)**

Ans. addition

Q.20 .... will give acetylene gas when treated with water. (CaC_2/CO)

Ans. CaC_2

Q.21 .... burns with a luminous and smoky flame. (Acetylene/Ethane)

Ans. Acetylene

Q.22 Alkynes undergo .... (addition/substitution) reactions. **(ICSE Specimen 2025)**

Ans. addition

Q.23 Hydrocarbon *X* decolourises bromine in carbon tetrachloride, and hydrocarbon *Y* does not decolourise bromine water. Both of the compounds burn with a sooty flame. The molecular formula of *X* and *Y* is ....(C_5H_{12} and C_4H_8/C_5H_8 and C_4H_{10}). **(Competency Based Que.)**

Ans. C_5H_8 and C_4H_{10}

TYPE - 4 01 Mark

Correct the Incorrect Statement

Q.1 Alkanes and alkenes are saturated hydrocarbon and alkynes are unsaturated hydrocarbon.

Ans. **Alkanes** are **saturated hydrocarbon** and **alkenes and alkynes** are **unsaturated hydrocarbons**.

Q.2 Cyclic hydrocarbons are also called aliphatic compounds.

Ans. Cyclic hydrocarbons are also called **alicyclic** compounds.

Q.3 Compounds with different functional groups show similar physical and chemical properties.

Ans. Compounds with different functional groups show **different** physical and chemical properties.

Q.4 The general molecular formula of alcohol is $C_nH_{2n}OH$.

Ans. The general molecular formula of alcohol is $C_nH_{2n+1}OH$.

Q.5 Members of the homologous series have different chemical properties.

Ans. Members of the homologous series have **same** chemical properties.

Q.6 Compounds having different molecular formula but same structural formula are known as isomers.

Ans. Compounds having **same molecular formula** but **different structural formula** are known as isomers.

Q.7 There are four chain isomers of pentane.

Ans. There are **three** chain isomers of pentane.

Q.8 Hexan-2-one and hexan-3-one are the chain isomers.

Ans. Hexan-2-one and hexan-3-one are the **position** isomers.

TYPE - 5 01 × 05 = 05 Marks

Matching Type Question

Q.1 Match the column I with column II.

	Column I (Name)		Column II (Functional group)
A.	Aldehyde	1.	$>C=O$
B.	Alcohol	2.	—COOH
C.	Ether	3.	—OH
D.	Carboxylic acid	4.	—O—
E.	Ketone	5.	—CHO

Ans. A→(5), B→(3), C→(4), D→(2), E→(1).

TYPE - 6 01 Mark

Identify the Following

Q.1 Give one word for "the tendency of an element to form chains of identical atoms." **(ICSE 2023, 2018)**

Or Name the property of elements by virtue of which atoms of the element can link to each other in the form of a long chain or ring structure. **(ICSE 2015)**

Ans. Catenation.

Q.2 Name the organic compounds having the same molecular formula but different structural formula. **(ICSE 2025, 2023)**

Ans. Isomers.

Q.3 Name the first homologue whose general formula is C_nH_{2n}. **(ICSE 2019)**

Ans. C_2H_4 (Ethyne)

Q.4 Identify the compound formed where two alkyl groups are linked by $—\overset{O}{\overset{||}{C}}—$ group. **(ICSE 2017)**

Ans. Ketone

Q.5 How many electrons are present in one molecule of CH_4? **(Competency Based Que.)**

Ans. 10

Q.6 Which group is obtained by removing one hydrogen atom from the parent alkane? **(ICSE 2024)**

Ans. Alkyl group

Q.7 Identify a reaction in which the hydrogen of an alkane is replaced by a halogen. **(ICSE Specimen 2025, 2024)**

Ans. Substitution reaction

Q.8 Which compound can be used to prepare ethylene by the dehydration of ethanol?

Ans. Concentrated sulphuric acid or Al_2O_3

Q.9 Name a gas evolved when ethene undergoes hydrogenation reaction. **(ICSE 2019)**

Ans. Ethane

Q.10 Which addition product is formed when ethylene reacts with chlorine?

Ans. $C_2H_4Cl_2$

Q.11 Name a reagent which can be used to distinguish between ethane and ethene.

Ans. Alkaline potassium permanganate solution

Q.12 What is the empirical formula of ethyne? **(ICSE 2024)**

Ans. CH

Q.13 Name the first member of alkyne series.

Ans. Ethyne

Q.14 Identify the hydrocarbon containing a triple bond used for welding purposes. **(ICSE 2017)**

Ans. Ethyne

TYPE - 7 — 02 Marks

Short Answer Type I Questions

Q.1 (i) Draw an isomer of the given structure

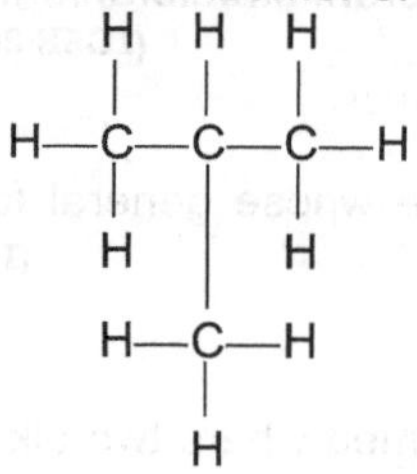

(ii) Draw the chain isomer for the following organic compound.

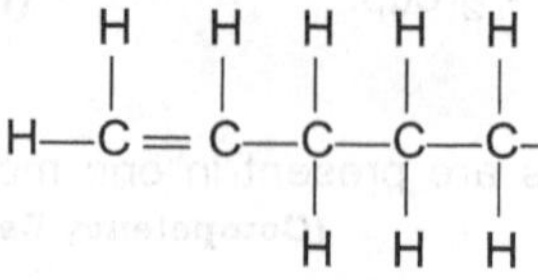

(Competency Based Que.)

Ans. (i)

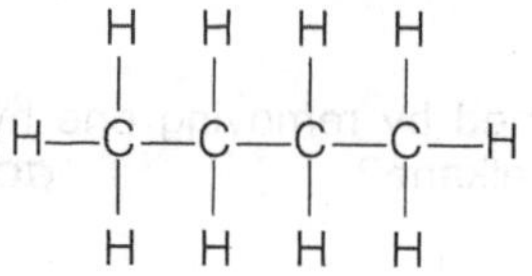

(1)

(ii)

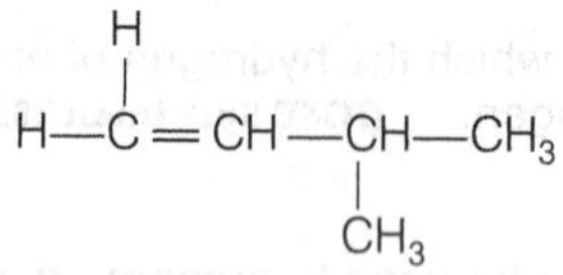

(1)

Q.2 (i) Give the IUPAC name of the compound represented below:

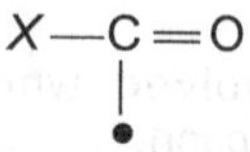

Where, C stands for Carbon, O for oxygen, *X* for hydrogen and • for ethyl group.

(ii) Give the IUPAC name of the following organic compounds.

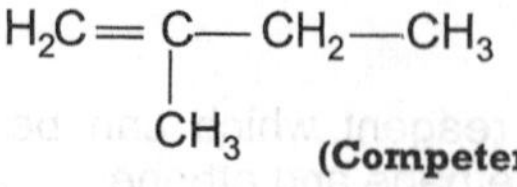

(Competency Based Que.)

Ans. (i) Propanal

(ii) 2-methylbut-1-ene **(1 × 2 = 2)**

Q.3 Give the IUPAC name of the following organic compounds. **(ICSE Specimen 2025, 2024)**

(i)

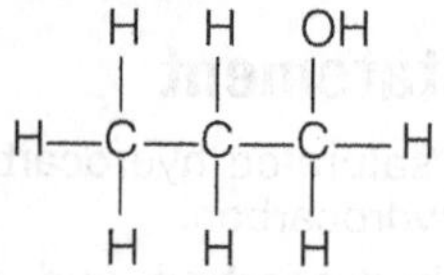

(ii)

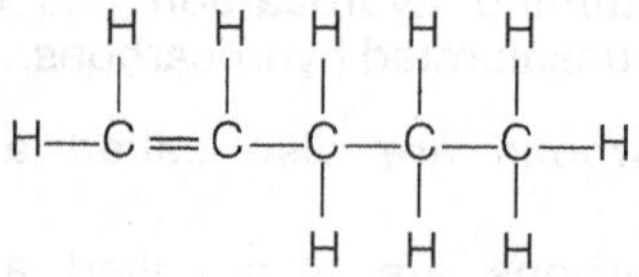

Ans. (i) Propanol (ii) Pent-1-ene **(1 × 2 = 2)**

Q.4 Give the IUPAC name for each of the following. **(ICSE 2018)**

(i)

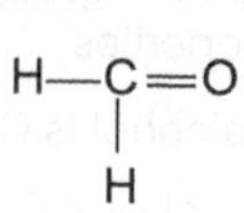

(ii)

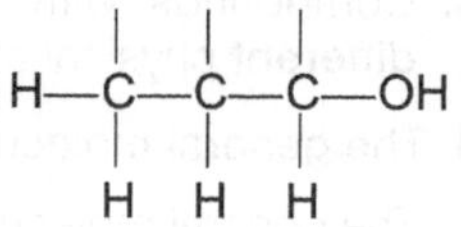

(iii)

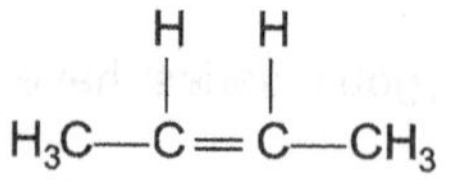

(iv)

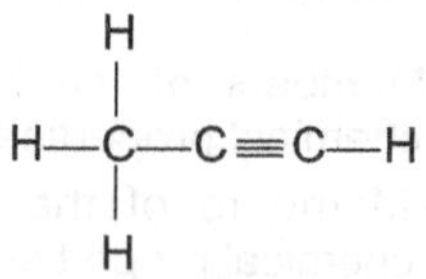

Ans.

S. No.	Structure	IUPAC name
(i)	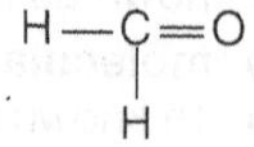	Methanal
(ii)	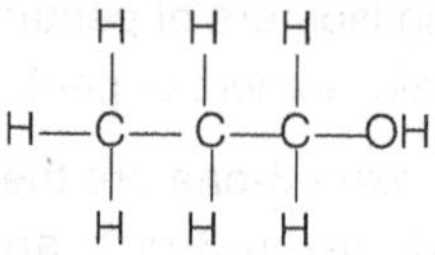	Propan-1-ol
(iii)	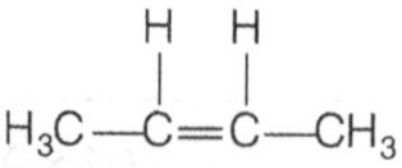	But-2-ene
(iv)	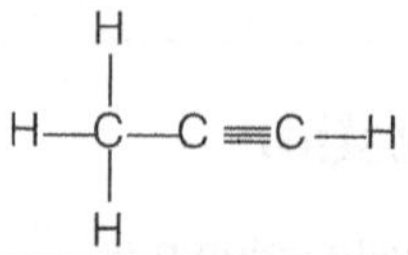	Prop-1-yne

(½ × 4 = 2)

Q.5 Give the correct IUPAC name and the functional group for each of the compounds whose structural formulae are given below.

(i)

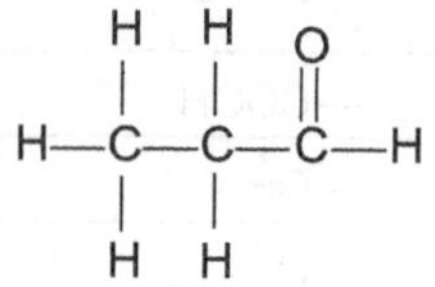

(ii)

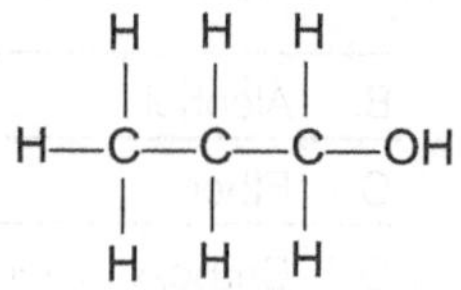

Ans. IUPAC name — Functional group

(i) Propanal — —CHO or —C(=O)—H **(1)**

(ii) Propanol — —OH **(1)**

Q.6 Write the IUPAC name for the following compounds.

(i) Acetaldehyde

(ii) Acetylene **(ICSE 2020)**

Ans. (i) IUPAC name of acetaldehyde is **ethanal.**

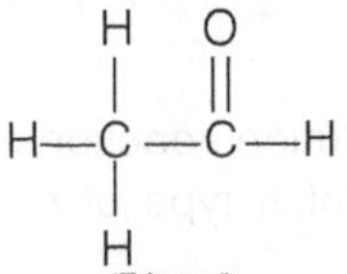

(Ethanal) **(1)**

(ii) IUPAC name of acetylene is **ethyne.**

H—C≡C—H **(1)**

(Ethyne)

Q.7 (i) Identify the longest carbon chain and mention the number of carbons present in it.

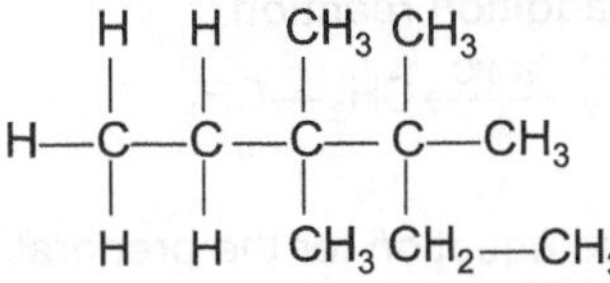

(ii) Draw the structure of 2-methylbutane. **(Competency Based Que.)**

Ans. (i) 6 (ii)

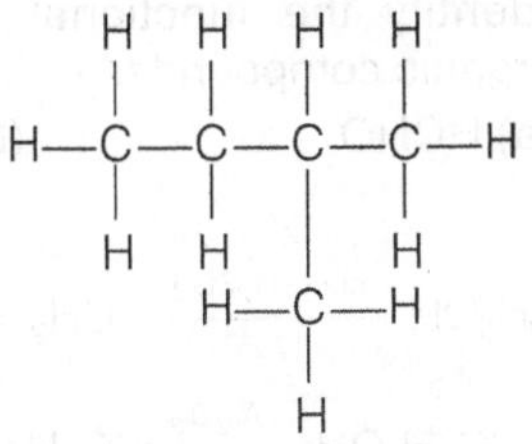

(1 × 2 = 2)

Q.8 Using their structural formulae, identify the functional group by circling them **(ICSE 2025)**

(i) Dimethyl ether (ii) Propanone

Ans. (i) Dimethyl ether, CH_3—O—CH_3

Functional group: —O— **(1)**

(ii) Propanone, CH_3—C(=O)—CH_3

Functional group: >C=O **(1)**

Q.9 Give the names and the structural formulae of

(i) a saturated hydrocarbon.

(ii) an unsaturated hydrocarbon with a double bond.

Ans. (i) Saturated hydrocarbon-**Ethane**

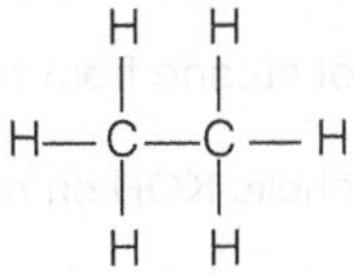

Ethane (C_2H_4) **(1)**

(ii) Unsaturated hydrocarbon-**Ethene**

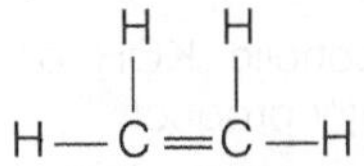

Ethene (C_2H_4) **(1)**

Q.10 (i) Draw the structural formula of ethyne.

(ii) How is the structure of alkynes different from that of alkenes?

Ans. (i) Ethyne, H—C≡C—H **(1)**

(ii) Alkynes possess a triple covalent bond between C—C atom, whereas alkenes possess a double covalent bond between carbon-carbon atoms. **(1)**

Q.11 Complete and balance the following equations:

(i) $C_2H_5COONa + NaOH \xrightarrow[CaO]{\Delta}$

(ii) $C_2H_4Br_2$ + Alc. KOH $\xrightarrow{\Delta}$ **(ICSE 2024)**

Ans. (i) $C_2H_5COONa + NaOH \xrightarrow[\Delta]{CaO} Na_2CO_3 + C_2H_6\uparrow$ **(1)**

(ii) $C_2H_4Br_2 + \underset{(Alc.)}{2KOH} \xrightarrow{Boiling} CH{\equiv}CH + 2KBr + 2H_2O$ **(1)**

Q.12 Give the involved reaction in following. **(ICSE 2020)**

(i) Producing ethane from bromoethane using Zn/Cu couple in alcohol.

(ii) Complete combustion of ethane. **(ICSE 2016)**

Ans. (i) Preparation of ethane from bromoethane by using Zn/Cu couple in alcohol.

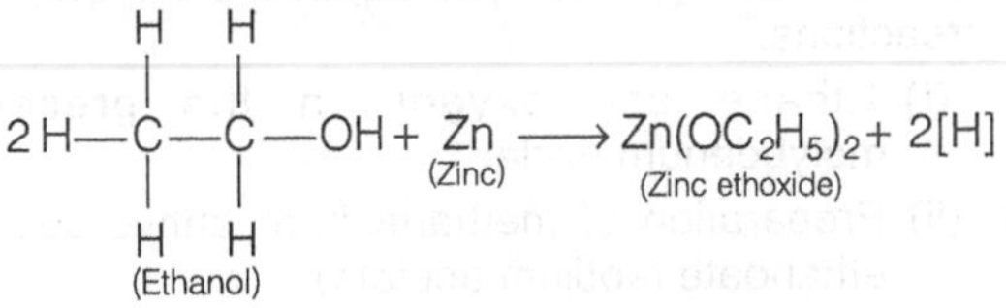

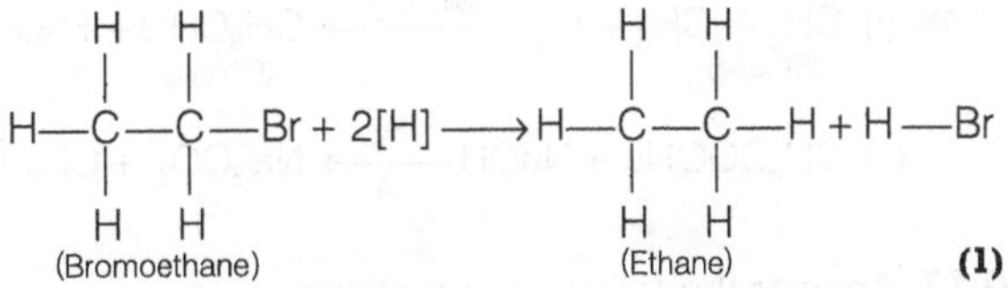

(1)

(ii) Complete combustion of ethane takes place as :

$$\underset{(Ethane)}{2C_2H_6} + \underset{\text{(In sufficient supply of oxygen)}}{7O_2} \longrightarrow \underset{\text{(Carbon dioxide)}}{4CO_2\uparrow} + \underset{(Water)}{6H_2O} + Heat$$ **(1)**

Q.13 Give a balanced chemical equation for each of the following. **(ICSE 2017)**

(i) Preparation of ethane from sodium propionate. **(ICSE 2014)**

(ii) Action of alcoholic KOH on bromoethane.

Ans. (i) $\underset{\text{(Sodium propionate)}}{C_2H_5COONa} + \underset{\text{(Soda lime)}}{NaOH} \xrightarrow[300°C]{CaO} Na_2CO_3 + \underset{\text{(Ethane)}}{C_2H_6} \uparrow$ **(1)**

(ii) Action of alcoholic KOH on bromoethane gives **ethene** as major product.

$\underset{\text{(Ethyl bromide)}}{C_2H_5Br} + Alc. KOH \longrightarrow \underset{\text{(Ethene)}}{C_2H_4} + KBr + H_2O$ **(1)**

Q.14 Give the structural formula and the name of the organic product formed when equal volumes of methane and chlorine react together. **(Competency Based Que.)**

Ans. 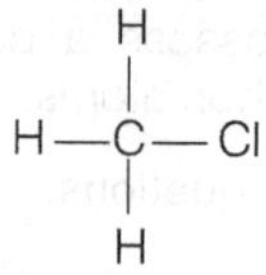

(1)

Chloromethane/ methyl chloride **(1)**

Q.15 Complete combustion of one mole of a hydrocarbon produced four moles of carbon dioxide and four moles of water only.

(i) Write the equation for the combustion reaction.

(ii) Draw the structure of the hydrocarbon. **(Competency Based Que.)**

Ans. (i) $C_4H_8 + 6O_2 \longrightarrow 4CO_2 + 4H_2O$ **(1)**

(ii) 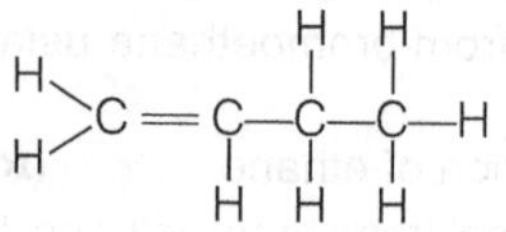

(1)

Q.16 Write balanced chemical equations for the following reactions.

(i) Ethane and oxygen in the presence of molybdenum oxide.

(ii) Preparation of methane from anhydrous sodium ethanoate (sodium acetate).

Ans. (i) $\underset{\text{(Ethane)}}{CH_3—CH_3} + O_2 \xrightarrow{Mo_2O_3} \underset{\text{(Ethanal)}}{CH_3CHO} + H_2O$ **(1)**

(ii) $CH_3COONa + NaOH \xrightarrow[\Delta]{CaO} Na_2CO_3 + CH_4 \uparrow$ **(1)**

Q.17 Answer the following questions.

(i) Using appropriate catalysts, ethane can be oxidised to an alcohol, an aldehyde and an acid. Name the alcohol, aldehyde and acid formed when ethane is oxidised.

(ii) Give balanced equations for the laboratory preparation of saturated hydrocarbon from iodomethane.

Ans. (i) When ethane is oxidised, then **ethanol** (C_2H_5OH), **ethanal** (CH_3CHO) and **ethanoic acid** (CH_3COOH) are formed. **(1)**

(ii) $2CH_3I + 2Na \xrightarrow[ether]{Dry} \underset{\text{Ethane}}{C_2H_6} + 2NaI$

Or $CH_3I + 2[H] \longrightarrow \underset{\text{Methane}}{CH_4} + HI$

[H], nascent hydrogen is produced by the action of Zn and dilute HCl. **(1)**

Q.18 Addition reactions and substitution reactions are the types of organic reactions. Which type of reaction is shown by

(i) ethane

(ii) ethene

Ans. (i) Ethane shows **substitution reaction.**

$\underset{\text{(Ethane)}}{C_2H_6} + Cl_2 \xrightarrow{Sunlight} \underset{\text{(Chloroethane)}}{C_2H_5Cl} + HCl$ **(1)**

(ii) Ethene shows **addition reaction.**

$\underset{\text{(Ethene)}}{CH_2{=}CH_2} + H_2 \xrightarrow[Ni]{200°C} \underset{\text{(Ethane)}}{CH_3—CH_3}$ **(1)**

Q.19 (i) Write balanced equation for the preparation of the following.

Ethene from ethanol.

(ii) Identify the functional group in the following organic compounds. **(ICSE Specimen 2023)**

(a) HCHO (b) C_2H_5COOH

Ans.

(i) $C_2H_5OH \xrightarrow[170°C]{conc. H_2SO_4} CH_2{=}CH_2 + H_2O$

or $C_2H_5OH \xrightarrow[350°C]{Al_2O_3} C_2H_4 + H_2O$ **(1)**

(ii) (a) Aldehyde (b) Carboxylic acid **(1)**

Q.20 (i) Give the chemical equations for the formation of ethene from iodoethane.

(ii) Write the equation for the reaction taking place between 1, 2-dibromoethane and alcoholic potassium hydroxide.

Ans. (i) $\underset{\text{(Iodoethane)}}{CH_3CH_2I} + \underset{\text{(Alc.)}}{KOH} \longrightarrow \underset{\text{Ethene}}{C_2H_4} + KI + H_2O$ **(1)**

(ii) $\underset{\text{(Ethylene dibromide)}}{CH_2Br—CH_2Br} + \underset{\text{(Alc.)}}{2KOH} \longrightarrow CH{\equiv}CH + 2KBr + 2H_2O$

or $\underset{\text{(Ethyne)}}{C_2H_2}$ **(1)**

Q.21 Equation for the reaction when compound *A* is bubbled through bromine dissolved in carbon tetrachloride is as follows **(ICSE 2016)**

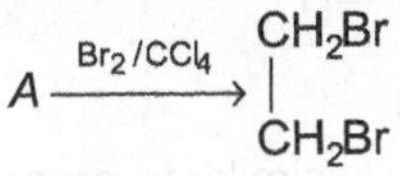

(i) Draw the structure of *A*.
(ii) State your observation during this reaction.

Ans. (i)

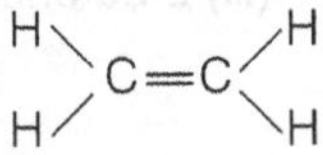

Ethene (*A*) **(1)**

(ii) Ethene undergoes **addition reaction** to give 1, 2-dibromoethane. **Reddish brown colour of bromine solution gets decolourised.** **(1)**

Q.22 $C_2H_4 + H_2 \xrightarrow[A]{200°C} X$

Given above is the representation of the conversion of ethene to a saturated hydrocarbon *X*, where '*A*' stands for the catalyst.

(i) Identify '*A*'.
(ii) Give the complete chemical equation for the conversion of C_2H_4 to *X*. **(Competency Based Que.)**

Ans. (i) Nickel

(ii) $C_2H_4 + H_2 \xrightarrow[Ni]{200°C} C_2H_6$ **(1 × 2 = 2)**

Q.23 Give balanced chemical equations for the following conversions: **(ICSE 2015)**

(i) Calcium carbide to ethyne. **(ICSE Specimen 2025, ICSE 2016)**
(ii) Sodium ethanoate to methane.

Ans. (i) $\underset{\text{(Calcium carbide)}}{CaC_2} + 2H_2O \longrightarrow \underset{\text{(Calcium hydroxide)}}{Ca(OH)_2} + \underset{\text{(Ethyne)}}{C_2H_2} \uparrow$ **(1)**

(ii) $\underset{\text{(Sodium ethanoate)}}{CH_3COONa} + NaOH \xrightarrow[300°C]{CaO} \underset{\text{(Sodium carbonate)}}{Na_2CO_3} + \underset{\text{(Methane)}}{CH_4} \uparrow$ **(1)**

Q.24 Complete and balance the following chemical equations. **(ICSE Specimen 2021-22, Sem-I)**

(i) $C_2H_6 + O_2 \longrightarrow$
(ii) $C_2H_2 + I_2 \longrightarrow$

Ans. (i) $\underset{\text{(Ethane)}}{2C_2H_6} + \underset{\text{(Oxygen)}}{7O_2} \longrightarrow \underset{\text{(Carbon dioxide)}}{4CO_2} + \underset{\text{(Water)}}{6H_2O}$ **(1)**

(ii) $\underset{\text{(Ethyne)}}{C_2H_2} + \underset{\text{(Iodine)}}{I_2} \longrightarrow \underset{\text{(1, 2-diiodoethane)}}{ICH{=}CHI}$ **(1)**

TYPE - 8 — 03 Marks

Short Answer Type II Questions

Q.1 Write the IUPAC names for each of the following compounds. **(ICSE 2016)**

(i) 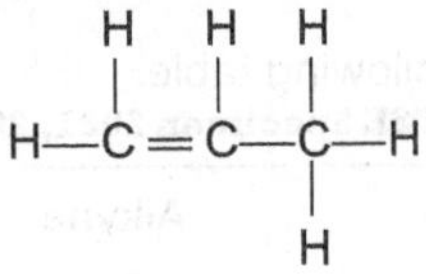 (ii) 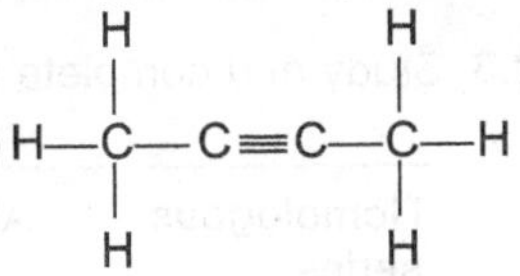

(iii) 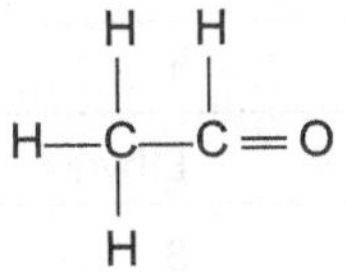

Ans. (i) 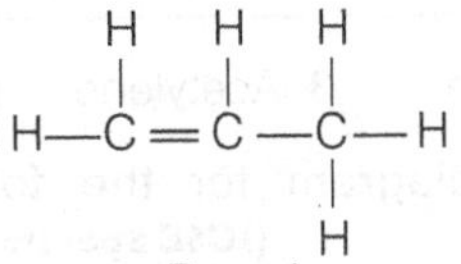

(Propene)

(ii) 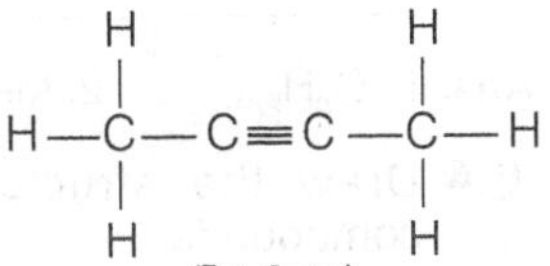

(But -2-yne)

(iii) 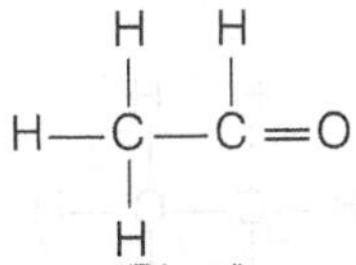

(Ethanal) **(1 × 3 = 3)**

Q.2 Give the IUPAC name for the following. **(ICSE 2021-22, Sem-II)**

(i) 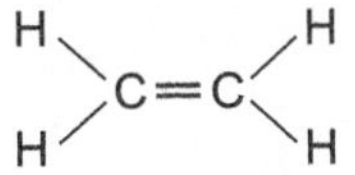 (ii) 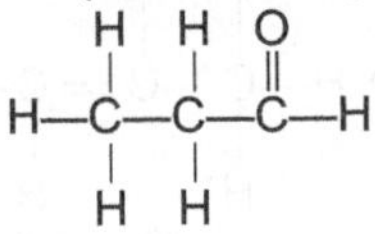

(iii) 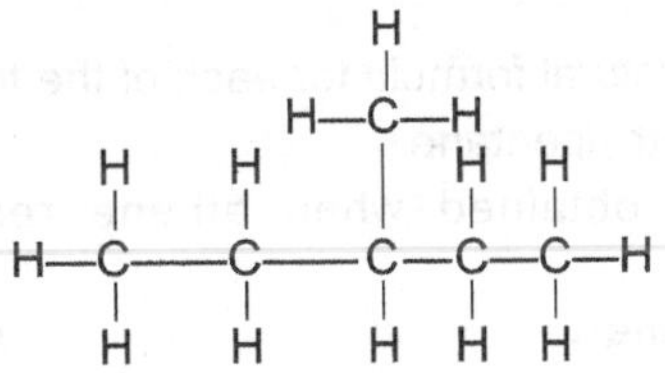

Ans. (i) 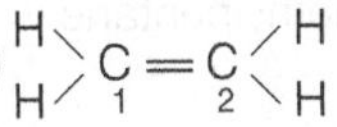 (double bond present)

IUPAC name: **Ethene** **(1)**

(ii) 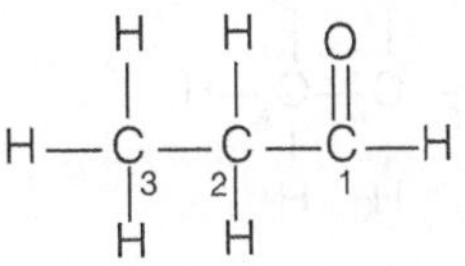 (aldehyde (—CHO) group present)

IUPAC name: **Propanal** **(1)**

(iii) 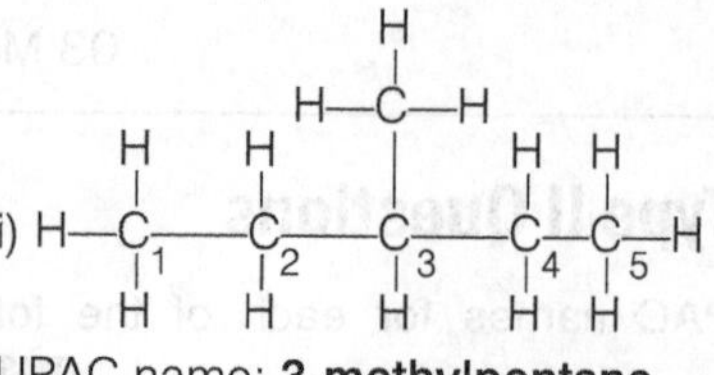

IUPAC name: **3-methylpentane** **(1)**

Q.3 Study and complete the following table. **(ICSE Specimen 2021, 22, Sem-II)**

Homologous series	Alkane	Alkyne
General formula	C_nH_{2n+2}	1. ....
IUPAC name	2.	Ethyne
Common name	Marsh gas	3. ....

Ans. 1. C_nH_{2n-2} 2. Methane 3. Acetylene **(1 × 3 = 3)**

Q.4 Draw the structural diagram for the following compounds **(ICSE Specimen 2024)**

(i) 1-propanal (ii) 1, 2-dichloroethane

(iii) But-2-ene

Ans. (i) 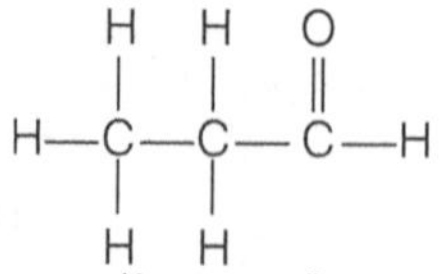

(1-propanal)

(ii) 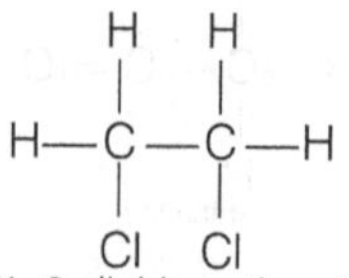

(1, 2-dichloroethane)

(iii) 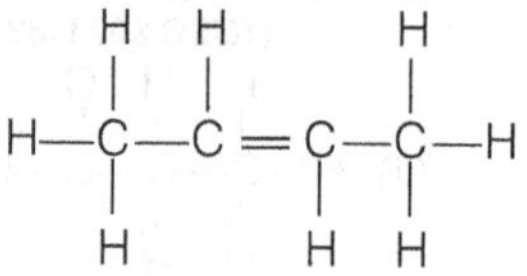

(But -2-ene)

(1 × 3 = 3)

Q.5 Draw the structural formula for each of the following.

(i) 2, 2-dimethylpentane

(ii) Product obtained when ethene reacts with chlorine.

(iii) *Iso*-propane **(ICSE 2020)**

Ans. (i) Structural formula of 2, 2-dimethylpentane is

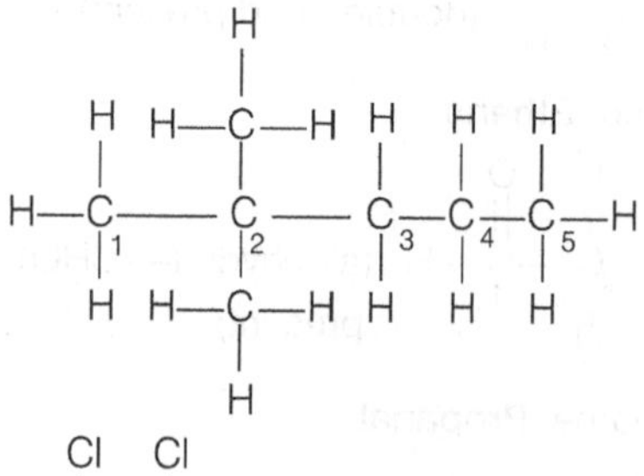

(1)

(ii) 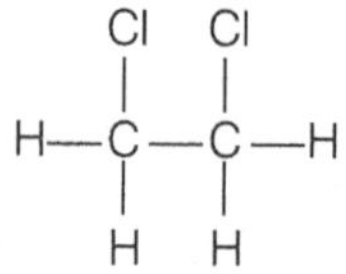

(1)

(iii) Structural formula of *iso*-propane is

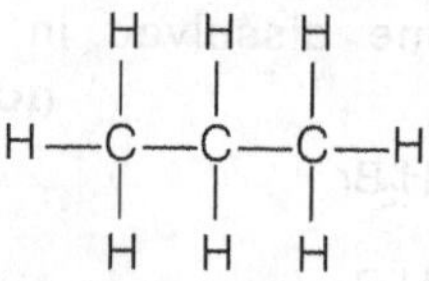

i.e. *iso*-propane is similar to propane. **(1)**

Q.6 Draw the structural diagram of **(ICSE 2021-22, Sem-II)**

(i) pentanal (ii) propanol (iii) 2-butene

Ans. Structural diagram

(i) Pentanal

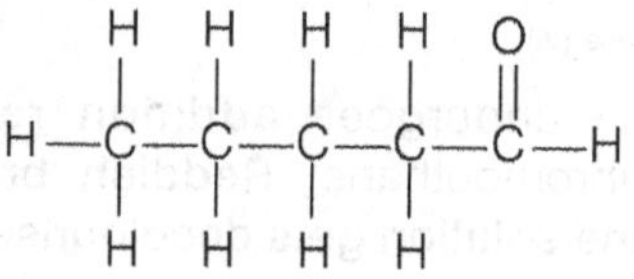

(1)

(ii) Propanol

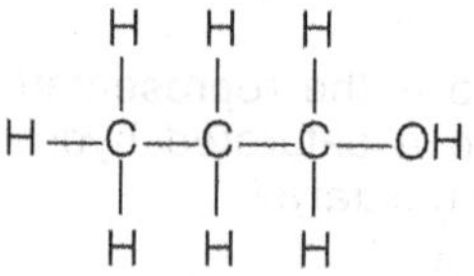

(1)

(iii) 2-butene

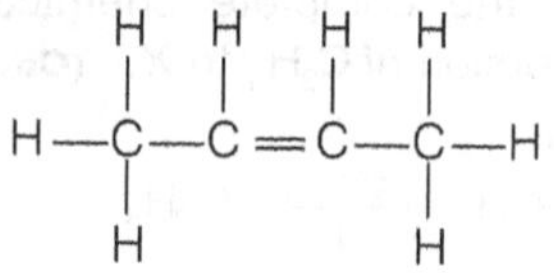

(1)

Q.7 Draw the structural formula for each of the following.

(i) 2, 3-dimethylbutane (ii) Diethyl ether

(iii) Propanoic acid **(ICSE 2017)**

Ans. (i) 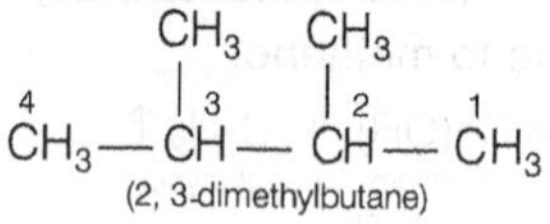

(2, 3-dimethylbutane) **(1)**

(ii) $C_2H_5OC_2H_5$ **(1)**

(Diethyl ether)

(iii) $\overset{3}{C}H_3\overset{2}{C}H_2\overset{1}{C}OOH$

(Propanoic acid) **(1)**

Q.8 Give the structural formulae for each of the following

(i) 2-methylpropane (ii) Ethanoic acid

(iii) Butan-2-ol **(ICSE 2016)**

Ans. (i) 2-methylpropane

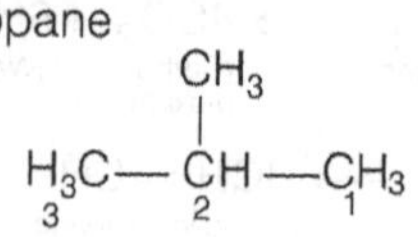

(1)

(ii) Ethanoic acid

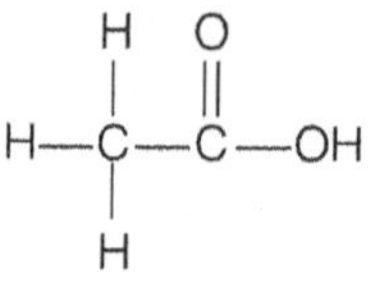

(1)

(iii) Butan-2-ol

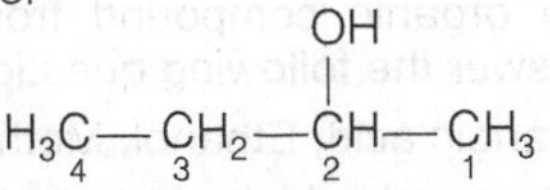

(1)

Q.9 Give the structural formulae for the following.

(i) An isomer of *n*-butane (ii) 2-propanol **(ICSE 2013)**

(iii) Diethyl ether

Ans. (i) An isomer of *n*-butane is **isobutane** (2-methylpropane).

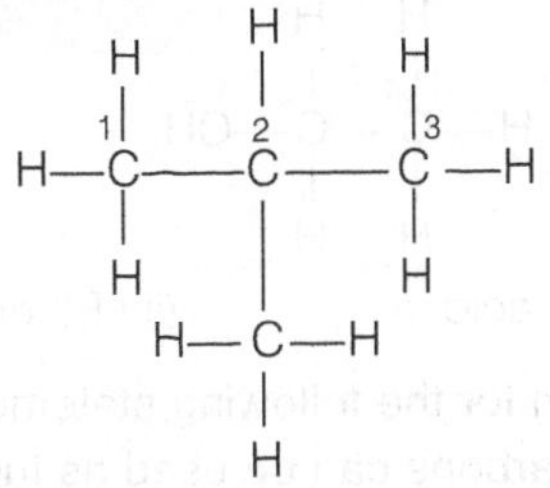

(1)

(ii) 2-propanol

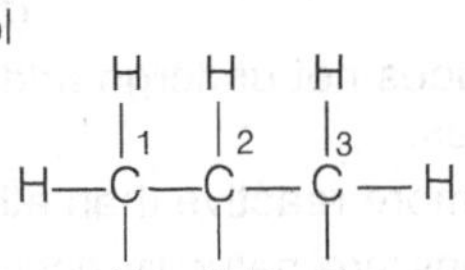

(1)

(iii) Diethyl ether

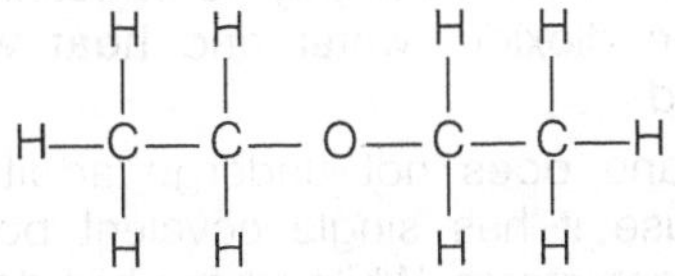

(1)

Q.10 Draw the structural formula of a compound with two carbon atoms in each of the following cases.

(i) An alkane with a carbon to carbon single bond.

(ii) An alcohol containing two carbon atoms.

(iii) An unsaturated hydrocarbon with a carbon to carbon triple bond.

Ans. (i) **Ethane** (An alkane)

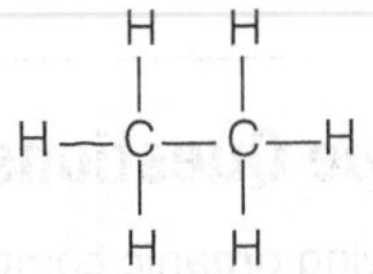

(1)

(ii) CH_3CH_2OH **(Ethanol)**

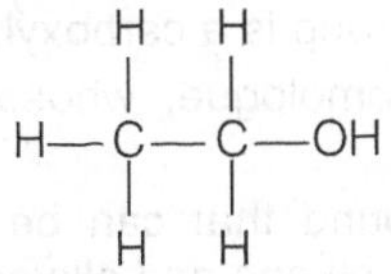

(1)

(iii) **Ethyne** H—C≡C—H (1)

Q.11 (i) A hydrocarbon, C_3H_y, burns in air to form carbon dioxide and water.

$$C_3H_y(g) + 5O_2(g) \longrightarrow 3CO_2(g) + \frac{y}{2}H_2O(g)$$

What is the value of y?

(ii) Which hydrocarbon ($X = C_2H_6$ and $Y = C_3H_6$) will burn completely in oxygen to give equal numbers of moles of carbon dioxide and water?

(iii) If 1 mole of each alkane is completely burned in oxygen, which will provide 7 moles of products? Choose from bracket.

[CH_4, C_2H_6, C_3H_8, C_4H_{10}]

Ans. (i) 5 moles of O_2 or 10 moles of O atom are used on reactant side. Six moles of oxygen atoms are used in producing $3CO_2$. Four moles of oxygen must be present in $\frac{y}{2}H_2O$.

$$\frac{y}{2} = 4$$

$$\Rightarrow \quad y = 8.$$ (1)

(ii) **C_3H_6 (Y)** will produce three moles of CO_2 and three moles of water. (1)

(iii) $CH_4 + 2O_2 \longrightarrow CO_2 + 2H_2O$

$C_2H_6 + \frac{7}{2}O_2 \longrightarrow 2CO_2 + 3H_2O$

$C_3H_8 + 5O_2 \longrightarrow 3CO_2 + 4H_2O$

$C_4H_{10} + \frac{13}{2}O_2 \longrightarrow 4CO_2 + 5H_2O$

It can be seen that 7 moles of products are formed by only **C_3H_8**. (1)

Q.12 Write a balanced chemical equation for the preparation of **(ICSE 2019)**

(i) ethene from bromoethane.

(ii) ethyne using calcium carbide.

(iii) methane from sodium acetate.

Ans. (i) By **dehydrohalogenation**.

$$\underset{\text{(Bromoethane)}}{C_2H_5Br} + \underset{\text{(Alcoholic)}}{KOH} \longrightarrow \underset{\text{(Ethene)}}{C_2H_4} + KBr + H_2O$$ (1)

(ii) $$\underset{\text{(Calcium carbide)}}{CaC_2} + 2H_2O \longrightarrow \underset{\text{(Calcium hydroxide)}}{Ca(OH)_2} + \underset{\text{(Ethyne)}}{C_2H_2}\uparrow$$

(iii) $$\underset{\text{(Sodium acetate)}}{CH_3CO\overset{-}{O}\overset{+}{Na}} + NaOH \xrightarrow[300°C]{CaO} Na_2CO_3 + \underset{\text{(Methane)}}{CH_4}\uparrow$$ (1)

Q.13 Give the chemical equation for

(i) the laboratory preparation of methane from sodium acetate.

(ii) the reaction of one mole of ethene with one mole of chlorine gas.

(iii) the preparation of ethyne from 1, 2-dibromoethane.

Ans. (i) $\underset{\text{(Sodium acetate)}}{CH_3COO^-Na^+} + NaOH \xrightarrow[300^\circ C]{CaO} Na_2CO_3 + \underset{\text{(Methane)}}{CH_4} \uparrow$

(ii) $\underset{\text{(Ethene)}}{C_2H_4} + Cl_2 \longrightarrow \underset{\text{(Dichloroethane)}}{C_2H_4Cl_2}$

(iii) $\begin{array}{l} CH_2Br \\ | \\ CH_2Br \end{array} + \underset{\text{(alc.)}}{2KOH} \longrightarrow CH \equiv CH + 2KBr + 2H_2O$ **(1 × 3 = 3)**

Q.14 Complete and balance the following chemical equations. **(ICSE 2021-22, Sem-II)**

(i) $H_2C = CH_2 + Cl_2 \xrightarrow[\text{Inert solvent}]{CCl_4}$

(ii) $C_2H_6 + O_2$ [excess] $\longrightarrow$

(iii) $CH_4 + O_2$ [excess] $\longrightarrow$

Ans. (i) $H_2C = CH_2 + Cl_2 \xrightarrow{CCl_4} \begin{array}{cc} H_2C & - CH_2 \\ | & | \\ Cl & Cl \end{array}$
(1,2-dichloroethane)

(ii) $2C_2H_6 + 7O_2$ [excess] $\longrightarrow \underset{\text{(Carbon dioxide)}}{4CO_2} + \underset{\text{(Water)}}{6H_2O}$

(iii) $CH_4 + 2O_2$ [excess] $\longrightarrow \underset{\text{(Carbon dioxide)}}{CO_2} + \underset{\text{(Water)}}{2H_2O}$ **(1 × 3 = 3)**

Q.15 Give a balanced chemical equation for the following conversions with conditions. **(ICSE 2023)**

(i) Ethene from ethanol

(ii) Ethyne from calcium carbide **(ICSE Specimen 2024)**

(iii) Monochloromethane from methane

Ans. (i) $\underset{\text{(Ethanol)}}{CH_3CH_2OH} \xrightarrow[160\text{-}170^\circ C]{Conc.H_2SO_4} \underset{\text{(Ethene)}}{CH_2 = CH_2} + \underset{\text{(Water)}}{H_2O}$

(ii) $CaC_2 + 2H_2O \longrightarrow Ca(OH)_2 + C_2H_2 \uparrow$

(iii) $CH_4 + Cl_2 \xrightarrow{h\nu \text{ or } 600\text{ K}} CH_3Cl + HCl$ **(1 × 3 = 3)**

Q.16 Name the following. **(ICSE 2015)**

(i) Process by which ethane is obtained from ethene.

(ii) A hydrocarbon which contributes towards the greenhouse effect.

(iii) Reaction when an alkyl halide is treated with alcoholic potassium hydroxide.

Ans. (i) **Hydrogenation** (addition of hydrogen).

(ii) **Methane** (CH_4) gas.

(iii) **Dehydrohalogenation.** **(1 × 3 = 3)**

Q.17 Choose the organic compound from the list given below to answer the following questions. **(ICSE 2024)**

Ethene, Ethanoic acid, Ethanol, Methanal

(i) The compound which does not have a double bond in its structure.

(ii) The compound which in its pure form turns into an ice like solid on cooling.

(iii) The compound which is used for artificial ripening of fruits.

Ans. (i) Ethanol, $\begin{array}{ccccc} & H & & H & \\ & | & & | & \\ H - & C & - & C & - OH \\ & | & & | & \\ & H & & H & \end{array}$

(ii) Ethanoic acid (iii) Ethene **(1 × 3 = 3)**

Q.18 Give reason for the following statements.

(i) Hydrocarbons can be used as fuels. **(ICSE Specimen 2024)**

(ii) Methane does not undergo addition reactions, but ethene does.

(iii) Ethyne is more reactive than ethane.

Ans. (i) Hydrocarbons are naturally occurring and form the basis of crude oil, coal and other important energy sources. They are **highly combustible** and produce carbon dioxide, water and **heat** when they are burned. **(1)**

(ii) Methane does not undergo addition reactions, because it has single covalent bonds with four hydrogen atoms. While ethene has **double covalent bond**. Double bond in ethene breaks and provides site for **addition**. **(1)**

(iii) Ethyne ($H - C \equiv C - H$) has **triple covalent bond**, which is **less stable**. Hence, it is **more reactive** than single covalent bond in ethane. **(1)**

TYPE - 9

04/05 Marks

Long Answer Type Questions

Q.1 Name the following organic compounds. **(ICSE 2019)**

(i) The compound with 3 carbon atoms whose functional group is a carboxyl. **(ICSE Specimen 2023)**

(ii) The first homologue, whose general formula is C_nH_{2n}.

(iii) The compound that can be used to distinguish between an alkene and alkyne.

(iv) The compound formed by complete chlorination of ethyne.

Ans. (i) Compound with 3 carbon atoms whose functional group is a carboxyl is **propanoic acid**. The formula is $CH_3 - CH_2 - COOH$. **(1)**

(ii) First homologue, whose general formula is C_nH_{2n} is C_2H_4. The name includes eth (root word) and suffix (ene), i.e., **ethene**. **(1)**

(iii) The compound that can be used to distinguish between alkene and alkyne is **ammoniacal cuprous chloride** or **ammoniacal silver nitrate**. **(1)**

(iv) The compound formed by complete chlorination of ethyne is **1,1,2,2-tetrachloroethane**. **(1)**

Q.2 Copy and complete the following paragraph using the options given in brackets. **(ICSE 2020)**

Alkenes are a homologous series of (i) .... (saturated/unsaturated) hydrocarbons characterised by the general formula (ii) .... (C_nH_{2n+2} / C_nH_{2n}). Alkenes undergo (iii) .... (addition/substitution) reactions and also undergo (iv) .... hydrogenation/dehydrogenation) to form alkanes.

Ans. (i) unsaturated

(ii) C_nH_{2n}

(iii) addition

(iv) hydrogenation **(1 × 4 = 4)**

Q.3 Give the structural formula for each of the following.

(i) Ethanol (ii) Butanal

(iii) Pentanoic acid

(iv) 1, 2-dichloropropane

Ans. (i) Ethanol (C_2H_5OH)

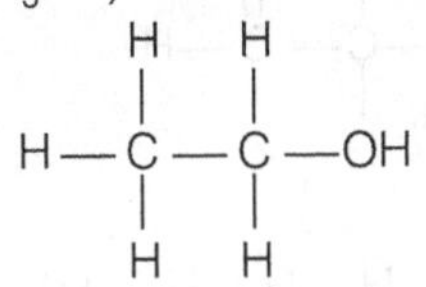

(ii) Butanal (C_3H_7CHO)

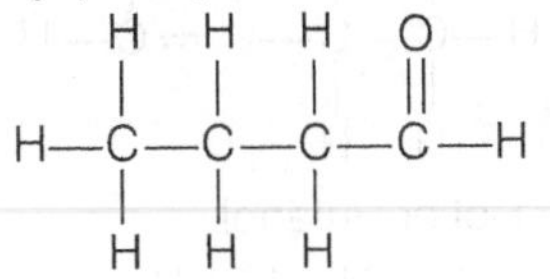

(iii) Pentanoic acid (C_4H_9COOH)

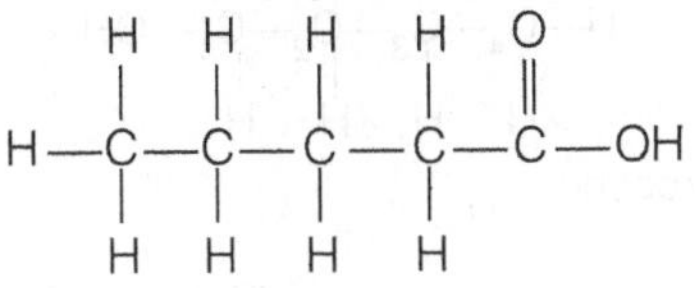

(iv) 1, 2-dichloropropane

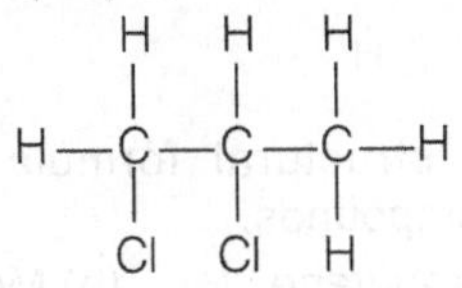

(1 × 4 = 4)

Q.4 (i) Draw the structural diagram for the following organic compounds:

(a) 2-methylpropene (b) butanal

(ii) Give IUPAC name for the following organic compounds.

(a) 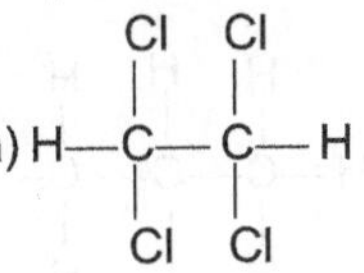

(b) 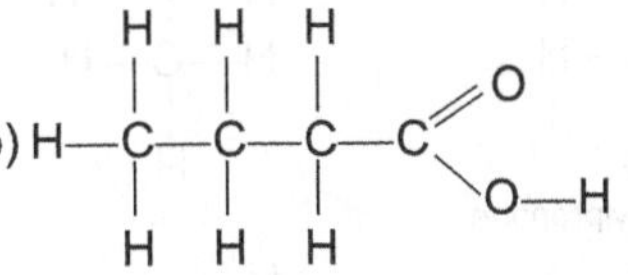

(c) 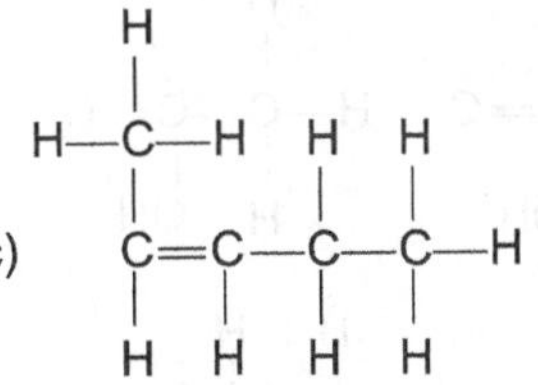

(ICSE 2025)

Ans. (i) (a) 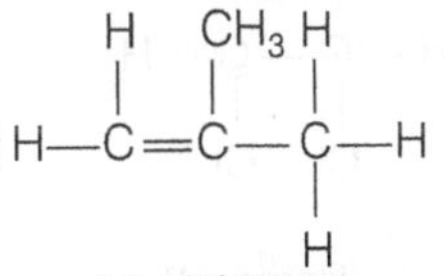

2–methylpropene **(1)**

(b) 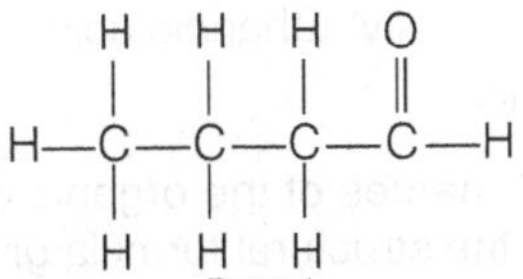

Butanal **(1)**

(ii) (a) 1, 1, 2, 2-tetrachloroethane **(1)**

(b) Butanoic acid **(1)**

(c) Pent-2-ene **(1)**

Q.5 Give the IUPAC names of the following compounds numbered (i) to (v). The IUPAC names of the compounds on the left are to guide you into giving the correct IUPAC names of the compounds on the right.

(i) 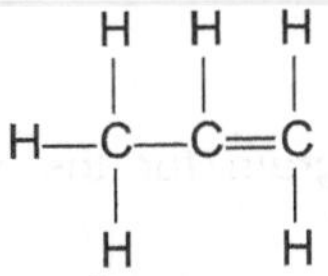 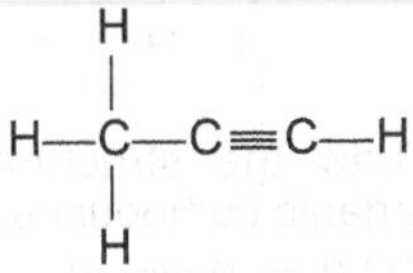

Propene

(ii) 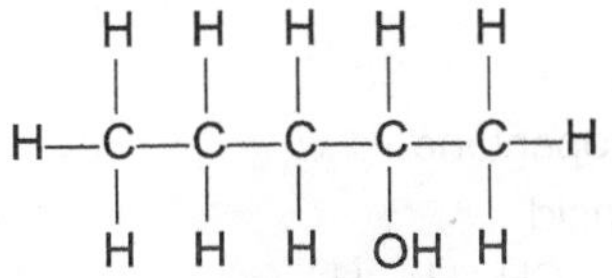

Pentan-2-ol

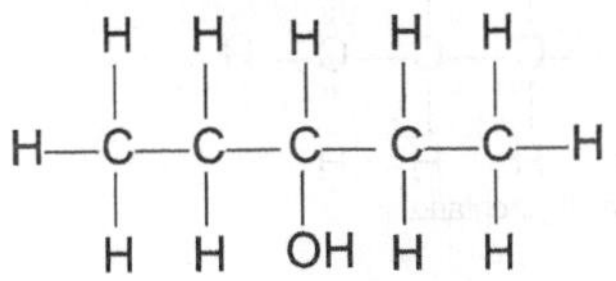

(iii) 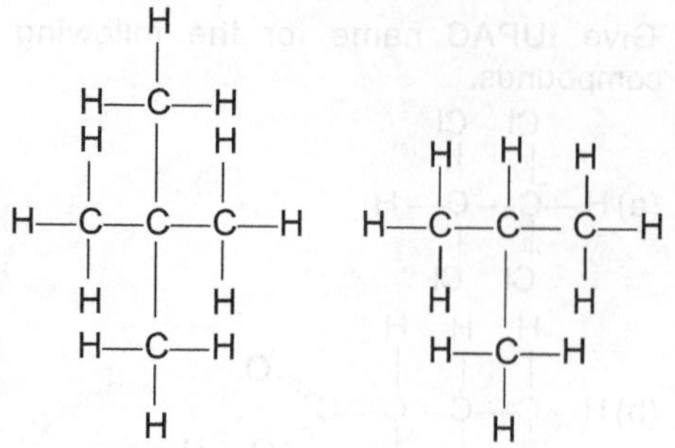

2, 2-dimethylpropane

(iv) 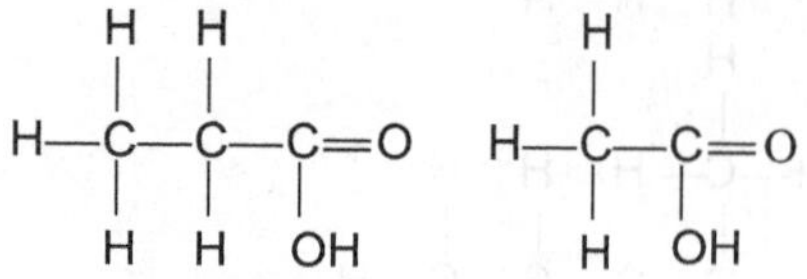

Propanoic acid

(v) 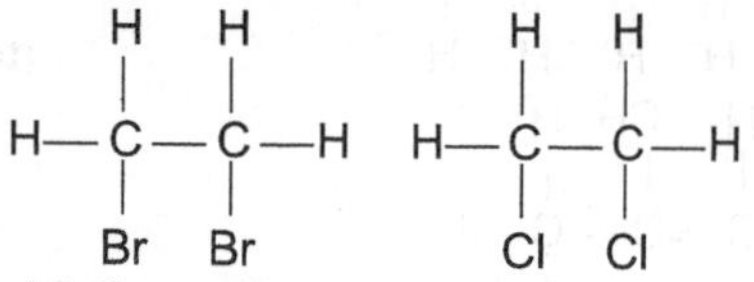

1,2-dibromoethane

Ans. (i) Propyne (ii) Pentan-3-ol

(iii) 2-methylpropane (iv) Ethanoic acid

(v) 1, 2-dichloroethane **(1 × 5 = 5)**

Q.6 (i) Give the IUPAC names of the organic compounds represented by the structural formula given below. **(ICSE 2024)**

(a) 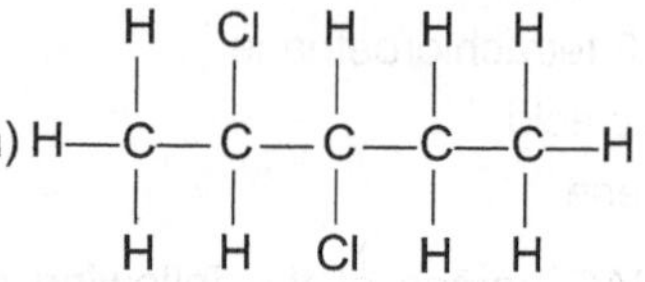

(b) 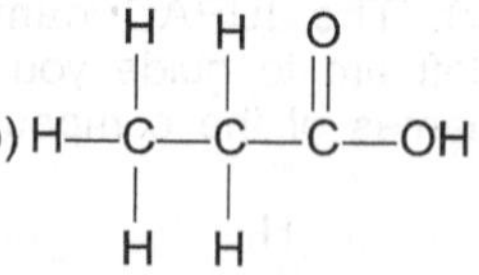

(ii) Draw the structural diagram for the following organic compounds

(a) 3-methylpentane

(b) Propyne

(c) Methanal

Ans. (i) (a) 2, 3-dichloropentane

(b) Propanoic acid **(1 × 2 = 2)**

(ii) (a) 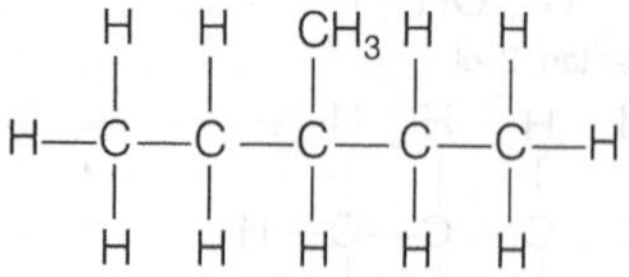

3-methylpentane

(b) 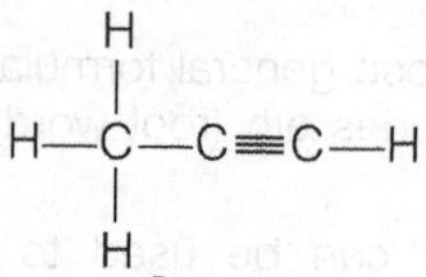

Propyne

(c) 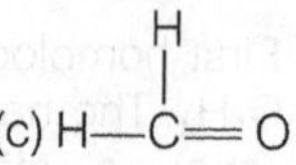

Methanal

(1 × 3 = 3)

Q.7 (i) Draw the structural formula for the following.

(a) 2-pentanol (b) ethanal (c) 1-butene

(ii) Name the following organic compounds in IUPAC system. **(ICSE Specimen 2023)**

(a) 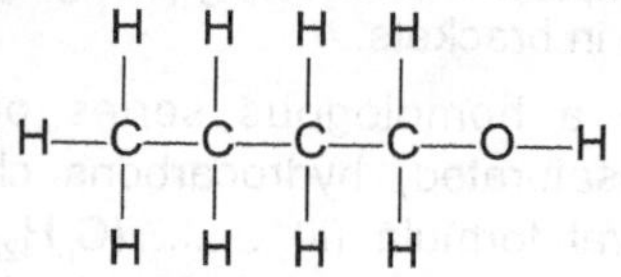

(b) 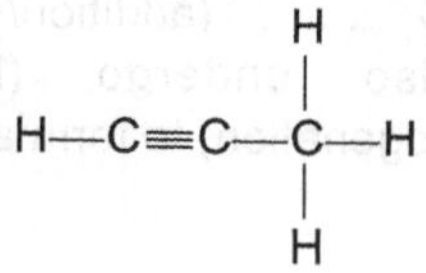

Ans. (i) (a) 2-pentanol

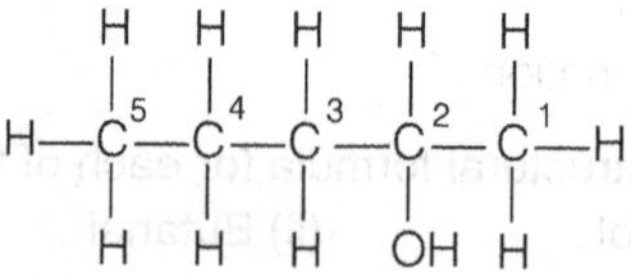

(b) Ethanal

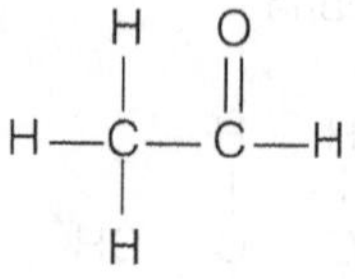

(c) 1-butene

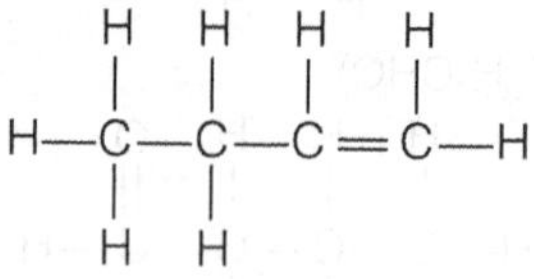

(1 × 3 = 3)

(ii) (a) Butan-1-ol or Butanol

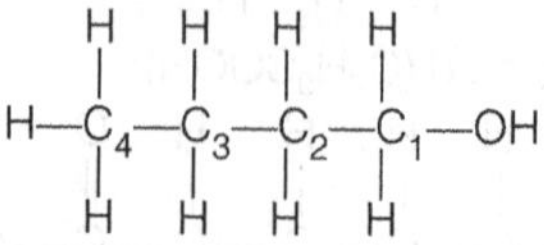

(b) 1-propyne

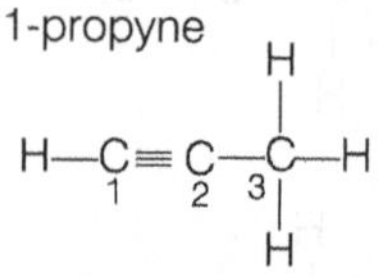

(1 × 2 = 2)

Q.8 (i) Give the structural formula of the following organic compounds. **(ICSE 2023)**

(a) 2-chlorobutane (b) Methanol

(c) But-2-yne

(ii) Give IUPAC name of the following organic compounds.

(a) 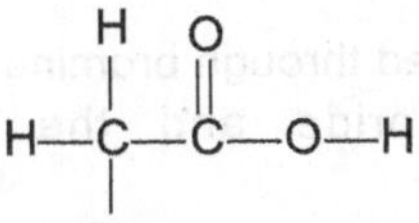

(b) 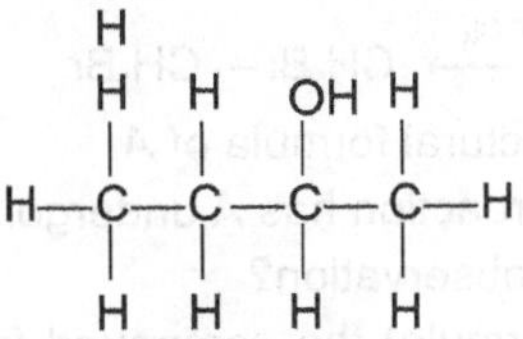

Ans. (i)

(a) 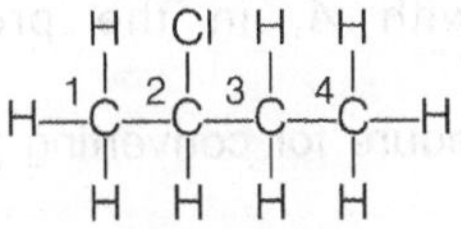

(2-chloro-butane)

(b) 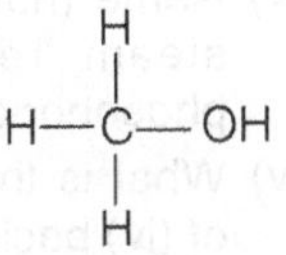

Methanol

(c) $CH_3—C\equiv C—CH_3$

But-2-yne **(1 × 3 = 3)**

(ii) (a) Ethanoic acid (b) Butan-2-ol **(1 × 2 = 2)**

Q.9 (i) **Give the IUPAC name of the following organic compounds.** **(ICSE 2019)**

(a) 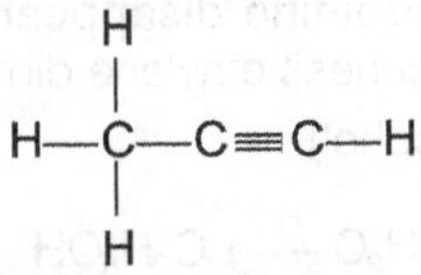 (b) 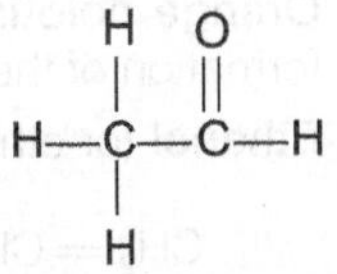

(ii) **What is the special feature of the structure of ethyne?**

(iii) **Name the saturated hydrocarbon containing two carbon atoms.**

(iv) **Give the structural formula of acetic acid.**

Ans. (i) (a) IUPAC name of 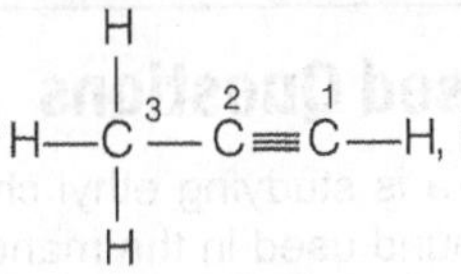, i.e.,

$CH_3—C\equiv CH$ or C_3H_4 is **propyne.**

(b) 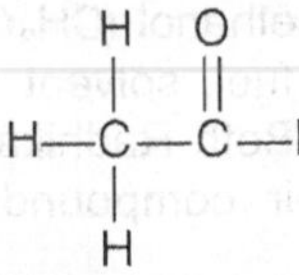, i.e. $CH_3—CHO$ is **ethanal.** **(2)**

(ii) **Structure of ethyne** In ethyne molecule there is **one triple bond** between two carbon atoms, each of which is singly bonded to one other hydrogen atom.

Ethyne molecule is **linear** in shape.

$H—C\equiv C—H$ (Linear structure) **(1)**

Ethyne

(iii) The name of saturated hydrocarbon containing two carbons is '**ethane**', as, 'eth' is used for two-carbons and suffix '-ane' for saturated hydrocarbon (alkane).

Structure of ethane $H_3C—CH_3$. **(1)**

(iv) **Structural formula of acetic acid** Acetic acid is also known as **ethanoic acid.**

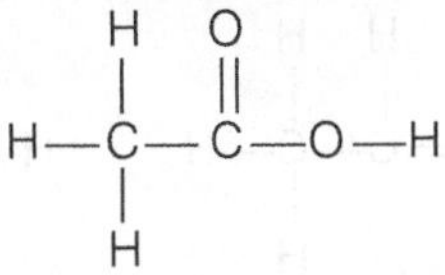

(1)

Q.10 (i) **Draw the structural diagram for the following compounds:** **(ICSE Specimen 2025)**

(a) Propanoic acid

(b) Pentan-2-ol

(c) 2,2-dibromobutane

(ii) **Give the IUPAC name of the following organic compounds:**

(a) 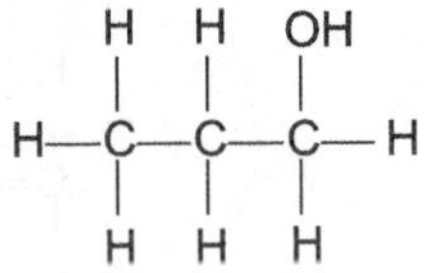

(b) 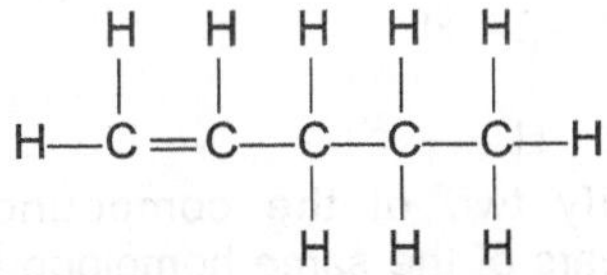

Ans. (i) (a) Propanoic acid is represented as

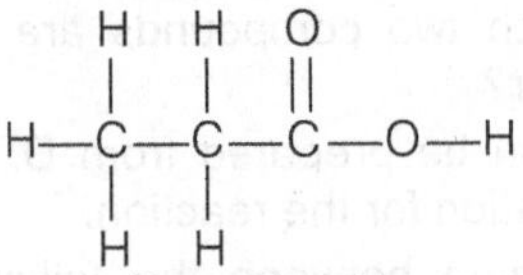

Propanoic acid

(b) The structure of pentan-2-ol is represented as

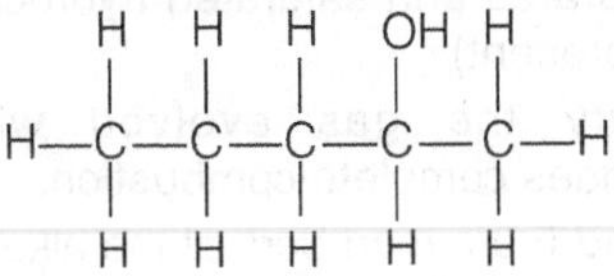

Pentan-2-ol

(c) The structure of 2, 2-dibromobutane is represented as

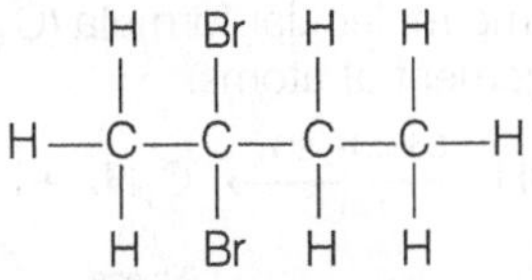

2,2-dibromobutane **(1 × 3 = 3)**

(ii) IUPAC name of the given organic compounds are:

(a) Propan-1-ol

(b) Pentene/pent-1-ene **(1 × 2 = 2)**

Q.11 (i) The structure of six organic compounds are shown: **(ICSE Specimen 2025)**

A

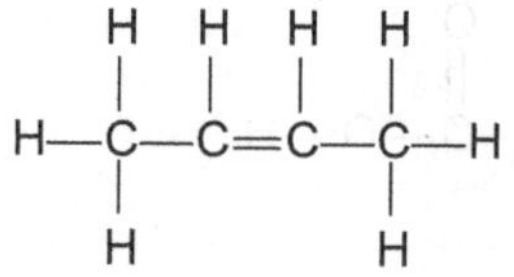

B

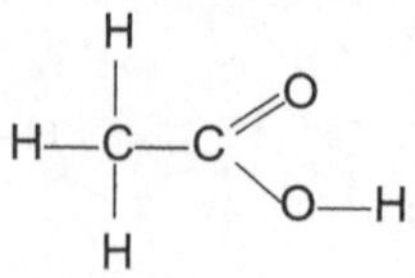

C

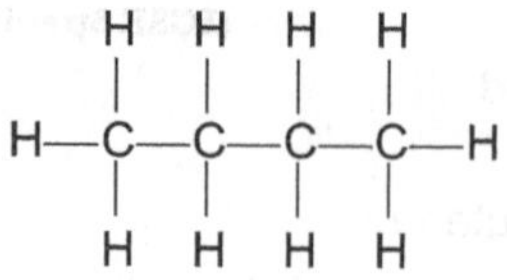

D

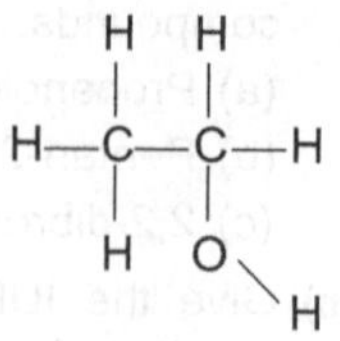

E

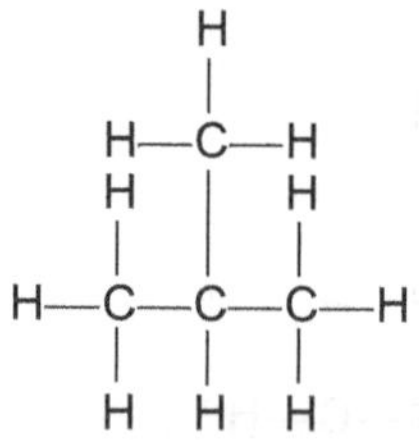

F

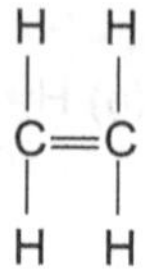

(a) Identify two of the compounds that are members of the same homologous series but are not isomers.

(b) Which two compounds are isomers of each other?

(c) F can be prepared from D. Give a chemical equation for the reaction.

(ii) Differentiate between the following pair on the criteria given:
Unsaturated and saturated hydrocarbons (type of bond present). **(ICSE 2024)**

(iii) Identify the gas evolved when methane undergoes complete combustion. **(ICSE 2024)**

Ans. (i) (a) **A and F** are members of the alkene homologous series, but they are not isomers as they have different molecular formula.

(b) **C and E** are isomers of each other as they have the same molecular formula (C_4H_{10}), but different arrangement of atoms.

(c) $\underset{\text{(Ethanol)}}{\underset{\text{(D)}}{C_2H_5OH}} \xrightarrow[170°C]{\text{Conc. } H_2SO_4} \underset{\text{(Ethene)}}{\underset{\text{(F)}}{C_2H_4}} + H_2O$ **(1 × 3 = 3)**

(ii) In saturated hydrocarbons, all carbon atoms are linked by **only single covalent bonds** whereas, in unsaturated hydrocarbons, atleast **one double or triple bond** is present along with single bonds. **(1)**

(iii) **CO_2 gas** is released on complete combustion of methane.

$$CH_4 + 2O_2 \longrightarrow CO_2\uparrow + 2H_2O + \text{Heat}$$ **(1)**

Q.12 Compound *A* is bubbled through bromine dissolved in carbon tetrachloride and the product is $CH_2Br—CH_2Br$.

$$A \xrightarrow{Br_2/CCl_4} CH_2Br—CH_2Br$$

(i) Draw the structural formula of *A*.

(ii) What type of reaction has *A* undergone?

(iii) What is your observation?

(iv) Name (not formula) the compound formed, when steam reacts with *A*, in the presence of phosphoric acid.

(v) What is the procedure for converting the product of (iv) back to *A*?

Ans. (i) *A* is **ethene**.

Structural formula is

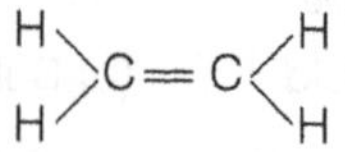

(ii) **Addition** reaction.

(iii) **Orange colour of bromine disappears** due to the formation of the colourless ethylene dibromide.

(iv) **Ethanol** (or ethyl alcohol).

$$CH_2{=}CH_2 + H_2O \xrightarrow{H^+} C_2H_5OH$$

(v) **Dehydration** of ethanol by conc. H_2SO_4 at 170°C **(1 × 5 = 5)**

TYPE - 10 — 03 Marks

Case-Based Questions

Q.1 Radhika is studying ethyl chloride (C_2H_5Cl), an organic compound used in the manufacture of refrigerants and as a solvent in some industrial processes. Priya, on the other hand, is studying methanol (CH_3OH), a type of alcohol that is used as a fuel, solvent, and in the production of formaldehyde. Both Radhika and Priya are fascinated by how their compounds differ in structure.

(i) What do you mean by functional group in an organic compound?

(ii) What is the functional group present in ethyl chloride and methanol?

(iii) Do both ethyl chloride and methanol exhibit the same chemical properties? Why or why not?

Ans. (i) **Functional group** is an atom or a group of atoms that defines the structure and properties of organic compounds. **(1)**

(ii) Ethyl chloride contains a **halide (–Cl) functional group**, making it a **haloalkane**. Methanol contains a **hydroxyl (—OH) functional group**, making it an **alcohol**. **(1)**

(iii) The chemical properties of compounds of different functional groups are **different**. Therefore, both ethyl chloride and methanol do not exhibit the same chemical properties. **(1)**

Q.2 Ramesh is studying alkanes and alkenes as a part of his chemistry syllabus. While going through his textbook, he learns that these groups of compounds form homologous series, which are groups of related compounds with similar properties. He becomes curious about how the compounds in these series are related and what makes them behave similarly.

(i) What is a homologous series in organic chemistry?

(ii) Do all the members of a homologous series share the same general formula? Why or why not?

(iii) What is the general formula of alkanes and alkenes?

Ans. (i) A **homologous series** is a group of organic compounds having a similar structure and similar chemical properties in which the successive compounds differ by a CH_2 group. **(1)**

(ii) **Yes**, all the members of a homologous series share the same general formula, as they have the same elements and the same functional group. **(1)**

(iii) The general formula of alkane is C_nH_{2n+2} and general formula of alkenes is C_nH_{2n}. **(1)**

Q.3 Ravi is studying two pairs of compounds: but-1-yne and but-2-yne, and pentane and isopentane. He learns that both pairs of compounds show isomerism. He is curious about what isomerism is and wants to understand which type of isomerism applies to these pairs of compounds.

(i) What is isomerism in organic chemistry and what are the two main types of isomerism?

(ii) Which type of isomerism is shown by the pairs but-1-yne and but-2-yne, and pentane and isopentane?

(iii) Define both the isomerism mentioned in the above part.

Ans. (i) Compounds having the same molecular formula but different structural formula are known as **isomers** and the phenomenon is known is **isomerism**.

Isomerism is of two types: structural and stereo isomerism. **(1)**

(ii) Both pairs show **structural isomerism**. Specifically, pentane and *iso*-pentane exhibits **chain isomerism** whereas, but-1-yne and but-2-yne shows **position isomerism**.

$$\underset{\text{Pentane}}{CH_3CH_2CH_2CH_2CH_3} \text{ and } \underset{\substack{\textit{iso}\text{-pentane} \\ \text{(2-methylbutane)}}}{CH_3\overset{\overset{\displaystyle CH_3}{|}}{C}HCH_2CH_3}$$

$$\underset{\text{But-1-yne}}{CH_3-CH_2C\equiv C-H} \text{ and } \underset{\text{But-2-yne}}{CH_3-C\equiv C-CH_3} \quad \textbf{(1)}$$

(iii) **Chain isomerism** occurs when compounds have the same molecular formula but they differ in the arrangement of the carbon chain, i.e. they have different carbon backbone structures.

Position isomerism occurs when compounds have the same molecular formula but they differ in the position of the functional group or multiple bonds (such as double or triple bonds) along the carbon chain. **(1)**

Q.4 Nita's father bought a basket of ripe mangoes. While opening it she found a small sachet containing a white crystalline powder along with the mangoes. She was told that it is a chemical that releases a gas when it comes in contact with moisture, that induces ripening of fruits. **(Competency Based Que.)**

(i) Name the chemical powder in the sachet.

(ii) Name the gas.

(iii) Give a balanced chemical equation for the reaction that results in the evolution of this gas.

Ans. (i) Calcium carbide.

(ii) ethyne/acetylene.

(iii) $CaC_2 + 2H_2O \longrightarrow Ca(OH)_2 + C_2H_2\uparrow$ **(1 × 3 = 3)**

ALCOHOLS AND CARBOXYLIC ACIDS

Alcohols

Alcohols are the organic compounds containing **hydroxyl group** (—OH) attached to a carbon atom. An alcohol is actually a hydroxyl derivative of an alkane.

$$\underset{\text{Methane}}{CH_4} \xrightarrow[\text{by OH}]{\text{Replace one H}} \underset{\substack{\text{Methyl alcohol}\\ \text{(Methanol)}}}{CH_3—OH}$$

The general molecular formula for homologous series of alcohol is **$C_nH_{2n+1}OH$.**

Types of Alcohol

(i) **Monohydric alcohol** (contains one —OH group) e.g. Methyl alcohol (CH_3OH), ethyl alcohol (C_2H_5OH).

(ii) **Dihydric alcohol** (contains two —OH groups) e.g. $\begin{matrix} CH_2OH \\ | \\ CH_2OH \end{matrix}$ (glycol).

(iii) **Trihydric alcohol** (contains three —OH groups) e.g. Glycerol or 1, 2, 3-propane triol $\left(\begin{matrix} CH_2 & — & CH & — & CH_2 \\ | & & | & & | \\ OH & & OH & & OH \end{matrix}\right)$.

Ethanol [C_2H_5OH]

It is also known as **ethyl alcohol**. This alcohol is an essential constituent of all wines. Thus, it is called **'Spirit of Wine'**. It is obtained from starchy grain, so, it is also known as **'grain alcohol'**.

Laboratory Preparation of Ethanol

Ethanol can be prepared by the **hydrolysis of alkyl halides.**

The reaction occurs with a **hot dilute alkali** like potassium hydroxide (KOH) or sodium hydroxide (NaOH).

$$\underset{\text{Ethyl bromide}}{C_2H_5Br} + NaOH(aq) \xrightarrow{\text{Boil}} \underset{\text{Ethanol}}{C_2H_5OH} + NaBr$$

$$\underset{\text{Ethyl chloride}}{C_2H_5Cl} + KOH(aq) \xrightarrow{\text{Boil}} \underset{\text{Ethanol}}{C_2H_5OH} + KCl$$

Physical Properties of Ethanol

(i) Ethanol is **colourless**, have a **faint odour** and a **burning taste.**

(ii) It is an **inflammable volatile liquid.**

(iii) The **boiling point** of ethanol is **78.3°C**. However, in general the boiling point of alcohols increases with an increase in number of carbon atoms.

e.g.

$$CH_3OH = 64.5°C$$

$$CH_3CH_2OH = 78.3°C$$

(iv) It is **soluble in water as well as in organic solvents.**

(v) Ethanol is **lighter than water** as its **density is 0.79 g cm^{-3}** at 20°C.

Chemical Properties of Ethanol

(i) **Combustion (Burning)** Ethyl alcohol burns in air to produce **carbon dioxide** and **water vapour** with the generation of **large amount of heat** during the reaction.

$$\underset{\text{Ethanol}}{C_2H_5OH} + 3O_2 \longrightarrow 2CO_2 + 3H_2O + \text{Heat}$$

Ethanol burns with **pale blue flame.**

(ii) **Action with sodium** When sodium reacts with ethanol, **hydrogen gas** is evolved with the formation of **sodium ethoxide.**

$$\underset{\text{Ethanol}}{2C_2H_5OH} + 2Na \longrightarrow \underset{\text{Sodium ethoxide}}{2C_2H_5\overset{-}{O}\overset{+}{Na}} + H_2\uparrow$$

Note Hydrogen produces effervescence which helps in identification of alcohol.

(iii) **Reaction with acetic acid (Ester formation)** Ethanol reacts with acetic acid in the presence of concentrated sulphuric acid to give ester and the process is known as **esterification.**

$$\underset{\text{Ethanol}}{C_2H_5OH} + \underset{\text{Ethanoic acid}}{CH_3COOH} \xrightarrow[\Delta]{\text{Conc. } H_2SO_4} \underset{\substack{\text{Ethyl acetate}\\ \text{(Ester)}}}{CH_3COOC_2H_5} + H_2O$$

Note Esters can be detected by their fruity smell.

(iv) **Dehydration with concentrated sulphuric acid** When a mixture of ethyl alcohol and concentrated sulphuric acid is heated upto 170°C, dehydration of ethyl alcohol (ethanol) takes place and **ethene** is formed.

$$\underset{\text{Ethanol}}{C_2H_5OH} \xrightarrow[170^\circ C]{\text{Conc. } H_2SO_4} \underset{\text{Ethene}}{CH_2{=}CH_2} + H_2O$$

Different Commercial Forms of Ethanol

Spurious Alcohol

It is an illicit liquor made by improper distillation. It contains large proportion of methanol in a mixture of alcohols. It is used in paint industry as solvent and is fatal for human consumption.

Absolute Alcohol

It is 100% pure ethyl alcohol, which can be easily obtained by distilling moist alcohol with benzene. A wide range of organic compounds are soluble in ethyl alcohol, it is the most common industrial solvent.

Denatured Alcohol

To discourage the misuse of ethanol as beverage, 5% methyl alcohol is added to it, thus making it unfit for drinking. This mixture is called **denatured alcohol** or **methylated spirit**. Pyridine or copper sulphate is also used widely to denature the alcohol.

Uses of Ethanol

- In manufacturing of chemicals and synthetic products such as dyes, perfumes, etc.
- In alcoholic drinks like wine, beer and whisky, etc.
- As a preservative for biological specimen due to its low freezing point.
- As a good solvent for gums and resins.
- In thermometers and an antiseptic in hospitals.
- As a fuel in powdered form.
- As an antifreeze for automobile radiators.

Carboxylic Acids

Organic compounds containing the **carboxyl group** (—COOH) or 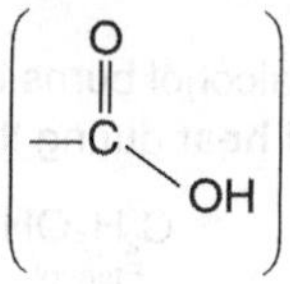 are known as carboxylic acids.

Their general formula is C_nH_{2n+1} COOH or *R*COOH.

Classification of Carboxylic Acid

These are classified into following types

- Compounds which contain one —COOH group are called **monocarboxylic acid.**

  e.g. HCOOH (Formic acid)

  CH_3COOH (Acetic acid)

- Compounds which contain two — COOH groups are called **dicarboxylic acid.**

  e.g. COOH | COOH (Oxalic acid)

Acetic Acid (CH_3COOH)

The name acetic acid is derived from Latin word 'ACETUM' means **vinegar. Vinegar** (known as Sirka) is a dilute (4-5%) solution of acetic acid.

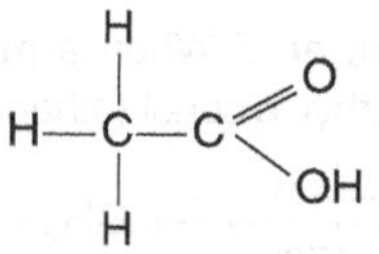

Preparation of Acetic Acid

Acetic acid can be prepared by the oxidation of ethyl alcohol or acetaldehyde with acidified potassium dichromate or sodium dichromate.

$$\underset{\text{Ethanol}}{CH_3CH_2OH} \xrightarrow[K_2Cr_2O_7/H^+]{[O]} \underset{\text{Ethanal}}{CH_3CHO} \xrightarrow[K_2Cr_2O_7/H^+]{[O]} \underset{\text{Ethanoic acid}}{CH_3COOH}$$

Physical Properties

- Ethanoic acid is a **colourless, pungent smelling** liquid. It has **vinegar like odour.**
- It is **sour** in taste.
- It is a **hygroscopic liquid.**
- Boiling point of ethanoic acid is **391 K.**
- It is **miscible** with **water, alcohol** and **ether** in all proportions.
- When pure ethanoic acid is cooled, it forms a crystalline mass, which looks like a glacier and has melting point of 17°C. That is why pure ethanoic acid is called **glacial acetic acid.**

Chemical Properties

(i) **Reaction on Litmus** Ethanoic acid is a weak acid and **turns moist blue litmus red.**

(ii) **Reaction with Alkalis (Sodium Hydroxide)** It reacts with sodium hydroxide to form **sodium acetate and water.**

$$\underset{\text{Acetic acid}}{CH_3COOH} + NaOH \longrightarrow \underset{\text{Sodium acetate}}{CH_3COONa} + H_2O$$

(iii) **Reaction with Alcohols (Esterification)** Ethanoic acid reacts with alcohols in the presence of concentrated sulphuric acid to form esters, which are sweet fruity smelling compounds. The reaction is called **esterification.**

$$\underset{\text{Ethanoic acid}}{CH_3COOH} + \underset{\text{Ethanol}}{C_2H_5OH} \xrightarrow{\text{Conc. } H_2SO_4} \underset{\text{Ethyl ethanoate}}{CH_3COOC_2H_5} + H_2O$$

Note Acetic acid liberates brisk effervescence of carbon dioxide with carbonates or hydrogen carbonates.

e.g. $2CH_3COOH + Na_2CO_3 \longrightarrow 2CH_3COONa + H_2O + CO_2\uparrow$

Uses of Acetic Acid

- As vinegar in cooking.
- In the production of dyes, perfumes, esters, etc.
- For coagulating rubber from latex.
- As a laboratory reagent.
- For the manufacturing of cellulose acetate, which is used for making packaging materials, varnishes, rayons, etc.
- In the manufacture of acetic anhydride, which is used in aspirin.

Examiner's Favourite Top 10 Equations

1. $CH_3{-}I + KOH(aq) \xrightarrow{\text{Boil}} CH_3OH + KI$

2. $CH_3CH_2OH \xrightarrow[170°C]{\text{Conc. } H_2SO_4} C_2H_4 + H_2O$

3. $CH_3COOH + C_2H_5OH \xrightarrow[\Delta]{H_2SO_4} CH_3COOC_2H_5 + H_2O$

4. $C_2H_5Cl + KOH(aq) \xrightarrow{\text{Boil}} C_2H_5OH + KCl$

5. $C_2H_4 + H_2O \xrightarrow{H^+} C_2H_5OH$

6. $C_2H_5OH + 2[O] \xrightarrow{K_2Cr_2O_7/H^+} CH_3COOH + H_2O$

7. $2C_2H_5OH + 2Na \longrightarrow 2C_2H_5ONa + H_2$

8. $C_2H_6 \xrightarrow[K_2Cr_2O_7/H^+]{[O]} C_2H_5OH \xrightarrow[K_2Cr_2O_7/H^+]{2[O]} CH_3COOH + H_2O$

9. $C_2H_5Cl + NaOH(aq) \xrightarrow{\text{Boil}} C_2H_5OH + H_2O$

10. $C_2H_5OH + 3O_2 \longrightarrow 2CO_2 + 3H_2O + \text{Heat}$

EXAM ORIENTED QUESTIONS

TYPE - 1 — 01 Mark

Multiple Choice Questions

Q.1 The general molecular formula for alcohols is

(a) $C_nH_{2n}OH$ (b) $C_nH_{2n-1}OH$
(c) $C_nH_{2n+1}OH$ (d) $C_nH_{2n+2}OH$

Ans. (c) $C_nH_{2n+1}OH$

Q.2 The IUPAC name for the given structural formula is

$$H_3C-\underset{}{\overset{OH}{\overset{|}{C}H}}-CH_3$$

(a) propan-2-ol (b) propan-1-ol
(c) propan-2-al (d) propane

Ans. (a) Propan-2-ol

Q.3 The IUPAC name for the given structural formula is

$$\underset{OH}{\underset{|}{CH_2}}-\underset{OH}{\underset{|}{CH}}-\underset{OH}{\underset{|}{CH_2}}$$

(a) 1,2,3-propane triol (b) propanol
(c) propanal (d) tri-propanol

Ans. (a) 1,2,3- propane triol

Q.4 The diagram below represents the molecule of an organic compound. **(Competency Based Que.)**

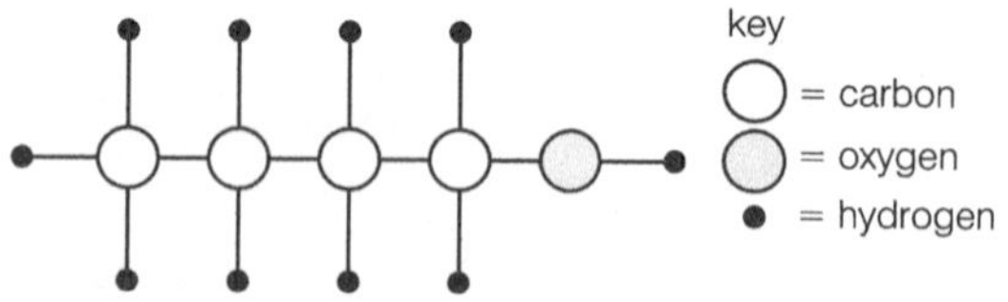

What is the name of this compound?

(a) Pentanol
(b) Butanol
(c) Butanoic acid
(d) Pentanoic acid

Ans. (b) Butanol

Q.5 Which of the following is not the property of alcohol?

(a) Inflammable volatile liquids.
(b) Insoluble in water.
(c) Soluble in organic solvents.
(d) Colourless and burning taste.

Ans. (b) Insoluble in water.

Q.6 Reaction of an alcohol with a carboxylic acid in the presence of concentrated H_2SO_4 is termed as **(ICSE 2024)**

(a) halogenation (b) esterification
(c) hydrogenation (d) dehydrohalogenation

Ans. (b) Esterification

$$\underset{\text{Ethanol (Alcohol)}}{C_2H_5OH} + \underset{\text{Ethanoic acid (Carboxylic acid)}}{CH_3COOH} \xrightarrow{\text{Conc. } H_2SO_4} \underset{\text{Ethyl acetate (Ester)}}{CH_3COOC_2H_5} + H_2O$$

Q.7 The organic compound prepared when ethanol undergoes dehydration. **(ICSE Specimen 2023)**

(a) Methane (b) Ethane (c) Acetylene (d) Ethene

Ans. (d) Ethene

$$\underset{\text{Ethanol}}{CH_3CH_2OH} \xrightarrow[170°C]{\text{Conc. } H_2SO_4} \underset{\text{Ethene}}{CH_2=CH_2} + H_2O$$

Q.8 Wine is an alcoholic drink that contains ethanol. If wine is left exposed to the air for too long, it can become acidic.

This is because the ethanol is ......1...... to the acid ......2...... .

Which word and formula correctly complete gaps 1 and 2?

	1	2
(a)	oxidised	CH_3COOH
(b)	oxidised	CH_3CH_2COOH
(c)	reduced	CH_3COOH
(d)	reduced	CH_3CH_2COOH

Ans. (a) Alcohols oxidise to carboxylic acid in the presence of an oxidising agent.

$$CH_3CH_2OH \xrightarrow{[O]} CH_3COOH$$

Q.9 The diagram shows a reaction scheme.

$$\text{Ethene + Steam} \xrightarrow{\text{Catalyst}} \text{Compound } X$$

$$\text{Compound } X \xrightarrow{\text{Acidified potassium dichromate(VI)}} \text{Compound } Y$$

$$\text{Compound } Y \xrightarrow{\text{Compound } X} \text{Compound } Z$$

What is the final compound Z ?

(a) A carboxylic acid (b) An alcohol
(c) An alkene (d) An ester

Ans. (d) Ethene reacts with water to produce **alcohol** which is **oxidised to an acid**. An acid and an alcohol react to produce an **ester**, therefore ***Z* is an ester** given in option (d).

Q.10 **When two organic compounds *A* and *B* react together in the presence of conc. H_2SO_4, a fruity smell evolved from one of the products. If *A* has the functional group [—O—H], which of the following stands for the functional group of *B*?**

(a) —C(H)=O (b) —C=O

(c) —C(=O)—OH (d) —O—

Ans. (c) *B* has —C(=O)—OH functional group.

Q.11 **The organic compound mixed with ethanol to make it spurious is**

(a) methanol (b) methanoic acid
(c) methanal (d) ethanoic acid

Ans. (a) Methanol

Q.12 **The general molecular formula for carboxylic acid is**

(a) $C_nH_{2n}COOH$ (b) $C_nH_{2n-1}COOH$
(c) $C_nH_{2n+1}COOH$ (d) $C_nH_{2n+2}COOH$

Ans. (c) $C_nH_{2n+1}COOH$

Q.13 **The functional group present in acetic acid is**

(a) ketonic (C=O) (b) hydroxyl (—OH)
(c) aldehydic (—CHO) (d) carboxyl (—COOH)

Ans. (d) Carboxyl (—COOH)

Q.14 **Formic acid and acetic acid are ......carboxylic acid.**

(a) mono (b) di (c) tri (d) aromatic

Ans. (a) mono

Q.15 **Vinegar is 4-5% solution of which acid?**

(a) Acetic acid (b) Sulphuric acid
(c) Nitric acid (d) Formic acid

Ans. (a) Acetic acid

Q.16 **Which of the following are the correct properties of carboxylic acids?**

(i) Smell of vinegar. (ii) Hygroscopic liquid.
(iii) Insoluble in water. (iv) Insoluble in alcohol.
(a) (i) and (iii) (b) (i) and (ii)
(c) (i) and (iv) (d) (ii) and (iv)

Ans. (b) (i) and (ii)

Q.17 **Baking soda ($NaHCO_3$), when added to vinegar, evolves a gas. Which of these statements is true about the evolution of gas? (Competency Based Que.)**

(i) It turn limewater milky.
(ii) It extinguishes the burning splinter.
(iii) It acts as a non-metallic oxide.
(iv) It has a pungent odour.
(a) I and IV (b) I and II
(c) I, II and III (d) III and IV

Ans. (c) Vinegar reacts with baking soda to produce carbon dioxide gas.

$$CH_3COOH + NaHCO_3 \longrightarrow CH_3COONa + H_2O + CO_2 \uparrow$$

Carbon dioxide is an odourless gas. It extinguishes the burning splinter (as it does not support combustion) and it turns limewater milky. It also acts as a non-metallic oxide.

Q.18 **The alcohol C_4H_9OH on oxidation with acidified potassium dichromate (VI) will give a carboxylic acid *X*. Which acid is *X*?**

(a) C_4H_9COOH
(b) C_3H_7COOH
(c) C_2H_5COOH
(d) CH_3COOH

Ans. (b) C_4H_9OH can be written as $C_3H_7CH_2OH$. A primary alcohol (R—CH_2OH) is oxidised to a carboxylic acid (R—CO_2H). Thus, $C_3H_7CH_2OH$ will be oxidised to **$C_3H_7CO_2H$**.

Q.19 **Which statements would be true for the compound which has the formula shown?**

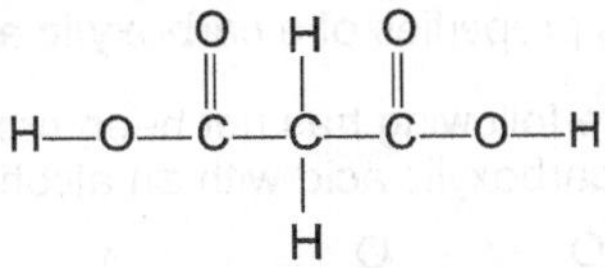

(i) It would react with excess aqueous sodium hydroxide in a 1:1 molar ratio.
(ii) In aqueous solution, it would have a pH of 9.5.
(iii) It would react with an alcohol to form an ester.
(a) Only (i) (b) (i) and (ii)
(c) (ii) and (iii) (d) Only (iii)

Ans. (d) The compound shown is a **dibasic carboxylic acid**. It would react with aqueous sodium hydroxide in a **1:2 molar ratio**. It would have a **pH lesser than 7** in aqueous solution and would react with an alcohol to **form an ester**.

Q.20 **What are the reactions of compounds *W*, *X*, *Y* and *Z*?**

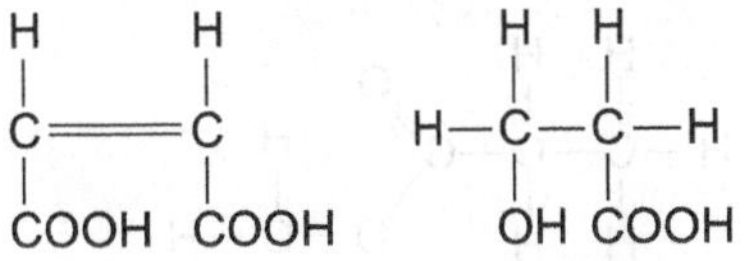

(*W*) (*X*)

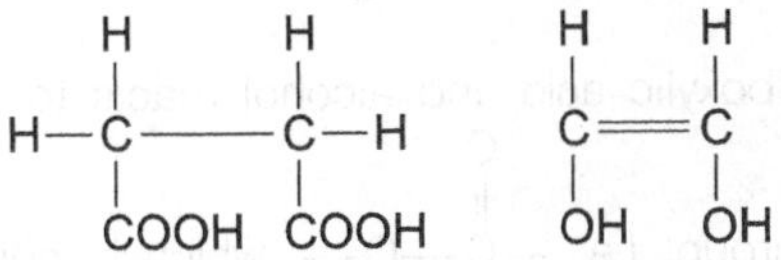

(*Y*) (*Z*)

	Decolourises aqueous bromine	Has a pH of less than 7	Reacts with a carboxylic acid to form an ester
(a)	*X* and *Y*	*W*, *X* and *Y*	*W*,*X*, *Y* and *Z*
(b)	*X* and *Y*	*X* and *Z*	*X* and *Z*
(c)	*W* and *Z*	*W*, *X* and *Y*	*X* and *Z*
(d)	*W* and *Z*	*X* and *Z*	*W*, *X*, *Y* and *Z*

Ans. (c) ***W* and *Z*** both have a carbon-carbon double covalent bond which **decolourises aqueous bromine.** ***W*, *X*, *Y* have a —COOH group** which causes them to have a **pH of lesser than 7**. ***X* and *Z* have a —OH group** which can react with a carboxylic acid to form an ester.

Q.21 Some properties of compound ***J*** are listed.

(i) It reacts with potassium carbonate to produce carbon dioxide.

(ii) It reacts with ethanol to produce a sweet-smelling liquid.

(iii) It reacts with sodium hydroxide to produce a salt.

What is a possible identity of ***J*** ?

(a) Ethanoic acid (b) Ethanol

(c) Ethyl ethanoate (d) Ethyl methanoate

Ans. (a) ***J*** shows properties of a **carboxylic acid**.

Q.22 Which of the following has not been prepared by reacting a carboxylic acid with an alcohol?

(a) 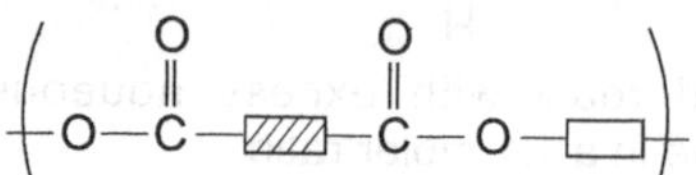

(b) 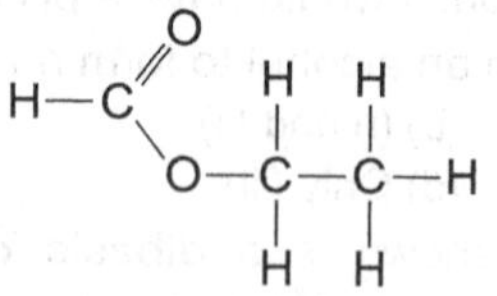

(c) 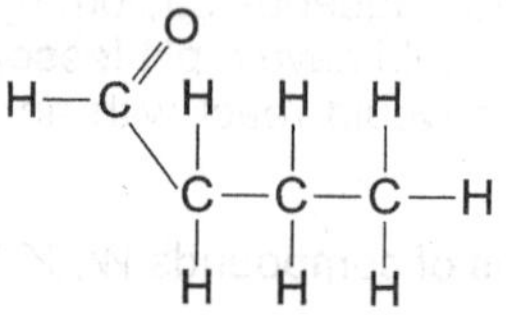

(d) 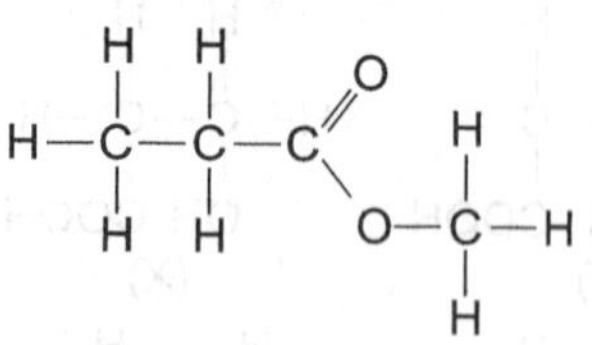

Ans. (c) Carboxylic acid and alcohol reacts to produce an ester group, i.e. $-\overset{\overset{O}{\|}}{C}-O-$, which is not present in option (c).

Q.23 Which statement about ethanoic acid is correct?

(a) It contains three carbon atoms per molecule.

(b) It contains five hydrogen atoms per molecule.

(c) It is insoluble in water.

(d) It reacts with ethanol to form a sweet-smelling compound.

Ans. (d) Ethanoic acid reacts with ethanol (an alcohol) to produce an **ester** which is a sweet-smelling compound.

Q.24 Carboxylic acids react with alcohols to form esters. Which acid and alcohol react together to form the following ester?

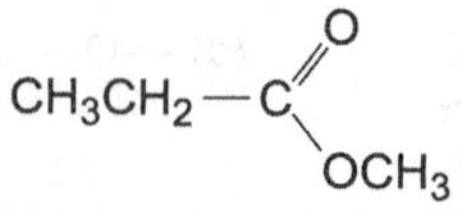

(a) Propanoic acid and ethanol

(b) Propanoic acid and methanol

(c) Ethanoic acid and ethanol

(d) Ethanoic acid and methanol

Ans. (b) To produce required ester, an acid containing three carbon atoms and an alcohol containing one carbon atom are needed.

Therefore, option (b) is correct.

TYPE - 2 01 Mark

Assertion-Reason Questions

Directions (Q. Nos. 1-5) In the following questions, a statement of Assertion (A) is followed by a statement of Reason (R). Choose the answer based on the codes given below.

(a) Both (A) and (R) are true and (R) is the correct explanation of (A).

(b) Both (A) and (R) are true but (R) is not the correct explanation of (A).

(c) (A) is true but (R) is false.

(d) (A) is false but (R) si true.

Q.1 Assertion (A) Methyl alcohol if taken in excess may cause blindness and even death.

Reason (R) Methyl alcohol is toxic in nature.

Ans. (a) Methanol or methyl alcohol if consumed in excess causes blindness and even death because it is toxic in nature. Thus, both (A) and (R) are true and (R) is the correct explanation of (A).

Q.2 Assertion (A) Oxalic acid is a dicarboxylic acid.

Reason (R) Oxalic acid has one carbon in it.

Ans. (c) Oxalic acid is a dicarboxylic acid because it contains two —COOH groups in it. Thus, (A) is true, but (R) is false.

Q.3 Assertion (A) Ethanoic acid is a hygroscopic liquid.
Reason (R) It does not absorb moisture easily.

Ans. (c) Ethanoic acid is hygroscopic in nature as it has ability to adsorb and absorb moisture or water from the surrounding environment. Thus, (A) is true but (R) is false.

Q.4 Assertion (A) Carboxylic acid reacts with alcohol in presence of concentrated H_2SO_4 to produce a fruity smell.
Reason (R) It is due to the formation of an alcohol.

Ans. (c) Carboxylic acid reacts with alcohol in the presence of concentrated H_2SO_4 to produce a fruity smell. The fruity smell is due to the formation of ester in the reaction. Thus, (A) is true but (R) is false.

Q.5 Assertion (A) On adding ethanoic acid to carbonates and bicarbonates, the carbon dioxide is evolved.
Reason (R) This release of CO_2 can be used as the test for the acids.

Ans. (a) On adding ethanoic acid to carbonates and bicarbonates, CO_2 is evolved with brisk effervescence and thus, this can be used as test for acids.
Thus, both (A) and (R) are true and (R) is the correct explanation of (A).

TYPE - 3 01 Mark

Fill in the Blanks

Q.1 Glycerol is .... (dihydric/trihydric) alcohol.

Ans. trihydric

Q.2 The product formed when ethene gas reacts with water in the presence of sulphuric acid is ..... (ethanol/ethanoic acid).

Ans. ethanol

Q.3 The compound formed when ethanol reacts with sodium is .... (sodium ethanoate/sodium ethoxide). **(ICSE 2014)**

Ans. sodium ethoxide

$$2C_2H_5OH + 2Na \longrightarrow \underset{\text{(Sodium ethoxide)}}{2C_2H_5ONa} + H_2 \uparrow$$

Q.4 The conversion of ethanol to ethene is an example of .... (dehydration/dehydrogenation).

Ans. dehydration

Q.5 Converting ethanol to ethene requires the use of .... (concentrated nitric acid/concentrated sulphuric acid).

Ans. concentrated sulphuric acid

Q.6 100% pure ethanol is called .... (denatured alcohol/absolute alcohol).

Ans. absolute alcohol

Q.7 .... is used widely to denature the alcohol. (Pyridine/Sodium sulphate)

Ans. Pyridine

Q.8 The carbon compounds containing .... (carboxyl/alkyl) group are known as carboxylic acids.

Ans. carboxyl (—COOH)

Q.9 The name of carboxylic acid is derived by the combination of carbonyl group and the .... (hydroxyl/halide) group.

Ans. hydroxyl

Q.10 .... (Methyl/Ethyl) is an alkyl component of acetic acid. **(Competency Based Que.)**

Ans. (Methyl) (—CH_3)

Q.11 IUPAC name for formic acid is .... (methanoic acid/acetaldehyde).

Ans. methanoic acid

Q.12 ....(Vinegar/Butyric acid) is used for flavouring and preserving foods.

Ans. Vinegar

TYPE - 4 01 Mark

Correct the Incorrect Statement

Q.1 Methanol and ethanol both exhibits the property of isomerism.

Ans. Methanol and ethanol **do not** show isomerism as alcohols with more than three carbons have the property to show isomerism.

Q.2 Alcohols can be prepared by boiling alkyl halide with aqueous acids.

Ans. Alcohols can be prepared by boiling alkyl halide with aqueous **alkalis**.

Q.3 Boiling point of alcohols decreases with increase in molecular weight.

Ans. Boiling point of alcohols **increases** with increase in molecular weight.

Q.4 Copper sulphate is added to ethyl alcohol in order to make it more tasty.

Ans. Copper sulphate is added to ethyl alcohol in order to make it **undrinkable**.

Q.5 Pure ethanoic acid is a yellow liquid.

Ans. Pure ethanoic acid is a **colourless** liquid.

Q.6 Acetic acid has fruity smell.

Ans. Acetic acid posses the **pungent smell** (smell of vinegar).

TYPE – 5 — 01 × 05 = 05 Marks

Matching Type Question

Q.1 Match the organic reaction in *X* with the type of reaction in *Y*.

X	Y
A. $C_2H_5OH + O_2$	1. Hydration
B. $C_2H_5OH + CH_3COOH$, Conc. H_2SO_4	2. Combustion
C. Ethanol + Al_2O_3 at 350°C	3. Esterification
D. $C_2H_4 + H_2O$	4. Denaturation
E. C_2H_5OH + Pyridine	5. Dehydration

Ans. A → 2, B → 3, C → 5, D → 1, E → 4

TYPE – 6 — 01 Mark

Identify the Following

Q.1 Which alcohol is called as spirit of wine?

Ans. Ethyl alcohol

Q.2 Name the gas evolved when ethanol reacts with sodium. **(ICSE 2018)**

Ans. Hydrogen (H_2) gas

Q.3 Which organic compound is used as a thermometric liquid?

Ans. Ethanol

Q.4 Name the undistilled alcohol containing a large amount of methanol. **(ICSE 2025)**

Ans. Spurious alcohol

Q.5 Identify the organic compound containing —COOH functional group. **(ICSE 2017)**

Ans. Carboxylic acid

Q.6 Which functional group is present in C_2H_5COOH? **(ICSE Specimen 2023)**

Ans. —COOH (Carboxyl group)

Q.7 What do you call ice like crystals which are formed on cooling an organic acid sufficiently? **(ICSE 2017)**

Ans. Glacial acetic acid

Q.8 Is acetic acid a weak or strong acid?

Ans. Weak acid

Q.9 Name the distinctive reaction that takes place when ethanol in presence of conc. H_2SO_4 is treated with acetic acid. **(ICSE 2015)**

Ans. Esterification

Q.10 Which acid is used for the manufacture of cellulose acetate which is used in making packaging material, varnishes, etc.

Ans. Acetic acid

TYPE – 7 — 02 Marks

Short Answer Type I Questions

Q.1 Draw the structural formula for the following.

(i) Methanol (ii) Ethanol **(ICSE 2020, 2014)**

Ans. (i) Structural formula of methanol is

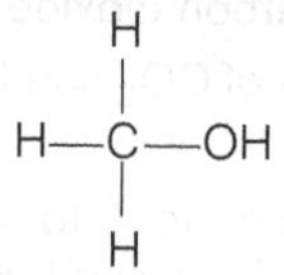

(1)

(ii) Structural formula of ethanol is

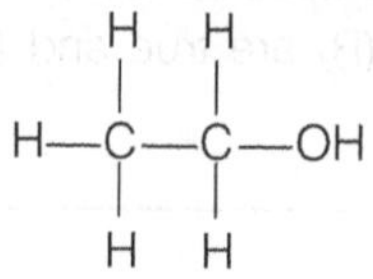

(1)

Q.2 Draw the structural formula for the following.

(i) Glycol (ii) Glycerol

Ans. (i) Structural formula of glycol is

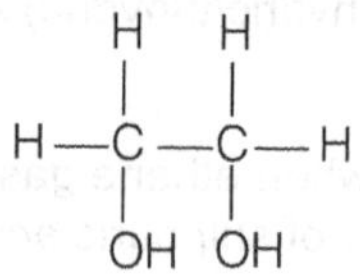

(1)

(ii) Structural formula of glycerol is

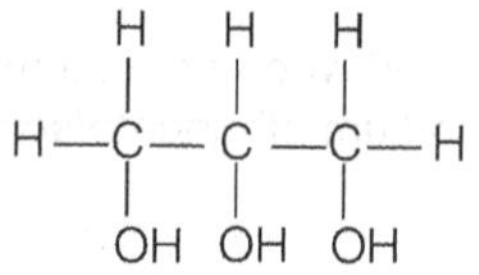

(1)

Q.3 The IUPAC name for the following structural formula. **(Competency Based Que.)**

(i)

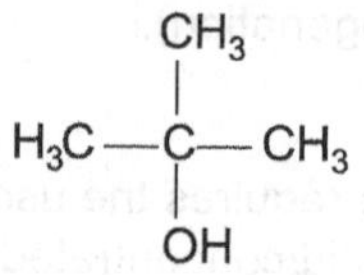

(ii)

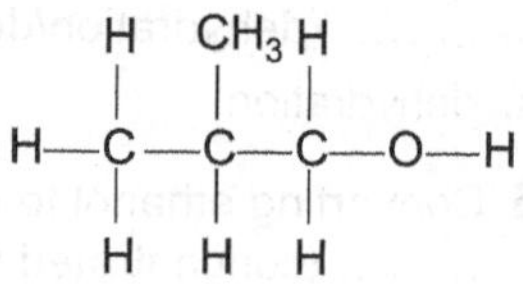

Ans. (i) 2-methylpropan-2-ol

(ii) 2-methylpropanol **(1 × 2 = 2)**

Q.4 The description of an organic compound is as follows

(i) Molecular formula is C_3H_8O.

(ii) Functional group is attached to the first carbon atom.

(iii) Reacts with sodium at room temperature with brisk effervescence, releasing hydrogen gas.

Identify the compound and draw its structure.

(Competency Based Que.)

Ans. The compound is **propanol.** **(1)**

Structure of propanol is 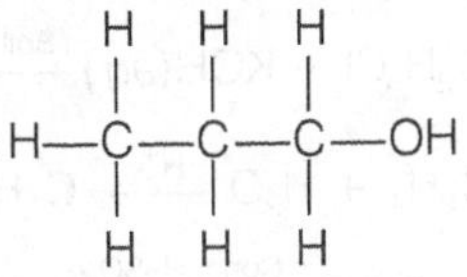

(1)

Q.5 Heating an alcohol with concentrated sulphuric acid results in the dehydration of the alcohol to give the ethene as shown by the reaction of ethanol to give ethene.

$$CH_3CH_2OH \xrightarrow{\text{Hot conc. sulphuric acid}} CH_2{=}CH_2$$

Pramila heated 2-butanol (shown below) with concentrated sulphuric acid.

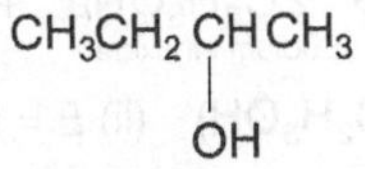

Write the structural formulae of all the possible products of the reaction.

Ans. The reaction is as follows

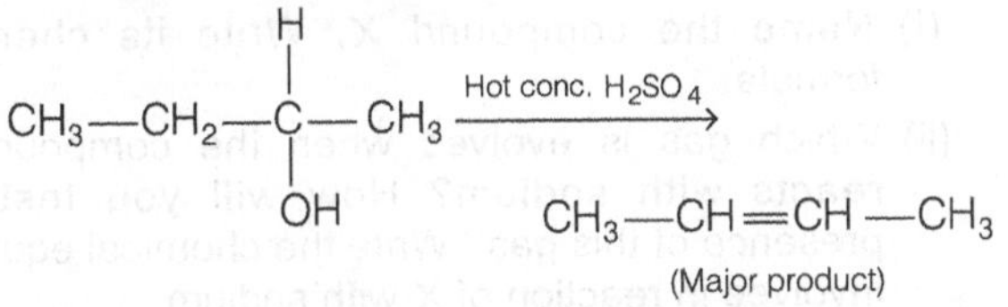

The structural formulae of all the possible products of the reaction are

(i) 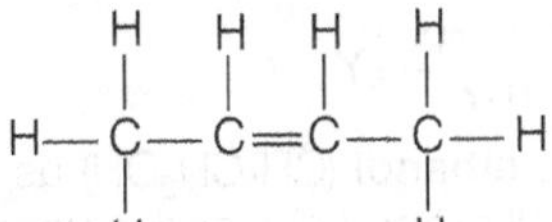

(ii) 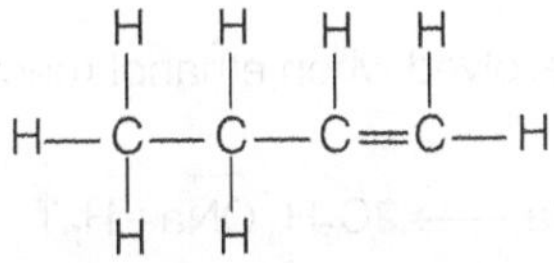

(1)

Q.6 Draw the structural formula for the following acids.

(i) Formic acid (ii) Acetic acid

Ans. (i) Structural formula of formic acid is

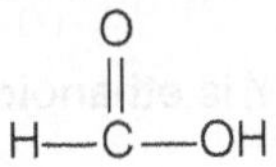

(1)

(ii) Structural formula of acetic acid is

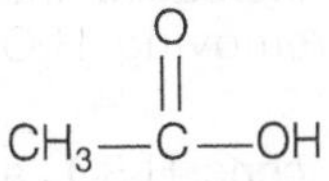

(1)

Q.7 (i) Ethyl alcohol is a colourless liquid. It is used as a major constituent in alcoholic beverages and also in the manufacture of many chemicals. When a chemical manufacturing unit ordered ethyl alcohol, they were supplied with a purple-coloured alcohol instead of a colourless one.

State the reason and the purpose of this colour change.

(ii) An organic acid on cooling below 16.5°C crystallises out in the pure form, forming a crystalline mass resembling ice. Draw the structural diagram of this carboxylic acid.

(Competency Based Que.)

Ans. (i) The purple colour of the alcohol is due to addition of a **coloured dye**. It is added to ethyl alcohol to **denature** it so as to prevent the misuse (consumption) of alcohol.

(ii) The carboxylic acid is **acetic acid** and its structural diagram is 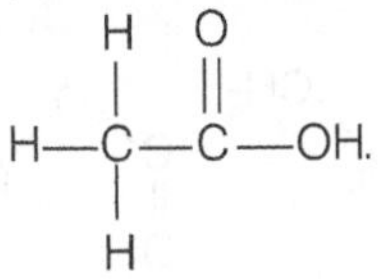

Q.8 (i) Why is pure acetic acid known as glacial acetic acid?

(ii) Give a chemical equation for the reaction between ethyl alcohol and acetic acid.

Ans. (i) The pure acid, i.e. anhydrous acid on cooling forms crystalline mass resembling ice (melting point 17°C) and for this reason, it is called **glacial acetic acid.** **(1)**

(ii) $\underset{\text{Ethanol}}{C_2H_5OH} + \underset{\text{Acetic acid}}{CH_3COOH} \xrightarrow{\text{Conc. } H_2SO_4} \underset{\text{Ethyl acetate}}{CH_3COOC_2H_5} + H_2O$ **(1)**

Q.9 Complete and balance the following equations.

(i) $CH_3COONa + NaOH \xrightarrow[\Delta]{CaO}$

(ii) $CH_3COOH + Mg \longrightarrow$ **(ICSE 2025)**

Ans. (i) $CH_3COONa + NaOH \xrightarrow[\Delta]{CaO} CH_4\uparrow + Na_2CO_3$ **(1)**

(ii) $2CH_3COOH + Mg \longrightarrow (CH_3COO)_2Mg + H_2\uparrow$ **(1)**

Q.10 What is the role of metal or reagents written on arrow in the given chemical reactions?

(i) $CH_3COOH + CH_3CH_2OH \xrightarrow{\text{Conc. } H_2SO_4} CH_3COOC_2H_5 + H_2O$

(ii) $CH_3CH_2OH \xrightarrow[\text{Heat}]{\text{Alk. } KMnO_4} CH_3COOH$

Ans. (i) Conc. H_2SO_4 increases the rate of the forward reaction by removing H_2O formed during the reaction.

In other words, conc. H_2SO_4 acts as a **dehydrating agent.** **(1)**

(ii) Alkaline $KMnO_4$ acts as an **oxidising agent** and oxidises ethanol to ethanoic acid. **(1)**

Q.11 The photograph shows a model of an ester molecule.

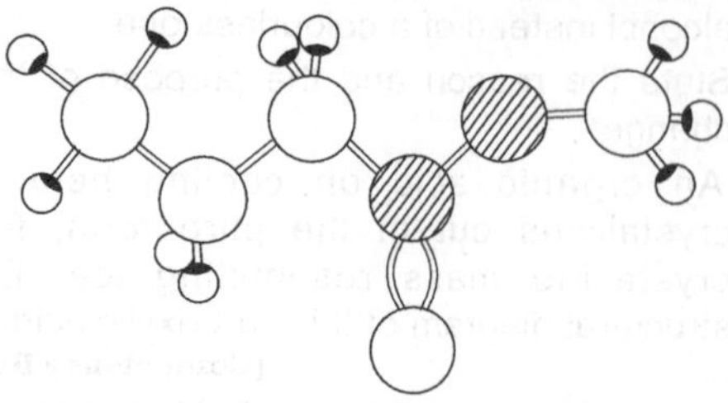

[Where, ◓ = H, ○ = C and ● = O]

(i) Write the structure of the given compound.

(ii) Which fragrance is produced by this ester?

Ans. (i) The model shows the structure of the compound given below.

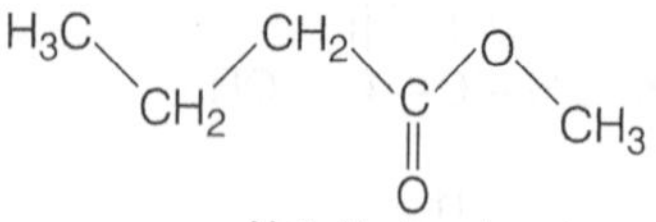

Methyl butanoate **(1)**

(ii) The ester produces a fragrance of an apple. **(1)**

Q.12 The formula of an ester is

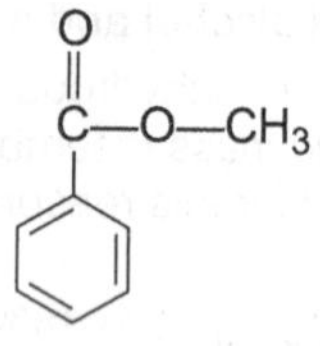

(i) Write the structural formula of the corresponding alcohol from given ester produced?

(ii) Which acid do we get back by the decomposition of this ester?

Ans. (i)

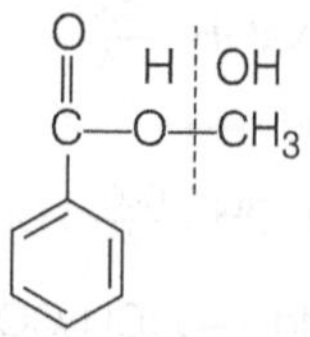

So, alcohol = CH_3OH **(1)**

(ii)

Benzoic acid =

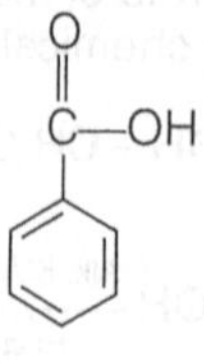

(1)

TYPE - 8

03 Marks

Short Answer Type II Questions

Q.1 State how the following conversions can be carried out? **(ICSE 2016)**

(i) Ethyl chloride to ethyl alcohol.

(ii) Ethene to ethyl alcohol.

(iii) Ethyl alcohol to ethene.

Ans. (i) $C_2H_5Cl + KOH(aq) \xrightarrow{\text{Boil}} C_2H_5OH + KCl$ **(1)**

(ii) $C_2H_4 + H_2O \xrightarrow{H^+} C_2H_5OH$ **(1)**

(iii) $C_2H_5OH \xrightarrow[160\text{-}170°C]{\text{Conc. } H_2SO_4} C_2H_4 + H_2O$ **(1)**

Q.2 A compound 'X' reacts with element 'E' to form sodium ethoxide and release the gas 'G'.

(i) The compound X is

(ii) The element E is

(iii) The gas G is

Ans. The given reaction takes place as follows

$$\underset{(X)}{2C_2H_5OH} + \underset{(E)}{2Na} \longrightarrow \underset{\text{Sodium ethoxide}}{2C_2H_5O\overset{-}{}\overset{+}{Na}} + \underset{(G)}{H_2\uparrow}$$

$\therefore$ (i) X = **Ethanol (C_2H_5OH)** (ii) E = **Na (Sodium)**

(iii) G = **H_2 (Hydrogen gas)** **(1 × 3 = 3)**

Q.3 A compound X is used in cough syrups and many tonics. It is also soluble in water in all proportions.

(i) Name the compound X. Write its chemical formula.

(ii) Which gas is evolved when the compound X reacts with sodium? How will you test the presence of this gas? Write the chemical equation involved in reaction of X with sodium.

(iii) Complete the following equation for X and identify Y.

$$X \xrightarrow[\text{Heat}]{\text{Alk. KMnO}_4} Y$$

Ans. (i) The compound X is **ethanol** (CH_3CH_2OH) as it is soluble in water in all proportions and is used in cough syrups. **(1)**

(ii) **Hydrogen gas** is evolved when ethanol reacts with sodium.

$$2C_2H_5OH + 2Na \longrightarrow 2C_2H_5\overset{-}{O}\overset{+}{Na} + H_2\uparrow$$ **(1)**

On bringing a matchstick near to the gas, it burns with a **pop sound.**

(iii) $\underset{\substack{\text{Ethanol}\\(X)}}{CH_3CH_2OH} \xrightarrow[\text{Heat}]{\text{Alk. KMnO}_4} \underset{\substack{\text{Ethanoic acid}\\(Y)}}{CH_3COOH}$

The compound Y is **ethanoic acid.** **(1)**

Q.4 Define the following.

(i) Denatured spirit

(ii) Spurious alcohol

(iii) Absolute alcohol

Ans. (i) Addition of 5% methyl alcohol to ethanol makes it unfit for drinking. This is called **denatured spirit**. **(1)**

(ii) **Spurious alcohol** is an illicit liquor made by distillation and contains a large proportion of methanol in a mixture of alcohols. **(1)**

(iii) **Absolute alcohol** is 100% pure ethyl alcohol which can be easily obtained by distilling moist alcohol with benzene. **(1)**

Q.5 Write the IUPAC name for the following structural formula. **(ICSE Specimen 2024)**

(i) 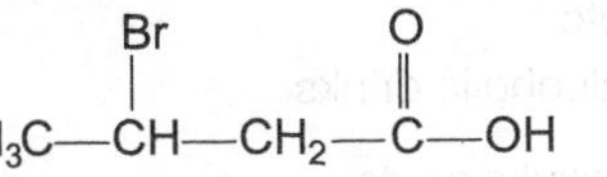

(ii) 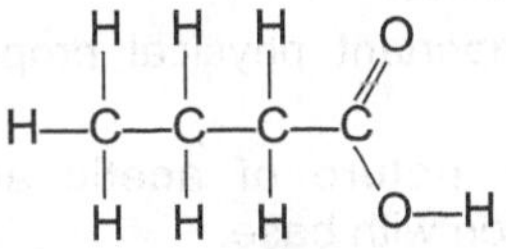

(iii) 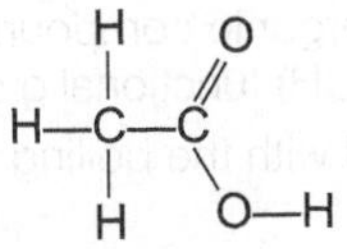

Ans. (i) 3-bromobutanoic acid **(1)**

(ii) Butanoic acid **(1)**

(iii) Ethanoic acid **(1)**

Q.6 (i) What is the effect of acetic acid on litmus paper?

(ii) Give the reactions of acetic acid with sodium carbonate and sodium hydrogen carbonate.

Ans. (i) Being acidic in nature, it turns **blue litmus paper** to red. **(1)**

(ii) $2CH_3COOH + Na_2CO_3 \longrightarrow 2CH_3COONa + H_2O + CO_2$

$CH_3COOH + NaHCO_3 \longrightarrow CH_3COONa + H_2O + CO_2$ **(2)**

Q.7 (i) Complete the given reactions.

(a) $CH_3COOH \xrightarrow{LiAlH_4} ......$

(b) $CH_3COOH \xrightarrow[P_2O_5]{\Delta} ......$

(ii) Write the method to prepare ethanoic acid from ethane.

Ans. (i) (a) $\underset{\text{Acetic acid}}{CH_3COOH} \xrightarrow[4[H]]{LiAlH_4} \underset{\text{Ethanol}}{C_2H_5OH} + H_2O$ **(1)**

(b) $2CH_3COOH \xrightarrow[P_2O_5]{\Delta} \underset{\text{Acetic anhydride}}{(CH_3CO)_2O} + H_2O$ **(1)**

(ii) $\underset{\text{Ethane}}{C_2H_6} \xrightarrow[K_2Cr_2O_7/H^+]{[O]} \underset{\text{Ethanol}}{C_2H_5OH} \xrightarrow[K_2Cr_2O_7/H^+]{[O]} \underset{\text{Ethanal}}{CH_3CHO}$

$\xrightarrow[K_2Cr_2O_7/H^+]{[O]} \underset{\text{Ethanoic acid}}{CH_3COOH}$ **(1)**

Q.8 In an experiment, 10.8 g of the carboxylic acid is reacted with an excess of the alcohol. The experimental yield of ethyl propenoate is 9.45 g.

[The relative formula mass of the carboxylic acid is 72.]

(i) Show that the maximum possible yield of ethyl propenoate is 15.0 g.

(ii) Calculate the percentage yield of ethyl propenoate in this experiment.

Ans. (i) Moles of carboxylic acid $= \frac{10.8}{72} = 0.15$ mol

Molecular mass of ethyl propanoate = 100

Since, acid reacted and ester produced are in 1:1 molar ratio.

$\therefore$ Maximum mass of ester that can form $= 0.15 \times 100 = 15$ g **(2)**

(ii) Percentage yield $= \frac{9.45}{15} \times 100 = 63\%$ **(1)**

Q.9 Given below are organic compounds labelled *A* to *F*.

A. 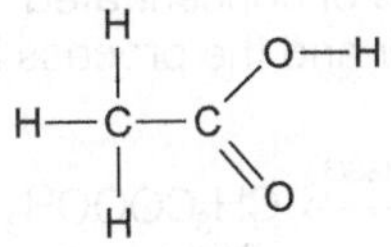

B. 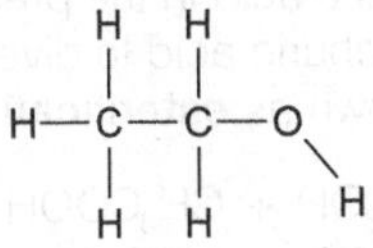

C. 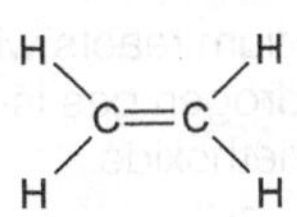

D. 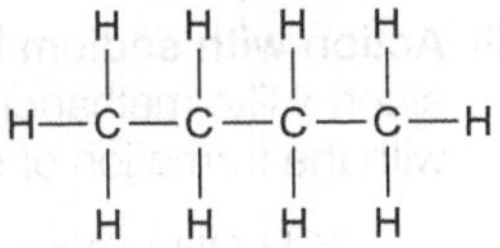

E. 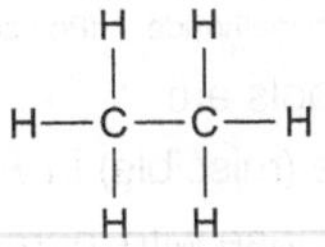

F. 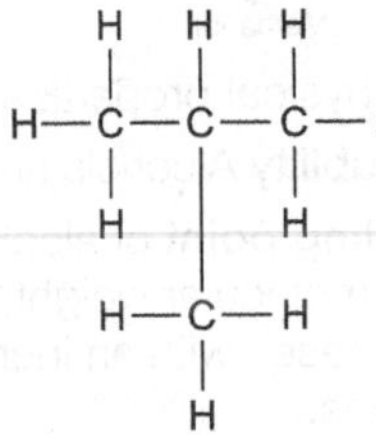

Answer the questions that follow:

(i) Which compound forms a single product with bromine?

(ii) Which two compounds have the same molecular formula?

(iii) Which two compounds will react together in the presence of concentrated H_2SO_4 to form a product with a fruity smell? **(ICSE 2025)**

Ans. (i) **Compound** *C* forms a single product with bromine. Ethene (*C*) reacts with Br_2 to form 1, 2-dibromoethane, as the two bromine atoms add across the double bond.

$$\underset{(C)}{CH_2{=}CH_2} + Br_2 \longrightarrow \underset{Br}{CH_2}{-}\underset{Br}{CH_2}$$

(ii) **Compounds *D* and *F*** have the same molecular formula (C_4H_{10}).

(iii) **Compounds *A* (acid) and *B* (alcohol)** reacts together in the presence of conc. H_2SO_4 to form **ester**, with a fruity smell. This reaction is called **esterification.**

$$\underset{(A)}{CH_3COOH} + \underset{(B)}{CH_3CH_2OH} \xrightarrow{\text{Conc. } H_2SO_4} \underset{\text{(Ester)}}{CH_3COOCH_2CH_3} \quad \textbf{(1)}$$

TYPE - 9 — 04/05 Marks

Long Answer Type Questions

Q.1 Give two chemical and two physical properties of alcohols.

Ans. Two chemical properties of alcohols are

(i) **Reaction with acetic acid** Alcohols react with acetic acid in the presence of concentrated sulphuric acid to give ester and the process is known as **esterification**.

$$\underset{\text{Methanol}}{CH_3OH} + \underset{\text{Acetic acid}}{CH_3COOH} \xrightarrow{\text{Conc.} H_2SO_4} \underset{\text{Methyl acetate}}{CH_3COOCH_3} + H_2O \quad \textbf{(1)}$$

(ii) **Action with sodium** When sodium reacts with any alcohol like methanol, then hydrogen gas is evolved with the formation of sodium methoxide.

$$\underset{\text{Methanol}}{2CH_3OH} + 2Na \longrightarrow \underset{\text{Sodium methoxide}}{2CH_3\overset{-}{O}\overset{+}{Na}} + \underset{\text{(Pop sound)}}{H_2\uparrow} \quad \textbf{(1)}$$

Two physical properties of alcohols are

(i) **Solubility** Alcohols are soluble (miscible) in water. **(1)**

(ii) **Boiling point** of alcohols increase with increase in the molecular weight, i.e. the boiling point of alcohol increases with an increase in number of carbon atoms. **(1)**

Q.2 When an organic compound (*A*) is heated with concentrated H_2SO_4, it forms a compound (*B*) which is able to form compound (*C*), when one mole of hydrogen in the presence of Ni is added to it. When one mole of compound (*C*) undergoes combustion, it forms two moles of CO_2 and three moles of H_2O. Identify the compounds *A*, *B* and *C* and also write the chemical equations involved in it.

Ans. Since, one mole of compound *C* on combustion forms two moles of CO_2 and three moles of H_2O, the compound is a hydrocarbon with molecular formula, C_2H_6, which is **ethane**. **(1)**

The compound *B* which forms C_2H_6 upon addition of hydrogen is **ethene** (C_2H_4). **(1)**

The organic compound *A* which forms ethene upon acidic dehydration is **ethanol**. The chemical equations for the reactions involved are **(1)**

$$\underset{\text{Ethanol }(A)}{C_2H_5OH} \xrightarrow[\text{Heat}]{\text{Conc.}H_2SO_4} \underset{\text{Ethene }(B)}{CH_2{=}CH_2} \xrightarrow[\text{Heat}]{H_2/Ni} \underset{\text{Ethane }(C)}{CH_3{-}CH_3}$$

$$\underset{(C)}{C_2H_6} + 7/2\,O_2 \xrightarrow{\text{Combustion}} 2CO_2 + 3H_2O \quad \textbf{(1)}$$

Q.3 Give four uses of ethyl alcohol.

Ans. Four uses of ethyl alcohol are as follows:

(i) It is used as a solvent.

(ii) It is used in the manufacture of thermometers.

(iii) It is used in the manufacture of dyes, perfumes, antiseptics, etc.

(iv) It is used in alcoholic drinks. **(1 × 4 = 4)**

Q.4 (i) **Define carboxylic acids.**

(ii) **Write any two important physical properties of acetic acid.**

(iii) **State the acidic nature of acetic acid with reference to reaction with base.**

Ans. (i) **Carboxylic acids** are the organic compounds containing carboxyl (—COOH) functional group. **(1)**

(ii) (a) It is a hygroscopic liquid with the boiling point of 391 K. **(1)**

(b) Pure ethanoic acid or acetic acid on cooling forms crystalline mass, which looks like a glacier. That is why, pure solid ethanoic acid is called glacial acetic acid. **(1)**

(iiii) Acetic acid is acidic in nature as it reacts with bases (alkalies) to form their respective salts and water.

$$\underset{\text{Acetic acid}}{CH_3COOH} + \underset{\text{Sodium hydroxide}}{NaOH} \longrightarrow \underset{\text{Sodium acetate}}{CH_3CO\overset{-}{O}\overset{+}{Na}} + H_2O \quad \textbf{(1)}$$

Q.5 A compound *X* (having vinegar like smell) when treated with ethanol in the presence of the acid, *Z*, gives a compond *Y* which has a fruity smell. The reaction is **(ICSE 2018)**

$$C_2H_5OH + X \xrightarrow{Z} Y + H_2O$$

(i) **Identify *Y* and *Z*.**

(ii) **Write the structural formula of *X*.**

(iii) **Give the structural formula of *Y*.**

Ans. Since, compound *X* has vinegar like smell, thus it must be an **acetic acid** or ethanoic acid (CH_3COOH).

(i) Now, in the given reaction,

$$C_2H_5OH + X \xrightarrow{Z} Y + H_2O$$

where, *X* is carboxylic acid.

Therefore, *Y* must be an **ester** and *Z* can be **conc. H_2SO_4**.

This can be justified by the following reaction.

$$\underset{\substack{\text{Ethyl}\\\text{alcohol}}}{C_2H_5OH} + \underset{\substack{\text{Ethanoic acid}\\(X)}}{CH_3COOH} \xrightarrow{\text{Conc. } H_2SO_4(Z)} \underset{\substack{\text{Ethyl}\\\text{ethanoate }(Y)}}{CH_3COOC_2H_5} + H_2O$$ **(2)**

(ii) Structural formula of (X) is

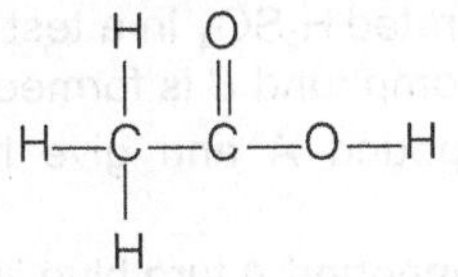

(1)

(iii) The structural formula of Y is

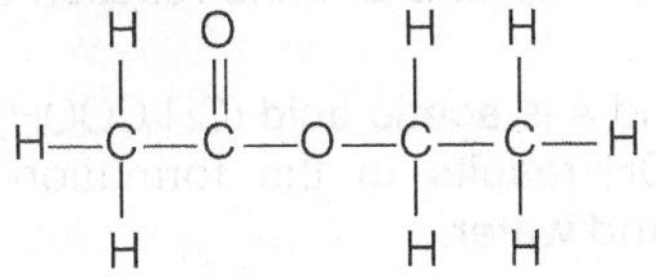

(1)

Q.6 **Write the balanced chemical equations for the following.**

(i) Monochloro ethane is hydrolysed with aqueous KOH.

(ii) Ethanol reacts with sodium at room temperature.

(iii) Preparation of propanol from propyl chloride

(iv) Heating of ethanol at 170°C in the presence of conc. sulphuric acid. **(ICSE 2016)**

(v) Methanol from iodomethane.

Ans. (i) $C_2H_5Cl + KOH(aq) \xrightarrow{\text{Boil}} \underset{\text{Ethanol}}{C_2H_5OH} + KCl$ **(1)**

(ii) $2C_2H_5OH + 2Na \longrightarrow \underset{\text{Sodium ethoxide}}{2C_2H_5ONa} + H_2\uparrow$ **(1)**

(iii) $\underset{\substack{\text{Propyl}\\\text{chloride}}}{C_3H_7Cl} + KOH(aq) \xrightarrow{\text{Boil}} \underset{\text{Propanol}}{C_3H_7OH} + KCl$ **(1)**

(iv) $\underset{\text{Ethanol}}{CH_3CH_2OH} \xrightarrow[170°C]{\text{Conc. } H_2SO_4} \underset{\text{Ethene}}{CH_2{=}CH_2} + H_2O$ **(1)**

(v) $\underset{\text{Iodomethane}}{CH_3I} + KOH(aq) \xrightarrow{\text{Boil}} \underset{\text{Methanol}}{CH_3OH} + KI$ **(1)**

Q.7 **(i) Ethanoic acid turns blue litmus to which colour?**

(ii) Give balanced equations for each of the following. **(ICSE Specimen 2025)**

(a) Laboratory preparation of ethanol by using chloroethane and aqueous sodium hydroxide.

(b) Conversion of acetic acid to ethyl acetate. **(ICSE 2015)**

(iii) Give structural formula of propionic acid

Ans. (i) Ethanoic acid is a **weak acid** and it turns blue litmus to red. **(1)**

(ii) (a) $C_2H_5Cl + NaOH(aq) \xrightarrow{\text{Boil}} C_2H_5OH + NaCl$ **(1)**

(b) $\underset{\text{Ethyl alcohol}}{C_2H_5OH} + \underset{\text{Acetic acid}}{CH_3COOH} \xrightarrow{\text{Conc. } H_2SO_4} \underset{\text{Ethyl acetate}}{CH_3COOC_2H_5} + H_2O$ **(1)**

(iii)

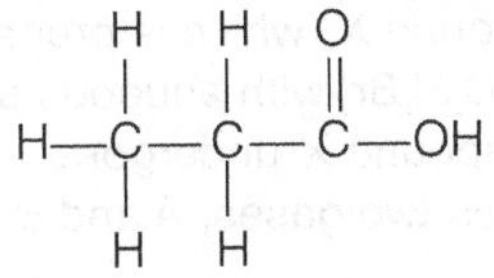

(1)

Q.8 **Look at the figure and answer the following questions.**

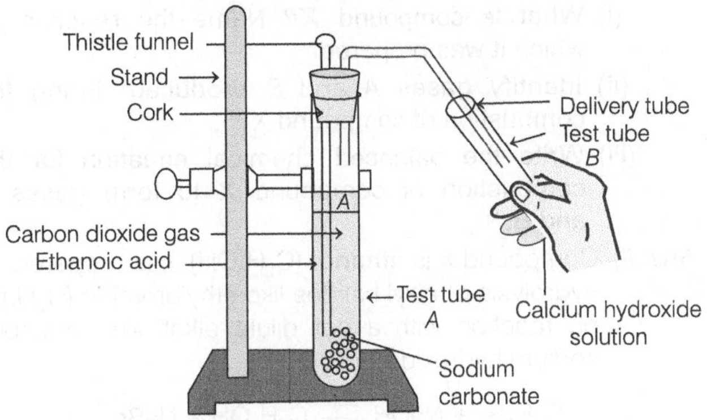

(i) What change would you observe in the calcium hydroxide solution taken in test tube *B*?

(ii) Write the reactions involved in test tubes *A* and *B* respectively.

(iii) If ethanol is given instead of ethanoic acid, would you expect the same change?

(iv) How can a solution of lime water be prepared in the laboratory?

Ans. (i) The calcium hydroxide solution taken in test tube *B* will turn **milky** due to the reaction with carbon dioxide. **(1)**

(ii) In test tube *A*,

$$\underset{\text{Ethanoic acid}}{2CH_3COOH} + \underset{\substack{\text{Sodium}\\\text{carbonate}}}{Na_2CO_3} \longrightarrow 2CH_3CO\overset{-}{O}\overset{+}{Na} + H_2O + CO_2\uparrow$$

In test tube *B*,

$$CO_2 + \underset{\text{Calcium hydroxide}}{Ca(OH)_2} \longrightarrow \underset{\text{Milky ppt.}}{CaCO_3\downarrow} + H_2O$$ **(2)**

(iii) **No**, the same change would not be expected. **(1)**

(iv) Lime water is obtained when **quicklime (CaO) is dissolved in water**. It produces $Ca(OH)_2$ which is a white powder and the resulting solution of calcium hydroxide in water is filtered. The filtrate is called lime water.

$$CaO + H_2O \longrightarrow Ca(OH)_2 + \text{Heat}$$ **(1)**

TYPE - 10 03 Marks

Case Based Questions

Q.1 Ravi is studying a compound *X*, which is prepared by reacting ethyl bromide (C_2H_5Br) with aqueous sodium hydroxide (NaOH). Compound *X* undergoes combustion and produces two gases, *A* and *B*.

Ravi is curious about the identity of compound *X* and the nature of the combustion reaction.

(i) What is compound *X*? Name the reaction by which it was prepared.

(ii) Identify gases *A* and *B* produced during the combustion of compound *X*.

(iii) Write the balanced chemical equation for the combustion of compound *X* to form gases *A* and *B*.

Ans. (i) Compound *X* is **ethanol** (C_2H_5OH). It is prepared by hydrolysis of alkyl halides like ethylbromide (C_2H_5Br) on reaction with a hot dilute alkali like, aqueous sodium hydroxide (NaOH).

$$C_2H_5Br + NaOH \xrightarrow{\text{Boil}} C_2H_5OH + NaBr$$ **(1)**

(ii) Gases *A* and *B* are **carbon dioxide** (CO_2) and **water vapour** (H_2O), respectively. **(1)**

(iii) The balanced chemical equation of combustion of ethanol is

$$C_2H_5OH + 3O_2 \longrightarrow 2CO_2 + 3H_2O.$$ **(1)**

Q.2 Priya took a compound *A* in two test tubes. She puts a blue litmus paper in the first test tube containing compound *A*, and it turns red. In another test tube, she adds NaOH solution to compound *A*, which results in the formation of sodium acetate.

Then, Priya puts compound *A*, ethanol and a few drops of concentrated H_2SO_4 in a test tube, and a sweet-smelling compound *B* is formed.

(i) Identify compound *A* and give its reaction with NaOH.

(ii) Why does compound *A* turn blue litmus paper red?

(iii) Name compound *B* and the reaction by which it is formed.

Ans. (i) Compound *A* is **acetic acid** (CH_3COOH). Its reaction with NaOH results in the formation of **sodium acetate and water.**

$$CH_3COOH + NaOH \longrightarrow CH_3COONa + H_2O$$ **(1)**

(ii) Acetic acid turns **blue litmus paper red** because it is an **acidic compound** (weak acid) that releases H^+ ions in solution, which turns the blue litmus paper red. **(1)**

(iii) Compound *B* is **ethyl acetate** ($CH_3COOC_2H_5$). It is formed by the reaction of acetic acid and ethanol in the presence of concentrated sulphuric acid. This reaction is known as reaction of **esterification.**

$$CH_3COOH + C_2H_5OH \xrightarrow{H_2SO_4} CH_3COOC_2H_5 + H_2O$$ **(1)**

ICSE Specimen Paper 2025

Latest ICSE Specimen Paper

Sample Question Paper

ICSE EXAMINATION PAPER 2025
CHEMISTRY (SOLVED)

General Instructions

Maximum Marks : 80

Time allowed : Two hours

- You will not be allowed to write during the first **15** minutes. This time is to be spent in reading the question paper.
- The time given at the head of this paper is the time allowed for writing the answers.

Section A is compulsory. Attempt **any four** questions from **Section B**.

- The intended marks for questions or parts of questions are given brackets [ ].

Section A

(Attempt **all** questions from this section) **(40 Marks)**

Question 1

Choose the correct answers to the questions from the given options. **[15]**

(i) Which gas decolourises potassium permanganate ($KMnO_4$) solution?

(a) Sulphur dioxide (b) Ammonia (c) Hydrogen chloride (d) Carbon dioxide

(ii) Which formula represents a saturated hydrocarbon?

(a) C_4H_8 (b) C_5H_{12} (c) C_4H_6 (d) C_5H_{10}

(iii) The metal whose oxide can be reduced by common reducing agents

(a) Copper (b) Sodium (c) Aluminium (d) Potassium

(iv) An organic compound has a vapour density of 22. The molecular formula of the organic compound is [Atomic weight: C = 12, H = 1]

(a) CH_4 (b) C_2H_4 (c) C_2H_6 (d) C_3H_8

(v) In the reaction given below sulphuric acid acts as a/an

$$S + 2H_2SO_4 \longrightarrow 3SO_2 + 2H_2O$$

(a) Non-volatile acid (b) Dibasic acid

(c) Oxidising agent (d) Reducing agent

(vi) **Assertion** (A) The tendency of losing electrons increases down the Group.

Reason (R) The most reactive metal is placed at the top of Group 1.

(a) Both (A) and (R) are true, and (R) is the correct explanation of (A).

(b) Both (A) and (R) are true, and (R) is not the correct explanation of (A).

(c) (A) is true but (R) is false.

(d) (A) is false but (R) is true.

(vii) The ore that can be concentrated by using magnetic separation

(a) Corundum (b) Haematite

(c) Calamine (d) Bauxite

(viii) The diagram given below shows the bonding in the covalent molecule AB_2

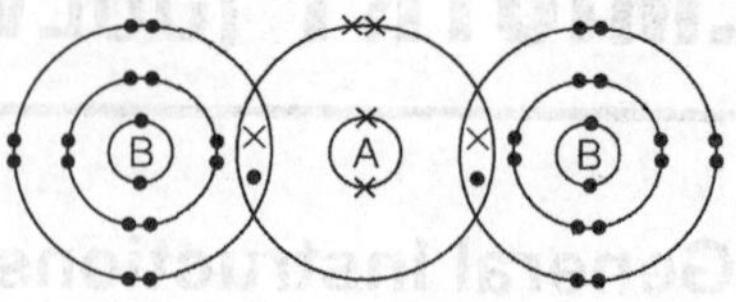

Which option represents the correct electronic configuration of atoms A and B before combining together to form the above molecule?

	A	B
(a)	2, 4	2,8,6
(b)	2,4	2,8,7
(c)	2, 8	2,8,8
(d)	2,6	2,8,7

(ix) Which of the following options has all the compounds which are members of the same homologous series?

(a) CH_4, C_2H_6, C_3H_8 (b) CH_4, C_2H_6, C_3H_6

(c) C_3H_4, C_3H_6, C_3H_8 (d) $C_2H_4, C_3H_6, C_4H_{10}$

(x) **Assertion** (A) In the contact process SO_3 gas is not directly dissolved in water to obtain sulphuric acid.

Reason (R) Dense fog or misty droplets of sulphuric acid are formed which is difficult to condense.

(a) Both (A) and (R) are true, and (R) is the correct explanation of (A).

(b) Both (A) and (R) are true, and (R) is not the correct explanation of (A).

(c) (A) is true but (R) is false.

(d) (A) is false but (R) is true.

(xi) Given below are four ions

Cl^-, Li^+, Al^{3+}, K^+

Identify the pair of ions which have the same electronic configuration.

[Atomic number: Cl = 17, Li = 3, Al = 13, K = 19]

(a) Cl^- and Li^+ (b) Al^{3+} and K^+ (c) Cl^- and K^+ (d) Li^+ and K^+

(xii) Which pair of reactants can be best used to produce lead (II) sulphate?

(a) Sulphuric acid + Lead (b) Sulphuric acid + Lead hydroxide

(c) Sodium sulphate + Lead nitrate (d) Potassium sulphate + Lead oxide

(xiii) Aqueous copper (II) sulphate is electrolysed using copper electrodes. Which statement about the electrolysis is not correct?

(a) An oxidation reaction occurs at the positive electrode.

(b) The current is carried through the electrolyte by ions.

(c) The positive electrode loses mass.

(d) The number of copper (II) ions in the electrolyte decreases.

(xiv) X, Y and Z are three metallic atoms in successive order belonging to the same group such that atomic radii of 'X' is the smallest. Which of the three atoms is the best reducing agent?

(a) X (b) Y

(c) Z (d) All three have the same reducing power.

(xv) 40 cm^3 of methane (CH_4) is reacted with 60 cm^3 of oxygen.

The equation for the reaction is given below

$$CH_4 + 2O_2 \longrightarrow CO_2 + 2H_2O$$

All volumes are measured at room temperature.

What is the total volume of the gases remaining at the end of the reaction?

(a) 60 cm^3 (b) 40 cm^3 (c) 45 cm^3 (d) 50 cm^3

Question 2

(i) A student was instructed by the teacher to prepare and collect ammonia gas in the laboratory by using aluminium nitride. The student had set up the apparatus as shown in the diagram below. Study the given diagram and answer the following questions. **[5]**

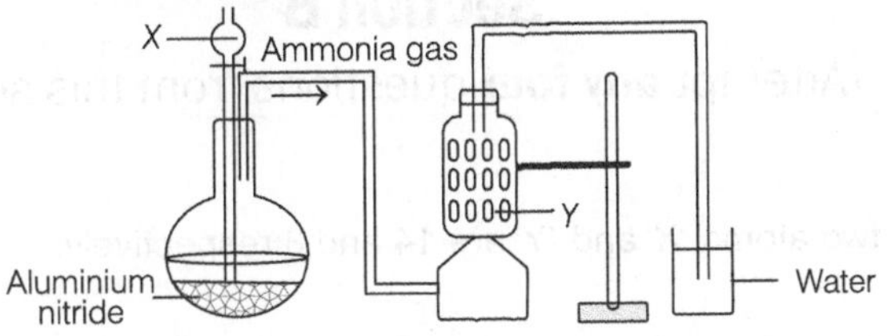

(a) Name the substance *X* added through the thistle funnel by the student.

(b) Write a balanced equation for the reaction occurring between aluminium nitride and substance *X*.

(c) Identify the substance *Y*.

(d) State the function of *Y*.

(e) Why could the student not collect ammonia gas at the end of the experiment?

(ii) State the terms for the following **[5]**

(a) Undistilled alcohol containing a large amount of methanol.

(b) A salt formed by the partial replacement of the hydroxyl group of a di-acidic or a tri-acidic base by an acid radical.

(c) Organic compounds having the same molecular formula but different structural formula.

(d) The tendency of an atom to attract the shared pair of electrons towards itself when combined in a compound.

(e) The type of covalent bond in which electrons are shared unequally between the combining atoms.

(iii) Complete the following sentences by choosing the correct word(s) from the brackets. **[5]**

(a) .... solution forms a coloured precipitate with ammonium hydroxide which is soluble in excess of ammonium hydroxide.
[Ferrous chloride/Copper nitrate]

(b) Zinc blende is converted to zinc oxide by .... [Calcination/Roasting]

(c) .... conducts electricity by the movement of ions. [Molten iron/Molten sodium chloride)

(d) The reaction that takes place at the anode during the electrolysis of aqueous sodium argentocyanide with silver electrodes is .... [$Ag \rightarrow Ag^+ + e^-$/$Ag^+ + e^- \rightarrow Ag$]

(e) The salt formed when ZnO reacts with hot concentrated NaOH is .... [sodium zincate/zinc hydroxide]

(iv) Match the Column A with Column B. **[5]**

Column A	Column B
(a) $N_2 + 3H_2 \rightleftharpoons 2NH_3$	1. Vanadium pentoxide
(b) $4NH_3 + 5O_2 \longrightarrow 4NO + 6H_2O$	2. Nickel
(c) $2SO_2 + O_2 \rightleftharpoons 2SO_3$	3. Iron
(d) $C_2H_4 + H_2 \longrightarrow C_2H_6$	4. Concentrated sulphric acid
(e) $CuSO_4 \cdot 5H_2O \longrightarrow CuSO_4 + 5H_2O$	5. Platinum

(v) (a) Draw the structural diagram for the following organic compounds **[5]**

1. 2-methyl propene 2. butanal

(b) Give IUPAC name for the following organic compounds.

1. 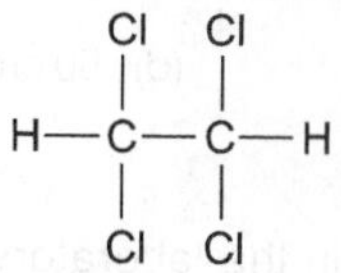

2. 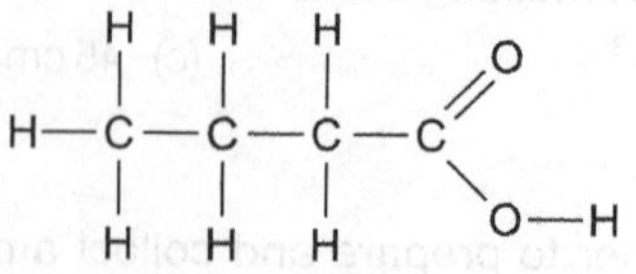

3. 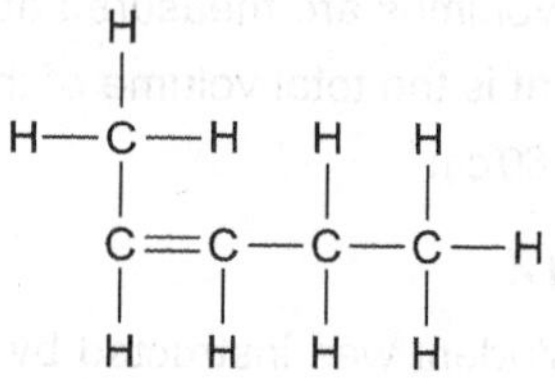

Section B

(Attempt **any four** questions from this section) **(40 Marks)**

Question 3

(i) The atomic number of two atoms '*X*' and '*Y*' are 14 and 8 respectively. **[2]**

State

(a) the period to which '*X*' belongs.

(b) the formula of the compound formed between '*X*' and '*Y*'.

(Do not identify X and Y)

(ii) Justify the following statements. **[2]**

(a) Anode is known as the oxidising electrode.

(b) Graphite electrodes are preferred in the electrolysis of molten lead bromide.

(iii) The reaction between concentrated sulphuric acid and magnesium can be represented by the equation given below. **[3]**

$$Mg + 2H_2SO_4 \longrightarrow MgSO_4 + 2H_2O + SO_2$$

If 60 g of magnesium is used in the reaction, calculate the following.

(a) The mass of sulphuric acid needed for the reaction.

(b) The volume of sulphur dioxide gas liberated at STP.

[Atomic weight Mg = 24, H = 1, S = 32, O = 16]

(iv) Give one significant observation when **[3]**

(a) a solution of barium chloride is added to zinc sulphate solution.

(b) lead nitrate is heated in a test tube.

(c) chlorine gas is passed over moist starch iodide paper.

Question 4

(i) A gas cylinder can hold 150 g of hydrogen under certain conditions of temperature and pressure. If an identical cylinder with the same capacity can hold 450 g of gas '*G*' under the same conditions of temperature and pressure, find **[2]**

(a) the vapour density of the gas '*G*'.

(b) the molecular weight of gas '*G*'.

(ii) Complete and balance the following equations. **[2]**

(a) $CH_3COONa + NaOH \xrightarrow[\Delta]{CaO}$ (b) $CH_3COOH + Mg \longrightarrow$

(iii) Name the gas produced during each of the following reactions. **[3]**

(a) When copper is treated with hot, concentrated nitric acid.

(b) When ammonia is burnt in an atmosphere of oxygen.

(c) When ferrous sulphide reacts with dilute hydrochloric acid.

(iv) Study the table given below. Use only the letters given in the table to answer the questions. Do not identify the elements. **[3]**

IA	IIA	IIIA	IVA	VA	VIA	VIIA	0
			E		*J*		Q
	L			*G*			
	M	*D*				*P*	
	N						

(a) State the valency of element '*G*'.

(b) Which element can exhibit catenation?

(c) Write the formula of the compound formed between '*M*' and '*P*'.

Questions 5

(i) Given below are two sets of elements from two different periods. **[2]**

Name the element with the highest ionisation potential in each of the following sets

(a) Al, Cl, Mg (b) Ne, O, F

(ii) Ammonia gas is passed over heated copper (II) oxide in a combustion tube. **[2]**

(a) Name the gas evolved.

(b) What will be the colour of the residue that is left in the combustion tube at the end of the reaction?

(iii) Give balanced equations for the following. **[3]**

(a) Action of dilute hydrochloric acid on ammonium carbonate.

(b) Oxidation of sulphur with hot concentrated nitric acid.

(c) Reaction of concentrated sulphuric acid with carbon.

(iv) Rohit took two different salt solutions in test tubes *C* and *D* as shown in the figure below. He added dilute HCl to each of the two test tubes. The products formed in the test tubes *C* and *D* are silver chloride and lead chloride respectively. **[3]**

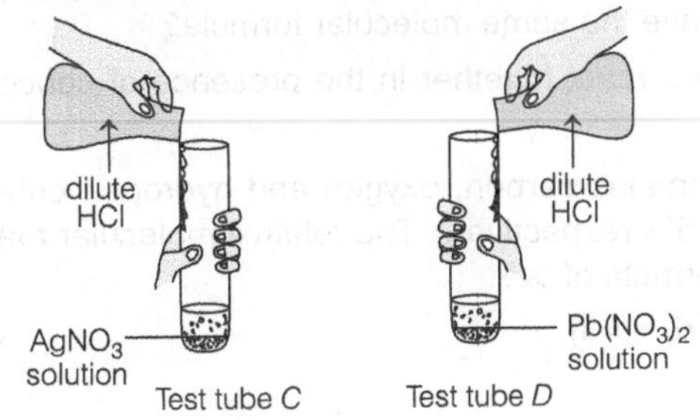

State

(a) One common observation made by Rohit in both the reactions.

(b) The observations made by him on addition of excess of ammonium hydroxide to the products formed in

1. test tube *C* 2. test tube *D*

Questions 6

(i) Given below is a diagram showing the placement of five different oxides. With respect to the given diagram answer the following questions: **[3]**

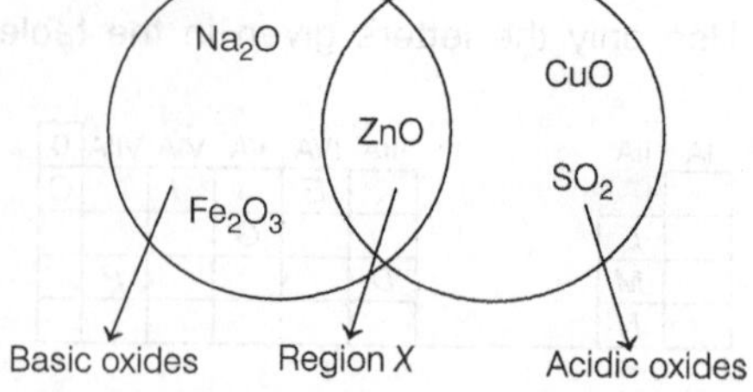

(a) Name the type of oxide represented in region *X* in the diagram.

(b) Identify the oxide which has been incorrectly placed in the above diagram.

(c) Name the oxide from the above diagram which will form an alkali when dissolved in water.

(ii) Given below are organic compounds labelled *A* to *F*. **[3]**

Answer the questions that follow:

A.
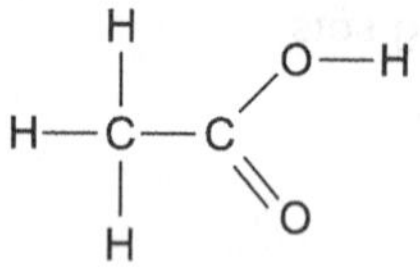

B.
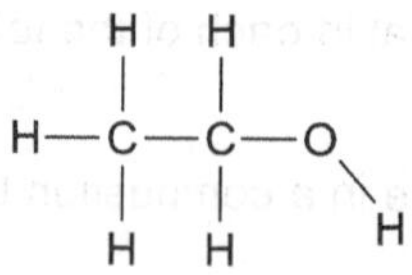

C.
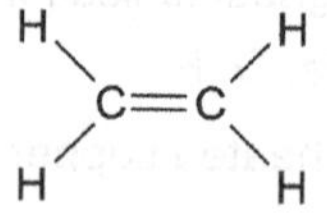

D.
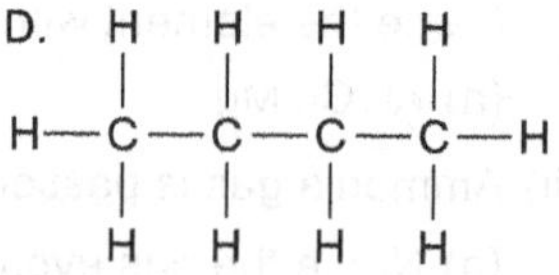

E.
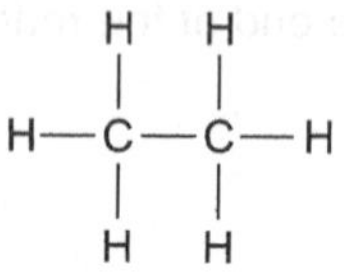

F.
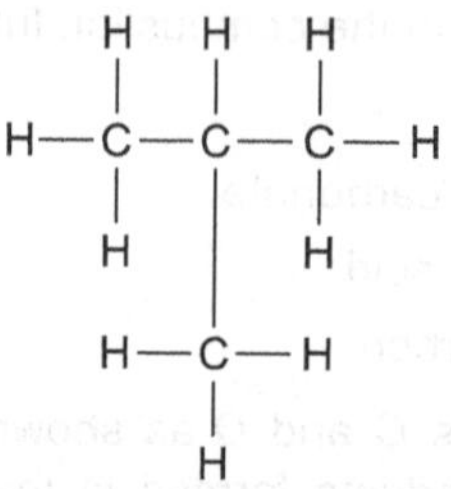

(a) Which compound forms a single product with bromine?

(b) Which two compounds have the same molecular formula?

(c) Which two compounds will react together in the presence of concentrated H_2SO_4 to form a product with a fruity smell?

(iii) An organic compound *'X'* contains carbon, oxygen and hydrogen only. The percentage of carbon and hydrogen are 47.4% and 10.5% respectively. The relative molecular mass of *'X'* is 76. Find the empirical formula and the molecular formula of *'X'*.

[Atomic weight : C = 12, O = 16, H = 1] **[4]**

Questions 7

(i) Seema added a few pieces of copper turnings to a test tube containing concentrated acid *P* and she noticed that a reddish-brown gas evolved.

(a) Name the acid *P* used by Seema.

(b) Write a balanced chemical equation for the reaction that took place. **[2]**

(ii) Answer the following questions with reference to the concentration of bauxite ore. **[2]**

(a) Name the process used to concentrate the ore.

(b) Give a balanced chemical equation for the conversion of aluminium hydroxide to pure alumina.

(iii) Draw the dot and cross structure of the following. **[3]**

(a) An ionic compound formed when Mg reacts with the dilute HCl.

(b) A covalent compound formed when H_2 reacts with Cl_2.

(c) The positive ion produced when ammonia gas is dissolved in water.

[Atomic number: Mg = 12, Cl = 17, H = 1, N = 7]

(iv) Acidulated water is electrolysed using platinum electrodes. **[3]**

Answer the following questions.

(a) Why is dilute sulphuric acid added to water?

(b) Write the reaction taking place at the cathode.

(c) What is the observation at the anode?

Questions 8

(i) (a) State Avogadro's Law. **[2]**

(b) Define Co-ordinate bond.

(ii) Differentiate between the following pairs of compounds using the reagent given in the bracket.

(a) Ammonium chloride and sodium chloride (using an alkali).

(b) Zinc nitrate solution and calcium nitrate solution. (using excess sodium hydroxide solution) **[2]**

(iii) You are provided with some compounds in the box. **[3]**

PbO, CH_4, PbO_2, CO_2, HCl, NCl_3, SO_2

Choose the most appropriate compound which fits the descriptions (a) to (c) given below.

(a) A colourless gas which turns acidified $K_2Cr_2O_7$ from orange to green.

(b) A yellow explosive oily liquid formed when excess chlorine gas reacts with ammonia gas.

(c) A yellow metallic oxide formed on thermal decomposition of $PbCO_3$.

(iv) *P*, *Q*, *R* and *S* are the different methods of preparation of salts. **[3]**

P — Simple displacement

Q — Neutralisation by titration

R — Precipitation

S — Direct combination

Choose the most appropriate method to prepare the following salts:

(a) $PbCl_2$ (b) $FeCl_3$ (c) Na_2SO_4

Answers

1\. (i) (a) **Sulphur dioxide** decolouries pink potassium permanganate ($KMnO_4$) solution.

$$\underset{\text{(Pink)}}{2KMnO_4} + 5SO_2 + 2H_2O \longrightarrow \underset{\text{(Colourless)}}{K_2SO_4} + 2MnSO_4 + 2H_2SO_4$$

In this reaction, $KMnO_4$ is reduced and the pink colour of the solution changes to colourless.

(ii) (b) C_5H_{12} represents a saturated hydrocarbon as they are represented by the general formula C_nH_{2n+2}.

(iii) (a) **Copper** can be obtained by the reduction of copper oxide with common reducing agents like carbon, carbon monoxide, hydrogen, etc.

Sodium, potassium and aluminium are highly active metals and have great affinity for oxygen so their oxides cannot be reduced by common reducing agents.

(iv) (d) Molecular mass = 2 × Vapour density = 2 × 22 = 44

Molecular mass of CH_4 = 12 + (4 × 1) = 16

Molecular mass of C_2H_4 = (2 × 12) + (4 × 1) = 28

Molecular mass of C_2H_6 = (2 × 12) + (6 × 1) = 30

Molecular mass of C_3H_8 = (3 × 12) + (8 × 1) = 44

Thus, the molecular formula of the organic compound is C_3H_8.

(v) (c) In the given reaction, sulphuric acid acts as an **oxidising agent** as it oxidises sulphur to sulphur dioxide.

(vi) (c) The most reactive metal is not placed at the top of Group I because **reactivity increases down the group**. The reason behind this trend is the increase in tendency to lose electrons down the group to form positive ions. Thus, (A) is true but (R) is false.

(vii) (b) **Haematite** can be concentrated by using magnetic separation as it is magnetic in nature and it can be separated from the non-magnetic gangue particles.

(viii) (d) To form the above molecule, the electronic configuration of the atoms A and B before combining is

A = 2, 6

B = 2, 8, 7

(ix) (a) The successive members of a homologous series differ by a —CH_2 group. Thus, CH_4, C_2H_6, C_3H_8 belong to the same homologous series.

(x) (a) In Contact process, SO_3 gas is not directly dissolved in water as it gives a **lot of heat** on dissolution and forms misty droplets of sulphuric acid, which are difficult to condense.

Thus, both (A) and (R) are true and (R) is the correct explanation of (A).

(xi) (c) **Cl^- and K^+** have the same electronic configuration.

Electronic configuration of Cl^- = 2, 8, 8

Electronic configuration of Li^+ = 2

Electronic configuration of Al^{3+} = 2, 8

Electronic configuration of K^+ = 2, 8, 8

(xii) (c) Insoluble lead (II) sulphate can be prepared by treating lead nitrate with sodium sulphate.

$$Pb(NO_3)_2 + Na_2SO_4 \longrightarrow \underset{\text{(Lead (II) sulphate)}}{PbSO_4\downarrow} + 2NaNO_3$$

(xiii) (d) The number of copper (II) ions does not decrease in the electrolyte, but it **remains the same.** This is because, for every copper ion discharged at the cathode to form copper metal, a Cu^{2+} ion is added to the solution by the anode. Thus, the blue colour of the solution also does not fade during electrolysis.

(xiv) (c) A metal with larger atomic radii and lower ionisation energy will readily lose electrons, and act as a stronger reducing agent. Among the three metals, Z has largest atomic radii (as atomic radii increases, down the group) and it has lowest ionisation energy. Thus, **atom Z will be the strongest reducing agent.**

(xv) (b) $\underset{1\ Vol}{CH_4} + \underset{2\ Vol}{2O_2} \longrightarrow \underset{1\ Vol}{CO_2} + 2H_2O$

According to the reaction,

1 vol of CH_4 reacts with 2 vol of O_2

$\therefore$ 40 cm^3 of CH_4 will react with

$(40 \times 2) = 80\ cm^3$ of O_2.

But, we have 60 cm^3 of oxygen. Therefore, **oxygen is the limiting reagent.**

$\because$ 2 vol of O_2 reacts with 1 vol of CH_4.

$\therefore$ 60 cm^3 of O_2 will react with $\left(\frac{60}{2}\right) = 30\ cm^3$ of CH_4

Volume of methane remaining at the end of the reaction $= (40 - 30)\ cm^3 = 10\ cm^3$

Also, 2 vol of O_2 gives 1 vol of CO_2

So, 60 cm^3 of O_2 will give 30 cm^3 of CO_2.

Thus, the total volume of the gases at the end of the reaction.

$= (10 + 30)\ cm^3 = 40\ cm^3$

2. (i) (a) The substance X added through thristle funnel by the student is **water.**

(b) $AlN + 3H_2O \longrightarrow Al(OH)_3 + NH_3 \uparrow$

(c) The substance Y is **quicklime (CaO).**

(d) Y (CaO) acts as the **drying agent.**

(e) The student could not collect ammonia gas at the end of the experiment because it is **highly soluble in water** and cannot be collected.

(ii) (a) Spurious alcohol

(b) Basic salt

(c) Isomers

(d) Electronegativity

(e) Non-planar covalent bond

(iii) (a) Copper nitrate

(b) Roasting

(c) Molten sodium chloride

(d) $Ag \longrightarrow Ag^+ + e^-$

(e) Sodium zincate

(iv) (a) 3 (b) 5 (c) 1

(d) 2 (e) 4

(v) (a) 1. 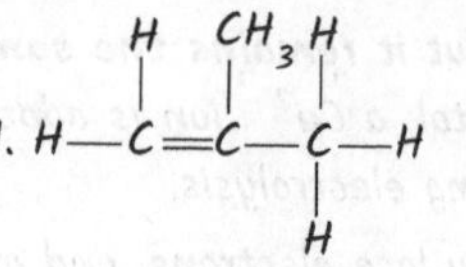

2 - methylpropene

2. 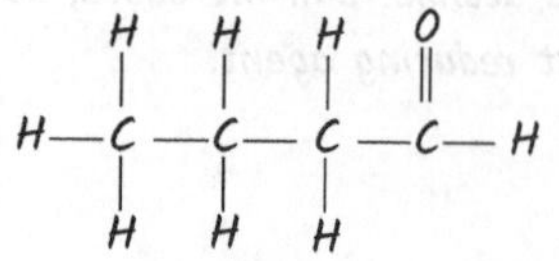

Butanal

(b) 1. 1,1,2,2-tetrachloroethane

2. Butanoic acid

3. Pent-2-ene

3. (i) Atomic number of X is 14. So, its electronic configuration is 2, 8, 4. Whereas, atomic number of Y is 8 and its electronic configuration is 2, 6.

(a) X belongs to **period 3** as its electrons occupy three shells.

(b) The valency of X is 4. Y has 6 valence electrons, so it needs two more electrons to complete its octet, thus its valency is 2.

Therefore, according to the valencies, X and Y combines to form **XY_2 compound**. (Here, electrons are shared to complete the octet.)

(ii) (a) Anode is known as the oxidising electrode because **oxidation**, i.e. loss of electrons, occurs at the anode during electrolysis.

(b) Graphite anode is preferred in the electrolysis of molten lead bromide because graphite is an **inert electrode** and it does not react with the electrolyte and the bromine produced at the anode.

(iii) $\underset{24\ g}{Mg} + \underset{\substack{2\ (2\times 1+32+4\times 16)\\ =196\ g}}{2H_2SO_4} \longrightarrow MgSO_4 + 2H_2O + \underset{22.4\ L}{SO_2}$

(a) From the reaction, 24 g Mg reacts with 196 g H_2SO_4.

$\therefore$ 60 g Mg will react with $\dfrac{60 \times 196}{24} = 490$ g H_2SO_4

Thus, the mass of sulphuric acid needed for the reaction is 490 g.

(b) 1 mol of Mg gives 1 mol of SO_2 and at STP, 1 mol of SO_2 occupies 22.4 L volume.

$\Rightarrow$ 1 mol or 24 g Mg gives 22.4 L SO_2.

$\therefore$ 60 g Mg will give $\dfrac{60 \times 22.4}{24} = 56$ L SO_2

Thus, the volume of SO_2 gas liberated at S.T.P is **56 L**.

(iv) (a) When a solution of barium chloride is added to zinc sulphate solution, a **white precipitate** of barium sulphate is formed.

$$BaCl_2(aq) + ZnSO_4(aq) \longrightarrow ZnCl_2(aq) + \underset{\text{(White ppt.)}}{BaSO_4(s)\downarrow}$$

(b) When lead nitrate is heated in a test tube, the formation of **yellow lead oxide** and the release of **reddish-brown fumes of nitrogen dioxide gas** takes place.

$$2Pb(NO_3)_2(s) \longrightarrow \underset{\text{(Yellow residue)}}{2PbO(s)} + \underset{\text{(Reddish brown fumes)}}{4NO_2(g)} + O_2(g)$$

(c) When chlorine gas is passed over moist starch iodide paper, the paper turns **blue-black**. This is because chlorine **oxidises iodide ions to iodine**, and then iodine reacts with starch to form a blue-black complex.

4. (i) (a) Vapour density of gas 'G' $= \dfrac{\text{Mass of gas 'G' under similar conditions}}{\text{Mass of hydrogen gas under similar conditions}}$

Vapour density of gas 'G' $= \dfrac{450}{150} = 3$

(b) Molecular weight of gas 'G' = 2 × Vapour density

$= 2 \times 3 = 6$

(ii) (a) $CH_3COONa + NaOH \xrightarrow[\Delta]{CaO} CH_4 \uparrow + Na_2CO_3$

(b) $2CH_3COOH + Mg \longrightarrow (CH_3COO)_2Mg + H_2\uparrow$

(iii) (a) When copper is treated with hot, concentrated nitric acid, **nitrogen dioxide gas** is produced.

$$Cu + 4HNO_3 \longrightarrow Cu(NO_3)_2 + 2H_2O + 2NO_2 \uparrow$$

(b) When ammonia is burnt in an atmosphere of oxygen, it gives **nitrogen gas and water vapour.**

$$4NH_3 + 3O_2 \longrightarrow 2N_2 \uparrow + 6H_2O \uparrow$$

(c) When ferrous sulphide reacts with dilute hydrochloric acid, **hydrogen sulphide gas** is evolved, which has a rotten egg like smell.

$$FeS + \underset{(dil.)}{2HCl} \longrightarrow FeCl_2 + H_2S \uparrow$$

(iv) (a) Since, 'G' belongs to group VA (Group 15). Elements in this group has 5 valence electrons, and it needs three electrons to complete its octet, thus its **valency is 3.**

(b) The element which can exhibit catenation is 'E'.

(c) Element 'M' belongs to group IIA, so it has a valency of two as it can lose two electrons to complete its octet. While, element 'P' belongs to group VII A, so it has a valency of one as it can gain one electron to achieve octet.

Thus, M and P can combine to form **MP_2** where, 'M' loses two electrons and two 'P' atoms gains each electron.

5. (i) (a) **Cl** has the highest ionisation potential as the ionisation potential generally increases from left to right across a period.

(b) **Ne** has the highest ionisation potential as it has a fully filled electronic configuration, making it very stable and difficult to remove an electron.

(ii) (a) $2NH_3 + 3CuO \longrightarrow 3Cu \downarrow + 3H_2O + N_2\uparrow$

Nitrogen gas and **water vapour** are evolved.

(b) **Reddish-brown residue of copper** is left in the combustion tube at the end of the reaction.

(iii) (a) $(NH_4)_2CO_3 + \underset{(Dil.)}{2HCl} \longrightarrow 2NH_4Cl + H_2O + CO_2 \uparrow$

(b) $S + \underset{(conc.)}{6HNO_3} \longrightarrow H_2SO_4 + 2H_2O + 6NO_2 \uparrow$

(c) $C + \underset{(Conc.)}{2H_2SO_4} \longrightarrow CO_2 + 2H_2O + 2SO_2$

(iv) (a) In both the test tubes, a **white precipitate** is formed.

(b) 1. In test tube C, the white precipitate of silver chloride **dissolves in excess ammonium hydroxide** and forms a complex salt called diammine silver (I) chloride.

$$AgCl + 2NH_4OH \longrightarrow [Ag(NH_3)_2]^+Cl^- + 2H_2O$$

2. In test tube D, the white precipitate of lead chloride **does not dissolve in excess ammonium hydroxide.**

6. (i) (a) Region X in the diagram represents **amphoteric oxides**.

(b) CuO is a **basic oxide**, but it is incorrectly placed in acidic oxides in the above diagram.

(c) Na_2O reacts with water to form an alkali (NaOH).

$$Na_2O + H_2O \longrightarrow \underset{\text{(Alkali)}}{2NaOH}$$

(ii) (a) **Compound** C forms a single product with bromine ethene (C) reacts with Br_2 to form 1,2-dibromoethane, as the two bromine atoms add across the double bond.

$$\underset{\text{(C)}}{CH_2{=}CH_2} + Br_2 \longrightarrow \underset{Br}{CH_2} - \underset{Br}{CH_2}$$

(b) **Compound D and F** have the same molecular formula (C_4H_{10}).

(c) **Compound A (acid) and B (alcohol)** reacts together in the presence of conc. H_2SO_4 to form **ester**, with a fruity smell. This reaction is called **esterification**.

$$\underset{\text{(A)}}{CH_3COOH} + \underset{\text{(B)}}{CH_3CH_2OH} \xrightarrow{\text{conc. } H_2SO_4} \underset{\text{(Ester)}}{CH_3COOCH_2CH_3}$$

(iii)

Element	Percentage composition	Atomic mass	Atomic ratio	Simplest ratio	Whole number ratio
C	47.4	12	$\frac{47.4}{12} = 3.95$	$\frac{3.95}{2.63} = 1.5$	$1.5 \times 2 = 3$
H	10.5	1	$\frac{10.5}{1} = 10.5$	$\frac{10.5}{2.63} = 4$	$4 \times 2 = 8$
O	$100 - (47.4 + 10.5) = 42.1$	16	$\frac{42.1}{16} = 2.63$	$\frac{2.63}{2.63} = 1$	$1 \times 2 = 2$

The empirical formula is $C_3H_8O_2$.

Empirical formula mass

$$= (3 \times 12) + (8 \times 1) + (2 \times 16) = 76$$

Molecular mass = 76 (Given)

$$n = \frac{\text{Molecular mass}}{\text{Empirical formula mass}} = \frac{76}{76} = 1$$

$\therefore$ Molecular formula = Empirical formula $\times$ n = $C_3H_8O_2$

7. (i) (a) The acid **P** is **nitric acid**. When a few pieces of copper turnings are added to a test tube containing conc. HNO_3, reddish-brown gas of nitrogen dioxide are evolved.

(b) $$Cu + \underset{\text{(Conc.)}}{4HNO_3} \longrightarrow Cu(NO_3)_2 + 2H_2O + \underset{\text{Reddish - brown gas}}{2NO_2 \uparrow}$$

(ii) (a) **Baeyer's process** is used to concentrate the bauxite ore.

(b) $$\underset{\text{Aluminium hydroxide}}{2Al(OH)_3} \xrightarrow[1000^\circ C]{\text{Heat}} \underset{\text{Pure alumina}}{Al_2O_3} + 3H_2O$$

(iii) (a) When Mg reacts with the dilute HCl, $MgCl_2$ is formed as an ionic compound.

$$Mg + \underset{\text{(dil.)}}{2HCl} \longrightarrow MgCl_2 + H_2 \uparrow$$

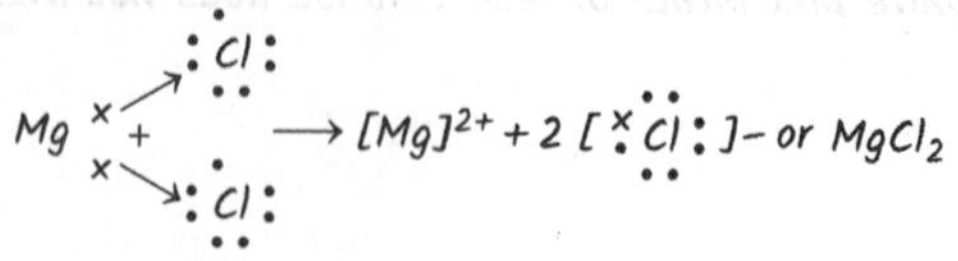

(b) When H_2 reacts with Cl_2, a covalent compound HCl is formed.

$$H_2 + Cl_2 \longrightarrow 2HCl$$

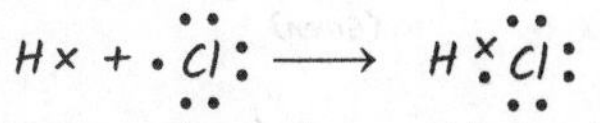

(Before combination) (After combination)

(c) When ammonia gas is dissolved in water, **ammonium ion (NH_4^+)** is formed as the positive ion.

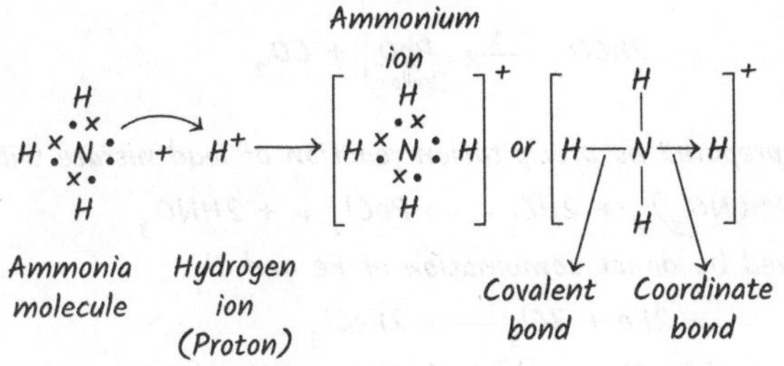

(iv) (a) Dilute sulphuric acid **catalyses** the ionisation of water.

(b) At cathode,

$$H^+ + e^- \longrightarrow H$$

$$H + H \longrightarrow H_2$$

(c) At anode, **oxygen gas** is liberated with the formation of water.

$$OH^- \longrightarrow OH + e^-$$

$$OH + OH \longrightarrow H_2O + O$$

$$O + O_2 \longrightarrow O_2$$

8. (i) (a) **Avogadro's law** states that "equal volumes of all gases under similar conditions of temperature and pressure contain the same number of molecules."

(b) The bond formed between two atoms by sharing a pair of electrons, provided entirely by one of the combining atoms, but shared by both is called a **coordinate bond** or **dative bond**.

(ii) (a) When ammonium chloride is heated with sodium hydroxide (alkali), a pungent smelling **ammonia gas** is produced. Whereas, no such reaction takes place when sodium chloride and sodium hydroxide (alkali) are heated together.

$$\underset{\text{(Ammonium chloride)}}{NH_4Cl} + \underset{\text{(Alkali)}}{NaOH} \xrightarrow{\Delta} NaCl + H_2O + \underset{\text{(Ammonia)}}{NH_3} \uparrow$$

(b) Zinc nitrate solution when reacted with sodium hydroxide solution forms a **gelatinous white precipitate**. This precipitate is **soluble in excess of NaOH** as it forms soluble sodium zincate.

$$\underset{\text{Zinc nitrate}}{Zn(NO_3)_2} + 2NaOH \longrightarrow \underset{\text{Zinc hydroxide White, gelatinous ppt.}}{Zn(OH)_2} \downarrow + 2NaNO_3$$

$$Zn(OH)_2 + \underset{\text{(excess)}}{2NaOH} \longrightarrow \underset{\text{Sodium zincate (Colourless)}}{Na_2ZnO_2} + H_2O$$

Whereas, calcium nitrate forms **calcium hydroxide (white precipitate)** when reacted with NaOH. This precipitate is **sparingly soluble in excess NaOH**.

$$\underset{\text{Calcium nitrate}}{Ca(NO_3)_2} + 2NaOH \longrightarrow \underset{\text{Calcium hydroxide (White ppt.)}}{Ca(OH)_2} + 2NaNO_3$$

(iii) (a) SO_2

$$\underset{\text{(Orange)}}{K_2Cr_2O_7} + H_2SO_4 + 3SO_2 \longrightarrow \underset{\text{(Green)}}{Cr_2(SO_4)_3} + K_2SO_4 + H_2O$$

(b) NCl_3

$$NH_3 + \underset{\text{(excess)}}{3Cl_2} \longrightarrow 3HCl + NCl_3$$

(c) PbO

$$PbCO_3 \xrightarrow{\Delta} \underset{\text{(Yellow)}}{PbO} + CO_2$$

(iv) (a) **R** — $PbCl_2$ can be prepared by precipitation reaction of lead nitrate with hydrochloric acid.

$$Pb(NO_3)_2 + 2HCl \longrightarrow PbCl_2 \downarrow + 2HNO_3$$

(b) **S** — $FeCl_3$ is prepared by direct combination of Fe and Cl_2.

$$2Fe + 3Cl_2 \longrightarrow 2FeCl_3$$

(c) **Q** — Na_2SO_4 is prepared by the method of neutralisation by titration of H_2SO_4 (an acid) and NaOH (a soluble base).

$$H_2SO_4 + 2NaOH \longrightarrow Na_2SO_4 + 2H_2O$$

LATEST ICSE SPECIMEN PAPER
CHEMISTRY

General Instructions

Maximum Marks : 80

Time allowed : Two hours

- You will not be allowed to write during the first **15** minutes.

  This time is to be spent in reading the question paper.

- The time given at the head of this paper is the time allowed for writing the answers.

  Section A is compulsory. Attempt **any four** questions from **Section B**.

- The intended marks for questions or parts of questions are given brackets [ ].

Section A

(Attempt **all** questions from this section)

Question 1

Choose the correct answers to the questions from the given options. **[15]**

(i) An aqueous solution of copper sulphate turns colourless on electrolysis.

Which of the following could be the electrodes?

P. anode: copper; cathode: copper

Q. anode: platinum; cathode: copper

R. anode: copper; cathode: platinum

(a) Only P
(b) Only Q
(c) Only R
(d) Both Q and R
• *Understanding*

(ii) A compound P is heated in a test tube with sodium hydroxide solution. A red litmus paper held at the mouth of the test tube turns blue. Which of the following could compound P be?

(a) Zinc sulphate
(b) Copper sulphate
(c) Ferrous sulphate
(d) Ammonium sulphate
• *Understanding*

(iii) Which of the following would weigh the least? (Atomic masses : C = 12, O = 16, Na = 23)

(a) 2 gram atoms of oxygen
(b) one mole of sodium
(c) 22.4 litres of carbon dioxide at STP
(d) 6.023×10^{22} atoms of carbon
• *Application*

(iv) The equation below shows the reaction between element 'X' and dilute sulphuric acid.

$$X(s) + H_2SO_4(aq) \longrightarrow XSO_4(aq) + H_2(g)$$

Which particles are responsible for conducting electricity in dilute sulphuric acid and compound XSO_4?

(a) Electrons
(b) Only positive ions
(c) Only negative ions
(d) Both positive and negative ions
• *Understanding*

(v) **Assertion** (A) Dry hydrogen chloride gas is collected by the upward displacement of air.

Reason (R) Hydrogen chloride gas is lighter than air.

(a) Both A and R are true and R is the correct explanation of A.
(b) Both A and R are true but R is not the correct explanation of A.
(c) A is true but R is false.
(d) A is false but R is true.

• *Understanding*

(vi) The structures of four hydrocarbons are shown below:

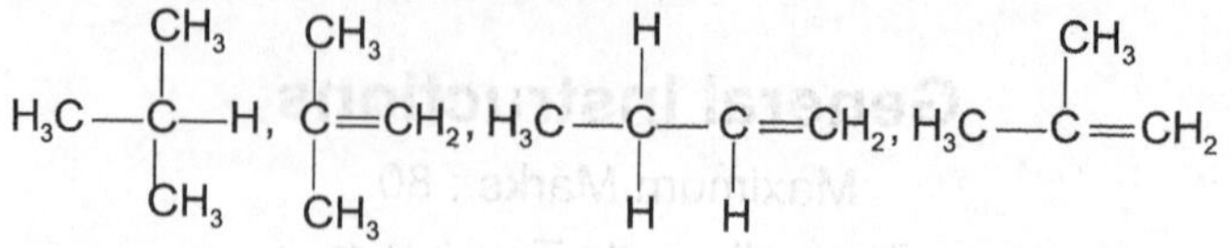

How many isomers of butene are there?

• *Analysis*

(a) 1 (b) 2 (c) 3 (d) 4

(vii) Element '*P*' has electronic configuration 2, 8, 8, 1. The number of chlorine atoms present in the chloride of '*P*' is:

(a) 2 (b) 1 (c) 3 (d) 4

• *Understanding and Application*

(viii) $_1H^2$ is an isotope of hydrogen. In the modern periodic table it will

(a) be placed before hydrogen
(b) be placed after hydrogen
(c) be placed at the same position as hydrogen
(d) not have any position in the periodic table

• *Understanding*

(ix) A nitrate which forms a precipitate with ammonium hydroxide and is also soluble in excess of it

(a) ferrous nitrate
(b) ferric nitrate
(c) lead nitrate
(d) copper nitrate

• *Understanding*

(x) Which of the following electronic configuration represents the most electropositive element?

(a) 2, 1
(b) 2, 8, 1
(c) 2, 2
(d) 2, 8, 2

• *Understanding*

(xi) **Assertion** (A) Alkali metals do not form dipositive ions.

Reason (R) After loss of one electron alkali metals achieve stable electronic configuration of noble gases.

(a) Both A and R are true and R is the correct explanation of A.
(b) Both A and are true but R is not the correct explanation of A.
(c) A is true but R is false.
(d) A is false but R is true.

• *Understanding*

(xii) The ratio between the volumes occupied by 4.4 grams of carbon dioxide and 2 grams of hydrogen gas is

(a) 2.2 :1
(b) 1:2.2
(c) 1:10
(d) 10 : 1

• *Application*

(xiii) Aqueous lead (II) nitrate can be distinguished from aqueous zinc nitrate by adding any of the following solution in excess, except

(a) aqueous potassium chloride
(b) aqueous sodium sulphate
(c) dilute sulphuric acid
(d) sodium hydroxide solution

• *Understanding*

(xiv) Which of the following about oxides is correct?

(a) A basic oxide is an oxide of a non-metal.
(b) Acidic oxides contain ionic bonds.
(c) Amphoteric oxides contain a metal.
(d) Basic oxides are always gases.

• *Understanding*

(xv) A student takes Cu, Al, Fe and Zn strips, separately in four test tubes labelled as I, II, III and IV respectively. He adds 10 ml of freshly prepared ferrous sulphate solution to each test tube and observes the colour of the metal residue in each case.

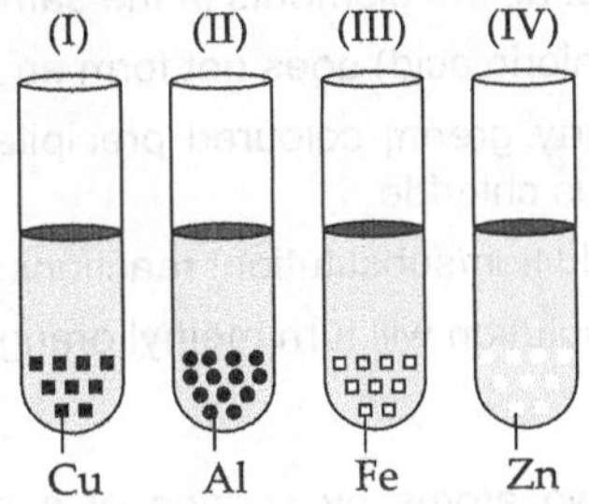

He would observe a black residue in the test tubes:

(a) (I) and (II)
(b) (I) and (III)
(c) (II) and (III)
(d) (II) and (IV) • *Understanding and Application*

Question 2

(i) Electroplating steel objects with silver involves a three-step process. **[5]**

Step 1 : A coating of copper is applied to the object.

Step 2 : A coating of nickel is applied to the object.

Step 3 : The coating of silver is applied to the object.

(a) A diagram of the apparatus used for step 1 is shown.

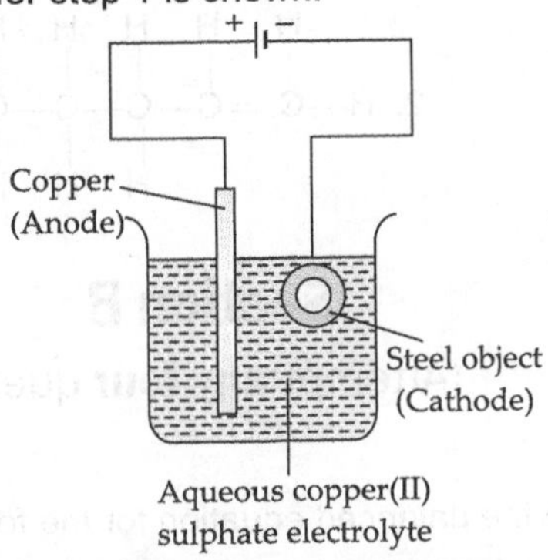

A. The chemical process taking place on the surface of the object is

$$Cu^{2+}(aq) + 2e^- \longrightarrow Cu(s)$$

What is the observation seen on the surface of the object?

B. Explain why the concentration of copper ions in the electrolyte remains constant throughout step 1.

(b) Give two changes which would be needed in order to coat nickel onto the object in step 2.

(c) Write down the reaction taking place at the positive electrode during step 3. • *Analysis and Application*

(ii) Match the following Column A with Column B. • *Recall and Understanding* **[5]**

Column A	Column B
(a) Aluminium	1. Covalent compound
(b) Sulphuric acid	2. Carbonate ore
(c) Calcination	3. Hall Heroult's process
(d) Calcium chloride	4. Contact process
(e) Carbon tetrachloride	5. Electrovalent compound

(iii) Complete the following by choosing the correct answers from the bracket: **[5]**

(a) If an element has one electron in the outermost shell, then it is likely to have the ...... [smallest/largest] atomic size amongst all the elements in the same period.

(b) ...... [sulphuric acid/hydrochloric acid) does not form an acid salt.

(c) A .... [reddish brown/dirty green] coloured precipitate is formed when ammonium hydroxide is added to a solution of ferrous chloride.

(d) Alkynes undergo .... [addition/substitution] reactions.

(e) An .... [alkaline/acidic] solution will turn methyl orange solution pink or red. • *Recall and Understanding*

(iv) Identify the following: **[5]**

(a) A bond formed between two atoms by sharing of a pair of electrons, with both electrons being provided by the same atom.

(b) A salt formed by the complete neutralisation of an acid by a base.

(c) A reaction in which the hydrogen of an alkane is replaced by a halogen.

(d) The energy required to remove an electron from a neutral gaseous atom.

(e) A homogeneous mixture of two or more metals or a metal and a non- metal in a definite proportion in their molten state. • *Recall*

(v) (a) Draw the structural diagram for the following compounds: **[5]**

1. Propanoic acid   2. Pentan-2-ol   3. 2, 2-dibromobutane

(b) Give the IUPAC name of the following organic compounds:

1. 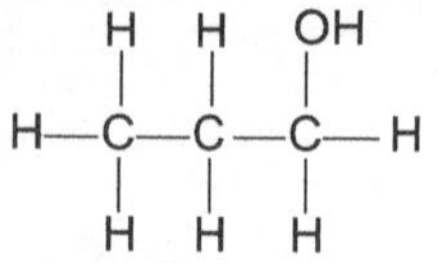

2. 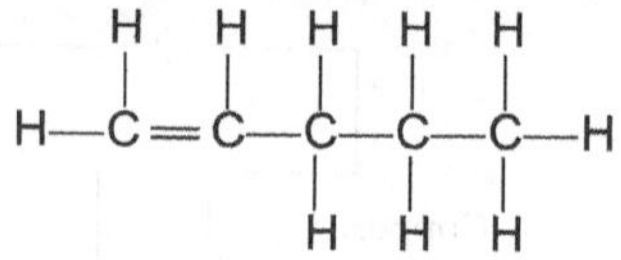

• *Understanding*

Section B

(Attempt **any four** questions)

Question 3

(i) Identify the reactant and write the balanced equation for the following: **[2]**

Nitric acid reacts with compound Q to give a salt $Ca(NO_3)_2$, water and carbon dioxide. • *Understanding*

(ii) What property of sulphuric acid is exhibited in each of the following cases? **[2]**

(a) In the preparation of HCl gas when it reacts with sodium chloride.

(b) When concentrated sulphuric acid reacts with copper to produce sulphur dioxide gas. • *Understanding*

(iii) The electron affinity of an element *X* is greater than that of element *Y*. **[3]**

(a) How is the oxidising power of *X* likely to compare with that of *Y*?

(b) How is the electronegativity of *X* likely to compare with that of *Y*?

(c) State whether *X* is likely to be placed to the left or to the right of *Y* in the periodic table? • *Application*

(iv) You are provided with the list of chemicals mentioned below in the box: **[3]**

Sodium hydroxide solution, copper carbonate, zinc, hydrochloric acid, copper, dilute sulphuric acid, chlorine, iron

Using suitable chemicals from the list given, write balanced chemical equation for the preparation of the salts mentioned below:

(a) Copper sulphate   (b) Sodium zincate   (c) Ferric chloride • *Understanding and Application*

Question 4

(i) The following questions relate to the extraction of aluminium by electrolysis. **[2]**

(a) Name the other aluminium containing compound added to alumina.

(b) Give a balanced equation for the reaction that takes place at the cathode. • *Recall*

(ii) Pratik heated 11.2 grams of element '*M*' (atomic weight 56) with 4.8 grams of element '*N*' (atomic weight 16) to form a compound. Find the empirical formula of the compound obtained by Pratik. • *Application* **[2]**

(iii) Give balanced equations for each of the following: **[3]**

(a) Action of warm water on aluminium nitride.

(b) Oxidation of carbon with conc. nitric acid.

(c) Laboratory preparation of ethanol by using chloroethane and aqueous sodium hydroxide.

• *Recall and Understanding*

(iv) The diagram given below is a representation of the industrial preparation of nitric acid by Ostwald's process. With respect to the process answer the following questions: **[3]**

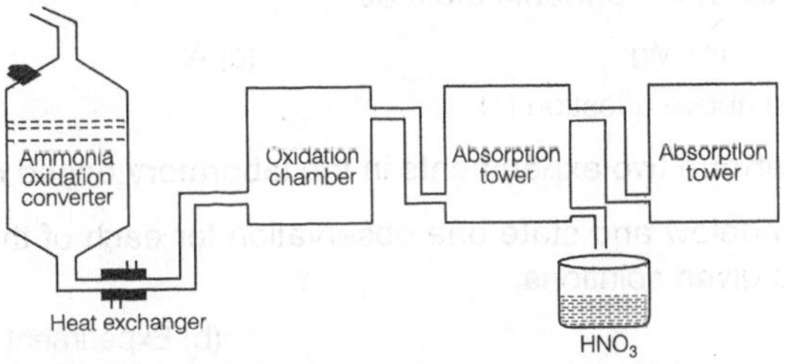

(a) Write the temperature and the catalyst required during the catalytic oxidation of ammonia.

(b) Give balanced chemical equation for the reaction occurring during the conversion of nitrogen dioxide to nitric acid. • *Recall*

Question 5

(i) (a) Ranjana wants to prove that ammonia is a reducing agent. To demonstrate this, she passes ammonia gas over heated copper oxide. What will she observe? **[2]**

(b) Write a balanced chemical equation for the above reaction. • *Understanding*

(ii) Name the alloy which is made up of **[2]**

(a) copper, zinc and tin

(b) lead and tin • *Recall*

(iii) Abhishek was given a salt '*X*' which was white in colour for analysis. On strong heating it produced a yellow residue, a colourless gas and also a reddish-brown gas. The solution of the salt '*X*' when tested with excess of ammonium hydroxide produced a chalky white insoluble precipitate. **[3]**

(a) Name the coloured gas evolved when Abhishek heated the salt strongly.

(b) Which cation was present in the sample given to Abhishek?

(c) Identify the salt given to Abhishek for analysis. • *Understanding*

(iv) Given below in column A is a schematic diagram of the electrolytic reduction of alumina. Identify the parts labelledasA,BandCwiththecorrectoptionsfromtheColumnB. **[3]**

Column A	Column B
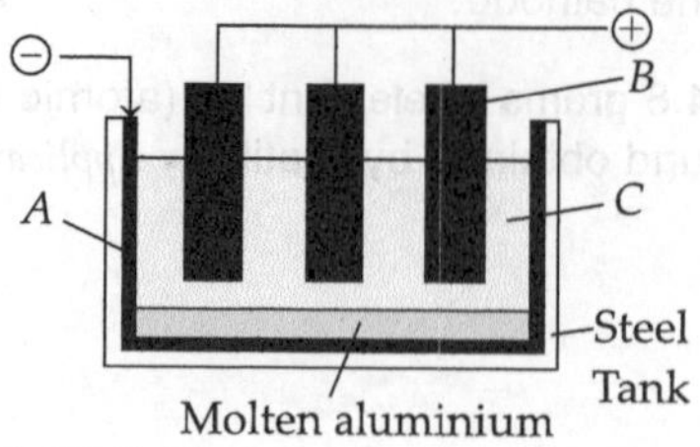	1. Platinum
	2. Anode
	3. Cathode
	4. Electrolyte mixture
	5. Bauxite

• *Understanding*

Question 6

(i) Element '*X*' forms an oxide with the formula X_2O_3 which is a solid with high melting point. '*X*' would most likely be placed in the group of the periodic table as **[2]**

1. (a) Na (b) Mg (c) Al (d) Si
2. Justify your answer in the above question (1). • *Application*

(ii) A student was asked to perform two experiments in the laboratory based on the instructions given: **[2]**

Observe the picture given below and state one observation for each of the experiments 1 and 2 that you would notice on mixing the given solutions.

(a) Experiment 1

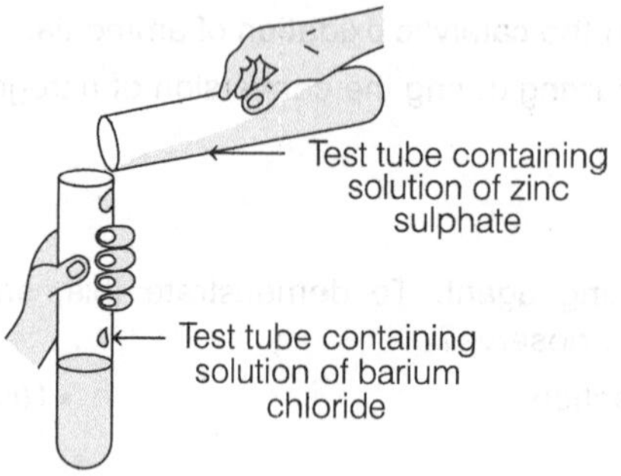

(b) Experiment 2

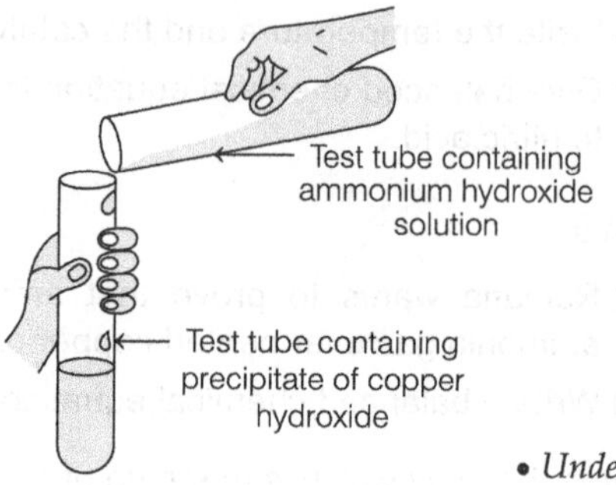

• *Understanding*

(iii) Copper sulphate solution is electrolysed using copper electrodes. **[3]**

(a) Which electrode [cathode or anode] is the oxidising electrode? Why?

(b) Write the equation for the reaction occurring at the above electrode. • *Understanding*

(iv) *X* [2, 8, 7] and *Y* [2, 8, 2] are two elements. Using this information complete the following: **[3]**

(a) .... is the metallic element.

(b) Metal atoms tend to have a maximum of .... electrons in the outermost shell.

(c) ...... is the reducing agent. • *Understanding*

Question 7

(i) One variety of household fuel is a mixture of propane (60%) and butane (40%). If 20 litres of this mixture is burnt, find the total volume of carbon dioxide added to the atmosphere. The combination reactions can be represented as

$$C_3H_8 + 5O_2 \longrightarrow 3CO_2 + 4H_2O$$

$$2C_4H_{10} + 13O_2 \longrightarrow 8CO_2 + 10H_2O$$

• *Application* **[3]**

(ii) Rohit has solution X, Y and Z that has pH 2, 7 and 13 respectively. Which solution **[3]**

(a) will liberate sulphur dioxide gas when heated with sodium sulphite ?

(b) will liberate ammonia gas when reacted with ammonium chloride ?

(c) will not have any effect on litmus paper? • *Application*

(iii) 8.2 grams of calcium nitrate is decomposed by heating according to the equation **[4]**

$$2Ca(NO_3)_2 \longrightarrow 2CaO + 4NO_2 + O_2$$

Calculate the following:

(a) Volume of nitrogen dioxide obtained at STP.

(b) Mass of CaO formed. [Atomic weights: Ca-40, N-14, O-16] • *Understanding*

Question 8

(i) State giving reasons if: • *Understanding* **[2]**

(a) Zinc and aluminium can be distinguished by heating the metal powder with concentrated sodium hydroxide solution.

(b) Calcium nitrate and lead nitrate can be distinguished by adding ammonium hydroxide solution to the salt solution.

(ii) Draw the electron dot diagram of ammonium ion. • *Recall and Understanding* **[2]**

(iii) Give balanced equations for the following: **[3]**

(a) Laboratory preparation of ethyne from calcium carbide.

(b) Conversion of acetic acid to ethyl acetate.

(c) Laboratory preparation of nitric acid. • *Recall*

(iv) The structures of six organic compounds are shown: **[3]**

(*A*)

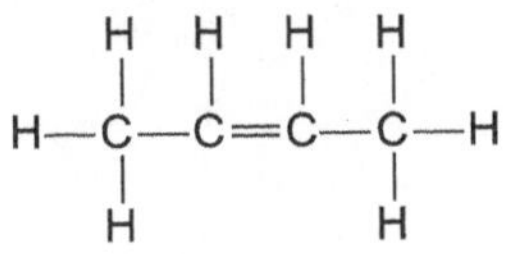

(*B*)

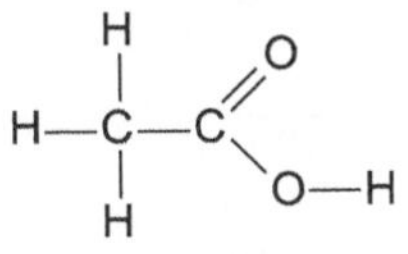

(*C*)

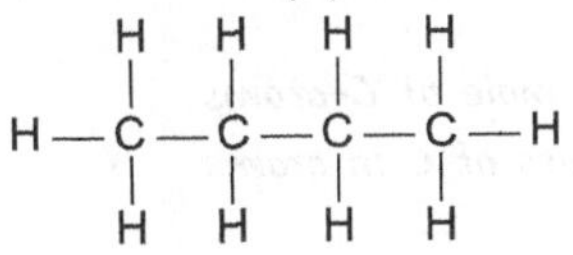

(*D*)

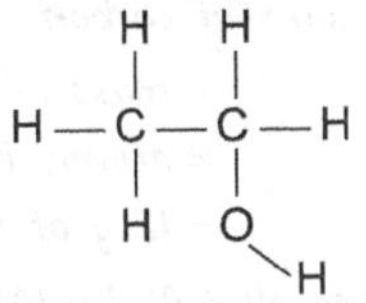

(*E*)

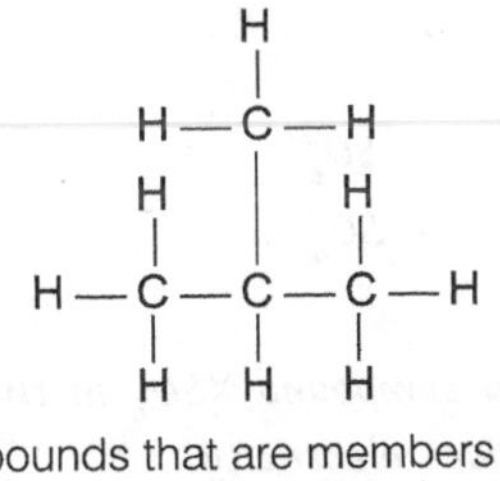

(*F*)

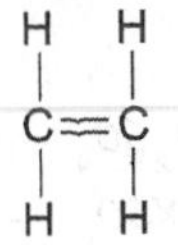

(a) Identify two of the compounds that are members of the same homologous series but are not isomers.

(b) Which two compounds are isomers of each other?

(c) F can be prepared from D. Give a chemical equation for the reaction. • *Understanding and Application*

Answers

1. (i) (b) Only Q.

On electrolysis of copper sulphate solution cathode is copper and anode is platinum.

(ii) (d) Ammonium sulphate

The reaction is represented as

$$\underset{\text{Ammonium sulphate (P)}}{(NH_4)_2SO_4} + \underset{\text{Sodium hydroxide}}{2NaOH} \longrightarrow \underset{\text{Sodium sulphate}}{Na_2SO_4} + 2H_2O + \underset{\text{Ammonia}}{2NH_3}$$

As, ammonia is alkaline in nature. When red litmus paper held at the mouth of the test tube, it changes the colour of the red litmus paper to blue.

(iii) (d) 6.023×10^{22} atoms of carbon.

Because, 1 g atoms of O = 1 mole of atoms of O

2 g atoms of O = 2 moles of atoms of O

2 g atoms of O = mass of 2 moles of O

2 g atoms of O = $2 \times 16 = 32$ g

Mass of one mole of sodium

= atomic mass of sodium in grams

= 23 g of sodium

22.4 L of CO_2 at STP = 1 mole of CO_2

= atomic mass of CO_2 in g

= 44 g of CO_2

6.023×10^{22} atoms of carbon

= mass of 1 mole of C-atoms

= atomic mass of C in gram

= 12 g of C

Therefore, among all 6.023×10^{22} atoms of carbon weigh least.

(iv) (d) Both positive and negative ions.

Ionisation of :

$$H_2SO_4 \longrightarrow 2H^+ + SO_4^{2-}$$
$$XSO_4 \longrightarrow X^{2+} + SO_4^{2-}$$

SO_4^{2-} ions migrate to the anode.

H^+ or X^{2+} ions migrate to the cathode. As both H_2SO_4 and compound XSO_4 in their aqueous solution dissociate into ions, thus both positive and negative ions help to conduct electricity.

(v) (c) Assertion is true but Reason is false.

Dry hydrogen chloride (HCl) gas is collected by the upward displacement of air, as it is 1.28 times heavier than air.

(vi) (c) 3

The molecular formula of butene is C_4H_{10}, thus isomers of butene are

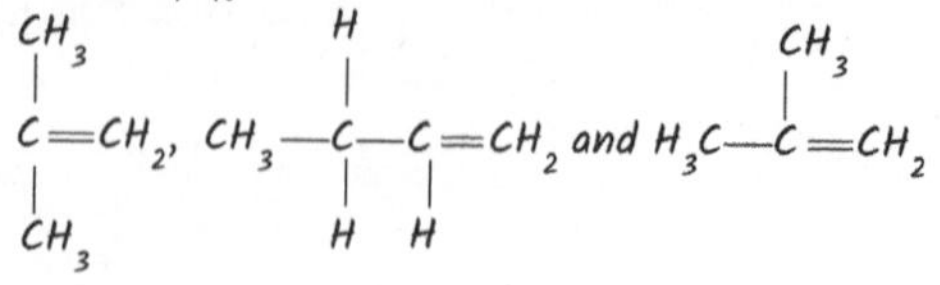

(vii) (b) 1

Electronic configuration of P = 2, 8, 8, 1

Valency of P = 1

Electronic configuration of Cl = 2, 8, 7

Valency of Cl = 1

Formula of the chloride of P = PCl

Thus, only one atom of chlorine is present in PCl.

(viii) (c) Be placed at the same position as hydrogen.

Elements in periodic table are arranged according to their atomic number. Since, isotopes have same atomic number but differ in mass number.

$\therefore {}_1H^2$ is with one atomic no. be placed at the same position as hydrogen.

(ix) (d) Copper nitrate

When NH_4OH is added to $Cu(NO_3)_2$ solution in small quantity then ppt. of $Cu(OH)_2$ is formed, but when excess of NH_4OH is added then, the ppt. turns into a solution of tetraamine copper nitrate.

(x) (b) 2, 8, 1

Tendency to lose electron to form a negatively charged ion is called electropositivity.

Electropositivity increases from top to bottom in a group and decreases from left to right in a period.

Thus, 2, 8, 1 (Na) is most electropositive element among all options.

(xi) (a) Both A and R are true and R is the correct explanation of A.

Alkali metals are present in group 1, has valency 1 and form monopositive ions.

Also, alkali metals can loose only one electron to become stable.

(xii) (c) 1 : 10

Volume occupied by 1 mole of gas = 22.4 litre at STP

No. of moles of $CO_2 = \frac{4.4}{44} = 0.1$

No. of moles of $H_2 = \frac{2}{2} = 1$

$$\therefore \frac{\text{Volume occupied by 4.4 g } CO_2}{\text{Volume occupied by 2 g } H_2} = \frac{0.1 \times 22.4}{1 \times 22.4} = 1 : 10$$

(xiii) (d) Sodium hydroxide solution

Both $Pb(NO_3)_2$ and $Zn(NO_3)_2$ form white precipitate with NaOH. So, we cannot distinguish these on adding NaOH.

$$\underset{\text{Lead (II) nitrate}}{Pb(NO_3)_2} + 2NaOH \longrightarrow \underset{\text{White ppt.}}{Pb(OH)_2} \downarrow + 2NaNO_3$$

$$\underset{\text{Zinc (II) nitrate}}{Zn(NO_3)_2} + 2NaOH \longrightarrow \underset{\text{White ppt.}}{Zn(OH)_2} \downarrow + 2NaNO_3$$

(xiv) (c) Amphoteric oxides contain a metal, e.g. Al_2O_3 and ZnO.

The corrected form of other statements are

Basic oxide is an oxide of a metal.

Acidic oxide contains covalent bonds.

Basic oxides are not always gases.

(xv) (d) (II) and (IV)

$$2Al + 3FeSO_4 \longrightarrow Al_2(SO_4)_3 + 3Fe$$
$$Zn + FeSO_4 \longrightarrow ZnSO_4 + Fe$$

In both reactions, Al and Zn are more reactive than Fe.

2. (i) (a) A. On the surface of the object pink or reddish brown deposit of copper takes place.

B. As, anode released copper ions the concentration of copper ions does not decrease.

(b) Anode should be made up of nickel so, that, reaction at anode

$$Ni - 2e^- \longrightarrow Ni^{2+}$$

and the electrolyte nickel sulphate solution or any salt solution of nickel should be used.

$$NiSO_4 \longrightarrow Ni^{+2} + SO_4^{2-} \quad \text{(Dissociation of electrolyte)}$$

(c) At anode, $Ag \longrightarrow Ag^+ + e^-$

If anode is a plate of pure silver.

(ii)

	Column A	Column B
(a)	Aluminium	3. Hall-Heroult's process
(b)	Sulphuric acid	4. Contact process
(c)	Calcination	2. Carbonate ore
(d)	Calcium chloride	5. Electrovalent compound
(e)	Carbon tetrachloride	1. Covalent compound

(iii) (a) largest

(b) hydrochloric acid

(c) dirty green

(d) addition

(e) acidic

(iv) (a) Coordinate bond

(A bond formed by two atoms by sharing of a pair of electrons, with both electrons being provided by the same atom.)

(b) Normal salt

e.g. $(HCl + NaOH \longrightarrow NaCl + H_2O)$

or $(H_2SO_4 + 2NaOH \longrightarrow Na_2SO_4 + 2H_2O)$

(c) Substitution reaction

e.g. $(CH_4 + Cl_2 \xrightarrow[\text{sunlight}]{\text{Diffused}} CH_3Cl + HCl)$

(d) Ionisation energy.

(e) Alloy

(v) (a) Structural diagram of

(I) Propanoic acid is represented as

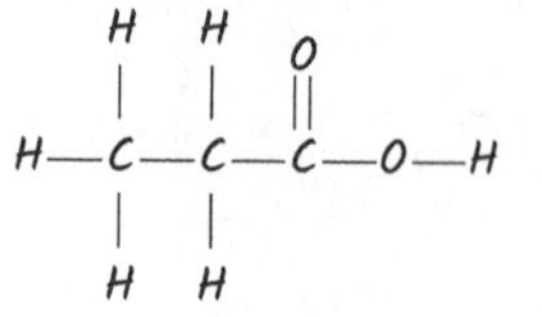

Propanoic acid

(2) The structure of pentan-2-ol is represented as

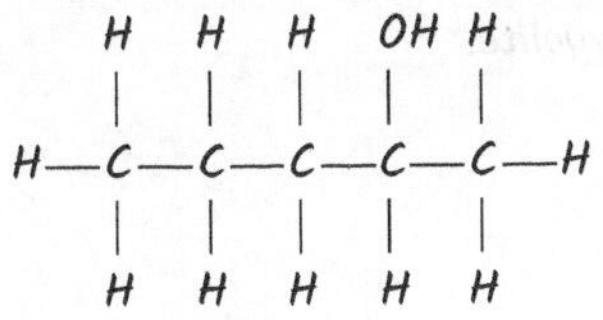

Pentan - 2 - ol

(3) The structure of 2, 2-dibromobutane is represented as

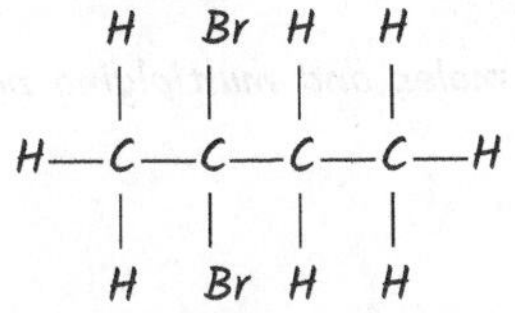

2, 2 -dibromobutane

(b) IUPAC name of the given organic compounds are

(1) Propan-1-ol (2) Pentene/pent-1-ene

3. (i) Reactant Q is $CaCO_3$ [Calcium carbonate] or $Ca(HCO_3)_2$ [Calcium bicarbonate].

Balanced equation are

$$\underset{Q}{CaCO_3} + 2HNO_3 \longrightarrow Ca(NO_3)_2 + H_2O + CO_2$$

Or

$$\underset{Q}{Ca(HCO_3)_2} + 2HNO_3 \longrightarrow Ca(NO_3)_2 + 2H_2O + 2CO_2$$

(ii) (a) In the preparation of HCl gas, H_2SO_4 is used to react with NaCl, because it is non-volatile in nature. Thus, **non-volatile property**, is exhibited by sulphuric acid used.

$$NaCl + H_2SO_4 \xrightarrow{< 200°C} NaHSO_4 + HCl\uparrow$$

(b) When conc. H_2SO_4 reacts with copper, it produces SO_2 gas.

$$Cu + 2H_2SO_4(conc.) \longrightarrow CuSO_4 + 2H_2O + SO_2\uparrow$$

Conc. H_2SO_4 shows oxidising property.

(iii) (a) As, the electron affinity increases, the amount of energy released when an electron is added to an atom increases which makes an atom stable, and the tendency to gain electrons increases.

So, oxidising property increases with an increase in electron affinity.

Hence, oxidising power of X is greater than Y.

(b) An element with high electron affinity has large electronegativity.

So, 'X' will be more electronegative than 'Y'.

(c) 'X' will be placed to the right of 'Y' because oxidising power is increases from left to right.

(iv) Balanced chemical equation for salts are

(a) $$\underset{\text{Copper carbonate}}{CuCO_3} + \underset{\text{(Dil. sulphuric acid)}}{H_2SO_4} \longrightarrow \underset{\text{Copper sulphate}}{CuSO_4} + H_2O + CO_2$$

(b) $$\underset{\text{Zinc}}{Zn(s)} + \underset{\text{Sodium hydroxide solution}}{2NaOH(aq)} \longrightarrow \underset{\text{Sodium zincate}}{Na_2ZnO_2} + H_2$$

(c) $$\underset{\text{Iron}}{2Fe} + \underset{\text{Chlorine}}{3Cl_2} \longrightarrow \underset{\text{Ferric chloride}}{2FeCl_3}$$

4. (i) (a) The other aluminium containing compound added to alumina is cryolite.

(b) The reaction that takes place at the cathode is

$$Al^{3+} + 3e^- \longrightarrow Al$$

(ii) No. of moles of element M $= \frac{w}{M} = \frac{11.2}{56} = 0.2$

No. of moles of element N $= \frac{w}{M} = \frac{4.8}{16} = 0.3$

By dividing the number of moles of each element by smallest number of moles and multiplying by 2.

For M $= \frac{0.2}{0.2} = 1 \times 2 = 2$

For N $= \frac{0.3}{0.2} = 1.5 \times 2 = 3$

∴ The empirical formula will be $= M_2N_3$

(iii) The given reaction is represented as

(a) $\underset{\text{Aluminium nitride}}{AlN} + \underset{\text{Warm water}}{3H_2O} \longrightarrow \underset{\text{Aluminium hydroxide}}{Al(OH)_3} + \underset{\text{Ammonia}}{NH_3}$

(b) $\underset{\text{Carbon}}{C} + \underset{\text{Nitric acid}}{4HNO_3}\ (\text{Conc.}) \longrightarrow \underset{\text{Carbon dioxide}}{CO_2} + \underset{\text{Nitrogen dioxide}}{4NO_2} + \underset{\text{Water}}{2H_2O}$

(c) $\underset{\text{Chloroethane}}{C_2H_5Cl} + \underset{\text{Sodium hydroxide}}{NaOH(aq)} \longrightarrow \underset{\text{Ethanol}}{C_2H_5OH} + \underset{\text{Sodium chloride}}{NaCl}$

(iv) (a) $4NH_3 + 5O_2 \xrightarrow[800°C]{Pt} 4NO + 6H_2O + \text{Heat}$

Temperature required is 800°C and the catalyst required is platinum.

(b) Balanced chemical equation for the conversion of NO_2 to HNO_3 is

$\underset{\text{Nitrogen dioxide}}{4NO_2(g)} + 2H_2O(l) + O_2(g) \longrightarrow \underset{\text{Nitric acid}}{4HNO_3(aq)}$

5. (i) (a) When ammonia is passed over heated copper oxide, the black colour copper oxide will change to reddish pink copper. It shows that ammonia is a reducing agent as it reduces cupric oxide to copper metal.

(b) The reaction is as follows

$$\underset{\text{Cupric oxide}}{3CuO} + 2NH_3 \longrightarrow \underset{\text{Copper}}{3Cu} + N_2 + 3H_2O$$

(ii) (a) Alloy made up of copper, zinc and tin is bronze.

(b) Solder is an alloy of lead and tin.

(iii) (a) $\underset{\text{Salt white in colour}}{2Pb(NO_3)_2} \xrightarrow{\Delta} \underset{\text{Yellow residue}}{2PbO} + \underset{\text{Reddish brown gas}}{4NO_2} + O_2$

The gas evolved is nitrogen dioxide which is reddish-brown in colour.

(b) Lead ions are present in the sample with salt 'X'.

(c) Salt is lead nitrate $Pb(NO_3)_2$, which was given to Abhishek for analysis.

(iv) The correct labels are

A = Cathode (3)

B = Anode (2)

C = Electrolyte mixture (4)

6. (i) 1. (c) The element 'X' is aluminium.

2. Aluminium has atomic number 13 and electronic configuration = 2, 8, 3

So, it has 3 electrons in the outermost shell and has valency 3.

So, Valency of Al = 3 Valency of O = 2

Formula of 'X' oxide is = Al_2O_3

(ii) (a) In experiment I,

$$\underset{\text{Zinc sulphate}}{ZnSO_4} + \underset{\text{Barium chloride}}{BaCl_2} \longrightarrow \underset{\text{Zinc chloride}}{ZnCl_2} + \underset{\text{Barium sulphate (White ppt.)}}{BaSO_4 \downarrow}$$

Observation White ppt. is formed.

(b) $$\underset{\text{Copper hydroxide (Pale blue ppt.)}}{Cu(OH)_2} + \underset{\text{Ammonium hydroxide}}{4NH_4OH} \longrightarrow \underset{\text{Tetraa min e copper hydroxide (deep blue solution)}}{[Cu(NH_3)_4](OH)_2} + 4H_2O$$

Observation Blue precipitate of $Cu(OH)_2$ dissolves to form an inky blue or deep blue solution.

(iii) (a) Anode electrode is the oxidising electrode because copper atoms lose electrons at this electrode.

(b) The reaction is as follows

$$CuSO_4 \rightleftharpoons Cu^{2+} + SO_4^{2-}$$

(i) Reaction at the anode

$$Cu \longrightarrow Cu^{2+} + 2e^-$$

(ii) Reaction at the cathode

$$Cu^{2+} + 2e^- \longrightarrow Cu$$

(iv) (a) Y (b) 3 (c) Y

7. (i) 20 litre of mixture

60% of 20 L → 12 L of propane

40% of 20 L → 8 L of butane

$$\underset{\text{1 vol.}}{C_3H_8} + \underset{\text{5 vol.}}{5O_2} \longrightarrow \underset{\text{3 vol.}}{3CO_2} + \underset{\text{4 vol.}}{4H_2O}$$

1 volume of propane gives 3 vol of CO_2

$$= 12 \times 3 = 36 \text{ L of } CO_2$$

$$\underset{\text{2 vol.}}{2C_4H_{10}} + \underset{\text{13 vol.}}{13O_2} \longrightarrow \underset{\text{8 vol.}}{8CO_2} + \underset{\text{10 vol.}}{10H_2O}$$

2 volume of butane gives 8 volume of CO_2

$$= \frac{8 \times 8}{2} = 32 \text{ L of } CO_2$$

Total volume of CO_2 = 36 + 32 = 68 litre of CO_2

(ii) (a) Sodium sulphite can react with dilute H_2SO_4 to release SO_2 gas.

$$\underset{\text{Sodium sulphite}}{Na_2SO_3(s)} + \underset{(pH = 2)}{H_2SO_4(l)} \longrightarrow Na_2SO_4 + \underset{\text{Sulphur dioxide gas}}{SO_2(g)} + H_2O$$

Thus, X will liberate sulphur dioxide gas when heated with sodium sulphite.

(b) Ammonia will be liberated from ammonium salts like ammonium chloride by addition of an alkaline solution like Z (pH = 13).

(c) Since, solution Y having pH 7 is neither acidic nor basic, so it will have no effect on either of the litmus papers.

(iii) (a) $2Ca(NO_3)_2 \longrightarrow 2CaO + 4NO_2 + O_2$

Molar mass of 2 × $Ca(NO_3)_2$

$$= 2 \times [40 + 2(14) + 6(16)]$$
$$= 2 \times 164$$
$$= 328 \text{ g}$$

328 g of $Ca(NO_3)_2$ liberated = 4 × 22.4 lit of NO_2

8.2 g of $Ca(NO_3)_2$ liberated $= \frac{4 \times 22.4 \times 8.2}{328}$

$$= 0.224 \text{ Litres of } NO_2$$

(b) Molar mass of CaO = 40 + 16 = 56

328 grams of $Ca(NO_3)_2$ produce

= 112 grams of CaO

1 gram of $Ca(NO_3)_2$ produce

$= \frac{112}{328}$ gram of CaO

8.2 grams of $Ca(NO_3)_2$ produce

$= \frac{8.2 \times 112}{328}$ grams of CaO

= 2.8 g of CaO formed

8. (i) (a) No

Metals like zinc and aluminium react with sodium hydroxide to produce gas. Zinc (Zn) reacts with NaOH to form sodium zincate with the evolution of hydrogen gas.

The reaction of aluminium with a NaOH gives a salt and hydrogen gas.

So, Zn and Al cannot be distinguish because both will form a white ppt. which is soluble in excess of sodium hydroxide.

(b) Yes

Calcium nitrate does not react with ammonium hydroxide because the concentration of OH^- ions produced by the ionisation of NH_4OH is very low, that cannot form ppt. of calcium hydroxide.

$$Ca(NO_3)_2 + NH_4OH \longrightarrow \text{No ppt.}$$

When ammonium hydroxide is added ~ drop by drop to a solution of lead nitrate, a white ppt. is formed which is soluble in excess of sodium hydroxide.

$$Pb(NO_3)_2 + 2NH_4OH \longrightarrow \underset{\text{White ppt.}}{Pb(OH)_2} \downarrow + 2NH_4NO_3$$

(ii)

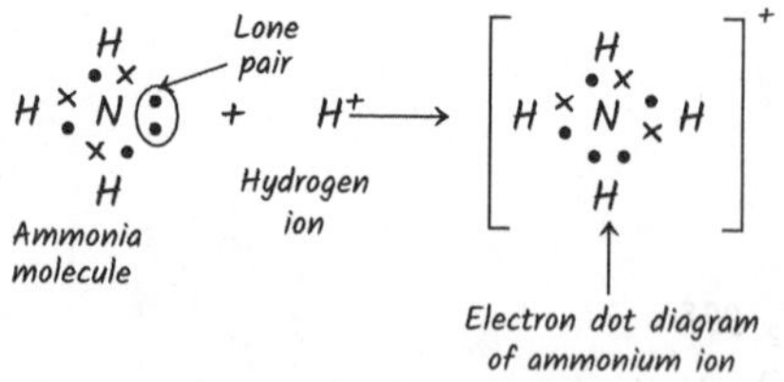

(iii) (a) Laboratory preparation of ethyne from calcium carbide is

$$\underset{\text{Calcium carbide}}{CaC_2(s)} + 2H_2O(l) \longrightarrow Ca(OH)_2(s) + \underset{\text{Ethyne}}{C_2H_2(g)}$$

(b) CH_3COOH + C_2H_5OH $\xrightarrow[H_2SO_4]{Conc.}$ $CH_3COOC_2H_5$ + $H_2(g)$

Acetic acid → Ethyl acetate

(c) KNO_3 + H_2SO_4 $\xrightarrow{\Delta}$ $KHSO_4$ + HNO_3

Potassium nitrate → Nitric acid

(iv) (a) **A and F**

A and F both are alkenes, therefore belongs to same homologous series, they are not isomers because their molecular formula is not same.

(b) C and E are isomers.

Because, they are having same molecular formula but different structure.

(c) F ⇒ Ethene [C_2H_2], D ⇒ Ethanol [C_2H_5OH]

$$\underset{\text{(Ethanol) (D)}}{C_2H_5OH} \xrightarrow[\text{Conc. } H_2SO_4]{170°C} \underset{\text{(Ethene) (E)}}{C_2H_4} + H_2O$$

SAMPLE QUESTION PAPER
CHEMISTRY

General Instructions

Maximum Marks : 80

Time allowed : Two hours

- You will not be allowed to write during the first **15** minutes.

This time is to be spent in reading the question paper.

- The time given at the head of this paper is the time allowed for writing the answers.

Section A is compulsory. Attempt **any four** questions from **Section B**.

- The intended marks for questions or parts of questions are given brackets [ ].

Section A

(Attempt **all** questions from this section) **(40 Marks)**

Questions 1

Choose the correct answers to the questions from the given options. **[15]**

(i) Which of the following statements are true for sulphuric acid?

I. Conc. H_2SO_4 acts as an oxidising agent.

II. Dilute H_2SO_4 acts as an dehydrating agent.

III. It is a strong electrolyte.

IV. It is a reducing agent.

(a) I and III (b) II and III (c) II and IV (d) III and IV

(ii) The diagram below represents the molecule of a compound.

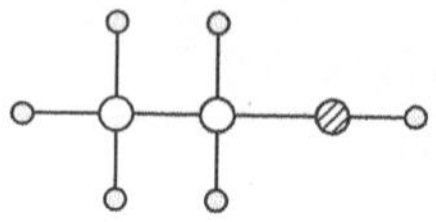

If, ○ represent carbon.

◍ represent oxygen

○ represent hydrogen

What is the name of this compound?

(a) Ethane

(b) Ethanol

(c) Ethanoic acid

(d) Ethene

(iii) Which graph shows the number of electrons in the outer shell of an atom, plotted against the proton (atomic number) for the first ten elements in the periodic table?

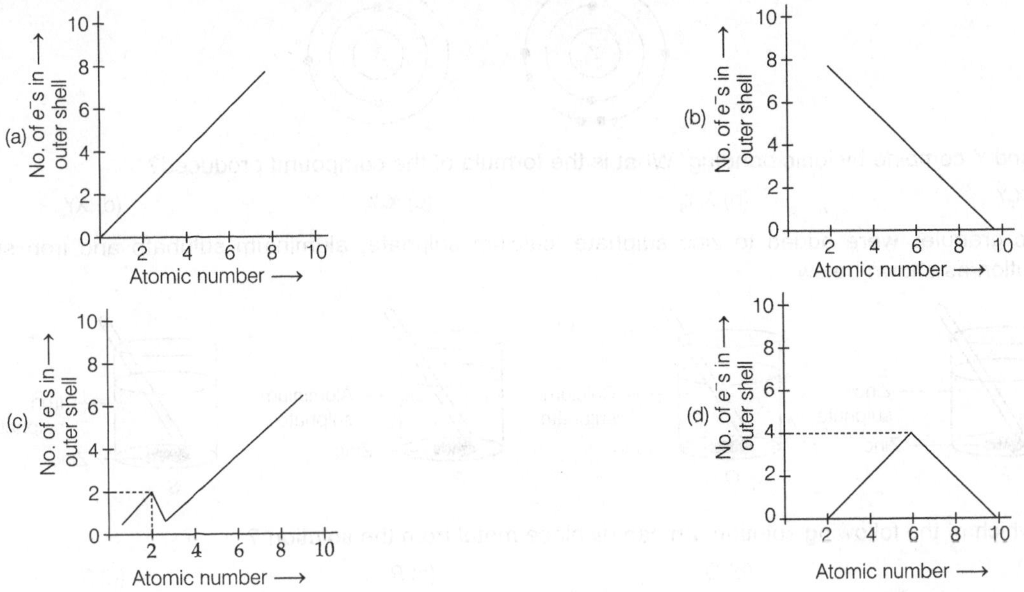

(iv) In the given reaction, what volume of oxygen would be required to burn completely 200 mL of C_2H_2?

$$C_2H_2 + O_2 \longrightarrow CO_2 + H_2O$$

(a) 400 mL
(b) 200 mL
(c) 500 mL
(d) 100 mL

(v) During the electrolysis of aqueous copper sulphate using copper electrodes, copper ions are generated at the anode, that go into the copper sulphate solution used as electrolyte.

Which of the following is correct regarding the mass of anode.

P. Mass of anode remain same.

Q. Mass of anode gradually decreases.

R. Mass of anode gradually increases.

(a) Only P
(b) Only Q
(c) Both P and Q
(d) P, Q and R

(vi) **Assertion** (A) During the extraction of aluminium, cryolite and fluorspar are added in the electrolyte.

Reason (R) Cryolite and fluorspar increases the conductivity since pure alumina is almost a non-conductor of electricity.

(a) Both A and R are true and R is the correct explanation of A.
(b) Both A and R are true but R is not the correct explanation of A.
(c) A is true but R is false.
(d) A is false but R is true.

(vii) A gas *P* is produced when ammonium sulphate is heated with sodium hydroxide solution.

Which of the following could gas *P* be?

(a) Hydrogen chloride gas
(b) Ammonia
(c) Sulphuric acid
(d) Chlorine

(viii) The electronic structures of atoms X and Y are shown :

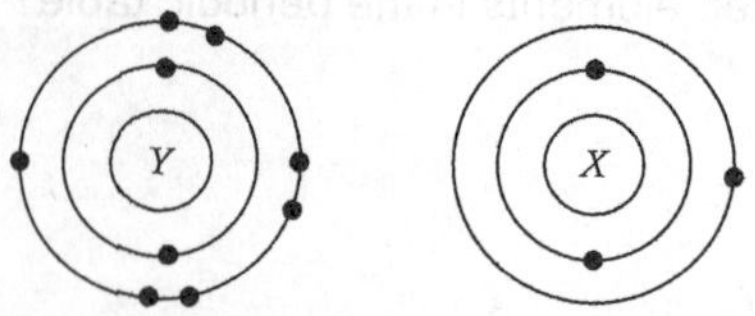

X and Y combine by ionic bonding. What is the formula of the compound produced?

(a) X_2Y (b) X_2Y_3 (c) X_3Y_2 (d) XY

(ix) Zinc granules were added to zinc sulphate, calcium sulphate, aluminium sulphate and iron sulphate solution as shown below.

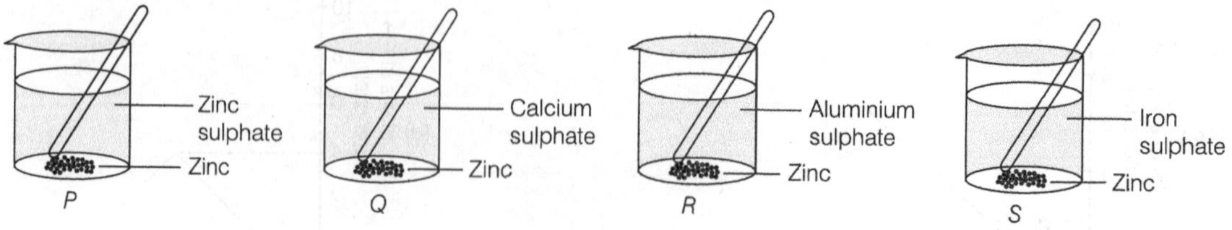

In which of the following solution, Zn can displace metal from the solution ?

(a) P (b) Q (c) R (d) S

(x) **Assertion** (A) In laboratory preparation of nitric acid, concentrated HCl is not used in place of conc. H_2SO_4.

Reason (R) HCl is volatile and hence, nitric acid vapours will carry HCl vapours during preparation of nitric acid.

(a) Both A and R are true and R is the correct explanation of A.
(b) Both A and R are true but R is not the correct explanation of A.
(c) A is true but R is false.
(d) A is false but R is true.

(xi) Four hydrocarbons are given below.

$$C_3H_4, C_3H_6, C_3H_8, C_4H_{10}$$

How many hydrocarbons have triple bond in them?

(a) 1 (b) 2 (c) 3 (d) 4

(xii) Pooja carried experiments separately in chemistry laboratory in different test tubes, labelled as (I), (II), (III) and (IV).

I. Mg + dil. HCl
II. Al + dil. H_2SO_4
III. Cu + dil. HCl
IV. Mn + dil. HNO_3

In which test tube, Pooja did not observed hydrogen gas?

(a) Only test tube (IV)
(b) Both test tubes (III) and (IV)
(c) Only test tube (III)
(d) Both test tubes (II) and (III)

(xiii) The equation below shows the thermal decomposition of metal nitrate. When 'X' is the metal.

$$X(NO_3)_2(s) \xrightarrow{\Delta} XO(s) + NO_2(g) + O_2(g)$$

Metal oxide appears yellow when it is hot and white when it is cold.

Which of the following metal 'X' could be?

(a) Lead (b) Sodium (c) Copper (d) Zinc

(xiv) On adding a few drops of universal indicator to three unknown colourless solutions *P*, *Q*, *R* and *S* taken separately in three test-tubes shown in the following diagrams. A student observed the changes in colour as green in *P*, red in *Q*, violet in *R* and dark blue in *S*. Which test-tubes is more acidic?

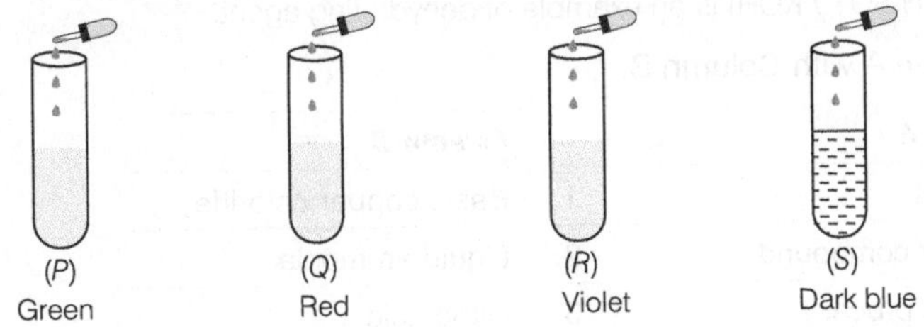

(a) *P* (b) *Q* (c) *R* (d) *S*

(xv) The atomic masses of nitrogen (N), oxygen (O), and neon (Ne) are approximately 14, 16 and 20.18 respectively.

Which of the following statements regarding the number of atoms in 14 g of nitrogen, 16 g of oxygen and 20 g of neon is correct?

P. 14 g of nitrogen contains double of atoms as 20 g of neon.

Q. 16 g of oxygen contains two times the number of atoms as 14 g of nitrogen.

(a) Only P (b) Only Q (c) Both P and P (d) Neither P nor Q

Question 2

(i) The diagram shows an experimental set up of a chemical *X* known as king of chemicals.

Study the diagram and answer the following. **[5]**

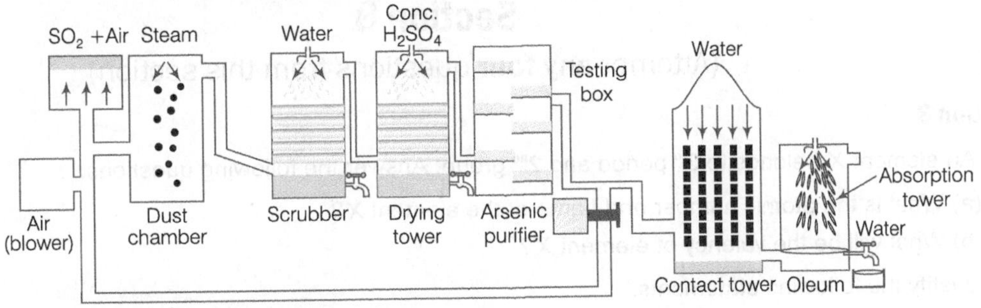

(a) Name the catalyst that is used during the process.

(b) Explain the process that is used to prepare chemical *X*.

(c) Write the chemical reactions involved during the process.

(d) SO_3 formed in catalytic chamber is not directly absorbed in water. Why?

(e) What property of conc. H_2SO_4 is used in the action when sugar turn black in its presence?

(ii) Identify the following. **[5]**

(a) An ore of zinc containing its sulphide.

(b) A hydrocarbon which on catalytic hydrogenation gives a saturated hydrocarbon.

(c) The gas produced when excess ammonia reacts with chlorine.

(d) A hydrocarbon which contributes towards greenhouse effect.

(e) A solution which gives brown colour with ammonium salts.

(iii) Complete the following sentences by choosing the correct word(s) from the brackets: **[5]**

(a) .... (Sulphuric acid/Hydrochloric acid) is used in lead storage battery.

(b) The compounds which conducts electricity only when dissolved in water or in molten state are called .... (electrolytes/conductors).

(c) Higher the pH value of a solution, the solution is more .... (acidic/alkaline) in nature.

(d) The salt which are formed by the partial replacement of hydroxyl radicals of a di-acidic or tri-acidic base with an acid radical is known as .... (acidic/basic) salt.

(e) .... (Conc. H_2SO_4 / KOH) is an example of dehydrating agent.

(iv) Match the Column A with Column B. **[5]**

	Column A		Column B
(a)	Acidic salt	1.	Basic copper chloride
(b)	Non-polar compound	2.	Liquid ammonia
(c)	Ostwald's process	3.	Nitric acid
(d)	Used as refrigerant	4.	Sodium hydrogen sulphite
(e)	Basic salt	5.	Carbon tetrachloride

(v) (a) Draw the structural formula for the following organic compounds. **[5]**

1. Propene 2. Pentan-2-ol

(b) Give IUPAC name for the following organic compounds

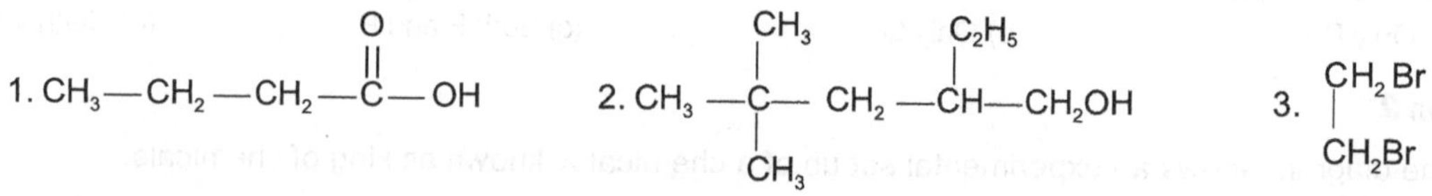

Section B

(Attempt **any four** questions from this section) **(40 Marks)**

Question 3

(i) An element *X* belongs to 3rd period and 2nd group. Answer the following questions. **[2]**

(a) What is the atomic number and name of the element *X*?

(b) What will be the valency of element *X*?

(ii) Justify the following statements. **[2]**

(a) A graphite anode is preferred to other inert electrodes during electrolysis of fused lead bromide.

(b) Name the gas released at the cathode when acidulated water is electrolysed.

(iii) The equation for the action of heat on calcium nitrate is **[3]**

$$2Ca(NO_3)_2 \longrightarrow 2CaO + 4NO_2 \uparrow + O_2 \uparrow$$

Calculate the following.

(a) How many moles of NO_2 are produced when 1 mole of $Ca(NO_3)_2$ decomposes?

(b) What volume of O_2 at STP will be produced on heating 65.6 g of $Ca(NO_3)_2$?

(iv) Give one significant observation when: **[3]**

(a) a mixture of calcium hydroxide and ammonium chloride heated.

(b) a solution of sodium nitrate and ammonium chloride is heated.

(c) crystals of copper nitrate are heated in a test tube.

Question 4

(i) Calculate. **[2]**

(a) An organic compound on analysis was found to contain 10.06% carbon, 0.84% hydrogen and 89.10% chlorine. What will be the empirical formula of the substance?

(b) Determine the molecular formula of the compound which has empirical formula C_5H_5N and the vapour density is 39.5.

(ii) Complete and balance the following equations : **[2]**

(a) $CH_3COO^-Na^+ + NaOH \xrightarrow[300\,°C]{CaO}$

(b) $CH_3CH_2OH \xrightarrow[170\,°C]{Conc.\ H_2SO_4}$

(iii) Name the gas evolved during each of the following reactions. **[3]**

(a) Magnesium reacts with hydrochloric acid.

(b) Ethene burns in sufficient supply of air.

(c) A colourless gas liberated on decompositon of nitric acid.

(iv) Study the extract of the periodic table given below and answer the questions that follow. Give the alphabet corresponding to the element in question. Do not repeat any element. **[3]**

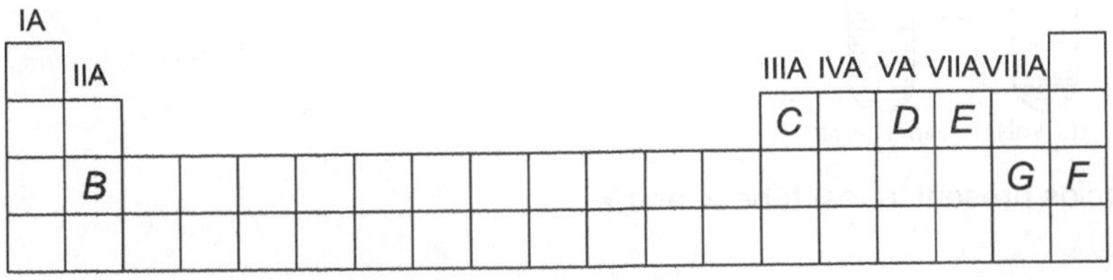

(a) Which element forms electrovalent compound with *G*?

(b) The ion of which element will migrate towards the cathode during electrolysis?

(c) Which non-metallic element has the valency of 2?

Question 5

(i) Identify the substances *P* and *Q* from the observations given below. **[2]**

(a) The deliquescent salt '*P*' turns yellow on dissolving in water and gives a reddish brown precipitate with sodium hydroxide solution.

(b) The white crystalline solid '*Q*' is soluble in water. It liberates a pungent smelling gas when heated with sodium hydroxide solution.

(ii) What happens when the following are added to ethene? Give reaction and name the reaction also. **[2]**

(a) Hydrogen at 200°C with nickel as catalyst.

(b) Water in presence of acids.

(iii) Write the balanced chemical equations for the following reactions. **[3]**

(a) Lead nitrate with sodium hydroxide.

(b) Concentrated hydrochloric acid with nitric acid.

(c) Calcium carbonate with silica.

(iv) The position of aluminium in the reactivity series of metals is shown below : **[3]**

Mg, Al, Zn, Cu

Aluminium is extracted by the electrolysis of its molten oxide.

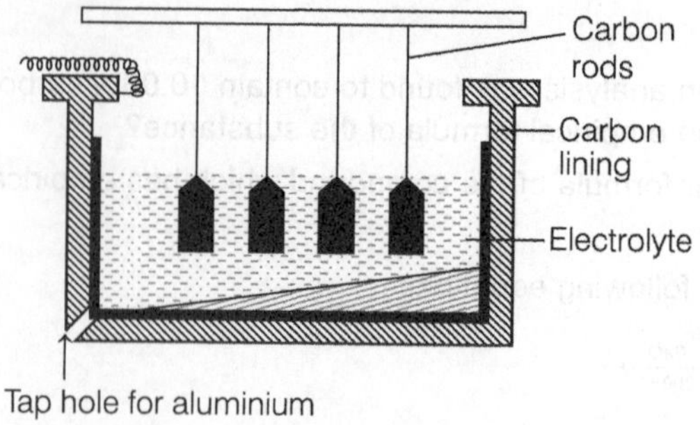

(a) Name the main ore of aluminium.

(b) Why does the molten electrolyte contain cryolite?

(c) Oxygen is produced at the anode. Name another gas which is given off at this electrode.

Question 6

(i) (a) **[3]**

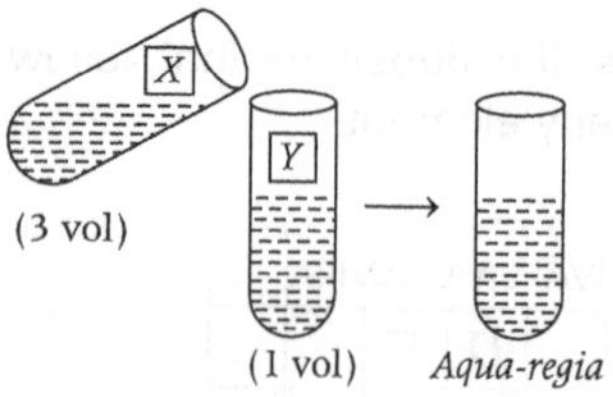

Name the acids present in test tube *X* and *Y*.

(b)

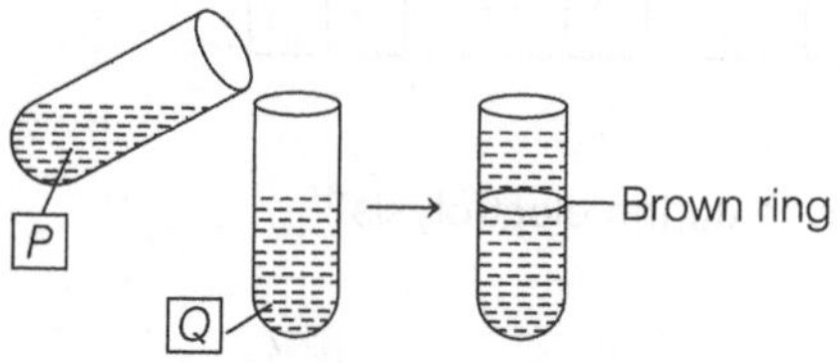

Name the substance/compounds present in *P* and *Q*.

(c) What do you observe when nitric acid decomposes on heating?

(ii) Consider the structures I to VI and answer the following questions (a) to (c). **[3]**

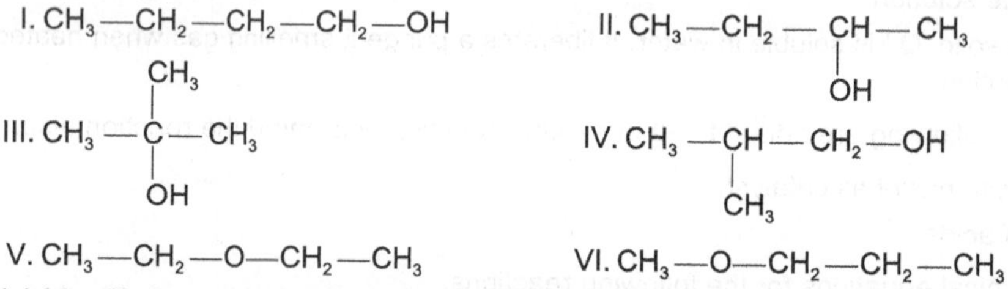

(a) Identify the pairs of compounds which are functional group isomers.

(b) Identify the pairs of compounds that represent position isomerism.

(c) Identify the pairs of compounds that represent chain isomerism.

(iii) Copper on reacting with concentrated H_2SO_4 produces copper sulphate. If 0.64 g copper is to be converted to copper sulphate, find **[4]**

(a) The weight of copper sulphate formed.

(b) Weight of sulphuric acid required.

[Cu = 64, S = 32, O = 16]

Questions 7

(i) Seema performs an experiment by adding a few drops of ethanoic acid to solid sodium hydrogen carbonate **[2]**

(a) What would she observed?

(b) Write the chemical reaction of above experiment.

(ii) Following questions are regarding the electrolysis. Answer each of them **[2]**

(a) The substance in which alumina is dissolved before subjecting it to electrolysis.

(b) The products formed at cathode and anode during electrolysis of alumina.

(iii) Draw the **dot and cross** structure of the following: **[3]**

(a) An ionic compound formed when Na reacts with the dil. HCl.

(b) A covalent compound formed when H_2 reacts with O_2.

(c) The positive ion produced when a hydrogen ion (H^+) reacts with a water molecule (H_2O).

(iv) Sonu has four containers of gases *A*, *B*, *C* and *D*. **[3]**

The volume of gases *A*, *B*, *C* and *D* are in the ratio, 1: 2 : 2 : 4 under the same conditions of temperature and pressure.

(a) Which sample of gas contains the maximum number of molecules?

(b) If the temperature and the pressure of gas *A* are kept constant, then what will happen to the volume of *A* when the number of molecules is doubled?

(c) If this ratio of gas volume refers to the reactants and products of a reaction, which gas law is being observed?

Question 8

(i) (a) State Gay-Lussac's law. (b) Define Non-electrolytes. **[2]**

(ii) Differentiate between the following pairs of compounds using the **reagent** given in the bracket. **[2]**

(a) Calcium sulphite and calcium carbonate (using dil. HCl).

(b) Lead nitrate solution and zinc nitrate solution (using an alkali).

(iii) Choose the substances given in the box below to answer the following questions. **[3]**

Acid salts	Neutralisation reaction	Calcium oxide
Decomposition reaction	Basic salts	Aluminium oxide

(a) Name the metal oxide which can react with an acid as well as base.

(b) Which reaction involves the formation of salts?

(c) Which type of salt is $NaHSO_3$?

(iv) The electronic configuration of 4 elements are shown: **[3]**

$P \rightarrow 2, 8, 2$

$Q \rightarrow 2, 8, 8, 1$

$R \rightarrow 2, 4$

$S \rightarrow 2, 8$

(a) Which element belongs to 3rd period?

(b) Which element belong to 1st group?

(c) Which is an inert element among the given?

Answers

1. (i) (a) Statement I and III are true as H_2SO_4 is a strong electrolyte and it also acts as an oxidising agent.

(ii) (b) **Ethanol**, it represents the structural formula of ethanol as,

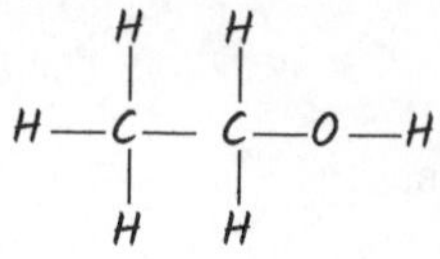

where, —OH is the functional group of alcohol.

(iii) (c)

Atomic no	No of e^- in outer shell
H = 1	1
He = 2	2
Li = 3	1
Be = 4	2
B = 5	3
C = 6	4
N = 7	5
O = 8	6
F = 9	7
Ne = 10	8

(iv) (c) $2C_2H_2 + 5O_2 \longrightarrow 4CO_2 + 2H_2O$

2 vol. of C_2H_2 requires 5 vol. of O_2

200 mL of C_2H_2 will require $= \frac{5}{2} \times 200 = 500$ mL of O_2

Thus, volume of oxygen required to burn 200 mL of C_2H_2 completely is **500 mL.**

(v) (b) The mass of the anode decreases because copper atoms from the anode get oxidised into copper ions and become part of the solution.

At anode $Cu - 2e^- \longrightarrow Cu^{2+}$

(vi) (a) Both (A) and (R) are true, and (R) is the correct explanation of (A).

During extraction of aluminium cryolite and fluorspar are added in the electrolyte to increase the conductivity of the electrolyte, which is necessary because pure alumina is almost a non-conductor of electricity.

(vii) (b) On heating ammonium sulphate with sodium hydroxide, we get **ammonia gas**

$$(NH_4)_2SO_4 + 2NaOH \longrightarrow Na_2SO_4 + 2NH_3 + 2H_2O$$

(viii) (d) XY is the formula of compound produced because electronic configuration of Y is 2, 7 so it can gain one electron whereas electronic configuration of X is 2, 1 so it can lose one electron to form an ionic bond.

(ix) (d) In **beaker** S, zinc will displace iron from iron sulphate as zinc is more reactive than iron.

(x) (a) Both (A) and (R) are true and (R) is the correct explanation of (A).

HCl is not used in place of conc. H_2SO_4 because HCl is volatile in nature, and thus HCl vapour will contaminate the nitric acid vapour obtained from the reaction.

(xi) (a) The general formula of compounds having a triple bond is C_nH_{2n-2}. So, among the given compounds the hydrocarbon having a triple bond is $\mathbf{C_3H_4}$.

(xii) Copper does not liberate H_2 from dil. HCl as any of those metals which are placed below hydrogen in the electrochemical series cannot displace hydrogen from a dilute acid.

(xiii) (d) Zinc nitrate decomposes to give yellow residue of oxide it turns white after being cold.

$$2Zn(NO_3)_2(s) \xrightarrow{\Delta} 2ZnO(s)+4NO_2(g) + O_2(g)$$

(xiv) (b) Test tube shown green colour has a pH of 7, test tube showing red colour has a pH of 1, test tube showing violet colour has a pH of 13 and test tube showing dark blue colour has a pH of 10. As numbers less than 7, i.e. pH 6, 5, 4, ... on the pH scale indicate that acidic nature is increasing as the numbers decrease. Therefore, test tube (Q) is most acidic.

(xv) (b) In case of oxygen (O_2)

$\because$ Moles of $O_2 = \dfrac{\text{Given mass}}{\text{Molar mass}} = \dfrac{16}{32} = \dfrac{1}{2}$

Number of molecules $= \dfrac{1}{2} \times N_A$ $\quad$ [$N_A = 6.022 \times 10^{23}$ moles]

Number of atoms $= 2 \times \dfrac{1}{2} \times N_A = 6.022 \times 10^{23}$ atoms

Similarly,

In case of nitrogen,

Moles of N $= \dfrac{\text{Given mass}}{\text{Molar mass}} = \dfrac{14}{28} = 0.5$ moles

Number of atoms $= 0.5 \times 6.022 \times 10^{23} = 3.011 \times 10^{23}$ atoms

In case of neon,

No. of moles $= \dfrac{20}{20.18} = 0.99$ moles

No. of atoms $= 0.99 \times 6.022 \times 10^{23} = 5.96 \times 10^{23}$ atoms

Thus, 16 g of oxygen contains two times the number of atoms as 14 g of nitrogen.

2. (i) (a) **Vanadium pentoxide (V_2O_5)** is used as a catalyst in this process.

(b) **Contact process** is used to prepare the chemical commonly called as king of chemicals, i.e. H_2SO_4.

(c) $S + O_2 \longrightarrow SO_2$

$$\underset{\text{Sulphur dioxide}}{2SO_2} + O_2 \underset{450°C}{\overset{V_2O_5}{\rightleftharpoons}} \underset{\text{Sulphur trioxide}}{2SO_3}$$

$$SO_3 + \underset{\text{Sulphuric acid}}{H_2SO_4} \longrightarrow \underset{\text{Oleum/pyrosulphuric acid}}{H_2S_2O_7}$$

$$H_2S_2O_7 + H_2O \longrightarrow \underset{\text{Sulphuric acid}}{2H_2SO_4}$$

(d) SO_3 formed in catalytic chamber is not directly absorbed in water because of its highly **exothermic nature**.

(e) Dehydrating property

(ii) (a) Zinc blende (ZnS) $\quad$ (b) Ethene $\quad$ (c) Nitrogen gas

(d) Methane $\quad$ (e) K_2HgI_4 (Nessler's reagent)

(iii) (a) Sulphuric acid $\quad$ (b) electrolytes $\quad$ (c) alkaline

(d) basic $\quad$ (e) Conc. H_2SO_4

(iv) The correct match is (a)-(4), (b)-(5), (c)-(3), (d)-(2), (e)-(1)

(v) (a) 1. 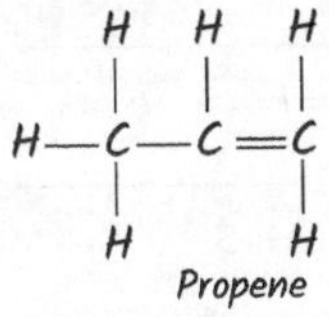

Propene

2. 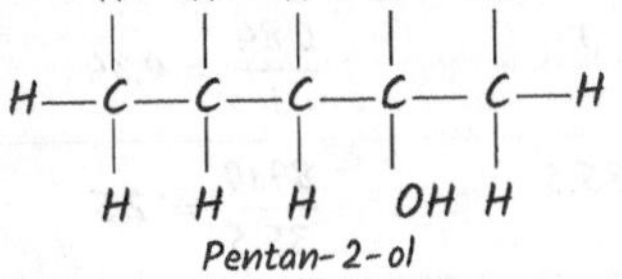

Pentan-2-ol

(b) (1)

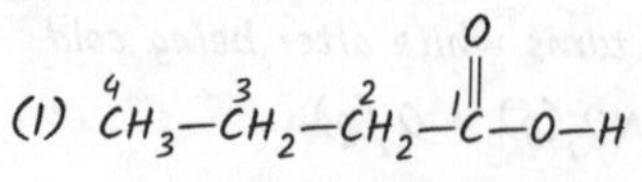

Butan-l-oic acid

(2)

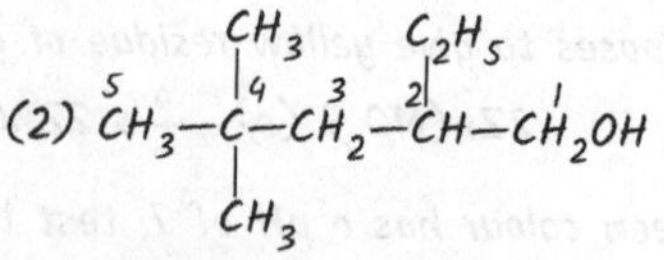

2-ethyl -4, 4-dimethyl-pentan-l-ol

(2)

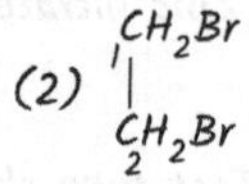

l, 2-Dibromoethane

3. (i) (a) The element belongs to 3rd period and 2nd group have 3 shell and valency 2.

Its electronic configuration will be 2, 8, 2. Hence, the atomic number of element is **12** and the element is **magnesium.**

(b) The outermost shell of magnesium contains 2 electrons. Hence, its valency is **2.**

(ii) (a) Graphite anode is preferred over other inert electrode because graphite is unaffected by reactive bromine vapours.

(b) When acidulated water is electrolysed, **hydrogen (H_2) gas** is evolved at cathode.

(iii) (a) From the given reaction, we can observe that 2 moles of $Ca(NO_3)_2$ produces 4 moles of NO_2.

So, one mole of $Ca(NO_3)_2$ will produce $\frac{4}{2}$ moles of $NO_2 = 2$ moles

(b) Molar mass of $Ca(NO_3)_2 = 164$ g in the reaction, 2 moles of $Ca(NO_3)_2$ is consumed, molar mass of 2 moles of $Ca(NO_3)_2$ is $= 2 \times 164$ g.

2×164 g of $Ca(NO_3)_2$ produces 22.4 litres of O_2

1 g of $Ca(NO_3)_2$ produces $= \frac{22.4}{2 \times 164}$ litres

65.6 g of $Ca(NO_3)_2$ produces $= \frac{22.4}{2 \times 164} \times 65.6 = 4.48$ litres of oxygen is produced.

(iv) (a) When mixture of calcium hydroxide and ammonium chloride is heated, ammonia (NH_3) gas is evolved. The following reaction takes place.

$$\underset{\text{Calcium hydroxide}}{Ca(OH)_2} + \underset{\text{Ammonium chloride}}{2NH_4Cl} \xrightarrow{\Delta} \underset{\text{Calcium chloride}}{CaCl_2} + \underset{\text{Ammonia}}{2NH_3} \uparrow + 2H_2O$$

(b) When mixture of sodium nitrite and ammonium chloride are heated, **nitrogen (N_2) gas** is evolved. The following reactions takes place.

$$\underset{\text{Sodium nitrite}}{NaNO_2} + \underset{\text{Ammonium chloride}}{NH_4Cl} \xrightarrow{\Delta} \underset{\text{Sodium chloride}}{NaCl} + \underset{\text{Nitrogen}}{N_2} \uparrow + 2H_2O$$

(c) When crystals of copper nitrate are heated in a test tube then reddish brown fumes on **nitrogen dioxide gas (NO_2)** are observed.

$$\underset{\text{Copper nitrate}}{2Cu(NO_3)_2} \xrightarrow{\Delta} \underset{\text{Copper oxide}}{2CuO} + \underset{\text{Nitrogen dioxide (Reddish brown)}}{4NO_2} + \underset{\text{Oxygen}}{O_2}$$

4. (i) (a)

Element	%	Atomic mass	Molar ratio	Simpler molar ratio
C	10.06%	12	$\frac{10.06}{12} = 0.84$	$\frac{0.84}{0.84} = 1$
H	0.84%	1	$\frac{0.84}{1} = 0.84$	$\frac{0.84}{0.84} = 1$
Cl	89.10%	35.5	$\frac{89.10}{35.5} = 2.5$	$\frac{2.5}{0.84} = 3$

$\therefore$ Empirical formula of compound $=$ **$CHCl_3$**

(b) Empirical formula (E.F.) = C_5H_5N

$n \times$ mass of E.F = $2 \times$ Vapour density

$n \times 79 = 2 \times$ Vapour density

$n \times 79 = 2 \times 39.5$

$\Rightarrow \quad n = 1$

$\therefore$ Molecular formula = C_5H_5N

(ii) (a) $\underset{\text{Sodium acetate}}{CH_3COO^-Na^+} + \underset{\text{Sodium hydroxide}}{NaOH} \xrightarrow[300°C]{CaO} \underset{\text{Sodium carbonate}}{Na_2CO_3} + \underset{\text{Methane}}{CH_4} \uparrow$

(b) $\underset{\text{Ethanol}}{CH_3CH_2OH} \xrightarrow[170°C]{\text{Conc. } H_2SO_4} \underset{\text{Ethene}}{CH_2=CH_2} + \underset{\text{Water}}{H_2O}$

(iii) (a) Magnesium reacts with hydrochloric acid to form metal chlorides and **hydrogen gas** is liberated.

$$\underset{\text{Magnesium}}{Mg} + \underset{\text{Hydrogen chloride}}{2HCl} \longrightarrow \underset{\text{Magnesium dichloride}}{MgCl_2} + \underset{\text{Hydrogen gas}}{H_2} \uparrow$$

(b) Ethene burns in sufficient supply of air to produce **CO_2 gas** and H_2O.

$$\underset{\text{Ethene}}{C_2H_4} + 3O_2 \longrightarrow \underset{\text{Carbon dioxide}}{2CO_2} \uparrow + 2H_2O + \text{Heat}$$

(c) **Oxygen (O_2)** gas is liberated on decomposition of nitric acid.

$$\underset{\text{Nitric acid}}{4HNO_3} \xrightarrow{\text{Decomposition}} \underset{\text{Nitrogen dioxide (reddish brown)}}{4NO_2} + \underset{\text{Oxygen (colourless)}}{O_2} \uparrow + \underset{\text{Water}}{2H_2O}$$

(iv) (a) As element G belongs to group-17 (halogen family), it will form electrovalent compound with the element of group 2, i.e. [B]. It forms BG_2 compound.

(b) During electrolysis (+) ve ions move towards cathode and get reduced.

As ion of **[A]** i.e, [A^+] is highly electropositive, in solution, it will migrate towards cathode during electrolysis.

(c) **'E'** is the non-metallic element having a valency of 2. 'E' element belongs to group 16 having 6 valence electrons. So, valency is $8 - 6 = 2$.

5. (i) (a) P = Ferric chloride

(b) Q = Ammonium chloride

(ii) (a) $C_2H_4 + H_2 \xrightarrow[Ni]{200°C} \underset{\text{(Ethane formed)}}{C_2H_6}$

Addition of hydrogen called as **hydrogenation**.

(b) $H_2C=CH_2 + H_2O \xrightarrow{H^+} \underset{\text{(Alcohol ethanol is formed)}}{C_2H_5OH}$

Addition of water is called as **hydration**.

(iii) (a) $\underset{\text{(Colourless)}}{Pb(NO_3)_2} + \underset{\text{(Colourless)}}{2NaOH} \longrightarrow \underset{\text{(White ppt.)}}{Pb(OH)_2} \downarrow + \underset{\text{(Colourless)}}{2NaNO_3}$

(b) $\underset{\text{Hydrochloric acid (Conc.)}}{3HCl} + \underset{\text{Nitric acid (Conc.)}}{HNO_3} \longrightarrow \underset{\text{Nitrosyl chloride}}{NOCl} + 2H_2O + \underset{\text{Nascent chlorine}}{2[Cl]}$

(c) $\underset{\text{Calcium carbonate}}{CaCO_3} + \underset{\text{Silicon dioxide}}{SiO_2} \longrightarrow \underset{\text{Calcium silicate}}{CaSiO_3} + \underset{\text{Carbon dioxide}}{CO_2} \uparrow$

(iv) (a) The main ore of aluminium (Al) is **bauxite**.

(b) The molten cryolite is used in electrolyte

- to reduce the melting point.
- to improves/enhances conductivity.

(c) Another gas is CO_2 **or** CO.

The elecrodes are made from carbon, the oxygen that formes there reacts with carbon to form carbon monoxide, which further forms carbon dioxide.

6. (i) (a) $X = HCl$, $Y = HNO_3$

(b) P = Conc. sulphuric acid

Q = Nitrate and Iron (II) sulphate solution

(c) $2HNO_3 \xrightarrow{\Delta} 2H_2O + 4NO_2 + O_2$

Brown fumes of **nitrogen dioxide** observed.

(ii) (a) I and V; I and VI; II and V; II and VI; III and V; IV and V; IV and VI are all functional group isomers.

(b) I and II; III and IV represent position isomerism.

(c) I and III; I and IV; II and III; II and IV represent chain isomerism.

(iii) $\underset{\substack{\text{1 mole}\\ 64\text{ g}}}{Cu} + \underset{\substack{\text{2 moles}\\ 2\times 98 = 196\text{ g}}}{2H_2SO_4(\text{Conc.})} \longrightarrow \underset{\substack{\text{1 mole}\\ 160\text{ g}}}{CuSO_4} + 2H_2O + SO_2$

(a) 64 g of Cu produces $CuSO_4 = 160$ g

0.64 g of Cu will produce $CuSO_4 = \frac{160}{64} \times 0.64 = 1.6$ g

(b) 64 g of Cu requires $H_2SO_4 = 196$ g

0.64 g of Cu requires $H_2SO_4 = \frac{196}{64} \times \frac{0.64}{1} = 1.96$ g

7. (i) (a) When ethanoic acid reacts with $NaHCO_3$ (Sodium bicarbonate), **CO_2 gas** is evolved with brisk effervescence.

(b) $\underset{\text{(Ethanoic acid)}}{CH_3COOH} + \underset{\text{(Sodium bicarbonate)}}{NaHCO_3} \longrightarrow \underset{\text{(Sodium ethanoate)}}{CH_3COONa} + CO_2 \uparrow + H_2O$

(ii) (a) Alumina is dissolved in cryolite because cryolite lowers the fusion temperature from 2050°C to 950°C and enhances conductivity.

(b) **At cathode** Aluminium

At anode Oxygen which is further oxidised to CO and then CO_2.

(iii) (a) **NaCl** is formed when Na reacts with the dil. HCl. The dot and cross structure of NaCl is

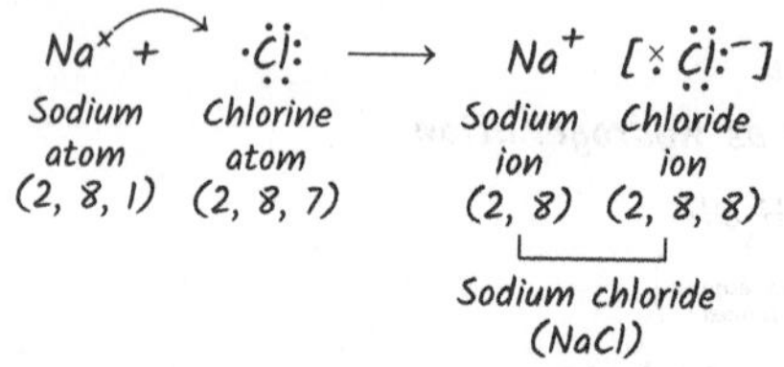

(b) **H_2O** is formed when H_2 reacts with O_2.

The dot and cross structure of H_2O is

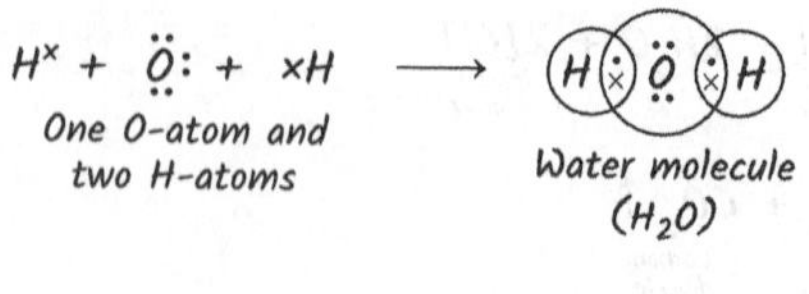

(c) H_3O^+ is formed when H^+ reacts with water molecule (H_2O). The dot and cross structure of H_3O^+ is

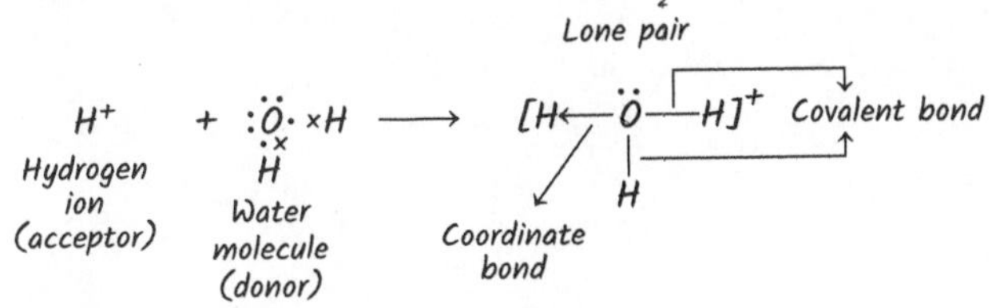

(iv) (a) Sample of **gas D** contains the maximum number of molecules.

(b) When the number of molecules is doubled, then the volume of the gas A will also get **doubled**.

(c) **Gay-Lussac's law** of combining volumes.

8. (i) (a) **Gay-Lussac's law of combining volumes** states that when gases react, they do so in volumes which bear a simple ratio to one another and to the volume of the gaseous product, provided that all the volumes are measured at the same temperature and pressure.

(b) Chemical compounds which do not conduct electricity in fused state or in aqueous solution are called as **non-electrolytes**. e.g. Glucose, urea, etc.

(ii) (a) On adding dil. HCl to calcium carbonates, bubbles of **carbon dioxide** will appears.

$$\underset{\text{Calcium carbonate}}{CaCO_3} + \underset{\text{Hydrogen chloride}}{2HCl}\ (dil.) \longrightarrow \underset{\text{Calcium chloride}}{CaCl_2} + \underset{\text{Carbon dioxide}}{CO_2}\uparrow + \underset{\text{Water}}{H_2O}$$

Calcium sulphite on reacting with dil. HCl produces **sulphur dioxide gas** and bubbles are not observed.

$$\underset{\text{Calcium sulphite}}{CaSO_3} + \underset{\text{Hydrogen chloride}}{2HCl}\ (dil.) \longrightarrow \underset{\text{Calcium chloride}}{CaCl_2} + \underset{\text{Water}}{H_2O} + \underset{\text{Sulphur dioxide}}{SO_2}$$

(b) When ammonium hydroxide (an alkali) is added to zinc nitrate a **white gelatinous precipitate** of zinc hydroxide is observed which then dissolves in excess ammonium hydroxide forming a colourless solution of a complex.

$$\underset{\text{Ammonium hydroxide}}{2NH_4OH} + \underset{\text{Zinc nitrate}}{Zn(NO_3)_2} \longrightarrow \underset{\text{Zinc hydroxide (White gelatinous ppt.)}}{Zn(OH)_2}\downarrow + \underset{\text{Ammonium nitrate}}{2(NH_4)NO_3}$$

When ammonium hydroxide is added to lead nitrate, a chalky white precipitate of lead hydroxide is observed which are insoluble in excess ammonium hydroxide.

$$\underset{\text{Lead nitrate (colourless)}}{Pb(NO_3)_2} + 2NH_4OH \longrightarrow \underset{\text{(Chalky white ppt.)}}{Pb(OH)_2}\downarrow + 2NH_4NO_3$$

(iii) (a) **Aluminium oxide** is the metal oxide which can react with an acid as well as base due to its amphoteric nature.

(b) **Neutralisation reaction** involves the formation of salts.

(c) $NaHSO_3$ is a type of **acidic salt**.

(iv) (a) Element P belong to 3 period as it has 3 shells.

(b) Element Q belong to group I as it has I electron in its valence shell.

(c) Element S is inert because it has electronic configuration with complete octet.